me Dependent territories of Commonwealth states (in brackets) SCALE 1 : 88,000,000

Learning English

GREEN LINE NEW E2 5

Englisch 2. Fremdsprache

von

Stephanie Ashford
Rosemary Hellyer-Jones
Marion Horner

Ernst Klett Verlag
Stuttgart • Leipzig

Learning English – Green Line New E2, Band 5
Englisch 2. Fremdsprache

Autoren: Stephanie Ashford M.Sc., Brigachtal; Rosemary Hellyer-Jones M.A., Ehingen (Donau); Marion Horner M.A., Cambridge; sowie Peter Lampater, Ehingen (Donau)

Beratende Mitarbeit: Dr. Thomas Becker, Nürnberg; Anne Marie Deißenböck, München; Waltraud Gschwendner, München; Gerhard Nickl, Nürnberg; Uli Nürnberger, München; Wolfgang Poeppel, Augsburg

CDs:

[01] Begleit-CD zum Schülerbuch für zu Hause und für den Unterricht mit Texten, Liedern, Ausspracheübungen (Klettnummer 581858)

[01] CD mit den Hörtexten für den Unterricht (Klettnummer 581859)

Lernsoftware:
Zu diesem Band gibt es ein multitmediales Lernprogramm. Dieses Programm bietet schulbuchbegleitende Materialien mit dem Schwerpunkt Textarbeit, eine Wiederholungskomponente mit abwechslungsreichen Übungsformen zu Vokabular und Grammatik und ein Lexikon mit dem kompletten Wortschatz des Lehrwerks.

1. Auflage 1 5 4 3 2 1 | 2012 11 10 09 08

Alle Drucke dieser Auflage sind unverändert und können im Unterricht nebeneinander verwendet werden. Die letzte Zahl bezeichnet das Jahr des Druckes.

Internetadresse: www.klett.de

Redaktion: Peter Cole M.A., Monique Kunhar M.A.
Gestaltung: Marietta Heymann
Illustrationen: Dorothee Wolters, Köln; Christian Dekelver, Weinstadt (Landkarten)
Umschlagfotos: Avenue Images GmbH/Fancy, Hamburg; shutterstock/Mendenhall, NY
Reproduktion: Meyle + Müller, Medien-Management, Pforzheim
Druck: Himmer AG, Augsburg

Printed in Germany
ISBN 978-3-12-581850-7

9 783125 818507

Welcome to Learning English Green Line NEW E2, volume 5!

If you have already taken a quick look through your *Green Line NEW E2* textbook, you will have noticed that the familiar structure and layout have changed. Your English book now consists of the following sections:

- Topics
- Skills
- Grammar
- Vocabulary with Everyday English
- Dictionary
- Appendix

In the first section of the book, **Topics**, there are texts and listening, speaking, reading, writing and mediation exercises, but the Topics contain no grammar exercises. Some texts or exercises are optional. It does not matter in which order the Topics 1–5 are done.

In the **Skills** section you can quickly look up the most important information on all the skills that you have learned to apply so far – to remind you, for example, what to do when you are asked to analyse a text or make a presentation.

Additionally there are some new skills introduced in this book, which you can also find in the Skills section. They may contain exercises that help you to learn them.

The **Grammar** section gives you the most important information you need for speaking and writing correct English and the forms are grouped according to their function and usage. This section contains not only rules, but also exercises. It has its own foreword, which tells you exactly how to work with the Grammar.

There is no vocabulary progression in this book. The new words listed chronologically in each Topic in the **Vocabulary** section are based on the combined vocabulary of Books 1–4. The Vocabulary no longer contains definitions, as you should by now be able to keep your own word lists and write your own definitions and helpful notes, but it does provide you with a lot of useful exercises to give you ideas on how to do vocabulary work on your own.

As well as these exercise boxes, you will find a new kind of page in the Vocabulary section: an **Everyday English** page after each Topic dealing with common speaking situations. These pages always involve a listening part, so they are best done in class with your teacher.

The **Dictionary** section contains the alphabetical word list you are used to, while in the **Appendix** you will find the list of irregular verbs, a glossary of literary terms and solutions to the checking up exercises in the Grammar.

As you work through the Topics, you will find references to **Skills** →S1 and **Grammar** →G1. These references are designed to help you with a particular task or grammar point and you should follow them up. However you can look at the Skills and Grammar sections on your own at any time. You will be sure to profit from the information given there!

You will soon become familiar with the new structure of your *Green Line NEW E2* textbook. It provides everything you need for a successful study of the English language in grade 10 and will prepare you well for your final two years at school.

Symbols

[01] This text or exercise is on the *Schülerbuch-CD*. And the symbol ■ shows where a new track begins.

[01] This text or exercise is on the *Hörverstehens-CD*. The listening texts are not printed in your textbook.

⟨ ⟩ These brackets show that an text or exercise is optional.

[partner] This exercise should be done with a partner.

[group] This exercise should be done in a group.

[internet] Use the internet to prepare for this exercise.

→S29, p.110 This is a reference to the Skills section.

→G14, p.123 This is a reference to the Grammar section.

Contents

Topic 5 Living in a modern world

Scientific and technological progress: its advantages and disadvantages for the individual and society

Topic 1 Growing up

A Responsibility on

Minimum legal age limits

	USA	UK	Germany	Peru	Pakistan
Leaving school	16–18*	16	16–18*	18	at any time***
Employment	14	13	13	12	14
Age of consent (AOC)	14–18*	16	14	14	only in marriage
Marriage	18	16 (with parental consent)	18	14 females 16 males	16 females 18 males
Driving a car	14–17*	17	17–18*	18	18
Buying alcohol (MPA)	21	18	16, 18**	18	illegal for all
Smoking	18–19*	18	18	12	18
Voting in an election	18	18	18	18	18
Criminal responsibility	6–10*	10	14	12	7

*varies from state to state **18 for spirits ***no compulsory education

WORD BANK

Reacting and commenting

I was surprised to see that … • I never knew that … • In my opinion … • It depends … • On the one hand … on the other … • From the point of view of … • Obviously, … • Frankly, … • The reason for this is … • If you …, you should … • It may be …, but … • … could be dangerous • … should be protected

FACT FILE

The **age of consent (AOC)** refers to when people can legally have sex. In Germany it is 14 provided the older partner is younger than 18. In many countries, the AOC is lower for females than for males.

The **age of criminal responsibility** is when children can be taken to court, depending on the type of crime.

The **minimum purchasing age (MPA)** refers to the purchase of alcohol. This may differ from the **minimum drinking age (MDA)** for consuming alcohol in bars. China, for example, has an MPA of 18 but no MDA.

1 [group work] *Look at the photos, the figures and the fact file. Compare and comment on age limits in different countries, and discuss whether they make sense to you.* →S16, p.100, →S23, p.105

A student's opinion

Everyone is capable of being irresponsible at times. Older and younger drinkers alike can be irresponsible, whatever their age. This fact alone means we do not need a law dictating what a responsible age is. It also applies to other things on which there is an age limit: driving, smoking, R-rated movies, government office and voting. Having age limits puts child-raising in the hands of the government rather than the parents. Say, for example, parents don't care if their child smokes, despite the fact that their child happens to be 12 years old. Whether or not this is good parenting is beside the point; the point is that the law denies parents the privilege of making choices concerning the raising of their own children. Now they want to ban children from buying violent video and computer games. Where will it all stop? This isn't what I call a land of liberty!

Joseph Lemanski, student at Western University, Illinois

WORD BANK
Legal language
age limit • legal • consent • responsibility • to ban • compulsory • to take sb to court • law • to dictate • to deny • privilege • independence

2 *Write a response to Joseph Lemanski's comment.*

3 *Debate: "Violent computer games should be banned."* →S17, p. 100

4 [01] *Listening: My big brother Jerry* →S1, p. 88

a) *Say what Jerry's life was like before and after moving out.*

b) *Make a list of the things you think you would need to do if you lived on your own. Then work in groups and make surveys in different classes of your school to find out how many teenagers are able to do these things and do them regularly. Present and comment on the results.* →S29, p. 110

B Being a teenager

1 a) *Brainstorming: What do you think it means to be a teenage boy or a girl? Write a statement on a card, using one of the following patterns:*

teenage girls
»Girls always worry more than boys about how they look.«

teenage boys
»Boys never show their feelings.«

b) ***Discussion:*** *Get someone to read the statements out and someone else to write them on the board. Discuss whether they are true or simply clichés.* →S16, p.100

[01] Teenage voices

Annabel, 16 To me, being a girl means spending a lot of time in a group and talking about things. Girls seem to be more able to sort out situations by being supportive and sharing things with each other. I think they are able to sort out situations that arise amongst their friends better than boys do. Mind you, there is still a lot of bitchiness amongst girls. They might compliment each other but not really mean it because they really just want a compliment in return. I don't think boys judge as much. They find it much easier to just start up a conversation, whereas a girl would judge someone's personality by what they're wearing and then decide whether to talk to them or not.

■ **Bethany[1], 16** I'd rather be a girl than a boy. I'm generalising a bit but I think boys mask over who they really are just to impress friends, whereas girls are more individual and don't just follow the crowd to please others. Girls don't have a problem with comforting their friends but if a boy was seen doing this, other boys would jump to conclusions and tease him for being gay. But being a girl is not easy because there's a lot of pressure on us to look good. Girls judge each other more on appearance. Boys appear to be a lot more confident than girls. They get into fights a lot more than girls. I've never been in a fight. I'm far too timid and afraid to confront people. I run away from conflict.

[1] **Bethany** ['beθni]

■ **Gabriella, 17** Being a girl means that you have to work harder for everything. Girls are often seen as vulnerable and less able than boys, so you have to prove yourself. I find it unfair that I have to stay inside at night while boys are allowed to go out. I feel like I have to prove that I'm strong enough to be able to go out and look after myself. I think people often think of women who want to do well at work in a bad light but that is unfair because all they're trying to do is succeed in what still seems like a man's world. I feel like there's quite a bit of pressure on me to be able to balance still being seen as a "girl" but also being strong without acting masculine.

Adrian[2], 15 Boys commit suicide more because they don't tell people when they're ticked off, "big boys don't cry" kind of thing.

[2] **Adrian** ['eɪdriən]

Nick, 16 The girls in our class all seem to work harder and learn more, and they usually get better results. And they don't mess around as much as the boys. The boys get bored more easily. They tend to want to look cool. Some mess around to impress the girls, but there are some who do it if anyone's there, not just girls. The girls are all interested in older boys so none of them have boyfriends in our class. In the breaks we go around in a gang, but we don't talk about the girls, mainly about music and games and stuff like that. Some boys are obsessed with their appearance. They're always rushing off to put gel in their hair.

Tony, 15 I think boys and girls want the first time to mean something and not just be nothing. But after that, all boys seem to want is good sex. They talk about how good it was. Girls normally talk about the emotional side. There is pressure on boys to grow up quickly, especially on the sex side. Some boys want it because it makes them a man. Some girls, too, think it makes them grown-up.

2 a) *Collect information from the texts and put it in a grid.*

	Girls	Boys
Positive qualities	supportive, …	confident, …
Negative qualities	bitchiness, …	…
Pressures	…	…

b) ***Discussion:** Compare notes and discuss the views and the facts.* →S16, p.100

3 [02] ***Listening: Family life.** You will hear some scenes from the life of an English family with three teenage children – Roddy (17), Anne (15 ½) and Nick (14). Listen to the three parts separately.* →S1, p.88

a) ***Part 1:** Decide whether these statements are true or not.*
1. *Nick wants to have half a dozen friends to stay on Friday.*
2. *Nick's parents have nothing against sleepovers.*
3. *Roddy is going to spend three nights away from home.*
4. *When Nick hears that Roddy's room will be free, his problems are over.*

b) ***Part 2:** Explain the situation and list the things the children complain about. Then say what you think of the way Anne and Nick behave. What about the way the parents treat them?*

c) ***Part 3:** Continue the dialogue. How will Nick and Roddy solve their problems?*

WORD BANK

Part 1: to doss down • mattress • to sleep over

Part 2: to unload a car • to rent DVDs • to catch a train • swearword • to deduct • allowance • torch

Part 3: to pop out • supper • fridge (= refrigerator) • 20 quid

[07] I go along

■ *Is this a typical way to start a written story?*

■ *Tense?*

■ *What is usually the function of 'but' and 'and'? What is different in this text? Why? Find more examples.*

■ *Differences between the two classes?*

■ *Relationship teacher – students?*

■ *Watch out for more examples of body language.*

Anyway, Mrs. Tibbetts comes into the room for second period, so we all see she's still in school. This is the spring she's pregnant, and there are some people making some bets about when she's due. The smart money says she'll make it to Easter, and after that we'll have a sub teaching us. Not that we're too particular about who's up there at the front of the room, not in this class.

Being juniors, we also figure we know all there is to know about sex. We know things about sex no adult ever heard of. Still, the sight of a pregnant English teacher slows us down some. But she's married to Roy Tibbets, a plumber who was in the service and went to jump school, so that's okay. We see him around town in his truck.

And right away Darla Craig's hand is up. It's up a lot. She doesn't know any more English than the rest of us, but she likes to talk.

"Hey, Mrs. Tibbets, how come they get to go and we don't?"
She's talking about the first-period people, the Advanced English class.

"I hadn't thought," Mrs. Tibbetts says, rubbing her hand down the small of her back, which may have something to do with being pregnant. So now we're listening, even here in the back row. "For the benefit of those of you who haven't heard," she says, "I'm taking some members of the – other English class over to the college tonight, for a program."

The college in this case is Bascomb[1] College at Bascomb, a thirty-mile trip away.

"We're going to hear a poet read from his works."

Somebody halfway back in the room says, "Is he living?" And we all get a big bang out of this.

But Mrs. Tibbets just smiles. "Oh, yes," she says, "he's very much alive." She reaches for her attendance book, but this sudden thought strikes her. "Would anyone in this class like to go, too?" She looks up at us, and you see she's being fair, and nice.

Since it's only the second period of the day, we're all feeling pretty good. Also it's a Tuesday, a terrible TV night. Everybody in the class puts up their hands. Even Marty Crawshaw, who's already married. And Pink Hohenfield, who's in class today for the first time this month. I put up mine. I go along.

Mrs. Tibbetts looks amazed. She's never seen this many hands up in our class. She's never seen anybody's hand except Darla's. Her eyes get wide. Mrs. Tibbetts has really great eyes, and she doesn't put anything on them. Which is something Darla could learn from.

But then she sees we have to be putting her on. So she just says, "Anyone who would like to go, be in the parking lot at five-thirty. And eat first. No eating on the bus."

Then she opens her attendance book, and we tune out. And at five-thirty that night I'm in the parking lot. I have no idea why. Needless to say, I'm the only one here from second period. Marty Crawshaw and Pink Hohenfield will be out on the access highway about now, at 7-Eleven, sitting on their hoods. Darla couldn't make it either. Right offhand I can't think of anybody who wants to ride a school bus thirty miles to see a poet. Including me.

The advanced-English juniors are milling around behind school. I'm still in my car, and it's almost dark, so nobody sees me.

■ Then Mrs. Tibbetts wheels the school bus in. You can see the black letters along the yellow side: CONSOLIDATED SCHOOL DIST. She swings in and hits the brakes, and the doors fly open. The advanced class starts to climb aboard.

[1] **Bascomb** [ˈbæskəm]

They're more orderly than us, but they've got their groups, too. And a couple of smokers. I'm settling behind my dashboard. The last kid climbs in the bus. And I seem to be sprinting across the asphalt. I'm on the bus, and the door's hissing shut behind me. When I swing past the driver's seat, I don't look at Mrs. Tibbetts, and she doesn't say anything. I wonder where I'm supposed to sit.

They're still milling around in the aisle, but there are plenty of seats. I find an empty double and settle by the window, pulling my ball cap down in front. It doesn't take us long to get out of town, not this town. When we go past 7-Eleven, I'm way down in the seat with my hand shielding my face on the window side. Right about then, somebody sits down next to me. I flinch.

■ *Narrator's relationship with his classmates?*

"Okay?" she says, and I look up, and it's Sharon Willis.

I've got my knee jammed up on the back of the seat ahead of me. I'm bent double, and my hand's over half my face. I'm cool, and it's Sharon Willis.

■ *His feelings?*

"Whatever," I say.

"How are you doing, Gene[2]?"

I'm trying to be invisible, and she's calling me by name.

"How do you know me?" I ask her.

She shifts around. "I'm a junior, you're a junior. There are about fifty-three people in our whole year. How could I not?"

GRAMMAR
Participle with a subject of its own
'… with my hand shielding my face' (line 59)
→G14, p.123

Easy, I think, but don't say it. She's got a notebook on her lap. Everybody seems to, except me.

"Do you have to take notes?" I say, because I feel like I'm getting into something here.

"Not really," Sharon says, "but we have to write about it in class tomorrow. Our impressions."

I'm glad I'm not in her class, because I'm not going to have any impressions. Here I am riding the school bus for the gifted on a Tuesday night with the major goddess girl in school, who knows my name. I'm going to be clean out of impressions because my circuits are starting to fail.

■ *His opinion of Sharon?*

Sharon and I don't turn this into anything. When the bus gets out on the route and Mrs. Tibbetts puts the pedal to the metal, we settle back. Sharon's more or less in with a group of the top girls around school. They're not even cheerleaders. They're a notch above that. The rest of them are up and down the aisle, but she stays put. Michelle Burkholder sticks her face down by Sharon's ear and says, "We've got a seat for you back here. Are you coming?"

But Sharon just says, "I'll stay here with Gene." Like it happens every day.

I look out the window a lot. There's still some patchy snow out in the fields, glowing gray. When we get close to the campus of Bascomb College, I think about staying on the bus.

"Do you want to sit together," Sharon says, "at the program?"

■ *Sharon's character?*

I clear my throat. "You go ahead and sit with your people."

"I sit with them all day long," she says.

■ At Bascomb College we're up on bleachers in a curtained-off part of the

[2] **Gene** [dʒiːn]

gym. Mrs. Tibbetts says we can sit anywhere we want to, so we get very groupy. I look up, and here I am sitting in these bleachers. And I'm just naturally here with Sharon Willis.

We're surrounded mainly by college students. The dean of Bascomb College gets up to tell us about the grant they got to fund their poetry program. Sharon has her notebook flipped open. I figure it's going to be like a class, so I'm tuning out when the poet comes in.

■ *Compare expectations and reality.*

First of all, he's only in his twenties. Not even a beard, and he's not dressed like a poet. In fact, he's dressed like me: Levi's and Levi's jacket. Big heavy-duty belt buckle. Boots, even. A tall guy, about a hundred and eighty pounds. It's weird, like there could be poets around and you wouldn't realize they were there.

■ *Perspective and style?*

But he's got something. Every girl leans forward. College girls, even. Michelle Burkholder bobs up to zap him with her flash camera. He's got a few loose-leaf pages in front of him. But he just begins.

"I've written a poem for my wife," he says, "about her."

Then he tells us this poem. I'm waiting for the rhyme, but it's more like talking, about how he wakes up and the sun's bright on the bed and his wife's still asleep. He watches her.

"Alone," he says, "I watch you sleep
Before the morning steals you from me,
Before you stir and disappear
Into the day and leave me here
To turn and kiss the warm space
You leave beside me."

He looks up and people clap. I thought what he said was a little too personal, but I could follow it. Next to me Sharon's made a note. I look down at her page and see it's just an exclamation point.

■ *Gene's reaction to the poems?*

He tells us a lot of poems, one after another. I mean, he's got poems on everything. He even has one about his truck: "Old buck-toothed, slow-to-start mama," something like that. People laugh, which I guess is okay. He just keeps at it, and he really jerks us around with his poems. I mean, you don't know what the next one's going to be about. At one point they bring him a glass of water, and he takes a break. But mainly he keeps going.
He ends up with one called "High School."

"On my worst nights," he says, "I dream myself back.
I'm the hostage in the row by the radiator, boxed in,
Zit-blasted, and they're popping quizzes at me.
I'm locked in there, looking for words
To talk myself out of being this young
While every girl in the galaxy
Is looking over my head, spotting for a senior.
On my really worst nights it's last period
On a Friday and somebody's fixed the bell
So it won't ring:
And I've been cut from the team,
And I've forgotten my locker combination,
And I'm waiting for something damn it to hell
To happen."

And the crowd goes wild, especially the college people. The poet just gives us a wave and walks over to sit down on the bottom bleacher. People swarm down to get him to sign their programs. Except Sharon and I stay where we are.

GRAMMAR
Gerunds and participles
'I'm locked in there, looking for words/To talk myself out of being this young' (line 132)
→G13/14, p.123

"That last one wasn't a poem," I tell her. "The others were, but not that one." She turns to me and smiles. I've never been this close to her before, so I've never seen the color of her eyes.

"Then write a better one," she says.

We sit together again on the ride home.

"No, I'm serious," I say. "You can't write poems about zits and your locker combination."

"Maybe nobody told the poet that," Sharon says.

"So what are you going to write about him tomorrow?" I'm really curious about this.

"I don't know," she says. "I've never heard a poet reading before, not in person. Mrs. Tibbetts shows us tapes of poets reading."

"She doesn't show them to our class."

"What would you do if she did?" Sharon asks.

"Laugh a lot."

The bus settles down on the return trip. I picture all these people going home to do algebra homework, or whatever. When Sharon speaks again, I almost don't hear her.

"You ought to be in this class," she says.

I pull my ball cap down to my nose and lace my fingers behind my head and kick back in the seat. Which should be answer enough.

"You're as bright as anybody on this bus. Brighter than some."

We're rolling on through the night, and I can't believe I'm hearing this. Since it's dark, I take a chance and glance at her. Just the outline of her nose and her chin, maybe a little stubborn.

"How do you know I am?"

"How do you know you're not?" she says. "How will you ever know?"

But then we're quiet because what else is there to say? And anyway, the evening's over. Mrs. Tibbetts is braking for the turnoff, and we're about to get back to normal. And I get this quick flash of tomorrow, in second period with Marty and Pink and Darla, and frankly it doesn't look that good.

Richard Peck

VIP FILE

Richard Peck
- born 1934 in Decatur, Illinois
- worked as a teacher and editor after university in the USA and England and military service in Germany
- famous writer of fiction for young people
- has won several awards for his works

■ *Trying to keep up his image?*

■ *Change? Perspectives?*

4 *What are the main themes of this story?*

5 a) *__Text analysis:__ To show how they are presented, make notes about the plot, the characters (examine their main traits, hopes and expectations, the way they speak and behave), the narrator, the style and the title. The clues in the margin will give you an idea of how to work with a text. Each group can deal with one of the aspects. Always remember to refer to the Skills section when you need help with a task. These skills are important here: Text analysis* →S3, p. 89, *Characters* →S5, p. 91, *Narrative point of view* →S6, p. 92, *Narrative techniques* →S7, p. 93

b) *Use your notes to present your findings to the class and discuss these questions: How does the author want the story to affect the reader? Do you think he has been successful?* →S16, p. 100

6 *What does the text say about poetry?*

7 *__Creative writing:__ Write about the trip to Bascomb College from Sharon's point of view. It can be a diary entry, a letter or a poem – it's up to you!* →S6, p. 92

⟨8⟩ *Can you remember a situation where something unexpected happened to you and changed your way of seeing things? Talk or write about it.*

WORD BANK

author • narrator • reader • character • perspective • feelings • theme • style • setting • exposition • development • turning point • surprise • ending • intention • to show • to describe • to express • to stress • to make fun of • to act • to appear

C No risk – no fun?

Tombstoning: Dying to jump?

***Shout* investigates the teen jumpers risking their lives ...**

GRAMMAR
-*ing* form with a subject of its own
'... a deadly craze that involves people jumping off cliffs ...'
→G13, p.123

GRAMMAR
Participles
'Hidden obstacles lurking beneath the waves'
→G14, p.123

WHAT IS IT?

Tombstoning is a deadly craze that involves people jumping off cliffs, rocks and harbour walls into the sea. It has inspired a host of websites and an expanding band of daredevil followers who love to try out the best sites around the country. Tombstoning, so called because of the high level of fatalities and serious injuries, has grown in popularity among teenagers and is normally done when the sea is at its roughest and most dangerous.

KNOW THE RISKS!

- Hidden obstacles lurking beneath the waves
- Getting swept away by the current
- Not knowing how shallow or deep the water is
- Over-estimating how far you can jump
- Permanent disability
- Being swept onto rocks
- Possible boat collision
- Death

FACT!

Mark Nicholas, an 18-year-old tombstoner from Plymouth, jumped off a 60 ft cliff just three hours after he'd been discharged from hospital with a severely bruised heart and lung suffered at the same spot 24 hours earlier.

1 *Dictionary work: Find out where the word 'tombstoning' comes from. Do you think it describes the activity well? Explain why or why not. Try to think of a good word for it in German.* →S9, p.94

2 *Analysing the article:* →S14, p.98
a) *Identify the different parts of this article (the various pictures, headlines, texts, etc.) and explain the function of each one.*
b) *Analyse the style of the article. Think of the target group and the purpose for which it was written.*

REAL LIFE

Why do it?

Shout spoke to Christine, 14, who loves tombstoning ...

"I have been tombstoning with my mates for the last year and I've never been hurt. I absolutely love the buzz that you get from it. You spend the whole week doing boring stuff at school and doing a big jump at weekends brings some excitement. For that split second you forget about all your troubles and feel free. I know some people have died and others have been seriously injured tombstoning, but if there was no risk, there'd be no point doing it. My mates and I all know what we're doing and agree that it's the biggest rush you can get – and it doesn't cost a thing.

FACT!

Rescue services have to deal with at least one cliff jumping every week and police are threatening tombstoners with ASBOS!

Don't do it!

Deborah[1], 17, told *Shout* a very different story ...

"I'd been tombstoning for a couple of years and during that time I'd managed to escape with only a few cuts and bruises. I knew that it was dangerous but I suppose I always felt that nothing bad would happen to me. However, one day me and three mates decided to choose a new area to tombstone from. The drop looked bigger than our usual spot but, egged on by my mates, I decided to go for it. Unfortunately, on landing, I hit a hidden rock and shattered vertebrae in my back. I'm now paralysed from the waist down and doctors don't know if it's temporary or permanent. It's a terrible price to pay for a bit of 'fun' and I hope my story puts people off wanting to ruin their lives tombstoning."

21

[1] Deborah [ˈdebrə]

3 *Discussion: Have you ever done anything dangerous for fun?* →S16, p.100
Describe the experience and say whether you regret it or would like to do it again. Give your reasons.

4 [ååå] *Team projects* →S18, p.101: *Create a poster or double-page magazine article about another craze. Use the layout and style of this article as a model.* →S14, p. 98
OR Make a survey to find out how adventurous other people at your school are. Think of areas in life where people take risks and include questions about these in your survey. Compare your results with other groups. →S29, p.110

⟨Sierra Wave⟩

Joe asked Steve and Catherine to stop in for a beer. His home was high up on a hill. They sat on his porch and looked out over Echo Park.

Steve liked Echo Park because here, everything he enjoyed about Los Angeles was more extreme. The hills were steeper, the houses older. At night the streets still belonged to the gangs.

They talked for a while, about sports. Steve had been a big swimmer in college but hadn't talked to anyone about it for a long time. He missed sports.

"Let me show you something," Joe said. "I think you'll be interested."

Steve followed him into the garage. Hanging from the roof was a hang glider.

"This is what I'm into now," Joe said.

Then Joe told him about hang gliding up north, in the Sierras – not just floating along a hundred feet above the beach, but standing on a mountaintop and catching the Sierra Wave, a thermal that could take you up to fourteen thousand feet, or higher, so high you had to carry an oxygen bottle. He showed Steve a picture he'd taken of himself, the tops of the mountains far below. The moment Steve saw that picture, he knew he had to learn.

Joe gave Steve lessons on the beach near Palos Verdes. Steve ran down a dune, holding the glider. As in certain dreams, his steps got longer and longer until he left the ground. At first the feeling frightened him; but he learned to enjoy it. When he got home, he started to tell Catherine, but she said,

"I don't want to hear about it. You're going to get yourself killed. Or end up in a wheelchair for the rest of your life."

Steve went out in the garden and sat looking at the moon for a while. Of course it was dangerous. But in danger, you learned something about yourself.

Joe decided it was time for Steve to solo. So early one Sunday morning they put the hang glider into Joe's pickup and drove to the beach. Along the top of the cliff there was what Joe called a rotor, a rolling cylinder of air. By staying in it, you could fly a mile or two down the beach. Steve lifted the glider and hooked in. Standing on the edge of the dropoff, he wondered for a moment why he was doing this; then Joe's instructions took over and he ran forward until his feet left the ground. His body was tingling and his throat was hot. He could hear Joe shouting for him to get the nose down. Then Joe's voice disappeared. He moved his body to the left and made a turn to the south.

Now he was flying along the coast. He was beginning to lose his fear. He watched his shadow move along over rooftops, parking lots, telephone lines. He could see the ground in such detail it seemed that even if he fell, he could not be hurt. Steve felt sorry for the people on the ground, all in their ordered paths, like the cars following the grid of streets. On the way back, a seagull flew beside him for a time. Then he saw Joe's pickup and his heart began to beat faster again. Landing was the most difficult part. He hit the ground so hard he fell to his knees.

"How long was I up?" he asked.

"Six minutes."

It had seemed much longer.

In June, Joe started talking about taking a trip to the Owens Valley, so Steve could do some real soaring. They drove north in Joe's pickup until the Sierras rose up on their left. They spent that night in a campground. The wind woke Steve early. He stood and looked at the mountains, feeling today would be the day they had been waiting for. As they drove up the dirt road to the top of Gunter Peak, Joe said it was going to be a hot day, a good day for soaring. The mountaintop was a dry world of rock and bright sunlight. Steve walked around, stopping to watch a kid assemble his glider.

"How you doing?" the kid asked him.

"Fine," Steve said. "It's going to be a great day. Going to catch one of those big thermals today."

The kid gave Steve a long look. "You done much of this?" he said.

"No," Steve admitted. "Not a lot."

"Then you'd better be careful of those thermals. They're nothing to play around with."

Steve said he'd be careful and walked on.

They flipped a coin to see who would go first. Steve won, and Joe assembled the glider.

Joe was working slowly, as if he had second thoughts. "Maybe you'd better not try for a thermal yet," he said. "Just take a short hop. It's up to you."

"All right," Steve said.

"Then you won't be needing the oxygen bottle. Do you want the parachute?"

"No, I won't be needing the parachute."

They carried the glider to the dropoff and Steve hooked in. Then he felt warm air on his face. He ran forward until it caught the glider, and lifted off into space.

The sunlight was blinding. The mountaintop fell away. A mile ahead, he could see several gliders, and flew towards them. It was a thermal. He knew it the moment he felt it push him up. Forgetting everything, he gave himself to it completely. One by one the other gliders dropped out. Then there was only a bird, perhaps an eagle, and together they spiraled for thousands of feet, straight up into the sun.

When the cold began to bite, even through his jacket, Steve pulled the control bar back into his stomach. But the glider did not respond. The thermal was too strong. He tried everything, but the glider continued climbing. Then he did what he had been afraid to do until now. He looked down.

Thousands of square miles lay below him, like a map. He was higher than the highest mountains now. The little lakes between them were frozen. The detail was astonishing. Looking south, he saw Mount Whitney. He could follow the highway back down through the valley. He could see all the way to China Lake. But something was wrong. He saw everything as if through the wrong end of a telescope. Detailed, distant, in a circle of black. He had flown so high he was suffering from a lack of oxygen. He was losing consciousness. But he could see so far, and so much, that he felt a joy stronger than he had ever known. Hanging in the sun, he felt tears running down his face, and knew only that he was floating, he was flying.

William Hauptman (adapted)

5 *Is it clear to you how the story ends? Say what you think happens next. Use clues from the text (think of Steve's character, Catharine's attitude, Joe's advice, the way the story is structured, etc.) to support your opinion.* →S7, p. 93

6 ***Creative writing:*** *Choose one of these tasks.* →S11, p. 96

a) *Write a quick description (two minutes) of what you would see if you were hang-gliding above where you are now and compare your descriptions with a partner.*

b) *Use some aspect of Sierra Wave as an inspiration for a poem or song.*

c) *Write a leaflet giving warnings and safety tips for hang gliders.*

Hallo Benedikt. Ich schreibe aus der Vergangenheit. Was ist wohl aus dir geworden?

D I'm gonna be like you

Cartoons

Dad, why can't I have sensible shoes?

Move! You're blocking the TV.

1 *Compare the cartoons and talk about the relationship between father and son.* →S24, p.106

[10] Cat's in the cradle (Ugly Kid Joe)

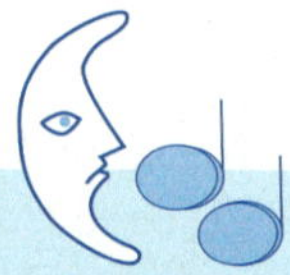

My child arrived just the other day, came to the world in the usual way, but there were planes to catch and bills to pay. He learned to walk while I was away. He was talking before I knew it. And as he grew, he said, "I'm gonna be like you, Dad. You know I'm gonna be like you."

Chorus: And the cat's in the cradle[1] and the silver spoon[2], little boy blue[3] and the man in the moon[4]. "When you coming home?" "Son, I don't know when. We'll get together then. You know we'll have a good time then."

Well, my son turned ten just the other day. He said, "Thanks for the ball, Dad. Come on, let's play. Could you teach me to throw?" I said, "Not today. I got a lot to do." He said, "That's okay." And he walked away and he smiled and he said, "You know, I'm gonna be like him, yeah. You know I'm gonna be like him."

Chorus

Well, he came from college just the other day, so much like a man I just had to say, "I'm proud of you. Could you sit for a while?" He shook his head and he said with a smile, "What I'd really like, Dad, is to borrow the car keys. See you later. Can I have them please?"

Chorus

I've long since retired, my son's moved away. I called him up just the other day. "I'd like to see you, if you don't mind." He said, "I'd love to, Dad, if I could find the time. You see my new job's a hassle and the kids have the flu. But it's sure nice talking to you, Dad. It's been sure nice talking to you."

And as I hung up the phone, it occurred to me, he'd grown up just like me. My boy was just like me.

Words: H. F. Chapin/S. Campbell Chapin

[1–4] expressions from common sayings, children's rhymes and games

GRAMMAR

Conditionals

'I'd love to, Dad, if I could find the time.' (line 36)

→G4, p.117

WORD BANK

should • to be supposed to • to be expected to • to argue • to need • to learn • to influence • to teach • values • to decide what is most important • to be busy • excuse • to care • to share • to spend quality time • to be proud of • personality • to be the same/different • expectation • to become independent • to obey • to rebel • to act/behave

2 *Role play: The father has just hung up the phone. His wife, the boy's mother, asks: "Who have you been talking to?" Act out a role play between the two.*

3 ***Discuss:*** *Do you think parents should be examples to their children?* →S16, p.100

Mediation: Mama ist die Beste

Vorbilder gab es immer. Die Definition hat sich bloß geändert. Ein Vorbild ist niemand, der für eine besondere Idee steht, sondern jemand, der gut aussieht, viel Geld hat oder schlicht so ist, wie wir auch gern wären. Die eigenen Eltern nennt sicher kein 16-Jähriger als Vorbild. Was war an denen schon besonders? Die gehen arbeiten, kochen, reden, putzen, lesen Zeitung und schlafen. Wie viel das ist, merkt man erst, wenn man es selbst tut. Erst dann überholen die Eltern die Popstars auf der Liste der am häufigsten genannten Vorbilder. Aber dafür muss man ein bisschen älter werden.

Mit 18 hatten wir genug von Individualisierung und gespielter Auflehnung gegen gar nichts. Zeit für Kate Moss. Sie vereinte uns alle wieder – in einer Diät. Ein paar Jahre mit dünnen, schönen und operierten Vorbildern folgten. Erst Abitur und Auszug aus der Parallelwelt Kinderzimmer brachten die Wende. Die Vorbilder mussten dringend überdacht werden. Das lief bei uns etwa so ab: Schauspielerin Angelina Jolie, die ihren Erfolg dem Ruhm ihres schauspielenden Vaters verdankt, wird ausgetauscht gegen Lehrertochter Franka Potente. Der junge Mann mit Ambitionen zum Unternehmer verabschiedet sich vom Vorbild Bill Gates und wendet sich dem eigenen Onkel zu, der erfolgreich Hörakustik vertreibt.

In diese Zeit etwa gehört auch die Studie mit dem grausamen Namen *null zoff & voll busy* der Universität Siegen, die als Erste wieder einen Trend zum Vorbild feststellt. Zwei von drei Jugendlichen hätten demnach wieder eines. Auf Platz eins der Jungs thront immer noch der Sportler, gefolgt von Papa. Bei den Mädchen belegen Popstars, Models und Schauspielerinnen nur Rang zwei, drei und vier. Vorbild Nummer eins ist Mama, fanden die Forscher um den Erziehungswissenschaftler Jürgen Zinnecker heraus. Das sollte sich auch nicht mehr ändern. Die aktuelle Shell-Studie 2006 besagt dasselbe: Eltern, Familie im weiteren Sinne und Bekannte der Eltern sind noch heute die häufigsten Vorbilder für junge Menschen.

Eltern sind die besten Vorbilder, weil ihre Vorgaben realistisch sind. Sie besitzen ähnliche Fähigkeiten wie man selbst. Der kanadische Psychologe Albert Bandura kam Anfang des 20. Jahrhunderts zu dem naheliegenden Schluss: Der Mensch sucht sich immer ein Vorbild, dessen Erfolge auch für einen selbst erreichbar scheinen. Wer liegt also näher als Mama und Papa? Dass die Vorbilder vorher immer Popstars waren, kann nur an jugendlicher Selbstüberschätzung liegen.

Und heute, mit Anfang 20, klingt der einst belächelte Tagesablauf „arbeiten gehen, kochen, reden, putzen, Zeitung lesen, sich zusammen schlafen legen" plötzlich ganz wunderbar. Viel besser als „alleine aufwachen, irgendwo jobben, shoppen, telefonieren und allein hinlegen". Was die Eltern geschafft haben, ist genau das, wonach wir uns sehnen, seit wir ausgezogen sind: Liebe, Treue und ein Zufluchtsort mit einer warmen Couch und einem vollen Kühlschrank. Da denken wir praktisch.

Lara Fritzsche, *Die Zeit*

4 ***Mediation:*** *Write a summary of the text in English. What do you think of the statements the author (23) makes about the different stages in the lives of young people?* →S28, p.108

5 [ååå] ***Debate:*** *Parents who try to stay young are the best role models for their children.* →S17, p.100

⟨E My child is starving herself to death⟩

1 ***Before you read:*** *Look at the pictures and comment on how the ideal of beauty has changed over the centuries.* →S23, p.105

The Three Graces by Peter Paul Rubens, c. 1636–39

Supermodels Alessandra Ambrosio, Heidi Klum and Izabel Goulart, 2006

⟨Joanne's story⟩

October, 2000: One day, a friend who is staying with us asks if anyone threw up in the bathroom. I ask Leon and the kids, all of whom say no. The next day, my friend says there's vomit in that bathroom again. I ask again. Same answer. A few days later, she tells me that a friend of Mara's has told her that Mara is purging. I go to Mara: "Are you throwing up?" "No, Mummy, I would tell you if I were." My daughter can't be bulimic. I don't diet. We don't talk about calories or fat or weight loss. Much of our family life centres around food. Look at my job as a restaurant critic! I tell Mara she's beautiful the way she is. We talk about body image and the tyranny of media images of skeletal women. Mara understands that, so it can't happen to her.

November, 2000: But it is. My whistle-blowing friend tells me. Thus begins a roller coaster of lies and deceit. I learn the first rule of eating disorders: They lie in order to protect themselves. I get advice from Sheena's Place, a support centre for people with eating disorders, who tell me not to accept the lies. They also say that Mara should be monitored by our family doctor.

February, 2001: Family dinners are a nightmare. She won't eat anything other than plain fish or chicken with boiled veg. If I put any fat on it, she screams at me and doesn't eat. I think she's eating carrot sticks for lunch at school; I beg her to eat more. She refuses. She pretends to take the subway, but I watch, and she's walking. She goes for a run often. Over-exercising is part of the illness. I watch, I worry, I sneak fat into meals.

FACT FILE

Eating disorders are widespread illnesses. They include, for example:

- Anorexia nervosa, in which you starve yourself because you think you are fat.
- Bulimia nervosa, involving periods of overeating followed by purging through vomiting or laxatives.

Eating disorders can lead to serious health problems and even death. Getting help early is important! Treatment must be individual and involves monitoring, psychotherapy, a nutritional plan and sometimes medicines.

May, 2001: The doctor says Mara's heart rate and blood pressure are dangerously low, and she is admitted to the Hospital for Sick Children. They tell us her life is in danger and put her on a heart monitor. I give up sleeping. Every morning, I phone to check how low her heart rate went at night. Mara is forced to eat. My heart is breaking. My baby, my beloved daughter – I feed her, I keep her alive. This is my fundamental job, to keep my child alive. And I can't do it. Mara is in Sick Kids for six weeks. We visit her every evening. We play cards, board games, read, pretend everything is all right, speak of nothing. She won't talk about her issues, so I feel useless and helpless.

October, 2001: She joins her school cross-country running team; her weight is dropping at weekly weigh-ins. She knows I watch her every mouthful. People are telling me that eating has to be her choice, but I can't stop watching. Am I the reason for this illness? She has always been such a good girl, overachieving at school, helpful and sweet at home, active in extracurriculars. When other 15-year-olds were doing drugs and alcohol instead of schoolwork, I congratulated myself that she wasn't. Is this her way of rebelling? We are very involved parents. We both work at home, we spend weekends alone with our kids, we have high expectations of them. Maybe her illness is a metaphor of refusal to be the daughter we control. That means we should let go. But we can't. We cannot let our daughter kill herself.

May, 2002: Homewood Health Centre offers her a bed in their eating disorder unit. It's a 16-week residential program for adults, 100 percent voluntary, more than an hour away. At 16, she would be the youngest person there. We hated the thought of Homewood. She'd be horribly homesick, need us desperately, and we wouldn't be able to visit except weekends. But she chooses to go. By letting her go to this program, I am accepting her decision to take charge of her life. For the first time, she has to decide to live. Or not.

December, 2002: It's a new relationship, with this almost grownup. I have relinquished control over her, and with it the folly of trying to be the perfect mother. I feel so lucky – that she chose to live, and that she came home to us.

2 *Describe in one or two sentences your first reactions to Joanne's story.*

3 ***Vocabulary work:*** *Make three mind maps with words that have to do with 1. food, 2. eating disorders, 3. control. There are a lot of them in the text.*

4 *Describe Joanne's problem and her feelings. How does she try to cope with the matter? Use quotes from the text to support your answers.*

5 [05 ◎] a) *Listen to what Mara, Joanne's daughter, says.*
b) *Take notes for each of the six paragraphs.*
c) *Listen again and match these statements with parts 1–6 of Mara's story.*

- I bet I could do more.
- I need help, but I won't admit it.
- I can't have an eating disorder.
- I wonder if I can make it through Grade 10.
- I have to let go of every way I know to deal with stress.
- I jump immediately into a normal lifestyle.

d) *Use the diagram to explain how she experiences her illness.* →S29, p.110

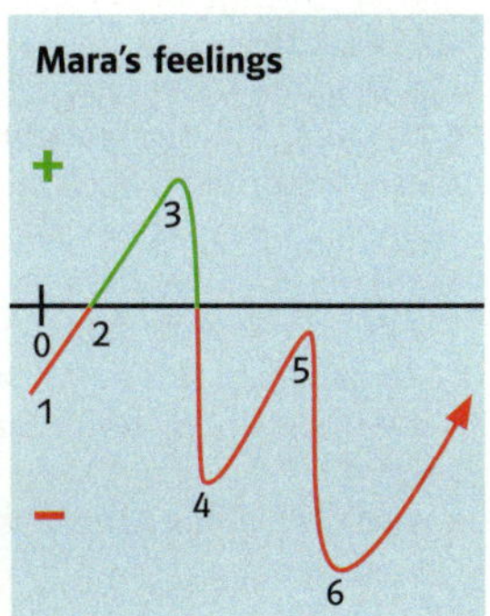

Topic 2 Major minorities

A Origins

US teenagers

New York City – a Harlem street scene

In the US ...

Total population: 281 million
(US Census 2000)

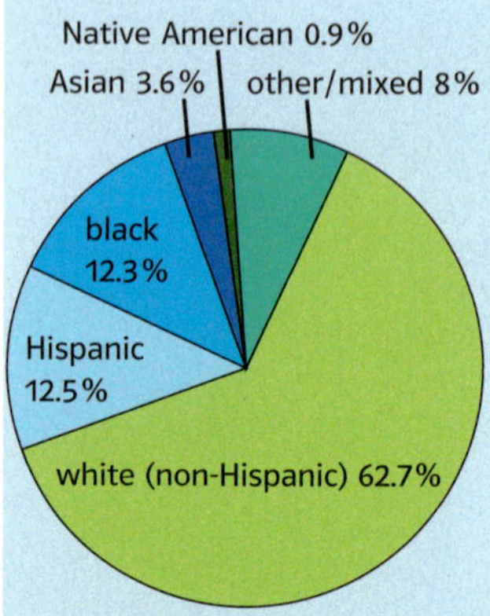

→S29, p.110

Most black Americans are descendants of the slaves that were transported from West Africa to work on plantations in the southern states.

Number of slaves

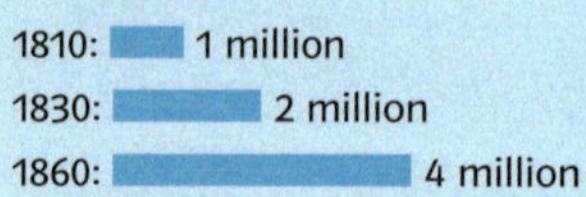

- new spinning machines invented in Britain
- great demand for cotton
- cotton grows well in the south-east of the USA
- cotton-picking is labour-intensive
- northern US states developed industries

The slave trade

FACT FILE

Blacks in the US

- 1619: first Africans brought to New World
- 1808: importation of slaves made illegal but slavery continues in southern states
- 1861–65: Civil War between North and South after southern states break away from the Union to protect their economy, which is based on slavery
- 1865: war won by North; slavery finally abolished in all states
- 1964: Civil Rights Act officially ends racial segregation and discrimination.

1 *Slavery: Use the material on this page to explain the reasons for the slave trade and how it worked.*

2 [11] ***Listening:*** *Charles Ball was a slave who managed to escape and later wrote about his experiences. Listen to this description of his first day in the cotton fields and discuss your reactions to it.* →S1, p.88

3 [ ] ***Research:*** *Find out when and why the Asian and Hispanic immigrants came to America.* →S30, p.111

A policeman in London

An Asian family on Blackpool Beach

Teens at a concert in South London

In the UK ...

The British population remained almost entirely white until the middle of the 20th century. After the Second World War, during which thousands of men from across the Empire had fought for Britain, labour shortages in the mother country and a lack of opportunities for these men on their return home led to the start of mass immigration of blacks from the Caribbean and Asians from the Indian subcontinent (Muslims from Pakistan and Bangladesh, Hindus and Sikhs from India). They settled mainly in London and in the industrial towns of the Midlands and the North of England. As Commonwealth citizens they were welcomed to the UK and their numbers were not restricted. Later, however, stricter controls began to limit immigration.

UK National Statistics Online

Total population: 60 million (2005)

Ethnic origin	%		%
White	**92.0**	**Black**	**2.0**
		Black Caribbean	1.0
Mixed	**1.2**	Black African	0.8
		Black Other	0.2
Asian	**4.0**		
Indian	1.8	**Chinese**	**0.4**
Pakistani	1.3		
Bangladeshi	0.5	**Other**	**0.4**
Other Asian	0.4		

4 *Asians and blacks in the UK:*

a) *Explain briefly where these two minority groups came from and why they came.*

b) *Compare their situation with that of the blacks and Hispanics in the US. Think of the historical background, the reasons for immigration, and the present-day situation.*

5 [👥] [💻] ***Research:*** *Use the Internet or other sources to find out more about the following topics. Work in groups and share the information in class.*
• Abraham Lincoln • the civil rights movement • the creation of Pakistan • the Commonwealth →S30, p.111

6 ***Thinking further:*** *What effect can minority groups have on a country? Think of both positive aspects and possible problems.*

7 [💻] ***Your country:*** *What parallels do you see with your own country? Collect information about minority groups in Germany for use later in this topic.*

WORD BANK

multi-ethnic society • political refugee • asylum seeker • to be aware of • cultural diversity • racial prejudice • discrimination/to discriminate against • (religious) tension • to be the victim of • race relations

B Black Power

[11] Rosa Parks and today's white youth

GRAMMAR
Participles
'Before rushing off to school, my seventh-grade daughter sat at the breakfast table scanning a newspaper story …' (line 1) →G14, p.123

Before rushing off to school, my seventh-grade daughter sat at the breakfast table scanning a newspaper story about Rosa Parks, the civil rights icon who died at age 92.

"Did you know who she was?" I asked. "Oh, Mom, what do you think?" she replied, a pre-teen's too-cool-for-you way of saying 'yes'.

Anna said she learned about Parks at school, during "that holiday for black people" – which turned out to be not Kwanzaa[1], but Black History Month (February). "You should write about her," she said, "because, you know, there is still segregation."

"Do you mean that black and white people don't live in the same neighbourhoods and don't hang out together?" I asked. "Yeah, write about that," she said.

So white suburban school children in the United States do learn about the contributions of courageous Americans like Rosa Parks. However, they learn about them in a bubble of time and space – within the context of a specific month, and often in schools with zero or few non-white classmates.

And it doesn't seem like that reality will change anytime soon. The de facto segregation of suburban America is stark and persistent. It prevails, even while white suburban teenagers enthusiastically borrow some aspects of urban black culture. Hip-hop music pulses from Volvo station wagons en route to soccer games. Everyone wears low-riding baggy jeans, and Beyonce[2] is a household word.

Lots of white kids believe it's cool to be black – only they don't know any black people. They know what they see on television, whether it is sports or music channels or reruns of *The Fresh Prince of Bel-Air*[3]. Their affect of black culture is also conveniently temporary; it can be shed whenever they or their parents are ready to move onto the next phase of their lives – high school graduation and college entrance exams and admissions interviews.

For those young people who watch the news, Hurricane Katrina[4] also brought black faces onto their wide-screen televisions. But if that level of poverty shocks adults, it is incomprehensible to the average white suburban teenager. Their schools will run Katrina relief drives, and then it is on to the next headliner cause.

Even though black athletes and entertainers greatly influence today's youth culture, contact with black peers is little different from their baby boomer parents' contact at that same age. We lived through the civil rights movement; to our children, it is a chapter in American history. But black and white children in America today still grow up in worlds that are more separate than shared.

[1] festival celebrating African-American culture (Dec 26–Jan 1)
[2] **Beyonce** [bi'ɒnsi:]
[3] TV series starring Will Smith
[4] The terrible floods caused by Hurricane Katrina in August 2005 were a disaster for poor blacks in the New Orleans area.

Of course, that does not diminish what Parks accomplished when she refused to give up her seat on a bus to a white man. That act of bravery and defiance on a city bus in Montgomery, Alabama, in 1955 inspired a movement that eventually ended officially sanctioned segregation in America. Changing the law of the land was not easy. If Rosa Parks is the acknowledged mother of the civil rights movement, it took many more like her who were willing to protest and, if necessary, die.

But tough as it was to change the law, changing the habits, attitudes and comfort level between the races is proving to be even tougher. America has learned that you can outlaw segregation, but you cannot force integration or even friendship. Today, adult conversations about race often devolve into bitter debates over affirmative action and quotas[5], as if those are the only forces that can bring blacks and whites together in the classroom or the workplace.

The next phase of race relations – living, working and playing together, by choice – is going to be up to the grandchildren of Parks's civil rights movement. Whites and blacks of my generation talked the talk, but in the end we really didn't walk the walk, into one another's living rooms and backyards.

Our children are smart enough to see the divide that still exists. Maybe they will also be smart enough to figure out how to reach across it. If they learn anything from Parks, it could be that change starts with tiny steps, not grand gestures. All Parks did was refuse to give up her seat. With that simple act of courage, she changed history.

Joan Venocchi, *International Herald Tribune*

GRAMMAR
Conditionals
'If they learn anything from Parks, it could be that change starts with tiny steps, …' (line 59)
→G4, p.117

[5] **affirmative action and quotas** giving an advantage to minority groups, especially in the context of education or employment

1 ***Mediation:*** *Explain in German how the article is structured and what each part is about.* →S28, p.108

2 ***Working with the text:***

a) *What does the text say about the influence of black culture on young white Americans and its relevance to them in their everyday lives?*

b) *Say what Rosa Parks's 'act of bravery and defiance' was. Then summarize what, according to the article, has or has not changed since that time.*

c) ***Vocabulary work:*** *Explain these expressions in your own words: civil rights icon (line 2); a bubble of time and space (line 15); headliner cause (line 33); comfort level (line 48); talk the talk (line 56); walk the walk (line 57)* →S8, p.94

3 ***Thinking about the future:*** *What changes need to occur for American society to become fully integrated? Do you think the younger generation will be able to overcome the divide that exists at present?*

[12] Sister Rosa (The Neville Brothers)

December 1st, 1955
Our freedom movement came alive
And because of Sister[1] Rosa you know
We don't ride on the back of the bus no more

Sister Rosa she was tired one day
After a hard day on her job
When all she wanted was a well deserved rest
Not a scene from an angry mob

A bus driver said Lady you got to get up
'Cause a white person wants that seat
But Miss Rosa she said no, not no more
I'm gonna stay right here and rest my feet

Chorus:
Yeah, thank you Miss Rosa
You were the spark
That started our freedom movement
Thank you Sister Rosa Parks

Now the police came without fail
And took Sister Rosa off to jail
And 14 dollars was her fine
Brother Martin Luther King knew it was our time

The people of Montgomery sat down to talk
It was decided all God's children should walk[2]
Until segregation was brought to its knees
And we obtain freedom and equality

Thank you Miss Rosa …

So we dedicate this song to thee
For being a symbol of our dignity

Thank you Sister Rosa

Words: C. G. Neville / D. A. Johnson / C. Moore, L. Neville

[1] Black people often call each other 'sister' or 'brother' to show a sense of togetherness.
[2] The black community decided to boycott the Montgomery buses in protest.
[3] **Montgomery** [mənt'gʌmri]

Rosa Parks, 72, back in Montgomery[3], Alabama, 30 years after the bus boycott

VIP FILE

Martin Luther King
- Baptist minister and civil rights leader
- 1955: organises the Montgomery bus strike
- 1963: leads 250,000 people in a march on Washington
- 1968: assassinated

4 *What story does this song tell and from whose point of view is it told?* →S6, p. 92

5 *Describe the mood of the song and the way it is performed.*

6 [pair work] *Creative writing:* →S11, p. 96
a) *Write a dialogue involving Rosa Parks. Either: A journalist interviews her. Or: She is questioned by the police.*
b) *Act out your dialogue with a partner.* →S15, p. 99

⟨7⟩ [computer] *Find another song that deals with an important event in history and present it to the class.* →S22, p. 104

I have a dream

Martin Luther King, who organized the boycott of buses to protest about the treatment of Rosa Parks, devoted his life to ending the segregation laws that stated that all citizens were equal but still allowed blacks and whites to be separated in schools and public places. After leading the 1963 March on Washington, King stood on the steps of the Lincoln Memorial and spoke to the crowd of 250,000 people.

FACT FILE

The Declaration of Independence (1776) states: 'We hold these truths to be self-evident that all men are created equal …'

The American Dream The idea of America as a land of opportunity in which everyone can hope to become rich and successful.

8 a) [12 ◎] *Listen to an extract from Martin Luther King's famous Washington speech and describe the atmosphere.* →S1, p.88

b) *Summarize in your own words what Martin Luther King says.* →S3, p.89

c) *What stylistic devices make the speech so moving?*

A different way

Black activist Malcolm X made a name for himself arguing that equal rights could only be gained by violence, not by peaceful protest. His ideas were adopted by the Black Panthers, a militant political group founded in 1966.

Athletes Tommie Smith and John Carlos give the Black Power salute after the Olympic 200m final in Mexico City in 1968. For this protest they were excluded from the games.

Malcolm X thought revenge on whites was justified, not least because of the violent activities of the Ku Klux Klan, a white anti-civil rights organization that terrorized blacks.

VIP FILE

Malcolm X
- Black nationalist leader
- born Malcolm Little, Nebraska 1925
- 1952: becomes a Muslim and changes name to X (to show that he has no inherited African name to replace his 'slave name')
- 1960s: makes a series of militant speeches
- 1965: assassinated

9 a) [13 ◎] *Listen to an extract from a speech by Malcolm X.*

b) *Say what he means when he calls Black Nationalism a 'self-help philosophy'. Why doesn't he like the 'sit-in' type of protest? What does he say about people in Africa and Asia?*

c) *Compare this speech with Martin Luther King's Washington speech.*

10 *Write a comment on whether you think violence can be justified as a way of achieving political aims.* →S13, p.97

⟨11⟩ a) [💻] *Find out more about the Black Panthers or the Ku Klux Klan. Or*

b) [💻] *Find an example of black American hip-hop or gangsta rap and compare the mood and attitude expressed with that of 'Sister Rosa'.*

VIP FILE

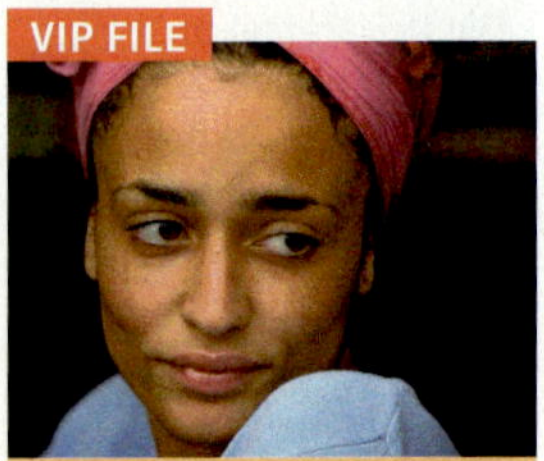

Zadie Smith
- born London 1975
- mother Jamaican, father English
- has won major prizes for 'White Teeth' (2000), 'Autograph Man' (2002), 'On Beauty' (2005)

[13] ⟨I get my culture where I can⟩

The following text is an extract from 'On Beauty' by Zadie[1] Smith. In this part of the story the Belseys – Howard, a white university lecturer, his black wife Kiki and their three teenage children Jerome, Zora and Levi[2] – are in a park in Boston, where a free open-air classical concert has just finished.

The family set off, continuing their debate. The black boy with the elegant neck who had been sitting next to Zora strained to hear the disappearing conversation. More and more these days he found himself listening to people talk, wanting to add something. But he wasn't in the habit of talking to strangers. He pulled his baseball cap down and checked in his pocket for his cell. He reached under his chair to retrieve his Discman[3] – it was gone. He swore violently, padded his hand around the area in the darkness and found something, a Discman. But not his. His had a sticky residue on the bottom, the remains of a long-gone sticker. Apart from that the two Discmans were identical. It took him a second to figure it out. He hurried as best he could after that girl with the glasses. With every step more people seemed to place themselves between him and her.

"Hey! *Hey!*"

But there was no name to put on the end of *Hey* and a six foot two athletic black man shouting *Hey* in a crowd does not create easiness.

"She's got my Discman, this girl, this lady – just up there – sorry, 'scuse me, man – yeah, can I just get by here – *Hey! Hey, sister!*"

"ZORA – wait!" came a voice loud by the side of him, and the girl he'd been trying to stop turned around and gave somebody the finger.

"Aw, fuck you too," said the voice resignedly. The young man turned and saw a boy a little shorter than him and several shades lighter.

"Hey, man – is that your girl?"

"What?"

"The girl with the glasses you was just calling? Is she your girl?"

"*Hell*, no – that's my sister, bro."

"Man, she's got my Discman, my music – she must have picked it up by mistake. See, I got hers. I been trying to call her, but I didn't know her name."

"For real?"

"This is hers, man. It ain't mine."

"Wait here –"

Levi pushed through the crowd, caught his sister by the arm and began to talk to her animatedly. The young man approached slowly, but got there in time to hear Zora say:

"Don't be ridiculous – I'm not giving some friend of yours my player –"

"You're not listening to me – it's *not* yours, it's his – *his*," repeated Levi, spotting the young man and pointing at him. The young man smiled weakly. Even so small a smile told you that his were perfect white teeth.

"Levi, if you and your friend want to be *gangstas*, piece of advice: you've got to take, not ask."

"Zoor – it's not yours –"

"I *know* my Discman – this is my Discman."

"Bro –" said Levi, "you got a disc in here?"

The young man nodded.

"Check the CD, Zora."

"Oh, for God's sake – see? It's a recordable disc. Mine. OK?"

"Mine's recordable too – it's my own mix," said the young man firmly.

"Levi … We've got to get to the car."

"Listen to it –" said Levi to Zora.

"No."

"Listen to the damn CD, Zoor."

"What's going on over there?" called Howard, twenty yards away.

[1] **Zadie** ['zeɪdi]
[2] **Levi** ['li:vaɪ]
[3] portable CD player

"Zora, you freak – just listen to the CD, settle this."

Zora made a face and pressed play. "Well, this isn't my CD. It's some kind of hip-hop," she said sharply, as if the CD itself were to blame.

The young man stepped forward cautiously. He turned the Discman over in her hand and showed her the sticky patch. He lifted his hoodie and drew a second Discman from his waistband. "This one's yours."

"They're *exactly* the same."

"Yeah, I guess that's where the confusion came from." He was grinning now and the fact that he was stupidly good-looking could no longer be ignored.

"Yeah, well, I put mine under *my* chair," she said tartly, and turned and walked off in the direction of her mother, who stood hands on hips another hundred yards away.

"Phew. Tough sister," said the young man, laughing lightly.

Levi sighed.

"Yo, thanks, man."

They clapped hands.

"Who you listening to anyway?" asked Levi.

"Just some hip-hop."

"Bro, can I check it out – I'm all into that."

"I guess …"

"I'm Levi."

"Carl."

How old is this boy, Carl wondered. And where'd he learn that you just ask some strange brother you never seen before in your life if you can listen to his Discman? Carl had figured a year ago that if he started going to events like this he would meet the kind of people he didn't usually meet – couldn't have been more right about that one.

"It's tight, man. There's a nice flow there. Who is it?"

"Actually, that track is me," Carl said, neither humbly nor proudly. "I got a very basic sixteen-track at home. I do it myself."

"You a rapper?"

"Well … more like Spoken Word[4]."

"Scene[5]."

They talked all the way towards the gates of the park. About hip-hop generally, and then about recent shows in the Boston area. Carl kept on trying to figure out what the deal was, but it seemed like there was no deal – some people just like to talk. Levi suggested they swap cell numbers, and they did so by a tree.

"Just, you know … next time you hear about a show in Roxbury[6] … You can call me or whatever," said Levi, rather too keenly.

"You live in Roxbury?" asked Carl doubtfully.

"Not really … but I'm there a lot – Saturdays, especially."

"What are you, fourteen?" asked Carl.

"No, man. I'm sixteen! How old are you?"

"Twenty."

This answer immediately inhibited Levi.

"You at college or … ?"

"Nah … I'm not an *educated* brother, although …" He had a theatrical, old-fashioned way of speaking, which involved his long, pretty fingers turning circles in the air. "I guess you could say I hit my own books in my own way."

"Scene."

"I get my culture where I can, you know – going to free shit like tonight, for example. Anything happening that's free and might teach me something, I'm *there*."

Levi's family were waving at him. He was hoping that Carl would go in another direction before they reached the gate, but of course there was only one way out of the park. *"Finally,"* said Howard, as they approached.

Now it was Carl's turn to grow inhibited. He pulled his baseball cap down low. He put his hands in his pockets.

GRAMMAR

Subjunctive

'Levi suggested they swap cell numbers …' (line 150)

→G15, p.125

[4] a performance, often to music, of lyrics, poetry or stories, with the emphasis on speaking rather than singing

[5] great, cool (street slang)

[6] neighborhood in Boston with a large African-American population

"Oh, hey," said Zora, embarrassed. Carl acknowledged her with a nod.
"So I'll call you," said Levi, trying to bypass the introduction. He was not quick enough.
"Hi!" said Kiki. "Are you a friend of Levi?"
Carl looked distraught.
"Er ... this is Carl. Zora stole his Discman."
"I didn't *steal* any –"
"Are you at Wellington[7]? Familiar face," said Howard distractedly. He was looking out for a taxi. Carl laughed, a strange artificial laugh that had more anger in it than good humour.
"Do I *look* like I'm at Wellington?"
"Not everybody goes to your stupid college," countered Levi, blushing. "People do other shit than go to college. He's a street poet."
"Really?" asked Jerome with interest.
"That ain't[8] really accurate, man ... I do some stuff, Spoken Word – that's all. I don't know if I be calling myself a street poet, exactly."
"Spoken Word?" repeated Howard.
Zora, who considered herself the bridge between Wellington's popular culture and her parents' academic culture, stepped in here. "It's like oral poetry ... it's in the African-American tradition – Claire Malcolm[9]'s all into it. She goes to the Bus Stop[10] to check it out with her little Cult of Claire groupies."
This last was sour grapes[11] on Zora's part; she had applied for, but not been accepted into, Claire's poetry workshop the previous semester.
"I've done the Bus Stop, several times," said Carl quietly. "It's about the only cool place for that stuff in Wellington." Now he put a thumb to his cap and lifted it so that he might get a good look at these people. Was the white guy the father?
"Claire Malcolm goes to a bus stop to hear poetry ..." began Howard, bewildered, busy looking up and down the street.
"Shut up, Dad," said Zora. "Do you know Claire Malcolm?"
"Nope ... can't say I do," replied Carl, releasing another one of his winning smiles, just nerves probably, but each time he did, you warmed to him further.
"She's like a *poet* poet," explained Zora.
"Oh ... A *poet* poet." Carl's smile disappeared.
"Shut up, Zoor," said Jerome.
"Rubens[12]," said Howard suddenly. "Your face. From the four African heads[13]. Nice to meet you, anyway."
Howard's family stared at him.
Howard stepped off the sidewalk to wave down a cab.
Carl pulled his hoodie over his cap and began to look around himself.

[7] city near Boston (Wellington College is a fictitious university modelled on Harvard)
[8] **ain't** = isn't
[9] poetry professor at Wellington College
[10] club for live music, poetry slams, etc.
[11] if you say something is worthless when you secretly want it but can't have it, that's called 'sour grapes'
[12] **Peter Paul Rubens** (1577–1640) Flemish painter

12 *Compare the reactions of Levi and Zora to Carl.*

13 *Comment on how Levi talks to Carl and to his family. What other elements or references stress the divide between Carl and the Belseys?*

14 *"I get my culture where I can." What idea of culture does each of these characters have: Levi, Carl, Zora and Howard?*

15 *Choose one of the characters and look at the way he or she is presented. Pick out relevant words and phrases used by the author to influence the reader's feelings towards that character.* →S5, p. 91

16 ***Creative writing:*** →S11, p. 96

a) *How could the story go on? Imagine what happens in the following week. Or:*
b) *Write an interview with Carl for a popular culture magazine.* →S15, p. 99

C Living together in the UK

1 a) [👥] *Pre-reading: First look at the pictures on this and the next page. Then decide with a partner what you think the three texts are about.*

b) *Read the texts carefully to find out if you were right. Then do the tasks on the next page.*

Asian voices

Poverty pervades the terraced houses of Wiltshire Street in one of Salford[1]'s Asian districts. Yet Ajeeta Naveed knows what has kept her here in the Higher Broughton[2] district. There is the strong sense of community among "the Pakistanis", good Asian stores, a nearby mosque and – most significant of all – no crime. "The Muslims are together so there's not the stick you get in Seedley[2]," she says, referring to the white racism she has been subjected to in that nearby district.

Jaz, 44, a local retailer, worries about that outlook. He sees the wealth being created at designer stores down on the vibrant Salford Quays[3] and fears none of that income will reach Higher Broughton while it is seen by whites as an Asian district. "It's not just about the Asian outlook. It's also about the white one," he said. "They [the whites] still tend to move out once a certain number of Asians move into a street. They're contributing to the ghettos too."

Ian Herbert in *The Independent*

For me, a British Pakistani, living in multicultural communities is less about easy access to halal[4] meat and more about the ability to disappear into crowds. Before I came to Easington[5] I had imagined I would be stepping back in time into a corner of England uncontaminated by multiculturalism. And yet here was Indus Kandola, 34, describing how he had recently become the first British Asian to manage a pub in the region. He also owns a shop as well as a takeaway. He lives with his wife and two children, his parents and his 90-year-old grandfather.

The family chose this corner of the northeast as they believed it offered more business potential,

with less competition from other Asians.

Easington may appear backwards in its racial diversity but the Kandolas seem impressively progressive. "Because this area isn't multicultural," Indus's wife Sukhvinder explains, "you are more open in whatever you try. There is no community judging you." With two young children at school in the district, Indus tells me he feels settled in Easington – but relatives who travel up to see him still think his family is strange. "We are known as the weirdos who live up north," agrees Sukhvinder. "To them it's like, 'Up north? Can you get curries there? Do you make chapatis[6]?' They feel sorry for us: whenever they come they just drive around asking 'Where are the Asians?'"

Sarfraz Manzoor in *The Guardian*

[1] city in the Greater Manchester area in northwest England
[2] inner-city area of Salford
[3] newly developed area on Manchester Ship Canal
[4] prepared according to Muslim law
[5] town in the northeast of England, officially the whitest place in the UK
[6] **chapati** a kind of Indian bread

It's a shocking figure: more than a hundred million pounds was spent in the past year for translating and interpreting for British residents who don't speak English. The financial cost is bad enough, but there is a wider problem about the confused signals we are sending to immigrant communities. We are telling them they don't have to learn English, let alone integrate.

The evidence is plain to anyone who visits Brick Lane[7] in the East End of London. In the Bangladeshi community from which I come, English is a foreign language. Even the street signs are in Bengali.

Every year Bangladeshis sit at the bottom of rankings of educational achievement. Their society persists in economic stagnation that locks many people into the catering industry. Drug abuse and crime are on the rise in the East End. Young Bangladeshi males, with no hope of employment, can choose between extremists in the mosques or the gangs in the streets.

"Awareness-raising[8] programmes" are all the rage[9] – we have to celebrate our diversity. But indulging differences can be harmful if it prevents communities from integrating. I believe we should reduce the translation and interpreting services and think about making English compulsory for all citizens.

Zia Haider Rahman in *The Sunday Times*

[7] street famous for its Bangladeshi curry houses; the area has become known as 'Banglatown'
[8] getting people to know and think more about a problem or situation
[9] **all the rage** [reɪdʒ] the latest fashion

2 a) ***The texts:*** *Think of a good headline for each of the three newspaper articles to sum up the content or view expressed. Compare your ideas in class.* →S14, p. 98

b) *Think about the pros and cons for minorities living in their own communities and start a list. Scan the texts for ideas to put on your list. Add your own ideas, too.* →S2, p. 88

3 ***Class debate:*** *Debate and then vote on this statement: "All residents of a country should be forced to learn the language of that country."* →S17, p. 100

4 [group] ***Project/Mediation:*** *Collect and present information you think is important or interesting about minority groups in Germany.* →S19, p. 101

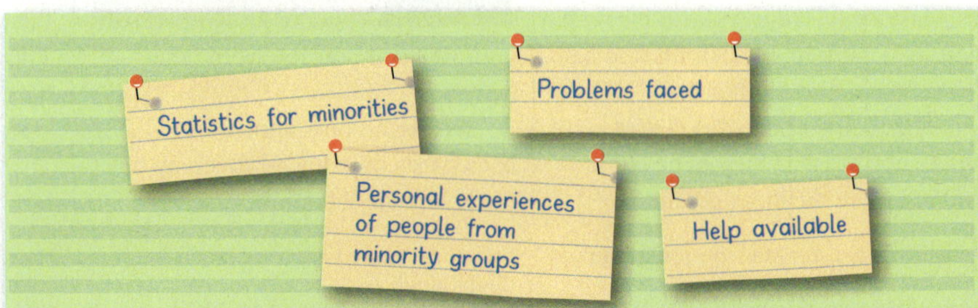

[16] A family drama

This text is an extract from 'The Buddha of Suburbia', a prize-winning novel by Hanif Kureishi[1] about a British Asian teenager growing up in the suburbs of London in the early 1980s.

Jamila[2] had started exercising every day, learning karate and judo, getting up early to stretch and run and do press-ups. She was preparing for the guerrilla war she knew would be necessary when the whites finally turned on the blacks and Asians.

This wasn't as crazy as it sounded. The area in which Jamila lived was closer to London than our suburbs, and much poorer. It was full of neo-fascist groups, and at night they wandered through the streets, beating Asians and throwing stones through their windows. Jamila and her parents, Anwar[3] and Jeeta[4], lived in constant fear of violence.

Anwar didn't like these training sessions of Jamila's. He thought she was meeting boys at these karate classes and long runs through the city. Soon Anwar started to lock himself in the living room with the phone for hours. The rest of the time the phone was locked. Anwar had secretly decided it was time Jamila got married.

Through these calls Anwar's brother in Bombay[5] had found a boy to come and live in London as Jamila's husband. Except that this boy wasn't a boy. He was thirty. As a dowry, he had demanded a warm winter coat, a colour television and the complete works of Conan Doyle[6].

Anwar had told Jamila what he'd decided; she should marry the Indian and he would come over, put on his winter coat and live happily ever after with his wife.

Then Anwar would rent a flat nearby for them. "Big enough for two children," he said to Jamila. He took her hand and added, "Soon you'll be very happy." Her mother said, "We're both very glad for you, Jamila."

Not surprisingly for someone with Jamila's feminist beliefs, she wasn't too pleased.

"What did you say to him?" I asked her.

"Creamy[7], I'd have walked out there and then. I'd have got the Council to take me into care. Anything. I'd have lived with friends. I'd have run away from home. Except for my mother. He takes it out on Jeeta. He abuses her."

"Hits her? Really?"

"He used to, yes, until I told him I'd cut off his hair with a kitchen knife if he did it again. But he knows how to make her life terrible without physical violence. He's had many years of practice."

"Well," I said, "in the end he can't make you do anything you don't want to do."

She turned on me. "But he can! You know my father well, but not that well. There's something I haven't told you. Come with me. Come on, Karim," she insisted.

We went back to their shop, where she quickly made me a kebab and chapati, this time with onions and green chillis.

"Bring it upstairs, will you, Karim?" she said.

Her mother called through to us from the till. "No, Jamila, don't take him up there!" And she banged down a bottle of milk and frightened a customer.

"What's wrong, Auntie Jeeta?" I asked. She was going to cry.

"Come on," Jamila said. She dragged me upstairs, her mother shouting after her. "Jamila, Jamila!"

By now I wanted to go home; I'd had enough of family dramas.

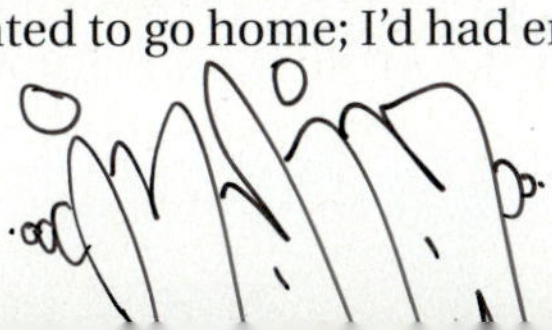

VIP FILE

Hanif Kureishi
- born 1954
- mother English, father Pakistani
- many plays, films and novels about multi-ethnic Britain

GRAMMAR
Past habits
'He used to, ...' (line 32) →G3, p.116

GRAMMAR
Modals
'Bring it upstairs, will you, ...?' (line 41) →G9, p.118

[1] **Hanif Kureishi** [hæˌniːf kʊˈreɪʃi]
[2] **Jamila** [dʒæˈmiːlə]
[3] **Anwar** [ˈʌnwɑː]
[4] **Jeeta** [ˈdʒiːtə]
[5] city in India, now called Mumbai
[6] British author (1859–1930), inventor of Sherlock Holmes
[7] another name for Karim, the narrator

Half-way upstairs I noticed a bad smell. Their flat was always a junk shop, with old furniture and fingerprints all over the doors and the wallpaper about a hundred years old and cigarette butts everywhere, but it never stank, except of Jeeta's wonderful cooking, which went on permanently in big burnt pans.

Anwar was sitting on a bed in the living room, which wasn't his normal bed in its normal place. He was wearing a dirty-looking pyjama jacket, and I noticed that his toenails looked like cashew nuts. He was unshaven, and thinner than I'd ever seen him. His lips were dry and flaking. His skin looked yellow and his eyes were sunken. Anwar was staring at my steaming kebab as though it were a torture instrument. I chewed quickly to get rid of it.

"Why didn't you tell me he's sick?" I whispered to Jeeta.

But I wasn't convinced he was simply sick, because of the anger in his face. Jamila was glaring at her father, but he wouldn't meet her eyes, nor mine after I'd walked in. He stared straight in front of him as he always did at the television screen, except that it wasn't on.

"He's not ill," she said.

"No?" I said, and then, to him, "Hallo, Uncle Anwar. How are you?"

His voice was changed: it was weak now. "Take that damn kebab out of my nose," he said. "And take that damn girl with you."

Jamila touched my arm. "Watch." She sat down on the edge of the bed and leaned towards him.

"Please, please stop all this."

"Get lost!" he shouted at her. "You're not my daughter. I don't know who you are."

"Please stop it, for all of us! Here, Karim who loves you –"

"Yes, yes!" I said.

"He's brought you a lovely tasty kebab!"

"Why is he eating it himself, then?" Anwar said, reasonably. She snatched the kebab from me and waved it in front of her father. Bits of meat and chilli and onion fell out of my poor kebab and onto the bed. Anwar ignored it.

"What's going on here?" I asked her.

"Look at him, Karim, he hasn't eaten or drunk anything for eight days! He'll die, Karim, won't he, if he doesn't eat anything!"

"Yes, you'll die, if you don't eat your food like everyone else."

"I won't eat. I will die. If Gandhi could shove out the English from India by not eating, I can get my family to obey me the same way."

"What do you want her to do?"

"To marry the boy I have chosen with my brother."

"But it's old-fashioned, Uncle, out of date," I explained. "No one does that kind of thing now. They just marry the person they like, if they bother to get married at all."

"That is not our way, boy. She must do what I say or I will die. She will kill me."

Jamila started to punch the bed. "It's so stupid! What a waste of time and life!"

Anwar was unmoved. I'd always liked him because he was so relaxed about everything, not like my parents. Now he was making a big fuss about a marriage and I couldn't understand it. I know it made me sad to see him do this to himself.

Jamila came outside while I unlocked my bike.

"What are you going to do, Jammie?"

"I don't know. What do you suggest?"

GRAMMAR

Conditionals
'If Gandhi could shove out the English …, I can get my family to obey me' (line 81)
→G4, p.117

VIP FILE

Mahatma Gandhi (1869–1948)
helped to end British rule in India through non-violent protest, including hunger strike

"I don't know either."

"No."

"But I'll think about it," I said. "I promise I'll come up with something."

"Thanks."

She started to cry openly, not covering her face or trying to stop. Usually I get embarrassed when girls cry. Sometimes I feel like hitting them for making a fuss. But Jamila really was in trouble. We must have stood there outside Paradise Stores[5] for at least half an hour, just holding each other and thinking about our futures.

[5] name of the shop run by Jamila's parents

Karim and his cousin Jamila

Karim and his parents (scenes from the TV version of *The Buddha of Suburbia*)

5 ***First reaction:*** *Which of the characters do you sympathize with most, and why?* →S5, p. 91

6 ***Reasons for the drama:*** *Explain the problem between Anwar and Jamila. Why do you think they behave the way they do?*

7 ***A step further:*** *Think about the relationship between the different characters and discuss ways in which the story might go on. Then do one of the following writing tasks:*

1. *A summary of the next chapter. If you like, you can invent more characters.*
2. *A letter from Jamila to one of her parents, or to both.* →S12, p. 96
3. *A dialogue between Jamila and Karim in which they discuss what to do.*

8 [ ] ***Film project:*** →S20, p. 102

a) *There are a number of films about the lives of British Asians ('East is East', 'Bend it like Beckham', the TV version of 'The Buddha of Suburbia', etc.). Choose one for your group, watch the DVD and find a scene that shows an important conflict between characters. Then present this scene to the class.*

b) ***Class discussion:*** *Compare the different scenes presented.* →S16, p. 100

[18] ⟨Half-caste⟩

VIP FILE

John Agard[1]
- born in Guyana 1949
- moved to England 1977
- writes and performs poetry celebrating Caribbean culture
- work sometimes also satirical

[1] **John Agard** [ˌdʒɒn ˈeɪgɑːd]
[2] **Pablo Picasso** (1881–1973) Spanish painter
[3] expression of anger
[4] **Peter Tchaikovsky** (1840–1893) Russian composer

Excuse me standing on one leg
I'm half-caste
Explain yuself
wha yu mean
when yu say half-caste
yu mean when picasso[2]
mix red an green
is a half-caste canvas/
explain yuself
wha yu mean
when yu say half-caste
yu mean when light an shadow
mix in de sky
is a half-caste weather/
well in dat case england weather
nearly always half-caste
in fact some o dem cloud
half-caste till dem overcast
so spiteful dem don't want de sun
to pass
ah rass[3]/
explain yuself
wha yu mean
when yu say half-caste
yu mean tchaikovsky[4]
sit down at dah piano
an mix a black key wid a white key
is a half-caste symphony/
Explain yuself
wha yu mean
Ah listening to yu wid de keen
half of mih ear
Ah looking at yu wid de keen
half of mih eye
an when I'm introduced to yu
I'm sure you'll understand
why I offer yu half-a-hand
an when I sleep at night
I close half-a-eye
consequently when I dream
I dream half-a-dream
an when moon begin to glow
I half-caste human being
cast half-a-shadow
but yu must come back tomorrow
wid de whole of yu eye
an de whole of yu ear
an de whole of yu mind
an I will tell yu
de other half
of my story

John Agard

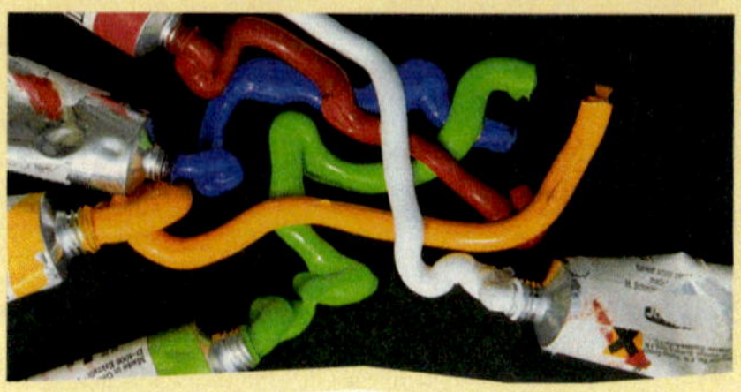

9 a) *Comment on the sound of the poem.* → S21, p.104
b) *What words show that the poem is written in Caribbean dialect? What would these words be in normal English?*

10 a) *In your own words, sum up the feelings of the speaker in the poem about the expression 'half-caste'.*
b) *What images, words and phrases does he use to get these feelings across and what is their effect?*

11 *Comment on the last seven lines of the poem. How does the focus change? What effect does this have?*

12 ***Creative tasks:*** *Choose one of the following, using ideas from the poem.*
a) *Draw a picture and present it to the class.*
b) [pair work] *Write a dialogue and perform it with your partner.*
c) *Tell the 'other half of the story'.*

FACT FILE

Caribbean English
- dialect of English influenced by African languages
- colonial background (slaves brought from Africa to work on sugar plantations)
- spoken with a 'sing-song' accent
- some sounds pronounced differently, e.g. 'th' = 'd'

Multi-ethnic Britain

Formula 1 racing driver Lewis Hamilton

Two British Asian women

Queen Elizabeth II visits the Islamic Centre in Scunthorpe

A lesson in English literature

Waiting for the Queen to arrive

Actress Parminder Nagra[1]

13 *Choose one of these pictures of people in Britain and do one task:* →S23, p.105

a) *Prepare an oral comment. (Explain what the picture shows, why you have chosen it, what it says about minorities in Britain, etc.)* →S18, p.101

b) [👥] *Work with a partner. Write a dialogue to go with the picture and perform it in class.* →S15, p.99

c) *Do some research on one of the celebrities in these pictures and write a profile of him/her.*

[1] **Parminder Nagra** [pɑːˌmɪndə ˈnɑːgrɑː]

Topic 3 Schooldays

A The question of what to wear

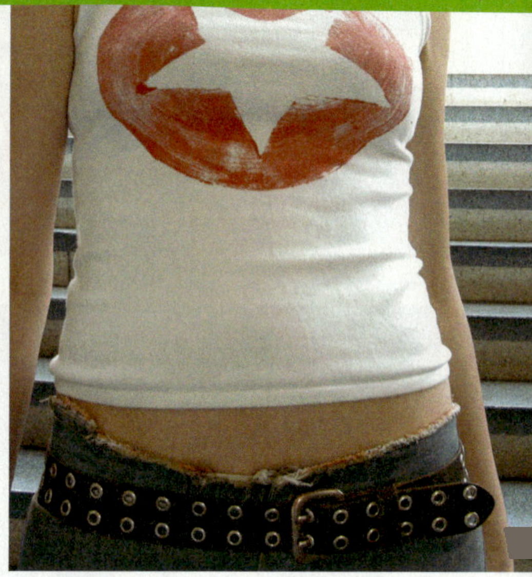

1 a) *Your opinion: Describe the way the students in the pictures are dressed. Do you think they are dressed appropriately for school?* →S23, p.105

b) [👥] *Now read the text below and discuss your reactions with your partner.*

Houston[1] County schools dress code policy (grades 6–12)

Students of the Houston County School System are expected to dress in a manner that is supportive of a positive learning environment that is free of distractions and disruptions. There is a direct connection between student dress and student behavior. Students are expected to observe styles of dress, hair, and personal grooming, which support the learning environment.

General Rules

Outer clothing which resembles pajamas, or underwear is prohibited. Styles in dress which differ extremely from conventionally accepted standards are prohibited. Any clothing that is viewed as distracting because of extremes in style, etc., shall not be permitted. Underwear may not be exposed at any time.

Specific Rules

Blouses / shirts should be constructed so that the top of the shoulder is covered (no spaghetti straps, etc.). Blouses / shirts which expose any part of the waist, hips, or midriff (or which are low-cut or see-through) are not allowed. Clothing which is cut, or has holes, is prohibited. Clothing shall be free of inappropriate writing, advertisement, or artwork. This includes offensive words and designs, violence, sex, hate groups, tobacco products, drugs, and alcohol. No clothing may be worn which may suggest membership in a gang at school. Pants, skirts, and dresses must be knee-length or longer. Shirts must be tucked in.

Shoes must be worn at all times. Male students may not wear earrings; female students may wear earrings. Neither male nor female students may wear ornaments (jewelry) which pierce the skin such as the nose, lips, tongue, etc. Students may not wear hats, caps, sunglasses, etc., inside the building.

Hair must be well groomed. Only conventional hair coloring will be permitted. Extreme hairstyles are prohibited. Well-groomed mustaches are permitted; beards are prohibited.

[1] **Houston** ['hju:stn]

Going to court over school dress code rules

Strict dress codes are common in US schools. Cases in which students protest against school rules (or feel the rules are interpreted unfairly) often end up in court. Here are just a few examples:

Case A A school in Texas prohibited students from wearing gang-related clothing as gangs were likely to cause a disruption to school activities. When local police officers identified rosaries as 'gang-related', the school decided to prohibit the wearing of rosaries as necklaces. Some students took the school to court, saying the school's new rule violated their First Amendment rights.

Case B Students in Massachusetts took their school to court to challenge its school dress code. The school had prohibited a student from wearing a T-shirt with the slogan 'Co-Ed Naked Band: Do It To The Rhythm'. This was considered inappropriate language and therefore a disruption to the school's basic educational message.

Case C A school in Indiana was challenged on its rule that earrings could only be worn by female students. The school argued that the wearing of earrings by males didn't follow 'community standards in the area'. It said the earring ban discouraged rebelliousness and served to prevent 'disrespect for authority and disrespect for discipline within the school'.

FACT FILE

The First Amendment
Part of the Constitution which guarantees US citizens certain rights such as 'free exercise of religion' and 'freedom of speech'.

2 *What did the court decide? Discuss each of the court cases. Who do you think is right? How do you think the case ended?* →S16, p.100

3 *Role play: Choose one of the young people in the photos on page 40 and act out a dialogue with your partner. One of you plays the student and the other plays a teacher who is not happy with the way the student is dressed.* →S15, p.99

WORD BANK

inappropiate dress • offensive message • bare midriff • prohibited/not permitted/banned • to show disrespect for authority • rebelliousness • self-expression • rights • freedom of speech

B Teachers and pupils

1 *Use a dictionary to prepare the text before you deal with it in class.* →S9/10, p. 94/95

[19] The sheep

In this extract from 'Teacher Man' by Frank McCourt, the author looks back at the start of his teaching career in New York in March 1958.

My life saved my life. On my second day at McKee[1] a boy asks a question that sends me into the past and colors the way I teach for the next thirty years. I am nudged into the past, the materials of my life.

Joey Santos calls out, Yo, teach …

You are not to call out. You are to raise your hand.

Yeah, yeah, said Joey, but …

They have a way of saying yeah yeah that tells you they're barely tolerating you. In the yeah yeah they're saying, We're trying to be patient, man, giving you a break because you're just a new teacher.

Joey raises his hand. Yo, teacher man …

Call me Mr. McCourt.

Yeah. OK. So, you Scotch[2] or somethin'?

Joey is the mouth. There's one in every class along with the complainer, the clown, the goody-goody, the beauty queen, the volunteer for everything, the jock, the intellectual, the momma's boy, the critic, the jerk, the religious fanatic who sees sin everywhere, the brooding one who sits in the back staring at the desk, the happy one, the saint who finds good in all creatures. It's the job of the mouth to ask questions, anything to keep the teacher from the boring lesson. I may be a new teacher but I'm on to Joey's delaying game. It's universal. I played the same game in Ireland. I was the mouth in my class in Leamy's National School. The master would write an algebra question or an Irish conjugation on the board and the boys would hiss, Ask him a question, McCourt. Get him away from the bloody lesson. Go on, go on.

I'd say, Sir, did they have algebra in olden times in Ireland?

Mr. O'Halloran[3] liked me, good boy, neat handwriting, always polite and obedient. He would put the chalk down, and you could see how happy he was to escape from algebra and Irish syntax. He'd say, Boys, you have every right to be proud of your ancestors. Long before the Greeks, even the Egyptians, your forefathers in this lovely land could capture the rays of the sun in the heart of winter and direct them to dark inner chambers for a few golden moments. They knew the ways of the heavenly bodies and that took them beyond algebra, beyond calculus, beyond, boys, oh, beyond beyond.

Sometimes, in the warm days of spring, he dozed off in his chair and we sat quietly, forty of us, waiting for him to wake, not even daring to leave the room if he slept past going-home time.

No. I'm not Scotch. I'm Irish.

Joey looks sincere. Oh, yeah? What's Irish? Like St. Patrick[4], right?

Well, no, not exactly. This leads to the telling of the story of St. Patrick, which keeps us away from the b-o-r-i-n-g English lesson, which leads to other questions.

Hey, mister. Everyone talk English over there in Ireland?

You all Catlics[5] in Ireland?

Don't let them take over the classroom. Stand up to them. Show them who's in charge. Be firm or be dead. Take no shit. Tell them, Open your notebooks.

VIP FILE

Frank McCourt
- Irish-American author
- born 1930 in New York
- grew up in Ireland
- returned to the USA at the age of 19
- taught in New York for 30 years
- his first novel 'Angela's Ashes' (1996) became a bestseller

GRAMMAR
Obligation
'You are not to call out.' (line 5) →G5, p. 118

GRAMMAR
Past habits
'The master would write …' (line 21) →G3, p. 116

[1] McKee High School, New York City
[2] = Scottish ('Scotch' normally means 'Scotch whisky')
[3] **O'Halloran** [əʊ'hælrən]
[4] **St. Patrick** (c. 398–461), born in Roman Britain; went to Ireland as a missionary. St. Patrick's Day (March 17) is still celebrated, especially in the USA
[5] Catholics (spoken with a New York accent)

Time for the spelling list.

Aw, teacher, aw, Gawd, aw man. Spelling. Spelling. Spelling. Do we haveta? They moan, B-o-r-i-n-g spelling list. They bury their faces in their folded arms. They beg for the pass[6]. Gotta go. Gotta go. Man, we thought you were a nice guy, young and all. Why do all these English teachers have to do the same old thing? Can't you tell us more about Ireland?

Yo, teacher man … Joey again. Mouth to the rescue.

Joey, I told you my name is Mr. McCourt, Mr. McCourt, Mr. McCourt.

Yeah, yeah. So, mister, did you go out with girls in Ireland?

No, dammit. Sheep. We went out with sheep. What do you think we went out with?

The class explodes. They laugh, elbow one another, pretend to fall out of their desks. This teacher. Crazy, man. Talks funny. Goes out with sheep. Lock up your sheep.

Excuse me. Open your notebooks, please. We have a spelling list to cover.

Hysterics. Will sheep be on the list? Oh, man.

That smart-ass response was a mistake. There will be trouble. The goody-goody, the saint and the critic will surely report me: Oh, Mom, oh, Dad, oh, Mr. Principal, guess what teacher said in class today. Bad things about sheep.

I'm not prepared, trained or ready for this. It's not teaching. It has nothing to do with English literature, grammar, writing. When will I be strong enough to walk into the room, get their immediate attention and teach? Around this school there are quiet industrious classes where teachers are in command. In the cafeteria older teachers tell me, Yeah, it takes at least five years.

Next day the principal sends for me. He sits behind his desk, talking into the telephone, smoking a cigarette. He keeps saying, I'm sorry. It won't happen again. I'll speak to the person involved. New teacher, I'm afraid.

He puts the phone down. Sheep. What is this about sheep?

Sheep?

I dunno[7] what I'm gonna do with you. There's a complaint you said "dammit" in class. I know you're just off the boat from an agricultural country and don't know the ropes, but you should have some common sense.

No, sir. Not off the boat. I've been here eight and a half years, including my two years in the army, not counting years of infancy in Brooklyn[8].

Well, look. Damn phone ringing off the hook. Parents up in arms. I have to cover my ass. Why the hell did you have to tell these kids about the sheep?

I'm sorry. They kept asking me questions, and I was exasperated. They were only trying to keep me away from the spelling list.

That's it?

I thought the sheep thing was a bit funny at the time.

Oh, yeah, indeed. You standing there advocating bestiality. Thirteen parents are demanding you be fired. There are righteous people on Staten Island[9].

I was only joking.

No, young man. No jokes here. There's a time and place. When you say something in class they take you seriously. You're the teacher. You say you went out with sheep and they're going to swallow every word. They don't know the mating habits of the Irish.

I'm sorry.

This time I'll let it go. I'll tell the parents you're just an Irish immigrant off the boat.

GRAMMAR
Subjunctive
'… you be fired.' (line 86)
→G15, p.125

[6] In US schools students who need to leave the classroom for any reason have to ask for a 'pass', which gives them official permission
[7] **dunno** = don't know
[8] part of New York City where the author was born
[9] part of New York City

FACT FILE
If you use **irony,** you say one thing but actually mean the opposite, sometimes as a joke: "That was a clever thing to do," she said with irony when I told her I'd forgotten my keys.

1 *Characters: Examine the relationships between the different characters in the text (teacher, pupils, principal, parents).* →S5, p. 91

2 *Point of view: How does the point of view chosen by the author affect the reader's feelings?* →S6, p. 92

3 *Language and style: Analyse the way the text is written, looking at the author's use of narrative and dialogue, formal and informal language, tenses, punctuation, etc. Then comment on their effect on the reader.* →S7, p. 93

4 *Creative tasks:*
a) [pair work] ***Role play:*** *Prepare a phone call between a parent and the principal, then act it out.* →S15, p. 99
b) *Draw a picture of one or more of the pupils in Frank McCourt's class.*

5 *Your opinion:*
a) *What do you think of Frank McCourt's 'mistake' and the way he deals with the lesson?*
b) *Should irony ever be used in the classroom?*
c) *How much influence should parents have on what goes on in schools?*

[21] ⟨How dare you?⟩

This is an extract from 'Who is Jesse[2] Flood?' by Malachy Doyle. The main character and narrator is a British schoolboy who is often in trouble with his headmaster, Mr Frost.

Typical. First day I go to school in ages, and Frostbite decides to clamp down on school uniform. You'd think he'd be glad to see me. Clap his arm around my shoulder and say, "Young Jesse Flood, it's great to have you back!"
But oh no! It's make-an-example day. Let-them-know-who's-in-charge day. Petty bloody officiousness, that's all it is. I mean, is it any wonder I've given up on all this crap?

"OUT! OUT OUT!"

Everyone who's wearing jeans, the wrong top, jewellery, Docs[3], dyed hair, anyone with the slightest ounce of individuality. Anyone with half a brain, basically. Anyone who dares to think for themselves, who can't bear to act like a complete robot for thirteen years while they pack your head full of stuff that's no use for nothing. Only so you can pass the odd exam to make their precious statistics look halfway good by the time you leave, and then they dump you in some mindless job, or on the scrapheap, like Dad.

So there we are in the corridor while Frostbite, the bloodless professor, is in the next-door classroom, turfing out half of that lot as well. People are unscrewing their nose studs, spitting on tissues to wash off their make-up, desperately composing their lies.

"I'm sorry, sir. My mum put it in the wash."

"Terribly sorry, sir. My younger brother took mine by mistake."

"I've an appointment at the hairdresser this very afternoon!"

And then Frostbite reaches me. And I'm so sick of all their sucking-up. So sick of him, even more, that something happens. Something weird. The words I'm thinking, the thoughts that usually stay deep in my subconscious, the sort of things I wouldn't ever even dream of actually saying, certainly not to Frostbite, rise up and out and into the air.

VIP FILE

Malachy Doyle[1]
- born 1954 in Northern Ireland
- author of children's and young adult literature
- lives in Wales

FACT FILE
According to their success rate in exams (e.g. at A Level) schools in Britain are placed in higher or lower positions in a national League Table. Parents naturally want to send their children to schools that are high up in the league.

[1] **Malachy Doyle** [ˌmæləki ˈdɔɪl]
[2] **Jesse** [ˈdʒesi]
[3] kind of boot

"Well, to tell you the truth," I find myself saying, looking him straight between the eyes. "I hadn't actually planned to come in today. I was going to spend it in the Town Library …" I carry on, ignoring the looks of horror on the faces of my classmates, some of whom had been in exactly the same situation but had no intention of saying so, "… but it was closed so I thought I might as well come up here and see what was happening."

Gasps from all around, Frostbite goes puce.

"I BEG your pardon?"

Help! I'm having some sort of emotional freak-out, right here and now, in front of everyone. But now I've started I can't seem to stop.

"As I said, sir, I wasn't coming in, I was planning to do some revision in the Town Library for my upcoming examinations, you know, but …"

It's true. The past few weeks they've only been going over the same old stuff in class, for the ones who didn't listen the first time. It's boring, so I've taken to spending my time down in the library, where they've got lots of little quiet spaces where you can get on with your work without any interference. I can get much more done there than I would in school, so what's he got to moan about?

But then Frostbite explodes. "This is insolence, boy! How DARE you? How DARE you talk to me like that! How DARE you come in here dressed like a tramp and then tell me that you had no intention to set foot in my school in the first place? How DARE you tell me that you consider the Town Library a more suitable educational establishment for fulfilling your puny academic aspirations!"

"Take it easy, sir," I say, trying to calm him down.

"TAKE IT EASY!" he yells, parroting me. "Where on earth do you children get such revolting phraseology? If you'd only spend more time at your studies, as I'm forever trying to drum into you, and less time watching cheap television, you wouldn't be coming out with all these inane mid-Atlantic clichés[4]. You wouldn't be losing all respect for authority. You …"

He's back on his favourite hobby-horse, but then he remembers me.

"And you, Jesse Flood! Just look at you! Your shoes are FILTHY!" he yells. He's got a point there, too. "There isn't a suspicion of school uniform anywhere on your disgusting body …"

"Steady on," I say. "I mean, there's no need to get personal."

Horrified sniggers up and down the line.

I don't quite know what's going on here, as a matter of fact. I was always as terrified of this guy as the next wimp. In fact, probably even more so. He'd come into class, whenever one of the teachers failed to turn up, and a deathly hush would descend on the place. Heads down, avoid eye contact, don't get singled out.

But somehow, somewhere, something changed. It's not as if I ever had any respect for him – he never did anything to earn it – but there was certainly fear. Fear of his power, his anger, his capacity to humiliate you, to make you feel worthless, to serve it up double by getting in touch with your parents and trying to get them to do the same. But all that's gone now. I don't know why but something's changed inside me, and I won't put up with all this crap any more.

"Look," I hear myself saying. It's like I'm standing outside myself, watching. "You've got it all wrong, here," I carry on. "If I was in your position, I'd much rather be told the truth, however unpleasant, than a pack of lies. If I had any influence, I'd want to use it to help people to think for themselves, instead of

[4] Mr Frost dislikes his pupils using 'fashionable' American expressions. →S30, p.111

GRAMMAR
Conditional sentences
'If you'd only spend …' (line 53) →G4, p.117

GRAMMAR
Inversion
'Not only have I …' (line 80) →G16, p.125

just turning them into mindless morons who only tell me what I want to hear rather than what they really believe …"

Now I've really gone and done it. Not only have I made inevitable my immediate expulsion, but by drawing his attention to the highly dubious nature of everyone else's excuses, I've alienated myself from just about everybody else in my year.

But I mean, it's sickening, all those fairy tales about little brothers and washing machines, all that crawling. Why can't they just come out with the truth, like me, and make old Frostbite face up to the fact that it's ridiculous in this day and age trying to force young adults into uniform, trying to force us to all look the same, think the same. Those days are over, mate. Look at America. Look at France, Australia, Germany. I mean, why does this stupid country always lag decades behind anywhere with any respect for the rights of young people? It's stupid, stupid, stupid!

6 *Analyse the way Jesse and Frostbite are characterized. Do you think they are realistic characters?* →S5, p.91

7 *Explain how the conflict between pupil and headmaster develops.*

8 *How appropriate is the language that they use?*

9 *Do you agree with Jesse? Comment on* a) *his reasons for missing school* b) *his honesty* c) *what he has to criticize about the school system.* →S13, p.97

10 *Compare this text with the text by Frank McCourt. Think of content, point of view and style. Say which text you prefer.* →S3, p.89

Two cartoons

History repeats itself. Which may explain why it's so boring.

"I can't wait to put this on my blog!"

11 *First look at the cartoons and make sure you understand them.* →S24, p.106
These questions may help you:
Cartoon 1: When is the phrase 'history repeats itself' normally used?
Cartoon 2: What does the letter F stand for? Why can't the student wait to put this on his blog?
Then say which of the two cartoons you prefer, and why.

[23] Geography lesson

Our teacher told us one day he would leave the school
And sail across a warm blue sea
To places he had only known from maps,
And all his life had longed to be.

The house he lived in was narrow and grey
But in his mind's eye he could see
Sweet-scented jasmine clambering up the walls,
And green leaves burning on an orange tree.

He spoke of the lands he longed to visit,
Where it was never drab or cold.
And I couldn't understand why he never left,
And shook off our school's stranglehold.

Then halfway through his final term
He took ill and he never returned.
And he never got to that place on the map
Where the green leaves of the orange trees burned.

The maps were pulled down from the classroom wall;
His name was forgotten, it faded away.
But a lesson he never knew he taught
Is with me to this day.

I travel to where the green leaves burn,
To where the ocean's glass-clear and blue,
To all those places my teacher taught me to love –
But which he never knew.

Brian Patten

12 *First reaction:* *Read the poem aloud, then listen to the recording, which you will hear being read by the poet himself. What are your first impressions?*

13 *Form and function:*

a) *Look for words and phrases in the poem which have to do with 'school', 'nature' and 'freedom'. What feelings do they express?*

b) *Examine the poem's imagery (pictures, colours, smells, sounds) and discuss its effect.*

c) *How important do you think rhythm and rhyme are in this poem?*

14 *Interpreting the poem:* →S21, p.104

a) *Discuss the teacher in the poem and the life he led. Would you call him a successful teacher?*

b) *Analyse the title of the poem.*

VIP FILE

Brian Patten
- born 1946 in Liverpool
- one of Britain's leading contemporary poets
- frequently performs his works

GRAMMAR

Relative clauses
'To places he had only known from maps' (line 3) →G12, p.121

C Why bother?

Addicted to fame

Celebrity status may be the modern-day addiction but it's schools that often have to pick up the pieces. Take Murat Ucar, a bright 16-year-old from Tottenham, north London, who craves fame as a model or actor or singer – he does not particularly mind which.

The BBC traced his efforts in a documentary called *The Wannabe,* in which we see Murat skip school for two weeks so he can go to Turkey and have a nose job. "A famous person turns up to school when he feels like turning up, not when he's told to," he explains to the camera.

No sooner is he back than he is busy auditioning for *The X-Factor*[1], a modelling agency and a theatre company. The problem is, the professionals say behind his back, he does not have the looks or the talent to match his enormous ambition.

His teachers, meanwhile, are exasperated that his lack of work and attendance – he turns up to one out of a possible 14 RE lessons – are hindering his academic potential.

It is a phenomenon that is mirrored across the UK. More than one in 10 young people would drop education to give fame a shot, according to a Learning and Skills Council survey. Even though the chances of being picked for a Big Brother-type reality show and going on to further fame are 30 million to one – even less likely than winning the lottery – about 16 per cent of teenagers believe they will be "the one".

Most of the 16 to 19-year-old respondents cited money and success as their main motivating factors, but many crave greater recognition and acceptance. More than a quarter of the 777 young people who responded said they saw fame as a way of "proving other people wrong", while 19 per cent said it would "let everyone know who they were". Roughly 9 per cent said fame would "help them to feel accepted", and 7 per cent said it would "make them appear more attractive".

Hannah Frankel in the *TES (Times Educational Supplement)*

[1] a singing talent show on British TV

GRAMMAR
Gerunds
'… when he feels like turning up, …'
(line 7) →G13, p.123

GRAMMAR
Inversion
'No sooner is he back than he is busy auditioning …'
(line 9) →G16, p.125

1 *Looking at the text:*
a) *How does Murat's view of himself compare with the way other people see him?*
b) *Scan the article for words and phrases which show that the author disagrees with Murat's attitude.* →S2, p.88

2 ***Your opinion:*** *Why do you think so many young people think school is less important than TV reality shows? The Word Bank may give you some ideas.*

3 [👥] ***Role play:*** *Prepare a dialogue between Murat and one of his parents or teachers and act it out with your partner.* →S15, p.99

WORD BANK
celebrities • more authority than teachers • success without working hard • money but no qualifications • role models

[01] Money for nothing (Dire Straits)

Now look at them yo-yos[1], that's the way you do it
You play the guitar on the MTV
That ain't workin'[2], that's the way you do it
Money for nothin' and your chicks[3] for free
Now that ain't workin', that's the way you do it
Lemme tell ya[4] them guys ain't dumb
Maybe get a blister on your little finger
Maybe get a blister on your thumb

Chorus: We gotta[5] install microwave ovens
Custom kitchen deliveries
We gotta move these refrigerators
We gotta move these colour TVs

See the little faggot[6] with the earring and the makeup
Yeah, buddy, that's his own hair
That little faggot got[7] his own jet airplane
That little faggot, he's a millionaire

Chorus

I shoulda[8] learned to play the guitar
I shoulda learned to play them drums
Look at that mama, she got it stickin' in the camera[9]
Man, we could have some fun
And he's up there, what's that? Hawaiian noises?
Bangin' on the bongoes like a chimpanzee
That ain't workin', that's the way you do it
Get your money for nothin', get your chicks for free

Chorus

Now that ain't workin', that's the way you do it
You play the guitar on the MTV
That ain't workin', that's the way you do it
Money for nothin' and your chicks for free
Money for nothin' and chicks for free

Words and music: Mark Knopfler/Sting

Informal language: →S30, p.111
[1] **them yo-yos** – those idiots
[2] **ain't workin'** – isn't working
[3] **chicks** – girls
[4] **lemme tell ya** – let me tell you
[5] **we gotta** – we've got to
[6] **faggot** – homosexual
[7] **(he) got** – (he) has got
[8] **I shoulda** – I should have
[9] **she got it stickin' in the camera** – she's showing her body to the camera

4 *The characters: How many different characters play a part in this song?*

5 *The setting: Explain the situation the song describes.*

6 *The point of view: What do we learn about the character who is singing the song (the 'lyrical I') from the language he uses and the views he expresses? Compare the views of the 'lyrical I' with those of the writers of the song.*
→S22, p.104, →S6, p.92

VIP FILE

Dire Straits
British rock band (active 1977–1995) which featured the lead guitar, lead vocals and songwriting of Mark Knopfler.

D School – and how to improve it

⟨The secrets of an inspirational headmistress⟩

GRAMMAR
Participles
'... a large teenager wearing a baseball cap.' (line 1) →G14, p.123

"Chill, man. Don't go there." The speaker is a large teenager wearing a baseball cap. He towers over me – not difficult as I'm only five feet three. I've asked him to pick up a piece of paper he's thrown on the ground. He has no intention of obeying me. As he saunters away, I become aware that someone else is watching me curiously – a tall girl wearing enormous earrings. "Would you like to pick that up?" I ask her. "F*** off, man," she replies. Welcome to St George's.

It's March 2000 and, at the age of 60, I have been asked to take the helm at St George's School in Maida Vale[1] – where head teacher Philip Lawrence was stabbed to death defending his pupils in 1995. Since that tragedy, St George's has descended into chaos. Order and discipline are said to have broken down, with physical attacks on teachers and fights between pupils. The school is now on "special measures", which means it's on the brink of permanent shutdown. I have just four terms to turn it round.

I arrive at St George's a day before the pupils return to school. The playground is a large expanse of tarmac pitted with chewing gum. Inside the school there are few posters or noticeboards. I wonder why my shoes seem to be sticking to the floor and looking down I realize the carpets are matted with chewing gum – ugh!

To help me in my seemingly impossible task, I've brought with me two of the best teachers from my last job: Sean Devlin and Tracey O'Leary. Both are brilliant at dealing with troublesome teenagers. The three of us decide to put up posters at strategic points along the corridors: Welcome Back, Respect Each Other, Walk Don't Run, Talk Don't Shout, Put Rubbish in the Bin. We've had the posters printed with Arabic, Spanish, Portuguese, Farsi[2] and Yoruba[3] translations underneath. More than half the children at St George's speak English only as a second language. Some are refugees who have arrived in Britain unaccompanied, knowing nobody.

We've decided to stagger the children's return, and today we have only Year 11s in, aged 15 and 16. Their response to us is crucial, because it will provide a template for the rest of the school. We walk purposefully into the school hall for our first assembly. They're a wonderful looking bunch of children, some watching me with interest, others making it clear they have better things to do. I move forward and sweep the room with a determined glance. "I'm going to say 'Good morning' to you, and I expect all of you to say 'Good morning, Headmistress' to me." I pause, then boom out: "Good morning, Year 11." The change in decibel level takes them by surprise – some of them actually jump – but it works. "Good morning, Headmistress," they chorus. I tell them that the past is over, and that from now on we will all pull together. After assembly, I am bombarded with questions. "What's this about prefects[4], Miss?" "Will we get badges, Miss?" "Come along now," I say. "Lessons, lessons. You mustn't be late."

GRAMMAR
Gerunds
'... the shock of being physically restrained ...' (line 46) →G13, p.123

One lunchtime in our second week, I hear shouts: "Fight! Fight!" I look out of the window and see a crowd of children swarming towards one corner of the playground. Two big 15-year-olds are in a fight: kicking, swearing, grabbing one another's hair. I rush out and grab one of them by the arm. Sean gets a grip on the other one. They separate easily – the shock of being physically restrained by a 60-year-old grandmother is enough. But the incident reminds me how little there is for the children to do in the playground. I ask one of the

[1] **Maida Vale** a road in northwest London and the area surrounding it
[2] a language spoken mainly in Iran and Afghanistan
[3] a West African language spoken mainly in Nigeria
[4] ['pri:fekts] pupils who are given special responsibilities and authority over others

technicians: "If I give you £200 from the Governors' Fund, would you spend it on the playground?"

I'm always keen to know what the children themselves want, and I put suggestion boxes around the school asking for their ideas. Some of the suggestions are just flippant – "Burn the place down", "More sex education" – but there are heartfelt messages, too: "Get more black teachers", "I'd like bigger dinners", "Can we have football teams?" Touchingly, some are thank-you messages. "I don't have any messages, but if I did, I know you would listen," one child wrote …

The new prefect system is helping with discipline. The older children love being given responsibility and wear their badges with pride. I see them insisting that other children get rid of chewing gum, and even telling them how stupid fighting is …

In no time at all Inspection Day is upon us. The future of the school rests on what the inspectors make of our changes. Nothing makes such a bond as a common enemy, and when the inspectors arrive, the children enter wholeheartedly into the wartime spirit. "I think they enjoyed that, Miss," a Year 9 whispers to me after assembly. "Don't run," I hear the prefects telling everyone. At lunchtime the inspectors wander round talking to the children, who respond in an open and friendly way.

The next day, I meet each year group in the hall to tell them what the inspectors have said. "We knew already," I say, "that St George's was doing well, because we've all been working so hard to improve it. Now the inspectors have told us that they agree. It's official: we're off Special Measures! Three cheers for us. Hip-hip-hooray!" And the roof is almost blown off by the cheers.

From: *Ahead of the Class* by Marie Stubbs

Head teacher Marie Stubbs

1 *Make a list of the problems facing Marie Stubbs when she takes over as head teacher of St George's School and discuss their causes.*

2 *Comment on the changes she and the other two new teachers made and their success in improving the situation.* →S13, p. 97

3 ***Your turn:*** *The above extract from Marie Stubbs's book does not cover all the problems that the school had. Discuss what you would do about:*
• the ugly playground • chewing gum on the carpets • dull paint on the walls inside • children from homes with no books • pupils arriving late for school • fighting in the lunch hour • rubbish dropped everywhere • bullies

Mediation: Visiting a public school

4 *Mediation: Herr and Frau Belz from Dresden would like to send their son Frank to school in England for a while. They are talking to the headmaster of Harrow, a famous public school. Frank's English is much better than his parents', so he does the interpreting. Act out the scene.* →S28, p.108

FACT FILE

Boarding schools: schools where some or all of the pupils 'board', i.e. they live at the school.

Boarding house: a large house, part of a boarding school, in which pupils live. Some schools have 'day houses' for pupils who do not board.

House master: a teacher who is responsible for a 'house'.

Sixth form: the last two years at school ending with the A-Level exam.

Herr Belz:	Frank, bitte frag, wie groß die Schule ist. (Frank: …)
Headmaster:	At Harrow we have 800 pupils. (Frank: …)
Frau Belz:	Und wie viele Schüler sitzen in einer Klasse? (Frank: …)
Headmaster:	Oh, the average class size is fifteen. (Frank: …)
Frau Belz:	Das hört sich gut an! Aber wie alt sind die Schüler, wenn sie hier anfangen? Unser Sohn ist bereits 16. (Frank: …)
Headmaster:	Well, most pupils come to Harrow at 13, but some do join the school in the sixth form when they're 16. (Frank: …)
Herr Belz:	Sie kommen also nur für zwei Jahre. Das geht? (Frank: …)
Headmaster:	Oh yes, many of these come from abroad to do the two-year A-Level course and get a university place. All our pupils are expected to go on to good universities. A lot make it to Oxbridge. (Frank: …)
Herr Belz:	Oxbridge? Nie gehört! Ich kenne aber Oxford. (Frank: …)
Headmaster:	Sorry, I mean Oxford and Cambridge, our two most famous universities. Harrow has a great tradition of sending pupils there. Of course there are lots of other good British universities. (Frank: …)
Frau Belz:	Und wo wohnen die Schüler? (Frank: …)
Headmaster:	Pupils live in one of the eleven boarding houses. There they are under the care of a "house master", who is also a teacher in the school. The house master is the person parents can speak to directly about their sons. (Frank: …)
Herr Belz:	Hmm, „house master" klingt wie unser „Hausmeister", bedeutet aber wohl was anderes. Und schlafen viele Schüler in einem großen Schlafsaal wie bei Harry Potter? (Frank: …)
Headmaster:	No. In the first two years there will be two to four boys together, but after that they have their own room. For sixth formers there's also a television room and a kitchen. (Frank: …)

Frau Belz: Hmm. Unser Sohn wird sich an das Leben in einem Internat gewöhnen müssen. (Frank: …)

Headmaster: I'm sure you'll enjoy it – boarding schools are able to offer small classes, highly motivated teachers who live in the school and a wealth of extra-curricular activities[1], so pupils with interests inside and outside the classroom are the ones who really profit. (Frank: …)

Herr Belz: Was sind die besonderen Stärken von Harrow? (Frank: …)

Headmaster: Well, there's our excellent exam results for a start. But we're also very strong in sport, music, acting and other cultural activities. Basically we're good at keeping teenage boys active, challenged and interested all day. (Frank: …)

Herr Belz: Warum hat Harrow keine Schülerinnen? (Frank: …)

Headmaster: Well, Harrow has always been a boys-only school and we aren't going to change now, especially as single-sex education is becoming popular again. Girls and boys together in the classroom can be a distraction to each other and in many cases this leads to underachievement. (Frank: …)

Frau Belz: Haben Ihre Jungs dann gar keine Gelegenheit, Mädchen zu treffen? (Frank: …)

Headmaster: Oh yes. A lot of activities such as acting, music and debating are run jointly with girls' schools. And in addition there are parties organized with girls' schools most Saturdays of the year. (Frank: …)

[1] after-school activities

5 ***What makes a good school?***

a) *Think about the advantages and disadvantages of boarding schools. Would you like to go to one? Say why or why not.*

(b)) *How does your own school compare to St George's and Harrow? Make a list of problems you feel need to be dealt with at your school. Discuss possible solutions.*

6 ***Writing:*** *Write an argumentative essay on one of the following topics.* →S13, p.97

1. *Many of the things that are learnt at school are useless in later life.*
2. *Of all the ways in which school could be improved, separating boys and girls is the least important.*
3. *You can learn more by doing your own research than by attending lessons.*

Just for fun

E Education in the US and the UK

Map of the US education system

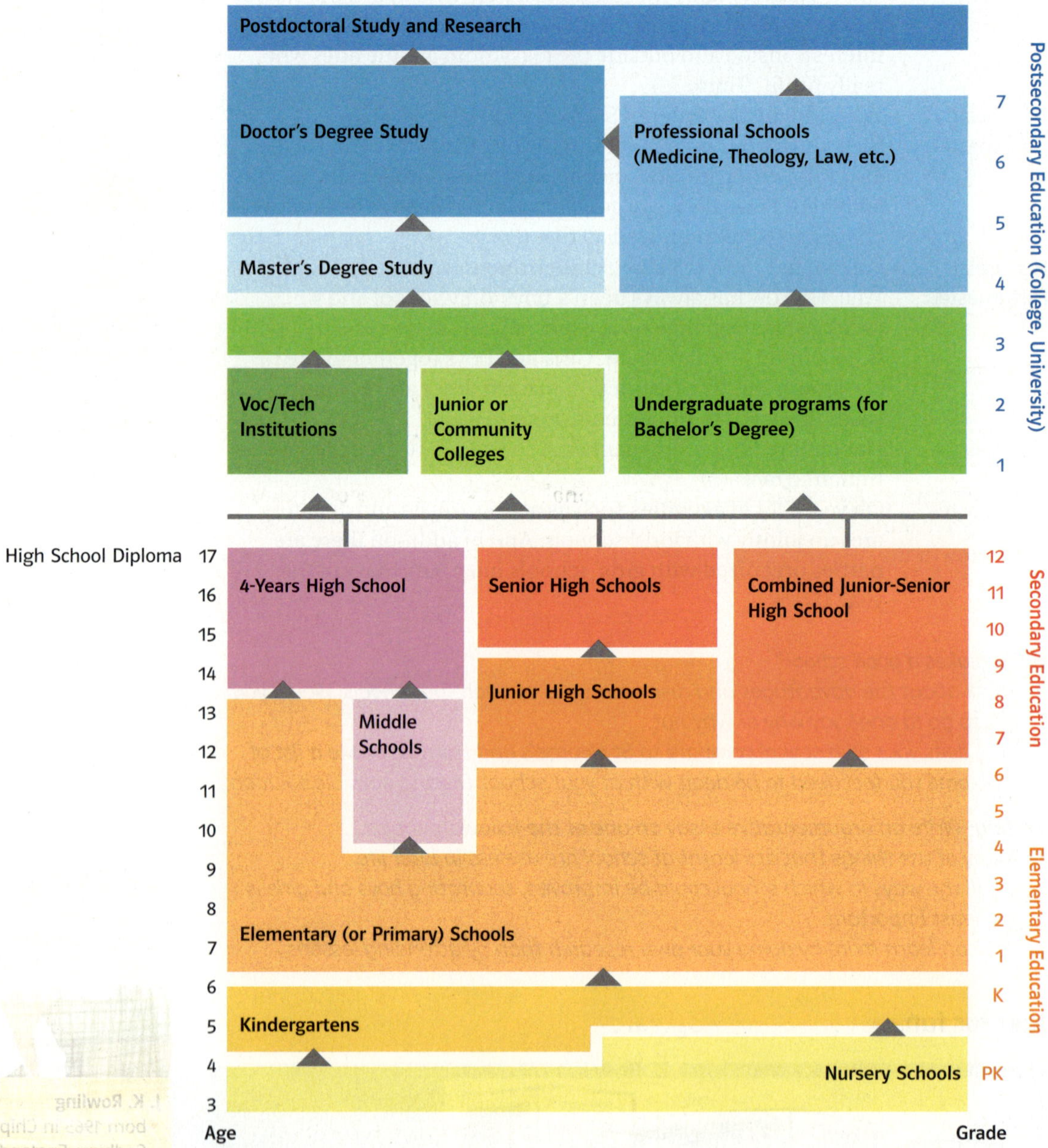

1 ***Understanding the diagram:*** *Use the information given in the diagram to answer the following questions.* →S29, p. 110

1. *John is 11, and is at Middle School. How old was he when he left his Elementary School? How old will he be when he starts High School?*
2. *What is the difference between Junior and Senior High School?*
3. *Marie is 16 and wants to be a doctor. What school is she at now? How will her education continue?*
4. *Sam, 17, has just started as an undergraduate at an American university. How many years will it take him to get his Bachelor[1]'s Degree?*

[1] **Bachelor** ['bætʃlə]

The UK education system

Children in the UK start primary school when they are five, usually after two years of nursery school. At age 11 they go on to secondary school. There are a few state grammar schools, but most pupils attend comprehensive schools. The first year classes at these schools are of mixed-ability, but after that they are usually divided into different groups for lessons in academic subjects. Some of these comprehensives are 'independent specialist schools', which put special emphasis on certain subjects like sports or IT and attract pupils who are particularly interested in this subject.

The National Curriculum has four 'key stages':

Key stage 1:	Key stage 2:	Key stage 3:	Key stage 4:
up to age 7	age 7–11	age 11–14	age 14–16
(Years 1/2)	(Years 3–6)	(Years 7–9)	(Years 10/11)

At the end of each key stage pupils are assessed by National Curriculum tests. The assessment at the end of Key stage 4 is called the GCSE (General Certificate of Secondary Education), a series of tests in different subjects. After taking GCSEs, pupils have a choice. They can leave school and look for a job. They can continue their education at vocational or technical colleges. Or they can stay at school in the sixth form and prepare for the AS-Level examinations at the end of the first year. If they want to go to a British university they must stay in the sixth form for two years and take A-Level examinations.

Most undergraduate courses at university take three years to complete and result in a Bachelor's Degree. Those who stay on for a fourth year as postgraduate students take a Master's Degree, in which they specialize in a certain area of study. A Doctor's Degree, also known as a PhD, can take another two or three years.

FACT FILE

UK:
- **Private schools** are fee-paying schools and are not run by the state. Many are **boarding schools.** They include the famous **public schools** (Eton, Harrow, etc.), which have a high academic standard. Over 7% of British pupils go to private schools.

US:
- **Private schools** are also popular in America.
- State schools in the US are known as **public schools.**

2 *Make a diagram: Take suitable information from the text to make a diagram explaining the British education system. Use the diagram on the opposite page as an example. Include as many facts as you can.*

3 *Different systems: Compare the US and UK systems with each other and with the one you know in Germany.*

The beginning of term at Hogwarts

Hogwarts, the wizarding school in J. K. Rowling's internationally successful *Harry Potter* novels, is modelled on the traditional British public school, with additional elements of magic. The following extract from *Harry Potter and the Goblet of Fire* is set at the beginning of the new school year, when everyone meets for dinner in the Great Hall.

4 [14] *Listening: An impressive appearance* →S1, p. 88
Look at these statements. Then listen and correct what is wrong.
1. *Professor Dumbledore is making an announcement when Mr Filch comes in.*
2. *He reads out the full list of things that must be brought to school by everyone.*
3. *Dumbledore is pleased to say that there will be no Quidditch Cup this year.*
4. *Professor Moody comes in quietly and sits down on Hagrid's right-hand side.*
5. *Moody has small blue eyes and a very ugly face.*
6. *The whole school gives Moody a warm welcome.*

VIP FILE

J. K. Rowling
- born 1965 in Chipping Sodbury, England
- started writing when she was a single mother on welfare
- lives in Scotland
- one of the wealthiest women in the world
- her *Harry Potter* novels have sold hundreds of millions of copies and been translated into more than 60 languages

Topic 4 South Africa

A The Rainbow Nation

See the best of South Africa

They call South Africa the Rainbow Nation. It's a kaleidoscope of colours, cultures and traditions; a land of great deserts, thundering oceans and golden bushveld with thousands of plant and animal species. Visit the Kruger and Hluhluwe/Umfolozi National Parks for the full safari experience. Trek through the dramatic mountain scenery of the Drakensberg. Take a walk on the wild side along the Wild Coast. Discover fascinating Cape Town, and look out across Table Bay from perhaps the most famous mountain in Africa. Become a connoisseur of wine in the famous winelands. South Africa is not called a world in one country for nothing!

Economy

South Africa is the wealthiest and fastest growing African country, with abundant natural resources and a highly developed infrastructure. It is a leading exporter of minerals and has very strong financial and manufacturing sectors. While tourism is a rapidly expanding industry and a key source of foreign exchange, most of the profits are made by international travel businesses rather than local communities. And in spite of the country's growth many South Africans remain poor and unemployment is high, particularly among black people.

FACT FILE

Full name: Republic of South Africa
Capital: Pretoria (Tshwane)
Population: 47.4 million (estimated 2006)
Ethnic groups: Black 79.5%, White 9.1%, Coloured (mixed race) 8.9%, Indian/Asian 2.5%
Language: English (11 official ethnic languages)
Area: 1.22 million sq km (470,693 sq miles)
Climate: mostly semi-arid; subtropical along east coast; sunny days, cool nights
Landscape: vast interior plateau surrounded by hills and narrow coastal plain
Agriculture/products: maize, wheat, sugar cane, fruits, vegetables, beef, poultry, mutton, wool, dairy products, wine
Natural resources and exports: gold, diamonds, other metals and minerals, machinery and equipment
Currency: 1 Rand (R) = 100 cents (c)

Colonial past

The Cape was an important point in the trade between Europe and the Far East. The first Europeans to settle there were the Dutch, in 1652. When the British took it over in 1806, many of the Dutch settlers (the Boers) moved inland to found their own republics. The discovery of diamonds in 1867 and gold in 1886 led to increased immigration and brought wealth, from which the native Africans were excluded. The Boers tried to stop British expansion, but were defeated in the Boer War (1899–1902). The Union of South Africa was formed in 1910 and racial segregation was generally accepted, though apartheid (separate development) didn't become the official policy until 1948, when the National Party came to power.

1 *Read the texts on pages 56–57 and look at the map at the back of the book. Then note down your impressions of South Africa, positive and negative, and discuss them in class.* →S25, p.106

2 *Collect expressions from the first text to show why it is different from the others. Write a text with the same purpose for your own region.* →S4, p.90

Languages

Of the 11 officially recognized languages, isiZulu is the mother tongue of 23.8 % of the population, followed by isiXhosa (17.6 %), Afrikaans (13.3 %), Sesotho sa Leboa (9.4 %), and English and Setswana (8.2 % each).
Although English is spoken at home by only 8.2 % of the population, it is the language most widely understood, and the second language of the majority of South Africans.

FACT FILE

Afrikaans developed from Dutch. It is the main language of the Afrikaners (descendants of the original Dutch settlers) and the Cape Coloureds (descendants of the slaves brought to the colony from the East Indies by the Dutch).

The flag
The current flag of the Republic of South Africa was adopted on April 27, 1994, after the first free elections and the end of apartheid.

3 [💻] *Research and give a short talk on one of these subjects: landscape and wildlife, people and languages, economy, Boer War, present government.* →S30, p.111

B Segregation

[02] Out of sight

In this extract from the short story 'What were you dreaming?' by Nadine Gordimer, set during apartheid, a white South African woman and a young newcomer from England have given a lift to a coloured man. The Englishman, who doesn't know much about the apartheid system, can hardly believe what the coloured man has told them.

"So you think it would at least be true that his family were kicked out of their home, sent away?"
"Why would anyone of them need to make that up? It's an everyday affair."
"What kind of place would they get, where they were moved?"
"Depends. A tent, to begin with. And maybe basic materials to build themselves a shack. Perhaps a one-room prefab. Always a tin toilet set down in the veld, if nothing else. Some industrialist must be making a fortune out of government contracts for those toilets. You build your new life round that toilet. His people are coloured, so it could be they were sent where there were houses of some sort already built for them; coloureds usually get something a bit better than blacks are given."
"And the house would be more or less as good as the one they had? People as poor as that – and they'd spent what must seem a fortune to them, fixing it up."
"I don't know what kind of house they had. We're not talking about slum clearance, my dear; we're talking about destroying communities because they're black, and white people want to build houses or factories for whites where blacks live. I told you. We're talking about loading up trucks and carting black people out of sight of whites."
"And even where he's come to work – Pietersburg, whatever-it's-called – he doesn't live in the town."
"Out of sight." She has lost the thought for a moment, watching to make sure the car takes the correct turning. "Out of sight. Like those mothers and grannies and brothers and sisters far away on the Cape Flats[1]."

VIP FILE

Nadine Gordimer
- born in Springs, South Africa, in 1923
- writer and political activist
- Nobel Prize in Literature in 1991

FACT FILE

Cape Town's District Six
1966: declared a whites-only area
1968–82: forced removals of more than 60,000 people from there to the Cape Flats[1] 25 km away

GRAMMAR

Past habits
'What kind of place would they get, …?' (line 4)
→G3, p.116

[1] flat area southeast of Cape Town, where non-white settlements were created by the government

Cape Town centre

Slums on the Cape Flats

[03] The development of townships around Johannesburg

Egoli[2] – Place of Gold

Up until the early 1900s most people lived in chiefdoms across South Africa where they produced all they needed through farming, trade or hunting and gathering. After the discovery of gold in the Rand[3] in 1886, more and more blacks were coming to Johannesburg to make a living. At first the poor were racially mixed and lived in the same neighbourhoods. The discovery of gold brought to the Rand not only gold seekers. From its early beginnings, some people realized the potential benefits of opening a business near the mines. Such people were the AmaWasha, Zulu laundry washers, Zulu 'houseboys' who worked for the middle classes, and prostitutes who worried the authorities by also sleeping with black mine workers.

The creation of townships

In 1905, a native area called Klipspruit outside Johannesburg was declared. Approximately 1,358 black people were moved to Klipspruit. Even though the government claimed that the removal was to improve the miserable conditions of people inhabiting slums, Klipspruit was not better than the shantytowns they were leaving behind. It was located about 300 meters from the City sewerage. The housing was a V shaped shack.

Moving to Klipspruit made life even more difficult. To maintain a 'respectable' distance between whites and blacks, it was far from the city centre, where most people worked, a distance of 13 kilometers. This meant that workers had to pay their transport fare each day, adding to their other costs.

Systematic resettlement after the Group Areas Act

Communities in Meadowlands and Diepkloof were grouped according to their ethnic identity. The purpose of dividing the communities along ethnic lines was that they could not express their worries as a unit.

Sophiatown, one of Johannesburg's original black suburbs, was gradually transformed into a mixed area inhabited by all races, becoming a symbol of how a non-racial South Africa could be made to work. This was not something which the Nationalist government could permit at a time when it had just introduced its programmes of social engineering and racial segregation. Therefore, in 1955, the land was declared a white area, its houses were bulldozed to the ground, and the area was redeveloped as a white residential suburb. Ironically, its new name was 'Triomf', which is Afrikaans for 'triumph'.

1 *Explain why so many people came to live in the cities. How and where did the coloureds and the blacks live before and after the Group Areas Act? What did the government want to achieve by forced removals and why?*

2 *How is the problem presented in the literary text and in the non-fictional one? Talk about the point of view. Which kind of text do you like better, and why?* →S4, p. 90

3 *Vocabulary work: Collect all the housing words you know and write definitions and example sentences to show what they mean.*

4 [group] [computer] *Find out more about Johannesburg and its suburbs (see the maps at the back of the book* →S25, p. 106*) to make up three short interviews about their everyday lives with these fictitious characters:*
a white businessman from Sandton, a black woman from Alexandra,
a black boy from a shantytown in Soweto. Act them out in class. →S15, p. 99

FACT FILE

Reasons for urbanisation
- discovery of gold (1886) and diamonds (1866): unskilled workforce needed
- hut tax (1890): to be paid in cash, which forced black farm workers into wage labour
- Land Act (1913): 87% of all land reserved for whites
- right to seek gold for whites only
- World War II (from 1939) and growth of manufacturing industry: labour shortage
- hope for access to schools and medical care

Group Areas Act (1950)
- races are assigned to different residential and business sections in urban areas by the apartheid government.

[2] Zulu name for Johannesburg
[3] Witwatersrand – an area with low mountains

Klipspruit housing

Soweto street scene

[06] Gimme hope, Jo'anna (Eddy Grant)

Well, Jo'anna she runs a country
She runs in Durban and the Transvaal
She makes a few of her people happy, oh
She don't care about the rest at all
She's got a system they call apartheid
It keeps a brother in subjection
But maybe pressure will make Jo'anna see
How everybody could live as one

Chorus: Gimme hope, Jo'anna
Hope, Jo'anna
Gimme hope, Jo'anna
'Fore the morning come
Gimme hope, Jo'anna
Hope, Jo'anna
Hope before the morning come

I hear she make all the golden money
To buy new weapons, any shape of guns
While every mother in black Soweto fears
The killing of another son
Sneakin' across all the neighbours' borders
Now and again having little fun
She doesn't care if the fun and games she play
Is dangerous to everyone

Chorus

She's got supporters in high up places
Who turn their heads to the city sun[1]
Jo'anna give them the fancy money
Oh, to tempt anyone who'd come[2] She even knows how to swing opinion
In every magazine and the journals
For every bad move that this Jo'anna make
They got a good explanation

Chorus

Even the preacher who works for Jesus
The Archbishop who's a peaceful man
Together say that the freedom fighters
Will overcome the very strong
I wanna know if you're blind Jo'anna
If you wanna hear the sound of drum
Can't you see that the tide is turning
Oh, don't make me wait till the morning come

Words and music: Eddy Grant

[1] Sun City is a tourist area in South Africa with hotels and casinos, similar to Las Vegas in the USA.
[2] South Africa tries to improve its image by attracting powerful people from abroad.

VIP FILE

Eddy Grant
- born in Plaisance, Guyana in 1948
- moved to London in 1960
- first band: the Equals in 1965
- musical influences: pop, funk, new wave, reggae, Caribbean, African, country
- top ten hits in the 80s: I don't wanna dance, Electric Avenue, Gimme hope, Jo'anna
- lives in Barbados today

5 *Explain how these ideas are expressed in the song:*
Johannesburg as a symbol of South Africa • one group of people holding all the power and exploiting the others • profits made by the mining industry • biased media • signs of a change coming • reversing the balance of power
Why does the author use these images?

6 *What is the perspective of the 'lyrical I' in the song? What points does he/she criticize? Find suitable headings and sum up his/her criticisms.* →S22, p.104

7 *The song appeared in 1988 and was an international hit. Think of the title and about what was happening in South Africa around that time. What could have been the author's intention?*

C The struggle against apartheid

Long walk to freedom

At the age of 75, Nelson Mandela became the first president of post-apartheid South Africa. A leading anti-apartheid activist, he had been committed to the politics of the African National Congress (ANC) since 1944. At first he supported peaceful resistance, like Gandhi in India. However, when the ANC was banned and he had to go underground, Mandela saw the need to use more violent tactics. He was later sentenced to life imprisonment. For the enemies of the apartheid regime, Mandela became a symbol of freedom and equality. The following paragraphs from his autobiography 'Long Walk to Freedom' describe some of the many state measures against non-whites and political activists.

In the 1940s, travelling for an African was a complicated process. All Africans over the age of sixteen were compelled to carry 'Native passes' issued by the Native Affairs Department, and were required to show that pass to any white policeman, civil servant or employer. Failure to do so could mean arrest, trial, a jail sentence or fine. The pass stated where the bearer lived, who his chief was, and whether he had paid the annual poll tax, which was a tax levied only on Africans. Later, the pass took the form of a booklet or 'Reference Book', as it was known, containing detailed information that had to be signed by one's employer every month. […]

It was a crime to walk through a Whites Only door, a crime to ride a Whites Only bus, a crime to use a Whites Only drinking fountain, a crime to walk on a Whites Only beach, a crime to be on the streets after 11 p.m., a crime not to have a pass book and a crime to have the wrong signature in that book, a crime to be unemployed and a crime to be employed in the wrong place, a crime to live in certain places and a crime to have no place to live. […]

My bans extended to meetings of all kinds, not only political ones. I could not, for example, attend my son's birthday party. I was prohibited from talking to more than one person at a time. This was part of a systematic effort by the government to silence, persecute and immobilize the leaders of those fighting apartheid and was the first of a series of bans on me that continued with brief intervals of freedom until the time I was deprived of all freedom some years later.

VIP FILE

Nelson Mandela
1918: born in Qunu, Eastern Cape
1944: becomes active for the ANC
1964–1990: in prison for anti-apartheid activism
1993: Nobel Peace Prize
1994: elected President of South Africa
1999: retires from politics; continues to fight for human rights and against HIV/AIDS

FACT FILE

ANC
1912: formed to bring all Africans together as one people
1960: banned
1994: becomes South Africa's governing social democratic party, supported by trade unions and the communist party

1 *Find headings for the paragraphs. What do you think the apartheid laws and regulations described by Mandela meant to the people? What was the purpose of these measures?*

2 *Find out more about Gandhi and make a short presentation comparing the biographies of the two political leaders.* →S18, p.101

3 ***Creative writing*** →S11, p.96: *Write a news report about* a) *Mandela's release from prison in 1990 or* b) *his coming to power in 1994.*

GRAMMAR

Obligation
"All Africans … were compelled to carry 'Native passes' …" (line 1)
→G5, p.118

[07] Soweto 1976: A schoolboy's memories

The Soweto uprising of 1976

Memorial to one of the first victims, Hector Pietersen, 13

It was one of the coldest winters in South Africa's history, and I was only 10 years old. It seemed like a normal Wednesday morning when I went to Belle Higher Primary School in Soweto's Orlando West neighbourhood. But suddenly, in the middle of Mrs Mofokeng's lesson, we heard her voice being drowned by a crowd singing outside the school yard. We looked through the windows. I saw thousands of high school students dressed in different school uniforms singing and shouting anti-apartheid songs and slogans.

We walked out of the classroom to investigate, only to find that the police had already drawn a cordon across the road, to prevent the marchers from going further. On the placards I read slogans such as: "Down with Afrikaans", "Black Power", "No to the language of the oppressor".

There was something different about the mood of the police: it was tense and they had guns at the ready. I noticed that there were more white policemen than usual. As the crowd grew bigger, the singing also grew louder. The police dogs were barking, police vans were revving higher and higher as they reinforced the cordon. For the first time in my life I saw teargas canisters, armoured personnel carriers (locally known as Hippos) and real live ammunition rifles at close range. There was a certain degree of excitement in the air. Then it all rose in a crescendo when the marchers did not disperse in "two minutes" as a police officer had ordered through a loud hailer.

I heard gunshots, people screaming and I looked right up into the sky as a teargas canister was flying high up followed by a white trail of smoke. I choked and began coughing uncontrollably, tears running down my cheeks.

Students were scattered across Orlando West as they ran for shelter. The police let their dogs loose on us. At that point students were stoning delivery vehicles and police cars, and the looters were at work too! It was chaos! I was scared, very scared. On my attempt to cross the main road, I came across one of our neighbours, Mbuyisa Makhubu, who was carrying a schoolboy in his arms. The boy was bleeding and Mbuyisa was shouting repeatedly in English: "Students, it's enough! It's enough, students!"

Milton Nkosi on the BBC website, 16 June 2006

GRAMMAR
Past progressive
'The police dogs were barking, …' (line 15)
→G1, p.114

FACT FILE
Soweto, 16 June 1976
- protest of 20,000 students against use of Afrikaans as main language in schools
- official number of deaths: 23; (estimated: over 100)
- riots begin to spread
- young people become militant
- world opinion made aware of brutality of apartheid state

Soweto statistics 1976
Population: 1.5 million
Electricity: 20% of homes
Hot water: 5% of homes
Hospitals: 1
Students per class: 60
Average income: 100 Rand per month
Cost of living: 140 Rand per month
Unemployment rate: over 50%

4 *Analysing the text* →S3, p.89: *From what perspective is this text written? How does the narrator experience the beginning of the Soweto riots? What were your main impressions of these events after reading the text? What expressions are used to create this picture?*

5 *Use the fact file to explain the anger in the townships which caused the riots.*

[08] In detention

He fell from the ninth floor
He hanged himself
He slipped on a piece of soap while washing
He hanged himself
He slipped on a piece of soap while washing
He fell from the ninth floor
He hanged himself while washing
He slipped from the ninth floor
He hung from the ninth floor
He slipped on the ninth floor while washing
He fell from a piece of soap while slipping
He hung from the ninth floor
He washed from the ninth floor while slipping
He hung from a piece of soap while washing

Christopher van Wyk[1]

[1] Christopher van Wyk [ˌkrɪstəfə fæn ˈvaɪk]

VIP FILE

Christopher van Wyk
- 1957 born in Soweto
- poet, novelist, editor, author of children's books
- has won several literary awards

WORD BANK

poetry: lyrical I • rhyme • rhythm • repetition • phrase • pattern • theme • imagery • title • to vary • author • intention • impression • reaction

6 *In the 1980s, the South African government detained thousands of political activists and held them without trial. Many died in detention. Use this background information to interpret the poem.* →S21, p. 104

Facing the past

South Africans reconciled?

The Truth and Reconciliation Commission (TRC) was set up to investigate political crimes committed during apartheid. Between 1996 and 1998 it took more than 20,000 statements from individual victims of human rights abuse, and received more than 7,000 applications for amnesty.

The aim of the commission and its chairman, Archbishop Desmond Tutu, was to achieve reconciliation in South Africa's divided society through truth about its dark past.

It has been an unprecedented experiment in trying to heal the wounds of the apartheid era, but some people are asking how much reconciliation has been achieved. Many black South Africans have been left feeling that apologies are not enough. Many are angry that the perpetrators of human rights abuse under South Africa's last white government can be granted amnesty if they admit to all of their crimes.

Much of the criticism of the commission comes from a basic misunderstanding about its purpose. It was never meant to punish people, just to expose their role in crimes committed under apartheid. Only by revisiting the trauma of the past can people look to a better future – but with the truth comes pain and a reminder that reconciliation may still be a distant goal in the new South Africa.

Greg Barrow, *BBC News*

7 *Explain the idea behind the TRC. Was it a success?*

8 *Do you think it makes sense to look into political crimes of the past and to keep their memory alive? Think of examples from German history.*

D Culture and sports

[09] *Tsotsi:* a film from South Africa

This South African film was adapted from a novel by Athol Fugard[1]. When it won the Academy Award for best foreign film last year, writer/director Gavin Hood was understandably elated.

And so was the country. South Africa now has a very good infrastructure for making films, and is attracting productions from America and Europe. It's the local stories, though, which are becoming more and more confident.

Tsotsi is filmed in one of the Johannesburg townships, home to Xhosa and Zulu peoples. 'Tsotsi', in the street slang of Johannesburg, means thug, or maybe what Americans call 'gangsta'. And as the film begins we see a bunch of these young thugs mark out a man stupid enough to flash his wallet at an automatic cash machine, and then get on the train with it. The gang follows him. One distracts him while another slashes his pocket. But when things go wrong, one of them knifes him and the man is left to bleed to death on the floor of the train.

Presley Chweneyagae[2] plays Tsotsi, and this knife attack has challenged his authority. He beats up the challenger in turn, and returns to his hut in the township to brood. He is the brains of the gang, which has been together since they were kids left to fend for themselves. Reluctantly he agrees to lead them on a burglary, which also goes wrong when a woman drives up in a car. To our horror, she too is violently assaulted. Tsotsi drives away with the car and is about to abandon it when he realises something. There is a baby on the back seat.

For reasons we don't at first understand, he can't abandon it. He turns back, grabs the child, puts it in a paper bag and walks across a field to the distant township.

About a third of the way through this film I began to think, oh no, this is an O. Henry[3] short story – bad man redeemed by tiny baby. But it turns out to be much more than that. There are layers in this film, and in the township life it shows, which say a lot about hope and despair in contemporary South Africa. Director Gavin Hood should know; he worked with gang members in those townships for three years.

[1] **Athol Fugard** [ˌæθl ˈfuːgɑːd]
[2] **Presley Chweneyagae** [ˌprezli ˌtʃwenəjəˈgaɪ]
[3] **O. Henry** pen name of William Sydney Porter, American short story writer (1862–1910)

1 a) *The text is from 'Movie Time', a radio show. First explain what is said about the state of the South African film industry. Then describe the presenter's feelings about the film 'Tsotsi'.*

b) [15] *Listen to the interview with writer/director Gavin Hood and summarize what he says about the film.*

2 [16] ***Listening: Kwaito music*** →S1, p. 88

The film's kwaito soundtrack helps to create an authentic township atmosphere. Among other artists, it features Zola, who also acts in the film. To find out more about kwaito, listen to the radio feature on kwaito music and make notes about the style: its origin and roots, the way it is performed, its political and social importance, the artists mentioned and the language they sing in.

Kwaito performer Zola

Mediation: Sport in Südafrika

Sport hat in Südafrika einen hohen Stellenwert. Grundsätzlich gibt es ein breites Angebot an Sportarten, vergleichbar mit den Sportarten in Europa, wenngleich Wintersportarten gänzlich fehlen. Wie in vielen ehemaligen britischen Kolonien sind Rugby und Cricket die – mit Abstand – wichtigsten Sportarten, zumindest gilt dies für die weiße Bevölkerung. Beide Sportarten werden an den Schulen intensiv unterrichtet und praktiziert, Rugby allerdings nicht in der Unterstufe wegen der zu großen Verletzungsgefahr. Am Wochenende schaut man sich nicht – wie in Deutschland – die Fußball-Ergebnisse an, sondern berauscht sich an den Rugby- und Cricket-Spielen, die im Fernsehen übertragen werden. Stolz ist man auf die „Springboks“, Südafrikas Rugby-Nationalmannschaft, die 1995 und 2007 die Rugby-Union-Weltmeisterschaft gewann sowie 1998 und 2004 die Tri-Nations-Turniere gegen Australien und Neuseeland.

Der Fußball wird von den weißen Südafrikanern nur zögernd angenommen, wenngleich sich dies seit der letzten Fußball-Weltmeisterschaft etwas geändert hat. An vielen Schulen gibt es mittlerweile zumindest AGs, in denen Fußball gespielt wird. In der schwarzen Bevölkerung ist der Fußball jedoch schon seit vielen Jahren die bei weitem populärste Sportart, und es gibt kaum ein schwarzes Kind, das nicht in der Freizeit Fußball spielt, und kaum eine Schwarzen-Siedlung, die keinen Fußballklub oder Fußballplatz hat.

Die südafrikanische Fußball-Nationalmannschaft „Bafana Bafana“ (bedeutet „The Boys“ in Zulu), ist der Stolz der Nation. Die noch junge Mannschaft wurde 1992 gegründet, und viele der Nationalspieler spielen heute in europäischen Klubs. Seit dem Ende der Apartheid und der Wiederaufnahme in die FIFA konnten sich die Südafrikaner zweimal für die Endrunde um die Fußball-Weltmeisterschaft qualifizieren (1998 und 2002), leider nicht 2006 bei der WM in Deutschland. 1996 gewann Bafana Bafana die Afrika-Meisterschaft. Südafrika erhielt als erste afrikanische Nation den Zuschlag für die Ausrichtung der WM 2010, und das Land schaut mit großer Erwartung auf dieses Ereignis.

WORD BANK
sports: football pitch • national team • to qualify (for) • finals • world cup • to host

3 *Mediation: You have found this text on a travel guide web page in German. Explain what it says about sport in South Africa and what has changed since apartheid was abolished.* →S28, p.108

4 [💻] *Research project: Find out about the unusual sporting career of Enos Mafokate and write a profile of him.* →S30, p.111

E Present-day challenges

Young ... and free!?

FACT FILE

Some figures:
- 30% unemployment (68% among under-30s)
- 20% HIV infection (10% between the age of 15–24)
- high crime rate: 21,995 murders, 53,008 rapes, 99,963 car thefts (2006)

After more than 10 years of democracy, South Africa still faces important challenges. It remains a land of contrasts. The following statements are summaries of positive and negative comments made by young South Africans.

“I appreciate living in a non-racial society. I can live and go where I want, I can study anywhere and go into any career. Education has improved and the government is now providing more bursaries. Democracy has also brought computers to my school.

There is freedom of expression and growing self-esteem among people of all cultural backgrounds. Young people's fresh ideas are exploding everywhere – in music, film, fashion, TV, theatre and the arts and poetry scene. I am proud of being South African!”

“This is a non-racial society only according to law. In reality, things are quite different. I'd love to study, but I can't afford to, and there aren't enough bursaries. Even if you get a chance to study, you might end up unemployed. Business and the government are definitely not doing enough to hire young people and provide work experience.

Another threat we are confronted with is HIV/Aids. Young people with no hope for the future face a greater risk of infection because they feel they have nothing to live for. And then there is the problem of crime ... I'm not surprised some people are thinking of leaving this country – well, those who can afford it, of course!”

1 *What opportunities do young people have in South Africa? Why are some people happy with recent developments? Why are others disappointed?*

2 ***Mediation:** What about your own country? Collect positive and negative aspects from German newspapers and write a comment about the chances young people have in present-day Germany.* →S13, p. 97

A cartoon

⟨F Out in the country⟩

⟨The wildlife trade⟩

The decision to strictly limit or outrightly ban trading in endangered species regularly puts governments and conservationists before a critical dilemma.

South Africa is one of many African countries which argue that a limited trade in wildlife product stockpiles should be allowed so that the proceeds can be used to pay for conservation. Governments and conservation groups that are hostile to this approach claim that any kind of sale will stimulate the illegal market, encourage more poaching and ultimately push species such as elephants and rhino closer to extinction.

Conservationists no longer oppose the idea of wildlife being exploited per se. If properly managed, they say, wildlife can provide food for impoverished rural populations and wildlife-based tourism can be an important source of income.

"Wildlife can be sold three times: to tourists, to sport hunters, and finally as ivory and hide," says Jon Hutton, director of Africa Resources Trust, an NGO involved in community conservation schemes in southern Africa. "The sale of wildlife products often brings in the most revenue."

Meanwhile, conservationists have been active in curtailing demand for some wildlife products. Education programmes in China have encouraged consumers to reject tiger bone remedies. Conservationists have also co-operated with Chinese medicinal practitioners to find alternatives to tiger bone and rhino horn, which are used in traditional medicines.

Trade bans probably need more time if they are to be made more effective through international pressure on governments and educating consumers.

FACT FILE

About 20 national parks protect South Africa's abundant flora and fauna.

Kruger National Park

- created in 1898
- size: about two million hectares
- world leader in environmental management techniques and policies
- huge number of different species, e.g. 507 birds and 147 mammals
- archaeological sites

GRAMMAR

Relative clauses

'… tiger bone and rhino horn, which are used in traditional medicines.' (line 18)

→G12, p.121

But some argue that trade or no trade, time is running out for wildlife. No matter how effective a trade ban, it cannot slow down the current rate of habitat loss or pay for wildlife protection. Trade which has the potential to save more wild areas and pay for their protection may ultimately be the preferred option.

Rolf Hogan in the *Daily Mail*

1 *List the problems and solutions mentioned in the article and discuss them. Do you agree with the conclusion? Write a letter to the editor with your opinion.* →S12, p.96

2 [17 ◎] ***Five kinds of safari:*** *Listen and take notes in a grid. Then say which is the best way to explore Kruger NP for what kind of target group and why. Which safari would you prefer and what would you like to see?*

Safari	1	2	3	4	5
freedom					
adventure					
money					
special features					

3 [💻] *Find out what South Africa's 'Big Five' are and what other interesting animals live there. Make a 'flora and fauna guide' for South Africa giving information on five animals and/or plants of your choice.* →S30, p.111

[10] ⟨The moment before the gun went off⟩

Marais Van der Vyver[1] shot one of his farm labourers, dead. An accident, there are accidents with guns every day of the week – children playing a fatal game with a father's revolver in the cities where guns are domestic objects, nowadays, hunting mishaps like this one, in the country – but these won't be reported all over the world. Van der Vyver knows his will be. He knows that the story of the Afrikaner farmer – regional Party leader and Commandant of the local security commando – shooting a black man who worked for him will fit exactly their version of South Africa, it's made for them. They'll be able to use it in their boycott and divestment campaigns, it'll be another piece of evidence in their truth about the country. The papers at home will quote the story as it has appeared in the overseas press, and in the back-and-forth he and the black man will become those crudely-drawn figures on anti-apartheid banners, units in statistics of white brutality against the blacks quoted at the United Nations – he, whom they will gleefully be able to call 'a leading member' of the ruling Party.

People in the farming community understand how he must feel. Bad enough to have killed a man, without helping the Party's, the government's, the country's enemies, as well. They see the truth of that. They know, reading the Sunday papers, that when Van der Vyver is quoted saying he is 'terribly shocked', he will 'look after the wife and children', none of those Americans and English, and none of those people at home who want to destroy the white man's power will believe him. And how they will sneer when he even says of the farm boy (according to one paper, if you can trust any of those reporters), 'He was my friend, I always took him hunting with me.' Those city and overseas people don't know it's true: farmers usually have one particular black boy they like to take along with them in the lands; you could call it a kind of friend, yes, friends are not only your own white people, like yourself, you take into your house, pray with in church and work with on the Party committee.

But how can those others know that? They don't want to know it. They think all blacks are like the big-mouth agitators in town. And Van der Vyver's face, in the photographs, strangely opened by distress – everyone in the district remembers Marais Van der Vyver as a little boy who would go away and hide himself if he caught you smiling at him, and everyone knows him now as a man who hides any change of expression round his mouth behind a thick, soft moustache, and in his eyes by always looking at some object in hand, leaf of a crop fingered, pen or stone picked up, while concentrating on what he is saying, or while listening to you. It just goes to show what shock can do; when you look at the newspaper photographs you feel like apologizing, as if you had stared in on some room where you should not be.

There will be an inquiry; there had better be, to stop the assumption of yet another case of brutality against farm workers, although there's nothing in doubt – an accident, and all the facts fully admitted by Van der Vyver. He made a statement when he arrived at the police station with the dead man in his bakkie[2].

Captain Beetge[3] knows him well, of course; he gave him brandy. He was shaking, this big, calm, clever son of Willem Van der Vyver, who inherited the old man's best farm. The black was stone dead, nothing to be done for him. Beetge will not tell anyone that after the brandy Van der Vyver wept. He sobbed, snot running onto his hands, like a dirty kid. The Captain was ashamed, for him, and walked out to give him a chance to recover himself.

[1] **Marais Van der Vyver** [mæ,reɪ fæn də ˈvaɪvə]
[2] pickup truck
[3] **Beetge** [ˈbeɪtʒə]

Marais Van der Vyver left his house at three in the afternoon to cull a buck from the family of kudu[4] he protects in the bush areas of his farm. He is interested in wildlife and sees it as the farmers' sacred duty to raise game as well as cattle. As usual, he called at his shed workshop to pick up Lucas, a twenty-year-old farmhand who had shown mechanical aptitude and whom Van der Vyver himself had taught to maintain tractors and other farm machinery. He hooted, and Lucas followed the familiar routine, jumping onto the back of the truck. He liked to travel standing up there, spotting game before his employer did. He would lean forward, braced against the cab below him.

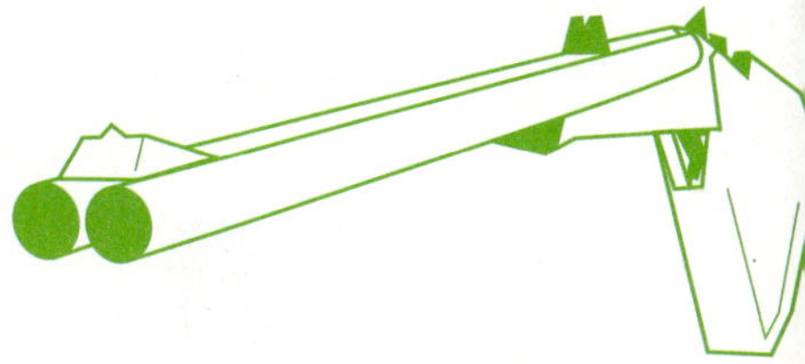

Van der Vyver had a rifle and .300[5] ammunition beside him in the cab. The rifle was one of his father's, because his own was at the gunsmith's in town. Since his father died (Beetge's sergeant wrote 'passed on') no one had used the rifle and so when he took it from a cupboard he was sure it was not loaded. His father had never allowed a loaded gun in the house; he himself had been taught since childhood never to ride with a loaded weapon in a vehicle. But this gun was loaded. On a dirt track, Lucas thumped his fist on the cab roof three times to signal: look left. Having seen the white-ripple-marked flank of a kudu, and its fine horns raking through disguising bush, Van der Vyver drove rather fast over a pot-hole. The jolt fired the rifle. Upright, it was pointing straight through the cab roof at the head of Lucas. The bullet pierced the roof and entered Lucas's brain by way of his throat.

That is the statement of what happened. Although a man of such standing in the district, Van der Vyver had to go through the ritual of swearing that it was the truth. It has gone on record, and will be there in the archive of the local police station as long as Van der Vyver lives, and beyond that, through the lives of his children, Magnus, Helena and Karel – unless things in the country get worse, the example of black mobs in the towns spreads to the rural areas and the place is burned down as many urban police stations have been. Because nothing the government can do will appease the agitators and the whites who encourage them. Nothing satisfies them, in the cities: blacks can sit and drink in white hotels, now, the Immorality Act[6] has gone, blacks can sleep with whites … It's not even a crime any more.

Van der Vyver has a high barbed security fence round his farmhouse and garden which his wife, Alida, thinks spoils completely the effect of her artificial stream with its tree-ferns beneath the jacarandas[7]. There is an aerial soaring like a flag-pole in the back yard. All his vehicles, including the truck in which the black man died, have aerials that swing their whips when the driver

[4] type of antelope
[5] **.300** (point-three-O-O) type of gun
[6] The Immorality Act (1950–1985), one of the first apartheid laws, made sexual relations between whites and non-whites illegal
[7] beautiful purple-blue flowering trees

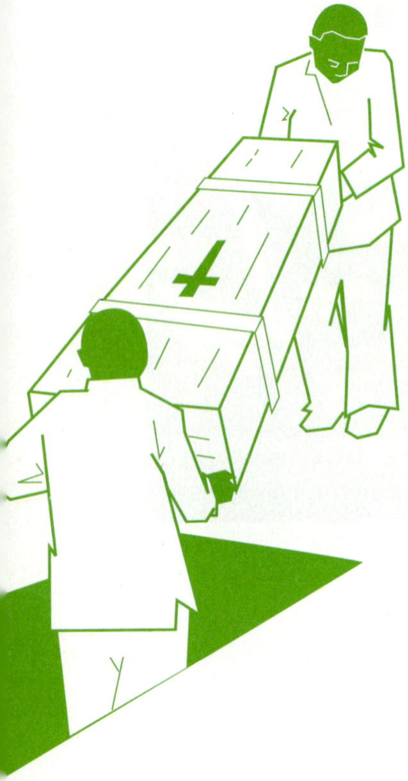

hits a pot-hole: they are part of the security system the farmers in the district maintain, each farm in touch with every other by radio, twenty-four hours out of twenty-four. It has already happened that infiltrators from over the border have mined remote farm roads, killing white farmers and their families out on their own property for a Sunday picnic. The pot-hole could have set off a land-mine, and Van der Vyver might have died with his farm boy. When neighbours use the communications system to call up and say they are sorry about 'that business' with one of Van der Vyver's boys, there goes unsaid: it could have been worse.

It is obvious from the quality and fittings of the coffin that the farmer has provided money for the funeral. And an elaborate funeral means a great deal to blacks; look how they will deprive themselves of the little they have, in their lifetime, keeping up payments to a burial society so they won't go in boxwood to an unmarked grave. The young wife is pregnant (of course) and another little one, wearing red shoes several sizes too large, leans under her jutting belly. He is too young to understand what has happened, what he is witnessing that day, but neither whines nor plays about; he is solemn without knowing why. Blacks expose small children to everything, they don't protect them from the sight of fear and pain the way whites do theirs. It is the young wife who rolls her head and cries like a child, sobbing on the breast of this relative and that.

All present work for Van der Vyver or are the families of those who work; and in the weeding and harvest seasons, the women and children work for him, too, carried – wrapped in their blankets, on a truck, singing – at sunrise to the fields. The dead man's mother is a woman who can't be more than in her late thirties (they start bearing children at puberty) but she is heavily mature in a black dress between her own parents, who were already working for old Van der Vyver when Marais, like their daughter, was a child. The parents hold her as if she were a prisoner or a crazy woman to be restrained. But she says nothing, does nothing. She does not look up; she does not look at Van der Vyver, whose gun went off in the truck, she stares at the grave. Nothing will make her look up; there need be no fear that she will look up; at him. His wife, Alida, is beside him. To show the proper respect, as for any white funeral, she is wearing the navy-blue-and-cream hat she wears to church this summer. She is always supportive, although he doesn't seem to notice it; this coldness and reserve – his mother says he didn't mix well as a child – she accepts for herself but regrets that it has prevented him from being nominated, as he should be, to stand as the Party's parliamentary candidate for the district. He does not let her clothing, or that of anyone else gathered closely, make contact with him. He, too, stares at the grave. The dead man's mother and he stare at the grave in communication like that between the black man outside and the white man inside the cab the moment before the gun went off.

The moment before the gun went off was a moment of high excitement shared through the roof of the cab, as the bullet was to pass, between the young black man outside and the white farmer inside the vehicle. There were such moments, without explanation, between them, although often around the farm the farmer would pass the young man without returning a greeting, as if he did not recognize him. When the bullet went off what Van der Vyver saw was the kudu stumble in fright at the report and gallop away. Then he heard the thud behind him, and past the window saw the young man fall out of the vehicle. He was sure he had leapt up and toppled – in fright, like the buck. The farmer was almost laughing with relief, ready to tease, as he opened his door, it did not seem possible that a bullet passing through the roof could have done harm.

The young man did not laugh with him at his own fright. The farmer carried him in his arms, to the truck. He was sure, sure he could not be dead. But the young black man's blood was all over the farmer's clothes, soaking against his flesh as he drove.

How will they ever know, when they file newspaper clippings, evidence, proof, when they look at the photographs and see his face – guilty! guilty! they are right! – how will they know, when the police stations burn with all the evidence of what has happened now, and what the law made a crime in the past. How could they know that they do not know. Anything. The young black callously shot through the negligence of the white man was not the farmer's boy; he was his son.

Nadine Gordimer

4 ***What happened?***

a) *Explain the plot of the story.*

b) *What does this mean in a political context?*

c) *What does this mean to Van der Vyver?*

5 ***Vocabulary work:*** *Make mind maps for the following word fields with words from the text: politics, life on a farm, feelings.*

6 ***How is the story told? Analyse:*** →S6, p.92, →S7, p.93

1. *the structure*
2. *the perspective*
3. *the characters, their feelings and relationships*
4. *the way whites and blacks live together*
5. *the title*

7 *What do you think of the story?*

8 [👥] *A black journalist comes to the farm to investigate Lucas's death. One of the people he/she questions is the young man's mother.*

a) *Make up the interview and act it out. OR*

b) *Write the news story the journalist wrote after doing his/her research.* →S14, p.98

Topic 5 Living in a modern world

A Robots – in science fiction and reality

Lieutenant Commander Data from *Star Trek* …

… and a Borg (short for cyborg = cybernetic organism)

Star Wars mates C3PO and R2D2

The film *I, Robot* is based on a series of stories by Isaac Asimov. Asimov wrote three laws which all robots in his books had to obey and which many other science fiction authors have adopted:

Three Laws of Robotics

1. A robot may not injure a human being or, through inaction, allow a human being to come to harm.
2. A robot must obey orders given to it by human beings except where such orders could conflict with the First Law.
3. A robot must protect its own existence as long as such protection does not conflict with the First or Second Laws.

1 *Robots in science fiction:*

a) *Talk about the robots in the pictures on this page. Say what you know or can find out about them and other robots from the world of science fiction. ([💻] Try the 'Robot Hall of Fame' website.)*

b) *Now compare them with robots in the real world. Use the information given on the opposite page.*

WORD BANK

robot/robotic (adj.) • to program • mechanical • repetitive work • artificial intelligence • remote-controlled

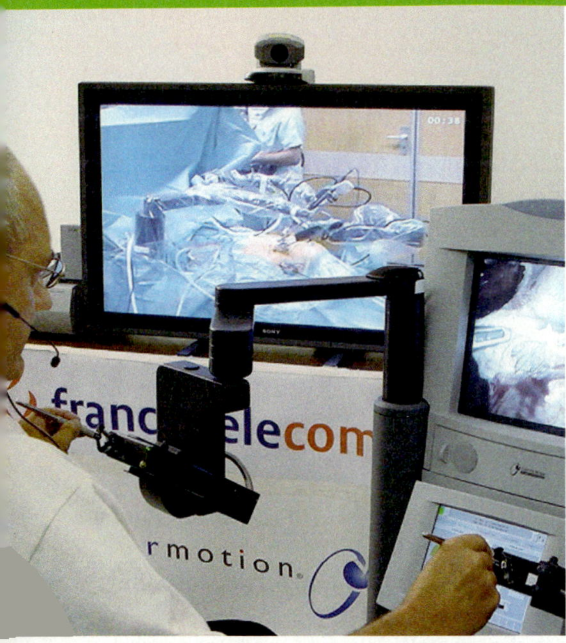

A surgeon uses a remote-controlled robot to operate on a patient 7000 km away

Robots welding automobile parts in a factory

At the RoboCup robots play football against each other – and against humans

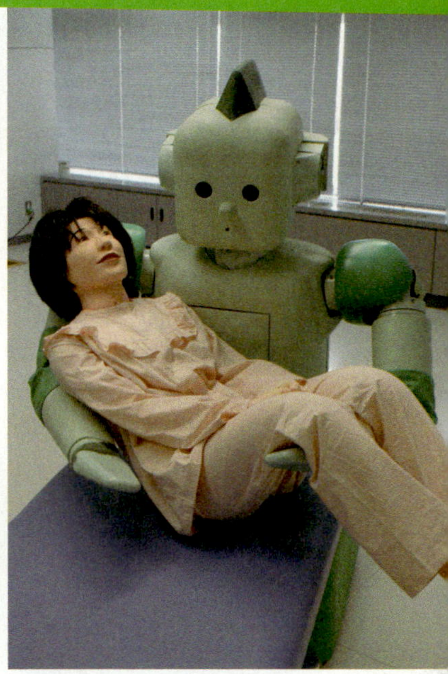

In Japan robots are being built to look after old people

2 *Robots and human beings:*

a) *What other tasks can robots be used for? Think of the strengths and weaknesses of robots/humans and say what kind of jobs suit each better.*

b) *Discuss the difference between robots and human beings, comparing science fiction and reality.*
→S16, p.100

3 [22] ***Listening:*** *Cathy and Ian are talking about the film 'I, Robot'. First look at the words in the word bank, then listen to the dialogue and summarise what each of them thinks of the film, and why.* →S1, p.88

WORD BANK
prejudiced against • to resemble • menace • homicidal • to approve • to abuse

⟨4⟩ ***Research:*** *Find out more about one of the things mentioned on this double page and do a presentation.*
→S18, p.101, →S30, p.111

FACT FILE

1206 Al-Jazari designs the first programmable robot, a boat with four automatic musicians

1495 Leonardo da Vinci creates a mechanical device that resembles a knight

1921 the first use of the word 'robot' (from the Czech 'robota' = hard labour) in a play by Karel Čapek

1966 Shakey, the first mobile robot able to navigate its own course

1969 Creation of the Stanford Arm, which becomes the standard for robotic arms

1977 the robotic spacecraft Voyager 1 is launched, visiting Jupiter and Saturn. It is the farthest man-made object from Earth

1981 Japanese factory worker Kenji Urada is killed by a robot he accidentally switches on while repairing

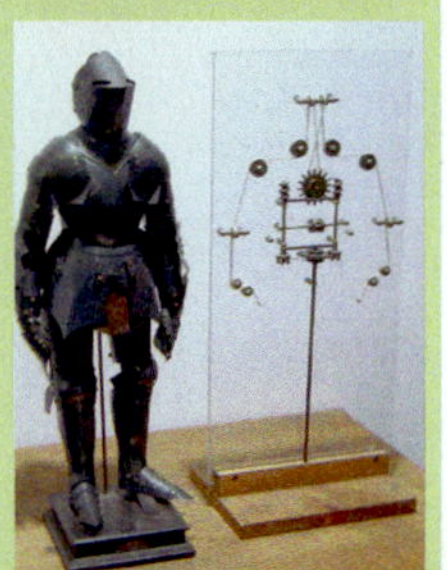

B Is there anybody out there?

I'm not an ambassador from my planet, I'm on my gap year.

1 *Before you read:* *Suggest why human beings through the ages have been fascinated by the idea of other worlds beyond their own.*

[13] They're made out of meat

"They're made out of meat."
"Meat?"
"Meat. They're made out of meat."
"Meat?"
"There's no doubt about it. We picked up several from different parts of the planet, took them aboard our recon vessels, and probed them all the way through. They're completely meat."
"That's impossible. What about the radio signals? The messages to the stars?"
"They use the radio waves to talk, but the signals don't come from them. The signals come from machines."
"So who made the machines? That's who we want to contact."
"They made the machines. That's what I'm trying to tell you. Meat made the machines."
"That's ridiculous. How can meat make a machine? You're asking me to believe in sentient meat."
"I'm not asking you, I'm telling you. These creatures are the only sentient race in that sector and they're made out of meat."
"Maybe they're like the orfolei. You know, a carbon-based intelligence that goes through a meat stage."
"Nope[1]. They're born meat and they die meat. We studied them for several of their life spans, which didn't take long. Do you have any idea what's the life span of meat?"
"Spare me. Okay, maybe they're only partly meat. You know, like the weddilei. A meat head with an electron plasma brain inside."
"Nope. We thought of that, since they do have meat heads, like the weddilei. But I told you, we probed them. They're meat all the way through."
"No brain?"
"Oh, there's a brain all right. It's just that the brain is *made out of meat!* That's what I've been trying to tell you."
"So … what does the thinking?"
"You're not understanding, are you? You're refusing to deal with what I'm telling you. The brain does the thinking. The meat."
"Thinking meat! You're asking me to believe in thinking meat!"
"Yes, thinking meat! Conscious meat! Loving meat. Dreaming meat. The meat is the whole deal! Are you beginning to get the picture or do I have to start all over[2]?"
"Omigod[3]. You're serious then. They're made out of meat."
"Thank you. Finally. Yes. They are indeed made out of meat. And they've been trying to get in touch with us for almost a hundred of their years."
"Omigod. So what does this meat have in mind?"
"First it wants to talk to us. Then I imagine it wants to explore the Universe, contact other sentiences, swap ideas and information. The usual."
"We're supposed to talk to meat."
"That's the idea. That's the message they're sending out by radio. 'Hello. Anyone out there? Anybody home?' that sort of thing."

GRAMMAR
Relative clauses
'…, which didn't take long.' (line 21)
→G12, p.121

[1] **nope** = no
[2] all over again (from the beginning)
[3] Oh my God!

"They actually do talk, then. They use words, ideas, concepts."

"Oh yes. Except they do it with meat."

"I thought you told me they used radio."

"They do, but what do you think is on the radio? Meat sounds. You know how when you slap or flap meat, it makes a noise? They talk by flapping their meat at each other. They can even sing by squirting air through their meat."

"Omigod. Singing meat. This is altogether too much. So what do you advise?"

"Officially or unofficially?"

"Both."

"Officially, we are required to contact, welcome, and log in any and all sentient races or multibeings in this quadrant of the Universe, without prejudice, fear, or favor. Unofficially, I advise that we erase the records and forget the whole thing."

"I was hoping you would say that."

"It seems harsh, but there is a limit. Do we really want to make contact with meat?"

"I agree one hundred percent. What's there to say? 'Hello, meat. How's it going?' But will this work? How many planets are we dealing with here?"

"Just one. They can travel to other planets in special meat containers, but they can't live on them. And being meat, they can only travel through C space, which limits them to the speed of light and makes the possibility of their ever making contact pretty slim. Infinitesimal, in fact."

"So we just pretend there's no one home in the Universe."

"That's it."

"Cruel. But you said it yourself, who wants to meet meat? And the ones who have been aboard our vessels, the ones you probed? You're sure they won't remember?"

"They'll be considered crackpots if they do. We went into their heads and smoothed out their meat so that we're just a dream to them."

"A dream to meat! How strangely appropriate, that we should be meat's dream."

"And we marked the entire sector unoccupied."

"Good. Agreed, officially and unofficially. Case closed. Any others? Anyone interesting on that side of the galaxy?"

"Yes, a rather shy but sweet hydrogen-core cluster intelligence in a class-nine star in G445 zone was in contact two galactic rotations ago, wants to be friendly again."

"They always come around."

"And why not? Imagine how unbearably, how unutterably cold the universe would be if one were all alone …"

Terry Bisson

GRAMMAR
Adverbs
'Officially, we are required …' (line 55)
→G10–11, p. 118

VIP FILE

Terry Bisson
- born 1942 in Owensboro, Kentucky
- award-winning author of science fiction short stories and novels

2 *Working with the text:* →S3, p. 89
a) *Explain the situation in which this dialogue takes place.*
b) *Compare the speakers' mission with the personal attitude they express.*
c) *Pick out images, comments or individual words that bring humour to the text.*
d) [👥] *With a partner, act the dialogue out. Use your creativity to bring it to life.*

3 *Creative writing:* *Choose three objects that are part of everyday life on earth and describe them from the point of view of an alien.* →S11, p. 96

C Big Brother

1 *What do you know about these men? Find out more about them.*

Josef Stalin, leader of the Soviet Union (1929–53)

Mao Zedong, China's Communist Party chairman (1949–76)

[14] Nineteen Eighty-four

George Orwell's 'Nineteen Eighty-four' was published in 1949, and portrays life in a future society. This is how the novel begins.

It was a bright cold day in April, and the clocks were striking thirteen. Winston Smith, his chin nuzzled into his breast in an effort to escape the vile wind, slipped quickly through the glass doors of Victory Mansions, though not quickly enough to prevent a swirl of gritty dust from entering along with him.

The hallway smelt of boiled cabbage and old rag mats. At one end of it a coloured poster, too large for indoor display, had been tacked to the wall. It depicted simply an enormous face, more than a metre wide: the face of a man of about forty-five, with a heavy black moustache and ruggedly handsome features. Winston made for the stairs. It was no use trying the lift. Even at the best of times it was seldom working, and at present the electric current was cut off during daylight hours. It was part of the economy drive in preparation for Hate Week. The flat was seven flights up, and Winston, who was thirty-nine and had a varicose ulcer above his right ankle, went slowly, resting several times on the way. On each landing, opposite the lift-shaft, the poster with the enormous face gazed from the wall. It was one of those pictures which are so contrived that the eyes follow you about when you move. BIG BROTHER IS WATCHING YOU, the caption beneath it ran.

Inside the flat a fruity voice was reading out a list of figures which had something to do with the production of pig-iron. The voice came from an oblong metal plaque like a dulled mirror which formed part of the surface of the right-hand wall. Winston turned a switch and the voice sank somewhat, though the words were still distinguishable. The instrument (the telescreen, it was called) could be dimmed, but there was no way of shutting it off completely. He moved over to the window: a smallish, frail figure, the meagreness of his body merely emphasized by the blue overalls which were the uniform of the party. His hair was very fair, his face naturally sanguine,

GRAMMAR
Participle with a subject of its own
'a smallish, frail figure, the meagreness of his body merely emphasized by the blue overalls' (line 24)
→G14. p.122

his skin roughened by coarse soap and blunt razor blades and the cold of the winter that had just ended.

Outside, even through the shut window pane, the world looked cold. Down in the street little eddies of wind were whirling dust and torn paper into spirals, and though the sun was shining and the sky a harsh blue, there seemed to be no colour in anything, except the posters that were plastered everywhere. The blackmoustachio'd face gazed down from every commanding corner. There was one on the house-front immediately opposite. BIG BROTHER IS WATCHING YOU, the caption said, while the dark eyes looked deep into Winston's own. Down at street level another poster, torn at one corner, flapped fitfully in the wind, alternately covering and uncovering the single word INGSOC[1]. In the far distance a helicopter skimmed down between the roofs, hovered for an instant like a bluebottle, and darted away again with a curving flight. It was the police patrol, snooping into people's windows. The patrols did not matter, however. Only the Thought Police mattered.

■ Behind Winston's back the voice from the telescreen was still babbling away about pig-iron and the overfulfilment of the Ninth Three-Year Plan. The telescreen received and transmitted simultaneously. Any sound that Winston made, above the level of a very low whisper, would be picked up by it; moreover, so long as he remained within the field of vision which the metal plaque commanded, he could be seen as well as heard. There was of course no way of knowing whether you were being watched at any given moment. How often, or on what system, the Thought Police plugged in on any individual wire was guesswork. It was even conceivable that they watched everybody all the time. But at any rate they could plug in your wire whenever they wanted to. You had to live – did live, from habit that became instinct – in the assumption that every sound you made was overheard, and, except in darkness, every movement scrutinized.

Winston kept his back turned to the telescreen. It was safer, though, as he well knew, even a back can be revealing. A kilometre away the Ministry of Truth, his place of work, towered vast and white above the grimy landscape. This, he thought with a sort of vague distaste – this was London, chief city of Airstrip One, itself the third most populous of the provinces of Oceania. He tried to squeeze out some childhood memory that should tell him whether London had always been quite like this. Were there always these vistas of rotting nineteenth-century houses, their sides shored up with baulks of timber, their windows patched with cardboard and their roofs with corrugated iron, their crazy garden walls sagging in all directions? And the bombed sites where the plaster dust swirled in the air and the willow-herb straggled over the heaps of rubble; and the places where the bombs had cleared a larger patch and there had sprung up sordid colonies of wooden dwellings like chicken-houses? But it was no use, he could not remember: nothing remained of his childhood except a series of bright-lit tableaux occurring against no background and mostly unintelligible.

The Ministry of Truth – Minitrue, in Newspeak – was startlingly different from any other object in sight. It was an enormous pyramidal structure of glittering white concrete, soaring up, terrace after terrace, 300 metres into the air. From where Winston stood it was just possible to read, picked out on its white face in elegant lettering, the three slogans of the Party:

WAR IS PEACE · FREEDOM IS SLAVERY · IGNORANCE IS STRENGTH

GRAMMAR

Participles

'another poster, torn at one corner, flapped fitfully in the wind, alternately covering and uncovering the single word INGSOC' (line 36) →G14, p.123

VIP FILE

George Orwell

- pseudonym of Eric Arthur Blair (1903–1950)
- writer of both fiction and non-fiction about inequalities in society
- famous satirical fable 'Animal Farm' (1945)
- criticized the Soviet Union under Stalin

[1] **INGSOC** English Socialism

2 ***The beginning of the story:*** *What is the effect of the first sentence? What do you learn about the setting, the characters and the theme of the novel from this extract?* →S7, p. 93

3 ***Looking at the language:***

a) *How would you describe the atmosphere in the world portrayed? What words and phrases help to create this feeling?* →S2, p. 88

b) *Compare the descriptions of 1. Big Brother and Winston*
2. The Ministry of Truth and the general view of London.

c) *Comment on the three slogans at the end of the extract.*

4 ***Then and now:*** *What references in the text would have seemed futuristic at the time when 'Nineteen Eighty-four' was written? In what ways would you say it was or wasn't a correct prediction of the future?*

5 ***Your opinion:*** *In what way is the theme of the novel still relevant today? Will it still be read in twenty years' time? Why?/Why not?*

6 ***Film project:*** *Watch a DVD of the film version of 'Nineteen Eighty-four' (it was actually filmed in the year 1984!) and explain why it does or doesn't fulfil your expectations. Also find and watch other films that portray future societies. Write reviews for a class 'film review' collection.* →S20, p. 102

A cartoon →S24, p.106

I'll tell you, Ed, this new technology is starting to really spook me out.

7 ***The situation:*** *Explain how the cartoon relates to the expression 'Big Brother'.*

8 ***Your reaction:*** *Say whether or not you would react like Carl. Give your reasons.*

9 ***Creative task:*** *Think of other captions for the cartoon.*

[16] Big Brother Britain

10 a) ***Before you read:*** *Make sure you understand all the expressions in the word bank.*

b) ***While you read:*** *Try to understand the gist. Decide whether a word is really important before you look it up in a dictionary.* →S9/10, p.94/95

WORD BANK
closed circuit television (CCTV) • surveillance cameras • footage • to track sb/to monitor sb • to breach guidelines • to break rules/regulations • evidence • reduction in crime rates

Four million CCTV cameras watch public. UK has the highest level of surveillance

More than four million surveillance cameras monitor our every move, making Britain the most-watched nation in the world, research has revealed.

The number of closed circuit television (CCTV) cameras has quadrupled in the past three years, and there is now one for every 14 people in the UK. The increase is happening at twice the predicted rate, and it is believed that Britain accounts for one-fifth of all CCTV cameras worldwide. Estimates suggest that residents of a city such as London can each expect to be captured on CCTV cameras up to 300 times a day, and much of the filming breaches existing data guidelines.

Civil liberties groups complain that the rules governing the use of the cameras in Britain are the most lax in the world. They say that, in contrast to other countries, members of the public are often unaware they are being filmed, and are usually ignorant of the relevant regulations. They also argue that there is little evidence to support the contention that CCTV cameras lead to a reduction in crime rates.

Professor Clive Norris[1], deputy director of the Centre for Criminological Research in Sheffield, presented the new research at an international conference on CCTV at Sheffield University on Saturday.

Professor Norris said: "We are the most-watched nation in the world. One of the surprising findings was how much more control there is in other countries, such as America and France, compared to Britain. Other countries

[1] Clive Norris [ˌklaɪv ˈnɒrɪs]

FACT FILE

Estimated number of CCTV cameras
- Western Europe excluding Britain: 6.5 million
- Britain: 4.2 million
- USA: 5 million
- Australia, Africa and the Middle East: 2 million

have been much more wary about CCTV, because of long-held concepts such as freedom of expression and assembly. These seem to be alien concepts here."

The Data Protection Act states that the public has to be informed that CCTV systems are in operation, and be told how they can exercise their legal right to see their own footage. But civil rights groups said many councils, shops and businesses were failing to provide this information, and they estimated that up to 70 per cent of CCTV camera operators were breaking the rules. Some shopping-centre security guards use the cameras to track "socially undesirable" people, such as groups of teenage boys or rough sleepers, around stores, and then eject them even if they have done nothing wrong.

Professor Norris warned: "The use of these practices represents a shift from formal and legally regulated measures of crime control towards private and unaccountable justice."

Footage from the cameras has also been passed to newspapers and television companies without people's permission. Professor Norris said: "CCTV is generally seen as benign rather than as Big Brother-style surveillance. We need to have a much wider debate about exactly what CCTV is doing in terms of our privacy and our society. It is about much more than crime. It enables people to be tracked and monitored and harassed and socially excluded on the basis that they do not fit into the category of people that a council or shopping centre wants to see in a public space."

Over the past decade, the Home Office has handed out millions of pounds to police forces and councils to install CCTV systems in the belief it will reduce and prevent crime. But Barry Hugill[2], of the human rights and civil liberties organisation Liberty, said: "All that CCTV does is shift the crime to another area for a bit, and then it returns. If you asked most people, they would rather see the Government spending the money on more police officers than on installing cameras, which do not appear to make much difference anyway."

Maxine Frith in *The Independent*

[2] **Hugill** ['hju:gɪl]

11 ***Pros and cons:*** *Discuss the arguments for and against CCTV cameras.*

12 ***Class debate:*** *Debate and vote on this statement: "Honest citizens have nothing to fear from CCTV surveillance." Use the ideas you have collected in Exercise 11 to help you prepare the debate.* →S17, p.100

13 [💻] ***CCTV and you:*** *Research the situation in Germany. Find out the statistics for CCTV cameras and what rules there are about where they can be installed and how images of the public can be used.*

D Digital culture

1 ***While you read:*** *As you read this article, note down the names of the people mentioned and the points they make.*

⟨The next step in brain evolution⟩

Emily Feld is a native of a new planet. While the 20-year-old student may appear to live in London, she actually spends much of her time in another galaxy – out there, in the digital universe of websites, e-mails, text messages and mobile phone calls. The behaviour of Feld and her generation, say experts, is being shaped by digital technology as never before. It may even be the next step in evolution, transforming brains and the way we think.

"The other day, I went to meet a friend in town, when I realised I'd left my mobile phone at home. I travelled the five miles back to collect it. I panicked. I need to have it on me at all times. I sound really sad, but everyone I know is the same. Technology is an essential part of my everyday social and academic life. I don't know where I'd be without it. I've never really been without it."

That's what makes Emily a 'digital native', one who has never known a world without instant communication. Her mother, Christine, on the other hand, is a 'digital immigrant', still coming to terms with a culture ruled by the ring of a mobile and the zip of e-mails. Though 55-year-old Christine happily shops online and e-mails friends, at heart she's still in the old world. "Children today are multitasking left, right and centre – downloading tracks, uploading photos, sending e-mails. It's nonstop," she says. "They find sitting down and reading, even watching TV, too slow and boring. I can't imagine many kids indulging in one particular hobby such as birdwatching, like they used to."

This generational divide has been evident for a while, but only now is its impact becoming clear. To some, a world flooded with endless info bits and constant stimuli is scary; to others it is full of possibility and fascinating questions. Are digital natives charting a new course for human intelligence? And if so, is it better, faster, smarter? Many parents still fear that children who spend hours glued to computer screens will end up nerdy zombies with the attention span of a gnat. But it need not be like that, say some experts.

GRAMMAR
Past habits
'like they used to' (line 20)
→G3, p.116

GRAMMAR
Inversion
'only now is its impact becoming clear' (line 21)
→G16, p.125

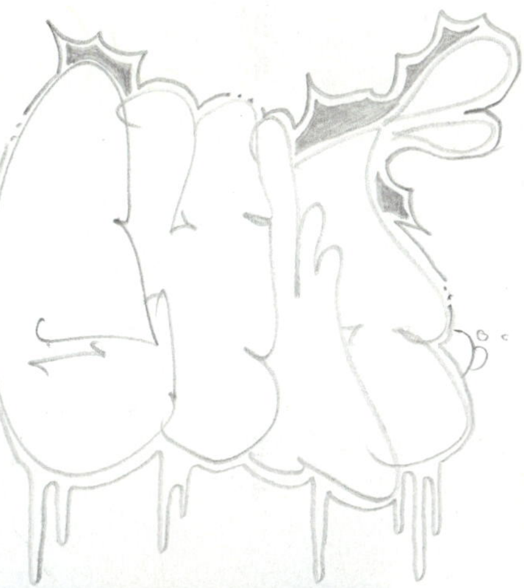

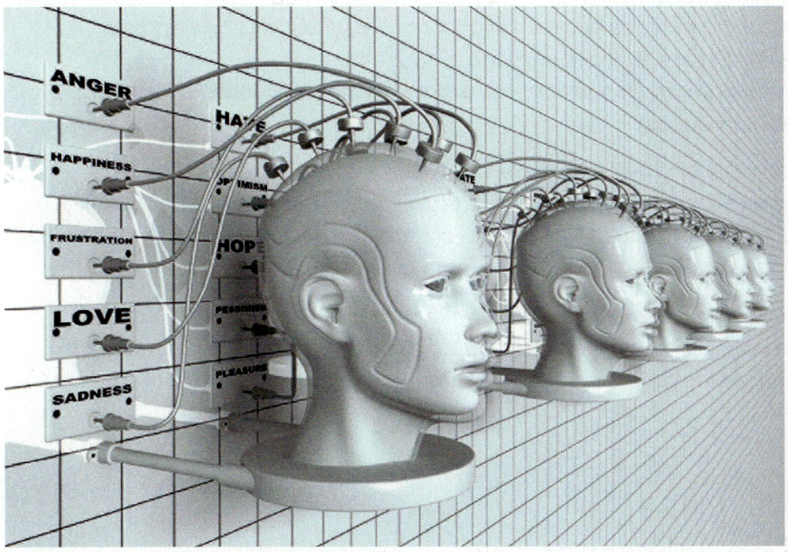

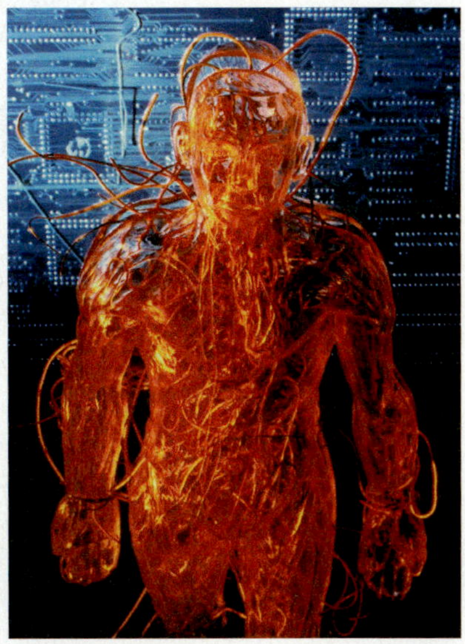

"Computer games can improve some aspects of attention, such as the ability to quickly count objects," says Dr Anders Sandberg, who is researching "cognitive enhancement" at Oxford University. "Is this a different way of thinking? Well, a bit. Being instantly able to itemise objects is a useful skill in this world. People are becoming more visual than verbal. Some people are claiming that once computers gain good language understanding and you can speak to them, then reading and writing are going to seem cumbersome." The mass of visual, auditory and verbal information in the modern world is forcing digital natives to make choices that those who grew up with only books and television did not. "Younger people filter more," says Helen Petrie, a professor of human-computer interaction at the University of York. "But I don't think attention spans are diminishing per se. If we find something that is engaging, then our attention span is just as long as it has always been."

The question, then, is how do digital natives learn to discriminate, and what determines the things that interest them? According to American consultant and author Marc Prensky, the reason why some children do not pay attention in school is that they find traditional teaching methods dull compared with their digital experiences. Digital natives draw on the experience and advice of online communities to shape their interests and boundaries. A telling symptom is blogging. Where once students confided in their diaries, now they write blogs on MySpace.com – where anyone can see and comment on them.

Where is it all leading? Only one thing seems clear: changes propelled by the digital world are just beginning. Indeed, one of the markers between the natives and the immigrants is the acceptance of rapid digital change. "My parents are as au fait with the internet as I am," says Nathan Midgely of the TheFishCanSing research consultancy, "but what they are not used to doing is upgrading. They got the internet seven years ago, but they bought it in the way you might have bought a TV 25 years ago: buy it and stick with it. People of my generation are much more used to the turnover of gadgetry." Faster broadband speeds, easier interfaces, smaller hardware – innovation is happening at such a pace that what was science fiction a few years ago is looming as fact.

Richard Woods in *The Sunday Times*

2 *Understanding the text:*

a) *Explain the difference between 'digital natives' and 'digital immigrants'. Make mind maps for each of them.*

b) *Summarize the main points of the article. The notes you made in Exercise 1 will help you.* →S3, p. 89

3 ***Vocabulary:*** *Explain the meaning of these words and phrases as they are used in the text: really sad (line 9); multitasking left, right and centre (line 17); generational divide (line 21); filter (line 37); markers (line 51); upgrading (line 55); stick with it (line 56)* →S8, p. 94

4 [group] ***Project: Do a survey*** a) *in your own class and* b) *among your parents/grandparents to find out what role digital technology plays in your/their daily lives. Evaluate the results according to group and gender and present them for discussion in class.* →S29, p. 110

Communicating online: Netiquette

We expect other drivers to observe the rules of the road. The same is true as we travel through cyberspace. That's where netiquette, a term coined for either network etiquette or Internet etiquette, comes in handy. Here are a few pointers to guide you through your online communications.

1. Avoid writing e-mail or posting messages in newsgroups, forums, blogs and other online venues using all capital letters. IT LOOKS LIKE YOU'RE SHOUTING! Not only that, it's difficult to read.

2. When you talk with someone, your tone of voice conveys great meaning. To add personality humor to your messages, use smileys, also known as emoticons, expressions you create from the characters on your keyboard. A few popular ones include:

:-)	Happy	:-@	Screaming	:-D	Laughing
:-(	Sad	:-l	Indifferent	;-)	Winking
:-o	Surprised	:-e	Disappointed	:-*	Kiss

3. Keep your communications to the point. Few people like reading text on a computer screen. Many people now receive e-mail on cell phones and other portable devices. The tiny screens make reading lengthy messages particularly challenging. This is true whether you send e-mail or post messages online.

4. To keep messages short, use some common abbreviations: <BTW> means By the Way. A <G> enclosed in brackets indicates grinning. A good one to keep handy in case you're worried about offending someone is <IMHO> – In My Humble Opinion. One of our favorites is <ROTFL>, which stands for Rolling on the Floor Laughing. A shortened version is <LOL> – Laughing Out Loud. And if you get called away while chatting online, try <BRB> – Be Right Back.

5. Remember that anything you post to a newsgroup, forum, blog or website and type during a public chat session is a public comment. You never know who's reading it or who may copy and spread it around. It could come back to haunt you.

5 ***Different forms:*** *What are the main differences in form between communicating electronically and writing to someone in the traditional way? Discuss whether you think it important for young people to learn the traditional forms.*

6 ***Emoticons:*** *Explain how the term 'emoticon' is typical of online language. What other emoticons not listed above do you know? See if your partner can guess their meaning.*

7 ***Discussion:*** *What are the advantages and dangers of using the internet? Use the cartoon as a starting point for your discussion.* →S16, p.100, →S24, p.106

8 *Read the report below quickly for the gist.* →S2, p.88 *Only use a dictionary for words you consider to be important.* →S9/10, p.94/95 *Then do these tasks:*

1. *Explain what RFID chips are and how they work.*
2. *Say what a couple did with RFID chips and why.*
3. *What questions would you ask the couple if you could interview them?*
4. *What do you think of this "grand gesture of love"? How far would you go in expressing love/attachment to another person?*
5. [ ] *Research: Find out what RFIDs are intended to be used for.*

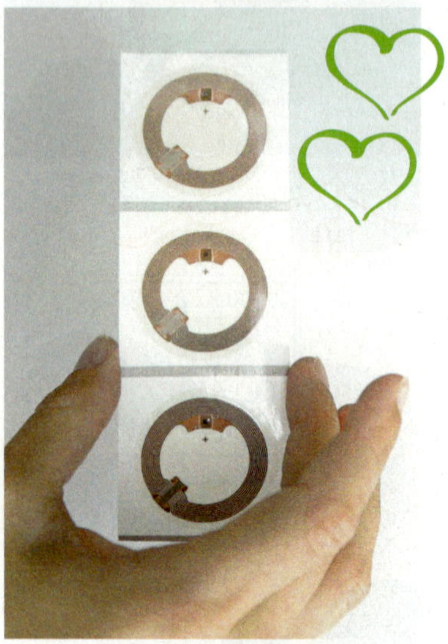

RFID chips are frequently used to store product data

[1] **Jennifer Tomblin** [ˌdʒenɪfə ˈtɒmblɪn]
[2] **Amal Graafstra** [ˌʌmɑːl ˈɡrɑːfstrə]

⟨Love chips⟩

Grand gestures of love take many forms on Valentine's Day – flowers, chocolate, romantic dinners – but a tech-savvy couple has taken it to a new level. Jennifer Tomblin[1] and Amal Graafstra[2] have made the most modern declaration of their affection for each other, with implanted electronic chips that allow them access to each other's lives.

It's called Radio Frequency Identification, or RFID. Both have had a small electronic chip embedded under their skin that grants access to each other's front doors and home computers. The system works like a key-card. A simple swipe of the wrist across an electronic sensor, and they're in.

The couple sees the decision as a modern declaration of love that also happens to be functional. "It's convenient and all of that. But it's definitely neat to have access to each other's things. Nobody else has that, definitely," Tomblin told CTV's Canada AM.

Tomblin, 23, lives in Vancouver, while Graafstra, 29, lives in Washington. Graafstra got interested in RFID several years ago, and began researching the possibilities. He works in remote server management, so it was a natural step to order his first chip, have it implanted by a cosmetic surgeon, then begin writing software to go along with it. "I got interested in RFID, essentially, as a way to replace my keys," Graafstra said.

He had a second chip put in later, and after witnessing his successful experiment, Tomblin got her own chip about six weeks ago. "He'd get into his house and car and computer with it, and I decided if I could do something like that too, it would be really neat," Tomblin said.

The chip itself is just two millimeters by 12 millimeters, and can be inserted under the skin with an injection needle. Graafstra's interest has continued to grow and he has now written several pieces of software to go along with the chip. That interest has developed into a book project called RFID Toys, which comes out later this month. The book will include the RFID programs he has written, and will reveal his self-implanting method.

The chip is in a tiny glass tube, and once implanted it is invisible. The chips are surprisingly inexpensive, not much more than a few US dollars, and can easily be ordered online, but come with a warning against doing what Graafstra and Tomblin did. "We do not advise users to implant the RFID tags we sell into humans or animals," reads the warning. "These tags are not sold as medical products." However, the trend is likely to gain momentum as Canadians seek new ways to implement technology into their daily lives, and just maybe, to demonstrate their love for each other.

E Technology and the environment

A farmer spraying crops

Traffic producing greenhouse gases that contribute to global warming

Using solar energy to produce electricity

A wind farm

A power station polluting the air

A car powered by electricity

1 ***The photos:*** *Use the photos to talk about the different ways in which science can have a positive or a negative effect on the environment. What other examples can you think of?* →S23, p.105

2 [23 ◎] ***Listening: FCC considers protecting birds from 'towerkill'*** →S1, p.88

a) *First check the words in the word bank. Then take notes while listening to this report from the Earth & Sky Radio Series with Deborah Byrd and Joel Block.*

WORD BANK
Federal Communications Commission (FCC) • to migrate/migratory (adj.) • to illuminate • overcast sky • collision/to collide with sth • to eliminate

Communications towers lit up at night

Birds killed in collisions with communications towers

b) *Now explain what the problem is, what causes it and what steps are being taken towards its solution.*

3 ***Mediation:*** *Some people who have listened to the Earth & Sky report are having a discussion about the problem of 'towerkill'. Sum up in German the point of view of each of the four people.* →S28, p.108

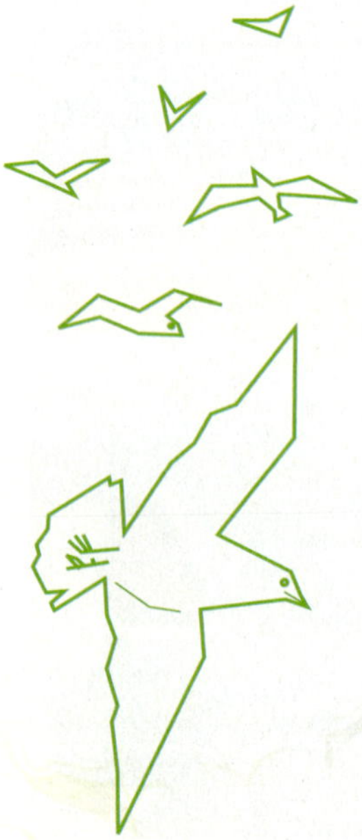

Adam: I know it's sad that birds get killed, but isn't it a question of them adapting? You can't stop human progress. Birds will simply have to get used to avoiding towers, won't they? If we solve the towerkill problem, it will just be something else that kills birds – or migrating frogs – or whatever.

Betty: Hold on there, Adam! Surely we have a duty to protect the animal world? We know they can't adapt at the speed with which we are developing our technology. We've got to help them before it's too late. That's obvious.

Carlos: I agree. Birds act on instinct. They use the light of stars to guide them. So if visibility is low and they can't see the stars, then they will be guided by the lights of towers. And they'll get killed unless these are made to look different.

Denise: Well, I'd say the safety of people in airplanes is more important than the lives of a few birds. The fact is, towers have to be illuminated properly.

Carlos: I'm not saying towers shouldn't be illuminated. I'm saying they should have lights that blink slowly. And anyway it's not "a few birds", it's millions that are being killed every spring.

Betty: And I don't think we humans should be saying that we are in any way more important than animals. Because we are all part of nature. We exist side by side. If all the animal species died, the earth wouldn't last very long, would it?

Denise: OK. But having blinking lights wouldn't save all the birds. I've heard that blinking lights are banned at night in some places. And I know for a fact that the lights on tall communications towers are not just turned on on cloudy or foggy nights as that report suggested. They're turned on every night.

Adam: Right. And I imagine more birds are killed by other human structures – you know, like bridges and power stations – than they are by communications towers.

Betty: That may be so. But what we all can agree on, I think, is that urban landscapes are a great threat to birds – and a major reason for the rapid decrease in the bird population worldwide. Incidentally, the city of Toronto, where I come from, recently brought out a booklet giving architects and city planners a list of options and strategies to reduce bird collisions in Toronto.

Carlos: Sounds like a good idea. I hope it catches on.

Denise: Yes, but let's face it – we all know that we aren't suddenly going to be able to live without communications towers and other bird-unfriendly structures.

Carlos: Of course not. That's why we need to do research into how birds behave when confronted by a lit tower or other obstacles. We have the technology, like radar and devices for seeing in the dark.

Adam: Huh! That's easier said than done. This kind of experiment is difficult because you need low visibility and bird migration to occur at the same time. And it's expensive to have equipment waiting night after night for such conditions to occur.

Toronto's guidelines for architects and city planners

[17] ⟨White coats (New Model Army)⟩

Well, we know what makes the flowers grow – but we don't know why
And we all have the knowledge of DNA – but we still die
We perch so thin and fragile here upon the land
And the earth that moves beneath us we don't understand

So we rush towards the Judgement Day, when She reclaims
A toast to the Luddite[1] martyrs then, who died in vain
Down at the lab they're working still, finishing off
How do we tell the people in white coats enough is enough?

Chorus:
Hey, hey, I listen to you pray as if some help will come
Hey, hey, She will dance on our graves when we are dead and gone

You and I we made no suicide pact – we didn't want to die
But we watch the wall, little darling, while the chemical trucks go by
This desperate imitation, now, of innocence
Those last few days at Jonestown[2] ain't got nothing on this

Chorus:
Hey, hey, I listen to you pray as if some help will come
Hey, hey, She will dance on our graves when we are dead and gone

Now beneath the fitted carpets, beyond the padded cells
Within these crimes of passion the naked truth She dwells
And this fury's just a part and this thunder's just a part
Desire is just a part – the cracking ice, the splitting rock

Chorus:
Hey, hey, I listen to you pray as if some help will come
Hey, hey, She will dance on our graves when we are dead and gone
Hey, hey, to the suicide day the blind man blunders on
Hey, hey, She will dance on our graves when we are dead and gone

As children learn about the world, we built that wall of sand
Along the beach we laboured hard with our bare hands
We worked until the sun went down beneath the waves
And the tide came rolling splashing in, washed the wall away
How do we tell the people in the white coats enough is enough?

Words: J. Sullivan/R. Heaton/J. Harris

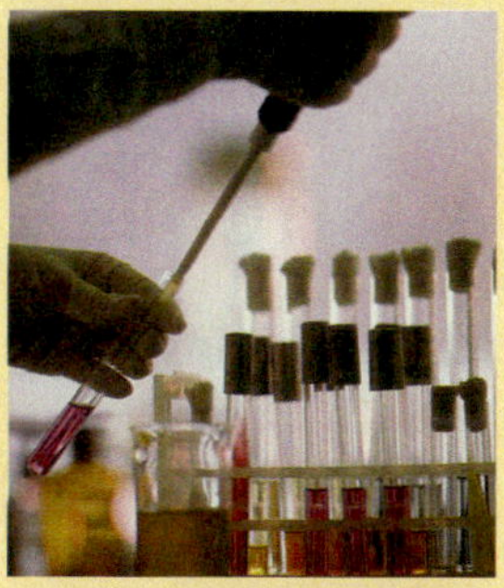

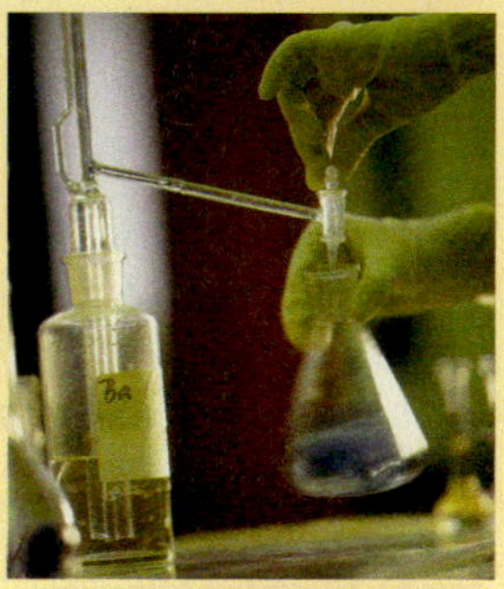

[1] **Luddites** were groups of workers in the early 19th century who destroyed machines they thought would take away jobs
[2] a settlement in Guyana where a cult from California organized the mass murder and suicide of over 900 adults and children in 1978

VIP FILE

New Model Army
- English rock band
- active 1980–present
- named after the Parliamentary army created in 1645 during the English Civil War

4 ***Listen to the song, then answer the questions:*** →S22, p.104
1. *How would you describe the feelings and atmosphere conveyed?*
2. *Explain how the title is linked to the 'message' of the song.*
3. *Comment on these images: 'Judgement Day' (line 5); 'She will dance on our graves' (line 11); 'we watch the wall' (line 13); 'the padded cells' (line 20); 'the blind man blunders on' (line 27); 'that wall of sand' (line 30)*
4. *Say whether you do or don't agree personally with how the future is portrayed in the song. Give your reasons.*
5. *Discuss whether scientists should be held responsible for discoveries or inventions that damage the environment.* →S16, p.100

Skills

A Text skills

S1 Listening

Common listening situations
- telephone conversations
- interpreting
- talks
- announcements
- radio and TV programmes

Listening tips

■ As with all comprehension situations, watch out for **key words** and **context** factors and try to **get the gist**. Key words are often names, times, numbers and places.

■ When you take part in a conversation, e.g. on the telephone or when you are asked to interpret for someone, you can always ask the speaker to **repeat** or **explain** anything that you haven't understood.

■ If you can see, as well as hear, the people you are talking to, look at their **body language**. It will help you to understand what they are saying.

■ When you listen to longer speeches, **take notes**.

■ Announcements contain important information, usually in clear, simple language. They are often **repeated** several times to make sure everyone understands them.

■ Following radio programmes is more difficult because the only help you can get is from the speakers' **intonation**.

■ Be aware of the most important differences between **American and British English**, and be prepared for other **regional pronunciation** differences when you make phone calls.

USEFUL PHRASES

Excuse me, can you say that again, please? • Could you repeat that for me, please? • Sorry, I don't understand the word ... What does it mean? • Can you spell that for me, please? • Have I got that right?

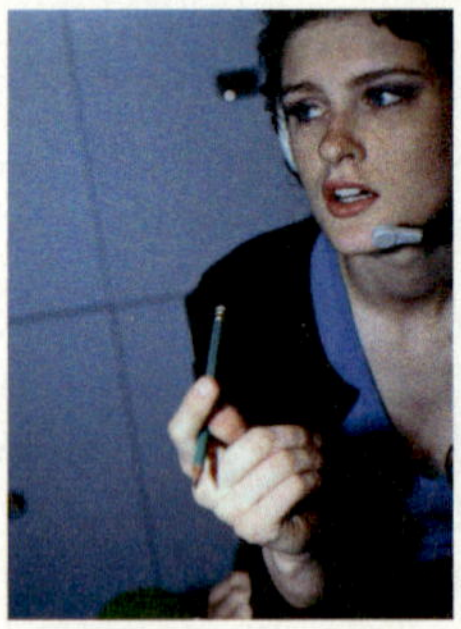

S2 Reading techniques

Skimming

■ Skimming means going through a text quickly and **getting the gist**.

■ Look out for headings, pictures and key words. Don't read every word, concentrate on beginnings and ends of paragraphs as well as key words.

Scanning

■ Scanning means going through a text quickly and finding particular **details**.

■ Headings and pictures give you an idea of what to expect from a text. What questions would you want the text to answer? Look out for relevant key words. Stop when you find one and read that part of the text carefully. Take notes if necessary.

S3 Text analysis

When you are asked to analyse a text, try to answer the following questions (choose the ones that are relevant for your text):

Questions for any text:
- What type of text is it?
- What purpose was it written for?
- What is the target group?
- Who wrote it?
- When was it written?
- What parts can it be divided into?
- What kind of language is used?
- How does the style relate to the content?
- What atmosphere is created?
- What else is special about the text?
- What effect does the text have on the reader?
- What is your personal impression?

Additional questions for fictional texts:
- Who is the narrator?
- What is the setting?
- Who are the characters?
- What is the main theme?
- What is the plot?
- Is there a turning point?
- What narrative techniques are used?

How to do it

- Make sure you understand what is in the text and what it is about. Looking for **key words** and **taking notes** will help you.
- Getting some **background information** about the text and its author can be helpful.
- Answer **questions** on the text **precisely** and to the point. Look carefully at the way the questions are phrased and do exactly as you are told, e.g. when you are asked to analyse, describe, discuss, compare or interpret things.
- It is often a good idea not just to describe things on their own, but to relate them to each other, e.g. by pointing out **contrasts** in the characters, the atmosphere, the language.
- Explain everything in your own words, but use **quotations** from the text to support your statements, marking them clearly as quotations and giving line references.
- Make clear what is **fact** and what is your **interpretation**. Do not repeat yourself.
- Only give your opinion if you are asked to and always give **reasons** for it.

REFERENCES

For a comparison between fictional and non-fictional texts and some important genres, e.g. novel, short story, essay, poem, play →S4, p.90. For narrator and point of view →S6, p.92. For characters →S5, p.91. For narrative techniques →S7, p.93. And for a list of important literary terms see the glossary on p. 200.

When you write about a text, think of using connectives and structuring devices (see also →S13, p.97) as well as adjectives and adverbs to give precise descriptions of characters, action and circumstances. Here are some useful phrases for text analysis and interpretation:

USEFUL PHRASES

The novel/short story/play/poem … was written in … by … • The author grew up in … • He/She is famous for … • The text is a typical example of … • It is about … • It tells the story of … from the point of view of … • It is set in … • The atmosphere is … • The main character/s is/are … • The narrator is … We get to know … by … • His/Her relationship with … is … • He/She feels … because … • There is a conflict between … Therefore … • On the one hand … on the other hand … • At the beginning … • Later he/she learns/changes … At the end … • This means … • The way … is presented suggests … • The author uses … in order to … He/she probably wants to show … • The text is special because …

S4 Literary genres

Extract from: Honey Bees and beekeeping

In January, the queen starts laying eggs in the center of the nest. Because stored honey and pollen are used to feed these larvae, colony stores may fall dangerously low in late winter when brood production has started but plants are not yet producing nectar or pollen. When spring 'nectar flows' begin, bee populations grow rapidly. By April and May, many colonies are crowded with bees, and these congested colonies may split and form new colonies by a process called 'swarming'. A crowded colony rears several daughter queens, then the original mother queen flies away from the colony, accompanied by up to 60 percent of the workers. These bees cluster on some object such as a tree branch while scout bees search for a more permanent nest site – usually a hollow tree or wall void. Within 24 hours the swarm relocates to the new nest. One of the daughter queens that was left behind inherits the original colony.

From: *The farm* website

The Rose and the Bee

If I were a bee and you were a rose,
Would you let me in when the gray wind blows?
Would you hold your petals wide apart,
Would you let me in to find your heart,
If you were a rose?

"If I were a rose and you were a bee,
You should never go when you came to me,
I should hold my love on my heart at last,
I should close my leaves and keep you fast,
If you were a bee."

Sara Teasdale (1884–1933)

1 *Examine the style, structure and purpose of the two texts, make notes and discuss what you suppose to be the author's intention and the effects produced in the reader. Then compare your findings with the information in the box below.*

Non-fictional texts

Important types:
newspaper article, informative text, essay, review, biography, instructions, legal document

Purpose:
giving truthful information about facts and opinions

Style:
informative, argumentative, usually clearly structured, simple and direct, prose

Fictional texts

Important genres:
novel, short story, fable, fairy tale, poem/song, play

Purpose:
transferring the reader into a different world; the author's intention is often a matter of interpretation

Style: Any kind of language or structure is possible, poetry or prose. Pictures in the reader's mind are produced to create a new reality. Atmosphere and emotions are more important than hard facts.

Typical features:
- interesting setting and characters
- conflicts within/between characters
- narrative techniques (perspective, order of events, suspense)
- imagery
- artful language (for a list of literary terms see the glossary on page 202)

S5 Characters

Topic 1: I go along First of all, he's only in his twenties. Not even a beard, and he's not dressed like a poet. In fact, he's dressed like me: Levi's and Levi's jacket. Big heavy-duty belt buckle. Boots, even. A tall guy, about a hundred and eighty pounds. It's weird, like there could be poets around and you wouldn't realize they were there.

Topic 2: I get my culture where I can "Nah … I'm not an *educated* brother, although …" He had a theatrical, old-fashioned way of speaking, which involved his long, pretty fingers turning circles in the air. "I guess you could say I hit my own books in my own way." … "I get my culture where I can, you know – going to free shit like tonight, for example. Anything happening that's free in this city and might teach me something, I'm there."

Topic 3: Teacher Man Don't let them take over the classroom. Stand up to them. Show them who's in charge. Be firm or be dead. Take no shit. Tell them, Open your notebooks. Time for the spelling list.

Topic 4: The moment before the gun went off … everyone in the district remembers Marais Van der Vyver as a little boy who would go away and hide himself if he caught you smiling at him, and everyone knows him now as a man who hides any change of expression round his mouth behind a thick, soft moustache, and in his eyes by always looking at some object in hand, leaf of a crop fingered, pen or stone picked up, while concentrating on what he is saying, or while listening to you.

1 *Compare the way characters in these excerpts are presented. Make a list of the people described. From whose point of view do we see them? What do we learn about them and how? Make notes. Use the grid below to help you. What effect do different ways of presenting characters have on the reader?*

2 *Choose one excerpt and go back to the topic to look at the full text. Analyse the development of the main characters throughout the story.*

3 *Choose a suitable scene from one of your favourite films that tells the viewers a lot about a main character. Play it in class and use it to practise analysing characters.*

4 [ååå] *Watch the film version of a novel you have read and compare the two. Why are they different? Do you think the actors are well chosen for their parts?*

Character grid:	• outward appearance	athletic, attractive, blonde, elegant, fat, tall, young, …
	• function in the constellation of characters	enemy, friend, rival, …
	• roles, social background	boss, daughter, girlfriend, broken home, criminal, lonely, married, rich, …
	• main traits	honest, intelligent, jealous, kind, show-off, shy, sympathetic, violent, …
	• actions, behaviour, mood	angry, embarrassed, emotional, irrresponsible, terrified, upset, …
	• language	excited, gentle, polite, rude, …

S6 Narrative point of view

The effect a story has on the reader or listener is strongly influenced by the point of view from which it is told. Basically there are three types of narrator that an author can use to tell a story, but the types can be mixed and the point of view can change in the course of the story. Make sure you don't confuse the author, the narrator and the characters when you talk about a text.

A Third-person omniscient[1] narrator

This type of narrator tells the story from the outside but knows about the characters' thoughts and feelings as well as the background of the story.

[1] **omniscient** [ɒm'nɪsiənt] knowing everything

B Third-person limited narrator

This type of narrator seems to tell the story from the outside, but knows only about the feelings and opinions of a particular character in the story. The narrator is not identical with this character, however.

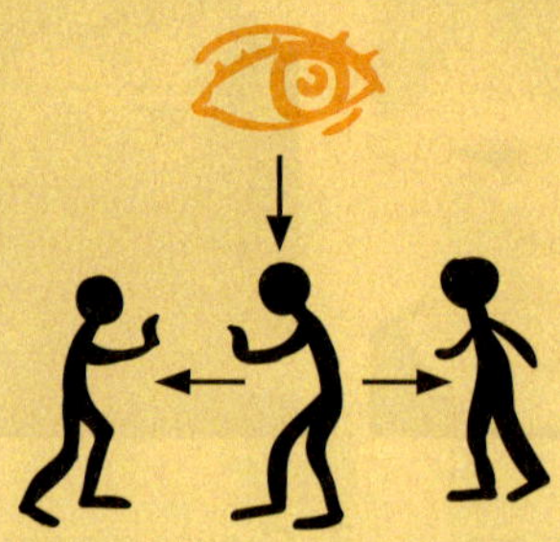

C First-person narrator

This type of narrator brings you close to the feelings and opinions of a particular character in the story because the narrator is identical with this character. You get to know only what this character knows.

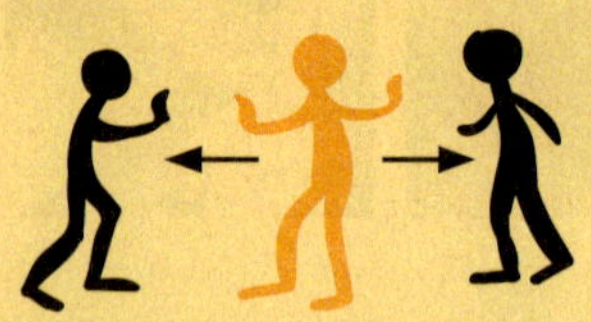

1 *Match the three examples with the types of narrator (A, B or C).*

1. Levi pushed through the crowd, caught his sister by the arm and began to talk to her animatedly. The young man approached slowly, but got there in time to hear Zora say: "Don't be ridiculous – I'm not giving some friend of yours my player – get off me" – "You're not listening to me – it's *not* yours, it's his – *his*," repeated Levi, spotting the young man and pointing at him. The young man smiled weakly. Even so small a smile told you that his were perfect white teeth.

(Topic 2, → page 30)

2. Jamila had started exercising every day, learning karate and judo, getting up early to stretch and run and do press-ups. She was preparing for the guerrilla war she knew would be necessary when the whites finally turned on the blacks and Asians.

This wasn't as crazy as it sounded. The area in which Jamila lived was closer to London than our suburbs, and much poorer. It was full of neo-fascist groups, and at night they wandered through the streets, beating Asians and throwing stones through their windows. Jamila and her parents, Anwar and Jeeta, lived in constant fear of violence.

(Topic 2, → page 35)

3. And how they will sneer when he even says of the farm boy (according to one paper, if you can trust any of those reporters), 'He was my friend, I always took him hunting with me.' Those city and overseas people don't know it's true: farmers usually have one particular black boy they like to take along with them in the lands; you could call it a kind of friend, yes, friends are not only your own white people, like yourself, you take into your house, pray with in church and work with on the Party committee. But how can those others know that? They don't want to know it. They think all blacks are like the big-mouth agitators in town.

(Topic 4, → page 68)

S7 Narrative techniques

Analysing a story (in literature or film) means not only looking at the story itself, but also at how it is told (see also the other Text skills pages). Narrative techniques can create interest and influence the way readers are affected by the story. Here are some important aspects of story-telling:

1. The relationship between author, narrator, reader and characters

The effect which a story has largely depends on the **relationship** between the **narrator**, the **characters** and the **reader**. How is it possible that the reader can **identify** with one or more of the characters? The following factors are important:

- **Point of view** →S6, p. 92: Who is the narrator and what is his/her attitude towards the characters? Does the narrator tell the reader everything, and is it really true? The point of view controls what the reader gets to know and when. Suspense can be created by not giving away too much information, a typical feature of crime or adventure stories.
- The **tense** may also influence the **distance** between the reader and the characters. If something is supposed to be happening while you read, you usually feel closer to it than if it happened long ago.
- Sometimes there is so much distance that the narrator does not even take the characters seriously, but treats them with **irony**. This means that what is said is not actually what is meant, or that the narrator and the reader know something the characters don't.
- As well as **descriptions** of events, characters or settings, there may also be **dialogues** which reveal characters' **thoughts and feelings**, or **comments** by the narrator or author (who are not necessarily the same person).
- In some stories you read or hear directly what a character says **(direct speech)** or thinks **(stream-of-consciousness)**. Stream-of-consciousness (like real thinking) is often unstructured and chaotic, so there is hardly any distance between the reader and the character.
  In other stories the narrator uses **indirect speech** to report what the characters are saying or thinking. This creates more distance.

2. Chronology

In what order are the events told? Is there a **back story** made up of the history of characters, objects, places or other elements in the story? The back story is extremely important in the 'Harry Potter' novels, for example.
In a **flashback** the narrative is taken back in time (a popular film technique), in a **flashforward** future events are revealed.
Foreshadowing means that there are clues early in the story that hint at a future development. This is typical of crime stories or tragedies.

3. Structure (exposition, main part, conclusion)

The main events and theme of a story are called the **plot**. Part of it can be told to the reader directly, other parts may be told by one character to another within the story.
A **frame story** may be provided to create one or more stories within a story. One famous example is the *Tales from the thousand and one nights.*

Children listening to a Native American story-teller

1 *Examine and comment on the narrative techniques in the stories you read. When you work on these texts, try to apply as many of the terms used above as you can. You can start with the short story 'I go along'* →page 12.

B Word skills

S8 Guessing new words

Don't be afraid of texts containing new words. You already know different ways of guessing their meanings. After you have tried these guessing techniques, there may still be some words you don't know, but don't worry, you will probably have understood the most important points in the text.

Guessable words

- words that are used in a **German** context
e.g. bestseller, boycott, clown, laptop, track

- words that are similar to **German** words
→ but watch out for false friends!
e.g. individuality, inner, install, parallel, to wander

- words that are similar to words you know from another **foreign language** (French, Latin, Spanish, Italian) → but watch out for false friends!
e.g. academic, announcement, artificial, descendant, dignity, disrespect, individuality, junior, minor, pasta, phase

- **compounds** of words you already know
e.g. handwriting, heartfelt, mixed ability, single-sex, washing machine, wholeheartedly

- words from a **word family** you already know
e.g. adventurous, announcement, importation, to mirror, nationalism, relevance

- words you already know, but which have another meaning that you can guess from the **context**
e.g. to admit, light, plain, pretty, to report sb, rubber, key (of a piano), (she was preparing for the war she knew would be necessary when the whites finally) turned on (the blacks and Asians)

- words whose meaning you can guess from the **context**
e.g. (he) dozed off (in his chair and we sat quietly, forty of us, waiting for him to wake); (it's old-fashioned,) out of date

S9 Working with a dictionary

As you already know, word-for-word translations do not always work. So be clever and use the additional information given in dictionaries to find the word that fits the context best.

English–German, German–English
This type of dictionary is best used for translating or understanding new words quickly.

- What part of speech is the word?
- What does it go together with?
- What topic or word field does it belong to?
- How is it pronounced?
- Does it have irregular forms?
- What translations are given?
- Which of the translations can only be used in a limited context (AE, formal, slang, etc.)?
- Which of the translations fits the context?

English–English
This type of dictionary is best used for writing an English text when you are not quite sure which is the best word in a given context. The more English you read, the more you will improve your language!

- What part of speech is the word?
- What does it go together with?
- What topic or word field does it belong to?
- How is it pronounced?
- Does it have irregular forms?
- What synonyms and/or definitions are given?
- Which of the given meanings fits the context?
- What examples show how the word is typically used?

S10 Practical dictionary work

A vampire's school report:

THE VAMP HIGHER SCHOOL – TRANSYLVANIA

Name of Pupil: Dracula, Count
Subject: Attendance and punctuality

Dracula's punctuality is appalling. What is the matter with the boy; can't he get up in the morning? To look at him, you would think he had been out all night.

I'm sure his health is suffering. He must get up so late he can't possibly have had time for a bite to eat.

Yesterday he missed the annual cricket match against our deadly rivals, Frankenstein's Middle School, a match we need not have lost had it not been for his absence. It made my blood boil, I can tell you. What chance have you got without your opening bat?

I really wonder whether Dracula's heart is in his school work. Does he not realise what is at stake? He makes me very cross. Unless he starts to put in a lot of effort he will end up without any qualifications at all; what a sucker he'll look then.

No, things must improve immediately. Every member of staff is fed up to the back teeth with Dracula's lateness. It used to be regarded as just a pain in the neck, but no longer. It's now a matter of grave concern.

I want to see him change: overnight.

Ilse Brunhilde Sauerkraut, *Form Mistress*

1 *Skim the text. What kind of text is it?*

2 *Look at the text in more detail. Use a dictionary to find out the correct meanings of all the unknown words in the context. Take your time to read through all the meanings for a word given in your dictionary. Watch out especially for idioms.*

3 *Use your knowledge about vampires to explain all the puns, word plays and allusions in the text.*

Dealing with a text using a monolingual dictionary

- First find out what the text is about. The **title**, **pictures** and **headings** – if there are any – and key words will help you when you skim it. Then try to find out who the text is aimed at and what the purpose of the text is. This knowledge will help to build up a meaningful context and make it easier to understand the text in detail.
- When you look up a word, make sure you know what part of speech it is (noun, verb, etc.). Then you only need to read the meanings related to this word category.
- Look at *all* the meanings and example sentences – for the appropriate part of speech – given for the word in the dictionary. Don't forget to consider other **words the word occurs with**. The word may be part of an **idiom**.
- Decide which meaning suits the given context best.
- Sometimes you think you know a word, but it means something completely different in a different **context**. So if you are unsure, look up more words than just the ones you don't know to make sure you get the meaning right.

C Writing skills

S11 Creative writing

Text-based writing

After reading a text, you may be asked to tell a part of the story that isn't in the text, use the same text type to write about a different subject, change the point of view, or transform one text type into another telling the same story.

- When you are asked to write something based on a text, first make sure you have understood the text properly. Then use your analysing skills and your knowledge about text types and style to create a new text that goes well with the original one.
- The content must fit: the characters and the way they talk or act must be convincing. The story must follow a certain logic. The form must also fit: the style of writing and the text type must either be like those of the original text or different, as the task requires.
- The basis of your new text could also be a cartoon, a film, a listening text or a picture.

Free writing

Before you start writing about a free topic, it is a good idea to brainstorm some ideas and organize them in a mind map.

- Decide on the target group, the genre/text type and purpose of the text, then think of the best way to express your ideas and suitable techniques to tell your story (for **point of view** and **narrative techniques** →S6/7, p. 92/93, how to present **characters** →S5, p. 91).
- If you decide to tell a story, introduce the main characters (who?), the setting (when? where?) and the theme (what?) in an exposition, write about the main action (how? why?) in the middle part and don't forget to think of an interesting conclusion.
- Use connectives and structuring devices to make your text logical. Keep to the same style level throughout the text. If you decide to write a poem, pay special attention to the form.

!
Check what you have written for common mistakes (tense, aspect, prepositions, word order, etc.) and improve your text where possible.

S12 Writing for special purposes

Unlike creative writing, writing for special purposes can mean presenting a lot of facts. Therefore the style should be clear, well-structured, formal, informative and to the point. Text types include letters, reports, reviews, summaries and essays. For news writing →S14, p. 98, for argumentative essays →S13, p. 97. Make sure you are polite when you address someone or give your opinion!

Tips for letter writing

1. Prepare by noting down the most important points you want to make.
2. Use formal and polite style.
3. Introduce your theme and say why you are writing.
4. Your points should be exact and in logical order and the structure should be clear.
5. At the end there should be a summary of what the most important point is.

USEFUL PHRASES

Dear Sir or Madam, • With reference to …, I'd like to … • In my opinion, … • As far as I know, … • In fact, … • That is why … • Therefore, … • Furthermore, … • I hope/wish to … • I would be glad/grateful if … • I wonder if you would be so kind as to … • Thank you very much in advance. • I look forward to … • Yours sincerely • Yours faithfully, …

Daniel Danello
Theatinerstr. 20
80333 München

Creative Concepts Ltd.
62 Denmark Street
London WC5 10B

24 November, 20…

Application for work placement

Dear Sir or Madam,

S13 Writing an argumentative essay

An argumentative essay discusses a controversial issue from more than one point of view. Its aim can either be to win someone over to one side or to present arguments for each side and leave the readers to decide for themselves.

Before you start: *Choose a clear issue that is can be argued about. Become an expert on the topic by using all kinds of sources of information. Decide if you want to persuade the reader to agree with you or if you want to remain neutral. An argumentative essay ending with your own opinion is also called a comment.*

Your essay should be made up of three different parts:

1. Introduction

- You present the issue. To attract the reader's attention, you can include:
  - facts about the history/background of the problem
  - information about its relevance today
  - a quotation
  - questions that you promise to give answers to

2. Main body

- There are two kinds of task:

A You are asked to present only one particular view of the topic. Then it is best to start with the weakest argument and end with the strongest.

B You are asked to present two or even more different views on the topic. Then you can either present the negative points first and then the positive, or the negative and positive points alternately. You can arrange the points according to their importance, from the weakest to the strongest or the other way round.

- Each statement must be supported by evidence (examples, statistics, etc.).
- If you want to persuade someone, it helps to use logic, good examples and good style.
- You can write about how the problem started, who is affected by it, how serious it is, what has been done about it so far, what can be expected if there is no solution, and so on.

3. Conclusion

- The presentation of your arguments should lead to a conclusion. What you can include here:
  - a summary of what you have found out
  - an outlook on further consequences
  - your own opinion
  - an appeal to the readers to reach their own conclusion

USEFUL PHRASES

Think of using connectives, emphasising techniques and structuring devices, such as:

Connectives: although • as … as … • as well • because • but • even if • however • in order to • in spite of • not … either • not until • provided that • since • so that • therefore • unless • whereas • while

Adverbs of comment: actually • after all • apparently • basically • fortunately • frankly • in fact • in my opinion • naturally • unfortunately • obviously • of course • perhaps • possibly • probably • sadly

Adverbs of degree: very • absolutely • almost • at all • at least • completely • drastically • extremely • hardly • most of all • particularly • quite • rarely • rather • really • utterly • virtually

Structuring devices: both … and … • consequently • either … or … • eventually • finally • first of all • furthermore • in the end • it is true that … but … • last but not least • on the one hand … on the other hand … • on top of that • secondly

S14 News writing

News reports or stories are supposed to inform the public about interesting and important events in an unbiased way. As total objectivity is not possible, they should at least be fair, with all the relevant points included, even if the writer does not like them. There are three basic types of news articles: reports (news), features (news and background) and commentaries (writer's opinion).

Writing a news report

- Remember the ABC of news writing: Accuracy (be exact, all the facts have to be correct), Brevity (keep it short and to the point), Clarity (make sure everyone understands). Remember also the five Ws: Who? What? When? Where? Why? (give answers to these questions) – and sometimes How? and So what?

- Attract the reader's attention with the headline and the lead, which is usually the first sentence or paragraph of the story. The lead contains the most important, most exciting point and makes the reader want to go on reading.

- The structure of a newspaper article is an inverted pyramid: The most important thing is at the top. More facts and additional details follow, the least important ones at the end, so that the reader can stop reading any time after the lead when he or she feels they have had enough information. If the story is written well, however, or if someone is interested in the details, they will read on till the end.

- Good news style is active, informative, to the point. Nothing is repeated and nothing unnecessary said. Everything is logical and easy to understand.

- Often news writing contains anecdotes, examples and quotes. If you use quotes, make sure they express the speaker's intention. Without the right context, they may be misunderstood. Only use them when they make a point clearer. A good ending rewards the reader for finishing the article by making some kind of reference to the lead.

1 *Most newspapers can be classified as either popular/tabloid (e.g. The Sun, The Daily Express, The Daily Mirror) or serious/quality papers (e.g. The Times, The Guardian, The Daily Telegraph). Buy some English newspapers or look at their websites. Compare the way the same issue is presented in different papers. Make notes about headlines, language, length, emotions, facts, opinions, pictures, etc.*

2 *Write a news article on a topic of your choice. Before you start, decide what kind of article you want to write and what kind of paper you want to write it for. Collect as much information as possible (through internet research, interviews, surveys, personal experience, etc.) and present it in a way that will interest your readers. Keep in mind why you think the topic is relevant to them.*

D Speaking skills

S15 Conversation

1 *Choose one of the pictures and describe the scene. What do you think the people are talking about? Write a short dialogue that goes with the picture and act it out with a partner.*

Factors influencing conversation

- **Situation** (when? where? for what purpose? formal?) → Make sure your language and behaviour fit the situation. If it's a formal situation and you know what will be talked about, prepare by looking up useful words and facts.
- **People** (age? role? relationships with each other?) → Depending on what kind of people you talk to, different degrees of politeness and indirectness are required. When you talk to older or more experienced people, you should use more polite phrases and not be too direct. When you are with people of your age or people you know really well, you can be a little more direct.
- **Message** (small talk? advice? discussion? argument?) → Give precise and clear information and remember to be tactful when you tell people something that affects them personally.

Tips for everyday conversation

- Be aware of what you say, put things clearly and make your arguments logical. Give good reasons for your opinion.
- Always pick up on what your conversation partners have said to show that you respect and sympathize with them, that you are listening carefully and judging fairly what they are saying. Use supportive intonation and body language as well as the following phrases, where appropriate:
- **Polite phrases:** *please* • *thank you* • *you're welcome* • *don't worry* • *not at all*
- **Short answers** (instead of just saying *yes* or *no*): *Yes, I will.* • *No, I don't.*
- **Modals** (instead of *I want* … or imperatives without *please*, to sound less direct): *Could I …?* • *Would you …?* • *May I …?* • *I'd like …*
- **Concessions** (instead of *No, that's not true* or *I disagree*): *Yes, that's true, but …* • *I agree, but …*
- **Downtoners** (to sound less direct): *not really* • *not exactly* • *slightly* • *maybe a little bit* • *rather* • *It's just …*
- **Emphatic devices** (to show interest and good will): *really* • *absolutely* • *I'd love to …*
- **Feedback phrases** (to show that you want to keep up a friendly atmosphere): *Oh, well* • *of course* • *I see* • *you know* • *I mean …* • *really?* • *Are you sure?* • *What a pity* • *That's very kind of you* • *I appreciate that*
- **Question tags** (to show that you want to keep up a friendly atmosphere): *…, are you?* • *…, can I?* • *…, isn't it?* • *…, shouldn't I?*

S16 Discussion

Tips for discussions

- Make sure you understand the issue that is to be discussed.
- Try to remember everything you know about the issue and make up your mind which side you are on.
- If there is time, note down arguments for the other side and decide in advance what you would say against them.
- When you present your arguments, arrange your points in a logical order. Always give reasons for your opinion and think of good examples to illustrate your argumentation.
- Speak in a way that is clear, precise and easy to follow.
- Be polite. Don't interrupt, and make sure you attack the arguments of the other side, but not the people.

USEFUL PHRASES

Introducing arguments: I'd like to begin with … • First of all … • Next … • I think … • I believe … • It's important to remember that … • Another point I'd like to make is … • It's a fact that … • Finally, … • Eventually, …
Reacting to others: I agree …, but … • It's true that …, but … • I admit that …, but … • I'm afraid I disagree strongly • The way I see it, … • In my opinion, … • But don't forget … • Surely you have to admit that … • You might think differently if … • But you probably remember … • Yes, but obviously you can't deny …

REFERENCES

For more connectives, emphasising techniques and structuring devices →S13, p. 97 'Writing an argumentative essay'

S17 Debate

A debate is a formalized discussion following certain rules. It is a contest between speakers for and against a statement, which ends in a vote. It can be organized like this:

1. The chairperson introduces the issue and presents the statement (also called 'motion') everyone will vote for or against at the end.
2. In a first round, four main speakers speak alternately for and against. They must not be interrupted. The audience (also called 'the floor') listen to the main speakers.
3. Then there is an open debating phase in which the floor may take part, raising their hands and making comments or asking questions when the chairperson allows them to.
4. At the end of the debate the positions are summarized again. Then the chairperson asks everyone to take a vote by raising their hands for or against.

All around the world there are debating societies and contests. Taking part in debates can help you to express opinions and arguments clearly and improve your English. How about setting up a debating club at your school?

S18 Giving a presentation

Increasingly you will be asked to give presentations on all kinds of topics and in different languages. Remember the most important steps for preparing and giving oral presentations:

1. Collect relevant information and material from all kinds of sources. For tips on internet research →S30, p.111.
2. Take notes. Mainly you will need to give the most important basic information on your topic. Additionally you should choose one or more points that are especially interesting, surprising or funny to keep your audience listening.
3. Prepare the material you want to use: maps, photos or videos and diagrams as well as a summary of key facts. You can include them in a handout, a power point file or transparencies that support your points visually. Everything should be clear and large enough for everyone to see.
4. The plan you want to use yourself will not contain a complete text, but just key words, facts and figures. Your presentation should be clearly structured (introduction, main part, conclusion), and the points should be in logical order.
5. Practise your talk using your notes to speak freely. Speak loudly and clearly and not too fast. Try to involve your audience at some point. Check the time you take and make sure it isn't too long.

S19 Project work

Working on a project is more complex than doing a presentation. You have to work in groups over a longer period of time. The results can be presented orally or in written form. Sometimes other school subjects are involved, e.g. Music, Art, History or Politics.

1. When you work in a group, you should get on well with each other. Decide who is going to do what, make a project plan and set deadlines. Everyone should know what their task is and when it should be completed. Your team should meet regularly to discuss the development of the project, whether everything is going to plan, and if not, what can be done about it.
2. Apart from looking for information in libraries or on the internet, you may need to do other kinds of research, e.g. making surveys →S29, p.110, writing to companies and organisations for support or watching developments outside school.
3. The results of a smaller project can be presented in an oral presentation (see above), but a bigger project that runs for a longer period during the school year may produce so much material that it is necessary to organize a project day or an exhibition at which all kinds of results are presented in various forms.

You could do an English history project, for example, involving History, Art and Music. At the end of your research and practice phase you could organize a kind of fair. You could dress up in costumes of the historical period (e.g. the Middle Ages, the Renaissance, the early colonisation of America or South Africa), sell food made to historical recipes, play music, read out poems, play games from that time and show arts and crafts you have made yourselves. A display with important dates, facts and pictures could give the visitors the necessary background information.

E Special skills

S20 Working with films

A feature film usually tells a story, so you can analyse the plot, setting, characters and narrative techniques exactly the way you do with a literary narrative.

In addition to the content, films have audiovisual aspects that must be considered.

By examining how the form is used to express the content, you can reach an interpretation of any work of fiction, be it a film or a novel. As you won't have enough time to analyse a film in full, you should concentrate on one scene and use it as an example of how the film works.

1 *To talk about films you need some knowledge of camera operations. The expressions in the box will help you to talk about stills or moving pictures. Use a dictionary if you need to.*

2 *Look at the film stills below and describe what can be seen and how the camera position and angle and the field size influence the viewers' emotions.*

3 [👥] ***Creative project:*** *Choose one of the stills and make up a scene that it could be part of. Think of a title, a setting, a set of characters, a plot and a dialogue. Then write a script for the scene. You can act it out and film it.*

USEFUL PHRASES

Important genres
action • adventure • comedy • crime • drama • epic/historical • horror • musical • science fiction • war • western • fantasy • romance • melodrama

Basic visual techniques
In the foreground/background there is … • The camera takes a long/medium/close-up/extreme close-up shot. • This brings us close to …/creates a distance between … • The camera position is … • The view of … is frontal/from above/below/behind. • The focus is on a … detail. • The camera zooms in/out of … • The camera pans from … to …/… is introduced in a panning shot. • The movement of … is followed in a tracking shot. • The shots follow each other quickly./The … shot lasts for a while. This creates a/an … atmosphere. • … is shown in slow/fast motion.

1

A scene from the French film *Gaspard et Robinson*

2

John Malkovich in *The Ogre*

3

Jodie Foster in *Contact*

4
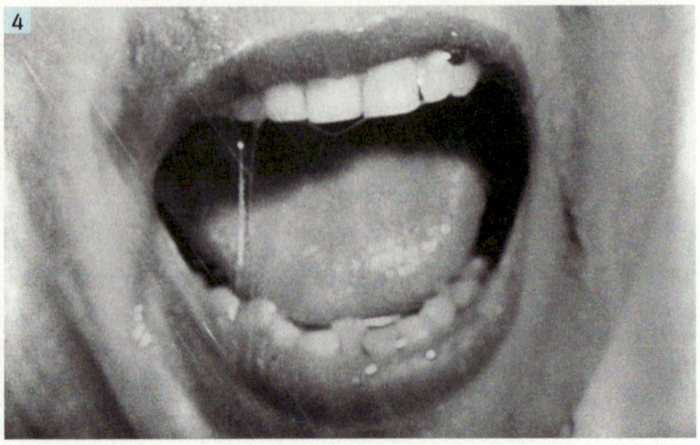
Janet Leigh in Alfred Hitchcock's classic thriller *Psycho*

Presenting a film in class

■ Start by giving your audience more information than just the title:
- Who directed it?
- Who acted in it?
- Who produced it?
- When was it made?
- Who wrote the music?
- Was it a success?
- If the film is based on a literary text, say what it is.

■ Then briefly introduce the setting and the characters and sum up the plot. Say what is good or bad about the film and why you like it or not.

■ Present a scene that has an important function in the film. The scene should enable you to say something about the characters, their relationship with each other, their role in the plot, their language and body language, the atmosphere of the film and what is typical of the way it tells its story. You should also be able to say at what point in the film it comes and what its function is.

You can use a grid like this to make notes about important aspects of one or more film scenes.

setting	characters	story and storyline	camera	light	cut	sound and music	special effects
contemporary/ historical? science fiction? city/country? exterior/interior?	how many? who? appearance? costumes? body language?	dialogue? interaction? fight? narrative structure?	field size? view? zooming? panning? tracking?	colours? brightness/ darkness? atmosphere?	tempo? rest? correspondence with actions?	voices? atmosphere?	animation? slow/fast motion?

4 *Present a film of your choice and get the rest of the class to analyse a scene from it. Discuss your results.*

5 *Further ideas for working with films:*

a) *Present a film that you like or hate • a film that is very exciting or very funny • a film that makes people cry • a film that has the latest special effects • a film with a frame story, flashbacks or unusual narrative techniques • a film that is typical of its genre.*

b) *Either compare two films with a similar plot or compare a film with the book it is based on.*

c) *Write a film review of a film you have seen. Make sure it is useful for someone who doesn't know the film.*

When you present shorter forms, you can use the same analysing techniques, but always keep in mind the purpose and the target group of the film.

Presenting video clips and commercials

■ When you analyse a music video clip, it's a good idea to do an interpretation of the song lyrics, research some background information about the artist, the musical genre and its fans, and find out if it is the artist or the song that plays the main part in the video.

■ When you analyse a commercial, you need to relate all the stylistic devices to its function (e.g. selling a product, creating or improving a company's image, etc.).

S21 Dealing with poetry

A poem is like a picture painted with words instead of paint. These words produce rhythms, sounds, pictures and meanings that you respond to when you read the poem. Like the different parts of a painting, every word in a poem is important. Every piece of the arrangement comes together to produce strong images and feelings in you. Don't worry about finding the 'correct' meaning. Often poems can be interpreted in different ways, so there may not be one.

- Take a close look at structure and form: stanzas, lines, verses.
- Look for rhyme, rhythm, repetitions, or other interesting sound, letter or word patterns. How does the poet treat language? Does he or she play with it or use it in any other unusual way?
- Look for comparison and contrasts. Identify images and symbols, and what impressions or ideas they give you.
- Find devices that are used to create a certain atmosphere and feelings, e.g. colours, sounds.
- Say what the 'lyrical I' is feeling and if a story is told. Sometimes more than one story is possible.
- For basic text analysis techniques →S3, p. 89. Remember that form is usually more important when you analyse a poem than when you analyse prose, and that sometimes a poem does not tell a story. It may just have a theme rather than a plot.

The Road Not Taken

Two roads diverged in a yellow wood,
And sorry I could not travel both
And be one traveler, long I stood
And looked down one as far as I could
To where it bent in the undergrowth;

Then took the other, just as fair,
And having perhaps the better claim
Because it was grassy and wanted wear,
Though as for that the passing there
Had worn them really about the same,

And both that morning equally lay
In leaves no step had trodden black.
Oh, I marked the first for another day!
Yet knowing how way leads on to way
I doubted if I should ever come back.

I shall be telling this with a sigh
Somewhere ages and ages hence:
Two roads diverged in a wood, and I,
I took the one less traveled by,
And that has made all the difference.

Robert Frost

S22 Dealing with songs

Songs are similar to poems, but their additional musical aspect is particularly important.

- As well as examining lyrics and structure (verses and chorus), look at the musical genre, the instruments used, the atmosphere and feelings produced by the sound and the rhythm, or by musical patterns that are repeated or arranged in a particular way.
- It is always useful to look for background information on the songwriter and/or the artist performing the song. Don't confuse these two, as they aren't necessarily the same person.

REFERENCES

For basic text analysis techniques →S3, p. 89.
For narrative techniques →S7, p. 93.
For analysing poetry, see above.

S23 Working with pictures

Visual elements, such as photographs, paintings, drawings, cartoons →S24, p.106 or diagrams →S26, p.107, have an effect on the viewer and can convey messages just like texts. To describe and analyse a picture and talk about its effect, follow these steps:

1. First impression
Talk about your first reaction to the picture and what emotions you felt. What does it show? What information do you have about who created it, and when and why it was created?s

2. Description
Describe in detail what can be seen in it. Starting with the most important elements, but not forgetting those in the background. Comment on people's body language and facial expressions and their relationship with each other. Say how light, colours and focus are used.

Sri Lanka, an armed Tamil Tiger child soldier, 2007

3. Interpretation
Try to answer these questions: What message is conveyed by the picture? Is it aimed at a particular target group? Did the person who created the picture intend it to have a certain effect on the viewer? If so, how is this achieved?

4. Evaluation
Say if you think the picture has the intended effect, and which elements are responsible for its success or failure. If it's a historical picture, compare the effect it must have had in its original context with the one it has now.

The Scream, expressionist painting by Edvard Munch (1893)

1 [partner work] *Work with a partner. One of you chooses the first picture, the other the second. Analyse your picture. Then discuss the quality and the effect of the picture with your partner.*

USEFUL PHRASES

My first thought when I saw the picture was … • The photograph is shocking/disgusting/amazing/spectacular/special … • The picture reminds me of … • It shows … • It was probably taken in/at … • The photograph looks as if it was staged to achieve a certain effect. • It is a realistic picture. • The picture was painted by … • It is a portrait/cartoon/still life/landscape/an oil/watercolour painting. • In the middle/centre of the picture there is … • at the top/bottom • to the left/right of … • in the top left-hand/bottom right-hand corner • in the background/foreground • There is a contrast between … • … is clearly visible • The focus is on … • The field size is a close-up/medium shot/long shot • The colours are bright/dark. • … is seen from above/below/the front/the back • This creates an … atmosphere. • The artist aims to present … • The picture is convincing because …

S24 Analysing cartoons

■ A cartoon is a special kind of visual text. It usually combines a drawing with a text. Cartoons often pick on one current news event and criticise people, institutions or developments in society and politics by making fun of them.

The following devices are often used to achieve this aim:
• exaggeration • irony • puns • symbols • contrast between picture and text

■ You can analyse cartoons according to the four steps introduced in →S23, p. 105 "Working with pictures", but paying special attention to the combination of text and picture.

■ In analysing a cartoon, you should consider its context (e. g. when it was drawn, where it first appeared, who the author and the target group are) before you talk about what is being criticised and why.

"We'll be back, after this commercial break, with more reasons why it's not safe to leave your house."

1 *Practise finding one or more of the elements in the cartoon above.*

S25 Working with maps

When you are asked to find information on a map, it is important to know what kind of map it is. Before you work with a map, look at it carefully to find out what type of map it is, and read the legend to understand the colour coding and all the symbols used. There are different types of maps for different purposes. These are the most important ones:

1. Physical maps
They show the surface of the earth or a specific area. Colours and shades show differences in altitude. You can see what the landscape is like and draw conclusions on what life is like there. They may contain additional information, e. g. on boundaries or capital cities.

2. Thematic maps
Thematic maps present a special topic in an area, e. g. climatic conditions, land utilisation, natural resources, or administrative units. Special symbols are used for these additional bits of information. This type of map is the most common one in your school books. Some contain special information about just one topic, others combine different interesting aspects of an area.

1 *Say what kind of map is shown here and what information you can find in it.*

2 *Look at the maps at the back of this book and say what information is given by each one.*

USEFUL PHRASES
The map shows • Is is divided into ... • It gives an outline of ... • The main road runs ... • ... is situated near the coast • in the valley • next to the river • along the mountain range • on the border with • forest • desert • plain • agriculture • cotton • wine • maize • coal • iron ore • The capital of the state/province/district/country is ... • It belongs to ... • There is a area where ... is grown/produced/mined.

S26 Interpreting diagrams

As you know, diagrams sum up a lot of statistics or information in very little space and can make information easier to understand. Before you interpret a diagram, look at it carefully, read the legend and make sure you understand all the information and the figures in the diagram. What kind of diagram is used (bar chart, pie chart, flow chart, line graph, etc.) depends on what you want to show.

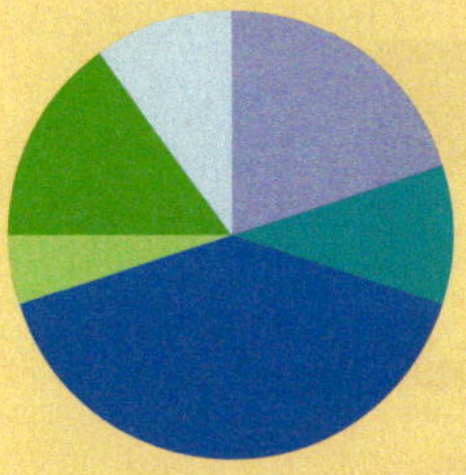

A **pie chart** shows percentages of 100%.

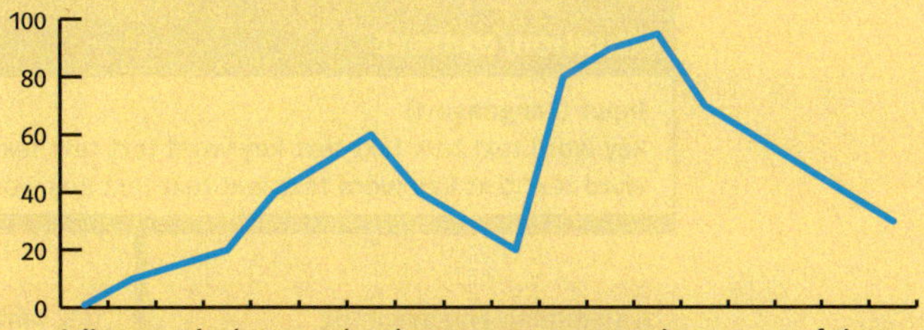

A **line graph** shows a development over a certain amount of time.

A **bar chart** is used to compare figures directly.

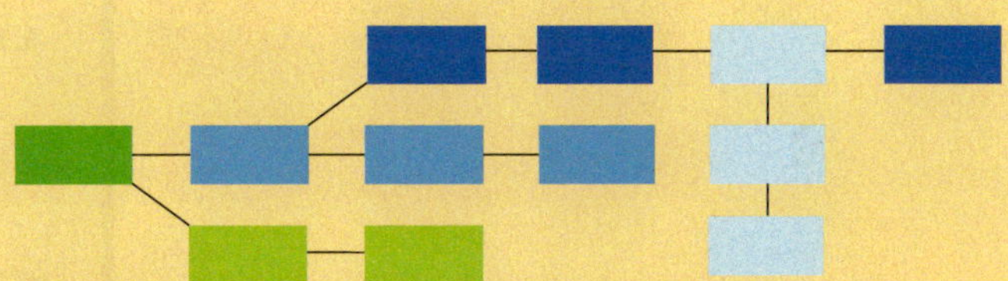

A **flow chart** shows the links between elements and their influence on each other. It is best used to describe processes that contain decisions at certain points where alternatives need to be shown.

USEFUL PHRASES

more/less/fewer than … • compared/in comparison with … • to rise/fall/grow/increase/decrease • percentage, amount, number, majority, minority • turning point • to lead to … • as a result of … • cause, effect, link, relation

S27 British English and American English

English is spoken and written all over the world, but there are lots of different varieties. Here is a list of examples of differences between British and American English:

	British English	American English
Spelling	centre, theatre colour, humour, neighbour programme dialogue travelling to fulfil	center, theater color, humor, neighbor program dialog traveling to fullfill
Pronunciation	[kɑː], [wɜːk], [hɑːf], ['letə], ['djuːti]	[kɑːr], [wɜːrk], [hæːf], ['ledər], ['duːdi]
Grammar	**I've** just come back. **Have** you **got** a car? She is still **at** school.	**I** just **came** back. **Do** you **have** a car? She is still **in** school.
Vocabulary	holiday, sweets, mobile, trousers, underground	vacation, candy, cellphone, pants, subway

S28 Mediation and translation

The diagram below shows the process of mediation and translation. To do it successfully several different skills need to be applied: For translation only the ones in the orange boxes are needed, and for mediation, all of them. Remember that when you mediate you should never try to translate word for word, but get the gist of the input from one language and express it in the other language.

situation/context

Input (Language 1)
key word text text text text **key word** text text text text text **key word key word** text text **key word** text text text text **key word** text text text text text

1. skimming and scanning
2. guessing new words
3. getting the gist
4. selecting the relevant points*
5. paraphrasing
6. summarizing*
7. dealing with idiomatic difficulties

*for mediation only

situation/context

Output (Language 2)
key word text **key word** text **key word** text text text **key word key word** text text **key word** text text text text **key word** text text text **key word** text

editing and polishing (written text)

situation/context

Improved output (Language 2)
key word text **key word** text **key word** text text text **key word key word** text text **key word** text text text text **key word** text text text **key word** text

You'll have to phrase it another way. They have no word for "fetch".

Mediation: The way you communicate is always influenced by the context. So before you start a mediation task, first analyse the situation in which you are mediating by asking yourself these questions.

1. *What text type is the input text? Oral or written language? What is its purpose?*
2. *Who is the author/speaker? Who is the reader/listener?*
3. *What is the relationship between author/speaker, mediator and reader/listener?*
4. *What is the purpose of the mediation?*

The next step is to apply the following techniques:

Mediation techniques

- **Skimming and scanning:** Look (or listen, if it is a spoken text) for important key words and interesting details.
- **Guessing new words:** The context, related or similar words, the body language of the speaker or pictures – if there are any – help you to understand the meaning of unknown words or phrases.
- **Getting the gist:** Find out what the most important information in the text is.
- **Selecting relevant points:** If you see that something isn't important to the reader/listener, feel free to leave it out.
- **Paraphrasing:** If you don't know the exact translation for a particular word or phrase, express it differently.
- **Summarizing:** Sum up the relevant points you have found in your own words, using language that is appropriate for the situation and your readers/listeners.
- **Dealing with idiomatic difficulties:** Try to avoid common mistakes caused by basic differences between the two languages. Remember how to deal with special grammar like gerund or participle constructions. If you don't know the translation for an idiom, try to explain its meaning. It is more important that the output text sounds natural than that it is close in style to the input text.
- **Editing and polishing:** Depending on the situation, you may have time to check if you can improve your text. Look at tense, aspect, prepositions, word order, and style. Watch out for false friends!

Translation: Most of the time you will need mediation skills rather than translation skills, but in some situations you will be asked to translate a text as exactly as possible. Usually in these situations you have more time than when you have to interpret in a dialogue or say what was in a listening text that you heard only once, and you are allowed to use a dictionary to look things up. So you get the chance to read your text again and do some editing and polishing. Use it well!

Translation tips

- Generally, you have to apply most of the techniques you need for mediation, only you must not leave anything out, and you are required to be more exact. However it is still very important that the output text is a good and natural-sounding text in the output language.
- Always keep the context in mind. The style of the output text should be the same as that of the input text.
- Apply skimming and scanning as well as guessing techniques to get the gist of the text before you start translating it.
- Paraphrase only if you can't find a suitable translation in the dictionary.
- Deal with idiomatic differences carefully.
- Use your dictionary for the final editing and polishing.

S29 Making a survey

You make a survey to find out about people's opinions or behaviour. Often you expect a certain result, and you need to prepare your questions carefully in order to find out if you were right. Decide what your target group is, e.g. you may either want to have a general impression of what people think, or compare the results of different age or interest groups. Make sure that the people who fill in your questionnaire know exactly what to do, and give them enough time.

Making up a questionnaire

Depending on what you want to know and how you want to present the results, there are different ways to ask questions.

1. Open-ended questions enable people to give any kind of answer. The results aren't easy to compare. You need to sum them all up to present them, which means a lot of work. Sometimes there is no other way, however, because you can't think of all the possible answers in advance.
   Example: What do you eat for breakfast?
2. If you ask yes/no questions, the results are easy to present, but this type of question only makes sense if the matter is absolutely clear.
   Example: Have you got your own computer?
   Yes/No
3. You can design multiple-choice questions. These are easy to answer.
   Example: **Where do you get information about what's going on in the world?**
   a) newspapers
   b) TV
   c) radio
   d) internet

4. You may want to ask people how they rate something. This means you have to give them a scale to refer to.
   Example: **How important is it for you to be able to speak a foreign language?**
   a) not important
   b) important in some situations
   c) very important

Presenting the results

Always think of your aims when you summarize and present your results:
- proving a certain expectation right or wrong?
- comparing the answers of different groups?
- giving the majority opinion?
- presenting the most surprising results?

Never forget to say how many and what kind of people took part in your survey!

Most answers can be turned into statistics straight away, so you can present your statistics as percentages and use diagrams to support the presentation visually.

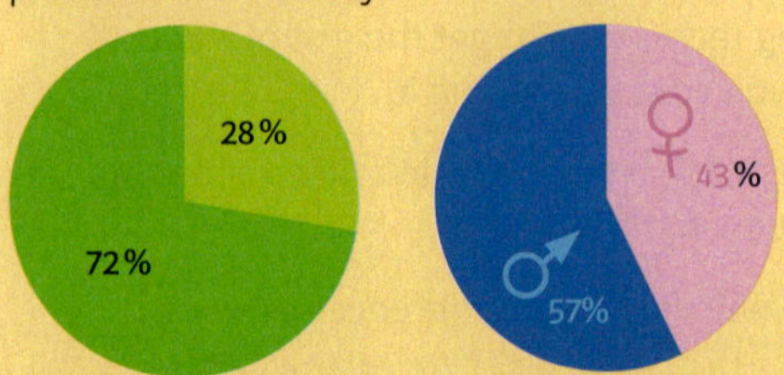

Of all the pupils in the tenth form at our school 72% have got their own computer, 57% of them are boys.

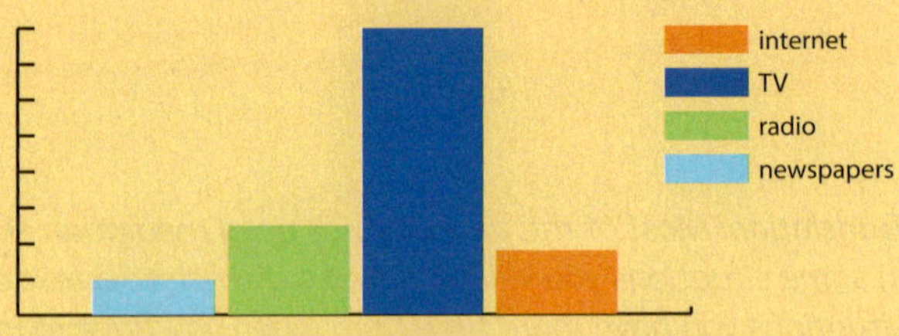

Popular sources of information for tenth graders

Ratings may require a different form of presentation, e.g.:

When asked about the importance of foreign languages 26 out of 30 people answered that foreign languages were generally very important to them, 3 out of 30 thought foreign languages were only important in some situations, and only 1 person said they were not important at all.

Presenting answers to open-ended questions, you may be able to make a top three, five or ten of similar answers or quote the most surprising ones.

The top three breakfast favourites among our class are:
1. rolls 2. cereals 3. jam.

S30 Internet search tips

1. Subject searches and key word searches
There are two ways of finding information on the internet:

- Using a **subject guide** or **directory**, e.g. Yahoo, you choose a category, then a subcategory and so on, e.g. *travel → travel guides → United States → Las Vegas.*

- Using a **search engine**, e.g. Google, you tell it to look for certain key words, e.g. *history apartheid mandela.*

- Generally, if you want information on a broad subject, use a subject guide. If you have exact topics with specific key words, use a search engine. There are even meta-search tools that can save time by doing a parallel search on several search engines simultaneously, e.g. *Metacrawler.*

2. Finding what you want
Most of the search engines use OR as a default. This means that you will get a list of sites that include any of the key words you have entered, e.g. you will get sites for *South Wales* (in Britain) as well as *New South Wales* (in Australia) if you enter *new south wales*.

- With most search engines you can use + or - signs in front of certain key words to make sure they are included or excluded from your search, e.g. *martin+luther+king*. If you look for a certain phrase, like the title of a book, put it in inverted commas, e.g. *"lord of the rings"*. Some search engines don't use these signs, so it's a good idea to check the help section first.
- To get better results, it may help to put the most unusual or relevant word first.
- Generally use lower case.
- If you don't get many hits, check your spelling, try similar key words or use fewer words.
- If you get too many hits, be more specific and add some words.

3. Bookmarks (Favoriten)
To make it easier to return to a site you like, you can add a bookmark either by clicking on the bookmarks (Favoriten) menu, by pressing Control-D (Strg-D) or by clicking on your right mouse button. If you forgot to add a bookmark, you can go back to sites you have visited during the last few sessions by using the forward or back buttons or by pressing Control-H (Strg-H) – *H* for *history*.

4. Finding something on a page
Apart from skimming and scanning →S2, p. 88 the texts on a page, you can use the find function in the edit (Bearbeiten) menu or Control-F (Strg-F) to find certain key words.

5. Evaluating your results
Don't believe everything you read! Remember that anyone can publish anything on the internet. Judge the reliability of a website before using information from it.

- Is it similar to *www.harvard.edu* or rather to *www.aol/users/joedoe*?
- Is it a commercial one? Then it might be interested in selling something rather than giving objective information.
- Does it contain facts or just opinions?
- Is the author someone who is likely to know something about a subject, e.g. a university teacher or a journalist?
- Also check if the website has been updated recently, especially when you look for the latest news on a topic.

6. Saving paper
Don't just print every document you find. Select relevant information only. If you just need part of a long document, use the Print preview (Druckvorschau) option in the File (Datei) menu to see which pages are relevant and print only those to make sure you don't waste any paper.

7. Summarizing and presenting your findings
Once you have selected relevant and reliable information for your topic, you can summarize it and present it in the form that is required, e.g. in a news article →S14, p. 98, a diagram →S29, p. 110, an argumentative essay →S13, p. 97 or a talk →S18, p. 101.

Remember: you should always be able to tell where your information came from!

Grammar

A Foreword

Welcome to the **Grammar** section of *Green Line NEW E2.* You will find that it differs in several ways from the grammar sections of your previous books.

First of all, it is in English throughout. This should not cause you any problems since you are now so familiar with the language. In fact it will make discussing matters of grammar and style in class much easier.

Secondly, this section not only provides grammar rules, it also contains all the grammar exercises in this book. In previous books, the Units introduced and practised new structures and these were explained in the **Grammar**. In *Green Line NEW E2,* there are no grammar exercises in the **Topics**. Instead there are references to the **Grammar**, which can be found in the blue boxes in the margins of the texts, as for example in Topic 1 on page 13:

> GRAMMAR
> **Participle with a subject of its own**
> '... with my hand shielding my face' (line 59)
> →G14, p.123

The box gives you the context in which a particular point of grammar occurs in the text. It also refers you to a paragraph and page in the **Grammar** where you will find the relevant rules and exercises.

This section consists of a number of important areas of grammar that are often a source of mistakes for language learners. They are arranged in a way which underlines their function: *Talking about the past, Expressing conditions and consequences,* etc. The exercises and rules will help you to revise these basic structures either in class or on your own.

If you want to revise on your own, a good idea would be to look at recent English tests or homework that your teacher has corrected and make a list of your most common mistakes. If, for example, you often get conditional sentences wrong or find it difficult to differentiate between the different past tenses, you can turn to the relevant pages in the **Grammar**.

You will notice that parts **B** to **F** follow the same pattern. Each part starts with **Checking up**, followed by **Basic rules** and **Practice**. To see whether you need to revise a certain grammar point, test yourself by doing **Checking up** and looking up the solutions on page 199. If you have got any of the answers wrong or if you find that you are at all unsure, you should go on to look at the **Basic rules** and then try one or two of the **Practice** exercises.

While parts **B** to **F** deal with basic areas of English grammar, most of which you are already familiar with, part **G** *(Advanced Style)* consists of two new structures that you may come across in English texts. This part simply explains these structures so that you will be able to recognize und understand them if you meet them in future. As these grammatical points are fairly uncommon, you won't find any exercises here requiring you to use them actively.

Checking up

These exercises introduce parts **B** to **F**. They are fairly easy and straightforward, and they will enable you to see how well you know a particular structure and the way it works. You can check your answers on page 201. If you find you have got them all right, you probably won't need to continue with that particular grammar point, but may prefer to concentrate on a different one.

Basic rules

These rules only cover the most essential grammar points. The rules are in simple English and the examples show you typical ways in which these structures are used. Some of these rules also include grammar points that are new to you. These are clearly marked ***NEW***. If you need more systematic or more detailed information on any of these structures, you should consult a grammar book.

Practice

This part consists of a number of different communicative exercises, from relatively straightforward exercises at the beginning to more demanding ones later on. In some exercises you are asked to spot the mistake or explain your choice of grammatical structure. This may be made easier by referring to the **Basic rules** again. In the more open and creative exercises you have the opportunity to bring in the structures you have revised in as natural a way as possible.

grammatical term	example	paragraph	page
adjective	an easy exercise, to look good	G10	120
adverb	easily, well, extremely, unfortunately	G11	120–122
adverbial	in the park, two days ago	G11	120–122
aspect	Look, Ben is playing tennis. That racket belongs to me.	G2	114
conditional sentences	If it rains, we'll go to the cinema.	G4	117
dynamic verbs	to play, to run, to sing	G2	114
for and *since*	for three years, since 4 o'clock	G2	114
gerunds	hang gliding, being a teenager, without stopping	G13	123
-ing form with a subject of its own	It involves people jumping off cliffs.	G13	123
inversion	No sooner had I arrived than the game began.	G16	125
modal auxiliaries	can, may, might, must, need, should, ought to	G5–G9	118
participles	walking/walked, while getting out of the car	G14	123–124
participle with a subject of its own	All things considered, she felt quite happy.	G14	124
past tense	She started surfing last year. I was watching TV when they came.	G1	114
past perfect	She had already left before I arrived. He had been working there for many years.	G1	114
position of adverbs and adverbials	Frankly, I never go to the cinema in the afternoon.	G11	120–122
present perfect	We haven't done it yet. They've been watching us for some time.	G1	114
relative clauses	Tom was the boy who phoned me. My aunt, who lives in America, is coming to stay next week.	G12	121
stative verbs	to know, to belong, to cost, to like	G2	114
subjunctive	They suggested that he go there. If only I were rich!	G15	125
used to + infinitive	We used to go there every year.	G3	116
would + infinitive	They would play football in the afternoons.	G3	116

B Talking about the past

Checking up

Which verb form is correct? Explain why.

Luke: Oh, there you are, Amy! At last! (1 **I've waited/I've been waiting**) for you for ages!

Amy: Sorry! But Josh (2 **rang/was ringing**) up while I (3 **got/was getting**) ready. And after (4 **we'd finished/we'd been finishing**) phoning, Sarah (5 **came/was coming**) round to give me a CD back. So when I finally (6 **arrived/was arriving**) at the bus stop, the bus (7 **just disappeared/was just disappearing**) round the corner!

Luke: Never mind. (8 **You got/You've got**) here now. Anyway, (9 **I've thought/I've been thinking**) for a while about which film to go to. (10 **Have you seen/Did you see**) the latest James Bond yet?

Amy: No, but Emma (11 **saw/has seen**) it last week. She (12 **had looked/had been looking**) forward to it for ages. Anyway, she (13 **was liking/liked**) it a lot. Everyone (14 **I've talked/I talked**) to so far says it's great!

Basic rules

G1 Past tenses

There are three tenses in English that refer to the past: **present perfect, past tense** and **past perfect**. Each of them has a simple and a progressive form.

Present perfect	
She has already seen the film.	▶ This stresses the result of an activity. Often with: *already, (not) yet, so far, ever, never*
You've been watching TV for hours.	▶ This indicates that an activity began in the past and has continued until now. Often with: *for, since* (→ !)

Past	
They read 'Romeo and Juliet' at school last year.	▶ This indicates that the event is over. Often with: *last …, … ago, yesterday, when, in 2006*, etc.
While we were watching the news, our TV suddenly broke down.	▶ This describes an activity that was in progress in the past. Often with: *while*

Past perfect	
After he had bought the book, he immediately started reading it.	▶ This describes an activity that happened before another activity in the past. Often with: *after, when*
I had only been reading a few pages, when I realized who the murderer was.	▶ This describes an activity that was in progress before another activity in the past. Often with: *for, since* (→ !)

G2 Aspect (dynamic verbs and stative verbs)

Most English verbs are **dynamic** ('action words' like *play, sing, walk*, etc.). You can use them in the **simple** and **progressive form**.

Some verbs are **stative** (describing 'states': *know, belong, cost, be, like, love, hate*, etc.). They are normally only used in the **simple form**.

!
For and since
- **For** is used for a period of time: *I've known him **for three years** now.*
- **Since** is used for a point in time: *They've been playing **since 4 o'clock**.*

Practice

1 [👥] *Do you know the answer? Ask questions in the correct tense: past tense or present perfect, simple or progressive form? Work with a partner, and take turns to ask and answer the questions.*

1. When • Industrial Revolution • begin • in Britain?
2. In which century • United States • become • independent country?
3. What European country • Britain • fight against • during the 1750s?
4. What city • be chosen • for the next Olympic Games?
5. Why • a dam • be built • in the Hetch Hetchy Valley • a century ago?
6. How long • Aborigines • live • in Australia?

2 *Travelling: Talk about the situation and explain what has happened.*
Example: John left home at 7.30 a.m. It's 11.45 now, and he's still at the wheel. → John has been driving since 7.30. He has been sitting at the wheel for over four hours so he's probably quite tired now.

1. Marion and Sue rush onto the station platform. But the train is just leaving.
2. Emma's parents arrived at the airport an hour ago, but Emma's flight home is delayed.
3. People's train tickets are being checked. Daniel is looking in all his pockets. He's worried.
4. Anna can't drive on because of the snow. It started three hours ago and the road is blocked.

3 *New in the New World: Decide which verb form is correct: present perfect? past tense? past perfect? simple or progressive? Sometimes there may be more than one possibility. If so, discuss which you think fits best.*

(1 . . . you hear) the story of the young man who **(2 emigrate)** to America in the 19th century? It **(3 be)** the time when millions of European immigrants **(4 come)** over to the United States, hoping to live happier lives there than they **(5 have)** in the countries they **(6 leave)** behind them. For some time, incredible stories about life in America **(7 go round)** in the young man's village, and some of them **(8 sound)** so fantastic that now he **(9 begin)** to think about going there himself. No wonder! People **(10 even tell)** him that the streets of New York **(11 be)** all paved[1] with gold! His family **(12 know)** for weeks that he **(13 want)** to go, and in the end, after he **(14 discuss)** it with them, he finally **(15 make)** the decision. He **(16 get)** on the next ship, and two weeks later he **(17 arrive)** in New York.

Ever since the start of the journey, he **(18 look)** forward to reaching dry land, and now that the ship **(19 arrive)**, he **(20 feel)** really great. The New World at last! While he **(21 walk)** along the street, he suddenly **(22 see)** a ten-dollar bill at his feet. Wow! Ten dollars **(23 be)** a lot of money in those days! But just as he **(24 bend)** down to pick up the money, he **(25 stop)** himself and **(26 think)** better of it. "Hell, no!" he **(27 say)** to himself. "Why hurry? I'm too tired now after the journey. I'll start tomorrow!"

[1] **paved** [peɪvd] gepflastert

4 *The party: Tell the story. Use tenses that refer to the past. You could start like this:* Mel had been going out with Dean for a few weeks, but she wasn't happy with their relationship. One afternoon Dean told Mel about a party that one of his friends, Luke, was giving …

G3 *NEW:* Expressing past habits with *used to* and *would*

a) You can use **used to + infinitive** to describe things that often happened in the past.

used to + infinitive	
We often used to go on holiday with our parents. Did you use to go camping? No, but we didn't use to stay at expensive hotels.	**Früher** machten wir oft mit unseren Eltern Urlaub. Habt ihr **immer** gezeltet? Nein, aber wir waren **nie** in teuren Hotels.

- There is only the past tense form **used to**. There is no present tense form.
- Questions are formed with **did … use to**; the negative forms are **didn't use to** (or **used not to**) and **never used to**.
- When you translate **used to** into German, you can sometimes use *früher* or *immer* to stress that this happened in the past and no longer happens now. But sometimes **used to** is not translated at all.

b) **Would + infinitive** can also be used to express a regular activity in the past.

would + infinitive	
Once a month we would have lunch together. Apart from that we wouldn't meet very often.	Einmal im Monat aßen wir zusammen zu Mittag. Ansonsten trafen wir uns nicht sehr oft.

- While **used to** can express activities and states and can be used with all verbs, the more literary form **would + infinitive** can only express activities and is therefore only used with dynamic verbs.

C Expressing conditions and consequences

Checking up

Make conditional sentences to fit each of these situations by putting in the correct verb forms.

1. You're lucky to live so near! If you **(still live)** in Oxford Road, you **(not be able)** to walk to school.
2. Don't worry about your exams next month. If you **(revise)** well, you **(pass)** easily.
3. It was just bad luck. If I **(not be)** ill last week, I **(not miss)** those important lessons.

Basic rules

G4 Conditional sentences

In conditional sentences the **if-clause** expresses a **condition** and the **main clause** describes the **consequence**. There are three basic types of conditional sentences.

Type 1 'realistic'	if-clause: **simple present** If she parks her car there,	main clause: **will-future** the neighbours will complain.
Type 2 'theoretical'	if-clause: **simple past** If I had enough money,	main clause: **conditional** I would buy myself a car.
Type 3 'no longer possible'	if-clause: **past perfect** If he had bought a new car last year,	main clause: **conditional perfect** it would have cost less than this year.

▶ Sometimes (according to the situation) there are mixed forms:
*If I **had saved** up enough money, I **would buy** that car today.*
*If I **had** a car, I **would have visited** you.*

! Do not use **will** or **would** in if-clauses unless they are modal auxiliaries (G9 willingness): *If you **would** only **listen**, you **would know** the answer.*

Practice

1 *Spot the error: In each of these conditional sentences, one of the verb forms is wrong. Find the mistakes, then correct them.*

1. If **I'd be** here next weekend, **I'd be able to** help you with your move.
2. **I'll come** to the cinema with you on Friday if **I'll have** time.
3. **I'd have got** Mark a present if you **told** me it was his birthday.
4. If we **had** a bigger garden, **I will invite** you all to a barbecue on my birthday.
5. If you **like** Indian food, **I make** a curry.
6. If these T-shirts **are cheaper**, **I'd buy** two of them.
7. If Jack **is invited**, he**'d be** here at the party.
8. If you **touch** that plate, you **burn** your fingers.
9. I **would have come** if I **didn't miss** my train.

2 *Think about it:*

a) *What else could the people in the cartoon say?*
b) *Would you do – or would you have done – the same as these people? Explain why (not).*

1. "Our neighbours' little boy is disabled. When they asked me to babysit last weekend, I said no, although the money would have been useful."
2. "I've been given quite a bit of money for my birthday, but I'm planning to put it all in my savings account."

See? If Mommy had worn her seat belt, that wouldn't have happened.

D Using modal auxiliaries

Checking up

Find different auxiliaries to fit each of these situations. Sometimes you will need substitute forms. More than one form may be correct.

1. "___ I borrow that book?" – "OK, but I ___ take it back to the library next week, so you ___ forget to give it back to me."
2. "Sorry I ___ come to the cinema last night." – "You ___ worry – the film wasn't worth seeing!"
3. "The menu was in Greek, so we ___ understand much of it. We ___ ask the waiter to translate it."
4. "If you take that big bag, you ___ take it on the plane with you. You ___ hand it in at the check-in counter."

Basic rules

Modal auxiliaries can express a wish or someone's personal atttitude.

G5 Obligation (müssen, sollen)

I really must start on that esssay now.
Luckily I needn't write more than five pages.
I had to do a lot of work last week.
I'll have to get down to some revision soon.

▶ **Must** expresses that something is necessary or should be done. **Needn't** expresses that something is not necessary. The substitute form is **have to**. (**Be forced to, be compelled to** and **be required to** also express obligation.)

We ought to discuss our plans for that project.
We're supposed to get it all ready by Monday.
Mr Cox says we're not to copy stuff from the net.

▶ ***NEW:*** **Ought to** means the same as **should**. **Be supposed to** and **be to** refer to what someone else has ordered or instructed.

G6 Possibility (können)

Can you give me Dave's phone number?
This can't be correct, can it?
It may be the wrong number. Amy might know.

▶ **Can, could, may** and **might** express that something is possible, or seems to be possible.

G7 Permission (dürfen)

May we bring our dog in here?
I'm sorry, but you can't. You mustn't bring him in, I'm afraid. When pets were allowed to come into the restaurant, lots of guests complained.

▶ **May** is used to ask politely for permission. **Mustn't, can't** and **may not** (more formal) are used to refuse permission. The substitute form is **be allowed to**. (**Be permitted** is also used.)

G8 Ability (können)

I can speak English, but I can't speak Spanish.
I couldn't understand what the waiter said.
Next year I'll go to America. Then I'll be able to communicate without any problems.

▶ **Can (cannot/can't)** and **could (couldn't)** express that someone (or something) is able or unable to do something. The substitute form is **be able to**.

G9 *NEW:* Willingness (wollen)

Will you help me? Take this bag, will you?
Oh, damn! The car won't start!
I asked Tom to drive, but he wouldn't.

▶ **Will** can be used in questions and question tags to ask if someone is willing to do something. **Won't** and **wouldn't** express refusal.

Practice

1 a) *How would you react? Look at these situations. Use auxiliaries in your reactions to them.*
Example: Your friend missed the bus to school. **(Express a criticism.)** →"You should have got up earlier." / "You mustn't always leave home so late."

1. You see some shoes you like in a shop, but you aren't sure if they'll fit. **(Ask permission.)**
2. Your uncle gets out a packet of cigarettes in a non-smoking café. **(Remind him of the rule.)**
3. Your brother wants to drive a friend's car to the disco, even though he hasn't passed his driving test yet. **(Mention risks/the law.)**
4. A friend of yours brings a bottle of wine to the party you're throwing. **(Say it wasn't necessary.)**
5. Your mother has cleared things up in your room – and now you can't find anything. **(Express a criticism.)**
6. Your father's always complaining about the cost of petrol, but he drives the short distance to work each day just the same. **(Give advice.)**
7. Your American visitors want to drive over a high pass in the Alps although the forecast is for heavy snow. **(Make a prediction/suggestion.)**
8. A friend of yours has been dumped by his girlfriend – because (according to her) he was always boasting about his achievements. **(Express a criticism and give advice.)**

b) [👥] *Choose one of the above situations and write a short dialogue around it. Then act it out with your partner.*

2 *Learning foreign languages: Fill in the gaps with suitable forms of auxiliaries. Whenever you think more than one form is possible, discuss which one you feel fits the context best.*

For many years, it was a tradition in Britain that secondary school students [1] learn at least one foreign language. At most schools everybody started with French, but at some schools it ([2] not) be French. Students [3] choose between French and German or Spanish – or they [4] learn all three. The logic behind it was simple: If you travelled to France, for example, or Germany, it was important to [5] speak the language.

Then, as English became globally more and more dominant, people started asking the question: "Why [6] we bother to learn other languages at all? We [7] any more, surely! After all, everybody else [8] speak English!" At the same time, foreign languages were becoming less popular in schools because many students found they ([9] not) get top grades in them as easily as they [10] in subjects like maths or science. So when the law was changed (in 2004) and 14–16-year-olds no longer [11] learn a foreign language, at last lots of young people [12] relax because they [13] finish school without [14] take exams in French or German!

[15] this be a mistake? It [16] be. Many people think so. [17] speak a foreign language [18] be a basic part of a good education, they say.

3 *Think of another caption for the cartoon. Use equivalents of the German 'sollen' – or other suitable auxiliaries.*

"We may need to work on your emergency stop."

E Describing things

Checking up

a) *Adjective or adverb? Decide on the correct form.*

1. "The concert was **(real) (fantastic)**. You played **(beautiful)**!" – "Thanks! I felt **(pretty) (nervous)** at the beginning. But **(lucky)** everything went **(good)**."
2. "Be **(careful)**! I **(absolute)** hate it when you drive so **(fast)**." – "Come on! You can't call me a **(dangerous)** driver. I just don't like driving **(slow)** for no **(real)** reason."

b) *Find the best word order.*

1. down on the beach • at the barbecue • had • last Saturday • we • a great time
2. always • on Sundays • have • we • breakfast • late • rather
3. never • I • a proper meal • cooked • have • frankly • on my own • actually

c) *Correct the mistakes in these sentences.*

1. I don't agree with everything what you said.
2. Most of the people which I talked to were Americans.
3. Jane and Mike, that were both at the meeting, came up to us afterwards.
4. Carlos spoke excellent English, what impressed me a lot.

Basic rules

You can use **adjectives** to say what someone or something is like. **Adverbs** describe the way something is done. **Relative clauses** give definitions or extra information.

G10 Adjective or adverb?

Have you tried 'Black Knights', the new interactive computer game?
No, but the title is good. It sounds interesting!
It starts dramatically with some really exciting scenes.
And the graphics are extremely well done.
Unfortunately, it's pretty expensive.

▶ Adjectives describe what someone or something is like. They can be used attributively *(**exciting** scenes)* or predicatively *(is **good**, sounds **interesting**)*.

▶ Adverbs describe the way something is done *(starts **dramatically**)*. They can modify adjectives *(**really** exciting)* and other adverbs *(**extremely** well)*. Adverbs like **unfortunately** comment on a whole sentence.

G11 Position of adverbs and adverbials

Front position

In London the new James Bond is already on in the cinemas.
This morning there was a report about it on TV.
Apparently, it's the best Bond film ever made.

▶ **Adverbs** and **adverbials of time and place** (e.g. *this morning, in London)* can appear in front position for emphasis. **Adverbs of comment** *(apparently, unfortunately, of course,* etc.) usually appear in front position.

Mid position

We never watch TV when we're having lunch.
I can easily find the programme in the TV guide.

▶ **Adverbs of frequency** *(never, often,* etc.) usually take mid position. **Adverbs of manner** *(easily, quickly,* etc.) appear in mid position when used descriptively (NOT for emphasis).

End position	
The actor who played Claudius played his part really well. I saw the play last year. At the moment it is on at Stratford. It was on TV a week ago.	▶ **Adverbs of manner** *(well)* usually appear in end position (after verb and object). **Adverbs and adverbials of time and place** *(last year, at Stratford)* mostly take end position. If there are two adverbials at the end of a sentence, the normal word order is place **before** time.

G12 Relative clauses

Defining relative clauses	
These days there aren't many Americans who don't own a car. The number seven is the only bus that goes to Southfield Park. Is that the bike (that) your parents gave you for Christmas?	▶ **Defining relative clauses** give necessary information. Without them the meaning of the main clause would be unclear. **Who, that** and **whose** are the relative pronouns used for people. **Which, that** and **whose** are used for things. The relative pronoun can be left out if it is the object of the relative clause **(= contact clause)**. There are **no commas**.

Non-defining relative clauses	
Life without a car would be a nightmare for most Americans, who are not used to relying on public transport. Los Angeles, which is the largest city in California, is well known for its traffic problems. California has a dry climate but a growing population, which means water must be carefully stored.	▶ **Non-defining relative clauses** add extra information. Without them the meaning of the main clause would still be understandable. **Who** and **whose** are used for people, **which** and **whose** for things. **That** is not used in non-defining relative clauses. **Which** can also be used to refer to the main clause as a whole, to express a comment on it. There are **commas** – and a pause in speaking – between main clause and relative clause.

Practice

1 *What's the difference? Adjectives and adverbs are often used differently in English from what you would expect in German. How would you express these ideas in English?*

1. Das Festival war toll organisiert, und alle Bands haben richtig gut gespielt.
2. Man hat als Rockstar einen gut bezahlten Job und muss nicht besonders hart arbeiten, meint Tim.
3. Denkt dein Bruder wirklich ernsthaft an eine Karriere als Rockstar?
4. Zum Glück ist er noch ziemlich jung, also hoffen wir, dass er langsam seine Meinung ändert.
5. Warum schaust du mich so seltsam an? Sehe ich so komisch aus?

2 *Explaining what's meant: Use relative clauses to explain these expressions. Use a dictionary if necessary.*
Example: A bad loser is someone who can't stand losing a game./… a person who behaves badly if they don't win.

1. a **fulfilling** job
2. a **brave** decision
3. a **revolutionary** idea
4. a **laidback** lifestyle
5. **liberal-minded** parents
6. a **convenient** arrangement
7. **suitable** clothing
8. a **professional** musician
9. a **fatal** accident
10. a **profitable** business
11. a **long-lost** friend
12. an **open** secret

3 ***Creative descriptions:*** *Add your own ideas to these basic sentences. Follow the suggestion for each sentence. Then compare your results with a partner's – and decide which you prefer.*
Example: I saw a turkey. *(Add an adjective, one adverbial of time and two of place.)*
→ I saw a huge turkey on the lawn in front of our neighbours' house yesterday afternoon!

1. I'm meeting one of my friends. *(Add an adjective, two adverbials of time and one of place.)*
2. There was a party. *(Add an adjective, and adverb of degree, an adverbial of time and one of place.)*
3. I prefer vegetables. *(Add an adverb of frequency, an adverb of comment – and a relative clause.)*
4. One of the girls plays the violin. *(Add a relative clause, an adverb of manner and one of degree.)*
5. I get up. *(Add an adverb of manner, one of degree, one of frequency – and one of comment.)*
6. The bike was stolen. *(Add a relative clause, an adjective, an adverbial of time, one of place and one of comment.)*

4 ***Adding extra interest and information:*** *The extra information on the right can be added to the text in the form of relative clauses.*
a) *Find a suitable detail for each sentence, and rewrite the text so that all the extra information is included.*

The people who come in and out of the UK

Up to 500 Britons leave the UK every day. Record numbers emigrated from Britain in 2005, most of them to Australia, Spain and France. At the same time, about 1,500 immigrants arrive in the UK daily. And another thousand leave the country to return to their original homes in the EU or other parts of the world.

Spain has become very popular with older Britons. The climate there is pleasantly warm in winter. Younger people are attracted by work opportunities abroad and a lower cost of living than in the UK. House prices are considerably lower in France than in Britain now.

High numbers of immigrants come from Asian countries. Thousands of Americans also settle in Britain. There are significant numbers of Germans, too. All these trends have had an effect on Britain's population.

- Most of these people come from Poland.
- Their dream is to live abroad.
- 1,000 have decided not to remain in Britain.
- These countries are the most popular destinations.

- This is especially interesting to young couples wanting to buy a home.
- Many young Britons move to Australia.
- This makes it particularly attractive.
- Many want to move away from the UK when they retire.

- Many of the Germans are doctors and other highly qualified people.
- The population increased by 185,000 in 2005, and passed 60 million.
- Most of these Americans come for work.
- These include India, Pakistan and Bangladesh.

b) *To make the text 'flow' even better, find suitable places for adding adverbs/adverbials of comment (e.g. naturally, of course, on the other hand, not surprisingly). Then read your text aloud to see how it sounds!*

F Linking ideas

Checking up

Use gerund or participle constructions to link these sentences. (Sometimes a preposition will help.)

1. He left the house. He didn't tell anyone where he was going.
2. We knew the weather would be cold. We packed warm clothing.
3. Several houses were destroyed in the floods. They had been built too near the river.
4. She's going to spend next year in Paris. She's looking forward to that.
5. I didn't use the underground. I decided to go by bus instead.

Basic rules

Both gerunds and participles can be used to connect sentence parts.

G13 Gerund constructions

Alternative to subordinate clause	
On leaving the plane, I switched on my mobile. **In spite of taking off** so late, our flight arrived on time.	▶ When a gerund is used after **on, before, after, for** and **in spite of**, the gerund construction corresponds to a subordinate clause *(On leaving = When I left).*

No corresponding subordinate clause	
Instead of helping us to clean up after the party, Tom and Lisa just went home. **Apart from breaking** a few glasses and **dropping** food all over the carpet, they behaved quite well.	▶ A gerund can also occur after **instead of, by, without, apart from, as well as, what about?, it's worth** and **it's no use**. Here there is no corresponding subordinate clause.

NEW: *-ing* form with a subject of its own	
I hate **people telling** me what to do. My father has nothing against **me studying** art. We can't do anything without **you complaining**.	▶ Sometimes a noun (e.g. *people*) or a pronoun *(me)* comes before the *-ing* form, giving it a 'subject of its own'. In these constructions it is not clear whether the *-ing* form is a gerund or a participle.

G14 Participle constructions

Participles used to shorten relative clauses	
The boy **standing near the counter** has stolen two CDs. (= **who is standing ...**) The CDs **found in his jacket pocket** were only worth a few pounds. (= **which were found ...**)	▶ Participle constructions can be an alternative to relative clauses. Present participles correspond to active verb forms in a relative clause, past participles correspond to passive forms.

Participle constructions used as adverbials	
Seeing the police car behind, she began to drive more slowly. I dropped my keys on the road **while getting out of the car**. The truck ran into the side of a bus, **injuring five passengers**.	▶ These correspond to adverbial clauses *(When she saw ...)*, but sound more formal. They can be introduced by a conjunction *(while, when, though, as if)*. In the last example the participle describes things happening at the same time ('accompanying circumstances').

NEW: Participle with a subject of its own

She walked onto the platform to receive the prize, **her heart beating fast**.
With so many people coming, extra seats had to be brought into the hall.
I can't concentrate properly **with all that noise going on in the background**.

▶ These 'absolute' participle constructions have their own subject *(her heart)*, which is different from the subject of the main clause *(she)*. These constructions sound very formal. When introduced by **with**, they are less formal and can also be used in colloquial English.

Practice

1 *Expressing things more fluently: Read what these people say. Think how to express their ideas more fluently – by using participle or gerund constructions. There may sometimes be more than one way of doing this.*

1. I earned a bit of money in the holidays. That was because I worked in my uncle's office.
2. My sister wants to go straight to university. She isn't going to do a gap year.
3. I can still play tennis once or twice a week. I can fit it in while I'm studying for my A Levels.
4. Are you taking part in that graphic design course? You know, the one that starts next week?
5. A lot of books were recommended to us by our German teacher. I'm afraid I haven't read any of them!
6. Sam goes to creative writing classes. He also does a lot of watercolour painting.
7. Why do volunteer work? What are the advantages?
8. I know you, Jamie! So I expect you'll study Maths!

2 *Where does your food come from? Complete the text with gerund or participle forms of suitable verbs. (You may also need passive forms of gerunds.)*

Most people **1** in the UK shop in enormous supermarkets **2** on the edge of towns. As well as **3** food, supermarkets offer their customers clothes, electrical goods and all sorts of other things. When **4** why they shop at these places, people mostly reply that apart from **5** so convenient, it's cheap.

But there is also another, quite different shopping experience: instead of **6** to one of these huge supermarkets, why not try **7** at your local farmers' market? There you'll find farmers, growers and producers from your local area **8** their own produce directly. There are also stalls **9** by local organizations like Fair Trade groups, and stalls where you can eat and sometimes even listen to music **10** by local musicians!

Unlike local food **11** within miles of your home and **12** fresh at a farmers' market, food **13** from supermarkets has a long 'history': after **14** in the country of origin, fruit and vegetables may have travelled thousands of miles before finally **15** on the supermarket shelves.

16 that it can't be right to buy food **17** in from countries on the other side of the world, people **18** in the health of the environment are happy to shop at farmers' markets – and also at any local shops still **19** in their towns and villages. And there's another advantage: food **20** at a farmers' market is often actually cheaper than in supermarkets – and the price **21** by the farmer fairer.

3 *Parents! Think of things that parents don't like their teenage children doing. Compare your experiences with other people's!*
Example: "My parents **hate me staying** out late. They also try to **stop me playing** computer games all the time." – "Really? Well, mine **don't mind me going** ... But they **don't like me** ..."

And another thing – you'll have to stop him drawing all over the walls.

G Advanced style

Here are two structures found mainly in formal English. The **present subjunctive** appears mostly in official statements and **inversion** is mainly used in written texts (for dramatic effect).

G15 ***NEW:*** **Subjunctive**

a) Present subjunctive	
In case of complaint, we recommend that the customer contact Customer Services. British politicians insist that strict new laws be made to confront climate change. We'll support you, come what may. God save the Queen.	▶ The form of the **present subjunctive** is the same for all persons. It is identical with the infinitive. It is mainly used in **that-clauses** after verbs expressing demands or suggestions *(recommend, request, demand, decide, suggest,* etc.*)* and in a few phrases that express a wish.

b) Were-subjunctive	
I wish I were/was better at tennis. If only my backhand were/was stronger. I remember the match as though it were/was yesterday.	▶ After **I wish, if only, as though, it's (high) time** the subjunctive form **were** is often used instead of **was**. It expresses a wish that is unlikely to be fulfilled. *(He/she/it **were** sounds more formal and is less common.)*

G16 ***NEW:*** **Inversion**

The normal word order in an English sentence is **subject – verb – object**. However, in certain cases the word order can be changed. This has a special stylistic effect.

Hardly had the battle **in the north ended,** when Harold heard of William of Normandy's landing. Not only did the Normans **conquer England,** but the French they spoke also changed the English language forever. No sooner had William **become king** than plans were begun for building castles all over the country. Never again was England **invaded** by a foreign power.	▶ If a sentence begins with **hardly (... when), scarcely (... when), not only (... but also), no sooner (... than), never, rarely, neither ... nor, the** subject *(the battle)* comes after the auxiliary *(had)* – as in questions. If there is no auxiliary in the sentence, a form of **do** is used *(**did** the Normans conquer)*. This construction is called **inversion**. It is sometimes used to make a written text sound more dramatic.

Vocabulary

Structure

In the *Vocabulary* section the new words and phrases from this volume that you cannot very easily guess are listed in chronological order, together with the information on pronunciation and meaning you need.

Words in **bold** print appear frequently, so you should be able to understand as well as use them. Words in regular print are important for dealing with certain texts and themes.
German translations or explanations are given in the right-hand column.

When related words come up shortly after one another in the same Topic, they will be given together. The second one will appear in black instead of blue print and with an indentation.

A large number of exercises provides opportunities for you to practise vocabulary learning and memorising techniques (looking up, collecting, organising, linking up and guessing the meaning of vocabulary) in on your own.

For more classroom practice, do the new *Everyday English* pages with your teacher. There is one after each Topic in the *Vocabulary* section, providing you with useful words and phrases that help you to get along in various everyday situations.

As usual, you will find an alphabetically arranged *Dictionary* section after the *Vocabulary* section, where you can look up words from all the volumes.

Abbreviations and symbols

pl. = plural	*etw.* = etwas	• word that is either similar to a German word or related to a word you already know
sg. = singular	*ugs.* = umgangssprachlich	* irregular verb (see page 202)
sb = somebody	*vulg* = vulgar (rude)	
sth = something	*AE* = American English	
jmdm = jemandem	*BE* = British English	
jmdn = jemanden	*fml* = formal	
jmds = jemandes	*infml* = informal	

Pronunciation

Here, once again, are the phonetic symbols used in *Green Line NEW E2:*

Consonants	Vowels	Diphthongs	Additional symbols
[ŋ] morning	[ɑː] father	[aɪ] I, my	[ˈ] Primary stress on the following syllable
[r] red	[ʌ] but	[aʊ] now, house	[ˌ] Secondary stress on the following syllable
[s] this	[e] pen	[eə] there, pair	[‿] Link between two words
[z] is	[ə] a sister	[eɪ] name, they	
[ʒ] television	[ɜː] girl	[ɪə] here, idea	
[dʒ] page	[æ] flat	[ɔɪ] boy	
[ʃ] she	[ɪ] it	[əʊ] hello	
[tʃ] lunch	[i] happy	[ʊə] sure	
[ð] the	[iː] teacher, she		
[θ] thanks	[ɒ] got		
[v] video	[ɔː] ball		
[w] wow, one	[ʊ] book		
	[u] January		
	[uː] too, two		

All other letters are pronounced roughly the way they are written, e. g [b], [j], [l] etc.

Topic 1 Growing up

A Responsibility only comes with age?

Minimum legal age limits

• **minimum** ['mɪnɪməm]	Minimum; Mindestmaß; minimal
• **limit** ['lɪmɪt]	Limit; Grenze; Beschränkung
consent [kən'sent]	Zustimmung; Einwilligung
• **marriage** ['mærɪdʒ]	Heirat; Ehe
• **parental** [pə'rentl]	elterlich; Eltern-
• **election** [ɪ'lekʃn]	Wahl
• **criminal** ['krɪmɪnl]	kriminell; verbrecherisch
• **spirits** *(pl.)* ['spɪrɪts]	Spirituosen
compulsory [kəm'pʌlsri]	verpflichtend; obligatorisch
• **sex** [seks]	Sexualität; Geschlecht
provided that ... [prəʊ'vaɪdɪd ðət]	vorausgesetzt, dass ...
• * to **take sb to court** [ˌteɪk tə 'kɔ:t]	jmdn verklagen
to **purchase** ['pɜ:tʃəs]	kaufen; erwerben
• to **differ** ['dɪfə]	sich unterscheiden; abweichen
• to **consume** [kən'sju:m]	konsumieren; verbrauchen
• **file** [faɪl]	Akte; Mappe; Datei
fake [feɪk]	Fälschung; gefälscht
ID card [ˌaɪ'di: ˌkɑ:d]	Ausweis; Personalausweis

A student's opinion

capable (of *+ gerund***)** ['keɪpəbl]	fähig, im Stande
• **irresponsible** [ˌɪrɪ'spɒntsəbl]	unverantwortlich; verantwortungslos
• alike [ə'laɪk]	gleichermaßen
• to **dictate** [dɪk'teɪt]	diktieren; vorschreiben
• to **happen to (be/do)** ['hæpn]	zufällig sein/tun
R-rated *(AE)* ['ɑ:ˌreɪtɪd]	frei ab 17
• parenting ['peərntɪŋ]	Kindererziehung
to **deny** [dɪ'naɪ]	abstreiten; verweigern
• **privilege** ['prɪvlɪdʒ]	Privileg; Vorrecht
to **concern** [kən'sɜ:n]	betreffen; beunruhigen
• to **ban** [bæn]	bannen; verbieten; sperren
violent ['vaɪəlnt]	gewaltsam; gewalttätig; brutal
liberty ['lɪbəti]	Freiheit
2 **response** [rɪ'spɒnts]	Antwort; Erwiderung; Rückmeldung

V1 Word families

■ 'New' words are very often **related** to words (and phrases) you already know. Remind yourself by writing them all down. Example: *marriage • to marry • to get married • to be married to someone*

■ Practise with families of the words (from A) given here, and collect more **word families** as you work through this book:
to consume • to differ • irresponsible • parenting • criminal • election • concerning

B Being a teenager

1 • **cliché** ['kli:ʃeɪ]	Klischee

Teenage voices

to **sort sth out** [ˌsɔ:t‿'aʊt]	etw. klären; etw. erledigen
supportive [sə'pɔ:tɪv]	unterstützend
* to **arise** [ə'raɪz]	aufkommen; entstehen
amongst [ə'mʌŋst]	unter (zwischen)
mind you [ˌmaɪnd 'ju:]	wohlgemerkt
bitchiness ['bɪtʃinəs]	Gehässigkeit
• to **compliment** ['kɒmplɪment]	Komplimente machen
compliment ['kɒmplɪmənt]	Kompliment
to **judge** [dʒʌdʒ]	beurteilen; bewerten
• **personality** [ˌpɜ:sn'æləti]	Persönlichkeit
• to **generalise** ['dʒenrlaɪz]	verallgemeinern
• to **impress** [ɪm'pres]	beeindrucken
to **comfort** ['kʌmpfət]	trösten; ermutigen
to **jump to conclusions** [ˌdʒʌmp tə kən'klu:ʒnz]	voreilige Schlüsse ziehen
to **tease** [ti:z]	necken; quälen
gay [geɪ]	homosexuell
• **appearance** [ə'pɪərnts]	Erscheinung; Aussehen; Auftritt
confident ['kɒnfɪdnt]	selbstsicher; überzeugt
timid ['tɪmɪd]	schüchtern; furchtsam
• to **confront** [kən'frʌnt]	konfrontieren; entgegentreten; sich stellen
vulnerable ['vʌlnrəbl]	verletzlich; verwundbar
• to **succeed (in** *+ noun or gerund***)** [sək'si:d]	Erfolg haben; nachfolgen
• to **balance** ['bæləns]	balancieren; ausgleichen; abwägen
• **masculine** ['mæskjəlɪn]	maskulin; männlich
to **commit suicide** [kəˌmɪt 'su:ɪsaɪd]	Selbstmord begehen
ticked off *(infml)* [ˌtɪkt 'ɒf]	verärgert
to **tend** to [tend]	(zu etw.) neigen
• **gel** [dʒel]	Gel
• **emotional** [ɪ'məʊʃnl]	emotional; gefühlsmäßig
3 dozen ['dʌzn]	Dutzend
• * to sleep over ['sli:p‿əʊvə]	übernachten
sleepover ['sli:pəʊvə]	Übernachtung
to **solve** [sɒlv]	lösen
to doss down *(infml)* [ˌdɒs 'daʊn]	sich aufs Ohr hauen
swearword ['sweəwɜ:d]	Schimpfwort
to deduct [dɪ'dʌkt]	abziehen
• **allowance** [ə'laʊənts]	Zuwendung; Unterhaltsgeld; Taschengeld
torch [tɔ:tʃ]	Fackel; Taschenlampe
to **pop in/out** *(infml)* [ˌpɒp‿'ɪn]	vorbeischauen
supper ['sʌpə]	spätes Abendessen
quid, *pl.* quid *(infml)* [kwɪd]	Pfund *(Währung)*

V2 Words to describe personality and character

■ Which of the words in B can be used to talk about **people's personality and character**?
Collect all the adjectives (or nouns/verbs) you can find (adding related words if you know them!). Then use them in short example sentences.

Example: *supportive* (to support)*:* A friend who is *supportive* is kind and helpful when you are having a difficult time.
■ Now add to your list any other words of this kind that you have learnt before (e.g. *helpful, fun to be with, to boast*). As you work through the book, collect more 'personality' words.

I go along

*to **go along** [ˌgəʊ_əˈlɒŋ]	mitmachen; mitziehen
pregnant [ˈpregnənt]	schwanger
due [djuː]	fällig
The smart money says … [ˈsmɑːt ˌmʌni]	Die meisten wetten, dass …
sub *(AE: substitute teacher)* [sʌb]	Aushilfslehrer(in)
junior [ˈdʒuːniə]	Mittelstufenschüler(in)
to **figure** [ˈfɪgə]	sich vorstellen; glauben
• to **slow (sb) down** [ˌsləʊ ˈdaʊn]	(jmdn) bremsen
plumber [ˈplʌmə]	Klempner(in); Installateur(in)
• **service** [ˈsɜːvɪs]	Militärdienst
• jump school [ˈdʒʌmp ˌskuːl]	Fallschirmspringerschule
• period [ˈpɪəriəd]	Unterrichtsstunde
advanced [ədˈvɑːntst]	fortgeschritten
to **rub** [rʌb]	reiben
the small of the back [ðə ˌsmɔːl_əv ðə ˈbæk]	Kreuz
• benefit [ˈbenɪfɪt]	Nutzen; Gewinn
* to get a big bang out of sth [ˌget_ə ˌbɪg ˈbæŋ]	einen Heidenspaß an etw. haben
• to **reach** [riːtʃ]	reichen; greifen
attendance book [əˈtendnts ˌbʊk]	Anwesenheitsliste; Klassentagebuch
* to **put sb on** [ˌpʊt ˈɒn]	jmdn auf den Arm nehmen
parking lot [ˈpɑːkɪŋ ˌlɒt]	Parkplatz
to tune out [ˌtjuːn_ˈaʊt]	abschalten
needless to say [ˈniːdləs tə ˌseɪ]	natürlich
hood *(AE)* [hʊd]	Motorhaube
offhand [ˌɒfˈhænd]	ohne Weiteres
to **mill around** [ˌmɪl əˈraʊnd]	umherlaufen
• to **wheel** [wiːl]	rollen
to **consolidate** [kənˈsɒlɪdeɪt]	vereinigen; zusammenlegen
• **district** [ˈdɪstrɪkt]	Distrikt; Bezirk
* to **swing** [swɪŋ]	schwingen; schwenken
brake [breɪk]	Bremse
• **aboard** [əˈbɔːd]	an Bord
orderly [ˈɔːdəli]	ordentlich
dashboard [ˈdæʃbɔːd]	Armaturenbrett
• to **sprint** [sprɪnt]	sprinten; spurten
• **asphalt** [ˈæsfælt]	Asphalt
to **hiss** [hɪs]	zischen; fauchen
aisle [aɪl]	Mittelgang
• to **shield** [ʃiːld]	beschirmen; schützen
to **flinch** [flɪntʃ]	zurückweichen; zusammenzucken
to **jam** [dʒæm]	klemmen
bent double [ˌbent ˈdʌbl]	zusammengekrümmt
to **shift** [ʃɪft]	verrutschen
• **notebook** [ˈnəʊtbʊk]	Notizbuch; Heft
lap [læp]	Schoß
• **impression** [ɪmˈpreʃn]	Impression; Eindruck
gifted [ˈgɪftɪd]	begabt
major [ˈmeɪdʒə]	Haupt-; wichtig; größer
• **goddess** [ˈgɒdes]	Göttin
* to be clean out of impressions [biː ˌkliːn_aʊt_əv_ɪmˈpreʃnz]	komplett frei sein von Eindrücken
circuit [ˈsɜːkɪt]	Schaltkreis
to **fail** [feɪl]	versagen; ausfallen; fehlschlagen
• **pedal** [ˈpedl]	Pedal
* to **be a notch above** [ˌbiː_ə ˌnɒtʃ_əˈbʌv]	eine Klasse besser sein als
to **stay put** [ˌsteɪ ˈpʊt]	an Ort und Stelle bleiben
patchy [ˈpætʃi]	ungleichmäßig; flickenartig
• **campus** [ˈkæmpəs]	Campus; Hochschulgelände
• to **clear one's throat** [ˌklɪə wʌnz ˈθrəʊt]	sich räuspern
bleachers *(pl. AE)* [ˈbliːtʃəz]	unüberdachte Tribüne
groupy [ˈgruːpi]	gruppenbezogen
dean [diːn]	Dekan
grant [grɑːnt]	Stipendium; Subvention; Zuwendung
to **fund** [fʌnd]	finanzieren; fördern
to **flip (a book) open** [ˌflɪp_ˈəʊpn]	aufschlagen (ein Buch)
heavy-duty [ˌheviˈdjuːti]	strapazierfähig
belt [belt]	Gürtel
buckle [ˈbʌkl]	Schnalle
weird [wɪəd]	sonderbar; merkwürdig
• **forward** [ˈfɔːwəd]	vorwärts
to bob up [ˌbɒb_ˈʌp]	auftauchen
to zap [zæp]	knipsen
flash [flæʃ]	Blitz
loose [luːs]	lose; locker
to **stir** [stɜː]	sich regen; (sich) rühren; umrühren
exclamation point *(AE)* [ekskləˈmeɪʃn ˌpɔɪnt]	Ausrufezeichen
buck-toothed [ˈbʌkˌtuːθt]	hasenzähnig
to **jerk sb around** [ˌdʒɜːk_əˈraʊnd]	jmdn hin und her werfen
hostage [ˈhɒstɪdʒ]	Geisel
• **radiator** [ˈreɪdieɪtə]	Heizkörper
• boxed in [ˌbɒkst_ˈɪn]	eingekeilt; eingekastelt
zit *(infml)* [zɪt]	Pickel
zit-blasted *(infml)* [ˈzɪtˌblɑːstɪd]	mit Pickeln übersät
• galaxy [ˈgæləksi]	Galaxie; Galaxis; Milchstraße
• **locker** [ˈlɒkə]	Schließfach; Spind
combination [ˌkɒmbɪˈneɪʃn]	Kombination

curious ['kjʊəriəs]	neugierig
to lace one's fingers [ˌleɪs wʌnz 'fɪŋgəz]	die Hände verschränken
bright [braɪt]	intelligent; gescheit
to **glance at** [glɑ:nts]	einen Blick werfen auf
outline ['aʊtlaɪn]	Kontur; Skizze; Überblick
chin [tʃɪn]	Kinn
stubborn ['stʌbən]	eigensinnig; störrisch
to **brake** [breɪk]	bremsen
5 • **analysis** [ə'næləsɪz]	Analyse
main trait [ˌmeɪn 'treɪt]	Haupteigenschaft
margin ['mɑ:dʒɪn]	Rand
entry ['entri]	Eintrag
It's up to you [ɪtsˌʌp tə 'ju:]	Wie du willst

V3 Develop your word power: Cars, bikes and traffic

In B, you will find a number of words – some of them new – to do with **traffic** and **driving**:
parking lot • *access highway* • *a thirty-mile trip*, etc.

■ Find any other words or phrases on this theme in B, and make a list. Then add any words you remember from before (e.g. *to ride a bike, saddle, car park, motorway*).

■ Try to guess what these English expressions mean, then check your dictionary:
speed limit • *dual carriageway* • *roundabout* • *headlights* • *roadworks* • *diversion*

■ Now use your dictionary to find the English equivalents of these (noting any differences between American and British English):
1. *Gaspedal, Gas geben* • 2. *Kupplung* • 3. *Lenken* • 4. *Kofferraum* • 5. *Gang, Gangschaltung, schalten* • 6. *Windschutzscheibe, Scheibenwischer* • 7. *Beifahrersitz, Fahrersitz* • 8. *Stoßstange* • 9. *Nummernschild* • 10. *Lenkstange* • 11. *Kette* • 12. *Reifen* • 13. *einen Platten haben, eine Panne haben* • 14. *Tankstelle* • 15. *Benzin* • 16. *Ampel*

C No risk – no fun?

Tombstoning: Dying to jump?

1 tombstone ['tu:mstəʊn]	Grabstein
craze [kreɪz]	Manie; Fimmel; fixe Idee
• **cliff** [klɪf]	Klippe; Kliff
• to **expand** [ɪk'spænd]	(sich) ausdehnen; erweitern; expandieren
daredevil ['deəˌdevl]	draufgängerisch; waghalsig
site [saɪt]	Ort; Gelände; Schauplatz
fatality [fə'tæləti]	Todesfall
• **injury** ['ɪndʒri]	Verletzung
obstacle ['ɒbstəkl]	Hindernis
to **lurk** [lɜ:k]	lauern
* to sweep away [ˌswi:pˌə'weɪ]	wegfegen; wegspülen
current ['kʌrnt]	Strömung
shallow ['ʃæləʊ]	seicht; flach
• **collision** [kə'lɪʒn]	Kollision; Zusammenstoß
to **discharge** [dɪs'tʃɑ:dʒ]	entlassen; freisetzen; entladen
severe [sɪ'vɪə]	ernst; schwerwiegend
to **bruise** [bru:z]	verletzen
bruise [bru:z]	Prellung; Quetschung; Bluterguss
lung [lʌŋ]	Lunge
buzz [bʌz]	Begeisterung; Kick
split second [ˌsplɪt 'seknd]	Sekundenbruchteil
rush [rʌʃ]	Rausch; Adrenalinstoß
ASBO (= anti-social behaviour order) *(BE)* ['æzbəʊ]	ASBO *(Verwarnung wegen antisozialen Verhaltens)*
• **cut** [kʌt]	Schnittverletzung; Platzwunde
to **suppose** [sə'pəʊz]	vermuten; annehmen
to **egg sb on** [ˌegˌ'ɒn]	jmdn anstacheln; jmdn antreiben
fortunately ['fɔ:tʃnətli]	zum Glück
to **shatter** ['ʃætə]	zerschlagen; zertrümmern
vertebra, *pl.* vertebrae ['vɜ:tɪbrə]	Wirbel
to **paralyse** ['pærlaɪz]	lähmen
waist [weɪst]	Bauch; Taille
• **temporary** ['temprəri]	vorübergehend; temporär
2 **various** ['veərɪəs]	verschieden(artig)
• **headline** ['hedlaɪn]	Schlagzeile
4 • **adventurous** [əd'ventʃrəs]	abenteuerlich; unternehmungslustig; wagemutig

⟨Sierra Wave⟩

Sierra Wave [sɪˌerə 'weɪv]	Sierra Wave *(ein in der Sierra Nevada auftretendes außergewöhnliches Thermikphänomen)*
sierra [sɪ'erə]	Gebirgskette
porch [pɔ:tʃ]	Veranda
• extreme [ɪk'stri:m]	extrem
hang glider ['hæŋ ˌglaɪdə]	Hängegleiter; Drachen
to float [fləʊt]	gleiten; treiben
thermal ['θɜ:ml]	Thermik
oxygen ['ɒksɪdʒən]	Sauerstoff
• dune [dju:n]	Düne
• to solo ['səʊləʊ]	einen Alleingang machen
• cliff [klɪf]	Klippe; Kliff
• rotor ['rəʊtə]	Rotor; Walze
• cylinder ['sɪlɪndə]	Zylinder; Walze
to lift [lɪft]	(sich) heben
to hook in [ˌhʊkˌ'ɪn]	einhaken; einhängen
edge [edʒ]	Rand; Kante
• dropoff ['drɒpɒf]	Abgrund; Abfall
• forward ['fɔ:wəd]	vorwärts
to tingle ['tɪŋgl]	prickeln
line [laɪn]	Leitung
• ordered ['ɔ:dəd]	geordnet
seagull ['si:gʌl]	Möwe
to soar [sɔ:]	aufsteigen; segeln
dirt [dɜ:t]	Schmutz; Dreck
to assemble [ə'sembl]	zusammenbauen; montieren
* to have second thoughts [hæv ˌseknd 'θɔ:ts]	Zweifel haben; es sich anders überlegen
thought [θɔ:t]	Gedanke
hop [hɒp]	Sprung; Hopser
parachute ['pærəʃu:t]	Fallschirm
eagle ['i:gl]	Adler

V4 Useful words for making your own comments

■ 'Needless to say, I'm the only one here …' (from *I go along*, p. 12, line 41)
■ What other words and phrases can you use for making comments?
■ Start a list *(Obviously; To tell you the truth; …)* and add to it every time you find new examples.

• to spiral ['spaɪərl]	spiralförmig aufsteigen
• control [kən'trəʊl]	Kontrolle; Steuerung
stomach ['stʌmək]	Magen
to respond [rɪ'spɒnd]	reagieren; erwidern; antworten
astonishing [ə'stɒnɪʃɪŋ]	erstaunlich; überraschend
• distant ['dɪstnt]	entfernt
lack (of) [læk]	Mangel (an); Fehlen (von)
consciousness ['kɒntʃəsnəs]	Bewusstsein
joy [dʒɔɪ]	Freude

D I'm gonna be like you

Cat's in the cradle

cradle ['kreɪdl]	Wiege
chorus ['kɔ:rəs]	Refrain
hassle ['hæsl]	Theater; Schwierigkeiten
4 **stage** [steɪdʒ]	Stadium
• **forever** [fə'revə]	für immer; ewig

⟨E My child is starving herself to death⟩

1 grace [greɪs]	Grazie; Anmut

Joanne's story

• medicine ['medsn]	Medizin
• ideal [aɪ'dɪəl]	Ideal
vomit ['vɒmɪt]	Erbrochenes
to purge [pɜ:dʒ]	abführen; reinigen
* to throw up [ˌθrəʊ‿'ʌp]	erbrechen
• bulimic [bʊ'lɪmɪk]	bulimisch; ess-/brechsüchtig
to diet [daɪət]	Diät halten
• calory; calorie ['kælri]	Kilokalorie
loss [lɒs]	Verlust
• to centre around ['sentər‿əˌraʊnd]	sich drehen um
• critic ['krɪtɪk]	Kritiker(in)
• tyranny ['tɪrni]	Tyrannei; Gewaltherrschaft
• skeletal ['skelɪtl]	skelettartig
whistle-blowing ['wɪslˌbləʊɪŋ]	verräterisch
roller coaster ['rəʊləˌkəʊstə]	Achterbahn
deceit [dɪ'si:t]	Täuschung; Betrug
• eating disorder ['i:tɪŋ dɪˌsɔ:də]	Essstörung
• support [sə'pɔ:t]	Unterstützung; Hilfe
• to monitor ['mɒnɪtə]	überwachen
• carrot ['kærət]	Karotte
to pretend [prɪ'tend]	vorgeben; vortäuschen
subway ['sʌbweɪ]	Unterführung *(BE)*; U-Bahn *(AE)*
over-exercising [ˌəʊvr'eksəsaɪzɪŋ]	übermäßige sportliche Betätigung
to sneak [sni:k]	schleichen; schmuggeln
to admit [əd'mɪt]	zulassen; aufnehmen
beloved [bɪ'lʌvd; bɪ'lʌvɪd]	geliebt
• fundamental [ˌfʌndə'mentl]	fundamental
• weekly ['wi:kli]	wöchentlich
weigh-in [ˌweɪ‿'ɪn]	Wiegeaktion
• to overachieve [ˌəʊvrə'tʃi:v]	mehr Leistung bringen als erwartet
extracurricular [ˌekstrəkə'rɪkjələ]	außerhalb des Lehrplans
• to congratulate [kən'grætʃʊleɪt]	gratulieren
• to rebel [rɪ'bel]	rebellieren
• metaphor ['metəfə]	Metapher; übertragener Ausdruck
• refusal [rɪ'fju:zl]	Ablehnung; Weigerung
* to let go [ˌlet 'gəʊ]	loslassen
• residential [ˌrezɪ'dentʃl]	Wohn-
• thought [θɔ:t]	Gedanke
homesick ['həʊmsɪk]	heimwehkrank
desperate ['desprət]	verzweifelt
to relinquish [rɪ'lɪŋkwɪʃ]	aufgeben
folly ['fɒli]	Verrücktheit; Torheit
4 to cope with [kəʊp]	bewältigen; fertig werden mit

V5 Word quiz

■ Which new words in Topic 1 are also synonyms of these words and phrases?
1. *expecting a baby* • 2. *shy, not sure of yourself* • 3. *intelligent, clever* • 4. *freedom* • 5. *not to allow any more* • 6. *to buy* • 7. *helpful and kind* • 8. *in spite of* • 9. *easily hurt* • 10. *money from the state* (e.g. to help students, fund projects) • 11. *something that stands in your way* • 12. *not deep* • 13. *unable to move parts of your body*, e.g. after an accident to your back • 14. *not permanent*

A At the doctor's

1 ***Reasons for going to the doctor:*** *Imagine situations when you are abroad and have to see a doctor.*

2 *What phrases might you need for these situations? Think of as many as you can. The pictures and phrases on this page will help.*

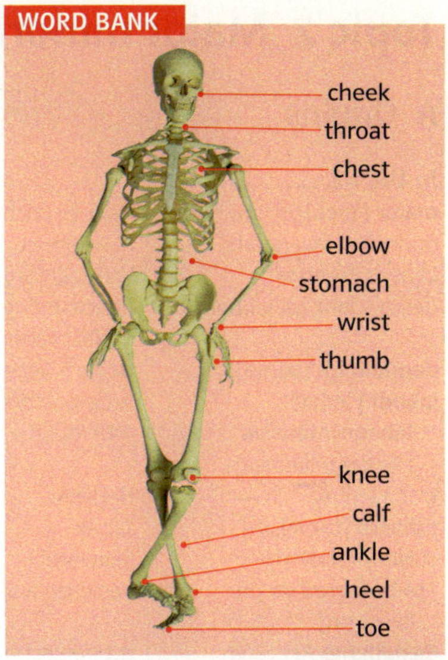

Patient: I need to see a doctor. Do I have to make an appointment[1]?
There's something the matter with my …
I've hurt my …/I've got pains in my …
I've got a stomach-ache/a headache/backache/earache/a sore throat[2].
(I think) I've broken …/sprained[3] my …
I've got a cut/bruise[4]/burn/rash[5] on my …
It won't heal up[6]. It's quite swollen/inflamed[7].
I feel sick./I've been sick.
I've got diarrhoea[8]/flu/hay fever[9].
My nose is blocked up[10].
I've been stung[11]/bitten by a … It's very painful.
Can you give me something for my …?
Should I stay in bed?
How long will it take to clear up[12]?
Do the pills have any side effects[13]?
Is there a chemist's[14] near here?

Doctor: Have you taken your temperature[15]?
You've caught an infection. It's going round.
You've torn[16] a muscle in your …
I'll give you some pills/ointment[17]/antibiotics/homeopathic[18] medicine/an injection[19].
We'd better have it X-rayed[20].
I'll have to do some tests/take a blood sample[21].
It looks like sinusitis[22].
You'll have to see a specialist.
If it's not better/cured in … days' time, come and see me again.
Here's your prescription[23].

3 [01 CD] ***Listening:*** *What seems to be the trouble? Listen to the dialogue between Lukas, who is on holiday in Greece, and a local doctor. Then answer these questions.*

1. *What is wrong with Lukas? Explain when and how his illness started, and what his symptoms are.*
2. *What is Dr Fotopoulos's diagnosis[24]? How does she want to treat the illness?*
3. *How does Lukas react to the doctor's suggestion for treatment? Why? What plan do they finally agree on?*

4 [pair work] ***Your turn:*** *Choose a situation (an illness, accident or other problem). Then use words and phrases from this page to write a dialogue between a patient and a doctor. Then act it out together.*

[1]Termin • [2]Halsweh • [3]verstaucht • [4]Prellung • [5]Ausschlag • [6]heilen • [7]entzündet • [8][ˌdaɪə'rɪə] Durchfall • [9]Heuschnupfen • [10]verstopft • [11]gestochen • [12]besser werden • [13]Nebenwirkungen • [14]Apotheke • [15]Fieber (gemessen) • [16]gerissen • [17]Salbe • [18][ˌhəʊmiəʊ'pæθɪk] • homöopathisch • [19]Spritze • [20]geröntgt • [21]Blutprobe • [22][ˌsaɪnə'saɪtɪs] Nebenhöhlenentzündung • [23]Rezept • [24][ˌdaɪəg'nəʊsɪs] Diagnose

Topic 2 Major minorities

A Origins

In the US ...

major ['meɪdʒə]	Haupt-; wichtig; größer
minority [maɪ'nɒrəti]	Minderheit
census ['sentsəs]	Volkszählung
descendant [dɪ'sendənt]	Abkömmling; Nachfahre; Nachfahrin
• **demand** [dɪ'mɑ:nd]	Bedarf; Verlangen
labour ['leɪbə]	Arbeit; Arbeitskraft; Mühe
labour-intensive [ˌleɪbər‿ɪn'tentsɪv]	arbeitsaufwändig
• **trade** [treɪd]	Handel
• **tobacco** [tə'bækəʊ]	Tabak
• **slavery** ['sleɪvri]	Sklaverei
* to **be based on** [bi: 'beɪst‿ɒn]	basieren auf; sich stützen auf
Civil Rights Act [ˌsɪvl 'raɪts‿ˌækt]	Bürgerrechtsgesetz
racial ['reɪʃl]	Rassen-
segregation [ˌsegrɪ'geɪʃn]	Trennung; Rassentrennung
• **discrimination** [dɪˌskrɪmɪ'neɪʃn]	Unterscheidung; Diskriminierung

In the UK ...

lack (of) [læk]	Mangel (an); Fehlen (von)
• **immigration** [ˌɪmɪ'greɪʃn]	Immigration; Einwanderung
• subcontinent [sʌb'kɒntɪnənt]	Subkontinent
• to **restrict** [rɪ'strɪkt]	begrenzen; beschränken
• **control** [kən'trəʊl]	Kontrolle; Steuerung
• to **limit** ['lɪmɪt]	limitieren; begrenzen; beschränken
• **ethnic** ['eθnɪk]	ethnisch; Volks-
• **Hindu** ['hɪndu:]	Hindu; hinduistisch
• **Muslim** ['mʊzlɪm]	Moslem(in); Muslim(in); moslemisch; muslimisch
• **multi-ethnic** [ˌmʌlti'eθnɪk]	Vielvölker-
refugee [ˌrefjʊ'dʒi:]	Flüchtling
asylum seeker [ə'saɪləm ˌsi:kə]	Asylbewerber(in)
• **diversity** [daɪ'vɜ:səti]	Vielfalt
prejudice ['predʒədɪs]	Vorurteil(e); Voreingenommenheit
• to **discriminate against** [dɪ'skrɪmɪneɪt‿əˌgentst]	diskriminieren; benachteiligen
victim ['vɪktɪm]	Opfer
race [reɪs]	Rasse
race relations [ˌreɪs rɪ'leɪʃnz]	Rassenbeziehungen

V6 Using the verb forms of nouns

■ Informative texts often contain nouns that tend to sound formal in English. Whereas in German it is quite common to use nouns rather than verbs, in English it is often best to express your ideas using the **verb forms** of these nouns to prevent your own style from sounding too formal.
Example: mass *importation* of slaves → Large numbers of slaves *were imported.*

■ Express these ideas in your own sentences, using verbs in place of nouns:

1. racial *discrimination* • 2. *immigration* of blacks • 3. the end of racial *segregation* • 4. fast economic *development* • 5. an incorrect *presentation* of the facts • 6. an excellent *performance* (of the play) • 7. an enormous *improvement* (in the standard of living) • 8. complete *amazement* (at someone's *achievement*).

■ Note down any other nouns you can think of that end in *'-ation'* or *'-ment'*, together with the verbs they are formed from.

V7 Compounds

■ Find the pairs that go together to make **compounds**. (They all appear in A.)

asylum • race • civil • minority • slave • Native • New • mother

relations • group • trade • seeker • American • World • country • rights

■ Now write your own example sentences explaining their meaning.

B Black Power

Rosa Parks and today's white youth

• to **scan** [skæn]	scannen; abtasten; nach Details durchsuchen
• icon ['aɪkɒn]	Ikone
to **turn out to be** [tɜ:n‿'aʊt tə ˌbi:]	sich herausstellen als
• **suburban** [sə'bɜ:bn]	Vorstadt-
• **courageous** [kə'reɪdʒəs]	mutig
bubble ['bʌbl]	Blase
• **specific** [spə'sɪfɪk]	spezifisch, speziell
zero ['zɪərəʊ]	null
• **classmate** ['klɑ:smeɪt]	Klassenkamerad(in); Mitschüler(in)
stark [stɑ:k]	krass
persistent [pə'sɪstnt]	hartnäckig; ausdauernd
to prevail [prɪ'veɪl]	vorherrschen; überwiegen
• enthusiastic [ɪnˌθju:zi'æstɪk]	enthusiastisch; begeistert
• to pulse [pʌls]	pulsieren
station wagon ['steɪʃn ˌwægən]	Kombi
low-riding ['ləʊˌraɪdɪŋ]	tiefsitzend; Hüft-
baggy ['bægi]	ausgebeult; bauschig
• **household** ['haʊshəʊld]	allgemein bekannt
rerun ['ri:rʌn]	Wiederholung
affect ['æfekt]	Affekt
• **temporary** ['temprəri]	vorübergehend; temporär
to shed [ʃed]	abwerfen
graduation [ˌgrædʒu'eɪʃn]	Schulabschluss

V8 Which preposition?

■ Knowing which preposition to use in English isn't always easy. Try to learn new words together with the preposition they take. Which one fits here?

across • against • for • on • of • to • with

1. *great demand … cotton* • 2. *a lack … opportunities* • 3. *to discriminate … minorities* • 4. *to be based … statistics* • 5. *parallels … your own country* • 6. *to reach … the divide* • 7. *relevance … Americans*

entrance ['entrənts]	Eingang; Eintritt
admission [əd'mɪʃn]	Zulassung; Aufnahme
• **hurricane** ['hʌrɪkən]	Hurrikan; Orkan; Wirbelsturm
• **incomprehensible** [ɪnˌkɒmprɪ'hentsəbl]	unverständlich; unbegreiflich
relief drive [rɪ'li:f ˌdraɪv]	Hilfsaktion
headliner cause [ˌhedlaɪnə 'kɔ:z]	schlagzeilenwürdiger Anlass
headline ['hedlaɪn]	Schlagzeile
peer [pɪə]	Gleichaltrige(r); gleichaltrig
baby boomer ['beɪbi ˌbu:mə]	Babyboomer *(Angehörige(r) eines geburtenstarken Jahrgangs)*
chapter ['tʃæptə]	Kapitel
to **diminish** [dɪ'mɪnɪʃ]	(sich) verringern
to **accomplish** [ə'kʌmplɪʃ]	vollbringen; erreichen
• **bravery** ['breɪvri]	Tapferkeit, Mut
defiance [dɪ'faɪənts]	Herausforderung; Trotz
eventually [ɪ'ventʃuəli]	schließlich, endlich
• to **sanction** ['sæŋktʃn]	sanktionieren; billigen
• to **acknowledge** [ək'nɒlɪdʒ]	anerkennen; einräumen
• * to **be willing to do sth** [bi: 'wɪlɪŋ]	gewillt sein, etw. zu tun
• **comfort** ['kʌmpfət]	Komfort; Behaglichkeit; Trost
• to **outlaw** ['aʊtlɔ:]	ächten; verbieten
• **integration** [ˌɪntɪ'greɪʃn]	Integration; Einbindung
to **devolve** [dɪ'vɒlv]	übergehen
• **force** [fɔ:s]	Macht
• **workplace** ['wɜ:kpleɪs]	Arbeitsplatz; Arbeitsstätte
* to **be up to sb** [bi:‿'ʌp tə]	liegen an; abhängen von; überlassen sein
backyard ['bækjɑ:d]	Garten; Hinterhof
smart [smɑ:t]	pfiffig; schlau
• **divide** [dɪ'vaɪd]	Kluft
to **figure out** [ˌfɪgər‿'aʊt]	herausfinden
• to **reach** [ri:tʃ]	reichen; greifen
tiny ['taɪni]	winzig
grand [grænd]	prächtig; großartig
gesture ['dʒestʃə]	Geste, Gebärde
1 • to **structure** ['strʌktʃə]	strukturieren; gliedern

Sister Rosa

to **deserve** [dɪ'zɜ:v]	verdienen
• **rest** [rest]	Rast
to **rest** [rest]	rasten; ausruhen; liegen
• **mob** [mɒb]	Mob; Pöbel
chorus ['kɔ:rəs]	Refrain
spark [spɑ:k]	Funke
without fail [wɪˌðaʊt 'feɪl]	unweigerlich; auf alle Fälle
jail [dʒeɪl]	Gefängnis
fine [faɪn]	Geldstrafe; Bußgeld
to **obtain** [əb'teɪn]	erlangen; bekommen
• **equality** [ɪ'kwɒləti]	Gleichberechtigung; Ebenbürtigkeit
to **dedicate** ['dedɪkeɪt]	widmen
thee [ði:]	dir; dich *(alt)*
dignity ['dɪgnəti]	Würde
Baptist ['bæptɪst]	Baptist(in)
minister ['mɪnɪstə]	Pfarrer(in)
• **strike** [straɪk]	Streik
to **assassinate** [ə'sæsɪneɪt]	ermorden
5 **mood** [mu:d]	Stimmung; Laune

I have a dream

to **devote** [dɪ'vəʊt]	widmen; verwenden
• **memorial** [mə'mɔ:riəl]	Denkmal; Gedenkstätte
8 **stylistic device** [staɪˌlɪstɪk dɪ'vaɪs]	Stilmittel

A different way

• **activist** ['æktɪvɪst]	Aktivist(in) *(jmd, der sich für etw. engagiert)*
• **peaceful** ['pi:sfl]	friedlich
• to **adopt** [ə'dɒpt]	übernehmen; annehmen; adoptieren
panther ['pæntθə]	Panther
• **militant** ['mɪlɪtnt]	militant; aggressiv
• **salute** [sə'lu:t]	Salut; Gruß
• to **terrorize** ['terəraɪz]	terrorisieren
9 • **sit-in** ['sɪtɪn]	Sitzstreik
10 to **justify** ['dʒʌstɪfaɪ]	rechtfertigen
to **inherit** [ɪn'herɪt]	erben

⟨I get my culture where I can⟩

lecturer ['lektʃrə]	Dozent(in)
• classical ['klæsɪkl]	klassisch
neck [nek]	Hals; Nacken
to strain [streɪn]	(sich) anstrengen; belasten
to retrieve [rɪ'tri:v]	zurückholen; wieder auffinden
to swear [sweə]	schwören; fluchen
to pad [pæd]	tappen; tasten
• sticky ['stɪki]	klebrig
sticker ['stɪkə]	Aufkleber
residue ['rezɪdju:]	Rückstand; Überrest
• remains [rɪ'meɪnz]	Rest(e); Überbleibsel
• identical [aɪ'dentɪkl]	identisch; gleich
• easiness ['i:zɪnəs]	Leichtigkeit; Lockerheit
* to get by [get 'baɪ]	vorbeikommen; durchkommen
* to give sb the finger [ˌgɪv sʌmbədi ðə 'fɪŋgə]	jmdm den Stinkefinger zeigen
• to resign [rɪ'zaɪn]	resignieren; zurücktreten
shade [ʃeɪd]	Schattierung; Schatten
light [laɪt]	hellhäutig
animated ['ænɪmeɪtɪd]	lebhaft; munter
to nod [nɒd]	nicken
for God's sake [fə ˌgɒdz 'seɪk]	um Gottes willen
• recordable disc [rɪ'kɔ:dəbl ˌdɪsk]	beschreibbare CD
firm [fɜ:m]	fest; standhaft

yard [jɑ:d] — Yard *(Längenmaß: 91,44 cm)*
freak [fri:k] — Missgeburt; eigenartiger Mensch
• to press [pres] — pressen; drücken
sharp [ʃɑ:p] — scharf; spitz
• forward ['fɔ:wəd] — vorwärts
cautious ['kɔ:ʃəs] — behutsam; vorsichtig
patch [pætʃ] — Fleck; Flicken; Stelle
to lift [lɪft] — (sich) heben
hoodie ['hʊdi] — Kapuzenpulli
* to draw [drɔ:] — ziehen
waistband ['weɪstbænd] — Bund
confusion [kən'fju:ʒn] — Verwirrung; Verwechslung
tart [tɑ:t] — scharf; herb; schroff
phew [fju:] — puh
light [laɪt] — leicht
tight *(infml)* [taɪt] — klasse; toll
• flow [fləʊ] — Fluss; Fließen; Strömung
track [træk] — Spur; Fährte; Musiktitel
neither … nor … ['naɪðə; 'ni:ðə … nɔ:] — weder … noch …
humble ['hʌmbl] — bescheiden; demütig
sixteen-track [ˌsɪksti:n'træk] — 16-Spur-Aufnahmegerät
deal [di:l] — Handel; Abmachung; Übereinkunft

to swap [swɒp] — tauschen
rather ['rɑ:ðə] — eher; eigentlich
to inhibit [ɪn'hɪbɪt] — hemmen; hindern
nah *(infml)* [næ] — nee
• to educate ['edʒʊkeɪt] — erziehen; bilden
• theatrical [θɪ'ætrɪkl] — theatralisch; Theater-
pretty ['prɪti] — hübsch
shit *(vulg)* [ʃɪt] — Scheiße; Scheißdreck
to bypass ['baɪpɑ:s] — umgehen
distraught [dɪ'strɔ:t] — bestürzt; zerstreut
to distract [dɪ'strækt] — ablenken
artificial [ˌɑ:tɪ'fɪʃl] — künstlich
to counter ['kaʊntə] — kontern; entgegnen
to blush [blʌʃ] — erröten
• accurate ['ækjərət] — akkurat; genau
previous ['pri:viəs] — vorherig; vorausgegangen
thumb [θʌm] — Daumen
bewildered [bɪ'wɪldəd] — verblüfft; verwirrt
* to shut up *(rude)* [ʃʌt‿'ʌp] — die Klappe halten
nope *(infml)* [nəʊp] — nee
to release [rɪ'li:s] — freigeben; herausgeben; freisetzen; loslassen
sidewalk *(AE)* ['saɪdwɔ:k] — Gehweg; Gehsteig
cab [kæb] — Taxi

V9 Useful new adjectives

■ What nouns would go well with these adjectives?
Get ideas from those given on the right – or choose others that you prefer.

temporary • suburban • courageous • persistent • incomprehensible • enthusiastic • smart • tiny

idea • decision • baby • smell • accommodation • area • dialect • applause

■ Now write definitions to go with the adjective/noun combinations you have chosen, or put them in example sentences.

C Living together in the UK

Asian voices

1 to pervade [pə'veɪd] — durchdringen; durchziehen
• **district** ['dɪstrɪkt] — Distrikt; Bezirk
mosque [mɒsk] — Moschee
• **significant** [sɪg'nɪfɪkənt] — signifikant; bedeutend; wesentlich
* to get stick *(infml)* [ˌget 'stɪk] — schikaniert werden
• **racism** ['reɪsɪzm] — Rassismus
to **subject (sb to sth)** [səb'dʒekt] — unterwerfen
retailer ['ri:teɪlə] — Einzelhändler(in)
outlook ['aʊtlʊk] — *hier:* Einstellung
vibrant ['vaɪbrənt] — dynamisch; lebhaft; pulsierend
to **tend** to [tend] — (zu etw.) neigen
• **multicultural** [ˌmʌlti'kʌltʃrl] — multikulturell
• to **contaminate** [kən'tæmɪneɪt] — kontaminieren; verseuchen
• **backwards** ['bækwədz] — rückwärts gewandt; rückständig
• **impressive** [ɪm'presɪv] — beeindruckend
to **judge** [dʒʌdʒ] — beurteilen; bewerten
weirdo *(infml)* ['wɪədəʊ] — Psychopath; komischer Kauz
• **financial** [faɪ'nænʃl] — finanziell
let alone [ˌlet‿ə'ləʊn] — geschweige denn

evidence ['evɪdnts] — Beweismaterial; Beleg
plain [pleɪn] — klar; schlicht; einfach
to **rank** [ræŋk] — einen Rang einnehmen; in eine Rangfolge einordnen
to **persist** [pə'sɪst] — verharren; beharren
• **catering** ['keɪtrɪŋ] — Gastronomie; Verpflegung
abuse [ə'bju:s] — Missbrauch
• **extremist** [ɪk'stri:mɪst] — Extremist(in)
to **indulge (in) sth** [ɪn'dʌldʒ] — nachgeben; sich etw. hingeben; sich in etw. ergehen
harmful ['hɑ:mfl] — schädlich
compulsory [kəm'pʌlsri] — verpflichtend; obligatorisch

A family drama

novel ['nɒvl] — Roman
to **stretch** [stretʃ] — strecken; dehnen
press-up ['presʌp] — Liegestütz
• guerrilla [gə'rɪlə] — Guerilla; Untergrundkämpfer(in)
to **turn on sb** ['tɜ:n‿ɒn] — sich gegen jmdn wenden; jmdn anfallen
dowry ['daʊri] — Mitgift; Aussteuer
they lived happily ever after [ðeɪ lɪvd ˌhæpɪli‿evər‿'ɑ:ftə] — und wenn sie nicht gestorben sind, dann leben sie noch heute
council ['kaʊntsl] — Gemeinderat; Stadtrat

V10 Discussing politics and society

■ Reading and talking about social and political issues is becoming more and more important in your school career.
Go through the vocabulary you know and collect useful words and phrases for these topics. According to what suits you best, organize them in **mind maps, grids, flow charts** or other forms of **lists**.

■ To start you off, here are some ideas on what topics you could look for:
1. *immigration* • *multi-ethnic society* • *racism* • *integration*
2. *government* • *political activism* • *revolution*
3. *colony* • *native* • *trade* • *independence*

■ Of course you can make other associations or link the words in another way. It's up to you.

* to **take sth out on sb** [ˌteɪk ɪt ˈaʊt ɒn]	etw. an jmdm auslassen
to **abuse** [əˈbjuːz]	beschimpfen; missbrauchen; misshandeln
• to **insist (on)** [ɪnˈsɪst]	insistieren; bestehen (auf)
till [tɪl]	Kasse
to **bang down** [ˌbæŋ ˈdaʊn]	hinknallen
junk shop [ˈdʒʌŋk ˌʃɒp]	Ramschladen
fingerprint [ˈfɪŋɡəprɪnt]	Fingerabdruck
• **wallpaper** [ˈwɔːlpeɪpə]	Tapete
• **cigarette butt** [sɪɡrˈet ˌbʌt]	Zigarettenstummel
• * to **stink** [stɪŋk]	stinken
toenail [ˈtəʊneɪl]	Zehennagel
nut [nʌt]	Nuss
to **flake** [fleɪk]	abblättern
as though [əz ˈðəʊ]	als ob
torture [ˈtɔːtʃə]	Folter
to **chew** [tʃuː]	kauen
sick [sɪk]	krank; unwohl
to **glare at sb** [ɡleə]	jmdn zornig anstarren
edge [edʒ]	Rand; Kante
• **reasonable** [ˈriːznəbl]	vernünftig; angemessen
to **snatch** [snætʃ]	schnappen; ergreifen
to **shove** [ʃʌv]	schieben; drängen
out of date [ˌaʊt əv ˈdeɪt]	veraltet
to **bother to do sth** [ˈbɒðə]	sich die Mühe machen, etw. zu tun
to **punch** [pʌntʃ]	mit der Faust schlagen; boxen
* to **make a fuss** [ˌmeɪk ə ˈfʌs]	viel Aufhebens machen
not … either [nɒt … ˈaɪðə; nɒt … ˈiːðə]	auch nicht
* to **come up with** [kʌm ˈʌp wɪð]	sich etw. einfallen lassen
5 • to **sympathize** [ˈsɪmpəθaɪz]	mitfühlen; sympathisieren
8 • **conflict** [ˈkɒnflɪkt]	Konflikt; Auseinandersetzung

⟨Half-caste⟩

half-caste [ˈhɑːfkɑːst]	Halbblut; Mischling
canvas [ˈkænvəs]	Leinwand
overcast [ˈəʊvəkɑːst]	bedeckt; bewölkt
spiteful [ˈspaɪtfl]	gehässig; schadenfroh
key [kiː]	Taste
keen [kiːn]	scharf; fein
consequently [ˈkɒntsɪkwəntli]	folglich; somit
to glow [ɡləʊ]	leuchten; glühen
* to cast [kɑːst]	werfen
• satirical [səˈtɪrɪkl]	satirisch; Spott-
• colonial [kəˈləʊniəl]	kolonial

Multi-ethnic Britain

formula, *pl.* formulae [ˈfɔːmjələ]	Formel
• Islamic [ɪzˈlæmɪk]	islamisch
13 **celebrity** [səˈlebrəti]	Prominente(r); berühmte Person

V11 Not always what you think

■ You already know a number of English words that look – and sound – like German words, but have a different meaning (e.g. *mist, brave, biscuit etc.*).
We call these **'false friends'**. Other words have several meanings (e.g. *argument* can mean both 'Argument' and 'Streit').
You might like to call these **'many-faced friends'**.
It can be a good idea to write down these words with your own examples (sometimes with the help of a dictionary).

■ *eventually* ≠ eventuell
We *eventually* reached the airport. = Wir kamen *schließlich* am Flughafen an.
We *may possibly* take a taxi. = *Eventuell* nehmen wir ein Taxi.

■ *control* = Herrschaft; Gewalt, Macht, Beherrschung, Leitung, Führung, Aufsicht, Kontrolle
We have no *control* over the weather. Mr Brown now has *control* of the company. The dog was out of *control*.

■ Now do the same with these new words from Topic 2:
labour • *comfort* • *figure (out)* • *minister* • *adopt* • *rest* • *fine* • *novel* • *punch* • *sympathize*

B Using public transport

1 ***Basic vocabulary:*** *Think of as many English words and expressions as you can that have to do with public transport. Collect them in a mind map.*

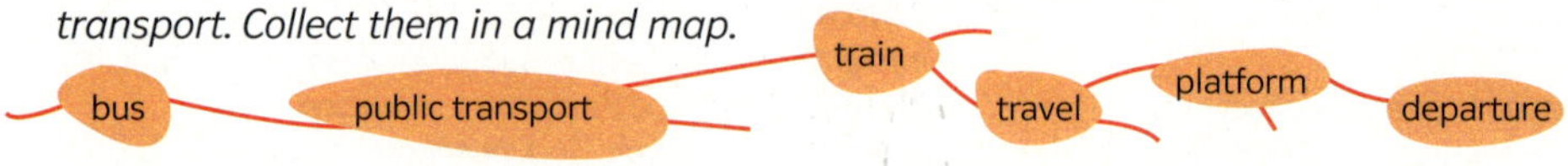

2 [02] ***Listening:*** *How to get there: You will hear three dialogues. Listen and choose the correct answers.*

a) At the Underground Station at Heathrow Airport
 1. The two women are staying near A Oxford Street B Piccadilly Circus C St James's Square.
 2. They buy Travelcards that are valid[1] for A one day B two days C a week.
 3. The A District B Central C Piccadilly Line goes to and from Heathrow Airport.

b) At a travel agent's in Thailand
 1. The two tourists want to travel to A Bangkok B Chiang Mai C Hualamphong.
 2. The assistant recommends[2] that they go by A plane B train C coach …
 3. … because it's A easier than by plane B safer than by coach C cheaper than by train.

c) At the ticket office of the main railway station in Munich
 1. The American tourist buys a ticket to A Neuschwanstein B Hohenschwangau C Füssen.
 2. He is told A the price of the bus B when the bus leaves C how long the bus takes.

3 ***Role play:***

a) *You are staying with a Scottish family in Glasgow and would like to take a day trip either to one of the Isles or into the Highlands. Use the information below to discuss the idea with your host family.*

ScotRail
Rail & ferry tickets to the Isles

Glasgow – Craignure (Mull)		**Glasgow – Armadale (Skye)**	
Cheap Day Return[3]: £29.70		**Cheap Day Return: £35**	
Depart[4] Glasgow	0821	Depart Glasgow	0851
Depart Oban	1122	Depart Mallaig	1505
Arrive Craignure	1241	Arrive Armadale	1535
Depart Craignure	1700	Depart Armadale	1705
Arrive Oban	1746	Arrive Mallaig	1735
Arrive Glasgow	2125	Arrive Glasgow	0014

Scottish Tours
One day coach tour from Glasgow (Glen Coe, Fort William, Ben Nevis, Fort Augustus, Loch Ness scenic[5] drive, Inverness, Spey Valley & Pitlochry)
Adult £31 (Child £26)
Leaves 08.15 hrs from Platform 6 Buchanan Bus Station Glasgow
Returns at 20.30 hrs

b) ***Internet research:*** *Choose a place you would like to visit and find out the best way to get there and the travel times.*

[1]gültig • [2][ˌrekəˈmendz] empfiehlt • [3]Rückfahrkarte • [4]ab(fahren) • [5]landschaftlich reizvoll

Topic 3 Schooldays

A The question of what to wear

appropriate [ə'prəʊpriət]	angemessen
inappropriate [ˌɪnə'prəʊpriət]	unangemessen

Houston County schools dress code policy (grades 6–12)

dress code ['dres kəʊd]	Kleiderordnung
policy ['pɒlɪsi]	Politik; politische Linie; Grundsatz
manner ['mænə]	(Art und) Weise
to **distract sb (from sth)** [dɪ'strækt]	jmdn (von etw.) ablenken
distraction [dɪ'strækʃn]	Ablenkung
to **disrupt** [dɪs'rʌpt]	stören; zerbrechen; sprengen
disruption [dɪs'rʌpʃn]	Störung; Bruch; Zerrüttung
to **observe** [əb'zɜ:v]	beobachten; beachten; befolgen
to **groom** [gru:m]	pflegen; putzen
to **resemble** [rɪ'zembl]	ähneln
pajamas *(pl.) (AE)* [pə'dʒɑ:məz]	Pyjama; Schlafanzug
underwear ['ʌndəweə]	Unterwäsche
to **prohibit** [prə'hɪbɪt]	untersagen; verbieten
• to **differ** ['dɪfə]	sich unterscheiden; abweichen
• **extreme** [ɪks'tri:m]	extrem
• **conventional** [kən'ventʃnl]	konventionell; herkömmlich; üblich
• to **permit** [pə'mɪt]	erlauben; genehmigen
to **expose** [ɪk'spəʊz]	ausstellen; entblößen; freilegen
• **specific** [spə'sɪfɪk]	spezifisch, speziell
• **blouse** [blaʊz]	Bluse
strap [stræp]	Träger; Gurt
waist [weɪst]	Bauch; Taille
midriff ['mɪdrɪf]	Taille
hole [həʊl]	Loch
• **artwork** ['ɑ:twɜ:k]	Illustrationen; Bebilderung
offensive [ə'fentsɪv]	anstößig; beleidigend
• **tobacco** [tə'bækəʊ]	Tabak
to **tuck in** [ˌtʌk‿'ɪn]	einstecken; einschlagen
neither … nor … ['naɪðə; 'ni:ðə … nɔ:]	weder … noch …
jewelry *(AE)* ['dʒu:əlri]	Schmuck
to **pierce** [pɪəs]	durchbohren; durchdringen

Going to court over school dress code rules

rosary ['rəʊzri]	Rosenkranz
necklace ['nekləs]	Halskette
* to **take sb to court** [ˌteɪk tə'kɔ:t]	jmdn verklagen
co-ed ['kəʊˌed]	gemischt *(Schule)*
therefore ['ðeəfɔ:]	deshalb; somit
• **ban** [bæn]	Bann; Verbot; Sperre
to **ban** [bæn]	bannen; verbieten; sperren
• to **discourage** [dɪs'kʌrɪdʒ]	abschrecken; entmutigen
rebelliousness [rɪ'beliəsnəs]	Aufsässigkeit
• **authority** [ɔ:'θɒrəti]	Autorität; Staatsgewalt; Behörde
• **discipline** ['dɪsɪplɪn]	Disziplin

V12 Different ways of expressing opposites

■ You already know a number of words which can be turned into their opposites simply by using the **prefix** *'un-'*.
Example: ***un**happy, to **un**pack.*
Other prefixes that can be used are:
– *'**in**-'* (*'**im**-'* before b, p, m; *'**il**-'* before l; *'**ir**-'* before r): ***in**dependence; **im**possible; **il**legal; **ir**regular*
– '**dis**-': *to **dis**respect*

■ Careful! The English prefixes *'un-'*, *'in-'*, etc. are not stressed when spoken. Compare with German: *un<u>happy</u> – <u>un</u>glücklich*

■ Decide which of the words in this list express negative ideas (opposites), and which do not:
1. *underwear* • 2. *inappropriate* • 3. *inside* • 4. *interpret* • 5. *discipline* • 6. *universe* • 7. *unbelievable* • 8. *unable* • 9. *disability* • 10. *disco* • 11. *discourage* • 12. *important* • 13. *impolite* • 14. *illness* • 15. *indefinite* • 16. *unknown*

■ Use prefixes to turn the following words into their opposites. Use a dictionary whenever you are unsure. Then check your answers with a partner's.
1. *honest* • 2. *legal* • 3. *relevant* • 4. *realistic* • 5. *to like* • 6. *responsible* • 7. *attractive* • 8. *logical* • 9. *likely* • 10. *advantage* • 11. *activity* • 12. *probable* • 13. *mobility* • 14. *married* • 15. *visible* • 16. *reliable* • 17. *replaceable* • 18. *to tie* • 19. *to agree* • 20. *personal* • 21. *direct*

■ Sometimes, of course, a completely different word is needed to express an opposite meaning. Do you (still) know the opposite of these?
1. *positive* • 2. *low* • 3. *well* (2 possible answers) • 4. *prohibited* • 5. *common* • 6. *against* • 7. *dressed* • 8. *winner* • 9. *to drop* • 10. *life* • 11. *male* • 12. *to save* (e.g. energy)

V13 Suffixes

■ By adding **suffixes**, lots of different words can be formed from the same root.
Examples: *move**ment**; dark**ness**; to short**en**; smel**ly***

■ Find the words in A which are formed from these roots, and underline the suffixes used. How many different suffixes did you find?
1. *support* • 2. *distract* • 3. *member* • 4. *connect* • 5. *react* • 6. *education* • 7. *disrupt* • 8. *rebellious* • 9. *advertise*

■ Collect four or five more words that end with each of the suffixes you found, e.g. suffix ***-ion**: invent**ion**; suffix: **-ness**: ill**ness**.*

■ Look out for more suffixes as you work through this book. Typical ones are:
-ence, -ance, -ity, -ation, -ision to form **nouns**
-ing, -able, -ible, -ical, -ful, -less to form **adjectives**
-ify, -ize to form **verbs**.

■ If you know the root, any new words with suffixes like these will be easily understandable.
Careful! Stress is often different from what you may expect,
Example: English: *re<u>ac</u>tion* – German: *Reak<u>tion</u>*.

B Teachers and pupils

The sheep

novel ['nɒvl]	Roman
to **nudge** [nʌdʒ]	stupsen; anstoßen
barely ['beəli]	kaum
• to **tolerate** ['tɒlreɪt]	tolerieren; dulden
patient ['peɪʃnt]	geduldig
* to **give sb a break** [ˌgɪv‿ə 'breɪk]	jmdn schonen; jmdm eine Chance geben
jock *(AE) (infml)* [dʒɒk]	Sportler(in)
• **intellectual** [ˌɪntl'ektʃuəl]	Intellektuelle(r)
• **critic** ['krɪtɪk]	Kritiker(in)
• **fanatic** [fə'nætɪk]	Fanatiker(in)
sin [sɪn]	Sünde
to **brood (over sth)** [bru:d]	brüten; (nach)grübeln (über)
saint [seɪnt]	Heilige(r)
• **creature** ['kri:tʃə]	Kreatur; Geschöpf
* to **be on to sth** [bi:‿'ɒn tə]	bekannt sein mit
to **delay** [dɪ'leɪ]	verzögern; aufschieben
• **universal** [ˌju:nɪ'vɜ:sl]	universell
master ['mɑ:stə]	Meister; Schulmeister; Lehrer
to **hiss** [hɪs]	zischen; fauchen
bloody *(rude)* ['blʌdi]	verdammt
in olden times [ɪn'əʊldən ˌtaɪmz]	anno dazumal
obedient [ə'bi:diənt]	gehorsam
chalk [tʃɔ:k]	Kreide
ancestor ['ænsestə]	Ahn; Vorfahr
• **Egyptian** [ɪ'dʒɪptʃn]	Ägypter(in)
forefather ['fɔ:ˌfɑ:ðə]	Ahne; Ahnin; Vorfahr
to **capture** ['kæptʃə]	ergreifen; erobern; einfangen
ray [reɪ]	Strahl
chamber ['tʃeɪmbə]	Kammer
heavenly body [ˌhevnli 'bɒdi]	Himmelskörper
beyond [bi'ɒnd]	jenseits; über etw. hinaus
calculus ['kælkjələs]	Differential- und Integralrechnung
to doze off [ˌdəʊz‿'ɒf]	einnicken; einschlafen
sincere [sɪn'sɪə]	aufrichtig; seriös
* to take no shit *(infml)* [ˌteɪk nəʊ 'ʃɪt]	sich nichts gefallen lassen
• **notebook** ['nəʊtbʊk]	Heft *(AE)*; Notizbuch; Notebook *(Computer)*
to fold [fəʊld]	falten; klappen
dammit *(rude)* ['dæmɪt]	verdammt
• **elbow** ['elbəʊ]	Ellenbogen; mit dem Ellenbogen anstoßen
to **pretend** [prɪ'tend]	vorgeben; vortäuschen
• hysterics [hɪ'sterɪks]	Hysterie; hysterischer Lachanfall
smart ass *(slang)* [ˌsmɑ:t‿'æs]	Klugscheißer(in)
response [rɪ'spɒnts]	Antwort; Erwiderung; Rückmeldung
• to **report** [rɪ'pɔ:t]	anzeigen; melden
industrious [ɪn'dʌstriəs]	fleißig
• * to **be in command** [bi:‿ɪn kə'mɑ:nd]	das Kommando haben; den Oberbefehl haben
• **cafeteria** [ˌkæfɪ'tɪəriə]	Cafeteria
• **complaint** [kəm'pleɪnt]	Beschwerde
* to know the ropes [ˌnəʊ ðə 'rəʊps]	die Spielregeln kennen
common sense [ˌkɒmən 'sents]	gesunder Menschenverstand
infancy ['ɪnfəntsi]	frühes Kindesalter
The phone is ringing off the hook. [ðə ˌfəʊn‿ɪz rɪŋɪŋ ɒf ðə 'hʊk]	Das Telefon klingelt ohne Unterlass.
* to be up in arms [bi:‿ʌp‿ɪn‿'ɑ:mz]	Sturm laufen; sich empören
to cover one's ass *(vulg)* [ˌkʌvə wʌnz‿'æs]	seine Haut retten
exasperated [ɪg'zæspreɪtɪd]	entnervt; außer sich
to advocate ['ædvəkeɪt]	befürworten; verteidigen; eintreten für
bestiality [ˌbesti'æləti]	Sodomie
• to **fire** [faɪə]	feuern; hinauswerfen
• righteous ['raɪtʃəs]	rechtschaffen
mating habits *(pl.)* ['meɪtɪŋ ˌhæbɪts]	Paarungsgewohnheiten
3 punctuation [ˌpʌŋktʃu'eɪʃn]	Zeichensetzung; Interpunktion
5 • **irony** ['aɪərəni]	Ironie

⟨How dare you?⟩

to clamp down [ˌklæmp 'daʊn]	strikter werden
petty bloody officiousness [ˌpeti ˌblʌdi‿ə'fɪʃəsnəs]	blöder kleinlicher Übereifer
crap *(vulg)* [kræp]	Scheiß
slight [slaɪt]	leicht; gering

V14 In the classroom

■ Joey Santos (in *The sheep*) talks to his teacher in a very **informal** way. How could he speak more appropriately? Put these phrases into language you think would sound more suitable for a pupil to use.

Example: *'Yo, teacher man …'* → *'Excuse me, Mr McCourt. May I ask a question?'*

1. *'Yeah. OK. So, you Scotch or somethin' ?'*
2. *'Oh yeah? What's Irish? Like St. Patrick, right?'*
3. *'Hey mister. Everyone talk English over there in Ireland?'*
4. *'You all Catlics in Ireland?'*
5. *'Aw, teacher … Spelling … Do we haveta? B-o-r-i-n-g spelling list.'*
6. *'Gotta go. Gotta go.'*

■ Imagine these situations. What could you ask? Think of how you might talk – politely, of course – to your teacher.

1. *You've run out of paper.* • 2. *Your mobile rings during the lesson.* • 3. *You don't understand a question.* • 4. *You're having trouble with an exercise.* • 5. *It's terribly hot in the classroom.* • 6. *You arrive late (the lesson has already started).* • 7. *You've left one of your books at home.* • 8. *You want to complain because you think you got an unfair grade in a test.* • 9. *The bell rings, but you aren't ready to hand your work in yet.* • 10. *You feel sick.*

ounce [aʊnts]	Unze *(Maßeinheit: 28,34952 Gramm)*
* to bear [beə]	(er)tragen; hervorbringen
• robot ['rəʊbɒt]	Roboter; Automat
the odd … [ði‿'ɒd]	das ein oder andere
precious ['preʃəs]	wertvoll; kostbar
to dump [dʌmp]	abladen
scrapheap ['skræphiːp]	Müllhaufen
to turf sb out *(BE) (slang)* [ˌtɜːf‿'aʊt]	hinauswerfen
to screw [skruː]	schrauben
stud [stʌd]	Ohrstecker
tissue ['tɪsjuː]	Taschentuch
desperate ['desprət]	verzweifelt; hoffnungslos
• to compose [kəm'pəʊz]	komponieren; verfassen; zusammensetzen
appointment [ə'pɔɪntmənt]	Termin
hairdresser ['heədresə]	Friseur(in)
this very afternoon [ðɪz ˌveri‿ɑːftə'nuːn]	noch heute Nachmittag
to suck up *(infml)* [ˌsʌk‿'ʌp]	kriechen; sich einschleimen
weird [wɪəd]	sonderbar; merkwürdig
subconscious [ˌsʌb'kɒnʃəs]	Unterbewusstsein
gasp [gɑːsp]	hörbares Einatmen
puce [pjuːs]	puterrot
I beg your pardon? [aɪ ˌbeg jə 'pɑːdn]	Wie bitte?
• emotional [ɪ'məʊʃnl]	emotional; gefühlsmäßig
to freak out [ˌfriːk‿'aʊt]	ausflippen
• examination [ɪgˌzæmɪ'neɪʃn]	Examen; Prüfung
* to take to *(+ gerund)* ['teɪk tə]	sich angewöhnen zu
interference [ˌɪntə'fɪərnts]	Störung; Beeinträchtigung; Einmischung
insolence ['ɪntslənts]	Anmaßung; Frechheit
tramp [træmp]	Landstreicher
in the first place [ɪn ðə 'fɜːst pleɪs]	von vornherein; überhaupt erst
establishment [ɪ'stæblɪʃmənt]	Einrichtung; Institution
puny [pjuːni]	kümmerlich; mickrig
aspiration [ˌæspɪ'reɪʃn]	Hoffnung; Streben
to yell [jel]	brüllen; laut schreien
to parrot ['pærət]	nachplappern
revolting [rɪ'vɒltɪŋ]	abscheulich
phraseology [ˌfreɪzɪ'ɒlədʒi]	Ausdrucksweise
• forever [fə'revə]	für immer; ewig
hobby horse ['hɒbi ˌhɔːs]	Steckenpferd
filthy ['fɪlθi]	schmutzig, dreckig

C Why bother?

Addicted to fame

to bother to do sth ['bɒðə]	sich die Mühe machen, etw. zu tun
* **to be addicted to sth** [biː‿ə'dɪktɪd]	abhängig sein von; süchtig sein nach
fame [feɪm]	Ruhm
celebrity [sə'lebrəti]	Prominente(r); berühmte Person
to pick up the pieces [ˌpɪk‿ʌp ðə 'piːsiːz]	etw. wieder in den Griff bekommen
bright [braɪt]	intelligent; gescheit
* to have a point [ˌhæv‿ə 'pɔɪnt]	nicht ganz Unrecht haben
suspicion [sə'spɪʃn]	*hier:* Hauch; Anflug
disgusting [dɪs'gʌstɪŋ]	ekelhaft; widerlich
steady on! [ˌstedi‿'ɒn]	Immer mit der Ruhe! Sachte!
snigger ['snɪgə]	Kichern
as a matter of fact [əz‿ə ˌmætər‿əv 'fækt]	in der Tat
wimp *(infml)* [wɪmp]	Weichei; Schlappschwanz
to fail to *(+ infinitive)* [feɪl]	versäumen zu; es nicht schaffen zu
to turn up [tɜːn‿'ʌp]	auftauchen; erscheinen
• deathly ['deθli]	tödlich; Todes-
hush [hʌʃ]	Schweigen, Stille
to descend [dɪ'send]	herabsteigen; sich herabsenken
to single sb out [ˌsɪŋgl‿'aʊt]	herausgreifen; aussondern
• capacity [kə'pæsɪti]	Kapazität; Vermögen
to humiliate [hjuː'mɪlieɪt]	demütigen; erniedrigen
to serve it up double [tə ˌsɜːv‿ɪt‿ʌp 'dʌbl]	es doppelt so schlimm machen
unpleasant [ˌʌn'pleznt]	unangenehm
moron ['mɔːrɒn]	Schwachkopf; Idiot(in)
inevitable [ɪn'evɪtəbl]	unvermeidlich; unabwendbar
expulsion [ɪk'spʌlʃn]	Ausschluss; Ausweisung
* to draw sb's attention to sth [ˌdrɔː sʌmbʌdiz‿ə'tentʃn tə]	jmds Aufmerksamkeit auf etw. lenken
• dubious ['djuːbiəs]	dubios; zweifelhaft; fragwürdig
excuse [ɪk'skjuːs]	Entschuldigung; Ausrede
to alienate ['eɪliəneɪt]	entfremden
to crawl [krɔːl]	kriechen
to lag [læg]	hinterherhinken; zurückbleiben
decade ['dekeɪd]	Jahrzehnt
7 • conflict ['kɒnflɪkt]	Konflikt; Auseinandersetzung
9 • honesty ['ɒnɪsti]	Ehrlichkeit; Ehrenhaftigkeit

Geography lesson

to long (for) [lɒŋ]	sich sehnen (nach); verlangen
scented ['sentɪd]	parfümiert
• jasmine ['dʒæzmɪn]	Jasmin
to clamber ['klæmbə]	klettern; erklimmen
drab [dræb]	düster; eintönig
stranglehold ['stræŋglhəʊld]	Würgegriff; Umklammerung
• * **to take ill** [ˌteɪk‿'ɪl]	krank werden
to fade away [ˌfeɪd‿ə'weɪ]	aus dem Gedächtnis schwinden; sterben
• **ocean** ['əʊʃn]	Ozean
12 • **impression** [ɪm'preʃn]	Impression; Eindruck
to crave [kreɪv]	sich sehnen nach
to trace [treɪs]	verfolgen; nachspüren
effort ['efət]	Mühe; Bemühung
wannabe *(infml)* ['wɒnəbiː]	Möchtegern
to skip sth [skɪp]	überspringen; auslassen; schwänzen
nose job *(infml)* ['nəʊz ˌdʒɒb]	Nasenkorrektur
to turn up [tɜːn‿'ʌp]	auftauchen; erscheinen
• **agency** ['eɪdʒəntsi]	Agentur
• the looks *(pl.)* [lʊks]	das Aussehen
meanwhile [ˌmiː'nwaɪl]	mittlerweile; in der Zwischenzeit

V15 What's that in everyday English?

■ You will find quite a number of words in this Topic that sound rather formal. Although they are commonly used in written English, they are less likely to appear in everyday spoken English.

■ Can you replace the words and phrases in *italics* so that the sentences sound less formal? Sometimes the whole sentence will need to be rephrased.

1. Any clothes *resembling* underwear are not *permitted* to be worn in this school.
2. *Clothing* which *suggests membership* in a gang is *prohibited*.
3. Noisy behaviour causing *disruption* during lessons cannot be tolerated.
4. Mr McCourt noticed that there were quiet *industrious* classes where teachers were *in perfect command*.
5. Murat's *lack of attendance* at school is *hindering* his *academic potential*.

lack (of) [læk]	Mangel (an); Fehlen (von)
attendance [ə'tendnts]	Anwesenheit; Teilnahme
• **to hinder** ['hɪndə]	behindern; erschweren
• **potential** [pəʊ'tentʃl]	Potenzial; Leistungsvermögen
• phenomenon, *pl.* phenomena [fə'nɒmɪnən]	Phänomen; Naturerscheinung
* to give sth a shot [ˌgɪv‿ə 'ʃɒt]	es mal probieren mit etw.; sein Glück versuchen mit etw.
to **pick** [pɪk]	auswählen; herauslesen
respondent [rɪ'spɒndnt]	Antwortende(r); Befragte(r)
to **respond** [rɪ'spɒnd]	reagieren; erwidern; antworten
to cite [saɪt]	anführen; zitieren
• **acceptance** [ək'septənts]	Akzeptanz; Zustimmung
to prove sb wrong [ˌpru:v 'rɒŋ]	beweisen, dass jmd Unrecht hat
rough [rʌf]	grob; rau; ungefähr
• **broken home** [ˌbrəʊkn 'həʊm]	nicht intakte Familie
role model ['rəʊl ˌmɒdl]	Vorbild

Money for nothing

thumb [θʌm]	Daumen
chorus ['kɔ:rəs]	Refrain
• **oven** ['ʌvn]	Backofen
custom ['kʌstəm]	maßgefertigt
• **delivery** [dɪ'lɪvri]	Lieferung
refrigerator [rɪ'frɪdʒreɪtə]	Kühlschrank
buddy *(infml)* ['bʌdi]	Kumpel
• **jet** [dʒet]	Düse; Düsenflugzeug
airplane ['eəpleɪn]	Flugzeug
to **bang** [bæŋ]	schlagen; fest (an)klopfen
• bongoes *(pl.)* ['bɒŋgəʊz]	Bongos *(kubanische Trommeln)*
chimpanzee [ˌtʃɪmpn'zi:]	Schimpanse

D School – and how to improve it

⟨The secrets of an inspirational headmistress⟩

inspirational [ˌɪntspɪ'reɪʃnəl]	inspiriert; fähig, andere zu begeistern
headmistress *(BE)* [ˌhed'mɪstrəs]	Schulleiterin
to chill [tʃɪl]	abkühlen; sich abregen
to tower [taʊə]	hoch aufragen
to saunter ['sɔ:ntə]	schlendern; bummeln
curious ['kjʊəriəs]	neugierig
* to take the helm [ˌteɪk ðə 'helm]	das Heft in die Hand nehmen
to stab (to death) [stæb]	(er)stechen
tragedy ['trædʒədi]	Tragödie
to descend [dɪ'send]	herabsteigen; sich herabsenken
measure ['meʒə]	Maßnahme
on the brink of [ɒn ðə 'brɪŋk]	am Rande von; kurz vor
• shutdown ['ʃʌtdaʊn]	Schließung; Stilllegung
expanse [ɪk'spænts]	Fläche
tarmac ['tɑ:mæk]	Asphalt
pitted ['pɪtɪd]	übersät
* to stick [stɪk]	kleben; stecken
matted ['mætɪd]	verfilzt; verklebt
troublesome ['trʌblsəm]	störend; lästig
bin [bɪn]	Abfalleimer
underneath [ˌʌndə'ni:θ]	unterhalb; unten
refugee [ˌrefjʊ'dʒi:]	Flüchtling
to stagger ['stægə]	staffeln
crucial ['kru:ʃl]	entscheidend; ausschlaggebend
template ['templeɪt]	Vorlage; Schablone; Muster
• purposeful ['pɜ:pəsfli]	entschlossen; zielgerichtet; zweckmäßig
bunch [bʌntʃ]	Bündel; Haufen; Packen
• forward ['fɔ:wəd]	vorwärts
* to sweep [swi:p]	fegen
determined [dɪ'tɜ:mɪnd]	entschlossen; entschieden; zielstrebig
glance [glɑ:nts]	Blick
to boom out [ˌbu:m‿'aʊt]	dröhnen
• decibel ['desɪbl]	Dezibel *(Einheit der Lautstärke)*
to jump [dʒʌmp]	erschrecken
• to bombard [bɒm'bɑ:d]	bombardieren
badge [bædʒ]	Abzeichen
to swarm [swɔ:m]	schwärmen; strömen; sich drängen
* to swear [sweə]	schwören; fluchen
* to get a grip on [ˌget‿ə 'grɪp]	in den Griff bekommen
to restrain [rɪ'streɪn]	zurückhalten; festhalten
incident ['ɪntsɪdnt]	Vorfall; Ereignis
• technician [tek'nɪʃn]	Techniker(in)
flippant ['flɪpnt]	nicht ernst gemeint
touching ['tʌtʃɪŋ]	rührend; ergreifend
• pride [praɪd]	Stolz
• to insist (on) [ɪn'sɪst]	insistieren; bestehen (auf)
• inspection [ɪn'spekʃn]	Inspektion; Kontrolle; Überprüfung
inspector [ɪn'spektə]	Inspektor(in); Prüfer(in); Schulrat; Schulrätin
• to rest [rest]	rasten; ausruhen; liegen

* to make of [ˌmeɪk_əv]	halten von
bond [bɒnd]	Bindung
spirit ['spɪrɪt]	Geist; Stimmung
three cheers for … [ˌθriː 'tʃɪəz fə]	ein dreifaches Hoch auf …
hip-hip-hooray [hɪp ˌhɪp hʊ'reɪ]	Hipp hipp hurra
4 **public school** [ˌpʌblɪk 'skuːl]	Privatschule *(BE)*; staatliche Schule *(AE)*
boarding school ['bɔːdɪŋ skuːl]	Internat
6 to **attend** [ə'tend]	teilnehmen; anwesend sein

V16 British and American English

■ Spelling: Start a list of words that are spelt differently in British and American English. Begin with words from Topic 3, and go on with words you have learned earlier.
What rules – if any – do you notice?
BE: jewellery – *AE:* jewelry
BE: moustache – *AE:* mustache

■ Different words and expressions: First write down all the words and expressions you find in Topic 3 that are different in British and American English.
Add any other examples you remember or get to know.
BE: exercise book – *AE:* notebook
BE: trousers – *AE:* pants

E Education in the US and the UK

Map of the US education system

• **medicine** ['medsn]	Medizin
1 **undergraduate** [ˌʌndə'grædjuət]	Student(in) vor dem ersten akademischen Grad
degree [dɪ'griː]	akademischer Grad; Hochschulabschluss

The UK education system

fee [fiː]	Gebühr; Abgabe
primary school ['praɪmri ˌskuːl]	Grundschule
nursery school ['nɜːsri ˌskuːl]	Vorschule; Kindergarten
secondary school ['sekəndri ˌskuːl]	weiterführende Schule
comprehensive school [kɒmprɪ'hentsɪv ˌskuːl]	Gesamtschule
curriculum, *pl.* curricula [kjə'rɪkjələm]	Lehrplan
stage [steɪdʒ]	Stadium
to assess [ə'ses]	bewerten; beurteilen; einschätzen
vocational [ˌvəʊ'keɪʃnl]	berufsbildend; beruflich
postgraduate [ˌpəʊst'grædjuət]	Doktorand(in); Student(in) im Aufbaustudium
PhD [ˌpiːeɪtʃ'diː]	Doktor der Philosophie

The beginning of term at Hogwarts

additional [ə'dɪʃnl]	zusätzlich
goblet ['gɒblət]	Kelch; Pokal
• **appearance** [ə'pɪərnts]	Erscheinung; Aussehen; Auftritt

V17 A word quiz

■ Find words (all new in Topic 3) that mean the same as:

1. (male) *teacher*
2. to *catch*
3. an *answer*
4. *hard-working*
5. to *choose*
6. to *go to* school
7. to *want very much* to do something
8. a *star* or *famous person*
9. *annoyed and frustrated*
10. *extra* or *added*

C Free-time activities

1 [05] ***Listening:*** *Planning a picnic. First listen to the dialogue, then read the questions below and listen again, making notes about the arrangements made.*

1. *Which of these things are Tony and Sharon not going to take?*
   Tony: something to drink, plates, sandwiches, a football;
   Sharon: peanuts[1], bananas, knives and forks, sandwiches.
2. *Say what the others are supposed to bring, where and when they are meeting.*

2 ***The picnic:*** *Write a dialogue to go with the cartoon on the right.*

It was a perfect day until a squirrel[2] stole his sandwich and ruined everything.

3 [ ] ***More plans:*** *Work with a partner and make arrangements for something you can do together one day next week.*

a) *First make a plan of all your commitments[3]. (Look at your diary if you keep one.)*
b) *Then decide what you want to do together and discuss details (looking up times, booking tickets, reserving a tennis court, where to meet, how to travel, what to take/wear, etc.)*

WORD BANK

Some useful phrases for making plans:
Shall I pick you up? Let's arrange to meet at …
Sorry, I can't manage Friday. I'm meeting … then.
I've got an appointment[4] with … at …
Thursday would suit me better/best.
That's no good, I'm afraid. What about …?
I've got a date[5] with … on … I'm seeing … then.
Shall we book seats/tickets/a court?
When does the performance start? It starts at …
If there's a problem, give me a ring[6].

4 *Saying the right thing: Jens is staying with the Hamiltons, an English family. His responses to some of their suggestions are a little unfortunate. Explain why and think of more appropriate ones.*

Mrs H.: Would you like to go sailing on Sunday, Jens? The weather forecast for the weekend's great.
Jens: Sailing? I don't know if I'd like it or not. I've never done any sailing before.

Mr H.: I'm going into town, Jens. Do you want to come? Or is there anything I can get for you?
Jens: No. Take me with you. I need some things which are indescribable.

Paul H.: The new 'Pirates of the Caribbean' film is on at the cinema. Shall we go this afternoon?
Jens: Good. I don't mind seeing a film.

Mrs H.: Are you sure you won't have another sandwich, Jens?
Jens: Thank you. I said before that I was full.

Mr H.: Is there anything you'd like to do today, Jens?
Jens: Yes. Going to the swimming pool would suit me fine.

Paul H.: Would you be interested in visiting Windsor Castle?
Jens: No, I wouldn't, because I've been there before.

[1]Erdnüsse • [2]Eichhörnchen • [3]Verpflichtung • [4]Termin • [5]Verabredung (privat) • [6]ruf mich an

Topic 4 South Africa

A The rainbow nation

See the best of South Africa

to **thunder** ['θʌndə]	donnern
thunder ['θʌndə]	Donner
• **ocean** ['əʊʃn]	Ozean
• **species**, *pl.* **species** ['spi:ʃi:z]	Spezies
bay [beɪ]	Bucht
connoisseur [ˌkɒnə'sɜ:]	Kenner(in)
interior [ɪn'tɪəriə]	innere(-r/-s); Innenaufnahme
• **maize** [meɪz]	Mais
segregation [ˌsegrɪ'geɪʃn]	Trennung; Rassentrennung

Economy

abundant [ə'bʌndnt]	im Überfluss; reichlich vorhanden
• **financial** [faɪ'nænʃl]	finanziell
• to **manufacture** [ˌmænjə'fæktʃə]	fertigen; fabrikmäßig herstellen
• **sector** ['sektə]	Sektor
• **rapid** ['ræpɪd]	rapide; schnell
• to **expand** [ɪk'spænd]	(sich) ausdehnen; erweitern; expandieren
expansion [ɪk'spænʃn]	Ausdehnung; Erweiterung; Expansion
foreign exchange [ˌfɒrɪn‿ɪks'tʃeɪndʒ]	Devisen
rather than ['rɑ:ðə ðən]	eher als
• **ethnic** ['eθnɪk]	ethnisch; Volks-
vast [vɑ:st]	ausgedehnt; riesig; unermesslich
• **coastal** ['kəʊstl]	Küsten-
sugar cane [ˌʃʊgə 'keɪn]	Zuckerrohr
poultry ['pəʊltri]	Geflügel
mutton ['mʌtn]	Hammelfleisch
wool [wʊl]	Wolle
• **export** ['ekspɔ:t]	Export; Ausfuhr
diamond ['daɪəmənd]	Diamant
• **machinery** [mə'ʃi:nri]	Maschinen
currency ['kʌrntsi]	Währung
racial ['reɪʃl]	Rassen-
race [reɪs]	Rasse
• to **adopt** [ə'dɒpt]	übernehmen; annehmen; adoptieren

Colonial past

• **colonial** [kə'ləʊniəl]	kolonial
• **inland** ['ɪnlænd]	landeinwärts
• **immigration** [ˌɪmɪ'greɪʃn]	Immigration; Einwanderung
to **defeat** [dɪ'fi:t]	besiegen
policy ['pɒlɪsi]	Politik; politische Linie; Grundsatz
descendant [dɪ'sendənt]	Abkömmling; Nachfahre; Nachfahrin

Languages

• **mother tongue** [ˌmʌðə 'tʌŋ]	Muttersprache
current ['kʌrnt]	aktuell; gegenwärtig
• **election** [ɪ'lekʃn]	Wahl

B Segregation

Out of sight

out of sight [ˌaʊt‿əv 'saɪt]	außer Sicht
* to **give sb a lift** [ˌgɪv‿ə 'lɪft]	jmdn im Auto mitnehmen
* to **make sth up** [ˌmeɪk‿'ʌp]	etw. erfinden; sich etw. ausdenken
• **affair** [ə'feə]	Affäre; Angelegenheit
shack [ʃæk]	Baracke; Bretterbude
prefab ['pri:fæb]	vorgefertigt; Fertighaus
tin [tɪn]	Blech
• **toilet** ['tɔɪlɪt]	Toilette
fortune ['fɔ:tʃu:n]	Vermögen; Reichtum; Schicksal; Glück
contract ['kɒntrækt]	Vertrag
slum clearance ['slʌm ˌklɪərnts]	Slumbereinigung; Slumsanierung
to **load** [ləʊd]	laden
to cart [kɑ:t]	karren; fahren
granny ['græni]	Oma
• **activist** ['æktɪvɪst]	Aktivist(in) *(jmd, der sich für etw. engagiert)*
activism ['æktɪvɪzm]	Aktivismus
• **district** ['dɪstrɪkt]	Distrikt; Bezirk
• to **declare** [dɪ'kleə]	erklären
removal [rɪ'mu:vl]	Beseitigung; Entfernung; Umzug

The development of townships around Johannesburg

township ['taʊnʃɪp]	Gemeinde; von Farbigen oder Schwarzen bewohnte städtische Siedlung *(Südafrika)*
• chiefdom ['tʃi:fdəm]	Stammesfürstentum
to **seek** [si:k]	suchen
• **potential** [pəʊ'tentʃl]	potenziell; möglich
• **benefit** ['benɪfɪt]	Nutzen; Gewinn
laundry ['lɔ:ndri]	Wäsche; Wäscherei
• **prostitute** ['prɒstɪtju:t]	Prostituierte

V18 Learning words in pairs or groups

■ Whenever possible, learn new words or phrases together with others you already know which are somehow connected – either as a **synonym**, an **opposite** or a **context-related** word or phrase. In this way, you revise 'old' vocabulary, and increase your ability to think in context.
Examples: *to expand* (a synonym?) → to grow; • *rapid* (an opposite?) → slow, gradual; • *foreign exchange* (context?) → money, economy, tourism

■ Now work with these words (all from A and B) in the same way:
1. *mother tongue* (a synonym?) • 2. *to give someone a lift* (a synonym?) • 3. *manufacturing* (context?) • 4. *to seek* (an opposite?) • 5. *to make something up* (a synonym?) • 6. *a shack* (context?) • 7. *benefit* (a synonym? and an opposite?) • 8. *fare* (context?)

• **authority** [ɔ:'θɒrəti]	Autorität; Staatsgewalt; Behörde
approximate [ə'prɒksɪmət]	ungefähr; circa
• to **inhabit** [ɪn'hæbɪt]	bewohnen
shantytown ['ʃæntitaʊn]	Elendsviertel; Barackensiedlung
sewerage ['sʊərɪdʒ]	Kanalisation
to **maintain** [meɪn'teɪn]	aufrechterhalten; instand halten
fare [feə]	Fahrpreis
act [ækt]	Gesetz
• to **transform** [træns'fɔ:m]	transformieren; umwandeln; verwandeln
• to **permit** [pə'mɪt]	erlauben; genehmigen
social engineering [ˌsəʊʃl endʒɪ'nɪərɪŋ]	Sozialplanung
therefore ['ðeəfɔ:]	deshalb; somit
• **residential** [ˌrezɪ'dentʃl]	Wohn-
• **ironical** [aɪər'ɒnɪkl]	ironisch
hut [hʌt]	Hütte
labour ['leɪbə]	Arbeit; Arbeitskraft; Mühe
to **assign** [ə'saɪn]	zuordnen; übertragen

2	• **fictional** ['fɪkʃnl]	fiktional; fiktiv
4	• **fictitious** [ˌfɪk'tɪʃəs]	fiktiv; erfunden; erdichtet

Gimme hope, Jo'anna

	chorus ['kɔ:rəs]	Refrain
	to **sneak** [sni:k]	schleichen; schmuggeln
	now and again [ˌnaʊ‿ənd‿ə'gen]	hin und wieder; ab und zu
	* to **swing** [swɪŋ]	schwingen; schwenken
	to **swing opinion** [ˌswɪŋ‿ə'pɪnjən]	eine Meinung ändern
	• **explanation** [ˌeksplə'neɪʃn]	Erklärung; Erläuterung
	preacher ['pri:tʃə]	Prediger(in)
	• **archbishop** [ɑ:tʃ'bɪʃəp]	Erzbischof
	• **peaceful** ['pi:sfl]	friedlich
	tide [taɪd]	Flut
5	• **mining industry** ['maɪnɪŋ ˌɪndəstri]	Bergbau
6	• **criticism** ['krɪtɪsɪsm]	Kritik

C The struggle against apartheid

Long walk to freedom

post [pəʊst]	danach
to **commit oneself to** [kə'mɪt]	sich (jmdm/etw.) verschreiben/verpflichten/widmen; sich binden an
• **politics** ['pɒlɪtɪks]	Politik
to **ban** [bæn]	bannen; verbieten; sperren
ban [bæn]	Bann; Verbot; Sperre
• **violent** ['vaɪəlnt]	gewaltsam; gewalttätig; brutal
to **sentence** ['sentənts]	verurteilen
sentence ['sentənts]	Verurteilung; Strafmaß
• **life imprisonment** [ˌlaɪf‿ɪm'prɪznmənt]	lebenslängliche Haftstrafe
• **equality** [ɪ'kwɒləti]	Gleichberechtigung; Ebenbürtigkeit
• **autobiography** [ˌɔ:təbaɪ'ɒgrəfi]	Autobiografie
measure ['meʒə]	Maßnahme
• **complicated** ['kɒmplɪkeɪtɪd]	kompliziert
• **process** ['prəʊsəs]	Prozess
to compel [kəm'pel]	zwingen
to issue ['ɪʃu:; 'ɪsju:]	ausstellen; herausgeben
civil servant [ˌsɪvl 'sɜ:vnt]	Beamter; Beamtin
failure ['feɪljə]	Versagen; Ausfall; Fehlschlag
trial [traɪəl]	Gerichtsverfahren; Gerichtsverhandlung
jail [dʒeɪl]	Gefängnis
fine [faɪn]	Geldstrafe; Bußgeld
* to **bear** [beə]	(er)tragen; hervorbringen
annual ['ænjuəl]	jährlich
• poll tax ['pəʊl ˌtæks]	Kopfsteuer
to levy ['levi]	erheben
fountain ['faʊntən]	Brunnen
• **unemployed** [ˌʌnɪm'plɔɪd]	arbeitslos
to **extend** [ɪk'stend]	(sich) ausdehnen; sich erstrecken
to **attend** [ə'tend]	teilnehmen; anwesend sein
to **prohibit** [prə'hɪbɪt]	untersagen; verbieten
effort ['efət]	Mühe; Bemühung
to **persecute** ['pɜ:səkju:t]	verfolgen
to immobilize [ɪ'məʊblaɪz]	unbeweglich machen; ruhig stellen
to **deprive sb of** [dɪ'praɪv]	berauben; entziehen
• to **govern** ['gʌvn]	regieren; verwalten
• **democratic** [ˌdemə'krætɪk]	demokratisch
democracy [dɪ'mɒkrəsi]	Demokratie

V19 Identical forms for noun and verb

■ English is full of examples of words that can be used both as a noun and as a verb. Some you are already familiar with: *rain, drink, help, interview*, etc.

■ The words below can all be used in this way.
Make sentences for each, once as a noun, once as a verb. (In some cases you will need to refer to a dictionary to be sure of the exact meaning.)
Example: *thunder* – Listen! Can you hear the *thunder*? – A heavy truck *thundered* past us.
defeat • *load* • *benefit* • *permit* • *labour* • *ban* • *swing* • *sentence* • *fine* • *release* • *arrest* • *silence* • *attempt* • *award*

■ Sometimes nouns referring to visible objects (e.g. *a mushroom, a chair, a bubble, a carpet, an eye, a finger*) can also be used (sometimes very descriptively!) as verbs.

■ Example: New houses and factories *mushroomed* everywhere.

Look up the words above to find out how they can be used as verbs. (If your English-English dictionary gives example sentences, you might like to note them down.)
Look out for more verbs of this kind as you read texts or listen to spoken English.

trade union [ˌtreɪd 'juːnjən]	Gewerkschaft
3 **release** [rɪ'liːs]	Freigabe; Herausgabe; Freisetzung

Soweto 1976: A schoolboy's memories

* to **draw** [drɔː]	ziehen
cordon ['kɔːdn]	Absperrkette
• **banner** ['bænə]	Banner; Spruchband; Transparent
oppressor [ɒ'presə]	Unterdrücker(in)
mood [muːd]	Stimmung; Laune
tense [tents]	angespannt; verkrampft
to rev [rev]	den Motor hochjagen; die Motordrehzahl erhöhen
to **reinforce** [ˌriːɪn'fɔːs]	verstärken
armoured personnel carrier [ˌɑːməd pɜːsˌnel 'kærɪə]	gepanzerter Mannschaftstransportwagen
hippo ['hɪpəʊ]	Nilpferd; Flusspferd
live [laɪv]	scharf
• **ammunition** [ˌæmjə'nɪʃn]	Munition
rifle ['raɪfl]	Gewehr
at close range [ət ˌkləʊs 'reɪndʒ]	aus nächster Nähe
degree [dɪ'griː]	Grad
crescendo *(ital., musikal.)* [krɪ'ʃendəʊ]	anwachsende Lautstärke
to disperse [dɪs'pɜːs]	(sich) zerstreuen; (sich) verteilen
loud hailer ['laʊd ˌheɪlə]	Megafon; Flüstertüte *(ugs.)*
trail [treɪl]	Spur; Schleppe; Schweif
to **choke** [tʃəʊk]	drosseln; würgen; sich verschlucken
to scatter ['skætə]	(sich) zerstreuen; auseinanderjagen
loose [luːs]	lose; locker; frei
• **vehicle** ['vɪəkl]	Fahrzeug; Vehikel
to loot [luːt]	plündern; erbeuten
attempt [ə'tempt]	Versuch
to **attempt** [ə'tempt]	versuchen
* to **come across (sb/sth)** [ˌkʌm‿ə'krɒs]	begegnen; antreffen; vorfinden
* to **bleed** [bliːd]	bluten
victim ['vɪktɪm]	Opfer
riot [raɪət]	Aufruhr; Ausschreitung; Unruhe
• **militant** ['mɪlɪtnt]	militant; aggressiv
• **brutality** [ˌbruː'tæləti]	Brutalität
4 • **impression** [ɪm'preʃn]	Impression; Eindruck

In detention

detention [dɪ'tentʃn]	Haft; Verhaftung
to **detain** [dɪ'teɪn]	verhaften; gefangen halten
• to **hang** [hæŋ]	(er)hängen
award [ə'wɔːd]	Preis; Auszeichnung

Facing the past

to reconcile ['reknsaɪl]	versöhnen
reconciliation [ˌreknˌsɪlɪ'eɪʃn]	Versöhnung
to **commit a crime** [kəˌmɪt‿ə 'kraɪm]	ein Verbrechen begehen
abuse [ə'bjuːs]	Missbrauch
human rights abuse [ˌhjuːmən 'raɪts‿əˌbjuːs]	Menschenrechtsverletzung
• **amnesty** ['æmnəsti]	Amnestie; Begnadigung
unprecedented [ʌn'presɪdentɪd]	beispiellos; noch nie da gewesen
• to **heal** [hiːl]	heilen
• **wound** [wuːnd]	Wunde; Verletzung
• **apology** [ə'pɒlədʒi]	Entschuldigung
perpetrator ['pɜːpətreɪtə]	Täter(in); Gesetzesübertreter(in)
to **grant** [grɑːnt]	gewähren; zusprechen
• **misunderstanding** [ˌmɪsʌndə'stændɪŋ]	Missverständnis
to **expose** [ɪk'spəʊz]	ausstellen; entblößen; freilegen
to **commit a crime** [kəˌmɪt‿ə 'kraɪm]	ein Verbrechen begehen
• **trauma**, *pl.* **traumata** ['trɔːmə]	Trauma; seelischer Schock
• **distant** ['dɪstnt]	entfernt

D Culture and sports

Tsotsi: a film from South Africa

elated [ɪ'leɪtɪd]	hocherfreut; überglücklich
confident ['kɒnfɪdnt]	selbstsicher; überzeugt
thug [θʌg]	Gangster; Schläger; Verbrecher
bunch [bʌntʃ]	Bündel; Haufen; Packen
to flash [flæʃ]	zeigen
wallet ['wɒlɪt]	Brieftasche; Geldbörse
to distract sb (from sth) [dɪ'strækt]	jmdn (von etw.) ablenken
to slash [slæʃ]	aufschlitzen

V20 Idioms with common verbs

■ Common verbs (*get, take, make, do, turn, give*, etc.) are often used together with prepositions and/or other words to make idioms, each with its own special meaning.

■ Make your own sentences to show the meaning of these:
1. to *make* (a story) *up* • 2. to *make it up* • 3. to *come across* sth • 4. to *come true* • 5. to *turn out to be* sth • 6. to *turn into* sth • 7. to *turn* sth *off* • 8. to *turn on* sb • 9. to *turn* sb *on* • 10. to *get over* sth • 11. to *give up* • 12. to *get rid of* sth • 13. to *take off*

■ Now use your dictionary to find out the meaning of these. (First guess – then check!)

1. What do you *make of* her strange behaviour? • 2. I *turned* the offer *down*. • 3. How did it *turn out*? • 4. Where are you *making for*? • 5. He *made off* with all the cash. • 6. Hasn't he *turned up* yet? • 7. *Give way* to cars on the main road. • 8. See what the children are *getting up to*, OK? • 9. I can't *get through* to anyone, I'm afraid. • 10. I'm *done in*! • 11. We've been *done out of* our share of the money. • 12. When he's angry about something, he always *takes it out on* other people.

• * to **beat sb up** [ˌbiːt‿ˈʌp]	zusammenschlagen
to **brood (over sth)** [bruːd]	brüten; (nach)grübeln (über)
to fend for oneself [fend]	alleine auskommen
reluctant [rɪˈlʌktnt]	zögernd; widerwillig
burglary [ˈbɜːgləri]	Einbruch
to **assault** [əˈsɔːlt]	tätlich angreifen; überfallen
to **abandon** [əˈbændən]	aufgeben; zurücklassen
to redeem [rɪˈdiːm]	erlösen
tiny [ˈtaɪni]	winzig
to **turn out to be** [tɜːn‿ˈaʊt tə ˌbiː]	sich herausstellen als
layer [ˈleɪə]	Schicht; Lage; Ebene
despair [dɪsˈpeə]	Hoffnungslosigkeit; Verzweiflung
contemporary [kənˈtemprəri]	zeitgenössisch; Gegenwarts-
2 • **artist** [ˈɑːtɪst]	Künstler(in)

E Present-day challenges

Young ... and free!?

bursary [ˈbɜːsri]	Stipendium
self-esteem [ˌselfɪsˈtiːm]	Selbstwertgefühl; Selbstachtung
to **afford** [əˈfɔːd]	sich leisten
threat [θret]	Bedrohung; Gefahr
• to **confront** [kənˈfrʌnt]	konfrontieren; entgegentreten; sich stellen
• **infection** [ɪnˈfekʃn]	Infektion
murder [ˈmɜːdə]	Mord
rape [reɪp]	Vergewaltigung
• **theft** [θeft]	Diebstahl
• **injury** [ˈɪndʒri]	Verletzung

V21 Crime and punishment

■ Topic 4 contains a lot of vocabulary that refers to violent behaviour, crime and punishment.

■ Make a list of all the new words and phrases of this kind that you can find.
Examples: *to sentence sb, life imprisonment, a victim*

■ Now add to the list words and phrases you have already learnt before (some of them will be in Topic 4, too).
How many can you think of?
Examples: *lawyer, to punish*

■ Can you name the crime? You can compare your answers with a partner's, to check.
1. *Someone breaks into a house with the intention of stealing something.* • 2. *A thug killed a woman in the street.* • 3. *A girl takes a DVD from a shop without paying for it.* • 4. *Someone attacks a person and beats them up.* (You know the verb – it is also used as a noun.) • 5. *Someone committed political crimes in South Africa during apartheid.* (A three-word phrase.)

⟨F Out in the country⟩

The wildlife trade

• to limit [ˈlɪmɪt]	limitieren; begrenzen; beschränken
outright [ˈaʊtraɪt]	vollständig; ganz und gar; ohne Umschweife
• endangered [ɪnˈdeɪndʒəd]	gefährdet
conservationist [ˌkɒntsəˈveɪʃnɪst]	Naturschützer(in); Umweltschützer(in)
conservation [ˌkɒntsəˈveɪʃn]	Naturschutz; Umweltschutz
• critical [ˈkrɪtɪkl]	kritisch
• dilemma [daɪˈlemə]	Dilemma; Zwangslage
stockpile [ˈstɒkpaɪl]	Vorrat; Stapelbestand
proceeds *(pl.)* [prəˈsiːdz]	Erlös; Einnahmen
hostile [ˈhɒstaɪl]	feindlich; ablehnend
• approach [əˈprəʊtʃ]	Annäherung; Ansatz; Vorgehensweise
• to stimulate [ˈstɪmjəleɪt]	stimulieren; anregen
to poach [pəʊtʃ]	wildern
• ultimately [ˈʌltɪmətli]	schließlich
• elephant [ˈelɪfənt]	Elefant
• rhino [ˈraɪnəʊ]	Rhinozeros; Nashorn
extinction [ɪksˈtɪŋkʃn]	Aussterben
• to oppose [əˈpəʊz]	ablehnen; sich entgegenstellen
per se [ˌpɜː ˈseɪ]	an sich
impoverished [ɪmˈpɒvrɪʃt]	verarmt
rural [ˈruːrl]	ländlich
* to be based on [biː ˈbeɪst‿ɒn]	basieren auf; sich stützen auf
ivory [ˈaɪvri]	Elfenbein
hide [haɪd]	Fell; Tierhaut
NGO *(non-governmental organisation)* [ˌendʒiːˈəʊ]	Nichtregierungsorganisation
scheme [skiːm]	Programm; Plan; Maßnahme
revenue [ˈrevnjuː]	Erlös; Einnahmen
meanwhile [ˌmiːnˈwaɪl]	mittlerweile; in der Zwischenzeit
to curtail [kɜːˈteɪl]	beschneiden; einschränken
to reject [rɪˈdʒekt]	zurückweisen; ablehnen
• tiger [ˈtaɪgə]	Tiger
remedy [ˈremədi]	Mittel; Abhilfe
• to cooperate [ˌkəʊˈɒprət]	kooperieren; zusammenarbeiten
• medicinal practitioner [meˈdɪsɪnl prækˈtɪʃnə]	Heilpraktiker(in)
medicine [ˈmedsn]	Medizin
• habitat loss [ˈhæbɪtæt ˌlɒs]	Verlust des Lebensraums
• flora and fauna [ˌflɔːrə‿ənd ˈfɔːnə]	Pflanzen- und Tierwelt
mammal [ˈmæml]	Säugetier
• site [saɪt]	Ort; Gelände; Schauplatz

The moment before the gun went off

fatal [ˈfeɪtl]	tödlich; verhängnisvoll
• nowadays [ˈnaʊədeɪz]	heutzutage
mishap [ˈmɪshæp]	Unglück; Missgeschick
security [sɪˈkjʊərəti]	Sicherheit; Schutz
to fit (in) [ˌfɪt‿ˈɪn]	(hinein)passen
divestment [ˌdaɪˈvestmənt]	Desinvestition
evidence [ˈevɪdnts]	Beweismaterial; Beleg
• to quote [kwəʊt]	zitieren

V22 Similar – but different!

■ Explain the link between each pair of words, then the difference in meaning, possibly with example sentences.
Example: *politics – policy*: Both words are used in a similar context, often to do with the government of a country or an organization.
Politics refers to activities and ideas about how to run a country or area. But a *policy* is a definite plan of what to do, which is agreed on by a government or business.

If you want to be a government minister, you have to go into ***politics****.*
I won't join that party because I don't agree with some of their ***policies****.*
1. *price – fare* • 2. *wallet – purse* • 3. *segregation – apartheid* • 4. *blacks – coloureds* • 5. *suburbs – townships* • 6. *poultry – chicken* • 7. *invention – discovery* • 8. *bus – coach* • 9. *country – land* • 10. *honest – true*

back-and-forth [ˌbæk_ənd ˈfɔːθ]	Auf und Ab; Hin und Her
crudely-drawn [ˈkruːdli ˌdrɔːn]	grob gezeichnet
gleeful [ˈgliːfl]	fröhlich; schadenfroh
• agitator [ˈædʒɪtəɪtə]	Agitator(in)
distress [dɪˈstres]	Bedrängnis; Notlage
It just goes to show … [ɪt ˌdʒʌst gəʊz tə ˈʃəʊ]	Das zeigt mal wieder …
• assumption [əˈsʌmpʃn]	Annahme; Voraussetzung
brandy [ˈbrændi]	Weinbrand
to inherit [ɪnˈherɪt]	erben
stone dead [ˌstəʊn ˈded]	mausetot
to sob [sɒb]	schluchzen
snot *(infml)* [snɒt]	Rotz
* to be ashamed [biː_əˈʃeɪmd]	sich schämen
to cull [kʌl]	(als überzählig) abschießen
buck [bʌk]	Bock
sacred [ˈseɪkrɪd]	heilig
game [geɪm]	Wild
• farmhand [ˈfɑːmhænd]	Landarbeiter(in)
aptitude [ˈæptɪtjuːd]	Geschick
to hoot [huːt]	hupen
• forward [ˈfɔːwəd]	vorwärts
to brace [breɪs]	aufstützen
cab [kæb]	Führerhaus
gunsmith [ˈgʌnsmɪθ]	Büchsenmacher(in)
dirt track [ˈdɜːt ˌtræk]	Feldweg; unbefestigte Straße
to thump [θʌmp]	klopfen
white-ripple-marked [ˌwaɪt rɪpl ˈmɑːkt]	mit weißer Wellenzeichnung
to rake [reɪk]	durchpflügen
pot-hole [ˈpɒthəʊl]	Schlagloch
jolt [dʒəʊlt]	Ruck
bullet [ˈbʊlɪt]	Geschoss; Kugel
to pierce [ˈpɪəs]	durchbohren; durchdringen
to enter [ˈentə]	eintreten; hereinkommen; betreten
of such standing [əv ˌsʌtʃ ˈstændɪŋ]	von solchem Ansehen
* to swear [sweə]	schwören; fluchen
beyond [biˈɒnd]	jenseits; über etw. hinaus
• mob [mɒb]	Mob; Pöbel
rural [ˈruːrl]	ländlich
to appease [əˈpiːz]	besänftigen
to satisfy [ˈsætɪsfaɪ]	zufriedenstellen
barbed [bɑːbd]	mit Stacheln versehen
to spoil [spɔɪl]	verderben
artificial [ˌɑːtɪˈfɪʃl]	künstlich
tree-fern [ˈtriːfɜːn]	Baumfarn
beneath [bɪˈniːθ]	unter, unterhalb
aerial [ˈeəriəl]	Antenne
to soar [sɔː]	aufsteigen; segeln
flag-pole [ˈflægpəʊl]	Fahnenmast
infiltrator [ˈɪnfɪltreɪtə]	Eindringling
to mine [maɪn]	verminen
remote [rɪˈməʊt]	fern; abgelegen
property [ˈprɒpəti]	Grundbesitz
• * to set off [ˌset_ˈɒf]	auslösen
communications [kəˌmjuːnɪˈkeɪʃnz]	Nachrichten; Fernmeldewesen
fitting [ˈfɪtɪŋ]	Beschlag
coffin [ˈkɒfɪn]	Sarg
funeral [ˈfjuːnrəl]	Beerdigung; Begräbnis
elaborate [ɪˈlæbrət]	aufwändig
• payment [ˈpeɪmənt]	Zahlung
burial society [ˌberiəl səˈsaɪəti]	Bestattungsverein
boxwood [ˈbɒkswʊd]	Buchsbaumholz
pregnant [ˈpregnənt]	schwanger
to jut [dʒʌt]	hervorragen
to witness [ˈwɪtnəs]	miterleben
neither … nor … [ˈnaɪðə; ˈniːðə … nɔː]	weder … noch …
to whine [waɪn]	quengeln
solemn [ˈsɒləm]	ernst; feierlich
breast [brest]	Brust
to weed [wiːd]	jäten
harvest [ˈhɑːvɪst]	Ernte
• puberty [ˈpjuːbəti]	Pubertät
mature [məˈtjʊə]	reif
to restrain [rɪˈstreɪn]	zurückhalten; festhalten
navy [ˈneɪvi]	Marine
supportive [səˈpɔːtɪv]	unterstützend
reserve [rɪˈzɜːv]	Reserviertheit
to mix well [ˌmɪks ˈwel]	gut mit Menschen auskommen
to stumble [ˈstʌmbl]	stolpern
fright [fraɪt]	Schreck
report [rɪˈpɔːt]	Knall
thud [θʌd]	dumpfer Schlag
* to leap [liːp]	springen
to topple [ˈtɒpl]	stürzen
relief [rɪˈliːf]	Erleichterung; Linderung
to tease [tiːz]	necken; quälen
* to do harm [hɑːm]	Schaden anrichten
to soak [səʊk]	tränken; durchweichen; durchnässen
flesh [fleʃ]	Fleisch
to file [faɪl]	ablegen; abheften
clipping [ˈklɪpɪŋ]	Ausschnitt
proof [pruːf]	Beweis
callous [ˈkæləs]	kaltschnäuzig
negligence [ˈneglɪdʒənts]	Fahrlässigkeit

D Holiday preparations

1 [ ] ***Advertisements:*** *You want to go on holiday together. Look at the advertisements below and discuss the advantages/disadvantages of each type of accommodation. Then make a decision.*

★ Homeleigh B&B ★

25 Exmouth Road, Budleigh Salterton

Comfortable Bed & Breakfast accommodation. Very quiet, off road, with sea views. Single, double/twin and family rooms. All rooms en-suite[1], with colour TV and tea & coffee making facilities[2]. Cosy[3] guest lounge[4] with open fire[5]. Central heating throughout[6].

★ One s/c[7] unit also available.
★ Children and dogs welcome.
★ Full English or continental breakfast.

Mrs Brenda Jackson ☎ 01395 443327

Walcott's Hotel

Rooms from £45 pppn[8]
Close to the seafront

Friendly, relaxed atmosphere, licensed restaurant open to non-residents Monday to Saturday, and for lunch on Sundays. The six double/twin rooms have en-suite facilities, while the single room has an adjacent[9] private shower and WC. All rooms have tea & coffee making facilities and colour televisions.
Non-smoking • Off-road parking

5 Long Road, Budleigh Salterton,
Devon EX9 6HS
Tel: 01395 434312
Fax: 01395 431223
E-mail: info@walcottshotel.co.uk

Bear Lane

Caravan[10] and Camping Park
Budleigh Salterton, Devon, EX9 7AQ

Telephone: 01395 453244
Mobile: 0797 0545474
E-mail: bearlane@beeb.net

- Touring caravans, motor vans, tents welcome.
- Small number of caravans and cottages to let[11].
- Outdoor[12] heated swimming pool.
- Facilities include: electricity, laundry[13], hot showers.
- Close to a number of beautiful beaches and rivers.
- Ten minutes walk from town.
- Reasonable prices.

The Hawthorns

(Self-catering)
Mrs Janet Freeman,
Yettington,
Budleigh Salterton,
Devon EX9 7PB
Tel: 01395 6584117

Two self-contained[14] cottages sleeping[15] 5 and 6. One with wheelchair access. Fully equipped[16]. Non-smoking. Large secluded[17] garden. Ample[18] off-street parking. Two miles from the sea.

2 [06] ***Listening:*** *Booking a room at a B&B place*

a) *Listen to the dialogue and answer the questions.*

1. *When – and for how long – are Markus and his friend coming to stay?*
2. *What is the difference between a double room and a twin?*
3. *What can you expect if a full English breakfast is offered?*
4. *Why can't Markus and his friend take the self-catering flat?*
5. *What is a deposit? Why do you think it is often required?*
6. *What arrangement does Markus come to with Mrs Jackson?*

b) [ ] ***Write a dialogue:*** *Markus gets in touch with his friend and tells him about the offer. They discuss whether to confirm the booking.*

[1]mit Bad/Dusche und WC • [2]Möglichkeiten • [3]gemütlich • [4][laʊndʒ] Aufenthaltsraum • [5]offener Kamin • [6]überall • [7]s/c (self catering) für Selbstversorger • [8]pppn = per person per night • [9][əˈdʒeɪsnt] *hier:* auf dem Flur • [10]Wohnwagen • [11]zu vermieten, [12]Frei(bad) • [13]Wäscherei • [14]abgeschlossen • [15]*hier:* für 5 und 6 Personen geeignet • [16]voll ausgestattet • [17]von außen nicht einsehbar • [18]reichlich

Topic 5 Living in a modern world

A Robots – in science fiction and reality

• **robot** ['rəʊbɒt]	Roboter; Automat
lieutenant commander [*AE:* luːˌtenənt kə'mɑːndə; *BE:* lefˌtenənt kə'mɑːndə]	Kapitänleutnant
cybernetic [ˌsaɪbə'netɪk]	kybernetisch
• organism ['ɔːgnɪzm]	Organismus
surgeon ['sɜːdʒn]	Chirurg(in)
• **patient** ['peɪʃnt]	Patient(in)
to **weld** [weld]	schweißen
* to **be based on** [biː 'beɪst‿ɒn]	basieren auf; sich stützen auf
• to **adopt** [ə'dɒpt]	übernehmen; annehmen; adoptieren
human being [ˌhjuːmən 'biːɪŋ]	menschliches Wesen
inaction [ɪn'ækʃn]	Untätigkeit
harm [hɑːm]	Schaden; Leid
• to **conflict** [kən'flɪkt]	kollidieren; im Widerspruch stehen
• **existence** [ɪg'zɪstnts]	Existenz; Dasein
• **protection** [prə'tekʃn]	Schutz
1 **hall of fame** [ˌhɔːl‿əv 'feɪm]	Ruhmeshalle
• **mechanical** [mə'kænɪkl]	mechanisch
• **repetitive** [rɪ'petətɪv]	sich wiederholend; monoton
artificial [ˌɑːtɪ'fɪʃl]	künstlich
• **intelligence** [ɪn'telɪdʒnts]	Intelligenz; Klugheit; Einsicht
remote [rɪ'məʊt]	fern; abgelegen
2 **strength** [streŋkθ]	Stärke
• **weakness** ['wiːknəs]	Schwäche
prejudiced ['predʒədɪst]	voreingenommen; befangen
to **resemble** [rɪ'zembl]	ähneln
menace ['menɪs]	Bedrohung; Gefahr
homicidal [ˌhɒmɪ'saɪdl]	menschenmörderisch
to **approve** [ə'pruːv]	anerkennen; genehmigen; gutheißen
to **abuse** [ə'bjuːz]	beschimpfen; missbrauchen; misshandeln
Czech [tʃek]	Tscheche; Tschechin; Tschechisch; tschechisch
labour ['leɪbə]	Arbeit; Arbeitskraft; Mühe
• to **navigate** ['nævɪgeɪt]	navigieren; steuern
spacecraft ['speɪskrɑːft]	Raumschiff
to **launch** [lɔːntʃ]	starten; abschießen; einführen
accidental [ˌæksɪ'dentl]	unbeabsichtigt; durch Unfall verursacht

V23 More related words

■ Always look out for words that are related in some way to words you already know. Write down any words you know that have the same root as the following words from A, adding the part of speech in brackets.

Example: *fame* (noun) – *famous* (adjective)
accidentally • *protection* • *existence* • *mechanical* • *repetitive* • *strength* • *to navigate* • *intelligence* • *to be based on*

B Is there anybody out there?

They're made out of meat

ambassador [æm'bæsədə]	Botschafter(in)
1 **beyond** [bi'ɒnd]	jenseits; über etw. hinaus
• **aboard** [ə'bɔːd]	an Bord
recon vessel [rɪ'kɒn ˌvesl]	Aufklärungsschiff
to probe [prəʊb]	untersuchen; sondieren
sentient ['sentʃnt]	empfindungsfähig
sentience ['sentʃnts]	empfindungsfähiges Wesen
• **creature** ['kriːtʃə]	Kreatur; Geschöpf
carbon-based ['kɑːbnˌbeɪst]	kohlenstoffbasiert
stage [steɪdʒ]	Stadium
• **span** [spæn]	Spanne
Spare me! [ˌspeə 'miː]	Verschonen Sie mich!
all right [ɔːl 'raɪt]	schon
conscious ['kɒntʃəs]	bewusst
the whole deal [ðə ˌhəʊl 'diːl]	alles
* to **have in mind** [ˌhæv‿ɪn 'maɪnd]	im Sinn haben
to **swap** [swɒp]	tauschen
• **concept** ['kɒnsept]	Begriff; Konzept
to **slap** [slæp]	schlagen; einen Klaps geben
to **flap** [flæp]	flattern; klappen; schlagen
to squirt [skwɜːt]	spritzen; sprühen
altogether [ˌɔːltə'geðə]	insgesamt; gänzlich; ganz und gar
to log in [ˌlɒg‿'ɪn]	eintragen; aufnehmen
• **prejudice** ['predʒədɪs]	Vorurteil(e); Voreingenommenheit
favor *(AE)* ['feɪvə]	Gefälligkeit; Begünstigung
to erase [ɪ'reɪz]	löschen; ausradieren
• **record** ['rekɔːd]	Aufzeichnung; Akte
harsh [hɑːʃ]	barsch; rau; unnachsichtig
• **limit** ['lɪmɪt]	Limit; Grenze; Beschränkung
speed [spiːd]	Geschwindigkeit
slim [slɪm]	dünn; schlank; gering
infinitesimal [ˌɪnfɪnɪ'tesɪml]	unendlich klein; winzig
to **pretend** [prɪ'tend]	vorgeben; vortäuschen
crackpot ['krækpɒt]	Verrückte(r)
to smooth out [ˌsmuːð‿'aʊt]	ausgleichen; glatt streichen
appropriate [ə'prəʊpriət]	angemessen
hydrogen-core ['haɪdrədʒən ˌkɔː]	Wasserstoffkern-
cluster ['klʌstə]	Klumpen; Anhäufung
* to come around [ˌkʌm‿ə'raʊnd]	einlenken
* to **bear** [beə]	(er)tragen; hervorbringen
unutterable [ʌn'ʌtrəbl]	unsagbar
award [ə'wɔːd]	Preis; Auszeichnung
novel ['nɒvl]	Roman

C Big Brother

1 Soviet Union [ˌsəʊviət ˈjuːnjən] Sowjetunion

Nineteen Eighty-four

to **portray** [pɔːˈtreɪ]	porträtieren, darstellen; schildern
chin [tʃɪn]	Kinn
to nuzzle [ˈnʌzl]	schmiegen
breast [brest]	Brust
effort [ˈefət]	Mühe; Bemühung; Versuch
vile [vaɪl]	gemein; widerwärtig
mansion [ˈmæntʃn]	Herrenhaus; Villa
swirl [swɜːl]	Wirbel; Strudel
to **swirl** [swɜːl]	wirbeln
gritty [ˈgrɪti]	kiesig
dust [dʌst]	Staub
to **enter** [ˈentə]	eintreten; hereinkommen; betreten
along with [əˈlɒŋ wɪð]	zusammen mit
cabbage [ˈkæbɪdʒ]	Kohl; Kraut
mat [mæt]	Matte
to **tack** [tæk]	heften
to depict [dɪˈpɪkt]	darstellen
rugged [ˈrʌgɪd]	rau; wild
handsome [ˈhændsəm]	attraktiv; gut aussehend
feature [ˈfiːtʃə]	Gesichtszug; Charakterzug; Merkmal
* to **make for** [ˈmeɪk fə]	auf etw. zuhalten
seldom [ˈseldəm]	selten
current [ˈkʌrnt]	Strom
economy drive [ɪˈkɒnəmi ˌdraɪv]	Sparprogramm
• **preparation** [ˌprepr'eɪʃn]	Vorbereitung
flight [flaɪt]	Treppe
varicose ulcer [ˌværɪkəʊs ˈʌlsə]	Krampfadergeschwür
ankle [ˈæŋkl]	Fußknöchel
• to **rest** [rest]	rasten; ausruhen; liegen
landing [ˈlændɪŋ]	Treppenabsatz
lift-shaft [ˈlɪftʃɑːft]	Aufzugschacht
to **gaze** [geɪz]	starren; blicken
to contrive [kənˈtraɪv]	ersinnen; ausklügeln
beneath [bɪˈniːθ]	unter, unterhalb
fruity [ˈfruːti]	fruchtig
pig iron [ˈpɪg ˌaɪən]	Roheisen
iron [aɪən]	Eisen
oblong [ˈɒblɒŋ]	länglich
plaque [plɑːk]	Tafel; Platte
surface [ˈsɜːfɪs]	Oberfläche
• **switch** [swɪtʃ]	Schalter
somewhat [ˈsʌmwɒt]	ein wenig; einigermaßen
to **distinguish** [dɪˈstɪŋgwɪʃ]	unterscheiden; klar erkennen
* to shut off [ʃʌt ˈɒf]	abschalten; herunterfahren
frail [freɪl]	schwächlich; zerbrechlich
meagreness [ˈmiːgənəs]	Magerkeit
mere [mɪə]	bloß
• to **emphasize** [ˈempfəsaɪz]	betonen
• **overalls** *(pl.)* [ˈəʊvrɔːlz]	Overall; Arbeitsanzug
sanguine [ˈsæŋgwɪn]	gesund *(Gesichtsfarbe)*
rough [rʌf]	grob; rau; ungefähr
coarse [kɔːs]	grob; rau
blunt [blʌnt]	stumpf
razor blade [ˈreɪzə ˌbleɪd]	Rasierklinge
window pane [ˈwɪndəʊ ˌpeɪn]	Fensterscheibe
eddy [ˈedi]	Wirbel; Strudel
to whirl [wɜːl]	wirbeln; sich drehen
to plaster [ˈplɑːstə]	kleben; vollpflastern
fitful [ˈfɪtfl]	ruckartig; launenhaft
to **skim** [skɪm]	überfliegen; abschöpfen
to **hover** [ˈhɒvə]	schweben
instant [ˈɪntstənt]	Augenblick; Moment
bluebottle [ˈbluːˌbɒtl]	Schmeißfliege
to **dart** [dɑːt]	schießen; stürzen
• to **curve** [kɜːv]	krümmen; biegen; kurven
to snoop [snuːp]	schnüffeln
• thought [θɔːt]	Gedanke
to babble [ˈbæbl]	plappern; schnattern; brabbeln
to **transmit** [trænzˈmɪt]	übertragen; senden
• **simultaneous** [ˌsɪmlˈteɪniəs]	simultan; gleichzeitig
moreover [mɔːrˈəʊvə]	überdies; außerdem
to **plug in** [ˌplʌg ˈɪn]	einstecken; einstöpseln
wire [waɪə]	Draht; Kabel
• guesswork [ˈgeswɜːk]	Rätselraten; Vermutung
conceivable [kənˈsiːvəbl]	denkbar; vorstellbar
at any rate [ət ˈeni ˌreɪt]	jedenfalls
• **assumption** [əˈsʌmpʃn]	Annahme; Voraussetzung
to scrutinize [ˈskruːtɪnaɪz]	eingehend untersuchen
to **reveal** [rɪˈviːl]	enthüllen; offenbaren; preisgeben
• **ministry** [ˈmɪnɪstri]	Ministerium
to tower [taʊə]	hoch aufragen
vast [vɑːst]	ausgedehnt; riesig; unermesslich
grimy [ˈgraɪmi]	rußgeschwärzt; schmutzig
vague [veɪg]	vage; unbestimmt; unklar
distaste [dɪˈsteɪst]	Abneigung; Ekel; Widerwillen
airstrip [ˈeəstrɪp]	Landestreifen

V24 Adjectives from verbs

■ The new adjectives *unbearable* (B) and *undesirable* (C) both come from common verbs (*to bear* = ertragen, *to desire* = wünschen). You already know other adjectives like these (e. g. *unforgettable, unbelievable*).

■ Now form adjectives in this way from these common verbs – and choose from them to fill the gaps in the sentences below.

imagine • accept • pronounce • beat • drink • approach • recognize • like • answer • adapt • explain • read

1. *Some people in developing countries live in … poverty.*
2. *Difficult? Some of the questions in the exam were …!*
3. *Sue doesn't like sudden changes of plan. She's very …*
4. *Some Welsh words are very long, and practically …!*
5. *If you play as well as this in the final, you'll be …!*
6. *Sam was really rude to me. I found his behaviour totally …*

■ Some adjectives of this type are spelt slightly differently – and may also be formed from a French or Latin root (e.g. *invisible*, to describe something that can't be seen). First try to guess the meanings of the following adjectives, then look them up in your dictionary to check.

incomprehensible • invincible • incredible • inaudible • inevitable • indestructible • inaccessible • inexplicable

populous ['pɒpjələs]	bevölkerungsreich
to **squeeze** [skwi:z]	pressen; quetschen
vista ['vɪstə]	Aussicht
• to **rot** [rɒt]	verrotten; verfaulen; verfallen
to shore up [ˌʃɔ:r‿'ʌp]	abstützen
baulk [bɔ:k]	Balken
timber ['tɪmbə]	(Bau-)Holz
to **patch** [pætʃ]	flicken
cardboard ['kɑ:dbɔ:d]	Pappe; Karton
corrugated iron [ˌkɒrəgeɪtɪd‿'aɪən]	Wellblech
crazy ['kreɪzi]	Naturstein-
to sag [sæg]	durchhängen; durchsacken; sich durchbiegen
• to **bomb** [bɒm]	zerbomben
site [saɪt]	Ort; Gelände; Schauplatz
willow-herb ['wɪləʊhɜ:b]	Weidenröschen
to straggle ['strægl]	umherstreifen
heap [hi:p]	Haufen; Halde
rubble ['rʌbl]	Geröll; Schutt
• * to **spring up** [ˌsprɪŋ‿'ʌp]	entspringen; hervorquellen
sordid ['sɔ:dɪd]	schäbig; schmutzig; erbärmlich
dwelling ['dwelɪŋ]	Behausung; Wohnstätte
tableau, *pl.* tableaux ['tæbləʊ]	Bild
intelligible [ɪn'telɪdʒəbl]	verständlich
startling ['stɑ:tlɪŋ]	alarmierend; verblüffend
• to glitter ['glɪtə]	glänzen; funkeln; glitzern
concrete ['kɒŋkri:t]	Beton
to soar [sɔ:]	aufsteigen; segeln
• **terrace** ['terɪs]	Terrasse; Absatz; Häuserreihe
• **slavery** ['sleɪvri]	Sklaverei
• **ignorance** ['ɪgnərnts]	Ignoranz; Unwissenheit
ignorant ['ɪgnərnt]	ignorant; unwissend
1 • pseudonym ['sju:dənɪm]	Pseudonym; Künstlername
• **satirical** [sə'tɪrɪkl]	satirisch; Spott-
4 • futuristic [ˌfju:tʃə'rɪstɪk]	futuristisch

A cartoon

to spook sb out [ˌspu:k‿'aʊt]	jmdm unheimlich werden

Big Brother Britain

10 CCTV (closed-circuit TV) [ˌsi:si:ti:'vi:]	Fernsehüberwachungsanlage
surveillance [sɜ:'veɪlənts]	Überwachung; Beobachtung; Beaufsichtigung
footage ['fʊtɪdʒ]	Filmmaterial
to **track sb** [træk]	aufspüren; verfolgen
• to **monitor** ['mɒnɪtə]	überwachen
to breach [bri:tʃ]	verletzen
• **guideline** ['gaɪdlaɪn]	Richtlinie
• **regulation** [ˌregjə'leɪʃn]	Regelung; Verordnung; Vorschrift
evidence ['evɪdnts]	Beweismaterial; Beleg
evident ['evɪdnt]	erwiesen; offensichtlich
• **reduction** [rɪ'dʌkʃn]	Reduzierung; Verminderung
to quadruple ['kwɒdrʊpl]	vervierfachen
to **account for** [ə'kaʊnt fə]	verantwortlich sein für
to **capture** ['kæptʃə]	ergreifen; erobern; einfangen
civil liberty [ˌsɪvl 'lɪbəti]	Bürgerrecht
• **lax** [læks]	lax; locker
contention [kən'tentʃn]	Behauptung
deputy ['depjəti]	Vize-; stellvertretend
• **control** [kən'trəʊl]	Kontrolle; Steuerung
wary ['weəri]	wachsam; misstrauisch
• **operation** [ˌɒpr'eɪʃn]	Operation; Betrieb; Einsatz
operator ['ɒpreɪtə]	Betreiber(in); Bediener(in)
council ['kaʊntsl]	Gemeinderat; Stadtrat
to **fail to** *(+ infinitive)* [feɪl]	versäumen zu; es nicht schaffen zu
security [sɪ'kjʊərəti]	Sicherheit; Schutz
guard [gɑ:d]	Wache; Wächter(in)
undesirable [ˌʌndɪ'zaɪərəbl]	unerwünscht
* to sleep rough [ˌsli:p 'rʌf]	auf der Straße leben; im Freien übernachten
to eject [ɪ'dʒekt]	hinauswerfen; vertreiben
shift [ʃɪft]	Wechsel; Verschiebung
measure ['meʒə]	Maßnahme
unaccountable [ˌʌnə'kaʊntəbl]	ohne rechtliche Grundlage
justice ['dʒʌstɪs]	Gerechtigkeit; Justiz
benign [bɪ'naɪn]	gütig; freundlich
in terms of [ɪn 'tɜ:mz‿əv]	bezüglich
• **privacy** ['prɪvəsi; 'praɪvəsi]	Privatsphäre
• to **enable** [ɪ'neɪbl]	befähigen; ermöglichen
• **basis**, *pl.* **bases** ['beɪsɪs; 'beɪsi:z]	Basis, Grundlage
to **fit (in)** [ˌfɪt‿'ɪn]	(hinein)passen
• **category** ['kætəgri]	Kategorie; Klasse
decade ['dekeɪd]	Jahrzehnt
Home Office *(BE)* ['həʊm‿ɒfɪs]	Innenministerium

V25 Verbs from adjectives

■ The new verb *to roughen* (Orwell: 'his skin roughened by coarse soap') comes from the adjective *rough*.
The same *'-en'* ending (*suffix*) can be added to form verbs from a large number of adjectives.
Example: *hard, soft, black, dark, sharp, flat, short, thick, tough, weak, wide, deep.*

■ Choose suitable verbs of this kind (in a suitable form) from the adjectives on the left to fit these sentences:
1. *These trousers are too long. They'll have to be …*
2. *The road is far less dangerous now it's been …*
3. *Butter … when it's put in a warm place.*
4. *The longer he knew her, the more his love for her …*

D Digital culture

⟨**The next step in brain evolution**⟩

• **digital** ['dɪdʒɪtl]	digital
• evolution [ˌi:və'lu:ʃn]	Evolution
• expert ['ekspɜ:t]	Experte, Expertin
to shape [ʃeɪp]	formen
• to transform [trænts'fɔ:m]	transformieren; umwandeln; verwandeln
• essential [ɪ'sentʃl]	essenziell; entscheidend; unverzichtbar
instant ['ɪntstənt]	sofortig

V26 Watch out for idioms!

■ *To come in handy* is a good example of an idiom commonly used in everyday English.
■ Can you put these idioms right? (The words in *italics* are all in the wrong place!)
1. to have something in *touch* • 2. to be on one's *fingers* • 3. to cross one's *foot* • 4. to have a *message* (with someone) about something • 5. to make a *row* out of (writing) • 6. to throw a *living* (for 50 guests) • 7. to pass on a *party* (to someone) • 8. to get in *ahead* with someone • 9. to go *common* (with a project) • 10. to put one's *own* down
■ Choose five of the idioms you found and make your own sentences with them, to show their meaning in a suitable context.

• communication [kəˌmju:nɪ'keɪʃn]	Kommunikation
* to come to terms with [ˌkʌm tə 'tɜ:mz wɪð]	zurechtkommen mit; sich arrangieren mit
zip [zɪp]	Schwirren
track [træk]	Spur; Fährte; Musiktitel
to indulge (in) sth [ɪn'dʌldʒ]	nachgeben; sich etw. hingeben; sich in etw. ergehen
impact ['ɪmpækt]	Auswirkung; Einfluss
stimulus, *pl.* stimuli ['stɪmjələs]	Stimulus; Reiz
to chart a course [ˌtʃɑ:t‿ə 'kɔ:s]	einen Kurs festlegen
smart [smɑ:t]	pfiffig; schlau
to glue [glu:]	kleben
nerdy *(slang)* ['nɜ:di]	intelligent, aber sozial unbeholfen
gnat [næt]	Stechmücke
ability [ə'bɪləti]	Fähigkeit
cognitive enhancement [ˌkɒgnətɪv‿ɪn'hɑ:ntsmənt]	Wahrnehmungssteigerung
to itemise ['aɪtəmaɪz]	aufschlüsseln; einzeln aufführen
cumbersome ['kʌmbəsəm]	mühsam; lästig
auditory ['ɔ:dɪtri]	auditiv
to diminish [dɪ'mɪnɪʃ]	abnehmen
per se [ˌpɜ: 'seɪ]	an sich
engaging [ɪn'geɪdʒɪŋ]	einnehmend; faszinierend
to discriminate [dɪ'skrɪmɪneɪt]	unterscheiden
to determine [dɪ'tɜ:mɪn]	bestimmen; entschließen
consultant [kən'sʌltnt]	Berater(in)
consultancy [kən'sʌltntsi]	Beratung; Beratungsunternehmen
* to pay attention to sth [ˌpeɪ‿ə'tentʃn]	seine Aufmerksamkeit auf etw. richten
* to draw (on sth) [drɔ:]	(etw.) heranziehen
boundary ['baʊndri]	grenze; Abgrenzung
telling ['telɪŋ]	aufschlussreich; vielsagend
• to blog [blɒg]	bloggen; ein Internettagebuch führen
to confide in sb [kən'faɪd‿ɪn]	sich jmdm anvertrauen
to propel [prə'pel]	antreiben; vorwärts treiben
* to be au fait with [bi:ˌ‿əʊ'feɪ wɪð]	vertraut sein mit
turnover ['tɜ:nˌəʊvə]	Absatz; Umsatz
gadgetry ['gædʒɪtri]	Geräte; technische Spielereien
interface ['ɪntəfeɪs]	Schnittstelle
pace [peɪs]	Geschwindigkeit; Gangart
to loom [lu:m]	sich abzeichnen
4 • to evaluate [ɪ'væljueɪt]	evaluieren; auswerten
• gender ['dʒendə]	Geschlecht

Communicating online: Netiquette

to **observe** [əb'zɜ:v]	beobachten; beachten; befolgen
to coin [kɔɪn]	prägen
• **network** ['netwɜ:k]	Netzwerk
* to **come in handy** [ˌkʌm‿ɪn 'hændi]	gelegen kommen
venue ['venju:]	Veranstaltungsort; Treffpunkt
capital letter [ˌkæpɪtl 'letə]	Großbuchstabe
to **convey** [kən'veɪ]	übermitteln; transportieren; ausdrücken
• **personality** [ˌpɜ:sn'æləti]	persönliche Note
indifferent [ɪn'dɪfrnt]	gleichgültig
to wink [wɪŋk]	zwinkern
• **portable** ['pɔ:təbl]	transportabel; tragbar
tiny ['taɪni]	winzig
lengthy ['leŋkθi]	langatmig; übermäßig lang
abbreviation [əˌbri:vi'eɪʃn]	Abkürzung
to indicate ['ɪndɪkeɪt]	anzeigen; angeben; kenntlich machen
to **offend** [ə'fend]	beleidigen; verletzen
humble ['hʌmbl]	bescheiden; demütig
to haunt [hɔ:nt]	spuken in; heimsuchen

V27 Word combinations

■ Find the right combinations to form compounds you recognize. If possible, also add other compounds that could be made (e.g. *police station*), checking your dictionary if necessary.

speed • Thought • remote • human • crime • Home • award-winning • security • online • capital • power • surveillance

■ Notice that as the English language develops more and more compounds come into existence. Some (like Orwell's 'Hate Week') are created new in novels and other forms of literature.

Police • control • rates • being • limit • Office • station • novel • guard • camera • communications • letters

V28 Technology

■ You may find it useful to start a collection of words and phrases you know that are connected with science and technology. Find a suitable way to organize them, e.g. in a **mind map**. Some you could start with: *information technology (IT)* • *to download* • *electronic device* • *screen …*

E Technology and the environment

• to **spray** [spreɪ]	sprühen
greenhouse ['gri:nhaʊs]	Gewächshaus
• to **contribute** [kən'trɪbju:t]	beitragen; mitwirken
power station ['paʊə ˌsteɪʃn]	Kraftwerk
• **communications tower** [ˌkəmju:nɪ'keɪʃnz ˌtaʊə]	Fernmeldeturm; Sendemast
• to migrate [maɪ'greɪt]	wandern; umziehen
migratory ['maɪgrətri]	Wander-; Zug-
to illuminate [ɪ'lu:mɪneɪt]	erleuchten
overcast ['əʊvəkɑ:st]	bedeckt; bewölkt
• **collision** [kə'lɪʒn]	Kollision; Zusammenstoß
to **collide** [kə'laɪd]	kollidieren; zusammenstoßen
• to **eliminate** [ɪ'lɪmɪneɪt]	elimineren; beseitigen

⟨White coats⟩

4 to perch [pɜ:tʃ]	sitzen
fragile ['frædʒaɪl]	schwächlich; zerbrechlich
Judgement Day ['dʒʌdʒmənt ˌdeɪ]	Tag des Jüngsten Gerichts
to reclaim a toast [rɪˌkleɪm‿ə 'təʊst]	*hier:* einen Toast aussprechen
• martyr ['mɑ:tə]	Märtyrer(in)
in vain [ɪn 'veɪn]	umsonst; vergeblich
• lab [læb]	Labor
chorus ['kɔ:rəs]	Refrain
• pact [pækt]	Pakt; Bündnis
darling ['dɑ:lɪŋ]	Liebling
desperate ['despərət]	verzweifelt; hoffnungslos
innocence ['ɪnəsnts]	Unschuld
fitted carpet *(BE)* [ˌfɪtɪd 'kɑ:pɪt]	Teppichboden
padded cell [ˌpædɪd 'sel]	Gummizelle
• passion ['pæʃn]	Passion; Leidenschaft
to dwell [dwel]	wohnen
fury ['fjʊəri]	Wut
thunder ['θʌndə]	Donner
desire [dɪ'zaɪə]	Begierde; Verlangen
* to split [splɪt]	spalten
to blunder ['blʌndə]	einen groben Fehler machen
tide [taɪd]	Flut

E On the telephone

1 [07] *Useful telephone phrases: Listen for these phrases. Try to use them in the tasks below.*

WORD BANK

The kind of things you may want to say:
Hello. Is that Mr Brown speaking?
Could I speak to Mr Brown, please?
This is ... I'm calling from Germany.
I'm calling about ...
I'd like to enquire about ...
I hope I'm not calling at an inconvenient time.
I've got a few questions/a complaint about ...
I'd like to make an appointment[1] to see the doctor/dentist ...
Shall I ring back later?
Could you take a message/give her a message, please?
What time would be most convenient?
Could you repeat that, please?
I'm afraid the line[2]'s very bad/we've got a bad connection.

What you may hear at the other end of the line:
Brown and Wilson Car Rentals. Can I help you?
Speaking!
I'll just fetch him. Hang on a moment, please.
I'm afraid he's not available/he's in a meeting.
I'm afraid the line is engaged at the moment.
Could you call back later?
Can I take a message?
I'll give you his extension[3].
I'll put you through to the ... department/...
I'll connect you. Please hold the line[4].
Sorry. I think you've got the wrong number.

The person you are calling is not available at the moment.
Please leave a message after the tone.
If you wish to contact the sales/complaints/customer service department, please press ONE/TWO/...

2 [ ] *Practising telephone conversations:*

a) [11] *Listen to Stéphanie calling the dental centre. Then imagine a scene in which the receptionist calls her back. Write a dialogue and play it through with a partner.*

b) [12] *Listen to three messages recorded on an answering machine. Then make up dialogues with your partner in which you answer the messages.*

c) *Think of more telephone conversations involving the people in the cartoons.* →S24, p.106

I'm just opening the mail – you should see the size of my mobile phone bill!

[1]Termin • [2]Leitung • [3]Durchwahl • [4]dran bleiben

Dictionary

The following alphabetical word list contains the entire vocabulary from Green Line NEW E2 I–V, except for the optional vocabulary from volumes I–IV. Irregular verbs, which you will find in the list on pages 202–203, are marked with an asterisk: *. The numbers and letters at the end of each entry tell you where a word or phrase occurs for the first time:
a(n) [ə; ən] ein(e) **I** occurs first in volume I.
alike [ə'laɪk] gleichermaßen ⟨**V T1**, 9⟩ occurs first in volume VI, Topic 1, page 9.
Angle brackets ⟨⟩ indicate that the word or phrase is optional.

A

a(n) [ə; ən] ein(e) **I**
a bit [ə 'bɪt] ein bisschen **I**
a couple of [ə 'kʌpl‿əv] einige, ein paar **IV**
a few [ə 'fju:] einige, ein paar **II**
a little [ə 'lɪtl] ein bisschen; ein wenig **III**
a lot of [ə 'lɒt‿əv] viele, eine Menge **I**
a pair of [ə 'peər‿əv] ein Paar **I**
a week [ə 'wi:k] pro Woche, in der Woche **II**
to **abandon** [ə'bændən] aufgeben; zurücklassen **VT4**, 64
abbreviation [əˌbri:vi'eɪʃn] Abkürzung **VT5**, 83
ability [ə'bɪləti] Fähigkeit ⟨**VT5**, 82⟩
able ['eɪbl] fähig, begabt **II**
to **be able to (do sth)** [bi:‿'eɪbl] fähig sein (zu); können; dürfen **II**
aboard [ə'bɔ:d] an Bord **VT1**, 12; **VT5**, 74
to **abolish** [ə'bɒlɪʃ] abschaffen **IV**
Aboriginal [ˌæbə'rɪdʒnl] Ureinwohner(in) Australiens **I**
Aborigine [ˌæbə'rɪdʒni] Ureinwohner(in) Australiens **III**
about [ə'baʊt] ungefähr, circa, etwa **II**; herum; umher; hier in der Gegend **III**
about [ə'baʊt] über; wegen **I**
above [ə'bʌv] oben, über, oberhalb **I**
*to **be a notch above** [ˌbi:‿ə ˌnɒtʃ‿ə'bʌv] eine Klasse besser sein als **VT1**, 13
abroad [ə'brɔ:d] im/ins Ausland **III**
absolutely [ˌæbsə'lu:tli] absolut; völlig **III**
absurd [əb'zɜ:d; əb'sɜ:d] absurd; widersinnig **IV**
abundant [ə'bʌndnt] im Überfluss; reichlich vorhanden **VT4**, 56
abuse [ə'bju:s] Missbrauch **VT2**, 34; **VT4**, 63
human rights abuse [ˌhju:mən 'raɪts‿əˌbju:s] Menschenrechtsverletzung **VT4**, 63
to **abuse** [ə'bju:z] beschimpfen; missbrauchen; misshandeln **VT2**, 35; **VT5**, 73
accent ['æksnt] Akzent **III**
to **accept** [ək'sept] akzeptieren; annehmen **III**
acceptance [ək'septənts] Akzeptanz; Zustimmung **VT3**, 48
access ['ækses] Zugang **IV**
accident ['æksɪdnt] Unfall **II**
accidental [ˌæksɪ'dentl] unbeabsichtigt; durch Unfall verursacht **VT5**, 73
accommodation [əˌkɒmə'deɪʃn] Unterbringung **IV**
to **accompany** [ə'kʌmpəni] begleiten **IV**
to **accomplish** [ə'kʌmplɪʃ] vollbringen; erreichen **VT2**, 27
according to [ə'kɔ:dɪŋ tə] laut, gemäß **III**
savings account ['seɪvɪŋz əˌkaʊnt] Sparkonto **IV**
to **account for** [ə'kaʊnt fə] verantwortlich sein für **VT5**, 79
accountant [ə'kaʊntənt] Buchhalter(in); Steuerberater(in) **IV**
accurate ['ækjərət] akkurat; genau ⟨**VT2**, 32⟩
to **achieve** [ə'tʃi:v] erringen; leisten; vollbringen **IV**
achievement [ə'tʃi:vmənt] Errungenschaft; Leistung **IV**
to **acknowledge** [ək'nɒlɪdʒ] anerkennen; einräumen **VT2**, 27
acrobat ['ækrəbæt] Akrobat(in) **II**
across [ə'krɒs] über, hinüber, quer durch/darüber **II**
act [ækt] Gesetz **VT4**, 59
Civil Rights Act [ˌsɪvl 'raɪts‿ækt] Bürgerrechtsgesetz **VT2**, 24
to **act** [ækt] handeln; sich verhalten **III**
to **act something out** [ˌækt sʌmθɪŋ‿'aʊt] etwas durchspielen **I**
action ['ækʃn] Aktion, Handlung **I**
active ['æktɪv] aktiv; Aktiv **III**
activism ['æktɪvɪzm] Aktivismus **VT4**, 58
activist ['æktɪvɪst] Aktivist(in) *(jmd, der sich für etw. engagiert)* **VT2**, 29; **VT4**, 58
activity [æk'tɪvəti] Aktivität **II**
activity centre [æk'tɪvəti ˌsentə] Jugendzentrum **II**
actor ['æktə] Schauspieler(in) **II**
actually ['æktʃuəli] eigentlich; tatsächlich **I**
ad [æd] Anzeige; Werbespot **IV**
AD (= Anno Domini) [eɪ'di:] nach Christus **II**
to **adapt** [ə'dæpt] (sich) anpassen; abstimmen; umarbeiten **IV**
to **add** [æd] hinzufügen, addieren **II**
*to **be addicted** to sth [bi:‿ə'dɪktɪd] abhängig sein von; süchtig sein nach **VT3**, 48
additional [ə'dɪʃnl] zusätzlich **VT3**, 55
address [ə'dres] Adresse **II**
adjective ['ædʒəktɪv] Adjektiv **II**
to **admire** [əd'maɪə] bewundern **IV**
admission [əd'mɪʃn] Zulassung; Aufnahme **VT2**, 26
to **admit** [əd'mɪt] zugeben **III**; zulassen; aufnehmen ⟨**VT1**, 23⟩
to **adopt** [ə'dɒpt] übernehmen; annehmen; adoptieren **VT2**, 29; **VT4**, 57; **VT5**, 72
adult ['ædʌlt] Erwachsene(r) **II**
in advance [ɪn‿əd'vɑ:nts] im Voraus **II**
advanced [əd'vɑ:ntst] fortgeschritten **VT1**, 12
advantage [əd'vɑ:ntɪdʒ] Vorteil **III**
adventure [əd'ventʃə] Abenteuer **II**
adventurous [əd'ventʃrəs] abenteuerlich; unternehmungslustig; wagemutig **VT1**, 17
adverb ['ædvɜ:b] Adverb **II**
adverb of manner [ˌædvɜ:b‿əv 'mænə] Adverb der Art und Weise **II**
adverbial [əd'vɜ:biəl] adverbiale Bestimmung **IV**
advert ['ædvɜ:t] Anzeige; Werbespot **IV**
to **advertise** ['ædvətaɪz] Werbung machen (für); anpreisen; inserieren **IV**
advertisement [əd'vɜ:tɪsmənt] Anzeige; Werbespot **III**
advice [əd'vaɪs] Rat **III**
to **advise (sb to do sth)** [əd'vaɪz] (jmdm) raten **III**
to **advocate** ['ædvəkeɪt] befürworten; verteidigen; eintreten für ⟨**VT3**, 43⟩
aerial ['eəriəl] Antenne ⟨**VT4**, 69⟩
affair [ə'feə] Affäre; Angelegenheit **VT4**, 58
affect ['æfekt] Affekt ⟨**VT2**, 26⟩
to **affect** [ə'fekt] beeinflussen; beeinträchtigen; betreffen **IV**

to afford [ə'fɔ:d] sich leisten **VT4,** 66
*to be **afraid** (of) [bi:‿ə'freɪd] (sich) fürchten, Angst haben (vor) **II**
African ['æfrɪkən] afrikanisch; Afrikaner(in) **I**
after ['ɑ:ftə] nach **I**
after all [ˌɑ:ftər‿'ɔ:l] schließlich; immerhin **III**
after ['ɑ:ftə] nachdem **II**
they lived happily ever after [ðeɪ lɪvd ˌhæpɪli‿evər‿'ɑ:ftə] und wenn sie nicht gestorben sind, dann leben sie noch heute ⟨**VT2,** 35⟩
afternoon [ˌɑ:ftə'nu:n] Nachmittag **I**
this very afternoon [ðɪz ˌveri‿ɑ:ftə'nu:n] noch heute Nachmittag ⟨**VT3,** 44⟩
aftershave ['ɑ:ftəʃeɪv] Aftershave, Rasierwasser **III**
afterwards ['ɑ:ftəwədz] danach; hinterher **IV**
now and **again** [ˌnaʊ‿ənd‿ə'gen] hin und wieder; ab und zu **VT4,** 60
again [ə'gen] wieder **I**
again and again [ə'gen‿ənd‿ə'gen] immer wieder **I**
against [ə'gentst] gegen **II**
age [eɪdʒ] Alter; Zeitalter **II**
for ages [fr‿'eɪdʒɪz] ewig lange **II**
Middle Ages [ˌmɪdl‿'eɪdʒɪz] Mittelalter **II**
aged [eɪdʒd] im Alter von **IV**
agency ['eɪdʒntsi] Agentur **VT3,** 48
agent ['eɪdʒnt] Agent(in), Vertreter(in) **II**
travel agent's ['trævl ˌeɪdʒnts] Reisebüro **II**
agitator ['ædʒɪteɪtə] Agitator(in) ⟨**VT4,** 68⟩
ago [ə'gəʊ] vor *(zeitlich)* **I**
to **agree** (with) [ə'gri:] zustimmen, (mit jmdm) einer Meinung sein **II**
to **agree (on)** [ə'gri:] sich einigen (auf) **II**
agricultural [ˌægrɪ'kʌltʃrl] landwirtschaftlich **IV**
agriculture ['ægrɪkʌltʃə] Agrikultur; Landwirtschaft **IV**
aim [eɪm] Ziel **II**
to **aim at** ['eɪm‿ət] zielen auf; sich richten an **III**
to **aim for** ['eɪm fə] anstreben; abzielen auf **IV**
air [eə] Luft **I**
airplane ['eəpleɪn] Flugzeug **VT3,** 49
airport ['eəpɔ:t] Flughafen **I**
airstrip ['eəstrɪp] Landestreifen ⟨**VT5,** 77⟩
aisle [aɪl] Mittelgang **VT1,** 13
alarm [ə'lɑ:m] Wecker **III**
alcohol ['ælkəhɒl] Alkohol **IV**
A Level ['eɪ levl] Abiturniveau; Abschluss auf Abiturniveau **IV**
to **alienate** ['eɪlɪəneɪt] entfremden ⟨**VT3,** 46⟩
alike [ə'laɪk] gleichermaßen ⟨**VT1,** 9⟩
*to be **alive** [ə'laɪv] lebendig sein; leben **I**

all [ɔ:l] alle(s); ganz **I**
after all [ˌɑ:ftər‿'ɔ:l] schließlich; immerhin **III**
all around [ˌɔ:l‿ə'raʊnd] überall; rundherum; rings umher **III**
all over [ˌɔ:l‿'əʊvə] überall **III**
all over the place [ɔ:l‿ˌəʊvə ðə 'pleɪs] überall verteilt **IV**
all right [ɔ:l 'raɪt] in Ordnung; alles klar **II**; schon ⟨**VT5,** 74⟩
all the time [ˌɔ:l ðə 'taɪm] die ganze Zeit **I**
at all [ət‿'ɔ:l] überhaupt **II**
most of all ['məʊst‿əv‿ɔ:l] am meisten **II**
allergic [æ'lɜ:dʒɪk] allergisch **II**
bowling **alley** ['bəʊlɪŋ‿æli] Bowlingbahn **III**
to **allow** [ə'laʊ] erlauben, gestatten **II**
to **allow for** [ə'laʊ fə] vorsehen; einplanen **IV**
to **be allowed to (do sth)** [bi:‿ə'laʊd] dürfen **II**
allowance [ə'laʊənts] Zuwendung; Unterhaltsgeld; Taschengeld **VT1,** 11
almost ['ɔ:lməʊst] fast, beinahe **I**
alone [ə'ləʊn] alleine **I**
let alone [ˌlet‿ə'ləʊn] geschweige denn **VT2,** 34
to **leave sb alone** [ˌli:v‿ə'ləʊn] jmdn in Ruhe lassen **III**
along [ə'lɒŋ] entlang **III**
to go along [ˌgəʊ‿ə'lɒŋ] mitmachen; mitziehen **VT1,** 12
along with [ə'lɒŋ wɪð] zusammen mit ⟨**VT5,** 76⟩
aloud [ə'laʊd] laut **IV**
alphabet ['ælfəbet] Alphabet **I**
already [ɔ:l'redi] schon **I**
also ['ɔ:lsəʊ] auch **I**
alternate [ɔ:l'tɜ:nət] abwechselnd **IV**
although [ɔ:l'ðəʊ] obwohl **II**
altogether [ˌɔ:ltə'geðə] insgesamt; gänzlich; ganz und gar **VT5,** 75
always ['ɔ:lweɪz] immer, ständig **I**
am [ˌeɪ'em] vormittags *(Uhrzeit)* **I**
amazed [ə'meɪzd] erstaunt, verblüfft **II**
amazement [ə'meɪzmənt] Erstaunen **III**
amazing [ə'meɪzɪŋ] erstaunlich **IV**
ambassador [æm'bæsədə] Botschafter(in) ⟨**VT5,** 74⟩
ambition [æm'bɪʃn] Ehrgeiz; Streben; Ambitionen *(pl.)*; Ziel **IV**
ambitious [æm'bɪʃəs] ehrgeizig **IV**
ambulance ['æmbjələnts] Krankenwagen **III**
American [ə'merɪkən] amerikanisch; Amerikaner(in) **I**
Native American [ˌneɪtɪv‿ə'merɪkən] Ureinwohner(in) Amerikas, Indianer(in); indianisch **II**
ammunition [ˌæmjə'nɪʃn] Munition **VT4,** 62

amnesty ['æmnəsti] Amnestie; Begnadigung **VT4,** 63
among [ə'mʌŋ] unter (zwischen) **IV**
amongst [ə'mʌŋst] unter (zwischen) **VT1,** 10
amount [ə'maʊnt] Betrag; Menge; Summe **IV**
to **amuse** oneself [ə'mju:z] sich amüsieren; sich die Zeit vertreiben **III**
amusing [ə'mju:zɪŋ] amüsant; unterhaltsam **IV**
to **analyse** ['ænlaɪz] analysieren **IV**
analysis [ə'næləsɪz] Analyse **VT1,** 15
ancestor ['ænsestə] Ahn; Vorfahr **VT3,** 42
ancient ['eɪntʃnt] alt; altertümlich; antik **IV**
and [ænd; ən(d)] und **I**
angel ['eɪndʒl] Engel **III**
anger ['æŋgə] Zorn; Wut **III**
angry ['æŋgri] verärgert, böse **I**
animal ['ænɪml] Tier **I**
animated ['ænɪmeɪtɪd] lebhaft; munter ⟨**VT2,** 30⟩
animator ['ænimeɪtə] Animator(in) **II**
ankle ['æŋkl] Fußknöchel **VT5,** 76
anniversary [ˌænɪ'vɜ:sri] Jubiläum; Jahrestag **IV**
to **announce** [ə'naʊnts] ankündigen; durchsagen **IV**
annoyed [ə'nɔɪd] verärgert **II**
annoying [ə'nɔɪɪŋ] ärgerlich, lästig **II**
annual ['ænjuəl] jährlich **VT4,** 61
anorak ['ænəræk] Anorak **I**
another [ə'nʌðə] noch ein(e); ein(e) andere(-r/-s) **I**
answer ['ɑ:ntsə] Antwort **I**
to **answer** ['ɑ:ntsə] (be)antworten **I**
antibiotic [ˌæntɪbaɪ'ɒtɪk] Antibiotikum **IV**
any ['enɪ] irgendein(-e/-er); irgendwelche **I**
at any rate [ət 'eni ˌreɪt] jedenfalls **VT5,** 77
not any better [ˌnɒt‿eni 'betə] (überhaupt) nicht besser **II**
not any more [ˌnɒt‿eni 'mɔ:] nicht mehr **II**
anybody ['eniˌbɒdi] irgendjemand; jeder (beliebige) **II**
anyone ['eniˌwʌn] irgendjemand; jeder (beliebige) **II**
anything ['eniθɪŋ] irgendetwas **II**
anyway ['eniweɪ] jedenfalls, sowieso **II**
anywhere ['eniweə] irgendwo; überall (egal, wo) **II**
apart [ə'pɑ:t] auseinander **IV**
apart from [ə'pɑ:t frəm] außer, abgesehen von **I**
apartment *(AE)* [ə'pɑ:tmənt] Apartment, Wohnung **I**
to **apologise** [ə'pɒlədʒaɪz] sich entschuldigen **III**
apology [ə'pɒlədʒi] Entschuldigung **VT4,** 63

apparently [ə'pærntli] anscheinend **IV**
to **appear** [ə'pɪə] erscheinen **III**
appearance [ə'pɪərnts] Erscheinung; Aussehen; Auftritt **VT1,** 10; **VT3,** 55
to **appease** [ə'pi:z] besänftigen ⟨**VT4,** 69⟩
appetite ['æpɪtaɪt] Appetit **II**
apple ['æpl] Apfel **I**
apple pie [ˌæpl 'paɪ] gedeckter Apfelkuchen **IV**
applicant ['æplɪkənt] Bewerber(in) **IV**
application [ˌæplɪ'keɪʃn] Bewerbung; Antrag; Anwendung **IV**
letter of application [ˌletər‿əv‿æplɪ'keɪʃn] Bewerbungsschreiben **IV**
to **apply (for)** [ə'plaɪ] sich bewerben **IV**
to **apply sth (to)** [ə'plaɪ] etw. anwenden (auf) **IV**
appointment [ə'pɔɪntmənt] Termin ⟨**VT3,** 44⟩
to **appreciate** [ə'pri:ʃieɪt] schätzen; anerkennen **IV**
approach [ə'prəʊtʃ] Annäherung; Ansatz; Vorgehensweise ⟨**VT4,** 67⟩
to **approach** [ə'prəʊtʃ] sich nähern **IV**
appropriate [ə'prəʊpriət] angemessen **VT3,** 40; **VT5,** 75
to **approve** [ə'pru:v] anerkennen; genehmigen; gutheißen **VT5,** 73
approximate [ə'prɒksɪmət] ungefähr; circa **VT4,** 59
apron ['eɪprən] Schürze **IV**
aptitude ['æptɪtju:d] Geschick ⟨**VT4,** 69⟩
aqueduct ['ækwɪdʌkt] Aquädukt; Wasserleitung **IV**
archaeologist [ˌɑ:ki'ɒlədʒɪst] Archäologe; Archäologin **IV**
archaeology [ˌɑ:ki'ɒlədʒi] Archäologie **II**
archbishop [ɑ:tʃ'bɪʃəp] Erzbischof **VT4,** 60
archery ['ɑ:tʃri] Bogenschießen **II**
area ['eəriə] Areal; Gebiet; Fläche **II**
to **argue** ['ɑ:gju:] argumentieren; streiten **IV**
argument ['ɑ:gjəmənt] Argument; Streit **II**
*to **arise, arose, arisen** [ə'raɪz] aufkommen; entstehen **VT1,** 10
arm [ɑ:m] Arm **I**
to **be up in arms** [bi:‿ʌp‿ɪn‿'ɑ:mz] Sturm laufen; sich empören ⟨**VT3,** 43⟩
armoured personnel carrier [ˌɑ:məd pɜ:sˌnel 'kæriə] gepanzerter Mannschaftstransportwagen ⟨**VT4,** 62⟩
army ['ɑ:mi] Armee **III**
around [ə'raʊnd] herum, umher **I**
all around [ˌɔ:l‿ə'raʊnd] überall; rundherum; rings umher **III**
to **hang around** [ˌhæŋ‿ə'raʊnd] herumhängen **II**
to **arrange** [ə'reɪndʒ] ausmachen; arrangieren **III**
arrangement [ə'reɪndʒmənt] Vereinbarung; Arrangement; Plan **IV**
to **arrest** [ə'rest] festnehmen; verhaften **III**
arrival [ə'raɪvl] Ankunft **III**
to **arrive (at)** [ə'raɪv] ankommen **I**
arrow ['ærəʊ] Pfeil **II**
art [ɑ:t] Kunst **II**
arts and crafts [ˌɑ:ts‿nd 'krɑ:fts] Kunsthandwerk **III**
article ['ɑ:tɪkl] Artikel *(in der Zeitung etc.)* **I**
artificial [ˌɑ:tɪ'fɪʃl] künstlich ⟨**VT2,** 32⟩; ⟨**VT4,** 69⟩; **VT5,** 72
artist ['ɑ:tɪst] Künstler(in) **VT4,** 64
artistic [ˌɑ:'tɪstɪk] künstlerisch; kunstvoll **IV**
artwork ['ɑ:twɜ:k] Illustrationen; Bebilderung **VT3,** 40
as [æz; əz] als **II**
as ... as [æz; əz] so ... wie ... **II**
as a matter of fact [əz‿ə ˌmætər‿əv 'fækt] in der Tat ⟨**VT3,** 45⟩
as a result of [əz‿ə rɪ'zʌlt‿əv] infolge (von) **III**
as far as [əz 'fɑ:r‿əz] bis **II**
As far as ... is/are concerned, ... [kən'sɜ:nd] Soweit es ... betrifft, ...; Was ... angeht, ... **IV**
as soon as [əz 'su:n‿əz] sobald **III**
as well [əz 'wel] auch **III**
... as well as ... [əz 'wel‿əz] sowohl ... als auch ... **IV**
as [æz; əz] da, weil **III**
ASBO (= anti-social behaviour order) *(BE)* ['æzbəʊ] ASBO *(Verwarnung wegen antisozialen Verhaltens)* ⟨**VT1,** 17⟩
ash [æʃ] Asche **III**
*to be **ashamed** [bi:‿ə'ʃeɪmd] sich schämen ⟨**VT4,** 68⟩
Asian ['eɪʃn] asiatisch; Asiat(in) **II**
as if [əz‿'ɪf] als ob **III**
to **ask** [ɑ:sk] fragen **I**
to **ask (for)** [ɑ:sk] bitten (um) **II**
aspect ['æspekt] Aspekt **II**
asphalt ['æsfælt] Asphalt **VT1,** 13
aspiration [ˌæspɪ'reɪʃn] Hoffnung; Streben ⟨**VT3,** 45⟩
smart **ass** *(slang)* [ˌsmɑ:t‿'æs] Klugscheißer(in) ⟨**VT3,** 43⟩
to **cover one's ass** *(vulg)* [ˌkʌvə wʌnz‿'æs] seine Haut retten ⟨**VT3,** 43⟩
to **assassinate** [ə'sæsɪneɪt] ermorden **VT2,** 28
to **assault** [ə'sɔ:lt] tätlich angreifen; überfallen **VT4,** 64
to **assemble** [ə'sembl] zusammenbauen; montieren ⟨**VT1,** 19⟩
Assembly [ə'sembli] Versammlung; Morgenappell **I**
to **assess** [ə'ses] bewerten; beurteilen; einschätzen ⟨**VT3,** 55⟩
to **assign** [ə'saɪn] zuordnen; übertragen **VT4,** 59
assignment *(AE)* [ə'saɪnmənt] Aufgabe **II**
shop **assistant** ['ʃɒp‿əˌsɪstnt] Verkäufer(in) **I**
to **assume** [ə'sju:m; ə'su:m] annehmen; voraussetzen **IV**
assumption [ə'sʌmpʃn] Annahme; Voraussetzung ⟨**VT4,** 68⟩; **VT5,** 77
as though [əz 'ðəʊ] als ob **VT2,** 36
astonishing [ə'stɒnɪʃɪŋ] erstaunlich; überraschend ⟨**VT1,** 19⟩
asylum seeker [ə'saɪləm ˌsi:kə] Asylbewerber(in) **VT2,** 25
at [æt; ət] in, auf, bei, an **I**
at all [ət‿'ɔ:l] überhaupt **II**
at any rate [ət 'eni ˌreɪt] jedenfalls **VT5,** 77
at close range [ət ˌkləʊs 'reɪndʒ] aus nächster Nähe ⟨**VT4,** 62⟩
at first [ət 'fɜ:st] zuerst; zunächst **II**
at home [ət 'həʊm] zu Hause **I**
at last [ət 'lɑ:st] endlich **I**
at least [ət 'li:st] mindestens, wenigstens **II**
at once [ət 'wʌnts] sofort, plötzlich **I**
at the Burtons' [ət ðə 'bɜ:tnz] bei den Burtons **II**
at the seaside [ət ðə 'si:saɪd] am Meer **I**
athlete ['æθli:t] (Leicht-)Athlet(in) **III**
athletic [æθ'letɪk] athletisch **II**
Atishoo! [ə'tɪʃu:] Hatschi! **II**
atmosphere ['ætməsfɪə] Atmosphäre; Stimmung **IV**
to **attack** [ə'tæk] angreifen **I**
attempt [ə'tempt] Versuch **VT4,** 62
to **attempt** [ə'tempt] versuchen **VT4,** 62
to **attend** [ə'tend] teilnehmen; anwesend sein **VT3,** 53; **VT4,** 61
attendance [ə'tendnts] Anwesenheit; Teilnahme **VT3,** 48
attendance book [ə'tendnts ˌbʊk] Anwesenheitsliste; Klassentagebuch **VT1,** 12
attention [ə'tentʃn] Aufmerksamkeit; Achtung **IV**
to **draw sb's attention to sth** [ˌdrɔ: sʌmbʌdiz‿ə'tentʃn tə] jmds Aufmerksamkeit auf etw. lenken ⟨**VT3,** 46⟩
to **pay attention to sth** [ˌpeɪ‿ə'tentʃn] seine Aufmerksamkeit auf etw. richten ⟨**VT5,** 82⟩
at the end [ˌət ði:‿'end] am Ende **II**
attitude (to/towards) ['ætɪtju:d] Haltung; Einstellung **IV**
to **attract** [ə'trækt] anziehen **IV**
attraction [ə'trækʃn] Attraktion, Sehenswürdigkeit **I**
attractive [ə'træktɪv] attraktiv **IV**
audience ['ɔ:diənts] Publikum **II**

auditory ['ɔ:dɪtri] auditiv ⟨**VT5,** 82⟩
*to be **au fait** with [bi:‿əʊ'feɪ wɪð] vertraut sein mit ⟨**VT5,** 82⟩
aunt [ɑ:nt] Tante **I**
au pair [ˌəʊ'peə] Au-pair(-Mädchen) **III**
Australian ['ɒstreɪliən] australisch; Australier(in) **I**
author ['ɔ:θə] Autor(in) **III**
authority [ɔ:'θɒrəti] Autorität; Staatsgewalt; Behörde **VT3,** 41; **VT4,** 59
autobiography [ˌɔ:təbaɪ'ɒgrəfi] Autobiografie **VT4,** 61
autograph ['ɔ:təgrɑ:f] Autogramm **II**
automatic [ˌɔ:tə'mætɪk] automatisch **IV**
autumn ['ɔ:təm] Herbst **II**
available [ə'veɪləbl] erhältlich; verfügbar; abkömmlich **IV**
an **average** of [ən‿'ævrɪdʒ‿əv] durchschnittlich; im Durchschnitt **IV**
to **avoid** *(+ noun/gerund)* [ə'vɔɪd] (ver)meiden **IV**
award [ə'wɔ:d] Preis; Auszeichnung **VT4,** 63; **VT5,** 75
*to be **aware** of [bi:‿ə'weə] sich ... bewusst sein **IV**
away [ə'weɪ] weg (von) **I**
right **away** [raɪt‿ə'weɪ] sofort, gleich **I**
awful ['ɔ:fl] schrecklich, furchtbar **III**

B

to **babble** ['bæbl] plappern; schnattern; brabbeln ⟨**VT5,** 77⟩
baby ['beɪbi] Baby, Säugling **II**
baby boomer ['beɪbi ˌbu:mə] Babyboomer *(Angehörige(r) eines geburtenstarken Jahrgangs)* **VT2,** 26
to **have a baby** [ˌhæv‿ə 'beɪbi] ein Kind bekommen **III**
back [bæk] Rücken **I**
the small of the back [ðə ˌsmɔ:l‿əv ðə 'bæk] Kreuz ⟨**VT1,** 12⟩
back [bæk] Hinter-, rückwärtig **II**
back [bæk] zurück **I**
back-and-forth [ˌbæk‿ənd 'fɔ:θ] Auf und Ab; Hin und Her ⟨**VT4,** 68⟩
background ['bækgraʊnd] Hintergrund **II**
backpack ['bækpæk] Rucksack **III**
backstage [bæk'steɪdʒ] backstage, hinter der Bühne **II**
backwards ['bækwədz] rückwärts gewandt; rückständig **VT2,** 33
backyard ['bækjɑ:d] Garten; Hinterhof **VT2,** 27
bacon ['beɪkn] Schinkenspeck **II**
bad [bæd] schlecht **I**
to **be in a bad way** [ɪn‿ə 'bæd ˌweɪ] in schlechter Verfassung sein **I**
badge [bædʒ] Abzeichen ⟨**VT3,** 50⟩
bag [bæg] Tasche **I**; Sack **II**
mixed bag [ˌmɪkst 'bæg] buntes Allerlei **I**
school bag ['sku:l bæg] Schultasche **I**
sleeping bag ['sli:pɪŋ ˌbæg] Schlafsack **III**
to **pack one's bags** [ˌpæk wʌnz 'bægz] seine Koffer packen; seine Sachen packen **IV**
baggy ['bægi] ausgebeult; bauschig **VT2,** 26
bagpipes *pl.* ['bægpaɪps] Dudelsack **I**
to **bake** [beɪk] backen **III**
to **balance** ['bæləns] balancieren; ausgleichen; abwägen **VT1,** 10
ball [bɔ:l] Ball **I**
bowling ball ['bəʊlɪŋ ˌbɔ:l] Bowlingkugel **III**
golf ball ['gɒlf ˌbɔ:l] Golfball **III**
ban [bæn] Bann; Verbot; Sperre **VT3,** 41; **VT4,** 61
to **ban** [bæn] bannen; verbieten; sperren **VT1,** 9; **VT3,** 41; **VT4,** 61
banana [bə'nɑ:nə] Banane **III**
band [bænd] Band, Kapelle **II**
bandage ['bændɪdʒ] Bandage; Verband **III**
*to get a big **bang** out of sth [ˌget‿ə ˌbɪg 'bæŋ] einen Heidenspaß an etw. haben ⟨**VT1,** 12⟩
to **bang** [bæŋ] schlagen; fest (an)klopfen **VT3,** 49
to **bang down** [ˌbæŋ 'daʊn] hinknallen **VT2,** 35
bank [bæŋk] Bank **IV**
banner ['bænə] Banner; Spruchband; Transparent **VT4,** 62
Baptist ['bæptɪst] Baptist(in) ⟨**VT2,** 28⟩
bar [bɑ:] Tafel; Riegel; Stück; Stange **I**
coffee bar ['kɒfi: ˌbɑ:] Café **III**
barbecue ['bɑ:bɪkju:] Grill(party) **III**
barbed [bɑ:bd] mit Stacheln versehen ⟨**VT4,** 69⟩
bare [beə] nackt; bloß; blank **IV**
barefoot [beə'fʊt] barfuß **IV**
barely ['beəli] kaum **VT3,** 42
to **bark** (at) [bɑ:k] (an)bellen **I**
barrel ['bærl] Fass, Tonne **II**
barrier ['bæriə] Barriere, Sperre **II**
*to be **based** on [bi: 'beɪst‿ɒn] basieren auf; sich stützen auf **VT2,** 24; ⟨**VT4,** 67⟩; **VT5,** 72
baseball ['beɪsbɔ:l] Baseball **I**
baseball bat ['beɪsbɔ:l ˌbæt] Baseballschläger **III**
baseball field ['beɪsbɔ:l ˌfi:ld] Baseballplatz **III**
basic ['beɪsɪk] grundlegend, Grund-, einfach **II**
basin ['beɪsn] Waschbecken **IV**
basis, *pl.* **bases** ['beɪsɪs; 'beɪsi:z] Basis, Grundlage **VT5,** 80
basket ['bɑ:skɪt] Korb, Körbchen **I**
basketball ['bɑ:skɪtbɔ:l] Basketball **II**
basketball court ['bɑ:skɪtbɔ:l ˌkɔ:t] Basketballplatz **III**
bass [beɪs] Bass **II**
bat [bæt] Schläger (Tischtennis-, Baseball-); Fledermaus **II**
baseball bat ['beɪsbɔ:l ˌbæt] Baseballschläger **III**
bath [bɑ:θ] Bad **I**; Badewanne **IV**
bathing suit ['beɪðɪŋ ˌsu:t] Badeanzug **IV**
bathroom ['bɑ:θrʊm] Badezimmer **I**; Toilette *(AE)* **III**
battery ['bætri] Batterie, Akku **II**
battle ['bætl] Schlacht **II**
baulk [bɔ:k] Balken ⟨**VT5,** 77⟩
bay [beɪ] Bucht **VT4,** 56
bazaar [bə'zɑ:] Bazar **II**
BC (= before Christ) [bi:'si:] vor Christus **II**
*to **be** [bi:] sein **I**
to **be able to (do sth)** [bi:‿'eɪbl] fähig sein (zu); können; dürfen **II**
to **be addicted to sth** [bi:‿ə'dɪktɪd] abhängig sein von; süchtig sein nach **VT3,** 48
to **be afraid (of)** [bi:‿ə'freɪd] (sich) fürchten, Angst haben (vor) **II**
to **be alive** [ə'laɪv] lebendig sein; leben **I**
to **be allowed to (do sth)** [bi:‿ə'laʊd] dürfen **II**
to **be a notch above** [ˌbi:‿ə ˌnɒtʃ‿ə'bʌv] eine Klasse besser sein als **VT1,** 13
to **be ashamed** [bi:‿ə'ʃeɪmd] sich schämen ⟨**VT4,** 68⟩
to **be as hungry as a horse** [əz ˌhʌŋgri‿əz‿ə 'hɔ:s] einen Bärenhunger haben **II**
to **be au fait with** [bi:‿əʊ'feɪ wɪð] vertraut sein mit ⟨**VT5,** 82⟩
to **be aware of** [bi:‿ə'weə] sich ... bewusst sein **IV**
to **be based on** [bi: 'beɪst‿ɒn] basieren auf; sich stützen auf **VT2,** 24; ⟨**VT4,** 67⟩; **VT5,** 72
to **be born** [bi: 'bɔ:n] geboren werden **II**
to **be called** [bi: 'kɔ:ld] heißen, genannt werden **II**
to **be clean out of impressions** [bi: ˌkli:n‿aʊt‿əv‿ɪm'preʃnz] komplett frei sein von Eindrücken ⟨**VT1,** 13⟩
to **be crazy about** [bi: 'kreɪzi‿əbaʊt] verrückt sein nach; abfahren auf **III**
to **be frightened (of)** ['fraɪtnd] Angst haben (vor) **I**
to **be going on** [bi: ˌgəʊɪŋ‿'ɒn] los sein **II**
to **be gone** [bi: 'gɒn] verschwunden sein **II**
to **be good at** ['gʊd‿ət] gut sein in **I**
to **be hurt** [bi: 'hɜ:t] verletzt sein/werden **I**
to **be in a bad way** [ɪn‿ə 'bæd ˌweɪ] in schlechter Verfassung sein **I**
to **be in charge (of)** [bi:‿ɪn 'tʃɑ:dʒ] die Verantwortung tragen (für); leiten **IV**
to **be in command** [bi:‿ɪn kə'mɑ:nd] das Kommando haben; den Oberbefehl haben **VT3,** 43

to **be in love (with)** [biː‿ɪn 'lʌv] verliebt sein (in) **II**
to **be interested in** [biː‿'ɪntrəstɪd‿ɪn] interessiert sein an, sich interessieren für **I**
to **be keen on** [biː 'kiːn‿ɒn] scharf sein auf, begeistert sein von **II**
to **be known as** [biː 'nəʊn‿əz] bekannt sein als **II**
to **be late** [biː 'leɪt] zu spät dran sein, zu spät kommen **I**
to **be likely (to)** [biː 'laɪkli] wahrscheinlich sein **III**
to **be located** [biː ləʊ'keɪtɪd] gelegen sein **II**
to **be lucky** ['lʌki] Glück haben **I**
to **be made of** [biː 'meɪd‿əv] hergestellt sein aus **II**
to **be married to** [biː 'mærid tə] verheiratet sein mit **I**
to **be obsessed (by/with)** [biː‿əb'sest] besessen sein (von) **IV**
to **be on** [ɒn] im Gange sein, laufen **I**
to **be on to sth** [biː‿'ɒn tə] bekannt sein mit **VT3,** 42
to **be out of one's mind** [biː‿aʊt‿əv wʌnz 'maɪnd] verrückt sein **II**
to **be pleased** [biː 'pliːzd] erfreut sein **III**
to **be related to** [biː rɪ'leɪtɪd] verwandt sein mit; sich beziehen auf **IV**
to **be scared** [biː 'skeəd] Angst haben, erschrocken sein **I**
to **be sick** [biː 'sɪk] sich übergeben **IV**
to **be sick of** *(+ noun/gerund)* [biː 'sɪk‿əv] satt haben, (einer Sache) überdrüssig sein **IV**
to **be stuck** [biː 'stʌk] stecken bleiben, festklemmen **II**
to **be suited (for/to)** [biː 'suːtɪd] geeignet sein (für) **IV**
to **be supposed to** *(+ infinitive)* [biː sə'pəʊzd tə] (etw. tun) sollen **IV**
to **be surprised** [sə'praɪzd] überrascht sein **I**
to **be tired of** *(+ gerund)* [biː 'taɪəd] es müde/leid sein/satt haben, etwas zu tun **III**
to **be to** *(+ infinitive)* ['biː tə] sollen **IV**
to **be trapped** [biː 'træpt] in der Falle sitzen **III**
to **be twinned with** [bi. 'twɪnd wɪð] Partnerstadt sein von **IV**
to **be unlikely (to)** [biː‿ʌn'laɪkli] unwahrscheinlich sein **III**
to **be up in arms** [biː‿ʌp‿ɪn‿'ɑːmz] Sturm laufen; sich empören ⟨**VT3,** 43⟩
to **be up to sb** [biː‿'ʌp tə] liegen an; abhängen von; überlassen sein **VT2,** 27
to **be used to** *(+ gerund)* [biː 'juːst tə] gewöhnt sein an; gewohnt sein **III**
to **be willing to do sth** [biː 'wɪlɪŋ] gewillt sein, etw. zu tun **VT2,** 27
to **be worried** ['wʌrid] besorgt, beunruhigt sein **I**
to **be worth** *(+ gerund)* [biː 'wɜːθ] (es) wert sein (zu) **III**
to **be wrong** [biː 'rɒŋ] Unrecht haben **II**
beach [biːtʃ] Strand **I**
beam [biːm] Strahl **IV**
black **bear** [ˌblæk 'beə] Schwarzbär **II**
teddy bear ['tedi ˌbeə] Teddybär **II**
*to **bear** [beə] (er)tragen; hervorbringen ⟨**VT3,** 44⟩; **VT4,** 61; **VT5,** 75
beard [bɪəd] (Voll-)Bart **IV**
*to **beat** [biːt] besiegen; schlagen **I**
to **beat sb up** [ˌbiːt‿'ʌp] zusammenschlagen **VT4,** 64
beautiful ['bjuːtɪfl] wunderschön, hübsch **I**
beauty ['bjuːti] Schönheit **IV**
because [bɪ'kɒz] weil **I**
*to **become** [bɪ'kʌm] werden **II**
bed [bed] Bett **I**
bed and breakfast [ˌbed‿n 'brekfəst] Zimmer mit Frühstück **I**
bedroom ['bedrʊm] Schlafzimmer **I**
beef [biːf] Rindfleisch **IV**
beer [bɪə] Bier **II**
before [bɪ'fɔː] vorher; zuvor; schon einmal **II**
before [bɪ'fɔː] vor **I**
before [bɪ'fɔː] bevor **I**
to **beg (for)** [beg] betteln (um); anflehen **III**
I beg your pardon? [aɪ ˌbeg jə 'pɑːdn] Wie bitte? ⟨**VT3,** 45⟩
*to **begin** [bɪ'gɪn] beginnen; anfangen **III**
beginning [bɪ'gɪnɪŋ] Anfang, Beginn **I**
to **behave** [bɪ'heɪv] sich verhalten, sich benehmen **II**
behaviour [bɪ'heɪvjə] Verhalten; Benehmen **IV**
behind [bɪ'haɪnd] hinten; im Rückstand **III**
behind [bɪ'haɪnd] hinter **II**
human **being** [ˌhjuːmən 'biːɪŋ] menschliches Wesen **VT5,** 72
belief [bɪ'liːf] Glaube **IV**
to **believe** [bɪ'liːv] glauben **II**
bell [bel] Glocke **II**
belly ['beli] Bauch **IV**
to **belong (to)** [bɪ'lɒŋ] gehören (zu) **IV**
beloved [bɪ'lʌvd; bɪ'lʌvɪd] geliebt ⟨**VT1,** 23⟩
below [bɪ'ləʊ] unterhalb, unten **I**
belt [belt] Gürtel **VT1,** 14
bent double [ˌbent 'dʌbl] zusammengekrümmt **VT1,** 13
to **bend over** [ˌbend‿'əʊvə] sich vorbeugen **III**
beneath [bɪ'niːθ] unter, unterhalb ⟨**VT4,** 69⟩; **VT5,** 76
benefit ['benɪfɪt] Nutzen; Gewinn ⟨**VT1,** 12⟩; **VT4,** 59
benign [bɪ'naɪn] gütig; freundlich ⟨**VT5,** 80⟩
berry ['beri] Beere **IV**
beside [bɪ'saɪd] neben **IV**
best [best] beste(-r/-s) **I**
Best wishes [ˌbest 'wɪʃɪz] Mit den besten Wünschen **IV**
bestiality [ˌbesti'æləti] Sodomie ⟨**VT3,** 43⟩
*to **bet** [bet] wetten **III**
better ['betə] besser **I**
between [bɪ'twiːn] zwischen **II**
in between [ˌɪn bɪ'twiːn] dazwischen **II**
bewildered [bɪ'wɪldəd] verblüfft; verwirrt ⟨**VT2,** 32⟩
beyond [bi'ɒnd] jenseits; über etw. hinaus **VT3,** 42; ⟨**VT4,** 69⟩; **VT5,** 74
biased ['baɪəst] voreingenommen; parteiisch **IV**
bible ['baɪbl] Bibel **III**
bicycle ['baɪsɪkl] Fahrrad **IV**
*to **bid** [bɪd] bieten **IV**
big [bɪg] groß; dick **I**
bike [baɪk] Fahrrad **I**
biking ['baɪkɪŋ] Radfahren **II**
mountain biking ['maʊntɪn ˌbaɪkɪŋ] Mountainbikefahren **II**
bill [bɪl] Banknote; Geldschein *(AE)* **III**; Rechnung **IV**
billion ['bɪljən] Milliarde *(tausend Millionen)* **IV**
bin [bɪn] Abfalleimer ⟨**VT3,** 50⟩
biology [baɪ'ɒlədʒi] Biologie **II**
bird [bɜːd] Vogel **I**
biro ['baɪrəʊ] Kugelschreiber, Kuli **I**
birth [bɜːθ] Geburt **IV**
birthday ['bɜːθdeɪ] Geburtstag **I**
biscuit ['bɪskɪt] Keks **II**
a **bit** [ə 'bɪt] ein bisschen **I**
not a bit of it [ˌnɒt‿ə 'bɪt‿əv‿ɪt] keine Spur davon **IV**
bitchiness ['bɪtʃinəs] Gehässigkeit **VT1,** 10
*to **bite** [baɪt] beißen; stechen **III**
bitter ['bɪtə] bitter **II**
black [blæk] schwarz **I**
black bear [ˌblæk 'beə] Schwarzbär **II**
blackboard, board ['blækbɔːd; bɔːd] Tafel **I**
razor **blade** ['reɪzə ˌbleɪd] Rasierklinge ⟨**VT5,** 77⟩
to **blame** [bleɪm] verantwortlich machen; beschuldigen **IV**
blanket ['blæŋkɪt] (Woll-)Decke **II**
zit-**blasted** *(infml)* ['zɪtˌblɑːstɪd] mit Pickeln übersät ⟨**VT1,** 14⟩
bleachers *(pl. AE)* ['bliːtʃəz] unüberdachte Tribüne ⟨**VT1,** 13⟩
*to **bleed** [bliːd] bluten **VT4,** 62
bless you ['bles juː] Gesundheit! **II**
blind [blaɪnd] Jalousie; Sonnenblende **III**
blind [blaɪnd] blind **III**
blister ['blɪstə] Blase **IV**
block [blɒk] (Häuser-)Block **III**
to **blog** [blɒg] bloggen; ein Internettagebuch führen ⟨**VT5,** 82⟩
blonde [blɒnd] blond **I**

blood [blʌd] Blut **III**
bloody *(rude)* ['blʌdi] verdammt **VT3,** 42
petty bloody officiousness [ˌpeti ˌblʌdi‿ə'fɪʃəsnəs] blöder kleinlicher Übereifer ⟨**VT3,** 44⟩
blouse [blaʊz] Bluse **VT3,** 40
blow [bləʊ] Hieb, Schlag **III**
*to **blow** [bləʊ] blasen **III**
blue [bluː] blau **I**
bluebottle ['bluːˌbɒtl] Schmeißfliege ⟨**VT5,** 77⟩
blues [bluːz] Blues **III**
to **blunder** ['blʌndə] einen groben Fehler machen ⟨**VT5,** 87⟩
blunt [blʌnt] stumpf **VT5,** 77
to **blush** [blʌʃ] erröten ⟨**VT2,** 32⟩
board [bɔːd] Brett **III**
board, blackboard ['blækbɔːd; bɔːd] Tafel **I**
to **board** [bɔːd] an Bord gehen, besteigen **II**
boarding school ['bɔːdɪŋ skuːl] Internat **VT3,** 52
boarding pass ['bɔːdɪŋ ˌpɑːs] Bordkarte **II**
to **boast** [bəʊst] angeben; prahlen **IV**
boat [bəʊt] Boot, Schiff **I**
to **bob up** [ˌbɒb‿'ʌp] auftauchen ⟨**VT1,** 14⟩
body ['bɒdi] Körper **I**
heavenly body [ˌhevnli 'bɒdi] Himmelskörper ⟨**VT3,** 42⟩
to **boil** [bɔɪl] kochen **III**
to **bomb** [bɒm] zerbomben **VT5,** 77
to **bombard** [bɒm'bɑːd] bombardieren ⟨**VT3,** 50⟩
bond [bɒnd] Bindung ⟨**VT3,** 51⟩
bone [bəʊn] Knochen **III**
bongoes *(pl.)* ['bɒŋgəʊz] Bongos *(kubanische Trommeln)* ⟨**VT3,** 49⟩
book [bʊk] Buch; Heft **I**
attendance book [ə'tendənts ˌbʊk] Anwesenheitsliste; Klassentagebuch **VT1,** 12
exercise book ['eksəsaɪz ˌbʊk] Übungsheft **I**
to **book** [bʊk] buchen, reservieren **II**
bookshop ['bʊkʃɒp] Buchhandlung **I**
to **boom out** [ˌbuːm‿'aʊt] dröhnen ⟨**VT3,** 50⟩
baby **boomer** ['beɪbi ˌbuːmə] Babyboomer *(Angehörige(r) eines geburtenstarken Jahrgangs)* **VT2,** 26
boot [buːt] Stiefel **II**
phone **booth** *(AE)* ['fəʊn ˌbuːð] Telefonzelle **III**
border ['bɔːdə] Grenze **III**
bored [bɔːd] gelangweilt **II**
boring ['bɔːrɪŋ] langweilig **I**
*to be **born** [biː 'bɔːn] geboren werden **II**
to **borrow** ['bɒrəʊ] (sich) ausleihen **III**
boss [bɒs] Boss, Chef **II**
both [bəʊθ] beide **I**

I can't be **bothered.** [aɪ ˌkɑːnt biː 'bɒðəd] Ich habe keine Lust.; Ich kann mich nicht dazu aufraffen. **IV**
to **bother to do sth** ['bɒðə] sich die Mühe machen, etw. zu tun **VT2,** 36; **VT3,** 48
bottle ['bɒtl] Flasche **I**
bottom ['bɒtəm] Boden; Grund; unterer Teil **IV**
boundary ['baʊndri] Grenze; Abgrenzung ⟨**VT5,** 82⟩
bow [bəʊ] Bogen **II**
bowl [bəʊl] Schale, Schälchen **I**
bowling alley ['bəʊlɪŋ‿ˌæli] Bowlingbahn **III**
bowling ball ['bəʊlɪŋ ˌbɔːl] Bowlingkugel **III**
box [bɒks] Kiste, Schachtel; Kasten **I**
boxed in [ˌbɒkst‿'ɪn] eingekeilt; eingekastelt ⟨**VT1,** 14⟩
boxwood ['bɒkswʊd] Buchsbaumholz ⟨**VT4,** 70⟩
boy [bɔɪ] Junge **I**
boycott ['bɔɪkɒt] Boykott **IV**
boyfriend ['bɔɪfrend] Freund **I**
to **brace** [breɪs] aufstützen ⟨**VT4,** 69⟩
bracket ['brækɪt] Klammer **IV**
braid [breɪd] Zopf **IV**
brain(s) [breɪn] Gehirn; Verstand **IV**
brake [breɪk] Bremse **VT1,** 12
to **brake** [breɪk] bremsen **VT1,** 15
branch [brɑːntʃ] Zweig, Ast **III**
brand [brænd] Marke **IV**
brandy ['brændi] Weinbrand ⟨**VT4,** 68⟩
brave [breɪv] tapfer, mutig **I**
bravery ['breɪvri] Tapferkeit, Mut **VT2,** 27
to **breach** [briːtʃ] verletzen ⟨**VT5,** 79⟩
bread [bred] Brot **II**
break [breɪk] Pause; Bruch **II**
to **give sb a break** [ˌgɪv‿ə 'breɪk] jmdn schonen; jmdm eine Chance geben **VT3,** 42
*to **break** [breɪk] (zer)brechen; kaputtmachen **II**
broken home [ˌbrəʊkn 'həʊm] nicht intakte Familie **VT3,** 48
to **break in** [breɪk‿'ɪn] einlaufen; einreiten **II**
to **break in(to)** [breɪk‿'ɪn] einbrechen (in) **III**
to **break it off** [ˌbreɪk‿ɪt‿'ɒf] Schluss machen **IV**
breakfast ['brekfəst] Frühstück **I**
bed and breakfast [ˌbed‿n 'brekfəst] Zimmer mit Frühstück **I**
breast [brest] Brust ⟨**VT4,** 70⟩; **VT5,** 76
breath [breθ] Atem; Atemzug **III**
to **breathe** [briːð] atmen **III**
bridge [brɪdʒ] Brücke **I**
brief [briːf] kurz **III**
bright [braɪt] leuchtend, strahlend **II**; intelligent; gescheit **VT1,** 15; **VT3,** 48

to **brighten** ['braɪtn] aufhellen; sich erhellen **IV**
brilliant ['brɪljənt] toll, prima; leuchtend **I**
*to **bring** [brɪŋ] bringen **I**
on the **brink** of [ɒn ðə 'brɪŋk] am Rande von; kurz vor ⟨**VT3,** 50⟩
Made in **Britain** [ˌmeɪd‿ɪn 'brɪtn] Hergestellt in Großbritannien **I**
British ['brɪtɪʃ] britisch **I**
Briton ['brɪtn] Brite, Britin **II**
broad [brɔːd] breit **II**
brochure ['brəʊʃə] Broschüre, Prospekt **II**
to **brood (over sth)** [bruːd] brüten; (nach)grübeln (über) **VT3,** 42; **VT4,** 64
brother ['brʌðə] Bruder **I**
brown [braʊn] braun **I**
bruise [bruːz] Prellung; Quetschung; Bluterguss **VT1,** 16
to **bruise** [bruːz] verletzen **VT1,** 16
brutality [ˌbruː'tælɪti] Brutalität **VT4,** 62
bubble ['bʌbl] Blase **VT2,** 26
buck [bʌk] Bock ⟨**VT4,** 69⟩
buck-toothed ['bʌkˌtuːθt] hasenzähnig ⟨**VT1,** 14⟩
buckle ['bʌkl] Schnalle ⟨**VT1,** 14⟩
buddy *(infml)* ['bʌdi] Kumpel ⟨**VT3,** 49⟩
budgie ['bʌdʒi] Wellensittich **I**
buffalo, *pl.* **buffalo** ['bʌfləʊ] Büffel **IV**
*to **build** [bɪld] bauen **II**
building ['bɪldɪŋ] Gebäude **I**
light **bulb** ['laɪt bʌlb] Glühbirne **IV**
bulimic [bʊ'lɪmɪk] bulimisch; ess-/brechsüchtig ⟨**VT1,** 22⟩
bullet ['bʊlɪt] Geschoss; Kugel ⟨**VT4,** 69⟩
bull's-eye ['bʊlsˌaɪ] Mittelpunkt der Zielscheibe **II**
bully ['bʊli] Rabauke, Rüpel, Tyrann **II**
*to give somebody the **bumps** [ˌgɪv ðə 'bʌmps] jemanden hochwerfen und wieder auffangen **I**
to **bump** [bʌmp] (an)stoßen, stoßen **I**
bumpy ['bʌmpi] holprig **II**
bun [bʌn] Brötchen **IV**
bunch [bʌntʃ] Bündel; Haufen; Packen ⟨**VT3,** 50⟩; **VT4,** 64
burger ['bɜːgə] Hamburger **I**
burglary ['bɜːgləri] Einbruch **VT4,** 64
burial society [ˌberiəl sə'saɪəti] Bestattungsverein ⟨**VT4,** 70⟩
*to **burn** [bɜːn] (ver)brennen **II**
bursary ['bɜːsri] Stipendium ⟨**VT4,** 66⟩
*to **burst** [bɜːst] bersten; platzen **III**
at the **Burtons'** [ət ðə 'bɜːtnz] bei den Burtons **II**
to **bury** ['beri] begraben; beerdigen **IV**
bus [bʌs] Bus **I**
by (bus) [baɪ] mit (dem Bus), per **I**
bush [bʊʃ] Busch, Strauch **I**
business ['bɪznɪs] Geschäft; Branche **I**
on business [ɒn 'bɪznɪs] geschäftlich **I**

busy ['bɪzi] beschäftigt; belebt; voller Menschen **I**
but [bʌt; bət] bis auf; außer **IV**
but [bʌt; bət] aber **I**
cigarette **butt** [sɪgr'et ˌbʌt] Zigarettenstummel **VT2,** 36
butter ['bʌtə] Butter **II**
butterfly ['bʌtəflaɪ] Schmetterling **IV**
*to **buy** [baɪ] kaufen **I**
buzz [bʌz] Begeisterung; Kick ⟨**VT1,** 17⟩
by [baɪ] von **I**; bei; an **I**; bis **III**
by (bus) [baɪ] mit (dem Bus), per **I**
by chance [baɪ 'tʃɑ:nts] zufällig **IV**
by mistake [ˌbaɪ mɪ'steɪk] versehentlich **III**
by oneself [ˌbaɪ‿wʌn'self] allein **III**
by the way [ˌbaɪ ðə 'weɪ] übrigens **III**
Bye! [baɪ] Tschüss! **I**
to **bypass** ['baɪpɑ:s] umgehen ⟨**VT2,** 32⟩

C

cab [kæb] Taxi ⟨**VT2,** 32⟩; Führerhaus ⟨**VT4,** 69⟩
cabbage ['kæbɪdʒ] Kohl; Kraut **VT5,** 76
cabin ['kæbɪn] Hütte **III**
cable ['keɪbl] Kabel **IV**
cactus ['kæktəs] Kaktus **III**
café ['kæfeɪ] Café **I**
cafeteria [ˌkæfɪ'tɪərɪə] Cafeteria **VT3,** 43
cake [keɪk] Kuchen **I**
calculus ['kælkjələs] Differential- und Integralrechnung ⟨**VT3,** 42⟩
calendar ['kæləndə] Kalender **I**
calf, *pl.* **calves** [kɑ:f; kɑ:vz] Kalb **II**
Californian [ˌkælɪ'fɔ:niən] kalifornisch; Kalifornier(in) **IV**
call [kɔ:l] Anruf **I**; Ruf **III**
to **call** [kɔ:l] (an)rufen; Bescheid geben **I**; nennen **II**
to **be called** [bi: 'kɔ:ld] heißen, genannt werden **II**
caller ['kɔ:lə] Anrufer(in) **II**
callous ['kæləs] kaltschnäuzig ⟨**VT4,** 71⟩
to **calm** down [ˌkɑ:m 'daʊn] sich beruhigen **IV**
calorie; calory ['kælri] Kilokalorie ⟨**VT1,** 22⟩
calory; calorie ['kælri] Kilokalorie ⟨**VT1,** 22⟩
camera ['kæmrə] Kamera, Fotoapparat **I**
camp [kæmp] Camp; Lager **III**
to **camp** [kæmp] campen, zelten, kampieren **III**
campaign [kæm'peɪn] Kampagne; Aktion **IV**
campfire ['kæmpfaɪə] Lagerfeuer **III**
camping ['kæmpɪŋ] Camping, Zelten **II**
campsite ['kæmpsaɪt] Campingplatz, Zeltplatz **III**
campus ['kæmpəs] Campus; Hochschulgelände **VT1,** 13

can [kæn] Dose; Büchse **IV**
trash can *(AE)* ['træʃ kæn] Mülleimer **IV**
can [kæn; kən] kann, können **I**
can't [kɑ:nt] nicht können **I**
I can't be bothered. [aɪ ˌkɑ:nt bi: 'bɒðəd] Ich habe keine Lust.; Ich kann mich nicht dazu aufraffen. **IV**
I can't face *(+ gerund)* [aɪ ˌkænt 'feɪs] Ich sehe mich außer Stande (zu …) **IV**
canal [kə'næl] Kanal **IV**
candle ['kændl] Kerze **I**
candy *(AE)* ['kændi] Süßigkeiten **II**
sugar **cane** [ˌʃʊgə 'keɪŋ] Zuckerrohr ⟨**VT4,** 56⟩
canoeing [kə'nu:ɪŋ] Kanufahren **II**
canvas ['kænvəs] Leinwand ⟨**VT2,** 38⟩
canyon ['kænjən] Canyon **II**
cap [kæp] Kappe, Mütze **II**
capable *(of + gerund)* ['keɪpəbl] fähig, im Stande **VT1,** 9
capacity [kə'pæsɪti] Kapazität; Vermögen ⟨**VT3,** 45⟩
capital ['kæpɪtl] Hauptstadt **I**
capital letter [ˌkæpɪtl 'letə] Großbuchstabe **VT5,** 83
capitalist ['kæpɪtlɪst] Kapitalist; kapitalistisch **IV**
caption ['kæpʃn] Untertitel; Bildunterschrift **III**
to **capture** ['kæptʃə] ergreifen; erobern; einfangen **VT3,** 42; **VT5,** 79
car [kɑ:] Auto **I**
car park ['kɑ: ˌpɑ:k] Parkplatz; Parkhaus **III**
carbon-based ['kɑ:bnˌbeɪst] kohlenstoffbasiert ⟨**VT5,** 74⟩
card [kɑ:d] Karte **I**
Valentine's card ['væləntaɪnz ˌkɑ:d] Valentinskarte **III**
cardboard ['kɑ:dbɔ:d] Pappe; Karton **VT5,** 77
care [keə] Pflege; Behandlung; Betreuung **IV**; Sorge **IV**
to **care** *(about/for)* [keə] sich kümmern (um); sich interessieren (für); wichtig nehmen **IV**
career [kə'rɪə] Beruf; Laufbahn **IV**
careful ['keəfl] vorsichtig; sorgfältig **II**
caretaker *(BE)* ['keəˌteɪkə] Hausmeister(in) **III**
cargo, *pl.* **cargoes** ['kɑ:gəʊ] Ladung, Fracht **IV**
Caribbean [ˌkærɪ'bi:ən] karibisch **IV**
carnival ['kɑ:nɪvl] Karneval **II**
carpet ['kɑ:pɪt] Teppich **IV**
fitted carpet *(BE)* [ˌfɪtɪd 'kɑ:pɪt] Teppichboden ⟨**VT5,** 87⟩
armoured personnel **carrier** [ˌɑ:məd pɜ:sˌnel 'kærɪə] gepanzerter Mannschaftstransportwagen ⟨**VT4,** 62⟩
carrot ['kærət] Karotte ⟨**VT1,** 22⟩
to **carry** ['kæri] tragen **I**

to **carry on** *(with/+ gerund)* [ˌkæri‿'ɒn] weiterführen; weitermachen (mit etw.) **IV**
to **carry out** [ˌkæri‿'aʊt] ausführen; durchführen **IV**
to **cart** [kɑ:t] karren; fahren ⟨**VT4,** 58⟩
carton ['kɑ:tn] Karton *(Verbundverpackung)* **III**
cartoon [kɑ:'tu:n] Cartoon; Zeichentrickfilm **I**
cartoonist [kɑ:'tu:nɪst] Karikaturist(in) **IV**
case [keɪs] Fall **IV**
in case [ɪn 'keɪs] falls; für den Fall, dass … **II**
pencil case ['pentsl ˌkeɪs] Federmäppchen **I**
cash [kæʃ] Bargeld **IV**
casino [kə'si:nəʊ] Casino **IV**
to **cast** [kɑ:st] Casting; Rollenbesetzung **IV**
*to **cast** [kɑ:st] werfen ⟨**VT2,** 38⟩
castle ['kɑ:sl] Schloss; Burg **I**
cat [kæt] Katze **I**
*to **catch** [kætʃ] fangen **II**
category ['kætəgri] Kategorie; Klasse **VT5,** 80
catering ['keɪtrɪŋ] Gastronomie; Verpflegung **VT2,** 34
Catholic ['kæθlɪk] Katholik(in); katholisch **III**
cattle *(pl. only)* ['kætl] (Rind-)Vieh **II**
cattle drive ['kætl ˌdraɪv] Viehtrieb **II**
cause [kɔ:z] Ursache; Grund **IV**
headliner cause [ˌhedlaɪnə 'kɔ:z] schlagzeilenwürdiger Anlass **VT2,** 26
to **cause** [kɔ:z] verursachen **III**
cautious ['kɔ:ʃəs] behutsam; vorsichtig ⟨**VT2,** 31⟩
CCTV (closed-circuit TV) [ˌsi:si:ti:'vi:] Fernsehüberwachungsanlage ⟨**VT5,** 79⟩
CD [si:'di:] CD **I**
CD player [ˌsi:'di: ˌpleɪə] CD-Spieler **I**
CD-ROM [ˌsi:di:'rɒm] CD-ROM **II**
ceiling ['si:lɪŋ] (Zimmer-)Decke **I**
to **celebrate** ['seləbreɪt] feiern **II**
celebration [ˌselə'breɪʃn] Feier **II**
celebrity [sə'lebrəti] Prominente(r); berühmte Person **VT2,** 39; **VT3,** 48
padded **cell** [ˌpædɪd 'sel] Gummizelle ⟨**VT5,** 87⟩
cellphone *(AE)* ['selfəʊn] Handy, Mobiltelefon **III**
Celtic ['keltɪk; 'seltɪk] keltisch **II**
census ['sentsəs] Volkszählung ⟨**VT2,** 24⟩
cent [sent] Cent *(Währung)* **IV**
central ['sentrl] zentral **IV**
centre ['sentə] Zentrum **I**
activity centre [æk'tɪvəti ˌsentə] Jugendzentrum **II**
city centre [ˌsɪti 'sentə] Stadtzentrum, Stadtmitte **I**

shopping centre ['ʃɒpɪŋ ˌsentə] Einkaufszentrum **I**
to **centre around** ['sentər‿əˌraʊnd] sich drehen um ⟨**VT1**, 22⟩
century ['sentʃri] Jahrhundert **II**
cereal ['sɪəriəl] Zerealie; Getreideprodukt *(z. B. Cornflakes oder Müsli)* **IV**
ceremony ['serɪməni] Zeremonie **IV**
certain ['sɜ:tn] bestimmt; sicher **III**
certificate [sə'tɪfɪkət] Zertifikat; Bescheinigung; Urkunde; Zeugnis **IV**
chain [tʃeɪn] Kette **IV**
chair [tʃeə] Stuhl **I**
chairperson ['tʃeəˌpɜ:sn] Vorsitzende(r) **IV**
chalk [tʃɔ:k] Kreide **VT3**, 42
challenge ['tʃælɪndʒ] Herausforderung **IV**
to **challenge** ['tʃælɪndʒ] herausfordern; in Frage stellen **IV**
chamber ['tʃeɪmbə] Kammer ⟨**VT3**, 42⟩
champion ['tʃæmpiən] Gewinner; Champion **I**
chance [tʃɑ:nts] Chance, Möglichkeit, Gelegenheit **II**
by chance [baɪ 'tʃɑ:nts] zufällig **IV**
change [tʃeɪndʒ] Wechsel, Änderung **II**
to **change** [tʃeɪndʒ] tauschen, wechseln; (sich) ändern **I**; umsteigen **II**
to **change sth into sth** [tʃeɪndʒ] in … verwandeln **II**
changing room ['tʃeɪndʒɪŋ ˌrʊm] Umkleideraum **III**
to **change one's mind** [tʃeɪndʒ] seine Meinung ändern **II**
channel ['tʃænl] Kanal; Programm **IV**
chaos ['keɪɒs] Chaos; Durcheinander **II**
chapter ['tʃæptə] Kapitel **VT2**, 26
character ['kærəktə] Charakter, Figur **II**
characteristic [ˌkærəktə'rɪstɪk] typisches Merkmal **III**
to **characterize** ['kærəktraɪz] charakterisieren **IV**
*to **be in charge (of)** [bi:‿ɪn 'tʃɑ:dʒ] die Verantwortung tragen (für); leiten **IV**
charity ['tʃærɪti] Wohltätigkeitsverein; tätige Nächstenliebe **II**
chart [tʃɑ:t] Diagramm; Tabelle; Grafik **IV**
pie chart ['paɪ ˌtʃɑ:t] Kuchendiagramm; Tortendiagramm **IV**
to **chart a course** [ˌtʃɑ:t‿ə 'kɔ:s] einen Kurs festlegen ⟨**VT5**, 81⟩
to **chase** [tʃeɪs] verfolgen, jagen **I**
to **chat** [tʃæt] chatten *(sich online unterhalten)*; plaudern **IV**
cheap [tʃi:p] billig **II**
to **cheat (on sb)** [tʃi:t] jmdn betrügen **IV**
to **check** [tʃek] (über)prüfen; kontrollieren **I**
Let's check! [lets 'tʃek] Lass(t) uns überprüfen! **I**
to **check sb/sth out** *(AE infml)* [ˌtʃek‿'aʊt] jmdn/etw. unter die Lupe nehmen **IV**
check-in ['tʃekɪn] Gepäckaufgabe **II**
cheek [tʃi:k] Wange **IV**
cheer [tʃɪə] Jubel **III**
three cheers for … [ˌθri: 'tʃɪəz fə] ein dreifaches Hoch auf … ⟨**VT3**, 51⟩
to **cheer** [tʃɪə] (zu)jubeln, anfeuern **II**
to **cheer up** [tʃɪer‿'ʌp] wieder guten Mutes sein **IV**
cheerleader ['tʃɪəˌli:də] Cheerleader *(Mädchen, das in einer Gruppe eine Sportmannschaft anfeuert)* **III**
cheese [tʃi:z] Käse **I**
chef [ʃef] Koch; Küchenchef **IV**
chemistry ['kemɪstri] Chemie **IV**
to **chew** [tʃu:] kauen **VT2**, 36
chewing gum ['tʃu:ɪŋ ˌgʌm] Kaugummi **IV**
chick [tʃɪk] Küken **I**
chicken ['tʃɪkɪn] Huhn, Hähnchen **I**
chief [tʃi:f] Häuptling **II**
chiefdom ['tʃi:fdəm] Stammesfürstentum ⟨**VT4**, 59⟩
child, *pl.* **children** ['tʃaɪld; 'tʃɪldrn] Kind **I**
only child [ˌəʊnli 'tʃaɪld] Einzelkind **IV**
chili ['tʃɪli] Chili **IV**
to **chill** [tʃɪl] abkühlen; sich abregen ⟨**VT3**, 50⟩
chimney ['tʃɪmni] Kamin **IV**
chimpanzee [ˌtʃɪmpn'zi:] Schimpanse ⟨**VT3**, 49⟩
chin [tʃɪn] Kinn **VT1**, 15; **VT5**, 76
Chinese [tʃaɪ'ni:z] chinesisch; Chinese, Chinesin **II**
chip *(AE)* [tʃɪp] Kartoffelchip **I**
chips pl. (BE) [tʃɪps] Pommes frites **I**
fish and chips [ˌfɪʃ‿n‿'tʃɪps] Fisch und Pommes frites **I**
chocolate ['tʃɒklət] Schokolade **I**
choice [tʃɔɪs] Wahl; Auswahl **IV**
to **choke** [tʃəʊk] drosseln; würgen; sich verschlucken **VT4**, 62
*to **choose** [tʃu:z; tʃəʊz] (aus)wählen **I**
chorus ['kɔ:rəs] Refrain **VT1**, 20; **VT2**, 28; **VT3**, 49; **VT4**, 60; ⟨**VT5**, 87⟩
Christian ['krɪstʃən] Christ(in) **II**
church [tʃɜ:tʃ] Kirche **I**
cigarette [ˌsɪgr'et] Zigarette **IV**
cigarette butt [sɪgr'et ˌbʌt] Zigarettenstummel **VT2**, 36
cinema ['sɪnəmə] Kino **I**
circle ['sɜ:kl] Kreis **I**
to **circle** ['sɜ:kl] kreisen **III**
circuit ['sɜ:kɪt] Schaltkreis ⟨**VT1**, 13⟩
circumstances *(pl.)* ['sɜ:kəmstæntsɪz] Umstände **IV**
to **cite** [saɪt] anführen; zitieren ⟨**VT3**, 48⟩
citizen ['sɪtɪzn] Bürger(in); Staatsangehörige(r) **IV**
city ['sɪti] Stadt; Großstadt **I**
city centre [ˌsɪti 'sentə] Stadtzentrum, Stadtmitte **I**
civil liberty [ˌsɪvl 'lɪbəti] Bürgerrecht **VT5**, 79
Civil Rights Act [ˌsɪvl 'raɪts‿ækt] Bürgerrechtsgesetz **VT2**, 24
civil servant [ˌsɪvl 'sɜ:vnt] Beamter; Beamtin **VT4**, 61
civil war [ˌsɪvl 'wɔ:] Bürgerkrieg **III**
civilization [ˌsɪvlaɪ'zeɪʃn] Zivilisation **IV**
to **claim** [kleɪm] behaupten; beanspruchen **IV**
to **clamber** ['klæmbə] klettern; erklimmen ⟨**VT3**, 47⟩
to **clamp down** [ˌklæmp 'daʊn] strikter werden ⟨**VT3**, 44⟩
to **clap** [klæp] klatschen **I**
class [klɑ:s] Schulklasse, Klasse **I**; Kurs, Unterricht **II**
in class [ɪn 'klɑ:s] in/vor der Klasse **I**
working class [ˌwɜ:kɪŋ 'klɑ:s] Arbeiterklasse **IV**
classic ['klæsɪk] klassisch; Klassiker **IV**
classical ['klæsɪkl] klassisch ⟨**VT2**, 30⟩
classmate ['klɑ:smeɪt] Klassenkamerad(in); Mitschüler(in) **VT2**, 26
classroom ['klɑ:srʊm] Klassenzimmer **I**
clause [klɔ:z] Satz *(Teil eines Satzgefüges)* **II**
contact clause ['kɒntækt ˌklɔ:z] *Relativsatz ohne Relativpronomen* **II**
defining relative clause [dɪˌfaɪnɪŋ ˌrelətɪv 'klɔ:z] notwendiger Relativsatz **IV**
non-defining relative clause [ˌnɒndɪfaɪnɪŋ ˌrelətɪv 'klɔ:z] nicht notwendiger Relativsatz **IV**
relative clause [ˌrelətɪv 'klɔ:z] Relativsatz **II**
to **clean** [kli:n] säubern, reinigen **I**
clean [kli:n] sauber **III**
to **be clean out of impressions** [bi: ˌkli:n‿aʊt‿əv‿ɪm'preʃnz] komplett frei sein von Eindrücken ⟨**VT1**, 13⟩
cleaner ['kli:nə] Raumpfleger(in), Putzkraft **III**
to **clear** [klɪə] frei machen; ausräumen; abräumen **IV**
to **clear one's throat** [ˌklɪə wʌnz 'θrəʊt] sich räuspern **VT1**, 13
clear [klɪə] klar **II**
slum **clearance** ['slʌm ˌklɪərnts] Slumbereinigung; Slumsanierung ⟨**VT4**, 58⟩
clerk [klɑ:k; klɜ:rk] Angestellte(r) **III**
clever ['klevə] schlau, klug, intelligent **II**
cliché ['kli:ʃeɪ] Klischee **VT1**, 10
to **click** [klɪk] klicken **IV**
client [klaɪənt] Klient(in); Kunde; Kundin **IV**
cliff [klɪf] Klippe; Kliff **VT1**, 16; ⟨**VT1**, 17⟩
climate ['klaɪmət] Klima **III**
climax ['klaɪmæks] Höhepunkt **IV**

to climb ['klaɪm] klettern, (be)steigen **II**
*__to cling (to)__ ['klɪŋ] sich festhalten (an), sich festklammern (an) **I**
video **clip** ['vɪdiəʊ klɪp] Videoclip **IV**
clipping ['klɪpɪŋ] Ausschnitt ⟨**VT4,** 71⟩
clock [klɒk] Uhr **II**
o'clock [ə'klɒk] Uhr *(Zeitangabe bei vollen Stunden)* **I**
to **close** [kləʊz] schließen **IV**
close [kləʊs] eng, knapp **II**
close (to) [kləʊs] nahe (bei) **III**
at close range [ət ˌkləʊs 'reɪndʒ] aus nächster Nähe ⟨**VT4,** 62⟩
closed [kləʊzd] geschlossen **I**
cloth [klɒθ] Tuch; Gewebe; Stoff **IV**
clothes *pl.* [kləʊðz] Kleider, Kleidung **I**
clothing ['kləʊðɪŋ] Kleidung **III**
cloud [klaʊd] Wolke **I**
club [klʌb] Club, Verein **II**
golf club ['gɒlf ˌklʌb] Golfschläger **III**
health club ['helθ ˌklʌb] Fitnessklub **II**
clue [klu:] Hinweis, Spur, Schlüssel **II**
cluster ['klʌstə] Klumpen; Anhäufung ⟨**VT5,** 75⟩
CO [ˌkɒlr'ɑ:dəʊ] Colorado *(Abkürzung)* **II**
coach [kəʊtʃ] Reisebus **III**; Trainer(in) **III**
coal [kəʊl] Kohle **II**
coarse [kɔ:s] grob; rau ⟨**VT5,** 77⟩
coast [kəʊst] Küste **I**
coastal ['kəʊstl] Küsten- **VT4,** 56
coat [kəʊt] Mantel **II**
co-ed ['kəʊˌed] gemischt *(Schule)* ⟨**VT3,** 41⟩
coffee ['kɒfi:] Kaffee **II**
coffee bar ['kɒfi: ˌbɑ:] Café **III**
coffin ['kɒfɪn] Sarg ⟨**VT4,** 70⟩
cognitive enhancement [ˌkɒgnətɪv‿ɪn'hɑ:ntsmənt] Wahrnehmungssteigerung ⟨**VT5,** 82⟩
coin [kɔɪn] Münze **III**
to **coin** [kɔɪn] prägen ⟨**VT5,** 83⟩
cola ['kəʊlə] Cola **III**
cold [kəʊld] Erkältung; Kälte **III**
cold [kəʊld] kalt **I**
collage [kɒ'lɑ:ʒ] Collage **I**
to **collapse** [kə'læps] kollabieren; zusammenbrechen **IV**
to **collect** [kə'lekt] sammeln **I**
college ['kɒlɪdʒ] College; Institut **II**
to **collide** [kə'laɪd] kollidieren; zusammenstoßen **VT5,** 85
collision [kə'lɪʒn] Kollision; Zusammenstoß **VT1,** 16; **VT5,** 85
colonial [kə'ləʊniəl] kolonial ⟨**VT2,** 38⟩; **VT4,** 57
colonist ['kɒlənɪst] Kolonist(in), Siedler(in) **II**
to **colonize** ['kɒlənaɪz] kolonisieren **III**
colony ['kɒləni] Kolonie **III**
colored *(AE)* ['kʌləd] bunt, farbig **II**
colour ['kʌlə] Farbe **I**
What colour is/are . . . ? [ˌwɒt 'kʌlər‿ɪz/ ɑ:] Welche Farbe hat/haben . . . ? **I**
to **comb** (one's hair) ['kəʊm] (sich) kämmen **IV**
combination [ˌkɒmbɪ'neɪʃn] Kombination **VT1,** 14
*to **come** [kʌm] kommen **I**
Come on! [kʌm‿'ɒn] Komm(t)! **I**
to **come across (sb/sth)** [ˌkʌm‿ə'krɒs] begegnen; antreffen; vorfinden **VT4,** 62
to **come around** [ˌkʌm‿ə'raʊnd] einlenken **VT5,** 75
to **come in** [kʌm‿'ɪn] hereinkommen **I**
to **come in handy** [ˌkʌm‿ɪn 'hændi] gelegen kommen **VT5,** 83
to **come to terms with** [ˌkʌm tə 'tɜ:mz wɪð] zurechtkommen mit; sich arrangieren mit ⟨**VT5,** 81⟩
to **come true** [ˌkʌm 'tru:] wahr werden; in Erfüllung gehen **III**
to **come up with** [kʌm‿'ʌp wɪð] sich etw. einfallen lassen **VT2,** 37
comedy ['kɒmədi] Komödie **IV**
comfort ['kʌmpfət] Komfort; Behaglichkeit; Trost **VT2,** 27
to **comfort** ['kʌmpfət] trösten; ermutigen **VT1,** 10
comfortable ['kʌmpftəbl] komfortabel; bequem **III**
comic ['kɒmɪk] Comic(heft) **I**
comma ['kɒmə] Komma **II**
command [kə'mɑ:nd] Befehl **III**
to **be in command** [bi:‿ɪn kə'mɑ:nd] das Kommando haben; den Oberbefehl haben **VT3,** 43
lieutenant **commander** [lu:ˌtenənt kə'mɑ:ndə; lefˌtenənt kə'mɑ:ndə] Kapitänleutnant ⟨**VT5,** 72⟩
comment ['kɒment] Kommentar **III**
to **comment (on)** ['kɒment] kommentieren **IV**
commercial [kə'mɜ:ʃl] Werbespot **III**
commission [kə'mɪʃn] Kommission; Provision; Auftrag **IV**
to **commit** oneself to [kə'mɪt] sich (jmdm/ etw.) verschreiben/verpflichten/ widmen; sich binden an **VT4,** 61
to **commit a crime** [kəˌmɪt‿ə 'kraɪm] ein Verbrechen begehen **VT4,** 63
to **commit suicide** [kəˌmɪt 'su:ɪsaɪd] Selbstmord begehen **VT1,** 11
common ['kɒmən] gebräuchlich; verbreitet **IV**
common sense [ˌkɒmən 'sents] gesunder Menschenverstand **VT3,** 43
to **have sth in common** [ˌhæv‿ɪn 'kɒmən] etw. gemeinsam haben **IV**
to **communicate** [kə'mju:nɪkeɪt] kommunizieren, sich verständigen **III**
communication [kəˌmju:nɪ'keɪʃn] Kommunikation ⟨**VT5,** 81⟩
communications tower [ˌkəmju:nɪ'keɪʃnz ˌtaʊə] Fernmeldeturm; Sendemast **VT5,** 85
community [kə'mju:nəti] Gemeinde; Gemeinschaft **I**
company ['kʌmpəni] Gesellschaft; Firma; Kompanie **II**
comparative [kəm'pærətɪv] Komparativ **II**
to **compare** (with/to) [kəm'peə] vergleichen (mit) **II**
comparison [kəm'pærɪsn] Vergleich **IV**
to **compel** [kəm'pel] zwingen ⟨**VT4,** 61⟩
to **compete (with)** [kəm'pi:t] konkurrieren (mit); sich messen (mit); in Wettbewerb treten (mit) **IV**
competition [ˌkɒmpə'tɪʃn] Wettbewerb, Turnier **II**
competitive [kəm'petɪtɪv] konkurrenzbetont; konkurrenzfähig **IV**
competitor [kəm'petɪtə] Teilnehmer(in); Mitbewerber(in) **II**
to **complain** [kəm'pleɪn] sich beschweren, sich beklagen **II**
complaint [kəm'pleɪnt] Beschwerde **VT3,** 43
to **complete** [kəm'pli:t] vervollständigen **II**
complete [kəm'pli:t] vollständig **II**
complicated ['kɒmplɪkeɪtɪd] kompliziert **VT4,** 61
compliment ['kɒmplɪmənt] Kompliment **VT1,** 10
to **compliment** ['kɒmplɪment] Komplimente machen **VT1,** 10
to **compose** [kəm'pəʊz] komponieren; verfassen; zusammensetzen ⟨**VT3,** 44⟩
compound ['kɒmpaʊnd] Kompositum *(zusammengesetztes Wort)* **II**
comprehension [ˌkɒmprɪ'hentʃn] Verständnis; Verstehen **IV**
comprehensive school [kɒmprɪ'hentsɪv ˌsku:l] Gesamtschule ⟨**VT3,** 55⟩
compulsory [kəm'pʌlsri] verpflichtend; obligatorisch **VT1,** 8; **VT2,** 34
computer [ˌkəm'pju:tə] Computer **I**
computer programmer [kəmˌpju:tə 'prəʊgræmə] Programmierer(in) **IV**
computer skills [kəm'pju:tə ˌskɪlz] EDV-Kenntnisse **IV**
conceivable [kən'si:vəbl] denkbar; vorstellbar ⟨**VT5,** 77⟩
to **concentrate** ['kɒntsntreɪt] (sich) konzentrieren **III**
concept ['kɒnsept] Begriff; Konzept **VT5,** 75
to **concern** [kən'sɜ:n] betreffen; beunruhigen **VT1,** 9
As far as . . . is/are concerned, . . . [kən'sɜ:nd] Soweit es . . . betrifft, . . .; Was . . . angeht, . . . **IV**
concert ['kɒnsət] Konzert **II**
conclusion [kən'klu:ʒn] Schluss; Schlussfolgerung **IV**

to **jump to conclusions** [ˌdʒʌmp tə kən'klu:ʒnz] voreilige Schlüsse ziehen **VT1**, 10
concrete ['kɒŋkri:t] Beton **VT5**, 77
condition [kən'dɪʃn] Kondition; Bedingung **III**
living conditions *(pl.)* ['lɪvɪŋ kənˌdɪʃnz] Lebensbedingungen **IV**
to **confide** in sb [kən'faɪd‿ɪn] sich jmdm anvertrauen ⟨**VT5**, 82⟩
confidence ['kɒnfɪdnts] Vertrauen; Zuversicht **IV**
confident ['kɒnfɪdnt] selbstsicher; überzeugt **VT1**, 10; **VT4**, 64
conflict ['kɒnflɪkt] Konflikt **III**
to **conflict** [kən'flɪkt] kollidieren; im Widerspruch stehen **VT5**, 72
to **confront** [kən'frʌnt] konfrontieren; entgegentreten; sich stellen **VT1**, 10; **VT4**, 66
confusion [kən'fju:ʒn] Verwirrung; Verwechslung ⟨**VT2**, 31⟩
to **congratulate** [kən'grætʃʊleɪt] gratulieren ⟨**VT1**, 23⟩
Congress ['kɒŋgres] Congress *(Parlament in den USA)* **IV**
conjunction [kən'dʒʌŋkʃn] Konjunktion **III**
to **connect (to)** [kə'nekt] verbinden (mit) **I**
connoisseur [ˌkɒnə'sɜ:] Kenner(in) ⟨**VT4**, 56⟩
to **conquer** ['kɒŋkə] erobern **II**
conscious ['kɒntʃəs] bewusst **VT5**, 74
consciousness ['kɒntʃəsnəs] Bewusstsein ⟨**VT1**, 19⟩
consent [kən'sent] Zustimmung; Einwilligung **VT1**, 8
consequently ['kɒntsɪkwəntli] folglich; somit ⟨**VT2**, 38⟩
conservation [ˌkɒntsə'veɪʃn] Naturschutz; Umweltschutz ⟨**VT4**, 67⟩
conservationist [ˌkɒntsə'veɪʃnɪst] Naturschützer(in); Umweltschützer(in) ⟨**VT4**, 67⟩
to **consider** [kən'sɪdə] betrachten; erwägen **IV**
considerable [kən'sɪdrəbl] beträchtlich **IV**
consideration [kənˌsɪdr'eɪʃn] Rücksicht **IV**
to **consolidate** [kən'sɒlɪdeɪt] vereinigen; zusammenlegen **VT1**, 12
to **construct** [kən'strʌkt] bauen; konstruieren **IV**
construction [kən'strʌkʃn] Konstruktion; Aufbau **IV**
consultancy [kən'sʌltntsi] Beratung; Beratungsunternehmen ⟨**VT5**, 82⟩
consultant [kən'sʌltnt] Berater(in) ⟨**VT5**, 82⟩
to **consume** [kən'sju:m] konsumieren; verbrauchen **VT1**, 8
consumer [kən'sju:mə] Konsument(in); Verbraucher(in) **IV**
contact ['kɒntækt] Kontakt **II**
contact clause ['kɒntækt ˌklɔ:z] *Relativsatz ohne Relativpronomen* **II**
to **contact** ['kɒntækt] kontaktieren **IV**
to **contain** [kən'teɪn] enthalten **IV**
to **contaminate** [kən'tæmɪneɪt] kontaminieren; verseuchen **VT2**, 33
contemporary [kən'temprəri] zeitgenössisch; Gegenwarts- **VT4**, 64
content ['kɒntent] Inhalt **IV**
contention [kən'tentʃn] Behauptung ⟨**VT5**, 79⟩
contest ['kɒntest] Wettbewerb **IV**
context ['kɒntekst] Kontext, Zusammenhang **II**
continent ['kɒntɪnənt] Kontinent, Erdteil **III**
to **continue** [kən'tɪnju:] fortfahren; andauern **IV**
contract ['kɒntrækt] Vertrag **VT4**, 58
contrast ['kɒntrɑ:st] Kontrast; Gegensatz **IV**
to **contribute** [kən'trɪbju:t] beitragen; mitwirken **VT5**, 85
contribution [ˌkɒntrɪ'bju:ʃn] Beitrag **IV**
to **contrive** [kən'traɪv] ersinnen; ausklügeln ⟨**VT5**, 76⟩
control [kən'trəʊl] Kontrolle; Steuerung ⟨**VT1**, 19⟩; **VT2**, 25; **VT5**, 79
to **control** [kən'trəʊl] kontrollieren; beherrschen **II**
convenient [kən'vi:niənt] bequem; zweckmäßig **IV**
conventional [kən'ventʃnl] konventionell; herkömmlich; üblich **VT3**, 40
conversation [ˌkɒnvə'seɪʃn] Konversation, Gespräch **II**
to **convey** [kən'veɪ] übermitteln; transportieren; ausdrücken **VT5**, 83
to **convince** [kən'vɪnts] überzeugen **IV**
to **cook** [kʊk] kochen **II**
cookie *(AE)* ['kʊki] Keks **II**
to **cool** [ku:l] kühlen **IV**
cool [ku:l] cool, prima **II**; kühl **III**
to **cooperate** [ˌkəʊ'ɒprət] kooperieren; zusammenarbeiten ⟨**VT4**, 67⟩
to **cope with** [kəʊp] bewältigen; fertig werden mit ⟨**VT1**, 23⟩
copy ['kɒpi] Kopie **II**
to **copy** ['kɒpi] abschreiben, kopieren **I**
cordon ['kɔ:dn] Absperrkette ⟨**VT4**, 62⟩
corn [kɔ:n] Korn; Mais **III**
corner ['kɔ:nə] Ecke **III**
to **correct** [kə'rekt] korrigieren, verbessern **I**
correct [kə'rekt] richtig, korrekt **I**
correspondence [ˌkɒrɪ'spɒndənts] Korrespondenz; Schriftwechsel **IV**
corrugated iron [ˌkɒrəgeɪtɪd‿'aɪən] Wellblech ⟨**VT5**, 77⟩
cosmetics *(pl.)* [kɒz'metɪks] Kosmetik **IV**
cost [kɒst] Preis; Kosten **IV**
*to **cost** [kɒst] kosten **III**
costume ['kɒstju:m] Kostüm **II**
cotton ['kɒtn] Baumwolle **IV**
couch [kaʊtʃ] Couch; Sofa **IV**
cougar ['ku:gə] Puma, Berglöwe **II**
to **cough** [kɒf] husten **IV**
could [kʊd] konnte(n) **II**; könnte(n) **II**
council ['kaʊntsl] Gemeinderat; Stadtrat **VT2**, 35; **VT5**, 80
to **count** [kaʊnt] zählen **III**
counter ['kaʊntə] Theke; Tresen; Schalter **IV**
to **counter** ['kaʊntə] kontern; entgegnen ⟨**VT2**, 32⟩
country ['kʌntri] Land; ländliche Gegend, Landschaft **I**; Countrymusik **III**
developing country [dɪˌveləpɪŋ 'kʌntri] Entwicklungsland **IV**
couple ['kʌpl] Paar **III**
a couple of [ə 'kʌpl‿əv] einige, ein paar **IV**
courage ['kʌrɪdʒ] Mut **IV**
courageous [kə'reɪdʒəs] mutig **VT2**, 26
course [kɔ:s] Gang **II**
golf course ['gɒlf ˌkɔ:s] Golfplatz **III**
of course [əv 'kɔ:s] natürlich, selbstverständlich **I**
to **chart a course** [ˌtʃɑ:t‿ə 'kɔ:s] einen Kurs festlegen ⟨**VT5**, 81⟩
court [kɔ:t] Hof; Gericht(shof) **IV**
basketball court ['bɑ:skɪtbɔ:l ˌkɔ:t] Basketballplatz **III**
to **take sb to court** [ˌteɪk tə 'kɔ:t] jmdn verklagen **VT1**, 8; **VT3**, 41
cousin ['kʌzn] Cousin, Cousine **I**
to **cover (up)** ['kʌvə] zudecken **III**
to **cover one's ass** *(vulg)* [ˌkʌvə wʌnz‿'æs] seine Haut retten ⟨**VT3**, 43⟩
cow [kaʊ] Kuh **I**
coward [kaʊəd] Feigling **IV**
cowboy ['kaʊbɔɪ] Cowboy, Rinderhirte **II**
to **crack** [kræk] anknacksen; einen Sprung in etw. machen/bekommen **IV**
crackpot ['krækpɒt] Verrückte(r) ⟨**VT5**, 75⟩
cradle ['kreɪdl] Wiege ⟨**VT1**, 20⟩
arts and crafts [ˌɑ:ts‿nd 'krɑ:fts] Kunsthandwerk **III**
craftsman, *pl.* **craftsmen** ['krɑ:ftsmən] Handwerker **IV**
crap *(vulg)* [kræp] Scheiß ⟨**VT3**, 44⟩
to **crash** [kræʃ] aufschlagen, gegen etwas krachen **I**
crash! [kræʃ] Krach! Bumm!; Zusammenstoß **I**
to **crave** [kreɪv] sich sehnen nach ⟨**VT3**, 48⟩
to **crawl** [krɔ:l] kriechen ⟨**VT3**, 46⟩
craze [kreɪz] Manie; Fimmel; fixe Idee ⟨**VT1**, 16⟩

crazy ['kreɪzi] verrückt **II**; Naturstein- ⟨**VT5,** 77⟩
to be crazy about [bi: 'kreɪzi‿əbaʊt] verrückt sein nach; abfahren auf **III**
cream [kri:m] Creme; Sahne **I**
ice cream [aɪs 'kri:m] Eis, Eiscreme **I**
to **create** [kri'eɪt] (er)schaffen **IV**
creative [kri'eɪtɪv] kreativ **II**
creature ['kri:tʃə] Kreatur; Geschöpf **VT3,** 42; **VT5,** 74
*to **creep** [kri:p] schleichen; kriechen **III**
crescendo *(ital., musikal.)* [krɪ'ʃendəʊ] anwachsende Lautstärke ⟨**VT4,** 62⟩
crew [kru:] Crew, Besatzung, Mannschaft **III**
crime [kraɪm] Verbrechen, Kriminalität **II**
to **commit a crime** [kəˌmɪt‿ə 'kraɪm] ein Verbrechen begehen **VT4,** 63
criminal ['krɪmɪnl] kriminell; verbrecherisch **VT1,** 8
crisis, *pl.* **crises** ['kraɪsɪs] Krise **IV**
crisp *(BE)* [krɪsp] Kartoffelchip **I**
crispy ['krɪspi] knusprig, kross **IV**
critic ['krɪtɪk] Kritiker(in) ⟨**VT1,** 22⟩; **VT3,** 42
critical ['krɪtɪkl] kritisch ⟨**VT4,** 67⟩
criticism ['krɪtɪsɪsm] Kritik **VT4,** 60
to **criticize** ['krɪtɪsaɪz] kritisieren **IV**
crocodile ['krɒkədaɪl] Krokodil **III**
crop [krɒp] Feldfrucht; Ernte **III**
cross [krɒs] Kreuz **III**
to **cross** one's fingers [ˌkrɒs wʌnz 'fɪŋgəz] die Daumen drücken **IV**
crossword (puzzle) ['krɒswɜ:d] Kreuzworträtsel **II**
crowd [kraʊd] Menschenmenge **II**
crowded ['kraʊdɪd] überfüllt **III**
crucial ['kru:ʃl] entscheidend; ausschlaggebend ⟨**VT3,** 50⟩
crudely-drawn ['kru:dli ˌdrɔ:n] grob gezeichnet ⟨**VT4,** 68⟩
cruel ['kru:əl] grausam **II**
crunchy ['krʌntʃi] knusprig; knackig **IV**
to **cry** [kraɪ] schreien, rufen; weinen **I**
to **cull** [kʌl] (als überzählig) abschießen ⟨**VT4,** 69⟩
cultural ['kʌltʃrl] kulturell **II**
culture ['kʌltʃə] Kultur **II**
cumbersome ['kʌmbəsəm] mühsam; lästig ⟨**VT5,** 82⟩
cup [kʌp] Tasse **I**; Pokal; Kelch **III**
cupboard ['kʌbəd] Küchenschrank, Schrank **I**
to **cure** [kjʊə] heilen; kurieren **III**
curious ['kjʊəriəs] neugierig **VT1,** 15; ⟨**VT3,** 50⟩
currency ['kʌrntsi] Währung **VT4,** 56
current ['kʌrnt] Strömung **VT1,** 16; Strom **VT5,** 76
current ['kʌrnt] aktuell; gegenwärtig **VT4,** 57
curriculum, *pl.* **curricula** [kjə'rɪkjələm] Lehrplan ⟨**VT3,** 55⟩
curry ['kʌri] Curry *(Gewürz oder Gericht)* **II**
to **curse** [kɜ:s] fluchen **III**
to **curtail** [kɜ:'teɪl] beschneiden; einschränken ⟨**VT4,** 67⟩
curtain ['kɜ:tn] Vorhang **III**
to **curve** [kɜ:v] krümmen; biegen; kurven **VT5,** 77
custom ['kʌstəm] Brauch, Sitte **II**
custom ['kʌstəm] maßgefertigt **VT3,** 49
customer ['kʌstəmə] Kunde, Kundin **I**
customs ['kʌstəmz] Zoll **IV**
cut [kʌt] Schnittverletzung; Platzwunde **VT1,** 17
short cut ['ʃɔ:t kʌt] Abkürzung **II**
*to **cut** (off) [kʌt‿'ɒf] (ab)schneiden **II**
cute [kju:t] niedlich; süß **III**
CV (= Curriculum Vitae) [ˌsi:'vi:] Lebenslauf **IV**
cybernetic [ˌsaɪbə'netɪk] kybernetisch ⟨**VT5,** 72⟩
to **cycle** ['saɪkl] Rad fahren **IV**
cylinder ['sɪlɪndə] Zylinder; Walze ⟨**VT1,** 18⟩
Czech [tʃek] Tscheche; Tschechin; Tschechisch; tschechisch **VT5,** 73

D

dad [dæd] Papa **I**
daily ['deɪli] täglich **II**
dairy ['deəri] Molkerei **IV**
dam [dæm] Damm; Staumauer **IV**
damage ['dæmɪdʒ] Schaden **III**
to **damage** ['dæmɪdʒ] schaden; beschädigen **III**
dammit *(rude)* ['dæmɪt] verdammt ⟨**VT3,** 43⟩
damn [dæm] verdammt **II**
damp [dæmp] feucht **IV**
dance [dɑ:nts] Tanz **II**
square dance ['skweə ˌdɑ:nts] Square Dance **II**
to **dance** [dɑ:nts] tanzen **II**
danger ['deɪndʒə] Gefahr **III**
dangerous ['deɪndʒrəs] gefährlich **I**
Danish ['deɪnɪʃ] dänisch **II**
to **dare** [deə] wagen **IV**
daredevil ['deəˌdevl] draufgängerisch; waghalsig ⟨**VT1,** 16⟩
dark [dɑ:k] dunkel **I**
darkness ['dɑ:knəs] Dunkelheit **II**
darling ['dɑ:lɪŋ] Liebling ⟨**VT5,** 87⟩
to **dart** [dɑ:t] schießen; stürzen **VT5,** 77
dashboard ['dæʃbɔ:d] Armaturenbrett **VT1,** 13
date [deɪt] Datum **I**
out of date [ˌaʊt‿əv 'deɪt] veraltet **VT2,** 36
to **date** from ['deɪt frəm] zurückgehen auf **II**
daughter ['dɔ:tə] Tochter **II**
day [deɪ] Tag **I**
a day/year off [ə ˌdeɪ‿'ɒf] ein freier Tag/ ein freies Jahr **IV**
every day [ˌevri 'deɪ] jeden Tag **I**
Judgement Day ['dʒʌdʒmənt ˌdeɪ] Tag des Jüngsten Gerichts ⟨**VT5,** 87⟩
some day ['sʌm deɪ] eines Tages **II**
the day before yesterday [ðə ˌdeɪ bɪfɔ: 'jestədeɪ] vorgestern **I**
the other day [ði‿ʌðə 'deɪ] neulich **IV**
these days ['ði:z ˌdeɪz] heutzutage **II**
dead [ded] tot **I**
stone dead [ˌstəʊn 'ded] mausetot ⟨**VT4,** 68⟩
deadline ['dedlaɪn] (Abgabe-)Termin **IV**
deadly ['dedli] tödlich **III**
deaf [def] gehörlos; schwerhörig **III**
deal [di:l] Handel; Abmachung; Übereinkunft ⟨**VT2,** 31⟩
the whole deal [ðə ˌhəʊl 'di:l] alles ⟨**VT5,** 74⟩
*to **deal** with ['di:l wɪð] sich befassen/ umgehen mit **II**
dean [di:n] Dekan ⟨**VT1,** 14⟩
Oh **dear!** ['əʊ ˌdɪə] Oje! **I**
dear [dɪə] lieb **I**
death [deθ] Tod **III**
deathly ['deθli] tödlich; Todes- ⟨**VT3,** 45⟩
debate [dɪ'beɪt] Debatte **IV**
to **debate** [dɪ'beɪt] debattieren **IV**
decade ['dekeɪd] Jahrzehnt ⟨**VT3,** 46⟩; **VT5,** 80
deceit [dɪ'si:t] Täuschung; Betrug ⟨**VT1,** 22⟩
decibel ['desɪbl] Dezibel *(Einheit der Lautstärke)* ⟨**VT3,** 50⟩
to **decide** [dɪ'saɪd] entscheiden **II**
decision [dɪ'sɪʒn] Entscheidung **III**
declaration [ˌdeklə'reɪʃn] Erklärung **III**
to **declare** [dɪ'kleə] erklären **VT4,** 58
to **decorate** ['dekreɪt] dekorieren, verzieren; tapezieren **IV**
decorated ['dekreɪtɪd] dekoriert, geschmückt **II**
decoration [ˌdek'reɪʃn] Dekoration **II**
decrease ['di:kri:s] Abnahme; Verminderung **IV**
to **decrease** [dɪ'kri:s] abnehmen; vermindern **IV**
to **dedicate** ['dedɪkeɪt] widmen **VT2,** 28
to **deduct** [dɪ'dʌkt] abziehen ⟨**VT1,** 11⟩
deep [di:p] tief **III**
deer, *pl.* **deer** [dɪə] Hirsch, Reh; Rotwild **II**
to **defeat** [dɪ'fi:t] besiegen **VT4,** 57
to **defend** [dɪ'fend] verteidigen **IV**
defiance [dɪ'faɪənts] Herausforderung; Trotz **VT2,** 27
defining relative clause [dɪˌfaɪnɪŋ ˌrelətɪv 'klɔ:z] notwendiger Relativsatz **IV**
definite ['defɪnət] definitiv, bestimmt, eindeutig **II**

definition [ˌdefɪ'nɪʃn] Definition; Festlegung **II**
degree [dɪ'gri:] akademischer Grad; Hochschulabschluss **VT3,** 54; Grad **VT4,** 62
to **delay** [dɪ'leɪ] verzögern; aufschieben **VT3,** 42
delayed [dɪ'leɪd] verspätet, verzögert **II**
delicious [dɪ'lɪʃəs] köstlich **II**
to **deliver** [dɪ'lɪvə] liefern **IV**
delivery [dɪ'lɪvri] Lieferung **VT3,** 49
demand [dɪ'mɑ:nd] Bedarf; Verlangen **VT2,** 24
to **demand** [dɪ'mɑ:nd] fordern; verlangen **III**
democracy [dɪ'mɒkrəsi] Demokratie **VT4,** 61
democratic [ˌdemə'krætɪk] demokratisch **VT4,** 61
dentist ['dentɪst] Zahnarzt; Zahnärztin **IV**
to **deny** [dɪ'naɪ] abstreiten; verweigern **VT1,** 9
department [dɪ'pɑ:tmənt] Abteilung **II**
departure [dɪ'pɑ:tʃə] Abflug, Abreise **II**
to **depend** (on) [dɪ'pend] abhängen (von); sich verlassen (auf) **III**
to **depict** [dɪ'pɪkt] darstellen ⟨**VT5,** 76⟩
depressed [dɪ'prest] deprimiert; bedrückt **III**
to **deprive** sb of [dɪ'praɪv] berauben; entziehen **VT4,** 61
deputy ['depjəti] Vize-; stellvertretend ⟨**VT5,** 80⟩
derby ['dɜ:bi] Derby **III**
to **descend** [dɪ'send] herabsteigen; sich herabsenken ⟨**VT3,** 45⟩; ⟨**VT3,** 50⟩
descendant [dɪ'sendənt] Abkömmling; Nachfahre; Nachfahrin ⟨**VT2,** 24⟩; **VT4,** 57
to **describe** [dɪ'skraɪb] beschreiben **II**
description [dɪ'skrɪpʃn] Beschreibung **II**
desert ['dezət] Wüste **IV**
to **deserve** [dɪ'zɜ:v] verdienen **VT2,** 28
design [dɪ'zaɪn] Design; Gestaltung **IV**
graphic design [ˌgræfɪk dɪ'zaɪn] Grafikdesign; grafische Gestaltung **IV**
to **design** [dɪ'zaɪn] entwerfen **II**
designer [dɪ'zaɪnə] Designer(in); Entwickler(in) **IV**
desire [dɪ'zaɪə] Begierde; Verlangen ⟨**VT5,** 87⟩
desk [desk] Schreibtisch **I**
despair [dɪs'peə] Hoffnungslosigkeit; Verzweiflung **VT4,** 64
desperate ['despərət] verzweifelt; hoffnungslos ⟨**VT1,** 23⟩; ⟨**VT3,** 44⟩; ⟨**VT5,** 87⟩
dessert [dɪ'zɜ:t] Dessert, Nachspeise **II**
to **destroy** [dɪ'strɔɪ] zerstören **IV**
detail ['di:teɪl] Detail, Einzelheit **II**
to **detain** [dɪ'teɪn] verhaften; gefangen halten ⟨**VT4,** 63⟩
detective [dɪ'tektɪv] Detektiv(in) **II**
detention [dɪ'tentʃn] Haft; Verhaftung ⟨**VT4,** 63⟩
to **determine** [dɪ'tɜ:mɪn] bestimmen; entschließen ⟨**VT5,** 82⟩
determined [dɪ'tɜ:mɪnd] entschlossen; entschieden; zielstrebig ⟨**VT3,** 50⟩
to **develop** [dɪ'veləp] (sich) entwickeln **IV**
developing country [dɪˌveləpɪŋ 'kʌntri] Entwicklungsland **IV**
development [dɪ'veləpmənt] Entwicklung **IV**
device [dɪ'vaɪs] Gerät, Vorrichtung **III**
stylistic device [staɪˌlɪstɪk dɪ'vaɪs] Stilmittel **VT2,** 29
to **devolve** [dɪ'vɒlv] übergehen **VT2,** 27
to **devote** [dɪ'vəʊt] widmen; verwenden **VT2,** 29
diagram ['daɪəgræm] Diagramm **II**
dialect ['daɪəlekt] Dialekt **I**
dialogue ['daɪəlɒg] Dialog, Gespräch **I**
diamond ['daɪəmənd] Diamant ⟨**VT4,** 56⟩
diary ['daɪəri] Tagebuch; Terminkalender **II**
to **dictate** [dɪk'teɪt] diktieren; vorschreiben **VT1,** 9
dictionary ['dɪkʃnri] Wörterbuch **I**
to **die** [daɪ] sterben **I**
to **diet** [daɪət] Diät halten ⟨**VT1,** 22⟩
to **differ** ['dɪfə] sich unterscheiden; abweichen **VT1,** 8; **VT3,** 40
difference ['dɪfrnts] Unterschied **II**
different ['dɪfrnt] anders, verschieden **I**
difficult ['dɪfɪklt] schwierig **II**
digital ['dɪdʒɪtl] digital **VT5,** 81
dignity ['dɪgnəti] Würde **VT2,** 28
dilemma [daɪ'lemə] Dilemma; Zwangslage ⟨**VT4,** 67⟩
to **diminish** [dɪ'mɪnɪʃ] (sich) verringern **VT2,** 27; abnehmen ⟨**VT5,** 82⟩
dinner ['dɪnə] Abendessen **I**
to **have dinner** [hæv 'dɪnə] zu Abend essen **I**
dip [dɪp] Dip *(cremige Sauce zum Einstippen)* **IV**
to **direct** [dɪ'rekt] leiten; anweisen; Regie führen **IV**
direct [dɪ'rekt] direkt **II**
direct speech [dɪˌrekt 'spi:tʃ] direkte Rede **III**
direction [dɪ'rekʃn] Richtung **III**
director [dɪ'rektə] Direktor(in); Regisseur(in) **III**
dirt [dɜ:t] Schmutz; Dreck ⟨**VT1,** 18⟩
dirt track ['dɜ:t ˌtræk] Feldweg; unbefestigte Straße ⟨**VT4,** 69⟩
dirty ['dɜ:ti] schmutzig **III**
disability [ˌdɪsə'bɪləti] Behinderung; Unfähigkeit **III**
disabled [dɪ'seɪbld] behindert **III**
disadvantage [ˌdɪsəd'vɑ:ntɪdʒ] Nachteil **IV**
disadvantaged [ˌdɪsəd'vɑ:ntɪdʒd] benachteiligt **IV**
to **disappear** [ˌdɪsə'pɪə] verschwinden **III**
disappointed [ˌdɪsə'pɔɪntɪd] enttäuscht **II**
disaster [dɪ'zɑ:stə] Desaster; Katastrophe **III**
recordable **disc** [rɪ'kɔ:dəbl ˌdɪsk] beschreibbare CD ⟨**VT2,** 30⟩
to **discharge** [dɪs'tʃɑ:dʒ] entlassen; freisetzen; entladen **VT1,** 16
discipline ['dɪsɪplɪn] Disziplin **VT3,** 41
disco ['dɪskəʊ] Disco, Diskothek **III**
to **discourage** [dɪs'kʌrɪdʒ] abschrecken; entmutigen **VT3,** 41
to **discover** [dɪ'skʌvə] entdecken **III**
discovery [dɪ'skʌvri] Entdeckung **IV**
to **discriminate** [dɪ'skrɪmɪneɪt] unterscheiden ⟨**VT5,** 82⟩
to **discriminate against** [dɪ'skrɪmɪneɪt‿əˌgentst] diskriminieren; benachteiligen **VT2,** 25
discrimination [dɪˌskrɪmɪ'neɪʃn] Unterscheidung; Diskriminierung **VT2,** 24
to **discuss** [dɪ'skʌs] diskutieren **II**
discussion [dɪ'skʌʃn] Diskussion **II**
disease [dɪ'zi:z] Krankheit **III**
disguise [dɪs'gaɪz] Verkleidung **II**
in disguise [ɪn dɪs'gaɪz] verkleidet **II**
disgusting [dɪs'gʌstɪŋ] ekelhaft; widerlich ⟨**VT3,** 45⟩
dish [dɪʃ] Gericht, Speise **II**
dislike [dɪ'slaɪk] Abneigung **II**
eating **disorder** ['i:tɪŋ dɪˌsɔ:də] Essstörung ⟨**VT1,** 22⟩
to **disperse** [dɪs'pɜ:s] (sich) zerstreuen; (sich) verteilen ⟨**VT4,** 62⟩
display [dɪ'spleɪ] Vorführung; Ausstellung; Schaukasten; Anzeige **IV**
to **disrupt** [dɪs'rʌpt] stören; zerbrechen; sprengen **VT3,** 40
disruption [dɪs'rʌpʃn] Störung; Bruch; Zerrüttung **VT3,** 40
distance ['dɪstnts] Distanz, Entfernung **III**
distant ['dɪstnt] entfernt ⟨**VT1,** 19⟩; **VT4,** 63
distaste [dɪ'steɪst] Abneigung; Ekel; Widerwillen ⟨**VT5,** 77⟩
to **distinguish** [dɪ'stɪŋgwɪʃ] unterscheiden; klar erkennen **VT5,** 76
to **distract sb (from sth)** [dɪ'strækt] jmdn (von etw.) ablenken ⟨**VT2,** 32⟩; **VT3,** 40; **VT4,** 64
distraction [dɪ'strækʃn] Ablenkung **VT3,** 40
distraught [dɪ'strɔ:t] bestürzt; zerstreut ⟨**VT2,** 32⟩
distress [dɪ'stres] Bedrängnis; Notlage ⟨**VT4,** 68⟩
district ['dɪstrɪkt] Distrikt; Bezirk **VT1,** 12; **VT2,** 33; **VT4,** 58
diversity [daɪ'vɜ:səti] Vielfalt **VT2,** 25
divestment [ˌdaɪ'vestmənt] Desinvestition ⟨**VT4,** 68⟩

divide [dɪ'vaɪd] Kluft **VT2,** 27
to **divide** [dɪ'vaɪd] teilen **II**
*to get **divorced** [ˌget dɪ'vɔ:st] sich scheiden lassen **III**
dizzy ['dɪzi] schwindlig **III**
*to **do** [du:] tun, machen **I**
It's nothing to do with me. [ɪts ˌnʌθɪŋ tə ˌdu: wɪð 'mi:] Ich habe damit nichts zu tun. **II**
to **do harm** [hɑ:m] Schaden anrichten ⟨**VT4,** 71⟩
to **do some revision** [ˌdu: səm rɪ'vɪʒn] lernen (wiederholen) **IV**
to **have sth done** [ˌhæv 'dʌn] etw. machen lassen **IV**
doctor ['dɒktə] Arzt, Ärztin **II**
documentary [ˌdɒkjə'mentri] Dokumentation **IV**
dog [dɒg] Hund **I**
dollar ['dɒlə] Dollar *(Währung)* **III**
dome [dəʊm] Kuppel **III**
door [dɔ:] Tür **I**
next door [nekst 'dɔ:] (von) nebenan **IV**
to **doss down** *(infml)* [ˌdɒs 'daʊn] sich aufs Ohr hauen ⟨**VT1,** 11⟩
double ['dʌbl] Doppel-, zweimal **I**
bent double [ˌbent 'dʌbl] zusammengekrümmt **VT1,** 13
to serve it up double [tə ˌsɜ:v‿ɪt‿ʌp 'dʌbl] es doppelt so schlimm machen ⟨**VT3,** 45⟩
to **doubt** [daʊt] bezweifeln **III**
down [daʊn] entlang; herunter, hinunter, nach unten **I**
the next size down [ðə ˌnekst saɪz 'daʊn] eine Größe kleiner **III**
to **download** ['daʊnləʊd] herunterladen *(aus dem Internet)* **IV**
downstairs [daʊn'steəz] (nach) unten; im Untergeschoss **II**
downtown *(AE)* [ˌdaʊn'taʊn] im Stadtzentrum **I**
dowry ['daʊri] Mitgift; Aussteuer ⟨**VT2,** 35⟩
dozen ['dʌzn] Dutzend ⟨**VT1,** 11⟩
to **doze off** [ˌdəʊz‿'ɒf] einnicken; einschlafen ⟨**VT3,** 42⟩
drab [dræb] düster; eintönig **VT3,** 47
to **drag** [dræg] ziehen; schleppen **IV**
drama ['drɑ:mə] Theater; Drama **II**
dramatic [drə'mætɪk] dramatisch **IV**
drastic ['dræstɪk] drastisch; einschneidend **IV**
crudely-**drawn** ['kru:dli ˌdrɔ:n] grob gezeichnet ⟨**VT4,** 68⟩
to **draw** [drɔ:] zeichnen **I**; ziehen ⟨**VT2,** 31⟩; **VT4,** 62
to **draw (on sth)** [drɔ:] (etw.) heranziehen ⟨**VT5,** 82⟩
to **draw sb's attention to sth** [ˌdrɔ: sʌmbʌdiz‿ə'tentʃn tə] jmds Aufmerksamkeit auf etw. lenken ⟨**VT3,** 46⟩
drawer [drɔ:] Schublade **I**
dream [dri:m] Traum **IV**
*to **dream** [dri:m] träumen **I**
dress [dres] Kleid **I**
to **dress** [dres] (sich) ankleiden **IV**
to **get dressed** [get 'drest] sich anziehen **IV**
dress code ['dres kəʊd] Kleiderordnung **VT3,** 40
drill [drɪl] Bohrer, Bohrmaschine **I**
electric drill [ɪˌlektrɪk 'drɪl] elektrische Bohrmaschine **I**
drink [drɪŋk] Getränk **I**
soft drink [ˌsɒft 'drɪŋk] alkoholfreies Getränk **IV**
*to **drink** [drɪŋk] trinken **I**
drive [draɪv] Autofahrt **III**
cattle drive ['kætl ˌdraɪv] Viehtrieb **II**
economy drive [ɪ'kɒnəmi ˌdraɪv] Sparprogramm ⟨**VT5,** 76⟩
relief drive [rɪ'li:f ˌdraɪv] Hilfsaktion **VT2,** 26
driving licence ['draɪvɪŋ ˌlaɪsnts] Führerschein **IV**
*to **drive** [draɪv] fahren **I**; treiben **IV**
driver ['draɪvə] Fahrer(in) **I**
to **drop** [drɒp] fallen (lassen) **II**
to **drop sb off** [ˌdrɒp‿'ɒf] jmdn absetzen; jmdn aussteigen lassen **IV**
dropoff ['drɒpɒf] Abgrund; Abfall ⟨**VT1,** 18⟩
drought [draʊt] Dürre; Trockenheit **IV**
to **drown** [draʊn] ertrinken; ertränken **IV**
drug [drʌg] Droge **IV**
drum [drʌm] Trommel, *pl.:* Schlagzeug **II**
drummer ['drʌmə] Schlagzeuger(in) **II**
drunk [drʌŋk] betrunken **IV**
to **dry** [draɪ] trocknen **III**
dry [draɪ] trocken **III**
dubious ['dju:biəs] dubios; zweifelhaft; fragwürdig ⟨**VT3,** 46⟩
duck [dʌk] Ente **I**
due [dju:] fällig **VT1,** 12
dull [dʌl] matt; stumpf; langweilig **IV**
dumb [dʌm] dumm, doof **III**
to **dump** [dʌmp] abladen ⟨**VT3,** 44⟩
to **dump sb** [dʌmp] mit jmdm Schluss machen; jmdm den Laufpass geben **IV**
dune [dju:n] Düne ⟨**VT1,** 18⟩
during *(+ noun)* ['djʊərɪŋ] während *(+ Nomen)* **II**
dust [dʌst] Staub **VT5,** 76
dusty ['dʌsti] staubig **III**
Dutch [dʌtʃ] Niederländisch; niederländisch **IV**
duty ['dju:ti] Pflicht **III**
heavy-duty [ˌhevi'dju:ti] strapazierfähig **VT1,** 14
DVD player [ˌdi:vi:di: 'pleɪə] DVD-Player **III**
to **dwell** [dwel] wohnen ⟨**VT5,** 87⟩
dwelling ['dwelɪŋ] Behausung; Wohnstätte ⟨**VT5,** 77⟩
to **dye** [daɪ] färben **IV**

E

each [i:tʃ] jede(-r/-s) **I**
each [i:tʃ] pro Person, pro Stück **II**
each other [ˌi:tʃ‿'ʌðə] sich gegenseitig **II**
eager ['i:gə] eifrig **III**
eagle ['i:gl] Adler ⟨**VT1,** 19⟩
ear [ɪə] Ohr **II**
early ['ɜ:li] früh **I**
to **earn** [ɜ:n] verdienen **I**
earring ['ɪərɪŋ] Ohrring **II**
earth [ɜ:θ] Erde **II**
earthquake ['ɜ:θkweɪk] Erdbeben **IV**
easiness ['i:zɪnəs] Leichtigkeit; Lockerheit ⟨**VT2,** 30⟩
east [i:st] Osten **I**
eastern ['i:stn] östlich **IV**
easy ['i:zi] einfach, leicht **I**
*to **eat** [i:t] essen **I**
eating disorder ['i:tɪŋ dɪˌsɔ:də] Essstörung ⟨**VT1,** 22⟩
economic [ˌi:kə'nɒmɪk] ökonomisch; wirtschaftlich **IV**
economy drive [ɪ'kɒnəmi ˌdraɪv] Sparprogramm ⟨**VT5,** 76⟩
economy [ɪ'kɒnəmi] Wirtschaft **III**
eddy ['edi] Wirbel; Strudel ⟨**VT5,** 77⟩
edge [edʒ] Rand; Kante **VT1,** 18; ⟨**VT2,** 36⟩
editor ['edɪtə] Herausgeber(in); Redakteur(in); Lektor(in) **IV**
letter to the editor [ˌletə tʊ ði‿'edɪtə] Leserbrief **IV**
to **educate** ['edʒʊkeɪt] erziehen; bilden ⟨**VT2,** 31⟩
education [edʒʊ'keɪʃn] Erziehung, Bildung **II**
Physical Education [ˌfɪzɪkl‿edʒʊ'keɪʃn] Sport *(Schulfach)* **II**
Religious Education [rɪˌlɪdʒəs‿edʒʊ'keɪʃn] Religionsunterricht **II**
educational [ˌedʒʊ'keɪʃnl] lehrreich; erzieherisch; Bildungs- **IV**
effect [ɪ'fekt] Effekt; Wirkung **IV**
efficient [ɪ'fɪʃnt] effizient; wirksam; wirtschaftlich; leistungsfähig **IV**
effort ['efət] Mühe; Bemühung; Versuch **VT3,** 48; **VT4,** 61; **VT5,** 76
egg [eg] Ei **I**
fried egg [fraɪd‿'eg] Spiegelei **II**
scrambled egg [ˌskræmbld‿'eg] Rührei **IV**
to **egg sb on** [ˌeg‿'ɒn] jmdn anstacheln; jmdn antreiben **VT1,** 17
Egyptian [ɪ'dʒɪptʃn] Ägypter(in) **VT3,** 42
eight-hundred-year-old [ˌeɪt hʌndrəd 'jɪər‿əʊld] achthundert Jahre alt **I**
either ... or ... ['aɪðə; 'i:ðə ... ɔ:] entweder ... oder ... **IV**

not … either [nɒt … 'aɪðə; nɒt … 'iːðə] auch nicht **VT2,** 37
to **eject** [ɪ'dʒekt] hinauswerfen; vertreiben ⟨**VT5,** 80⟩
elaborate [ɪ'læbrət] aufwändig ⟨**VT4,** 70⟩
elated [ɪ'leɪtɪd] hocherfreut; überglücklich ⟨**VT4,** 64⟩
elbow ['elbəʊ] Ellenbogen; mit dem Ellenbogen anstoßen **VT3,** 43
elderly ['eldəli] älter **IV**
to **elect** [ɪ'lekt] wählen **IV**
election [ɪ'lekʃn] Wahl **VT1,** 8; **VT4,** 57
electric [ɪ'lektrɪk] elektrisch **I**
electric drill [ɪˌlektrɪk 'drɪl] elektrische Bohrmaschine **I**
electricity [ˌelɪk'trɪsəti] Elektrizität; Strom **III**
electronic [ˌelek'trɒnɪk] elektronisch **IV**
electronics *(sg.)* [ˌelek'trɒnɪks] Elektronik **IV**
elegant ['elɪgnt] elegant **IV**
element ['elɪmənt] Element **III**
elementary [elɪ'mentri] elementar, grundlegend **II**
elementary school *(AE)* [elɪ'mentri ˌskuːl] Grundschule **II**
elephant ['elɪfənt] Elefant ⟨**VT4,** 67⟩
elevator *(AE)* ['elɪveɪtə] Aufzug, Lift **III**
eleven [ɪ'levn] elf **I**
to **eliminate** [ɪ'lɪmɪneɪt] elimineren; beseitigen **VT5,** 85
else [els] andere(-r/-s) **I**
what else [ˌwɒt‿'els] was sonst/noch **II**
e-mail ['iːmeɪl] E-Mail **I**
to **e-mail** ['iːmeɪl] mailen; E-Mail schreiben; per E-Mail schicken **IV**
embarrassed [ɪm'bærəst] verlegen **II**
embarrassing [ɪm'bærəsɪŋ] peinlich **III**
to **embrace** [ɪm'breɪs] umarmen; begeistert annehmen **IV**
emergency [ɪ'mɜːdʒntsi] Notfall, Notlage **I**
to **emigrate** ['emɪgreɪt] emigrieren; auswandern **III**
emotional [ɪ'məʊʃnl] emotional; gefühlsmäßig **VT1,** 11; ⟨**VT3,** 45⟩
emphasis ['empfəsɪs] Betonung **IV**
to **emphasize** ['empfəsaɪz] betonen **VT5,** 76
empire ['empaɪə] Reich; Kaiserreich **II**
to **employ** [ɪm'plɔɪ] einstellen; beschäftigen; gebrauchen **IV**
employee [ɪm'plɔɪiː] Angestellte(r); Mitarbeiter(in) **IV**
employment [ɪm'plɔɪmənt] Beschäftigung; Anstellung **IV**
empty ['empti] leer **I**
emu ['iːmjuː] Emu **III**
to **enable** [ɪ'neɪbl] befähigen; ermöglichen **VT5,** 80
to **enclose** [ɪn'kləʊz] beifügen **III**
to **encourage** [ɪn'kʌrɪdʒ] ermutigen; unterstützen **IV**

end [end] Ende, Schluss **I**
in the end [ˌɪn ðiː‿'end] schließlich, zum Schluss **II**
to **end** [end] enden **II**
endangered [ɪn'deɪndʒəd] gefährdet ⟨**VT4,** 67⟩
ending ['endɪŋ] Ende, Schluss *(einer Geschichte)* **I**
to **end up** [ˌend‿'ʌp] enden; landen **IV**
to **endure** [ɪn'djʊə] aushalten; überstehen **IV**
enemy ['enəmi] Feind(in) **II**
energy ['enədʒi] Energie; Kraft **IV**
solar energy [ˌsəʊlər‿'enədʒi] Solarenergie; Sonnenenergie **IV**
engaged [ɪn'geɪdʒd] besetzt, belegt **I**; verlobt **III**
engaging [ɪn'geɪdʒɪŋ] einnehmend; faszinierend ⟨**VT5,** 82⟩
engine ['endʒɪn] Motor **I**
steam engine ['stiːm‿ˌendʒɪn] Dampfmaschine **IV**
engineer [ˌendʒɪ'nɪə] Ingenieur(in); Techniker(in) **IV**
engineering [ˌendʒɪ'nɪərɪŋ] Maschinenbau; Technik **IV**
English ['ɪŋglɪʃ] englisch; Englisch **I**
What's … in English? [ˌwɒts … ɪn‿'ɪŋglɪʃ] Was heißt … auf Englisch? **I**
cognitive **enhancement** [ˌkɒgnətɪv‿ɪn'hɑːntsmənt] Wahrnehmungssteigerung ⟨**VT5,** 82⟩
to **enjoy** [ɪn'dʒɔɪ] genießen **II**
to enjoy oneself [ɪn'dʒɔɪ] Spaß haben; sich amüsieren **III**
enjoyable [ɪn'dʒɔɪəbl] angenehm; unterhaltsam **III**
enormous [ɪ'nɔːməs] enorm; gewaltig **IV**
enough [ɪ'nʌf] genug, genügend **I**
to **enter** ['entə] eintreten; hereinkommen; betreten ⟨**VT4,** 69⟩; **VT5,** 76
entertainment [ˌentə'teɪnmənt] Unterhaltung **IV**
enthusiastic [ɪnˌθjuːzi'æstɪk] enthusiastisch; begeistert ⟨**VT2,** 26⟩
entire [ɪn'taɪə] ganz **IV**
entrance ['entrənts] Eingang; Eintritt **VT2,** 26
entry ['entri] Eintrag **VT1,** 15
environment [ɪn'vaɪərnmənt] Umwelt; Umgebung **IV**
environmental [ɪnˌvaɪərn'mentl] Umwelt-; die Umwelt betreffend; umweltbedingt **IV**
environmentalist [ɪnˌvaɪərn'məntlɪst] Umweltschützer(in) **IV**
episode ['epɪsəʊd] Episode; Folge **IV**
equal ['iːkwəl] Gleichgestellte(r); Gleichwertige(r); Ebenbürtige(r) **III**
equality [ɪ'kwɒləti] Gleichberechtigung; Ebenbürtigkeit **VT2,** 28; **VT4,** 61
equipment [ɪ'kwɪpmənt] Ausstattung **IV**

er [ɜː] äh **I**
to **erase** [ɪ'reɪz] löschen; ausradieren ⟨**VT5,** 75⟩
erosion [ɪ'rəʊʒn] Erosion; Abtragung **IV**
to **escape** [ɪ'skeɪp] flüchten, entkommen **II**
especially [ɪ'speʃli] besonders, vor allem **I**
essential [ɪ'sentʃl] essenziell; entscheidend; unverzichtbar ⟨**VT5,** 81⟩
establishment [ɪ'stæblɪʃmənt] Einrichtung; Institution ⟨**VT3,** 45⟩
to **estimate** ['estɪmeɪt] schätzen **IV**
etc. [ɪt'setrə] usw., et cetera **II**
ethnic ['eθnɪk] ethnisch; Volks- **VT2,** 25; **VT4,** 56
European [ˌjʊərə'piːən] Europäer(in); europäisch **III**
to **evaluate** [ɪ'væljueɪt] evaluieren; auswerten ⟨**VT5,** 82⟩
even ['iːvn] sogar **II**
even *(+ comparative)* ['iːvn] noch *(+ Komparativ)* **II**
even if [ˌiːvn‿'ɪf] auch wenn **II**
even though [ˌiːvn‿'ðəʊ] auch wenn; obwohl **IV**
not even [nɒt‿'iːvn] nicht einmal **II**
evening ['iːvnɪŋ] Abend **I**
event [ɪ'vent] Ereignis **I**
eventually [ɪ'ventʃuəli] schließlich, endlich **VT2,** 27
ever ['evə] jemals **II**; immer **IV**
they lived happily ever after [ðeɪ lɪvd ˌhæpɪli‿evər‿'ɑːftə] und wenn sie nicht gestorben sind, dann leben sie noch heute ⟨**VT2,** 35⟩
every ['evri] jede(-r/-s) **I**
every day [ˌevri 'deɪ] jeden Tag **I**
everybody ['evribɒdi] jeder; alle **I**
everyday ['evrideɪ] alltäglich **III**
everyone ['evriwʌn] jeder **II**
everything ['evriθɪŋ] alles **I**
everywhere ['evriweə] überall **I**
evidence ['evɪdnts] Beweismaterial; Beleg **VT2,** 34; ⟨**VT4,** 68⟩; **VT5,** 79
evident ['evɪdnt] erwiesen; offensichtlich **VT5,** 79
evil ['iːvl] böse, schlecht **II**
evolution [ˌiːvə'luːʃn] Evolution ⟨**VT5,** 81⟩
exact [ɪg'zækt] exakt; genau **IV**
not exactly [ˌnɒt‿ɪg'zæktli] nicht gerade **III**
exactly [ɪg'zæktli] genau **II**
exam [ɪg'zæm] Examen; Prüfung **IV**
examination [ɪgˌzæmɪ'neɪʃn] Examen; Prüfung ⟨**VT3,** 45⟩
to **examine** [ɪg'zæmɪn] untersuchen, kontrollieren **I**
example [ɪg'zɑːmpl] Beispiel **I**
for example [fər‿ɪg'zɑːmpl] zum Beispiel **I**
exasperated [ɪg'zæspreɪtɪd] entnervt; außer sich **VT3,** 43

excellent ['ekslnt] exzellent, hervorragend **IV**
except [ɪk'sept] außer **I**
exchange [ɪks'tʃeɪndʒ] Austausch **III**
foreign exchange [ˌfɒrɪn‿ɪks'tʃeɪndʒ] Devisen ⟨**VT4,** 56⟩
to **excite** [ɪk'saɪt] aufregen; erregen **IV**
excited [ɪk'saɪtɪd] aufgeregt **I**
excitement [ɪk'saɪtmənt] Aufregung **IV**
exciting [ɪk'saɪtɪŋ] spannend, aufregend **I**
exclamation point *(AE)* [ekskləˈmeɪʃn ˌpɔɪnt] Ausrufezeichen **VT1,** 14
to **exclude** [ɪks'klu:d] ausschließen **IV**
excuse [ɪk'skju:s] Entschuldigung; Ausrede ⟨**VT3,** 46⟩
Excuse me! [ɪk'skju:z mi] Entschuldigung! Entschuldigen Sie! **I**
to **execute** ['eksɪkju:t] exekutieren; hinrichten **III**
exercise ['eksəsaɪz] Übung **I**
exercise book ['eksəsaɪz ˌbʊk] Übungsheft **I**
exhibition [ˌeksɪ'bɪʃn] Ausstellung; Vorführung **II**
to **exist** [ɪg'zɪst] existieren **III**
existence [ɪg'zɪstnts] Existenz; Dasein **VT5,** 72
exit ['eksɪt] Ausgang; Abgang; Ausfahrt **IV**
to **expand** [ɪk'spænd] (sich) ausdehnen; erweitern; expandieren **VT1,** 16; **VT4,** 56
expanse [ɪk'spænts] Fläche ⟨**VT3,** 50⟩
expansion [ɪk'spænʃn] Ausdehnung; Erweiterung; Expansion **VT4,** 56
to **expect** [ɪk'spekt] erwarten **II**
expectation [ˌekspek'teɪʃn] Erwartung **III**
expedition [ˌekspɪ'dɪʃn] Expedition; Forschungsreise **IV**
expensive [ɪk'spentsɪv] teuer **II**
experience [ɪk'spɪəriənts] Erfahrung; Erlebnis **II**
work experience ['wɜ:k‿ɪkˌspɪəriənts] Berufserfahrung **IV**
to **experience** [ɪk'spɪəriənts] erfahren, erleben **II**
experiment [ɪk'sperɪmənt] Experiment, Versuch **III**
expert ['ekspɜ:t] Experte, Expertin ⟨**VT5,** 81⟩
to **explain** [ɪk'spleɪn] erklären, erläutern **I**
explanation [ˌekspləˈneɪʃn] Erklärung; Erläuterung **VT4,** 60
to **explode** [ɪk'spləʊd] explodieren **III**
to **exploit** [ɪk'splɔɪt] ausbeuten **IV**
to **explore** [ɪk'splɔ:] erkunden; erforschen **III**
explorer [ɪk'splɔ:rə] Forscher; Forschungsreisender **III**
explosion [ɪk'spləʊʒn] Explosion **III**
export ['ekspɔ:t] Export; Ausfuhr **VT4,** 56
to **expose** [ɪk'spəʊz] ausstellen; entblößen; freilegen **VT3,** 40; **VT4,** 63
exposition [ˌekspəˈzɪʃn] Exposition **IV**
to **express** [ɪk'spres] ausdrücken **II**
expression [ɪk'spreʃn] Ausdruck **III**
expulsion [ɪk'spʌlʃn] Ausschluss; Ausweisung ⟨**VT3,** 46⟩
to **extend** [ɪk'stend] (sich) ausdehnen; sich erstrecken **VT4,** 61
extinction [ɪks'tɪŋkʃn] Aussterben ⟨**VT4,** 67⟩
extra ['ekstrə] extra, besonders **II**
extract ['ekstrækt] Extrakt; Auszug **III**
extracurricular [ˌekstrəkəˈrɪkjələ] außerhalb des Lehrplans ⟨**VT1,** 23⟩
extreme [ɪk'stri:m] extrem ⟨**VT1,** 18⟩; **VT3,** 40
extremist [ɪk'stri:mɪst] Extremist(in) **VT2,** 34
eye [aɪ] Auge **I**

F

face [feɪs] Gesicht **I**
to **face** [feɪs] gegenüber stehen; konfrontiert werden mit **IV**
I can't face *(+ gerund)* [aɪ ˌkænt 'feɪs] Ich sehe mich außer Stande (zu ...) **IV**
fact [fækt] Fakt, Tatsache **II**
as a matter of fact [əz‿ə ˌmætər‿əv 'fækt] in der Tat ⟨**VT3,** 45⟩
in fact [ɪn 'fækt] tatsächlich; eigentlich **II**
factory ['fæktri] Fabrik; Werk **III**
to **fade away** [ˌfeɪd‿əˈweɪ] aus dem Gedächtnis schwinden; sterben **VT3,** 47
without **fail** [wɪˌðaʊt 'feɪl] unweigerlich; auf alle Fälle **VT2,** 28
to **fail** [feɪl] versagen; ausfallen; fehlschlagen **VT1,** 13
to **fail to** *(+ infinitive)* [feɪl] versäumen zu; es nicht schaffen zu ⟨**VT3,** 45⟩; **VT5,** 80
failure ['feɪljə] Versagen; Ausfall; Fehlschlag **VT4,** 61
to **faint** [feɪnt] ohnmächtig werden **I**
fair [feə] Messe, Jahrmarkt **II**
fair [feə] gerecht, fair **I**
fairy ['feəri] Fee **II**
fairy tale ['feəri ˌteɪl] Märchen **II**
fall [fɔ:l] Sturz **III**
falls *(pl.)* [fɔ:lz] Wasserfall **I**
fall *(AE)* [fɔ:l] Herbst **II**
*to **fall** (over) [fɔ:l‿'əʊvə] (hin)fallen; umfallen **I**
to **fall asleep** [ˌfɔ:l‿əˈsli:p] einschlafen **IV**
to **fall in love (with)** [ˌfɔ:l‿ɪn 'lʌv] sich verlieben (in) **II**
false [fɔ:ls] falsch **I**
fame [feɪm] Ruhm **VT3,** 48
hall of fame [ˌhɔ:l‿əv 'feɪm] Ruhmeshalle **VT5,** 72
familiar [fəˈmɪliə] vertraut **III**
to **seem familiar** [ˌsi:m fəˈmɪliə] bekannt vorkommen **III**
family ['fæmli] Familie **I**
famous ['feɪməs] berühmt **II**
fan [fæn] Fan, Anhänger(in) **II**
fanatic [fəˈnætɪk] Fanatiker(in) **VT3,** 42
to **fancy** ['fæntsi] angetan sein von **III**
to **fancy** *(+ gerund) (infml) (BE)* ['fæntsi] Lust haben zu **IV**
fantastic [fæn'tæstɪk] fantastisch, großartig **I**
far [fɑ:] weit **I**
so far ['səʊ fɑ:] bis jetzt **II**
far [fɑ:] bei weitem; weitaus **IV**
further ['fɜ:ðə] weiter **IV**
far more interesting [ˌfɑ: mɔ:r‿'ɪntrəstɪŋ] weitaus interessanter **I**
fare [feə] Fahrpreis **VT4,** 59
farm [fɑ:m] Farm, Bauernhof **I**
to **farm** [fɑ:m] Landwirtschaft treiben **III**
farmer ['fɑ:mə] Farmer, Landwirt(in) **I**
farmhand ['fɑ:mhænd] Landarbeiter(in) ⟨**VT4,** 69⟩
farmyard ['fɑ:mjɑ:d] Hof *(auf einem Bauernhof)* **I**
fascinating ['fæsɪneɪtɪŋ] faszinierend **III**
fashion ['fæʃn] Mode **IV**
fashionable ['fæʃnəbl] modisch; elegant **IV**
fast [fɑ:st] schnell **I**
fat [fæt] fett, dick **III**
fatal ['feɪtl] tödlich; verhängnisvoll ⟨**VT4,** 68⟩
fatality [fəˈtæləti] Todesfall ⟨**VT1,** 16⟩
father ['fɑ:ðə] Vater **I**
(my) **fault** ['maɪ ˌfɔ:lt] (meine) Schuld **III**
flora and **fauna** [ˌflɔ:rə‿ənd 'fɔ:nə] Pflanzen- und Tierwelt ⟨**VT4,** 67⟩
favor *(AE)* ['feɪvə] Gefälligkeit; Begünstigung **VT5,** 75
favourite ['feɪvrɪt] Lieblings- **I**
fax [fæks] Fax **II**
fear [fɪə] Angst, Furcht **II**
feature ['fi:tʃə] Gesichtszug; Charakterzug; Merkmal **VT5,** 76
feature film ['fi:tʃə ˌfɪlm] Spielfilm **IV**
to **feature** ['fi:tʃə] jmdn in einer Hauptrolle haben **IV**
federal ['fedrl] Bundes-; föderalistisch **IV**
fee [fi:] Gebühr; Abgabe **VT3,** 55
*to **feed** [fi:d] füttern **I**
feedback ['fi:dbæk] Feedback, Rückmeldung **II**
*to **feel** [fi:l] (sich) fühlen **I**
to **feel like** *(+ gerund)* ['fi:l laɪk] Lust haben auf/zu **III**
to **feel sick** [ˌfi:l 'sɪk] Übelkeit verspüren; sich schlecht fühlen **III**
to **feel sorry for** [ˌfi:l 'sɒri] Mitleid haben mit; bedauern **II**
feeling ['fi:lɪŋ] Gefühl **II**
female ['fi:meɪl] weiblich; Weibchen **IV**
fence [fents] Zaun **II**
to **fend for oneself** [fend] alleine auskommen ⟨**VT4,** 64⟩

festival ['festɪvl] Festival, Fest **II**
to **fetch** [fetʃ] (ab)holen **I**
fever ['fi:və] Fieber **III**
few [fju:] wenige **III**
a few [ə 'fju:] einige, ein paar **II**
fictional ['fɪkʃnl] fiktional; fiktiv **VT4,** 59
fictitious [ˌfɪk'tɪʃəs] fiktiv; erfunden; erdichtet **VT4,** 59
field [fi:ld] Feld; Acker **I**
baseball field ['beɪsbɔ:l ˌfi:ld] Baseballplatz **III**
football field ['fʊtbɔ:l ˌfi:ld] Footballplatz **III**
track and field [ˌtræk‿ənd 'fi:ld] Leichtathletik **III**
fierce [fɪəs] grimmig; wild; kämpferisch **IV**
*to **fight** [faɪt] streiten, kämpfen **I**
figure ['fɪgə] Figur, Gestalt; Ziffer **II**
to **figure** ['fɪgə] sich vorstellen; glauben **VT1,** 12
to **figure out** [ˌfɪgər‿'aʊt] herausfinden **VT2,** 27
file [faɪl] Akte; Mappe; Datei **VT1,** 8
to **file** [faɪl] ablegen; abheften ⟨**VT4,** 71⟩
to **fill in** [fɪl‿'ɪn] ausfüllen **II**
film [fɪlm] Film **II**
feature film ['fi:tʃə ˌfɪlm] Spielfilm **IV**
to **film** [fɪlm] filmen; drehen **IV**
filthy ['fɪlθi] schmutzig, dreckig ⟨**VT3,** 45⟩
final ['faɪnl] Finale **II**
finally ['faɪnli] schließlich, endlich **II**
financial [faɪ'nænʃl] finanziell **VT2,** 34; **VT4,** 56
*to **find** [faɪnd] finden **I**
Find the odd word out! [ˌɒd wɜ:d‿'aʊt] Finde das Wort, das nicht in die Gruppe passt! *(Wortschatzübung)* **I**
fine [faɪn] Geldstrafe; Bußgeld **VT2,** 28; **VT4,** 61
fine [faɪn] gut, in Ordnung; schön **I**
I'm fine. [aɪm 'faɪn] Mir geht es gut. **I**
finger ['fɪŋgə] Finger **I**
to **cross one's fingers** [ˌkrɒs wʌnz 'fɪŋgəz] die Daumen drücken **IV**
to **give sb the finger** [ˌgɪv sʌmbədi ðə 'fɪŋgə] jmdm den Stinkefinger zeigen ⟨**VT2,** 30⟩
to **lace one's fingers** [ˌleɪs wʌnz 'fɪŋgəz] die Hände verschränken ⟨**VT1,** 15⟩
fingerprint ['fɪŋgəprɪnt] Fingerabdruck **VT2,** 36
fingertip ['fɪŋgətɪp] Fingerspitze **II**
to **finish** ['fɪnɪʃ] fertig machen; aufhören **I**
fire [faɪə] Feuer; Kamin; Ofen **II**
to **set fire to** [set 'faɪə tə] in Brand stecken **II**
to **fire** [faɪə] feuern; hinauswerfen **VT3,** 43
firework ['faɪəwɜ:k] Feuerwerkskörper; *Plural:* Feuerwerk **IV**

firm [fɜ:m] Firma; Unternehmen; Gesellschaft **IV**
firm [fɜ:m] fest; standhaft ⟨**VT2,** 30⟩
first [fɜ:st] erste(-r/-s); zuerst **I**
at first [ət 'fɜ:st] zuerst; zunächst **II**
first name ['fɜ:st ˌneɪm] Vorname **III**
in the first place [ɪn ðə 'fɜ:st pleɪs] von vornherein; überhaupt erst ⟨**VT3,** 45⟩
fish and chips [ˌfɪʃ‿n‿'tʃɪps] Fisch und Pommes frites **I**
fishing ['fɪʃɪŋ] Angeln, Fischen **II**
fist [fɪst] Faust **III**
fitted carpet *(BE)* [ˌfɪtɪd 'kɑ:pɪt] Teppichboden ⟨**VT5,** 87⟩
to **fit (in)** [ˌfɪt‿'ɪn] (hinein)passen ⟨**VT4,** 68⟩; **VT5,** 80
fit [fɪt] fit **III**
fitful ['fɪtfl] ruckartig; launenhaft ⟨**VT5,** 77⟩
fitting ['fɪtɪŋ] Beschlag ⟨**VT4,** 70⟩
to **fix** [fɪks] festlegen; fixieren; reparieren **IV**
to **fix sth up** [fɪks‿'ʌp] etw. herrichten; etw. anbringen **IV**
flag [flæg] Flagge **I**
flag-pole ['flægpəʊl] Fahnenmast ⟨**VT4,** 69⟩
to **flake** [fleɪk] abblättern **VT2,** 36
flame [fleɪm] Flamme **IV**
to **flap** [flæp] flattern; klappen; schlagen **VT5,** 75
flash [flæʃ] Blitz **VT1,** 14
to **flash** [flæʃ] blitzen; blinken **III**; zeigen ⟨**VT4,** 64⟩
flashlight *(AE)* ['flæʃlaɪt] Taschenlampe **IV**
flat [flæt] Wohnung **I**
flat [flæt] flach, platt **III**
flavor *(AE)* ['fleɪvə] Geschmack, Aroma **IV**
flesh [fleʃ] Fleisch ⟨**VT4,** 71⟩
flight [flaɪt] Flug **I**; Treppe ⟨**VT5,** 76⟩
to **flinch** [flɪntʃ] zurückweichen; zusammenzucken **VT1,** 13
to **flip (a book) open** [ˌflɪp‿'əʊpn] aufschlagen (ein Buch) **VT1,** 14
flippant ['flɪpnt] nicht ernst gemeint ⟨**VT3,** 51⟩
to **float** [fləʊt] gleiten; treiben ⟨**VT1,** 18⟩
flood [flʌd] Flut; Hochwasser; Überschwemmung **IV**
to **flood** [flʌd] überfluten; überschwemmen **IV**
floor [flɔ:] Fußboden; Stockwerk **I**
flora and fauna [ˌflɔ:rə‿ənd 'fɔ:nə] Pflanzen- und Tierwelt ⟨**VT4,** 67⟩
flow [fləʊ] Fluss; Fließen; Strömung ⟨**VT2,** 31⟩
to **flow** [fləʊ] fließen; strömen **IV**
flower ['flaʊə] Blume **II**
flu [flu:] Grippe **IV**
fly [flaɪ] Fliege **II**
*to **fly** [flaɪ] fliegen **I**
to **fly on** [flaɪ‿'ɒn] weiterfliegen **I**

focus ['fəʊkəs] Blickpunkt **I**
to **focus (on)** ['fəʊkəs] sich konzentrieren (auf) **IV**
fog [fɒg] Nebel **II**
foggy ['fɒgi] neblig **II**
to **fold** [fəʊld] falten; klappen **VT3,** 43
folder ['fəʊldə] Ordner, Mappe **I**
to **follow** ['fɒləʊ] hinterhergehen; (be)folgen **I**
folly ['fɒli] Verrücktheit; Torheit ⟨**VT1,** 23⟩
food [fu:d] Essen, Nahrung; Lebensmittel **I**
fool [fu:l] Narr, Dummkopf **II**
foot, *pl.* **feet** [fʊt; fi:t] Fuß **I**; Fuß *(Längenmaß: 30,48 cm)* **III**
on foot [ɒn 'fʊt] zu Fuß **IV**
footage ['fʊtɪdʒ] Filmmaterial **VT5,** 79
football ['fʊtbɔ:l] Fußball **I**
football field ['fʊtbɔ:l ˌfi:ld] Footballplatz **III**
football magazine ['fʊtbɔ:l mægəˌzi:n] Fußballzeitschrift **I**
footstep ['fʊtstep] Schritt **III**
for [fɔ:; fə] für **I**; wegen **II**; seit **III**
for example [fər‿ɪg'zɑ:mpl] zum Beispiel **I**
for many years [fə ˌmæni 'jɪəz] viele Jahre lang **II**
for their own good [fə ðər‿əʊn 'gʊd] zu ihrem Besten **III**
force [fɔ:s] Macht **VT2,** 27
to **force** [fɔ:s] zwingen **III**
forecast ['fɔ:kɑ:st] Vorhersage **II**
weather forecast ['weðə ˌfɔ:kɑ:st] Wettervorhersage **II**
forefather ['fɔ:ˌfɑ:ðə] Ahne; Ahnin; Vorfahr ⟨**VT3,** 42⟩
foreign ['fɒrɪn] ausländisch; fremd **III**
foreign exchange [ˌfɒrɪn‿ɪks'tʃeɪndʒ] Devisen ⟨**VT4,** 56⟩
forest ['fɒrɪst] Wald **I**
forever [fə'revə] für immer; ewig **VT1,** 21; ⟨**VT3,** 45⟩
*to **forget** [fə'get] vergessen **I**
fork [fɔ:k] Gabel **I**; Gabelung **II**
form [fɔ:m] Form **I**
to **form** [fɔ:m] formen; bilden **III**
formal ['fɔ:ml] formal; formell; förmlich **III**
formula, *pl.* **formulae** ['fɔ:mjələ] Formel ⟨**VT2,** 39⟩
fortunately ['fɔ:tʃnətli] zum Glück **VT1,** 17
fortune ['fɔ:tʃu:n] Vermögen; Reichtum; Schicksal; Glück **VT4,** 58
forward ['fɔ:wəd] vorwärts **VT1,** 14; ⟨**VT1,** 18⟩; ⟨**VT2,** 31⟩; ⟨**VT3,** 50⟩; ⟨**VT4,** 69⟩
to **found** [faʊnd] gründen **II**
fountain ['faʊntən] Brunnen ⟨**VT4,** 61⟩
fragile ['frædʒaɪl] schwächlich; zerbrechlich ⟨**VT5,** 87⟩
frail [freɪl] schwächlich; zerbrechlich ⟨**VT5,** 76⟩

frankly ['fræŋkli] ehrlich gesagt; offen gestanden **IV**
freak [fri:k] Missgeburt; eigenartiger Mensch ⟨**VT2,** 31⟩
to **freak out** [ˌfri:k‿'aʊt] ausflippen ⟨**VT3,** 45⟩
free [fri:] frei **I**; kostenlos **III**
freedom ['fri:dəm] Freiheit **III**
*to **freeze** [fri:z] erstarren; gefrieren **IV**
French [frentʃ] französisch; Französisch **I**
frequency ['fri:kwəntsi] Frequenz; Häufigkeit **IV**
fresh [freʃ] frisch **I**
freshness ['freʃnəs] Frische **IV**
Friday ['fraɪdeɪ] Freitag **I**
fried [fraɪd] in der Pfanne gebraten **II**
fried egg [fraɪd‿'eg] Spiegelei **II**
friend [frend] Freund(in) **I**
to **make friends (with)** [ˌmeɪk 'frendz] Freundschaft schließen (mit) **IV**
friendly ['frendli] freundlich, nett **II**
friendship ['frendʃɪp] Freundschaft **IV**
fries *pl. (AE)* [fraɪz] Pommes frites **I**
fright [fraɪt] Schreck ⟨**VT4,** 70⟩
to **frighten** ['fraɪtn] erschrecken, Angst machen **II**
*to be **frightened** (of) ['fraɪtnd] Angst haben (vor) **I**
frog [frɒg] Frosch **I**
from [frɒm; frəm] aus, von **I**
Where are you from? [ˌweər‿ə jə 'frɒm] Woher kommst du/kommt ihr/ kommen Sie? **I**
Where ... from? [ˌweə ... 'frɒm] Woher ... ? **I**
front [frʌnt] Vorderseite **II**
in front of [ɪn 'frʌnt‿əv] vor, davor **I**
fruit [fru:t] Frucht **III**
fruit *(pl.)* [fru:t] Obst **II**
fruity ['fru:ti] fruchtig ⟨**VT5,** 76⟩
fuel ['fju:əl] Treibstoff; Brennmaterial **IV**
to **fulfil** [fʊl'fɪl] erfüllen **III**
full [fʊl] voll **I**
fun [fʌn] Freude, Spaß **I**
fun to be with [ˌfʌn tə'bi: wɪð] lustig; witzig; fröhlich **IV**
to **make fun of** [ˌmeɪk 'fʌn‿əv] sich lustig machen über **IV**
function ['fʌŋkʃn] Funktion **IV**
to **fund** [fʌnd] finanzieren; fördern **VT1,** 14
fundamental [ˌfʌndə'mentl] fundamental ⟨**VT1,** 23⟩
funeral ['fju:nrəl] Beerdigung; Begräbnis ⟨**VT4,** 70⟩
funky ['fʌŋki] irre **III**
funny ['fʌni] komisch, lustig **I**
fur [fɜ:] Fell; Pelz **IV**
furious ['fjʊəriəs] wütend **III**
furniture *(singular noun with plural meaning)* ['fɜ:nɪtʃə] Möbel **IV**
furthermore [ˌfɜ:ðə'mɔ:] überdies; außerdem **IV**
fury ['fjʊəri] Wut ⟨**VT5,** 87⟩
*to **make a fuss** [ˌmeɪk‿ə 'fʌs] viel Aufhebens machen **VT2,** 36
future ['fju:tʃə] Zukunft **II**
futuristic [ˌfju:tʃə'rɪstɪk] futuristisch ⟨**VT5,** 78⟩

G

gadgetry ['gædʒɪtri] Geräte; technische Spielereien ⟨**VT5,** 82⟩
to **gain** [geɪn] gewinnen **IV**
galaxy ['gæləksi] Galaxie; Galaxis; Milchstraße ⟨**VT1,** 14⟩
gallery ['gæləri] Galerie **II**
gallon ['gælən] Gallone *(Hohlmaß, AE: 3,78 l, BE: 4,54 l)* **IV**
game [geɪm] Spiel **I**
game [geɪm] Wild ⟨**VT4,** 69⟩
gang [gæŋ] Gang, Bande **II**
gangster ['gæŋkstə] Gangster, Verbrecher **I**
gap [gæp] Lücke; Spalt; Abstand **IV**
garage ['gærɑ:ʒ] Garage **I**
garbage *(AE)* ['gɑ:bɪdʒ] Müll; Abfall **IV**
garden ['gɑ:dn] Garten **I**
gardener ['gɑ:dnə] Gärtner(in) **IV**
gas [gæs] Gas **III**
gasp [gɑ:sp] hörbares Einatmen ⟨**VT3,** 45⟩
gate [geɪt] Tor, Pforte **I**; Gate, Flugsteig, Ausgang **II**
to **gather** ['gæðə] (sich) sammeln; erfassen **IV**
gay [geɪ] homosexuell **VT1,** 10
to **gaze** [geɪz] starren; blicken **VT5,** 76
gear [gɪə] Ausrüstung, Zeug **II**
gel [dʒel] Gel **VT1,** 11
gender ['dʒendə] Geschlecht ⟨**VT5,** 82⟩
general ['dʒenrl] General **III**
general ['dʒenrl] allgemein **II**
the general public [ðə ˌdʒenrl 'pʌblɪk] die Allgemeinheit; die breite Öffentlichkeit **IV**
to **generalise** ['dʒenrlaɪz] verallgemeinern **VT1,** 10
generation [ˌdʒenə'reɪʃn] Generation **III**
gentle ['dʒentl] sanft, liebenswürdig **II**
gentleman, *pl.* **gentlemen** ['dʒentlmən] Gentleman, (feiner) Herr **II**
ladies and gentlemen [ˌleɪdiz‿n 'dʒentlmən] meine Damen und Herren **II**
geography [dʒi'ɒgrəfi] Geographie, Erdkunde **I**
German ['dʒɜ:mən] deutsch; Deutsche(r); Deutsch **I**
gesture ['dʒestʃə] Geste, Gebärde **VT2,** 27
*to **get** [get] (be)kommen; kriegen **I**; werden **II**
Get lost! *(infml)* [get 'lɒst] Hau ab!; Verzieh dich! **IV**
Get well soon! [get ˌwel 'su:n] Gute Besserung! **III**
I don't get it. [aɪ ˌdəʊnt 'get‿ɪt] Das kapiere ich nicht. **II**
to **get a big bang out of sth** [ˌget‿ə ˌbɪg 'bæŋ] einen Heidenspaß an etw. haben ⟨**VT1,** 12⟩
to **get a grip on** [ˌget‿ə 'grɪp] in den Griff bekommen ⟨**VT3,** 50⟩
to **get by** [get 'baɪ] vorbeikommen; durchkommen ⟨**VT2,** 30⟩
to **get divorced** [ˌget dɪ'vɔ:st] sich scheiden lassen **III**
to **get dressed** [get 'drest] sich anziehen **IV**
to **get into** [get‿'ɪntə] in etwas hineingelangen **I**
to **get in touch (with)** [ˌget‿ɪn 'tʌtʃ] in Verbindung treten (mit); kontaktieren **III**
to **get (sb) involved (in)** [ˌget‿ɪn'vɒlvd] sich (oder jmdn) beteiligen (an); sich engagieren (für); sich einlassen (auf) **III**
to **get lost** [get 'lɒst] verloren gehen, sich verirren **I**
to **get married** [get 'mærid] heiraten **II**
to **get off (the bus)** [get‿'ɒf] aussteigen (aus dem Bus) **I**
to **get on (the bus)** [get‿'ɒn] einsteigen (in den Bus) **I**
to **get over sth** [ˌget‿'əʊvə] über etw. hinwegkommen; mit etw. fertigwerden **IV**
to **get rid of** [get 'rɪd‿əv] loswerden **II**
to **get stick** *(infml)* [ˌget 'stɪk] schikaniert werden ⟨**VT2,** 33⟩
to **get the gist** [ˌget ðə 'dʒɪst] das Wesentliche erfassen **III**
to **get to know** [ˌget tə 'nəʊ] kennen lernen **III**
to **get up** [get‿'ʌp] aufstehen **I**
to **get used to** *(+ gerund)* [ˌget 'ju:st tə] sich gewöhnen an **III**
to **get well** [get 'wel] gesund werden **III**
to **get wet** [get 'wet] nass werden **I**
ghost [gəʊst] Geist **II**
giant [dʒaɪənt] Riese; Gigant **IV**
gifted ['gɪftɪd] begabt **VT1,** 13
girl [gɜ:l] Mädchen **I**
girlfriend ['gɜ:lfrend] Freundin *(in einer Paarbeziehung)* **III**
*to **get the gist** [ˌget ðə 'dʒɪst] das Wesentliche erfassen **III**
*to **give** [gɪv] geben; schenken **I**
to **give a talk** [ˌgɪv‿ə 'tɔ:k] einen Vortrag halten **II**
to **give sb a break** [ˌgɪv‿ə 'breɪk] jmdn schonen; jmdm eine Chance geben **VT3,** 42
to **give sb a lift** [ˌgɪv‿ə 'lɪft] jmdn im Auto mitnehmen **VT4,** 58
to **give somebody the bumps** [ˌgɪv ðə 'bʌmps] jemanden hochwerfen und wieder auffangen **I**

to **give sth a shot** [ˌgɪv‿ə ˈʃɒt] es mal probieren mit etw.; sein Glück versuchen mit etw. ⟨**VT3,** 48⟩
to **give up** [gɪv‿ˈʌp] aufgeben **I**
*to **give** sb the finger [ˌgɪv sʌmbədi ðə ˈfɪŋgə] jmdm den Stinkefinger zeigen ⟨**VT2,** 30⟩
glad [glæd] froh **III**
glance [glɑːnts] Blick ⟨**VT3,** 50⟩
to **glance at** [glɑːnts] einen Blick werfen auf **VT1,** 15
to **glare at sb** [gleə] jmdn zornig anstarren **VT2,** 36
glass [glɑːs] Glas **I**
glasses *pl.* [ˈglɑːsɪz] Brille **I**
gleeful [ˈgliːfl] fröhlich; schadenfroh ⟨**VT4,** 68⟩
hang **glider** [ˈhæŋ ˌglaɪdə] Hängegleiter; Drachen ⟨**VT1,** 18⟩
to **glitter** [ˈglɪtə] glänzen; funkeln; glitzern ⟨**VT5,** 77⟩
global [ˈgləʊbl] global **IV**
globalisation [ˌgləʊblaɪˈzeɪʃn] Globalisierung **IV**
glove [glʌv] Handschuh **III**
to **glow** [gləʊ] leuchten; glühen ⟨**VT2,** 38⟩
to **glue** [gluː] kleben ⟨**VT5,** 81⟩
gnat [næt] Stechmücke ⟨**VT5,** 81⟩
*to **go** [gəʊ] gehen **I**
to **go** *(+ adjective)* [gəʊ] werden **II**
It just goes to show … [ɪt ˌdʒʌst gəʊz tə ˈʃəʊ] Das zeigt mal wieder … ⟨**VT4,** 68⟩
Let's go! [lets ˈgəʊ] Lass(t) uns gehen! **I**
to **be going on** [biː ˌgəʊɪŋ‿ˈɒn] los sein **II**
to **be gone** [biː ˈgɒn] verschwunden sein **II**
to **go ahead** [ˌgəʊ‿əˈhed] fortfahren; vorangehen; loslegen **IV**
to **go along** [ˌgəʊ‿əˈlɒŋ] mitmachen; mitziehen **VT1,** 12
to **go down** [gəʊ ˈdaʊn] untergehen *(Sonne)* **II**
to **go for a walk** [ˌgəʊ fər‿ə ˈwɔːk] spazieren gehen **I**
to **go on** [gəʊ‿ˈɒn] weitermachen, weiterführen **I**
to **go on** *(+ gerund)* [gəʊ‿ˈɒn] etwas weiter/immer wieder tun **II**
to **go shopping** [ˌgəʊ ˈʃɒpɪŋ] einkaufen gehen **I**
to **go to sleep** [gəʊ tə ˈsliːp] einschlafen **I**
to **go wrong** [gəʊ ˈrɒŋ] schief gehen **II**
goal [gəʊl] Tor; Ziel **III**
goblet [ˈgɒblət] Kelch; Pokal ⟨**VT3,** 55⟩
God [gɒd] Gott **II**
for God's sake [fə ˌgɒdz ˈseɪk] um Gottes willen ⟨**VT2,** 30⟩
thank God [ˌθæŋk ˈgɒd] Gott sei Dank **II**
goddess [ˈgɒdes] Göttin **VT1,** 13
gold [gəʊld] Gold **II**
gold [gəʊld] golden **III**
golden [ˈgəʊldn] golden **III**
golf [gɒlf] Golf **III**
golf ball [ˈgɒlf ˌbɔːl] Golfball **III**
golf club [ˈgɒlf ˌklʌb] Golfschläger **III**
golf course [ˈgɒlf ˌkɔːs] Golfplatz **III**
for their own **good** [fə ðər‿ˌəʊn ˈgʊd] zu ihrem Besten **III**
good [gʊd] gut **I**
Best wishes [ˌbest ˈwɪʃɪz] Mit den besten Wünschen **IV**
I'd better = I had better [aɪd ˈbetə] Ich sollte lieber … **III**
no good [nəʊ ˈgʊd] nutzlos, wertlos **II**
not any better [ˌnɒt‿eni ˈbetə] (überhaupt) nicht besser **II**
to **be good at** [ˈgʊd‿ət] gut sein in **I**
Goodbye! [gʊdˈbaɪ] Auf Wiedersehen! **I**
goods *(pl.)* [gʊdz] Güter; Waren **III**
*to have **(got)** [hæv ˈgɒt] besitzen, haben **I**
to **govern** [ˈgʌvn] regieren; verwalten **VT4,** 61
government [ˈgʌvnmənt] Regierung **II**
governor [ˈgʌvnə] Gouverneur(in) **IV**
to **grab** [græb] greifen; schnappen **I**
grace [greɪs] Grazie; Anmut ⟨**VT1,** 22⟩
grade *(AE)* [greɪd] Klasse *(AE)*; Note *(AE)* **II**
grader *(AE)* [ˈgreɪdə] -Klässler(in) **II**
gradual [ˈgrædʒuəl] allmählich **II**
graduation [ˌgrædʒuˈeɪʃn] Schulabschluss **VT2,** 26
gram [græm] Gramm **IV**
grammar [ˈgræmə] Grammatik **I**
grammar school [ˈgræmə ˌskuːl] Gymnasium *(BE)* **IV**
grand [grænd] prächtig; großartig **VT2,** 27
grandma [ˈgrændmɑː] Oma **I**
grandpa [ˈgrændpɑː] Opa **I**
granny [ˈgræni] Oma ⟨**VT4,** 58⟩
grant [grɑːnt] Stipendium; Subvention; Zuwendung **VT1,** 14
to **grant** [grɑːnt] gewähren; zusprechen **VT4,** 63
grape [greɪp] Traube **III**
graph [grɑːf] Diagramm; Graph; Schaubild **IV**
graphic design [ˌgræfɪk dɪˈzaɪn] Grafikdesign; grafische Gestaltung **IV**
grass [grɑːs] Gras **II**
grateful [ˈgreɪtfl] dankbar **IV**
grave [greɪv] Grab **III**
gray *(AE)* [greɪ] grau **IV**
great [greɪt] großartig, toll **I**; groß **II**
greed [griːd] Gier **IV**
Greek [griːk] Griechisch; griechisch **IV**
green [griːn] grün **I**
greenhouse [ˈgriːnhaʊs] Gewächshaus **VT5,** 85
to **greet** [griːt] (be)grüßen **III**
grey [greɪ] grau **I**
grid [grɪd] Gitter, Tabelle **II**
to **grill** [grɪl] grillen **III**
grimy [ˈgraɪmi] rußgeschwärzt; schmutzig ⟨**VT5,** 77⟩
to **grin** [grɪn] grinsen **II**
*to get a **grip** on [ˌget‿ə ˈgrɪp] in den Griff bekommen ⟨**VT3,** 50⟩
gritty [ˈgrɪti] kiesig ⟨**VT5,** 76⟩
to **groan** [grəʊn] stöhnen **III**
to **groom** [gruːm] pflegen; putzen **VT3,** 40
ground [graʊnd] Boden; Grund **III**
group [gruːp] Klasse; Gruppe **I**
tutor group [ˈtjuːtə ˌgruːp] Klasse *(in einer englischen Schule)* **I**
groupy [ˈgruːpi] gruppenbezogen ⟨**VT1,** 14⟩
*to **grow** [grəʊ] anbauen; wachsen **I**
to **grow up** [grəʊ‿ˈʌp] aufwachsen, erwachsen werden **II**
grown-up [ˌgrəʊn‿ˈʌp] erwachsen **IV**
growth [grəʊθ] Wachstum **IV**
guard [gɑːd] Wache; Wächter(in) **VT5,** 80
guerrilla [gəˈrɪlə] Guerilla; Untergrundkämpfer(in) ⟨**VT2,** 35⟩
to **guess** [ges] raten, vermuten **I**
guesswork [ˈgeswɜːk] Rätselraten; Vermutung ⟨**VT5,** 77⟩
guest [gest] Gast **II**
guide [gaɪd] Führer(in) **III**
guideline [ˈgaɪdlaɪn] Richtlinie **VT5,** 79
guilty [ˈgɪlti] schuldig **IV**
guitar [gɪˈtɑː] Gitarre **I**
guitarist [gɪˈtɑːrɪst] Gitarrist(in) **II**
chewing **gum** [ˈtʃuːɪŋ ˌgʌm] Kaugummi **IV**
gun [gʌn] Schusswaffe **I**
gunsmith [ˈgʌnsmɪθ] Büchsenmacher(in) ⟨**VT4,** 69⟩
guy [gaɪ] Typ, Kerl; *pl.:* Leute **II**
Mr Nice Guy [ˌmɪstə ˈnaɪs gaɪ] der nette Mann von nebenan **IV**
gym(nasium) [dʒɪm; dʒɪmˈneɪziəm] Turnhalle **III**

H

habit [ˈhæbɪt] Gewohnheit **IV**
mating habits *(pl.)* [ˈmeɪtɪŋ ˌhæbɪts] Paarungsgewohnheiten ⟨**VT3,** 43⟩
habitat loss [ˈhæbɪtæt ˌlɒs] Verlust des Lebensraums ⟨**VT4,** 67⟩
hair [heə] Haar(e) **II**
hairdresser [ˈheədresə] Friseur(in) ⟨**VT3,** 44⟩
hairstyle [ˈheəstaɪl] Frisur **III**
half, *pl.* **halves** [hɑːf; hɑːvz] (die) Hälfte **III**
half past (two) [ˈhɑːf pɑːst] halb (drei) **I**
half-caste [ˈhɑːfkɑːst] Halbblut; Mischling ⟨**VT2,** 38⟩

half-time [ˌhɑːfˈtaɪm] Halbzeit **III**
hall [hɔːl] Flur, Diele, Korridor **I**; Halle, Saal **II**
hall of fame [ˌhɔːl‿əv ˈfeɪm] Ruhmeshalle **VT5,** 72
ham [hæm] Schinken **II**
hamburger [ˈhæmˌbɜːgə] Hamburger **IV**
hamster [ˈhæmstə] Hamster **I**
hand [hænd] Hand **I**
on the other hand [ɒn ðiˈʌðə ˌhænd] andererseits **III**
to **hand sth over** [hænd‿ˈəʊvə] etw. übergeben **III**
handle [ˈhændl] Griff **III**
handmade [ˌhændˈmeɪd] handgefertigt **IV**
handout [ˈhændaʊt] Informationsblatt **III**
handsome [ˈhændsəm] attraktiv; gut aussehend **VT5,** 76
*to come in **handy** [ˌkʌm‿ɪn ˈhændi] gelegen kommen **VT5,** 83
to **hang** [hæŋ] (er)hängen **VT4,** 63
*to **hang around** [ˌhæŋ‿əˈraʊnd] herumhängen **II**
to **hang out (with)** [hæŋ‿ˈaʊt] sich herumtreiben (mit) **II**
to **hang up** [hæŋ‿ˈʌp] aufhängen **III**
hang glider [ˈhæŋ ˌglaɪdə] Hängegleiter; Drachen ⟨**VT1,** 18⟩
to **happen** [ˈhæpn] geschehen, passieren **I**
to **happen to (be/do)** [ˈhæpn] zufällig sein/tun **VT1,** 9
happy [ˈhæpi] glücklich, froh **I**
they lived happily ever after [ðeɪ lɪvd ˌhæpɪli‿evər‿ˈɑːftə] und wenn sie nicht gestorben sind, dann leben sie noch heute ⟨**VT2,** 35⟩
to **harass** [ˈhærəs; həˈræs] belästigen; drangsalieren **IV**
harbour [ˈhɑːbə] Hafen **I**
hard [hɑːd] hart; schwer **II**
to **harden** [ˈhɑːdn] (ver)härten; hart machen **IV**
hardly [ˈhɑːdli] kaum **III**
hardness [ˈhɑːdnəs] Härte **IV**
harm [hɑːm] Schaden; Leid ⟨**VT5,** 72⟩
to **do harm** [hɑːm] Schaden anrichten ⟨**VT4,** 71⟩
harmful [ˈhɑːmfl] schädlich **VT2,** 34
harsh [hɑːʃ] barsch; rau; unnachsichtig **VT5,** 75
harvest [ˈhɑːvɪst] Ernte ⟨**VT4,** 70⟩
hassle [ˈhæsl] Theater; Schwierigkeiten **VT1,** 20
hat [hæt] Hut **II**
to **hate** [heɪt] hassen, nicht mögen **I**
to **haunt** [hɔːnt] spuken in; heimsuchen ⟨**VT5,** 83⟩
*to **have** [hæv] haben **II**; essen; trinken **II**
I'd better = I had better [aɪd ˈbetə] Ich sollte lieber … **III**
to **have (got)** [hæv ˈgɒt] besitzen, haben **I**
to **have a baby** [ˌhæv‿ə ˈbeɪbi] ein Kind bekommen **III**
to **have a look (at)** [ˌhæv‿ə ˈlʊk] anschauen **II**
to **have a point** [ˌhæv‿ə ˈpɔɪnt] nicht ganz Unrecht haben ⟨**VT3,** 45⟩
to **have a race** [ˌhæv‿ə ˈreɪs] ein Rennen veranstalten **I**
to **have a row** [ˌhæv‿ə ˈraʊ] streiten; Krach haben **IV**
to **have dinner** [hæv ˈdɪnə] zu Abend essen **I**
to **have in mind** [ˌhæv‿ɪn ˈmaɪnd] im Sinn haben **VT5,** 74
to **have on** [hæv‿ˈɒn] anhaben **II**
to **have second thoughts** [hæv ˌseknd ˈθɔːts] Zweifel haben; es sich anders überlegen ⟨**VT1,** 19⟩
to **have sth done** [ˌhæv ˈdʌn] etw. machen lassen **IV**
to **have sth in common** [ˌhæv‿ɪn ˈkɒmən] etw. gemeinsam haben **IV**
to **have to (do sth)** [hæv] etwas tun müssen **II**
Hawaiian [həˈwaɪən] Hawaiianer(in); hawaiianisch **IV**
hazard [ˈhæzəd] Gefahr; Risiko **IV**
he [hiː] er **I**
head [hed] Kopf **I**; Oberhaupt **III**
head teacher *(BE)* [ˌhed ˈtiːtʃə] Schulleiter(in) **III**
to **head (for)** [hed] zusteuern auf **II**
headache [ˈhedeɪk] Kopfweh **III**
heading [ˈhedɪŋ] Überschrift **I**
headline [ˈhedlaɪn] Schlagzeile **VT1,** 16; **VT2,** 26
headliner cause [ˌhedlaɪnə ˈkɔːz] schlagzeilenwürdiger Anlass **VT2,** 26
headmistress *(BE)* [ˌhedˈmɪstrəs] Schulleiterin ⟨**VT3,** 50⟩
to **heal** [hiːl] heilen **VT4,** 63
health [helθ] Gesundheit; Gesundheitslehre **II**
health club [ˈhelθ ˌklʌb] Fitnessklub **II**
healthy [ˈhelθi] gesund **III**
heap [hiːp] Haufen; Halde **VT5,** 77
*to **hear** [hɪə] hören **I**
heart [hɑːt] Herz **I**
to **heat** [hiːt] erhitzen; heizen **IV**
heavenly body [ˌhevnli ˈbɒdi] Himmelskörper ⟨**VT3,** 42⟩
heavy [ˈhevi] schwer **II**
heavy-duty [ˌheviˈdjuːti] strapazierfähig **VT1,** 14
height [haɪt] Höhe **II**
helicopter [ˈhelɪˌkɒptə] Helikopter, Hubschrauber **I**
hell [hel] Hölle **IV**
Hello! [həˈləʊ] Hallo! **I**
to **say hello** [seɪ həˈləʊ] Hallo sagen, sich begrüßen **I**
*to take the **helm** [ˌteɪk ðə ˈhelm] das Heft in die Hand nehmen ⟨**VT3,** 50⟩
helmet [ˈhelmət] Helm **III**
help [help] Hilfe, Rettung **I**
to **help** [help] helfen **I**
help yourself [ˌhelp jɔːˈself] bediene dich!/bedienen Sie sich! **II**
helpful [ˈhelpfl] hilfsbereit **IV**
helpless [ˈhelpləs] hilflos **I**
her [hɜː] ihr(e); sie; ihr **I**
herb [hɜːb] Kraut **IV**
here [hɪə] hier **I**
Here you are! [ˌhɪə juː‿ˈɑː] Hier bitte! Bitte schön! **I**
hero, *pl.* **heroes** [ˈhɪərəʊ] Held **II**
heroine [ˈherəʊɪn] Heldin **II**
herself [hɜːˈself] (sie) selbst; sich (selbst) **III**
Hey! [heɪ] He! **I**
Hi! [haɪ] Hi! Hallo! **I**
hide [haɪd] Fell; Tierhaut ⟨**VT4,** 67⟩
*to **hide** [haɪd] (sich) verstecken **II**
high [haɪ] hoch; groß **I**
high school [ˈhaɪ ˌskuːl] High School *(weiterführende Schule in den USA, Oberstufe)* **III**
highlight [ˈhaɪlaɪt] Highlight **III**
highway [ˈhaɪweɪ] Landstraße; Bundesautobahn *(AE)* **IV**
hike [haɪk] Wanderung **III**
to **hike** [haɪk] wandern **III**
hill [hɪl] Berg; Hügel **I**
him [hɪm] ihm; ihn **I**
himself [hɪmˈself] (er) selbst; sich (selbst) **III**
to **hinder** [ˈhɪndə] behindern; erschweren **VT3,** 48
Hindu [ˈhɪnduː] Hindu; hinduistisch **VT2,** 25
hip [hɪp] Hüfte **IV**
hip-hip-hooray [hɪp ˌhɪp hʊˈreɪ] Hipp hipp hurra ⟨**VT3,** 51⟩
hip-hop [ˈhɪp hɒp] Hip-Hop **II**
hippo [ˈhɪpəʊ] Nilpferd; Flusspferd **VT4,** 62
to **hire** [haɪə] einstellen **IV**
his [hɪz] sein(e) **I**
Hispanic [hɪˈspænɪk] hispanisch; lateinamerikanisch **IV**
to **hiss** [hɪs] zischen; fauchen **VT1,** 13; **VT3,** 42
historical [hɪˈstɒrɪkl] geschichtlich, historisch **III**
history [ˈhɪstri] Geschichte **II**
hit [hɪt] Hit **II**
*to **hit** [hɪt] schlagen; treffen; gegen etwas fahren **I**
hobby [ˈhɒbi] Hobby **II**
hobby horse [ˈhɒbi ˌhɔːs] Steckenpferd ⟨**VT3,** 45⟩

*to **hold** [həʊld] halten **II**
hole [həʊl] Loch **VT3,** 40
holiday ['hɒlədeɪ] Urlaub, Feiertag **I**
hollow ['hɒləʊ] hohl **II**
home [həʊm] Heim; nach Hause **I**
at home [ət 'həʊm] zu Hause **I**
broken home [ˌbrəʊkn 'həʊm] nicht intakte Familie **VT3,** 48
Home Office *(BE)* ['həʊm‿ɒfɪs] Innenministerium **VT5,** 80
old people's home [ˌəʊld pi:plz 'həʊm] Altersheim **II**
homeless ['həʊmləs] obdachlos **II**
homepage ['həʊmpeɪdʒ] Homepage **II**
homesick ['həʊmsɪk] heimwehkrank ⟨**VT1,** 23⟩
hometown ['həʊmtaʊn] Heimatstadt **III**
homework ['həʊmwɜ:k] Hausaufgaben **I**
homicidal [ˌhɒmɪ'saɪdl] menschenmörderisch ⟨**VT5,** 73⟩
honest ['ɒnɪst] ehrlich **IV**
honesty ['ɒnɪsti] Ehrlichkeit; Ehrenhaftigkeit ⟨**VT3,** 46⟩
honey ['hʌni] Honig; Schätzchen *(AE)* **IV**
hood *(AE)* [hʊd] Motorhaube **VT1,** 12
hoodie ['hʊdi] Kapuzenpulli ⟨**VT2,** 31⟩
The phone is ringing off the **hook.** [ðə ˌfəʊn‿ɪz rɪŋɪŋ ɒf ðə 'hʊk] Das Telefon klingelt ohne Unterlass. ⟨**VT3,** 43⟩
to **hook in** [ˌhʊk‿'ɪn] einhaken; einhängen ⟨**VT1,** 18⟩
to **hoot** [hu:t] hupen ⟨**VT4,** 69⟩
hop [hɒp] Sprung; Hopser ⟨**VT1,** 19⟩
hope [həʊp] Hoffnung **IV**
to **hope** [həʊp] hoffen **I**
hopefully ['həʊpfli] hoffentlich **IV**
hopeless ['həʊpləs] hoffnungslos **III**
horn [hɔ:n] Horn **IV**
horrified ['hɒrɪfaɪd] entsetzt **III**
horror ['hɒrə] Horror, Schrecken **II**
horse [hɔ:s] Pferd **I**
hobby horse ['hɒbi ˌhɔ:s] Steckenpferd ⟨**VT3,** 45⟩
to **be as hungry as a horse** [əz ˌhʌŋgri‿əz‿ə 'hɔ:s] einen Bärenhunger haben **II**
white horses [waɪt 'hɔ:sɪz] *hier:* Schaumkronen **I**
horseback riding [ˌhɔ:sbæk 'raɪdɪŋ] Reiten **II**
hospital ['hɒspɪtl] Hospital, Krankenhaus **II**
host [həʊst] Gastgeber(in); Talkmaster **III**
hostage ['hɒstɪdʒ] Geisel ⟨**VT1,** 14⟩
hostel ['hɒstl] Herberge **IV**
hostile ['hɒstaɪl] feindlich; ablehnend ⟨**VT4,** 67⟩
hot [hɒt] heiß **I**; scharf **III**
hotel [həʊ'tel] Hotel **II**
hour ['aʊə] Stunde **II**
opening hours ['əʊpnɪŋ‿aʊəz] Öffnungszeiten **I**
house [haʊs] Haus **I**
terraced house [ˌterɪst 'haʊs] Reihenhaus **IV**
household ['haʊshəʊld] allgemein bekannt **VT2,** 26
housing ['haʊzɪŋ] Unterkunft; Wohnungsbeschaffung **IV**
to **hover** ['hɒvə] schweben **VT5,** 77
how [haʊ] wie **I**
How about . . .? ['haʊ‿əˌbaʊt] Wie ist es mit . . .? **I**
How are you? [ˌhaʊ‿'ɑ: ju:] Wie geht es dir/euch/Ihnen? **I**
how many [haʊ 'meni] wie viele **I**
How much is/are . . . ? [ˌhaʊ 'mʌtʃ‿ɪz/ɑ:] Wie viel kostet/kosten . . . ? **I**
How old are you? [haʊ‿'əʊld‿ə ju:] Wie alt bist du/sind Sie? **I**
however [haʊ'evə] jedoch **II**
huge [hju:dʒ] riesig, gewaltig **I**
Huh? [hʌ; hə] Was? Hä? **I**
human ['hju:mən] menschlich **IV**
human being [ˌhju:mən 'bi:ɪŋ] menschliches Wesen **VT5,** 72
human rights abuse [ˌhju:mən 'raɪts‿əˌbju:s] Menschenrechtsverletzung **VT4,** 63
humble ['hʌmbl] bescheiden; demütig ⟨**VT2,** 31⟩; ⟨**VT5,** 83⟩
to **humiliate** [hju:'mɪlieɪt] demütigen; erniedrigen ⟨**VT3,** 45⟩
humour ['hju:mə] Humor; Komik; Stimmung **IV**
Hungarian [hʌŋ'geəriən] ungarisch; Ungar(in) **II**
hungry ['hʌŋgri] hungrig **I**
to **be as hungry as a horse** [əz ˌhʌŋgri‿əz‿ə 'hɔ:s] einen Bärenhunger haben **II**
to **hunt** [hʌnt] jagen **II**
hurricane ['hʌrɪkən] Hurrikan; Orkan; Wirbelsturm **VT2,** 26
to **hurry (up)** [ˌhʌri‿'ʌp] (sich) (be)eilen **II**
*to **hurt** [hɜ:t] verletzen, weh tun **II**
*to be **hurt** [bi: 'hɜ:t] verletzt sein/werden **I**
husband ['hʌzbənd] Ehemann **II**
hush [hʌʃ] Schweigen, Stille ⟨**VT3,** 45⟩
husky ['hʌski] Husky *(Schlittenhunderasse)* **II**
hut [hʌt] Hütte **VT4,** 59
hydrogen-core ['haɪdrədʒən ˌkɔ:] Wasserstoffkern- ⟨**VT5,** 75⟩
hydropower [ˌhaɪdrəʊ'paʊə] Wasserkraft **IV**
hysterics [hɪ'sterɪks] Hysterie; hysterischer Lachanfall ⟨**VT3,** 43⟩

I

I [aɪ] ich **I**
I beg your pardon? [aɪ ˌbeg jə 'pɑ:dn] Wie bitte? ⟨**VT3,** 45⟩
I can't be bothered. [aɪ ˌkɑ:nt bi: 'bɒðəd] Ich habe keine Lust.; Ich kann mich nicht dazu aufraffen. **IV**
I can't face *(+ gerund)* [aɪ ˌkænt 'feɪs] Ich sehe mich außer Stande (zu . . .) **IV**
I'd [aɪd] Ich würde **II**
I'd better = I had better [aɪd 'betə] Ich sollte lieber . . . **III**
I don't get it. [aɪ ˌdəʊnt 'get‿ɪt] Das kapiere ich nicht. **II**
I'd rather [aɪd 'rɑ:ðə] ich würde lieber **IV**
I'm fine. [aɪm 'faɪn] Mir geht es gut. **I**
I see. [aɪ 'si:] aha; ach so **II**
lyrical I [ˌlɪrɪkl‿'aɪ] lyrisches Ich **IV**
ice [aɪs] Eis **I**
ice cream [aɪs 'kri:m] Eis, Eiscreme **I**
icon ['aɪkɒn] Ikone ⟨**VT2,** 26⟩
idea [aɪ'dɪə] Einfall, Idee; Ahnung **I**
No idea! [ˌnəʊ‿aɪ'dɪə] Keine Ahnung! **I**
ideal [aɪ'dɪəl] Ideal ⟨**VT1,** 22⟩
identical [aɪ'dentɪkl] identisch; gleich ⟨**VT2,** 30⟩
to **identify (with)** [aɪ'dentɪfaɪ] (sich) identifizieren (mit) **IV**
identity [aɪ'dentəti] Identität **II**
idiom ['ɪdiəm] Redewendung; Idiom; Redensart **IV**
idiot ['ɪdiət] Idiot(in) **II**
if [ɪf] wenn, falls; ob **I**
ignorance ['ɪgnərnts] Ignoranz; Unwissenheit **VT5,** 77
ignorant ['ɪgnərnt] ignorant; unwissend **VT5,** 77
to **ignore** [ɪg'nɔ:] ignorieren **III**
ill [ɪl] krank **II**
to **take ill** [ˌteɪk‿'ɪl] krank werden **VT3,** 47
illegal [ɪ'li:gl] illegal; unrechtmäßig; rechtswidrig **IV**
illness ['ɪlnəs] Krankheit **III**
to **illuminate** [ɪ'lu:mɪneɪt] erleuchten ⟨**VT5,** 85⟩
image ['ɪmɪdʒ] Bild; Image **IV**
imagery ['ɪmɪdʒri] Bildsprache; Metaphorik **IV**
imaginative [ɪ'mædʒɪnətɪv] einfallsreich, fantasievoll **II**
to **imagine** [ɪ'mædʒɪn] sich (etwas) vorstellen **II**
to **imitate** ['ɪmɪteɪt] imitieren; nachahmen **IV**
immediately [ɪ'mi:diətli] sofort, gleich **I**
immigrant ['ɪmɪgrənt] Immigrant(in), Einwanderer; Einwanderin **III**
immigration [ˌɪmɪ'greɪʃn] Immigration; Einwanderung **VT2,** 25; **VT4,** 57

to immobilize [ɪ'məʊblaɪz] unbeweglich machen; ruhig stellen ⟨**VT4,** 61⟩
impact ['ɪmpækt] Auswirkung; Einfluss ⟨**VT5,** 81⟩
to import [ɪm'pɔ:t] importieren; einführen **IV**
importance [ɪm'pɔ:tnts] Bedeutung, Wichtigkeit **IV**
important [ɪm'pɔ:tnt] wichtig; einflussreich **I**
impossible [ɪm'pɒsəbl] unmöglich **III**
impoverished [ɪm'pɒvrɪʃt] verarmt ⟨**VT4,** 67⟩
to impress [ɪm'pres] beeindrucken **VT1,** 10
impression [ɪm'preʃn] Impression; Eindruck **VT1,** 13; **VT3,** 47; **VT4,** 62
  to **be clean out of impressions** [bi: ˌkli:n‿aʊt‿əv‿ɪm'preʃnz] komplett frei sein von Eindrücken ⟨**VT1,** 13⟩
impressive [ɪm'presɪv] beeindruckend **VT2,** 33
life **imprisonment** [ˌlaɪf‿ɪm'prɪznmənt] lebenslängliche Haftstrafe **VT4,** 61
to improve [ɪm'pru:v] (sich) verbessern **II**
improvement [ɪm'pru:vmənt] Verbesserung **IV**
in [ɪn] in; rein, herein **I**
  in advance [ɪn‿əd'vɑ:nts] im Voraus **II**
  in between [ˌɪn bɪ'twi:n] dazwischen **II**
  in case [ɪn 'keɪs] falls; für den Fall, dass … **II**
  in class [ɪn 'klɑ:s] in/vor der Klasse **I**
  in disguise [ɪn dɪs'gaɪz] verkleidet **II**
  in fact [ɪn 'fækt] tatsächlich; eigentlich **II**
  in front of [ɪn 'frʌnt‿əv] vor, davor **I**
  in my opinion [ɪn 'maɪ‿əˌpɪnjən] meiner Meinung nach **IV**
  in need [ɪn 'ni:d] bedürftig **IV**
  in order to [ɪn‿'ɔ:də tə] um … zu **III**
  in return [ɪn rɪ'tɜ:n] als Gegenleistung **IV**
  in spite of [ɪn 'spaɪt‿əv] trotz **III**
  in terms of [ɪn 'tɜ:mz‿əv] bezüglich **VT5,** 80
  in the end [ˌɪn ði:‿'end] schließlich, zum Schluss **II**
  in the first place [ɪn ðə 'fɜ:st pleɪs] von vornherein; überhaupt erst ⟨**VT3,** 45⟩
  in the late 1100s [leɪt] im späten 12. Jahrhundert **II**
  in time for [ɪn 'taɪm fə] rechtzeitig zu **II**
  in vain [ɪn 'veɪn] umsonst; vergeblich ⟨**VT5,** 87⟩
inaction [ɪn'ækʃn] Untätigkeit ⟨**VT5,** 72⟩
inappropriate [ˌɪnə'prəʊpriət] unangemessen **VT3,** 40
incident ['ɪntsɪdnt] Vorfall; Ereignis ⟨**VT3,** 50⟩

to include [ɪn'klu:d] einschließen; beinhalten; aufnehmen **IV**
income ['ɪnkʌm] Einkommen **IV**
incomprehensible [ɪnˌkɒmprɪ'hentsəbl] unverständlich; unbegreiflich **VT2,** 26
increase ['ɪnkri:s] Zunahme; Wachstum; Anstieg **IV**
to increase [ɪn'kri:s] zunehmen; vergrößern **IV**
indeed [ɪn'di:d] tatsächlich; in der Tat; allerdings **IV**
indefinite [ˌɪn'defɪnət] unbestimmt; indefinit **IV**
independence [ˌɪndɪ'pendənts] Unabhängigkeit **III**
independent (of/from) [ˌɪndɪ'pendənt] unabhängig (von) **III**
Indian ['ɪndiən] indisch; Inder(in); indianisch; Indianer(in) **I**
to indicate ['ɪndɪkeɪt] anzeigen; angeben; kenntlich machen ⟨**VT5,** 83⟩
indifferent [ɪn'dɪfrnt] gleichgültig **VT5,** 83
indirect speech [ˌɪndɪrekt 'spi:tʃ] indirekte Rede **III**
individual [ˌɪndɪ'vɪdʒuəl] individuell; einzeln **IV**
to indulge (in) sth [ɪn'dʌldʒ] nachgeben; sich etw. hingeben; sich in etw. ergehen **VT2,** 34; ⟨**VT5,** 81⟩
industrial [ɪn'dʌstriəl] industriell **IV**
industrious [ɪn'dʌstriəs] fleißig **VT3,** 43
industry ['ɪndəstri] Industrie **III**
  mining industry ['maɪnɪŋ ˌɪndəstri] Bergbau **VT4,** 60
inevitable [ɪn'evɪtəbl] unvermeidlich; unabwendbar ⟨**VT3,** 46⟩
infancy ['ɪnfəntsi] frühes Kindesalter ⟨**VT3,** 43⟩
infection [ɪn'fekʃn] Infektion **VT4,** 66
infiltrator ['ɪnfɪltreɪtə] Eindringling ⟨**VT4,** 70⟩
infinitesimal [ˌɪnfɪnɪ'tesɪml] unendlich klein; winzig ⟨**VT5,** 75⟩
infinitive [ɪn'fɪnətɪv] Infinitiv **II**
influence ['ɪnfluənts] Einfluss **III**
to influence ['ɪnfluənts] beeinflussen **III**
to inform [ɪn'fɔ:m] informieren **IV**
informal [ɪn'fɔ:ml] informell; zwanglos **III**
information [ˌɪnfə'meɪʃn] Information(en) **I**
  information technology [ɪnfəˌmeɪʃn tek'nɒlədʒi] Informatik; Informationstechnik **IV**
infrastructure ['ɪnfrəˌstrʌktʃə] Infrastruktur **IV**
to inhabit [ɪn'hæbɪt] bewohnen **VT4,** 59
inhabitant [ɪn'hæbɪtnt] Einwohner(in); Bewohner(in) **III**
to inherit [ɪn'herɪt] erben **VT2,** 29; ⟨**VT4,** 68⟩
to inhibit [ɪn'hɪbɪt] hemmen; hindern ⟨**VT2,** 31⟩

to injure ['ɪndʒə] verletzen **III**
injury ['ɪndʒri] Verletzung **VT1,** 16; **VT4,** 66
inland ['ɪnlænd] landeinwärts **VT4,** 57
innocence ['ɪnəsnts] Unschuld ⟨**VT5,** 87⟩
inquiry [ɪn'kwaɪəri] Ermittlung; Nachforschung; Anfrage **III**
insect ['ɪnsekt] Insekt **III**
inside [ɪn'saɪd] innen, drin; nach drinnen **I**
to insist (on) [ɪn'sɪst] insistieren; bestehen (auf) **VT2,** 35
insolence ['ɪntslənts] Anmaßung; Frechheit ⟨**VT3,** 45⟩
inspection [ɪn'spekʃn] Inspektion; Kontrolle; Überprüfung ⟨**VT3,** 51⟩
inspector [ɪn'spektə] Inspektor(in); Prüfer(in); Schulrat; Schulrätin ⟨**VT3,** 51⟩
inspirational [ˌɪntspɪ'reɪʃnəl] inspiriert; fähig, andere zu begeistern ⟨**VT3,** 50⟩
to inspire [ɪn'spaɪə] inspirieren; anregen **IV**
instant ['ɪntstənt] Augenblick; Moment **VT5,** 77
instant ['ɪntstənt] sofortig ⟨**VT5,** 81⟩
instead [ɪn'sted] stattdessen **III**
instead of [ɪn'sted‿əv] anstatt **III**
institution [ˌɪntstɪ'tju:ʃn] Institution; Einrichtung **IV**
instruction [ɪn'strʌkʃn] Instruktion, Anweisung **III**
instrument ['ɪntstrəmənt] Instrument **I**
to insult [ɪn'sʌlt] beleidigen **IV**
to integrate ['ɪntɪgreɪt] integrieren; einbinden **IV**
integration [ˌɪntɪ'greɪʃn] Integration; Einbindung **VT2,** 27
intellectual [ˌɪntl'ektʃuəl] Intellektuelle(r) **VT3,** 42
intelligence [ɪn'telɪdʒnts] Intelligenz; Klugheit; Einsicht **VT5,** 72
intelligent [ɪn'telɪdʒnt] intelligent; klug; vernünftig **IV**
intelligible [ɪn'telɪdʒəbl] verständlich ⟨**VT5,** 77⟩
to intend [ɪn'tend] beabsichtigen; intendieren **IV**
intention [ɪn'tentʃn] Absicht, Intention **II**
interactive [ˌɪntər'æktɪv] interaktiv **II**
interest ['ɪntrəst] Interesse **III**
*to be **interested** in [bi:‿'ɪntrəstɪd‿ɪn] interessiert sein an, sich interessieren für **I**
interesting ['ɪntrəstɪŋ] interessant **I**
  far more interesting [ˌfɑ: mɔ:r‿'ɪntrəstɪŋ] weitaus interessanter **I**
interface ['ɪntəfeɪs] Schnittstelle ⟨**VT5,** 82⟩
interference [ˌɪntə'fɪərnts] Störung; Beeinträchtigung; Einmischung ⟨**VT3,** 45⟩
interior [ɪn'tɪəriə] innere(-r/-s); Innenaufnahme **VT4,** 56

international [ˌɪntəˈnæʃnl] international **I**
Internet [ˈɪntənet] Internet **I**
internship *(AE)* [ˈɪntɜːnʃɪp] Praktikum **IV**
to **interpret** [ɪnˈtɜːprɪt] interpretieren; dolmetschen **IV**
to **interrupt** [ˌɪntəˈrʌpt] unterbrechen **II**
interview [ˈɪntəvjuː] Interview; Befragung **I**
to **interview** [ˈɪntəvjuː] interviewen **II**
into [ˈɪntu; ˈɪntə] in, hinein **I**
to **introduce** [ˌɪntrəˈdjuːs] vorstellen, einführen **II**
introduction [ˌɪntrəˈdʌkʃn] Einführung; Vorstellung **II**
to **invade** [ɪnˈveɪd] einmarschieren (in); überfallen **IV**
to **invent** [ɪnˈvent] erfinden **II**
invention [ɪnˈventʃn] Erfindung **IV**
inventor [ɪnˈventə] Erfinder(in) **IV**
to **invest** [ɪnˈvest] investieren **IV**
to **investigate** [ɪnˈvestɪgeɪt] ermitteln; untersuchen; Nachforschungen anstellen; recherchieren **IV**
invisible [ɪnˈvɪzəbl] unsichtbar **II**
invitation [ˌɪnvɪˈteɪʃn] Einladung **I**
to **invite** [ɪnˈvaɪt] einladen **I**
to **involve** [ɪnˈvɒlv] involvieren; einbeziehen; beteiligen **IV**
  to **get (sb) involved (in)** [ˌget‿ɪnˈvɒlvd] sich (oder jmdn) beteiligen (an); sich engagieren (für); sich einlassen (auf) **III**
Irish [ˈaɪrɪʃ] irisch; Irisch **I**
iron [aɪən] Eisen **VT5,** 76
  corrugated iron [ˌkɒrəgeɪtɪd‿ˈaɪən] Wellblech ⟨**VT5,** 77⟩
  iron ore [ˈaɪən‿ɔː] Eisenerz **IV**
  pig iron [ˈpɪg‿aɪən] Roheisen ⟨**VT5,** 76⟩
ironical [ˌaɪəˈrɒnɪkl] ironisch **VT4,** 59
irony [ˈaɪərəni] Ironie **VT3,** 44
irregular [ɪˈregjələ] unregelmäßig **I**
irresponsible [ˌɪrɪˈspɒntsəbl] unverantwortlich; verantwortungslos **VT1,** 9
Islamic [ɪzˈlæmɪk] islamisch ⟨**VT2,** 39⟩
island [ˈaɪlənd] Insel **I**
issue [ˈɪʃuː; ˈɪsjuː] Frage; Angelegenheit; Problem **IV**
to **issue** [ˈɪʃuː; ˈɪsjuː] ausstellen; herausgeben ⟨**VT4,** 61⟩
it [ɪt] es **I**
  It just goes to show ... [ɪt ˌdʒʌst gəʊz tə ˈʃəʊ] Das zeigt mal wieder ... ⟨**VT4,** 68⟩
  It's nothing to do with me. [ɪts ˌnʌθɪŋ tə ˌduː wɪð ˈmiː] Ich habe damit nichts zu tun. **II**
  It's no use *(+ gerund)* [ɪts ˈnəʊ juːs] Es nützt nichts ... **III**
  It's up to you [ɪts‿ʌp tə ˈjuː] Wie du willst **VT1,** 15
  It's your turn. [ˈjɔː tɜːn] Du bist/Sie sind dran. **I**

IT [ˌaɪˈtiː] Informatik; Informationstechnik **IV**
Italian [ɪˈtæliən] italienisch; Italiener(in); Italienisch **I**
to **itemise** [ˈaɪtəmaɪz] aufschlüsseln; einzeln aufführen ⟨**VT5,** 82⟩
its [ɪts] sein(e); ihr(e) **I**
ivory [ˈaɪvri] Elfenbein ⟨**VT4,** 67⟩

J

jacket [ˈdʒækɪt] Jacke **II**
jail [dʒeɪl] Gefängnis **VT2,** 28; **VT4,** 61
jam [dʒæm] Marmelade **II**; Gedränge; Klemme **II**
  traffic jam [ˈtræfɪk ˌdʒæm] Stau **II**
to **jam** [dʒæm] klemmen **VT1,** 13
Japanese [ˌdʒæpnˈiːz] japanisch; Japanisch **III**
jasmine [ˈdʒæzmɪn] Jasmin ⟨**VT3,** 47⟩
jazz [dʒæz] Jazz **II**
jealous (of) [ˈdʒeləs] eifersüchtig, neidisch **II**
jeans *pl.* [dʒiːnz] Jeans **I**
jelly [ˈdʒeli] Wackelpudding, Gelee **I**
jerk [dʒɜːk] Trottel **II**
to **jerk sb around** [ˌdʒɜːk‿əˈraʊnd] jmdn hin und her werfen **VT1,** 14
jet [dʒet] Düse; Düsenflugzeug **VT3,** 49
jewelry *(AE)* [ˈdʒuːəlri] Schmuck **VT3,** 40
job [dʒɒb] Arbeitsstelle, Job **I**; Tätigkeit; Arbeit; Aufgabe **IV**
  nose job *(infml)* [ˈnəʊz ˌdʒɒb] Nasenkorrektur ⟨**VT3,** 48⟩
jock *(AE) (infml)* [dʒɒk] Sportler(in) **VT3,** 42
jogging [ˈdʒɒgɪŋ] Jogging **I**
to **join** [dʒɔɪn] beitreten, sich anschließen; verbinden **II**
joke [dʒəʊk] Witz **II**
to **joke** [dʒəʊk] scherzen **II**
jolt [dʒəʊlt] Ruck ⟨**VT4,** 69⟩
journalist [ˈdʒɜːnlɪst] Journalist(in) **I**
journey [ˈdʒɜːni] Reise, Fahrt **II**
joy [dʒɔɪ] Freude ⟨**VT1,** 19⟩
to **judge** [dʒʌdʒ] beurteilen; bewerten **VT1,** 10; **VT2,** 33
Judgement Day [ˈdʒʌdʒmənt ˌdeɪ] Tag des Jüngsten Gerichts ⟨**VT5,** 87⟩
judo [ˈdʒuːdəʊ] Judo **III**
to **juggle** [ˈdʒʌgl] jonglieren **II**
juice [dʒuːs] Saft **II**
to **jump** [dʒʌmp] springen **I**; erschrecken ⟨**VT3,** 50⟩
  jump school [ˈdʒʌmp ˌskuːl] Fallschirmspringerschule ⟨**VT1,** 12⟩
  to **jump to conclusions** [ˌdʒʌmp tə kənˈkluːʒnz] voreilige Schlüsse ziehen **VT1,** 10
junior [ˈdʒuːniə] Mittelstufenschüler(in) **VT1,** 12

junk shop [ˈdʒʌŋk ˌʃɒp] Ramschladen **VT2,** 36
just [dʒʌst] gerade; nur **I**
justice [ˈdʒʌstɪs] Gerechtigkeit; Justiz **VT5,** 80
to **justify** [ˈdʒʌstɪfaɪ] rechtfertigen **VT2,** 29
to **jut** [dʒʌt] hervorragen ⟨**VT4,** 70⟩

K

kangaroo [ˌkæŋgrˈuː] Känguru **III**
kayaking [ˈkaɪækɪŋ] Kajakfahren **II**
keen [kiːn] scharf; fein ⟨**VT2,** 38⟩
  to **be keen on** [biː ˈkiːn‿ɒn] scharf sein auf, begeistert sein von **II**
*to **keep** [kiːp] (be)halten **II**
  to **keep** *(+ doing)* [kiːp] etwas weiter/immer wieder tun **II**
  to **keep up** [kiːp‿ˈʌp] aufrechterhalten **II**
keeper [ˈkiːpə] Wärter(in), Aufseher(in) **I**; Wächter(in), Aufpasser(in), Hüter(in) **II**
key [kiː] Schlüssel **II**; Taste ⟨**VT2,** 38⟩
  key ring [ˈkiː ˌrɪŋ] Schlüsselbund; Schlüsselanhänger **IV**
  key word [ˈkiː wɜːd] Stichwort; Schlüsselbegriff **II**
keyboard [ˈkiːbɔːd] Keyboard; Tastatur **III**
to **kick** [kɪk] kicken, treten **II**
  to **kick sb off a team** [kɪk‿ˈɒf] jmdn aus dem Team werfen **III**
kid [kɪd] Kind; Kitz **I**
to **kidnap** [ˈkɪdnæp] kidnappen; entführen **III**
kidnapper [ˈkɪdnæpə] Kidnapper(in); Entführer(in) **III**
to **kill** [kɪl] töten **II**
kilometre [ˈkɪləʊˌmiːtə; kɪˈlɒmɪtə] Kilometer **II**
kind [kaɪnd] Art, Sorte **II**
  kind of [ˈkaɪnd‿əv] ziemlich **III**
kind [kaɪnd] freundlich, nett **II**
kindergarten [ˈkɪndəgɑːtn] Kindergarten **I**
kindness [ˈkaɪndnəs] Freundlichkeit; Güte **IV**
king [kɪŋ] König **I**
kingdom [ˈkɪŋdəm] Königreich **II**
to **kiss** [kɪs] küssen **IV**
kitchen [ˈkɪtʃɪn] Küche **I**
knee [niː] Knie **III**
knife, *pl.* **knives** [naɪf; naɪvz] Messer **I**
knight [naɪt] Ritter **III**
knock [nɒk] Klopfen, Schlag **II**
to **knock out** [nɒk‿ˈaʊt] k.o. schlagen; umhauen **III**
  to **knock over** [ˌnɒk‿ˈəʊvə] umstoßen **II**
*to **know** [nəʊ] wissen; kennen **I**
  to **know the ropes** [ˌnəʊ ðə ˈrəʊps] die Spielregeln kennen ⟨**VT3,** 43⟩
knowledge [ˈnɒlɪdʒ] Wissen; Kenntnisse **IV**
*to **be known as** [biː ˈnəʊn‿əz] bekannt sein als **II**
koala [kəʊˈɑːlə] Koala **III**

L

lab [læb] Labor ⟨**VT5,** 87⟩
label ['leɪbl] Etikett; Beschriftung **IV**
labour ['leɪbə] Arbeit; Arbeitskraft; Mühe **VT2,** 24; **VT4,** 59; **VT5,** 73
labour-intensive [ˌleɪbər‿ɪn'tentsɪv] arbeitsaufwändig ⟨**VT2,** 24⟩
to **lace** one's fingers [ˌleɪs wʌnz 'fɪŋgəz] die Hände verschränken ⟨**VT1,** 15⟩
lack (of) [læk] Mangel (an); Fehlen (von) ⟨**VT1,** 19⟩; **VT2,** 25; **VT3,** 48
lad [læd] Junge **IV**
lady ['leɪdi] Dame, Frau **I**
ladies and gentlemen [ˌleɪdiz‿n 'dʒentlmən] meine Damen und Herren **II**
to **lag** [læg] hinterherhinken; zurückbleiben ⟨**VT3,** 46⟩
lake [leɪk] See **II**
lamb [læm] Lamm, Lämmchen **I**
lamp [læmp] Lampe; Leuchte **III**
land [lænd] Land **II**
to **land** [lænd] landen **I**
landing ['lændɪŋ] Treppenabsatz ⟨**VT5,** 76⟩
landmark ['lændmɑ:k] Wahrzeichen; Markstein **III**
landscape ['lændskeɪp] Landschaft **I**
landslide ['lændslaɪd] Erdrutsch **IV**
lane [leɪn] Gasse; Fahrspur **I**
language ['læŋgwɪdʒ] Sprache **I**
programming language ['prəʊgræmɪŋ ˌlæŋgwɪdʒ] Programmiersprache **IV**
lantern ['læntən] Laterne **II**
lap [læp] Schoß **VT1,** 13
large [lɑ:dʒ] groß, riesig **I**
largest ['lɑ:dʒɪst] (der, die, das) größte **I**
to **last** [lɑ:st] dauern, anhalten **II**
last [lɑ:st] letzte(-r/-s) **I**
at last [ət 'lɑ:st] endlich **I**
last night [lɑ:st 'naɪt] gestern Abend/Nacht **II**
late [leɪt] spät **I**
in the late 1100s [leɪt] im späten 12. Jahrhundert **II**
to **be late** [bi: 'leɪt] zu spät dran sein, zu spät kommen **I**
later ['leɪtə] später **I**
latest ['leɪtɪst] neueste(-r/-s) **II**
Latin ['lætɪn] Latein **II**
to **laugh** [lɑ:f] lachen **I**
to **launch** [lɔ:ntʃ] starten; abschießen; einführen **VT5,** 73
laundry ['lɔ:ndri] Wäsche; Wäscherei **VT4,** 59
law [lɔ:] Gesetz **III**; Jura; Recht **IV**
lawyer ['lɔɪə] Jurist(in); Anwalt, Anwältin **IV**
lax [læks] lax; locker **VT5,** 79
layer ['leɪə] Schicht; Lage; Ebene ⟨**VT4,** 64⟩
layout ['leɪaʊt] Layout, Anordnung **II**
lazy ['leɪzi] faul **I**
*to **lead** [li:d] führen **III**
leader ['li:də] Führer(in), Anführer(in) **II**
leaf, *pl.* **leaves** [li:f; li:vz] Blatt **II**
*to **lean** [li:n] (sich) lehnen **IV**
*to **leap** [li:p] springen ⟨**VT4,** 70⟩
*to **learn** [lɜ:n; lɜ:nt] lernen **I**
at **least** [ət 'li:st] mindestens, wenigstens **II**
leather ['leðə] Leder **III**
*to **leave** [li:v] (ver)lassen; abfahren **II**
to **leave out** [li:v‿'aʊt] auslassen **II**
to **leave sb alone** [ˌli:v‿ə'ləʊn] jemanden in Ruhe lassen **III**
lecturer ['lektʃrə] Dozent(in) ⟨**VT2,** 30⟩
left [left] links; linke(-r/-s) **I**
on somebody's right/left [ɒn ˌsʌmbədiz 'raɪt/'left] zur Rechten/zur Linken von jemandem **I**
left [left] übrig **II**
leg [leg] Bein **I**
legal ['li:gl] legal; rechtlich; Rechts- **IV**
legend ['ledʒənd] Legende, Sage **II**
lemonade [ˌlemə'neɪd] Limonade **IV**
*to **lend** [lend] (ver)leihen **III**
length [leŋkθ] Länge **IV**
lengthy ['leŋkθi] langatmig; übermäßig lang ⟨**VT5,** 83⟩
less [les] weniger **II**
lesson ['lesn] Unterrichtsstunde, Schulstunde **I**
*to **let** [let] lassen **I**
let alone [ˌlet‿ə'ləʊn] geschweige denn **VT2,** 34
Let's check! [lets 'tʃek] Lass(t) uns überprüfen! **I**
Let's go! [lets 'gəʊ] Lass(t) uns gehen! **I**
Let's start! [lets 'stɑ:t] Lass(t) uns anfangen **I**
to **let go** [ˌlet 'gəʊ] loslassen ⟨**VT1,** 23⟩
letter ['letə] Buchstabe; Brief **I**
capital letter [ˌkæpɪtl 'letə] Großbuchstabe **VT5,** 83
letter of application [ˌletər‿əv‿ˌæplɪ'keɪʃn] Bewerbungsschreiben **IV**
letter to the editor [ˌletə tʊ ði‿'edɪtə] Leserbrief **IV**
thank you letter ['θæŋk ju: ˌletə] Dankschreiben **I**
lettuce ['letɪs] Kopfsalat **IV**
level ['levl] Level, Höhe, Niveau **II**
poverty level ['pɒvəti ˌlevl] Armutsgrenze **IV**
to **levy** ['levi] erheben ⟨**VT4,** 61⟩
liberty ['lɪbəti] Freiheit **VT1,** 9
civil liberty [ˌsɪvl 'lɪbəti] Bürgerrecht **VT5,** 79
library ['laɪbri] Bibliothek **II**
licence ['laɪsnts] Lizenz; Erlaubnis **IV**
driving licence ['draɪvɪŋ ˌlaɪsnts] Führerschein **IV**
lie [laɪ] Lüge **IV**
to **lie** [laɪ] lügen **II**
*to **lie** [laɪ] liegen **I**
lieutenant commander [lu:ˌtenənt kə'mɑ:ndə; lefˌtenənt kə'mɑ:ndə] Kapitänleutnant ⟨**VT5,** 72⟩
life imprisonment [ˌlaɪf‿ɪm'prɪznmənt] lebenslängliche Haftstrafe **VT4,** 61
life, *pl.* **lives** [laɪf] Leben **I**
to **take one's own life** [ˌteɪk wʌnz‿əʊn 'laɪf] sich das Leben nehmen **II**
lifestyle ['laɪfstaɪl] Lebensart **III**
lift-shaft ['lɪftʃɑ:ft] Aufzugschacht ⟨**VT5,** 76⟩
to **give sb a lift** [ˌgɪv‿ə 'lɪft] jmdn im Auto mitnehmen **VT4,** 58
to **lift** [lɪft] (sich) heben ⟨**VT1,** 18⟩; ⟨**VT2,** 31⟩
light [laɪt] Licht **II**
light bulb ['laɪt bʌlb] Glühbirne **IV**
*to **light** [laɪt] anzünden; erhellen; beleuchten **IV**
light [laɪt] hellhäutig ⟨**VT2,** 30⟩; leicht ⟨**VT2,** 31⟩
lighthouse ['laɪthaʊs] Leuchtturm **I**
like [laɪk] Vorliebe **II**
to **like** [laɪk] mögen, gern haben **I**
Would you like . . .? [ˌwʊd jə 'laɪk] Möchtest du/möchten Sie/möchtet ihr . . .? **II**
What's it **like?** [ˌwɒts‿ɪt 'laɪk] Wie ist es? **II**
like (this/that) [laɪk 'ðɪs/ðæt] so wie (hier/dort) **I**
like [laɪk] als ob **IV**
*to be **likely** (to) [bi: 'laɪkli] wahrscheinlich sein **III**
limit ['lɪmɪt] Limit; Grenze; Beschränkung **VT1,** 8; **VT5,** 75
to **limit** ['lɪmɪt] limitieren; begrenzen; beschränken **VT2,** 25; ⟨**VT4,** 67⟩
line [laɪn] Zeile; Linie **I**; Leitung ⟨**VT1,** 18⟩
time line ['taɪm laɪn] Zeitstrahl **II**
link [lɪŋk] Link; Verbindung **II**
lion [laɪən] Löwe **III**
lip [lɪp] Lippe **IV**
list [lɪst] Liste **I**
to **list** [lɪst] auflisten **IV**
to **listen** (to) ['lɪsn] zuhören, (an)hören **I**
listening ['lɪsnɪŋ] Hören, *hier:* Hörübung **I**
literary ['lɪtrəri] literarisch **IV**
literature ['lɪtrətʃə] Literatur **III**
little [lɪtl] klein **I**
a little [ə 'lɪtl] ein bisschen; ein wenig **III**
to **live** [lɪv] wohnen, leben **I**
they lived happily ever after [ðeɪ lɪvd ˌhæpɪli‿evər‿'ɑ:ftə] und wenn sie nicht gestorben sind, dann leben sie noch heute ⟨**VT2,** 35⟩

to **live on sth** ['lɪv‿ɒn] von etw leben **III**
live [laɪv] scharf **VT4,** 62
living conditions *(pl.)* ['lɪvɪŋ kənˌdɪʃnz] Lebensbedingungen **IV**
living room ['lɪvɪŋ rʊm] Wohnzimmer **I**
standard of living [ˌstændəd‿əv 'lɪvɪŋ] Lebensstandard **IV**
to **make a living from sth** [ˌmeɪk‿ə 'lɪvɪŋ frəm] seinen Lebensunterhalt mit etw. bestreiten **IV**
to load [ləʊd] laden **VT4,** 58
lobster ['lɒbstə] Hummer **III**
local ['ləʊkl] lokal, örtlich **III**
*to be located [bi: ləʊ'keɪtɪd] gelegen sein **II**
lock [lɒk] (Fahrrad-)Schloss **I**
to lock [lɒk] abschließen **III**
locker ['lɒkə] Schließfach; Spind **VT1,** 14
to log in [ˌlɒg‿'ɪn] eintragen; aufnehmen ⟨**VT5,** 75⟩
logical ['lɒdʒɪkl] logisch **IV**
logo ['ləʊgəʊ] Logo; Firmenzeichen **IV**
Londoner ['lʌndənə] Londoner(in) **II**
lonely ['ləʊnli] einsam **III**
to long (for) [lɒŋ] sich sehnen (nach); verlangen **VT3,** 47
long [lɒŋ] lang; weit **I**
no longer [nəʊ 'lɒŋgə] nicht mehr, nicht länger **I**
loo *(infml)* [lu:] Klo **IV**
the looks *(pl.)* [lʊks] das Aussehen ⟨**VT3,** 48⟩
to **have a look (at)** [ˌhæv‿ə 'lʊk] anschauen **II**
to look [lʊk] (aus)sehen; schauen **I**
to **look after** [lʊk‿'ɑ:ftə] aufpassen auf; hüten **I**
to **look at** ['lʊk‿ət] anschauen **I**
to **look down on sb/sth** [lʊk 'daʊn] auf jmdn/etw. herabsehen **IV**
to **look forward to (+ doing)** [ˌlʊk 'fɔ:wəd] sich freuen auf **III**
to **look like** ['lʊk laɪk] aussehen wie **I**
to **look out for** [ˌlʊk‿'aʊt fə] Ausschau halten nach; sich in Acht nehmen vor **II**
to **look up** [lʊk‿'ʌp] nachschlagen, nachschauen **II**
to **look upon ... as ...** ['lʊk‿əˌpɒn] ansehen als **IV**
power loom [ˌpaʊə 'lu:m] mechanischer Webstuhl **IV**
to loom [lu:m] sich abzeichnen ⟨**VT5,** 82⟩
loose [lu:s] lose; locker; frei **VT1,** 14; **VT4,** 62
lord [lɔ:d] Lord, Herr **II**
*to lose [lu:z] verlieren **I**
Get lost! *(infml)* [get 'lɒst] Hau ab!; Verzieh dich! **IV**
to **get lost** [get 'lɒst] verloren gehen, sich verirren **I**

loss [lɒs] Verlust ⟨**VT1,** 22⟩
habitat loss ['hæbɪtət ˌlɒs] Verlust des Lebensraums ⟨**VT4,** 67⟩
a lot of [ə 'lɒt‿əv] viele, eine Menge **I**
lots of ['lɒts‿əv] viel(e) **I**
you lot ['ju: ˌlɒt] ihr alle **I**
lottery ['lɒtri] Lotterie **IV**
loud [laʊd] laut **I**
loud hailer ['laʊd ˌheɪlə] Megafon; Flüstertüte *(ugs.)* ⟨**VT4,** 62⟩
love [lʌv] Liebe; Herzliche Grüße *(am Briefende)* **I**
to **be in love (with)** [ˌbi:‿ɪn 'lʌv] verliebt sein (in) **II**
*to fall in love (with) [ˌfɔ:l‿ɪn 'lʌv] sich verlieben (in) **II**
to love [lʌv] lieben, gern mögen **I**
lovely ['lʌvli] schön, hübsch; herrlich **I**
low [ləʊ] niedrig **IV**
to lower ['ləʊə] absenken; verringern; herunterschrauben **IV**
low-paid [ˌləʊ'peɪd] schlecht bezahlt **IV**
low-riding ['ləʊˌraɪdɪŋ] tiefsitzend; Hüft- ⟨**VT2,** 26⟩
luck [lʌk] Glück **I**
*to be lucky ['lʌki] Glück haben **I**
lunch [lʌntʃ] Mittagessen **I**
lunchbox ['lʌntʃbɒks] Pausenbrotbehälter **I**
lunchroom *(AE)* ['lʌntʃrʊm] Speisesaal **II**
lung [lʌŋ] Lunge **VT1,** 16
to lurk [lɜ:k] lauern **VT1,** 16
lyrical I [ˌlɪrɪkl‿'aɪ] lyrisches Ich **IV**

M

MA [ˌmæsə'tʃu:sɪts] Massachusetts **II**
machine [mə'ʃi:n] Maschine **IV**
machinery [mə'ʃi:nri] Maschinen **VT4,** 56
mad [mæd] verrückt; wütend **II**
madam ['mædəm] Gnädige Frau *(Anrede)* **I**
magazine [mægə'zi:n] Zeitschrift, Magazin **I**
football magazine ['fʊtbɔ:l mægəˌzi:n] Fußballzeitschrift **I**
magic ['mædʒɪk] Magie, Zauberei **II**
magnificent [məg'nɪfɪsnt] großartig, prachtvoll **III**
mail [meɪl] Post **IV**
to mail [meɪl] mailen, per E-Mail schicken **II**
main [meɪn] Haupt- **II**
main trait [ˌmeɪn 'treɪt] Haupteigenschaft **VT1,** 15
mainstream ['meɪnstri:m] Durchschnitts-; Massen- **IV**
to maintain [meɪn'teɪn] aufrechterhalten; instand halten **VT4,** 59
maize [meɪz] Mais **VT4,** 56
major ['meɪdʒə] Haupt-; wichtig; größer **VT1,** 13; **VT2,** 24

majority [mə'dʒɒrəti] Mehrheit **IV**
*to make [meɪk] machen, tun **I**
Made in Britain [ˌmeɪd‿ɪn 'brɪtn] Hergestellt in Großbritannien **I**
to **be made of** [bi: 'meɪd‿əv] hergestellt sein aus **II**
to **make a fuss** [ˌmeɪk‿ə 'fʌs] viel Aufhebens machen **VT2,** 36
to **make a living from sth** [ˌmeɪk‿ə 'lɪvɪŋ frəm] seinen Lebensunterhalt mit etw. bestreiten **IV**
to **make a mess (of sth)** [ˌmeɪk‿ə 'mes] eine Schweinerei veranstalten; (etw.) zurichten **IV**
to **make for** ['meɪk fə] auf etw. zuhalten **VT5,** 76
to **make friends (with)** [ˌmeɪk 'frendz] Freundschaft schließen (mit) **IV**
to **make fun of** [ˌmeɪk 'fʌn‿əv] sich lustig machen über **IV**
to **make it** ['meɪk‿ɪt] es schaffen **III**
to **make it up** [ˌmeɪk‿ɪt‿'ʌp] sich wieder versöhnen **IV**
to **make of** [ˌmeɪk‿əv] halten von ⟨**VT3,** 51⟩
to **make sb do sth** [meɪk] jmdn veranlassen, etw. zu tun **II**
to **make sense** [ˌmeɪk 'sents] Sinn machen; einleuchten **III**
to **make sth up** [ˌmeɪk‿'ʌp] etw. erfinden; sich etw. ausdenken **VT4,** 58
to **make the most of** [ˌmeɪk ðə 'məʊst‿əv] ausnutzen **II**
male [meɪl] männlich; Männchen **IV**
mammal ['mæml] Säugetier ⟨**VT4,** 67⟩
man, *pl.* men [mæn; men] Mann **I**
to manage to (do sth) ['mænɪdʒ] schaffen (etw. zu tun) **III**
management ['mænɪdʒmənt] Management; Geschäftsführung; Verwaltung **IV**
manager ['mænɪdʒə] Manager(in), Geschäftsführer(in) **II**
manner ['mænə] (Art und) Weise **VT3,** 40
adverb of manner [ˌædvɜ:b‿əv 'mænə] Adverb der Art und Weise **II**
mansion ['mæntʃn] Herrenhaus; Villa **VT5,** 76
to manufacture [ˌmænjə'fæktʃə] fertigen; fabrikmäßig herstellen **VT4,** 56
many ['meni] viele **I**
how many [haʊ 'meni] wie viele **I**
map [mæp] Stadtplan, Landkarte **I**
mind map ['maɪnd mæp] Wörternetz *(eine Art Schaubild)* **I**
marathon ['mærəθn] Marathon **III**
to march [mɑ:tʃ] marschieren **III**
margin ['mɑ:dʒɪn] Rand **VT1,** 15
to mark [mɑ:k] markieren **I**
marked [mɑ:kt] markiert **II**
white-ripple-marked [ˌwaɪt rɪpl 'mɑ:kt] mit weißer Wellenzeichnung ⟨**VT4,** 69⟩

market ['mɑ:kɪt] Markt **I**
marketing ['mɑ:kɪtɪŋ] Marketing; Vermarktung; Vertrieb **IV**
marmalade ['mɑ:məleɪd] Marmelade von Zitrusfrüchten **II**
marriage ['mærɪdʒ] Heirat; Ehe **VT1,** 8
*to be **married** to [bi: 'mærid tə] verheiratet sein mit **I**
to **get married** [get 'mærid] heiraten **II**
to **marry** ['mæri] heiraten **II**
martyr ['mɑ:tə] Märtyrer(in) ⟨**VT5,** 87⟩
masculine ['mæskjəlɪn] maskulin; männlich **VT1,** 10
mask [mɑ:sk] Maske **II**
mass [mæs] Masse **III**
massacre ['mæsəkə] Massaker **IV**
to **massacre** ['mæsəkə] massakrieren **IV**
master ['mɑ:stə] Meister; Schulmeister; Lehrer **VT3,** 42
mat [mæt] Matte ⟨**VT5,** 76⟩
mouse mat ['maʊs mæt] Mauspad **I**
match [mætʃ] Wettkampf; Spiel; Match **I**; Streichholz **III**
to **match** [mætʃ] zusammenbringen, zusammenfügen **I**
mate [meɪt] Kamerad(in) **III**
mating habits *(pl.)* ['meɪtɪŋ ˌhæbɪts] Paarungsgewohnheiten ⟨**VT3,** 43⟩
material [mə'tɪəriəl] Material **II**
raw material [ˌrɔ: mə'tɪərɪel] Rohmaterial; Rohstoff **IV**
Math *(AE)* [mæθ] Mathematik **II**
Maths [mæθs] Mathematik **I**
matted ['mætɪd] verfilzt; verklebt ⟨**VT3,** 50⟩
as a **matter** of fact [əz‿ə ˌmætər‿əv 'fækt] in der Tat ⟨**VT3,** 45⟩
What's the matter? [ˌwɒts ðə 'mætə] Was ist los? Was hast du? **I**
to **matter** ['mætə] von Bedeutung sein **IV**
mattress ['mætrəs] Matratze **IV**
mature [mə'tjʊə] reif ⟨**VT4,** 70⟩
may [meɪ] könnte(n) vielleicht; mögen; dürfen **III**
maybe ['meɪbi] vielleicht **I**
me [mi:] mich; mir **I**
Me, too. [ˌmi: 'tu:] Ich auch. **II**
meagreness ['mi:gənəs] Magerkeit ⟨**VT5,** 76⟩
meal [mi:l] Mahlzeit **III**
*to **mean** [mi:n] bedeuten; meinen **I**
to **mean (to do sth)** [mi:n] beabsichtigen **IV**
mean [mi:n] gemein **II**
meaning ['mi:nɪŋ] Bedeutung, Sinn **II**
means, *pl.* **means** [mi:nz] Mittel **II**
means of transport *(sg. and pl.)* [ˌmi:nz‿əv 'træntspɔ:t] Transportmittel, Verkehrsmittel **II**
meanwhile [ˌmi:n'waɪl] mittlerweile; in der Zwischenzeit **VT3,** 48; ⟨**VT4,** 67⟩
measure ['meʒə] Maßnahme ⟨**VT3,** 50⟩; **VT4,** 61; **VT5,** 80
meat [mi:t] Fleisch **II**
mechanic [mə'kænɪk] (Kfz-)Mechaniker(in) **IV**
mechanical [mə'kænɪkl] mechanisch **VT5,** 72
medal ['medl] Medaille **IV**
media *pl.* ['mi:diə] Medien **I**
medical ['medɪkl] medizinisch; ärztlich **IV**
medicinal practitioner [me'dɪsɪnl præk'tɪʃnə] Heilpraktiker(in) ⟨**VT4,** 67⟩
medicine ['medsn] Medizin ⟨**VT1,** 22⟩; **VT3,** 54; ⟨**VT4,** 67⟩
*to **meet** [mi:t] (sich) treffen **I**
Nice to meet you. [ˌnaɪs tə 'mi:t ju:] Nett, dich/Sie/euch kennen zu lernen. **II**
meeting ['mi:tɪŋ] Meeting, Treffen **III**
*to **meet up** [ˌmi:t‿'ʌp] sich treffen **IV**
member ['membə] Mitglied **III**
memorial [mə'mɔ:riəl] Denkmal; Gedenkstätte **VT2,** 29
memory ['memri] Erinnerung; Gedächtnis **III**
menace ['menɪs] Bedrohung; Gefahr ⟨**VT5,** 73⟩
to **mend** [mend] flicken, reparieren **II**
to **mention** ['mentʃn] erwähnen **III**
Don't mention it. [ˌdəʊnt 'mentʃn‿ɪt] Bitte schön!; Gern geschehen. **III**
menu ['menju:] Speisekarte; Menü **II**
mere [mɪə] bloß ⟨**VT5,** 76⟩
merry ['meri] fröhlich **II**
mess [mes] Durcheinander; Schweinerei **II**
to **make a mess (of sth)** [ˌmeɪk‿ə 'mes] eine Schweinerei veranstalten; (etw.) zurichten **IV**
to **mess** sth up [ˌmes‿'ʌp] etw. durcheinanderbringen; etw. vergeigen **III**
message ['mesɪdʒ] Nachricht **I**
messenger ['mesɪndʒə] Bote; Botin **IV**
metal ['metl] Metall **IV**
metaphor ['metəfə] Metapher; übertragener Ausdruck ⟨**VT1,** 23⟩
method ['meθəd] Methode **IV**
metre ['mi:tə] Meter **I**
Mexican ['meksɪkən] mexikanisch; Mexikaner(in) **II**
microphone ['maɪkrəfəʊn] Mikrofon **II**
to **microwave** ['maɪkrəʊweɪv] in der Mikrowelle zubereiten **IV**
middle ['mɪdl] Mitte; Mittel- **I**
Middle Ages [ˌmɪdl‿'eɪdʒɪz] Mittelalter **II**
middle school ['mɪdl ˌsku:l] Mittelschule *(weiterführende Schule in den USA, Mittelstufe)* **II**
midnight ['mɪdnaɪt] Mitternacht **IV**
midriff ['mɪdrɪf] Taille ⟨**VT3,** 40⟩
might [maɪt] könnte(n) **III**
to **migrate** [maɪ'greɪt] wandern; umziehen ⟨**VT5,** 85⟩
migratory ['maɪgrətri] Wander-; Zug- ⟨**VT5,** 85⟩
mild [maɪld] mild **III**
mile [maɪl] Meile *(brit. Längenmaß)* **I**
militant ['mɪlɪtnt] militant; aggressiv **VT2,** 29; **VT4,** 62
milk [mɪlk] Milch **I**
to **milk** [mɪlk] melken **I**
milkman, *pl.* **milkmen** ['mɪlkmən] Milchmann **II**
Milky Way [ˌmɪlki 'weɪ] Milchstraße **II**
to **mill around** [ˌmɪl ə'raʊnd] umherlaufen **VT1,** 12
millennium, *pl.* **millennia** [mɪ'leniəm] Jahrtausend **II**
million ['mɪljən] Million **III**
millionaire [ˌmɪljə'neə] Millionär(in) **IV**
to **mince** [mɪnts] hacken **IV**
mind [maɪnd] Geist, Verstand **II**
mind map ['maɪnd mæp] Wörternetz *(eine Art Schaubild)* **I**
to **be out of one's mind** [bi:‿aʊt‿əv wʌnz 'maɪnd] verrückt sein **II**
to **change one's mind** [tʃeɪndʒ] seine Meinung ändern **II**
to **have in mind** [ˌhæv‿ɪn 'maɪnd] im Sinn haben **VT5,** 74
to **mind** [maɪnd] etwas dagegen haben; nichts ausmachen **I**
mind you [ˌmaɪnd 'ju:] wohlgemerkt **VT1,** 10
Never mind! [ˌnevə 'maɪnd] Mach dir nichts draus!; Macht nichts. **III**
mine [maɪn] Mine **II**
to **mine** [maɪn] verminen ⟨**VT4,** 70⟩
mining industry ['maɪnɪŋ ˌɪndəstri] Bergbau **VT4,** 60
mineral ['mɪnrl] Mineral **IV**
mineral water ['mɪnrl ˌwɔ:tə] Mineralwasser **III**
minimum ['mɪnɪməm] Minimum; Mindestmaß; minimal **VT1,** 8
minister ['mɪnɪstə] Pfarrer(in) ⟨**VT2,** 28⟩
ministry ['mɪnɪstri] Ministerium **VT5,** 77
minority [maɪ'nɒrəti] Minderheit **VT2,** 24
minus ['maɪnəs] minus; weniger **I**
minute ['mɪnɪt] Minute **I**
mirror ['mɪrə] Spiegel **III**
mischievous ['mɪstʃɪvəs] schelmisch, zu Streichen aufgelegt **II**
miserable ['mɪzrəbl] elend; armselig; jämmerlich **IV**
mishap ['mɪshæp] Unglück; Missgeschick ⟨**VT4,** 68⟩
to **miss** [mɪs] verpassen, verfehlen; vermissen **II**

What's missing? [ˌwɒts ˈmɪsɪŋ] Was fehlt? **I**
mission [ˈmɪʃn] Mission, Auftrag **II**
mistake [mɪˈsteɪk] Fehler **II**
by mistake [ˌbaɪ mɪˈsteɪk] versehentlich **III**
misunderstanding [ˌmɪsʌndəˈstændɪŋ] Missverständnis **VT4,** 63
to **mix** [mɪks] mixen; mischen **IV**
to **mix well** [ˌmɪks ˈwel] gut mit Menschen auskommen ⟨**VT4,** 70⟩
mixed [mɪkst] gemischt **II**
mixed bag [ˌmɪkst ˈbæg] buntes Allerlei **I**
to **moan** [məʊn] stöhnen; jammern; klagen **IV**
mob [mɒb] Mob; Pöbel **VT2,** 28; ⟨**VT4,** 69⟩
mobile [ˈməʊbaɪl] Handy, Mobiltelefon **I**
mobility [məʊˈbɪləti] Mobilität **IV**
model [ˈmɒdl] Model; Modell **III**
role model [ˈrəʊl ˌmɒdl] Vorbild **VT3,** 48
modern [ˈmɒdn] modern **II**
Mom *(AE)* [mɒm] Mama **II**
moment [ˈməʊmənt] Moment, Augenblick **I**
monarchy [ˈmɒnəki] Monarchie **III**
Monday [ˈmʌndeɪ] Montag **I**
money [ˈmʌni] Geld **I**
pocket money [ˈpɒkɪt ˌmʌni] Taschengeld **I**
The smart **money** says ... [ˈsmɑːt ˌmʌni] Die meisten wetten, dass ... ⟨**VT1,** 12⟩
monitor [ˈmɒnɪtə] Monitor **II**
to **monitor** [ˈmɒnɪtə] überwachen ⟨**VT1,** 22⟩; **VT5,** 79
monotonous [məˈnɒtnəs] monoton; eintönig **IV**
monster [ˈmɒnstə] Monster **I**
month [mʌnθ] Monat **I**
mood [muːd] Stimmung; Laune **VT2,** 28; **VT4,** 62
moon [muːn] Mond **IV**
moral [ˈmɒrl] moralisch **IV**
more [mɔː] mehr **I**
not any more [ˌnɒt‿eni ˈmɔː] nicht mehr **II**
moreover [mɔːrˈəʊvə] überdies; außerdem **VT5,** 77
morning [ˈmɔːnɪŋ] Morgen; Vormittag **I**
moron [ˈmɔːrɒn] Schwachkopf; Idiot(in) ⟨**VT3,** 46⟩
mosque [mɒsk] Moschee **VT2,** 33
most [məʊst] das meiste; die meisten **II**
most of all [ˈməʊst‿əv‿ɔːl] am meisten **II**
most of the time [ˈməʊst‿əv ðə ˌtaɪm] meistens **III**
to **make the most of** [ˌmeɪk ðə ˈməʊst‿əv] ausnutzen **II**
mother [ˈmʌðə] Mutter **I**
mother tongue [ˌmʌðə ˈtʌŋ] Muttersprache **VT4,** 57
motivation [ˌməʊtɪˈveɪʃn] Motivation; Beweggründe **IV**
motorway *(BE)* [ˈməʊtəweɪ] Autobahn **IV**
mountain [ˈmaʊntɪn] Berg **I**
mountain biking [ˈmaʊntɪn ˌbaɪkɪŋ] Mountainbikefahren **II**
Mountain Rescue [ˌmaʊntɪn ˈreskjuː] Bergwacht **II**
mouse, *pl.* **mice** [maʊs; maɪs] Maus **I**
mouse mat [ˈmaʊs mæt] Mauspad **I**
moustache [məˈstɑːʃ] Schnurrbart; Oberlippenbart **IV**
mouth [maʊθ] Mund **III**
to **move** [muːv] (sich) bewegen **I**; umziehen **III**
movement [ˈmuːvmənt] Bewegung **IV**
movie [ˈmuːvi] Film **II**
Mr [ˈmɪstə] Herr *(Anrede)* **I**
Mr Nice Guy [ˌmɪstə ˈnaɪs gaɪ] der nette Mann von nebenan **IV**
Mrs [ˈmɪsɪz] Frau *(Anrede)* **I**
Ms [mɪz] Frau *(Anrede)* **II**
MT [mɒnˈtænə] Montana **II**
much [mʌtʃ] viel **I**
How much is/are ... ? [ˌhaʊ ˈmʌtʃ‿ɪz/ɑː] Wie viel kostet/kosten ... ? **I**
mud [mʌd] Schlamm **III**
muddy [ˈmʌdi] schlammig **III**
muesli [ˈmjuːzli] Müsli **I**
mug [mʌg] Becher; Krug **I**
multicultural [ˌmʌltiˈkʌltʃrl] multikulturell **VT2,** 33
multi-ethnic [ˌmʌltiˈeθnɪk] Vielvölker- **VT2,** 25
multinational [ˌmʌltiˈnæʃnl] multinational **IV**
Mum [mʌm] Mama **I**
murder [ˈmɜːdə] Mord **VT4,** 66
muscle [ˈmʌsl] Muskel **III**
museum [mjuːˈziːəm] Museum **I**
mushroom [ˈmʌʃrʊm] Pilz **III**
music [ˈmjuːzɪk] Musik **I**
musical [ˈmjuːzɪkl] Musical **II**
musical [ˈmjuːzɪkl] musikalisch, Musik- **II**
musician [mjuːˈzɪʃn] Musiker(in) **IV**
Muslim [ˈmʊzlɪm] Moslem(in); Muslim(in); moslemisch; muslimisch **VT2,** 25
must [mʌst; məst] müssen **I**
mustang [ˈmʌstæŋ] Mustang **II**
mutton [ˈmʌtn] Hammelfleisch **VT4,** 56
my [maɪ] mein(e) **I**
(my) fault [ˈmaɪ ˌfɔːlt] (meine) Schuld **III**
My name is ... [maɪ ˈneɪm‿ɪz] Ich heiße ... **I**
(my) own [əʊn] (mein) eigen(-e/-r/-s) **I**
myself [maɪˈself] (ich) selbst; mich (selbst) **III**
mystery [ˈmɪstri] Mysterium, Rätsel, Geheimnis **II**
myth [mɪθ] Mythos **IV**

N

nah *(infml)* [næ] nee ⟨**VT2,** 31⟩
naked [ˈneɪkɪd] nackt **IV**
name [neɪm] Name **I**
first name [ˈfɜːst ˌneɪm] Vorname **III**
My name is ... [maɪ ˈneɪm‿ɪz] Ich heiße ... **I**
What's your name? [ˌwɒts jə ˈneɪm] Wie heißt du/heißen Sie? **I**
to **name** [neɪm] benennen **IV**
narrative [ˈnærətɪv] Erzählung; erzählerisch **IV**
narrator [neˈreɪtə] Erzähler(in) **III**
narrow [ˈnærəʊ] eng, schmal **II**
nasty [ˈnɑːsti] garstig, gemein; scheußlich **II**
nation [ˈneɪʃn] Nation **IV**
national [ˈnæʃnl] national, landesweit **I**
national park [ˌnæʃnl ˈpɑːk] Nationalpark, Naturpark **I**
nationality [ˌnæʃnˈæləti] Nationalität, Staatsangehörigkeit **II**
native [ˈneɪtɪv] eingeboren **II**
native speaker [ˌneɪtɪv‿ˈspiːkə] Muttersprachler(in) **IV**
Native American [ˌneɪtɪv‿əˈmerɪkən] Ureinwohner(in) Amerikas, Indianer(in); indianisch **II**
natural [ˈnætʃrl] natürlich, Natur- **II**
natural resource [ˌnætʃrl rɪˈzɔːs] Bodenschatz **IV**
nature [ˈneɪtʃə] Natur **III**
to **navigate** [ˈnævɪgeɪt] navigieren; steuern **VT5,** 73
navigation [ˌnævɪˈgeɪʃn] Navigation; Orientierung **III**
navy [ˈneɪvi] Marine ⟨**VT4,** 70⟩
near [nɪə] nahe, in der Nähe von **I**
nearby [ˌnɪəˈbaɪ] in der Nähe **IV**
nearly [ˈnɪəli] fast, annähernd **II**
neat [niːt] gepflegt; ordentlich; hübsch **IV**
necessary [ˈnesəsri] notwendig, nötig **III**
neck [nek] Hals; Nacken ⟨**VT2,** 30⟩
necklace [ˈnekləs] Halskette **VT3,** 41
need [niːd] Bedürfnis; Erfordernis **III**
in need [ɪn ˈniːd] bedürftig **IV**
to **need** [niːd] brauchen, benötigen **I**
needle [niːdl] Nadel **III**
needless to say [ˈniːdləs tə ˌseɪ] natürlich **VT1,** 12
negative [ˈnegətɪv] negativ, verneint **I**
negligence [ˈneglɪdʒənts] Fahrlässigkeit ⟨**VT4,** 71⟩
neighborhood *(AE)* [ˈneɪbəhʊd] Nachbarschaft **II**

neighbour ['neɪbə] Nachbar(in) **I**
neither ... nor ... ['naɪðə; 'ni:ðə ... nɔ:] weder ... noch ... ⟨**VT2,** 31⟩; **VT3,** 40; ⟨**VT4,** 70⟩
neither ['naɪðə; 'ni:ðə] keine(-r/-s) (von beiden) **IV**
nerdy *(slang)* ['nɜ:di] intelligent, aber sozial unbeholfen ⟨**VT5,** 81⟩
nervous ['nɜ:vəs] nervös, aufgeregt **I**
network ['netwɜ:k] Netzwerk **VT5,** 83
never ['nevə] nie, niemals **I**
Never mind! [ˌnevə 'maɪnd] Mach dir nichts draus!; Macht nichts. **III**
new [nju:] neu **I**
newcomer ['nju:ˌkʌmə] Neuling; Neuankömmling **IV**
news *(sg.)* [nju:z] Nachricht(en), Neuigkeit(en) **II**
newspaper ['nju:sˌpeɪpə] Zeitung **I**
next [nekst] nächste(-r/-s) **I**
next door [nekst 'dɔ:] (von) nebenan **IV**
next to ['nekst tə] neben **I**
the next size down [ðə ˌnekst saɪz 'daʊn] eine Größe kleiner **III**
next [nekst] als Nächstes **II**
NGO (non-governmental organisation) [ˌendʒi:'əʊ] Nichtregierungsorganisation ⟨**VT4,** 67⟩
nice [naɪs] nett **I**
Mr Nice Guy [ˌmɪstə 'naɪs gaɪ] der nette Mann von nebenan **IV**
Nice to meet you. [ˌnaɪs tə 'mi:t ju:] Nett, dich/Sie/euch kennen zu lernen. **II**
night [naɪt] Nacht **I**
last night [lɑ:st 'naɪt] gestern Abend/ Nacht **II**
nightmare ['naɪtmeə] Alptraum **IV**
nil [nɪl] null **II**
no [nəʊ] kein(e) **I**
no good [nəʊ 'gʊd] nutzlos, wertlos **II**
No idea! [ˌnəʊ‿aɪ'dɪə] Keine Ahnung! **I**
no longer [nəʊ 'lɒŋgə] nicht mehr, nicht länger **I**
No way! [ˌnəʊ 'weɪ] Auf keinen Fall! **III**
There's no point in *(+ gerund)* [ðeəz ˌnəʊ 'pɔɪnt] Es hat keinen Sinn, zu ... **IV**
no [nəʊ] nein **I**
nobody ['nəʊbədi] niemand **II**
to nod [nɒd] nicken ⟨**VT2,** 30⟩
noise [nɔɪz] Geräusch, Lärm **I**
noisy ['nɔɪzi] laut **I**
non-defining relative clause [ˌnɒndɪfaɪnɪŋ ˌrelətɪv 'klɔ:z] nicht notwendiger Relativsatz **IV**
none [nʌn] keine(r) **III**
nonsense ['nɒnsnts] Unsinn; Quatsch **IV**
noodle ['nu:dl] Nudel **IV**
nope *(infml)* [nəʊp] nee ⟨**VT2,** 32⟩
neither ... nor ... ['naɪðə; 'ni:ðə ... nɔ:] weder ... noch ... ⟨**VT2,** 31⟩; **VT3,** 40; ⟨**VT4,** 70⟩

normal ['nɔ:ml] normal **IV**
Norman ['nɔ:mən] Normanne, Normannin; normannisch **II**
north [nɔ:θ] Norden **I**
nose [nəʊz] Nase **I**
nose job *(infml)* ['nəʊz ˌdʒɒb] Nasenkorrektur ⟨**VT3,** 48⟩
not [nɒt] nicht **I**
not a bit of it [ˌnɒt‿ə 'bɪt‿əv‿ɪt] keine Spur davon **IV**
not any better [ˌnɒt‿eni 'betə] (überhaupt) nicht besser **II**
not any more [ˌnɒt‿eni 'mɔ:] nicht mehr **II**
not ... either [nɒt ... 'aɪðə; nɒt ... 'i:ðə;] auch nicht **VT2,** 37
not even [nɒt‿'i:vn] nicht einmal **II**
not exactly [ˌnɒt‿ɪg'zæktli] nicht gerade **III**
not until [nɒt‿ən'tɪl] nicht (be)vor; erst (wenn/als) **III**
*__to be a notch above__ [ˌbi:‿ə ˌnɒtʃ‿ə'bʌv] eine Klasse besser sein als **VT1,** 13
note [nəʊt] Notiz; Zettel **III**
notebook ['nəʊtbʊk] Heft *(AE)*; Notizbuch; Notebook *(Computer)* **VT1,** 13; **VT3,** 42
to note down [ˌnəʊt 'daʊn] notieren; aufschreiben **IV**
notes *pl.* [nəʊts] Notizen, Anmerkungen **I**
nothing ['nʌθɪŋ] nichts **II**
It's nothing to do with me. [ɪts ˌnʌθɪŋ tə ˌdu: wɪð 'mi:] Ich habe damit nichts zu tun. **II**
notice ['nəʊtɪs] Anschlag, Notiz **II**
to notice ['nəʊtɪs] bemerken **II**
noun [naʊn] Nomen **II**
novel ['nɒvl] Roman **VT2,** 35; **VT3,** 42; **VT5,** 75
now [naʊ] jetzt, nun **I**
now and again [ˌnaʊ‿ənd‿ə'gen] hin und wieder; ab und zu **VT4,** 60
right now [ˌraɪt 'naʊ] jetzt gleich **II**
nowadays ['naʊədeɪz] heutzutage ⟨**VT4,** 68⟩
nowhere ['nəʊweə] nirgendwo; nirgendwohin **II**
to nudge [nʌdʒ] stupsen; anstoßen **VT3,** 42
number ['nʌmbə] Zahl, Nummer **I**
nurse [nɜ:s] Krankenschwester, Krankenpfleger **II**
nursery school ['nɜ:sri ˌsku:l] Vorschule; Kindergarten ⟨**VT3,** 55⟩
nut [nʌt] Nuss **VT2,** 36
to nuzzle ['nʌzl] schmiegen ⟨**VT5,** 76⟩

O

o'clock [ə'klɒk] Uhr *(Zeitangabe bei vollen Stunden)* **I**
oak [əʊk] Eiche **II**

obedient [ə'bi:dɪənt] gehorsam **VT3,** 42
to obey [əʊ'beɪ] gehorchen **IV**
object ['ɒbdʒɪkt] Objekt; Gegenstand **III**
obligation [ˌɒblɪ'geɪʃn] Verpflichtung **IV**
oblong ['ɒblɒŋ] länglich ⟨**VT5,** 76⟩
to observe [əb'zɜ:v] beobachten; beachten; befolgen **VT3,** 40; **VT5,** 83
*__to be obsessed (by/with)__ [bi:‿əb'sest] besessen sein (von) **IV**
obstacle ['ɒbstəkl] Hindernis **VT1,** 16
to obtain [əb'teɪn] erlangen; bekommen **VT2,** 28
obvious ['ɒbviəs] offensichtlich **III**
to occupy ['ɒkjəpaɪ] besetzen; belegen; beschäftigen **IV**
to occur [ə'kɜ:] sich ereignen; vorkommen **IV**
to **occur to sb** [ə'kɜ:] jmdm einfallen; jmdm in den Sinn kommen **IV**
ocean ['əʊʃn] Ozean **VT3,** 47; **VT4,** 56
odd [ɒd] seltsam, nicht passend **I**
Find the odd word out! [ˌɒd wɜ:d‿'aʊt] Finde das Wort, das nicht in die Gruppe passt! *(Wortschatzübung)* **I**
the odd ... [ði‿'ɒd] das ein oder andere ⟨**VT3,** 44⟩
of [ɒv; əv] von **I**
of course [əv 'kɔ:s] natürlich, selbstverständlich **I**
of such standing [əv ˌsʌtʃ 'stændɪŋ] von solchem Ansehen ⟨**VT4,** 69⟩
off [ɒf] von ... weg/ab/herunter **I**
a day/year off [ə ˌdeɪ‿'ɒf] ein freier Tag/ ein freies Jahr **IV**
off to ['ɒf tə] auf nach **I**
Off to the USA! [ˌɒf tə ðə ˌju:es‿'eɪ] Auf in die USA! **I**
to offend [ə'fend] beleidigen; verletzen **VT5,** 83
offensive [ə'fentsɪv] anstößig; beleidigend **VT3,** 40
offer ['ɒfə] Angebot **I**
special offer [ˌspeʃl‿'ɒfə] Sonderangebot **I**
to offer ['ɒfə] anbieten **II**
offhand [ˌɒf'hænd] ohne Weiteres **VT1,** 12
office ['ɒfɪs] Büro **I**
Home Office *(BE)* ['həʊm‿ˌɒfɪs] Innenministerium **VT5,** 80
post office ['pəʊst‿ˌɒfɪs] Postamt **III**
officer ['ɒfɪsə] Beamter, Beamtin **III**
official [ə'fɪʃl] Beamter, Beamtin; Funktionär(in) **IV**
official [ə'fɪʃl] offiziell **IV**
petty bloody officiousness [ˌpeti ˌblʌdi‿ə'fɪʃəsnəs] blöder kleinlicher Übereifer ⟨**VT3,** 44⟩
often ['ɒfn] oft **I**
oh [əʊ] oh; null **I**
Oh dear! ['əʊ ˌdɪə] Oje! **I**
oil [ɔɪl] Öl **IV**
OK [əʊ'keɪ] OK **I**

old [əʊld] alt **I**
How old are you? [haʊ‿'əʊld‿ə ju:] Wie alt bist du/sind Sie? **I**
in olden times [ɪn'əʊldən ˌtaɪmz] anno dazumal **VT3,** 42
old people's home [ˌəʊld pi:plz 'həʊm] Altersheim **II**
old-fashioned [ˌəʊld 'fæʃnd] altmodisch **III**
omelette ['ɒmlət] Omelett **I**
*to be **on** [ɒn] im Gange sein, laufen **I**
on [ɒn] auf **I**
on business [ɒn 'bɪznɪs] geschäftlich **I**
on foot [ɒn 'fʊt] zu Fuß **IV**
on one's own [ɒn wʌnz‿'əʊn] allein; für sich **IV**
on purpose [ɒn 'pɜ:pəs] absichtlich **III**
on somebody's right/left [ɒn ˌsʌmbədiz 'raɪt/'left] zur Rechten/zur Linken von jemandem **I**
on the brink of [ɒn ðə 'brɪŋk] am Rande von; kurz vor ⟨**VT3,** 50⟩
on the other hand [ɒn ði‿'ʌðə ˌhænd] andererseits **III**
on the run [ɒn ðə 'rʌn] auf der Flucht **III**
on time [ɒn 'taɪm] pünktlich **II**
on top (of) [ɒn 'tɒp] obendrauf **II**
to **live on sth** ['lɪv‿ɒn] von etw leben **III**
once [wʌnts] einmal; einst **I**
at once [ət 'wʌnts] sofort, plötzlich **I**
onion ['ʌnjən] Zwiebel **I**
online [ˌɒn'laɪn] online **II**
only ['əʊnli] einzige(-r/-s) **II**
only child [ˌəʊnli 'tʃaɪld] Einzelkind **IV**
only ['əʊnli] nur; erst; bloß **I**
onto ['ɒntə] auf … hinauf **II**
Oops! [u:ps] Hoppla! Huch! **I**
to **open** ['əʊpn] öffnen, aufmachen **I**
open ['əʊpn] offen; geöffnet **I**
to **flip (a book) open** [ˌflɪp‿'əʊpn] aufschlagen (ein Buch) **VT1,** 14
opening hours ['əʊpnɪŋ‿ˌaʊəz] Öffnungszeiten **I**
opera ['ɒprə] Oper **III**
to **operate** ['ɒpreɪt] bedienen; operieren **IV**
operation [ˌɒpr'eɪʃn] Operation; Betrieb; Einsatz **VT5,** 80
operator ['ɒpreɪtə] Betreiber(in); Bediener(in) **VT5,** 80
opinion [ə'pɪnjən] Meinung **II**
in my opinion [ɪn 'maɪ‿əˌpɪnjən] meiner Meinung nach **IV**
to **swing opinion** [ˌswɪŋ‿ə'pɪnjən] eine Meinung ändern **VT4,** 60
opportunity [ˌɒpə'tju:nəti] Gelegenheit; Chance **III**
to **oppose** [ə'pəʊz] ablehnen; sich entgegenstellen ⟨**VT4,** 67⟩
opposite ['ɒpəzɪt] Gegenteil **II**
oppressor [ɒ'presə] Unterdrücker(in) **VT4,** 62
or [ɔ:] oder **I**
oral ['ɔ:rl] mündlich **IV**
orange ['ɒrɪndʒ] Orange **II**
orange ['ɒrɪndʒ] orange **I**
orchestra ['ɔ:kɪstrə] Orchester **IV**
order ['ɔ:də] Reihenfolge, Ordnung **II**; Befehl **IV**; Bestellung **IV**
in **order** to [ɪn‿'ɔ:də tə] um … zu **III**
to **order** ['ɔ:də] bestellen **II**; befehlen **II**
ordered ['ɔ:dəd] geordnet ⟨**VT1,** 18⟩
orderly ['ɔ:dəli] ordentlich **VT1,** 13
iron **ore** ['aɪən‿ɔ:] Eisenerz **IV**
organisation [ˌɔ:gnaɪ'zeɪʃn] Organisation **IV**
organism ['ɔ:gnɪzm] Organismus ⟨**VT5,** 72⟩
to **organize** ['ɔ:gənaɪz] organisieren **II**
origin ['ɒrɪdʒɪn] Ursprung **II**
original [ə'rɪdʒnl] original; ursprünglich **II**
other ['ʌðə] anders; andere(-r/-s) **I**
each other [ˌi:tʃ‿'ʌðə] sich gegenseitig **II**
the other day [ði‿ˌʌðə 'deɪ] neulich **IV**
otherwise ['ʌðəwaɪz] sonst **I**
ought to *(+ infinitive)* ['ɔ:t tə] sollte(n); sollte(s)t **IV**
ounce [aʊnts] Unze *(Maßeinheit: 28,34952 Gramm)* ⟨**VT3,** 44⟩
our ['aʊə] unser(e) **I**
out [aʊt] außerhalb, (nach) draußen, raus **I**
out of ['aʊt‿əv] aus … heraus **I**
out of date [ˌaʊt‿əv 'deɪt] veraltet **VT2,** 36
out of sight [ˌaʊt‿əv 'saɪt] außer Sicht **VT4,** 58
out of work [ˌaʊt‿əv 'wɜ:k] arbeitslos **III**
outback ['aʊtbæk] Outback *(australisches Hinterland)* **III**
outlaw ['aʊtlɔ:] Geächtete(r), Vogelfreie(r) **II**
to **outlaw** ['aʊtlɔ:] ächten; verbieten **VT2,** 27
outline ['aʊtlaɪn] Skizze **VT1,** 15
outlook ['aʊtlʊk] Einstellung **VT2,** 33
outright ['aʊtraɪt] vollständig; ganz und gar; ohne Umschweife ⟨**VT4,** 67⟩
outside [aʊt'saɪd] (nach) (dr)außen; außerhalb **I**
oven ['ʌvn] Backofen **VT3,** 49
over ['əʊvə] (hin)über **I**; vorüber **II**
all over [ˌɔ:l‿'əʊvə] überall **III**
over there [ˌəʊvə 'ðeə] da drüben **I**
to **overachieve** [ˌəʊvrə'tʃi:v] mehr Leistung bringen als erwartet ⟨**VT1,** 23⟩
overalls *(pl.)* ['əʊvrɔ:lz] Overall; Arbeitsanzug **VT5,** 76
overcast ['əʊvəkɑ:st] bedeckt; bewölkt ⟨**VT2,** 38⟩; **VT5,** 85
*to **overcome** [ˌəʊvə'kʌm] überwinden **III**
overcrowding [ˌəʊvə'kraʊdɪŋ] Überfüllung **IV**
over-exercising [ˌəʊvr'eksəsaɪzɪŋ] übermäßige sportliche Betätigung ⟨**VT1,** 22⟩
*to **overhear** [ˌəʊvə'hɪə] belauschen; zufällig mit anhören **IV**
*to **oversleep** [ˌəʊvə'sli:p] verschlafen **II**
overtime ['əʊvətaɪm] Überstunden **IV**
overweight [ˌəʊvə'weɪt] übergewichtig **II**
Ow! [aʊ] Autsch! **I**
to **own** [əʊn] besitzen **II**
on one's **own** [ɒn wʌnz‿'əʊn] allein; für sich **IV**
(my) own [əʊn] (mein) eigen(-e/-r/-s) **I**
ox, *pl.* **oxen** [ɒks; ɒksn] Ochse **IV**
oxygen ['ɒksɪdʒən] Sauerstoff ⟨**VT1,** 18⟩

P

pace [peɪs] Geschwindigkeit; Gangart ⟨**VT5,** 82⟩
pack [pæk] Packung **IV**
to **pack** [pæk] packen **II**
to **pack one's bags** [ˌpæk wʌnz 'bægz] seine Koffer packen; seine Sachen packen **IV**
package ['pækɪdʒ] Paket **III**
packet ['pækɪt] Packung **IV**
pact [pækt] Pakt; Bündnis ⟨**VT5,** 87⟩
to **pad** [pæd] tappen; tasten ⟨**VT2,** 30⟩
padded cell [ˌpædɪd 'sel] Gummizelle ⟨**VT5,** 87⟩
page [peɪdʒ] Seite **I**
pain [peɪn] Schmerz **II**
paint [peɪnt] Farbe **III**
to **paint** [peɪnt] (an)malen, streichen **II**
painting ['peɪntɪŋ] Gemälde **IV**
pair [peə] Paar **I**
a pair of [ə 'peər‿əv] ein Paar **I**
pajamas *(pl.) (AE)* [pə'dʒɑ:məz] Pyjama; Schlafanzug **VT3,** 40
pan [pæn] Pfanne; Kochtopf mit Stiel **III**
pancake ['pænkeɪk] Pfannkuchen **IV**
window **pane** ['wɪndəʊ ˌpeɪn] Fensterscheibe ⟨**VT5,** 77⟩
panic ['pænɪk] Panik **III**
panther ['pæntθə] Panther **VT2,** 29
pants *(AE) (pl.)* [pænts] Hose **III**
paper ['peɪpə] Papier **III**
parachute ['pærəʃu:t] Fallschirm ⟨**VT1,** 19⟩
parade [pə'reɪd] Parade, Umzug **II**
paragraph ['pærəgrɑ:f] Paragraph, Absatz **II**
to **paralyse** ['pærlaɪz] lähmen **VT1,** 17
to **paraphrase** ['pærəfreɪz] paraphrasieren; umschreiben **IV**
I beg your **pardon?** [aɪ ˌbeg jə 'pɑ:dn] Wie bitte? ⟨**VT3,** 45⟩
parental [pə'rentl] elterlich; Eltern- **VT1,** 8

parenting ['peərntɪŋ] Kindererziehung ⟨**VT1,** 9⟩
parents *pl.* ['peərənts] Eltern **I**
park [pɑ:k] Park **I**
car park ['kɑ: ˌpɑ:k] Parkplatz; Parkhaus **III**
national park [ˌnæʃnl 'pɑ:k] Nationalpark, Naturpark **I**
theme park ['θi:m ˌpɑ:k] Freizeitpark; Themenpark **IV**
parking lot ['pɑ:kɪŋ ˌlɒt] Parkplatz **VT1,** 12
parliament ['pɑ:ləmənt] Parlament **II**
to **parrot** ['pærət] nachplappern ⟨**VT3,** 45⟩
part [pɑ:t] Teil **I**; Rolle **II**
part of speech [ˌpɑ:t‿əv 'spi:tʃ] Wortart **IV**
to **take part (in)** [teɪk 'pɑ:t] teilnehmen (an) **II**
part [pɑ:t] teils **III**
participle ['pɑ:tɪsɪpl] Partizip **IV**
particular [pə'tɪkjələ] bestimmt **IV**
particularly [pə'tɪkjələli] besonders **IV**
partner ['pɑ:tnə] Partner(in) **I**
party ['pɑ:ti] Party, Feier **I**; Partei; Gruppe **IV**
to **throw a party** [ˌθrəʊ‿ə 'pɑ:ti] eine Party veranstalten **IV**
pass [pɑ:s] Ausweis, Pass **II**
boarding pass ['bɔ:dɪŋ ˌpɑ:s] Bordkarte **II**
to **pass** [pɑ:s] zupassen, zuspielen; reichen **III**; durchgehen; vorbeigehen; bestehen **III**
to **pass on** [ˌpɑ:s‿'ɒn] weitergeben **IV**
passenger ['pæsndʒə] Passagier(in); Beifahrer(in) **III**
passion ['pæʃn] Passion; Leidenschaft ⟨**VT5,** 87⟩
passive ['pæsɪv] Passiv **II**
past [pɑ:st] Vergangenheit **I**
past [pɑ:st] vorbei, vorüber **I**
half **past** (two) ['hɑ:f pɑ:st] halb (drei) **I**
pasta ['pæstə] Pasta, Nudeln **II**
patch [pætʃ] Fleck; Flicken; Stelle ⟨**VT2,** 31⟩
to **patch** [pætʃ] flicken **VT5,** 77
patchy ['pætʃi] ungleichmäßig; flickenartig **VT1,** 13
path [pɑ:θ] Pfad, Weg **II**
patient ['peɪʃnt] Patient(in) **VT5,** 73
patient ['peɪʃnt] geduldig **VT3,** 42
to **patrol** [pə'trəʊl] patrouillieren; Streife gehen/fahren **IV**
pattern ['pætn] Muster **IV**
to **pause** [pɔ:z] Pause machen; anhalten; verharren **II**
*to **pay for** [peɪ] bezahlen **II**
to **pay attention to sth** [ˌpeɪ‿ə'tentʃn] seine Aufmerksamkeit auf etw. richten ⟨**VT5,** 82⟩

payment ['peɪmənt] Zahlung ⟨**VT4,** 70⟩
PE [pi:‿'i:] Sportunterricht **II**
peace [pi:s] Frieden **IV**
peaceful ['pi:sfl] friedlich **VT2,** 29; **VT4,** 60
peasant ['peznt] Kleinbauer **II**
pedal ['pedl] Pedal **VT1,** 13
peer [pɪə] Gleichaltrige(r); gleichaltrig **VT2,** 26
pen [pen] Füller **I**
pencil ['pentsl] Bleistift; Buntstift **I**
pencil case ['pentsl ˌkeɪs] Federmäppchen **I**
penny, *pl.* **pence** ['peni; pents] Penny, Pence *(brit. Währungseinheit)* **I**
people ['pi:pl] Leute, Menschen **I**
old people's home [ˌəʊld pi:plz 'həʊm] Altersheim **II**
pepper ['pepə] Pfeffer; Paprikaschote **IV**
per [pɜ:; pə] pro **IV**
per se [ˌpɜ: 'seɪ] an sich ⟨**VT4,** 67⟩; ⟨**VT5,** 82⟩
percent, *pl.* **percent** [pə'sent] Prozent **II**
percentage [pə'sentɪdʒ] Prozentsatz; prozentualer Anteil **IV**
verb of **perception** [ˌvɜ:b‿əv pə'sepʃn] Verb der Wahrnehmung **IV**
to **perch** [pɜ:tʃ] sitzen ⟨**VT5,** 87⟩
perfect ['pɜ:fɪkt] perfekt, vollkommen **III**
to **perform** [pə'fɔ:m] aufführen, auftreten **II**
performance [pə'fɔ:mənts] Aufführung; Vorstellung **IV**
perhaps [pə'hæps] vielleicht **III**
period ['pɪəriəd] Periode; Zeitspanne **III**; Unterrichtsstunde ⟨**VT1,** 12⟩
permanent ['pɜ:mnənt] permanent; dauerhaft **III**
permission [pə'mɪʃn] Erlaubnis **IV**
to **permit** [pə'mɪt] erlauben; genehmigen **VT3,** 40; **VT4,** 59
perpetrator ['pɜ:pətreɪtə] Täter(in); Gesetzesübertreter(in) ⟨**VT4,** 63⟩
to **persecute** ['pɜ:səkju:t] verfolgen **VT4,** 61
to **persist** [pə'sɪst] verharren; beharren **VT2,** 34
persistent [pə'sɪstnt] hartnäckig; ausdauernd **VT2,** 26
person ['pɜ:sn] Person **I**
personal ['pɜ:snl] persönlich **IV**
personality [ˌpɜ:sn'æləti] Persönlichkeit **VT1,** 10; persönliche Note **VT5,** 83
personnel [ˌpɜ:sn'el] Personal **IV**
armoured personnel carrier [ˌɑ:məd pɜ:sˌnel 'kærɪə] gepanzerter Mannschaftstransportwagen ⟨**VT4,** 62⟩
perspective [pə'spektɪv] Perspektive, Blickwinkel **III**
to **persuade** [pə'sweɪd] überreden **II**
to **pervade** [pə'veɪd] durchdringen; durchziehen ⟨**VT2,** 33⟩
pet [pet] Haustier; Liebling **I**

petty bloody officiousness [ˌpeti ˌblʌdi‿ə'fɪʃəsnəs] blöder kleinlicher Übereifer ⟨**VT3,** 44⟩
PhD [ˌpi:eɪtʃ'di:] Doktor der Philosophie ⟨**VT3,** 55⟩
phenomenon, *pl.* **phenomena** [fə'nɒmɪnən] Phänomen; Naturerscheinung ⟨**VT3,** 48⟩
phew [fju:] puh ⟨**VT2,** 31⟩
phone [fəʊn] Telefon **II**
phone booth *(AE)* ['fəʊn ˌbu:ð] Telefonzelle **III**
The phone is ringing off the hook. [ðə ˌfəʊn‿ɪz rɪŋɪŋ ɒf ðə 'hʊk] Das Telefon klingelt ohne Unterlass. ⟨**VT3,** 43⟩
to **phone** [fəʊn] telefonieren **I**
photo ['fəʊtəʊ] Foto, Fotografie **I**
to **take photos** [teɪk 'fəʊtəʊz] fotografieren, Fotos machen **I**
photocopy ['fəʊtəʊˌkɒpi] Fotokopie **III**
photographer [fə'tɒgrəfə] Fotograf(in) **III**
phrasal verb [ˌfreɪzl 'vɜ:b] phrasal verb *(Verb + Präposition oder Partikel)* **IV**
phrase [freɪz] Redewendung, Ausdruck **I**
phraseology [ˌfreɪzɪ'ɒlədʒi] Ausdrucksweise ⟨**VT3,** 45⟩
physical ['fɪzɪkl] physisch, körperlich **II**
Physical Education [ˌfɪzɪkl‿edʒʊ'keɪʃn] Sport *(Schulfach)* **II**
piano [pi'ænəʊ] Klavier, Piano **II**
to **pick** [pɪk] pflücken **III**; auswählen; herauslesen **VT3,** 48
to **pick up** [pɪk‿'ʌp] aufheben; abholen **I**
to **pick up the pieces** [ˌpɪk‿ʌp ðə 'pi:si:z] etw. wieder in den Griff bekommen ⟨**VT3,** 48⟩
pickup ['pɪkʌp] Pickup **II**
picnic ['pɪknɪk] Picknick **I**
picture ['pɪktʃə] Bild **I**
pie [paɪ] Kuchen; Pastete **IV**
apple pie [ˌæpl 'paɪ] gedeckter Apfelkuchen **IV**
pie chart ['paɪ ˌtʃɑ:t] Kuchendiagramm; Tortendiagramm **IV**
piece [pi:s] Stück **II**
to **pick up the pieces** [ˌpɪk‿ʌp ðə 'pi:si:z] etw. wieder in den Griff bekommen ⟨**VT3,** 48⟩
to **pierce** ['pɪəs] durchbohren; durchdringen **VT3,** 40; ⟨**VT4,** 69⟩
pig [pɪg] Schwein **I**
pig iron ['pɪg‿aɪən] Roheisen ⟨**VT5,** 76⟩
pigsty ['pɪgstaɪ] Schweinestall **I**
pile [paɪl] Stapel; Haufen **IV**
pilgrim ['pɪlgrɪm] Pilger(in) **III**
pill [pɪl] Pille, Tablette **III**
pillow ['pɪləʊ] Kopfkissen **III**
pilot ['paɪlət] Pilot(in) **I**
pine (tree) [paɪn] Kiefer **III**
pink [pɪŋk] pink, rosa **I**
pint [paɪnt] Pinte *(engl. Hohlmaß: 0,57 l)* **II**

pioneer [ˌpaɪəˈnɪə] Pionier **IV**
pipe [paɪp] Rohr(leitung) **IV**
pirate [ˈpaɪərət] Pirat(in), Seeräuber(in) **III**
pitted [ˈpɪtɪd] übersät ⟨**VT3,** 50⟩
What a **pity!** [ˌwɒt‿ə ˈpɪti] Wie schade! **II**
place [pleɪs] Platz, Stelle, Ort **I**; Heim; Haus **III**
all over the place [ɔːl‿əʊvə ðə ˈpleɪs] überall verteilt **IV**
in the first place [ɪn ðə ˈfɜːst pleɪs] von vorne herein; überhaupt erst ⟨**VT3,** 45⟩
to **take place** [teɪk ˈpleɪs] stattfinden **II**
placement *(BE)* [ˈpleɪsmənt] Praktikum **IV**
plain [pleɪn] Ebene **II**
plain [pleɪn] klar; schlicht; einfach **VT2,** 34
plan [plæn] Plan **I**
to **plan** [plæn] planen **II**
plane [pleɪn] Flugzeug **I**
plant [plɑːnt] Pflanze **III**
to **plant** [plɑːnt] pflanzen **II**
plantation [plænˈteɪʃn] Plantage **IV**
plaque [plɑːk] Tafel; Platte **VT5,** 76
plaster [ˈplɑːstə] Gips **III**
to **plaster** [ˈplɑːstə] kleben; vollpflastern ⟨**VT5,** 77⟩
plate [pleɪt] Teller **I**
platform [ˈplætfɔːm] Plattform, Tribüne; Bahnsteig **II**
play [pleɪ] Spiel, Theaterstück **I**
role play [ˈrəʊl pleɪ] Rollenspiel **I**
to **play** [pleɪ] spielen **I**
to **play around** [ˌpleɪ‿əˈraʊnd] herumspielen **III**
player [ˈpleɪə] Spieler, Mitspieler **I**
CD player [ˌsiːˈdiː ˌpleɪə] CD-Spieler **I**
DVD player [ˌdiːviːdiː ˈpleɪə] DVD-Player **III**
playground [ˈpleɪɡraʊnd] Schulhof, Pausenhof **I**
please [pliːz] bitte **I**
pleased [pliːzd] erfreut; zufrieden **III**
to **be pleased** [biː ˈpliːzd] erfreut sein **III**
plenty [ˈplenti] eine Menge **IV**
plot [plɒt] Handlung **IV**
to **plug in** [ˌplʌɡ‿ˈɪn] einstecken; einstöpseln **VT5,** 77
plumber [ˈplʌmə] Klempner(in); Installateur(in) **VT1,** 12
plural [ˈplʊərl] Plural, Mehrzahl **I**
plus [plʌs] plus **I**
pm [ˌpiːˈem] nachmittags *(Uhrzeit)* **I**
to **poach** [pəʊtʃ] wildern ⟨**VT4,** 67⟩
pocket [ˈpɒkɪt] Hosen- oder Jackentasche **I**
pocket money [ˈpɒkɪt ˌmʌni] Taschengeld **I**
poem [ˈpəʊɪm] Gedicht **I**
poet [ˈpəʊɪt] Poet(in); Dichter(in) **IV**
poetry [ˈpəʊɪtri] Lyrik **IV**
point [pɔɪnt] Punkt **I**
exclamation point *(AE)* [ekskləˈmeɪʃn ˌpɔɪnt] Ausrufezeichen **VT1,** 14
point of view [ˌpɔɪnt‿əv ˈvjuː] Standpunkt; Perspektive **IV**
There's no point in *(+ gerund)* [ðeəz ˌnəʊ ˈpɔɪnt] Es hat keinen Sinn, zu ... **IV**
to **have a point** [ˌhæv‿ə ˈpɔɪnt] nicht ganz Unrecht haben ⟨**VT3,** 45⟩
to the point [tə ðə ˈpɔɪnt] zur Sache gehörig; treffend **IV**
turning point [ˈtɜːnɪŋ ˌpɔɪnt] Wendepunkt **III**
2.45 (point) [ˈtuː pɔɪnt ˌfɔː ˈfaɪv] Komma *(bei Zahlenangaben)* **I**
to **point out** [pɔɪnt‿ˈaʊt] hinweisen auf **III**
poison [ˈpɔɪzn] Gift **III**
poisonous [ˈpɔɪznəs] giftig **III**
police [pəˈliːs] Polizei **I**
policy [ˈpɒlɪsi] Politik; politische Linie; Grundsatz **VT3,** 40; **VT4,** 57
polite [pəˈlaɪt] höflich **III**
political [pəˈlɪtɪkl] politisch **IV**
politics [ˈpɒlɪtɪks] Politik **VT4,** 61
poll tax [ˈpəʊl ˌtæks] Kopfsteuer ⟨**VT4,** 61⟩
to **pollute** [pəˈluːt] verschmutzen **IV**
pony [ˈpəʊni] Pony **I**
pony trekking [ˈpəʊni ˌtrekɪŋ] Ponyreiten im Gelände **II**
Pooh! [puː] Pfui! Bäh! **I**
swimming **pool** [ˈswɪmɪŋ ˌpuːl] Schwimmbecken; Schwimmbad **I**
poor [pɔː; pʊə] arm **I**
pop [pɒp] Pop **II**
pop star [ˈpɒp stɑː] Popstar **I**
to **pop in/out** *(infml)* [ˌpɒp‿ˈɪn] vorbeischauen **VT1,** 11
popcorn [ˈpɒpkɔːn] Popcorn **II**
popular [ˈpɒpjələ] populär, beliebt **II**
popularity [ˌpɒpjəˈlærəti] Popularität; Beliebtheit **IV**
population [ˌpɒpjəˈleɪʃn] Bevölkerung **III**
populous [ˈpɒpjələs] bevölkerungsreich ⟨**VT5,** 77⟩
porch [pɔːtʃ] Veranda ⟨**VT1,** 18⟩
pork [pɔːk] Schweinefleisch **IV**
porridge [ˈpɒrɪdʒ] Haferbrei **IV**
port [pɔːt] Hafen **I**
portable [ˈpɔːtəbl] transportabel; tragbar **VT5,** 83
to **portray** [pɔːˈtreɪ] porträtieren, darstellen; schildern **VT5,** 76
position [pəˈzɪʃn] Position **III**
positive [ˈpɒzətɪv] positiv **II**
possibility [ˌpɒsəˈbɪləti] Möglichkeit **III**
possible [ˈpɒsəbl] möglich **III**
post [pəʊst] Post **I**; Pfosten, Mast **II**
post [pəʊst] Versandkosten **IV**
post office [ˈpəʊst‿ˌɒfɪs] Postamt **III**
to **post** [pəʊst] aufgeben *(einen Brief)*; abschicken **III**
post [pəʊst] danach **VT4,** 61
postcard [ˈpəʊstkɑːd] Postkarte **I**
poster [ˈpəʊstə] Poster **I**
postgraduate [ˌpəʊstˈɡrædjuət] Doktorand(in); Student(in) im Aufbaustudium **VT3,** 55
pot [pɒt] Topf **III**
potato, *pl.* **potatoes** [pəˈteɪtəʊ] Kartoffel **II**
potential [pəʊˈtentʃl] Potenzial; Leistungsvermögen **VT3,** 48
potential [pəʊˈtentʃl] potenziell; möglich **VT4,** 59
pot-hole [ˈpɒthəʊl] Schlagloch ⟨**VT4,** 69⟩
pottery [ˈpɒtri] Töpferei **III**
poultry [ˈpuːltri] Geflügel **VT4,** 56
pound [paʊnd] Pfund *(brit. Währungseinheit)* **I**
to **pour** [pɔː] einschenken; eingießen; schütten **IV**
poverty [ˈpɒvəti] Armut **IV**
poverty level [ˈpɒvəti ˌlevl] Armutsgrenze **IV**
power [ˈpaʊə] Kraft, Stärke, Macht **I**; Energie; Leistung **IV**
power loom [ˌpaʊə ˈluːm] mechanischer Webstuhl **IV**
power station [ˈpaʊə ˌsteɪʃn] Kraftwerk **VT5,** 85
Word power [ˈwɜːd ˌpaʊə] *Besondere Wortschatzübung* **I**
to **power** [ˈpaʊə] antreiben; mit Energie versorgen **IV**
powerful [ˈpaʊəfl] stark; mächtig; leistungsfähig **III**
practical [ˈpræktɪkl] praktisch **III**
practice [ˈpræktɪs] Übung **I**; Praxis; Verfahren **IV**
sound practice [ˈsaʊnd ˌpræktɪs] *Hör-/Ausspracheübung* **I**
to **practice** *(AE)* [ˈpræktɪs] üben, praktizieren **II**
medicinal **practitioner** [meˈdɪsɪnl prækˈtɪʃnə] Heilpraktiker(in) ⟨**VT4,** 67⟩
to **praise** [preɪz] loben; preisen **IV**
to **pray** [preɪ] beten **II**
prayer [preə] Gebet **II**
preacher [ˈpriːtʃə] Prediger(in) **VT4,** 60
precious [ˈpreʃəs] wertvoll; kostbar ⟨**VT3,** 44⟩
prediction [prɪˈdɪkʃn] Voraussage **II**
prefab [ˈpriːfæb] vorgefertigt; Fertighaus ⟨**VT4,** 58⟩
to **prefer** [prɪˈfɜː] vorziehen **II**
pregnant [ˈpreɡnənt] schwanger **VT1,** 12; ⟨**VT4,** 70⟩
prejudice [ˈpredʒədɪs] Vorurteil(e); Voreingenommenheit **VT2,** 25; **VT5,** 75
prejudiced [ˈpredʒədɪst] voreingenommen; befangen **VT5,** 73
Premiership [ˈpremiəʃɪp] *erste Division, vgl. Deutsche Bundesliga* **II**
preparation [ˌprepr'eɪʃn] Vorbereitung **VT5,** 76

to **prepare** [prɪ'peə] vorbereiten; zubereiten **II**
to **prepare (for)** [prɪ'peə] sich vorbereiten (auf) **III**
preposition [ˌprepə'zɪʃn] Präposition **II**
present ['preznt] Gegenwart, Präsens **I**; Geschenk **I**
to **present** [prɪ'zent] präsentieren **II**
presentation [ˌprezn'teɪʃn] Präsentation **III**
present-day [ˌpreznt'deɪ] heutig; Gegenwarts- **IV**
president ['prezɪdnt] Präsident(in) **IV**
press [pres] Presse **III**
to **press** [pres] pressen; drücken ⟨**VT2**, 31⟩
press-up ['presʌp] Liegestütz **VT2**, 35
pressure ['preʃə] Druck **III**
to **pretend** [prɪ'tend] vorgeben; vortäuschen ⟨**VT1**, 22⟩; **VT3**, 43; **VT5**, 75
pretty ['prɪti] hübsch ⟨**VT2**, 31⟩
pretty ['prɪti] ziemlich **III**
to **prevail** [prɪ'veɪl] vorherrschen; überwiegen ⟨**VT2**, 26⟩
to **prevent** sth from happening/sb from doing sth [prɪ'vent] verhindern, dass etwas passiert/dass jmd etw. tut **IV**
previous ['pri:viəs] vorherig; vorausgegangen ⟨**VT2**, 32⟩
price [praɪs] Preis **III**
pride [praɪd] Stolz ⟨**VT3**, 51⟩
primary school ['praɪmri ˌsku:l] Grundschule ⟨**VT3**, 55⟩
prince [prɪnts] Prinz **II**
principal *(AE)* ['prɪntsɪpl] Schulleiter(in) **II**
to **print** [prɪnt] drucken **III**
printer ['prɪntə] Drucker(in) **II**
printout ['prɪntaʊt] Ausdruck **III**
prison ['prɪzn] Gefängnis **III**
prisoner ['prɪznə] Gefangene(r) **II**
privacy ['prɪvəsi; 'praɪvəsi] Privatsphäre **VT5**, 80
private ['praɪvɪt] privat **III**
privilege ['prɪvlɪdʒ] Privileg; Vorrecht **VT1**, 9
prize [praɪz] Preis **IV**
probably ['prɒbəbli] wahrscheinlich **II**
to **probe** [prəʊb] untersuchen; sondieren ⟨**VT5**, 74⟩
problem ['prɒbləm] Problem, Schwierigkeit **I**
proceeds *(pl.)* [prə'si:dz] Erlös; Einnahmen ⟨**VT4**, 67⟩
process ['prəʊsəs] Prozess **VT4**, 61
to **produce** [prə'dju:s] herstellen, produzieren **III**
product ['prɒdʌkt] Produkt **III**
productive [prə'dʌktɪv] produktiv **IV**
professional [prə'feʃnl] professionell **IV**
professor [prə'fesə] Professor(in) **III**
profile ['prəʊfaɪl] Profil; Porträt; Steckbrief **II**
profit ['prɒfɪt] Profit; Gewinn **IV**
profitable ['prɒfɪtəbl] profitabel **IV**
program *(AE)* ['prəʊgræm] Programm **II**
programme *(BE)* ['prəʊgræm] Programm; Sendung **III**
programming language ['prəʊgræmɪŋ ˌlæŋgwɪdʒ] Programmiersprache **IV**
computer **programmer** [kəmˌpju:tə 'prəʊgræmə] Programmierer(in) **IV**
to **prohibit** [prə'hɪbɪt] untersagen; verbieten **VT3**, 40; **VT4**, 61
project ['prɒdʒekt] Projekt **II**
video **projector** [ˌvɪdiəʊ prəʊ'dʒektə] Beamer *(Projektionsgerät)* **III**
promise ['prɒmɪs] Versprechen **I**
to **promise** ['prɒmɪs] versprechen **II**
pronoun ['prəʊnaʊn] Pronomen **II**
relative pronoun [ˌrelətɪv 'prəʊnaʊn] Relativpronomen **II**
to **pronounce** [prə'naʊnts] aussprechen **III**
pronunciation [prəˌnʌntsi'eɪʃn] Aussprache **III**
proof [pru:f] Beweis ⟨**VT4**, 71⟩
-proof [pru:f] -sicher; -resistent **III**
to **propel** [prə'pel] antreiben; vorwärts treiben ⟨**VT5**, 82⟩
proper ['prɒpə] richtig; ordentlich; angemessen **IV**
property ['prɒpəti] Grundbesitz ⟨**VT4**, 70⟩
pros and cons [ˌprəʊz‿ənd 'kɒnz] Argumente für und gegen etw. **IV**
prose [prəʊz] Prosa **IV**
prostitute ['prɒstɪtju:t] Prostituierte **VT4**, 59
to **protect sb** (from) [prə'tekt] jmdn (be)schützen (vor) **II**
protection [prə'tekʃn] Schutz **VT5**, 72
protest ['prəʊtest] Protest **IV**
to **protest** [prəʊ'test] protestieren **II**
Protestant ['prɒtɪstnt] Protestant(in); protestantisch **III**
proud (of) [praʊd] stolz (auf) **IV**
to **prove** [pru:v] beweisen **III**
to **prove sb wrong** [ˌpru:v 'rɒŋ] beweisen, dass jmd Unrecht hat ⟨**VT3**, 48⟩
to **provide** sb with [prəʊ'vaɪd] jmdn versorgen mit **III**
provided that ... [prəʊ'vaɪdɪd ðət] vorausgesetzt, dass ... **VT1**, 8
pseudonym ['sju:dənɪm] Pseudonym; Künstlername ⟨**VT5**, 77⟩
pub [pʌb] Kneipe; Gasthaus **III**
puberty ['pju:bəti] Pubertät ⟨**VT4**, 70⟩
the general **public** [ðə ˌdʒenrl 'pʌblɪk] die Allgemeinheit; die breite Öffentlichkeit **IV**
public ['pʌblɪk] öffentlich **IV**
public school [ˌpʌblɪk 'sku:l] Privatschule *(BE)*; staatliche Schule *(AE)* **VT3**, 52
public works [ˌpʌblɪk 'wɜ:ks] öffentliche Bauarbeiten; staatliche Bauprojekte **IV**
to **publish** ['pʌblɪʃ] veröffentlichen; publizieren; verlegen **IV**
puce [pju:s] puterrot ⟨**VT3**, 45⟩
puddle ['pʌdl] Pfütze **IV**
to **pull** [pʊl] ziehen **II**
pullover ['pʊləʊvə] Pullover **IV**
to **pulse** [pʌls] pulsieren ⟨**VT2**, 26⟩
pump [pʌmp] Pumpe, Luftpumpe **I**
to **pump** [pʌmp] pumpen; aufblasen **IV**
pumpkin ['pʌmpkɪn] Kürbis **II**
to **punch** [pʌntʃ] mit der Faust schlagen; boxen **VT2**, 36
punctuation [ˌpʌŋktʃu'eɪʃn] Zeichensetzung; Interpunktion ⟨**VT3**, 44⟩
to **punish** ['pʌnɪʃ] bestrafen **II**
punk [pʌŋk] Punk **II**
puny [pju:ni] kümmerlich; mickrig ⟨**VT3**, 45⟩
pupil ['pju:pl] Schüler(in) **I**
to **purchase** ['pɜ:tʃəs] kaufen; erwerben **VT1**, 8
to **purge** [pɜ:dʒ] abführen; reinigen ⟨**VT1**, 22⟩
Puritan ['pjʊərɪtn] Puritaner(in); puritanisch **III**
purple ['pɜ:pl] lila, violett **I**
purpose ['pɜ:pəs] Zweck **III**
on purpose [ɒn 'pɜ:pəs] absichtlich **III**
purposeful ['pɜ:pəsfli] entschlossen; zielgerichtet; zweckmäßig ⟨**VT3**, 50⟩
purse [pɜ:s] Geldbeutel *(BE)*; Handtasche *(AE)* **IV**
to **push** [pʊʃ] stoßen, schieben, drücken **II**
*to **put** [pʊt] setzen, stellen, legen **I**
to **put in** [pʊt‿'ɪn] einsetzen **I**
to **put on** [pʊt‿'ɒn] anziehen **II**
to **put out** [pʊt‿'aʊt] ausmachen; löschen **IV**
to **put sb on** [ˌpʊt 'ɒn] jmdn auf den Arm nehmen **VT1**, 12
to **put up** [pʊt‿'ʌp] aufstellen; errichten **III**
to **put up with sth** [ˌpʊt‿'ʌp wɪð] sich mit etw. abfinden; etw. ertragen **IV**
puzzle ['pʌzl] Rätsel; Puzzle **I**
crossword (puzzle) ['krɒswɜ:d] Kreuzworträtsel **II**

Q

to **quadruple** ['kwɒdrʊpl] vervierfachen ⟨**VT5**, 79⟩
qualification [ˌkwɒlɪfɪ'keɪʃn] Qualifikation; Befähigung **IV**
qualifications *(pl.)* [ˌkwɒlɪfɪ'keɪʃnz] Befähigungsnachweise; Zeugnisse **IV**
quality ['kwɒləti] Qualität; Eigenschaft **IV**
quarter past/to ['kwɔ:tə pɑ:st/tə] Viertel nach/vor **I**

queen [kwi:n] Königin **II**
question ['kwestʃən] Frage **I**
question tag ['kwestʃən ˌtæg] Frageanhängsel, Bestätigungsfrage **I**
questionnaire [ˌkwestʃə'neə] Fragebogen **IV**
queue [kju:] (Warte-)Schlange **IV**
quick [kwɪk] schnell **II**
quid *pl.* **quid** *(infml)* [kwɪd] Pfund *(Währung)* ⟨**VT1,** 11⟩
quiet [kwaɪət] leise **I**; still **III**
quite [kwaɪt] ziemlich; ganz, völlig **I**
quite a ['kwaɪt‿ə] ein(e) ziemliche(-r/-s); ein(e) wirkliche(-r/-s) **III**
quiz [kwɪz] Quiz, Rätsel **I**
quotation [kwəʊ'təɪʃn] Zitat; Belegstelle **IV**
to **quote** [kwəʊt] zitieren ⟨**VT4,** 68⟩

R

rabbit ['ræbɪt] Kaninchen **I**
race [reɪs] Wettlauf, Rennen **I**; Rasse **VT2,** 25; **VT4,** 57
race relations [ˌreɪs rɪ'leɪʃnz] Rassenbeziehungen **VT2,** 25
to **have a race** [ˌhæv‿ə 'reɪs] ein Rennen veranstalten **I**
racial ['reɪʃl] Rassen- **VT2,** 24; **VT4,** 57
racism ['reɪsɪzm] Rassismus **VT2,** 33
racket ['rækɪt] Schläger **I**
radiator ['reɪdieɪtə] Heizkörper **VT1,** 14
radio ['reɪdiəʊ] Radio **I**
rag [ræg] Lumpen, Fetzen **II**
railroad ['reɪlrəʊd] Eisenbahn **IV**
railway ['reɪlweɪ] Eisenbahn **III**
rain [reɪn] Regen **I**
to **rain** [reɪn] regnen **I**
rainbow ['reɪnbəʊ] Regenbogen **II**
raindrop ['reɪndrɒp] Regentropfen **III**
to **raise** [reɪz] anheben, erhöhen, (Kinder) großziehen, (Geld) aufbringen **II**
to **rake** [reɪk] durchpflügen ⟨**VT4,** 69⟩
ranch [rɑ:ntʃ; ræntʃ] Ranch **II**
at close **range** [ət ˌkləʊs 'reɪndʒ] aus nächster Nähe ⟨**VT4,** 62⟩
to **rank** [ræŋk] einen Rang einnehmen; in eine Rangfolge einordnen **VT2,** 34
rap [ræp] Rap **I**
rape [reɪp] Vergewaltigung ⟨**VT4,** 66⟩
rapid ['ræpɪd] rapide; schnell **VT4,** 56
rare [reə] rar, selten **IV**
raspberry ['rɑ:zbri] Himbeere **IV**
rate [reɪt] Rate **IV**
at any rate [ət 'eni ˌreɪt] jedenfalls **VT5,** 77
to **rate** [reɪt] bewerten; einstufen **IV**
rather ['rɑ:ðə] ziemlich **III**; eher; eigentlich ⟨**VT2,** 31⟩
I'd rather [aɪd 'rɑ:ðə] ich würde lieber **IV**
rather than ['rɑ:ðə ðən] eher als **VT4,** 56
raw material [ˌrɔ: mə'tɪərɪel] Rohmaterial; Rohstoff **IV**
ray [reɪ] Strahl **VT3,** 42
razor blade ['reɪzə ˌbleɪd] Rasierklinge ⟨**VT5,** 77⟩
RE [ɑ:r‿'i:] Religion *(Schulfach)* **II**
to **reach** [ri:tʃ] erreichen **III**; reichen; greifen **VT1,** 12; **VT2,** 27
to **react** [ri'ækt] reagieren **III**
reaction [ri'ækʃn] Reaktion **II**
*to **read** [ri:d] lesen **I**
ready ['redi] fertig, bereit **I**
real [rɪəl] echt, richtig, wirklich **II**
realistic [ˌrɪə'lɪstɪk] realistisch **II**
reality [ri'æləti] Realität; Wirklichkeit **IV**
to **realize** ['rɪəlaɪz] erkennen, realisieren **II**
really ['rɪəli] wirklich **I**
reason ['ri:zn] Grund **II**
reasonable ['ri:znəbl] vernünftig; angemessen **VT2,** 36
to **rebel** [rɪ'bel] rebellieren ⟨**VT1,** 23⟩
rebellion [rɪ'beliən] Rebellion **II**
rebelliousness [rɪ'beliəsnəs] Aufsässigkeit ⟨**VT3,** 41⟩
to **receive** [rɪ'si:v] empfangen **IV**
recent ['ri:snt] kürzlich; neueste(-r/-s); letzte(-r/-s) **IV**
recently ['ri:sntli] kürzlich; neulich; in letzter Zeit **IV**
recipe ['resɪpi:] Rezept **II**
to **reclaim** a toast [rɪˌkleɪm‿ə 'təʊst] *hier:* einen Toast aussprechen ⟨**VT5,** 87⟩
recognition [ˌrekəg'nɪʃn] Erkennung; Anerkennung **IV**
to **recognize** ['rekəgnaɪz] erkennen **II**
recon vessel [rɪ'kɒn ˌvesl] Aufklärungsschiff ⟨**VT5,** 74⟩
to **reconcile** ['reknsaɪl] versöhnen ⟨**VT4,** 63⟩
reconciliation [ˌrekn̩ˌsɪlɪ'eɪʃn] Versöhnung ⟨**VT4,** 63⟩
record ['rekɔ:d] Rekord **IV**; Aufzeichnung; Akte **VT5,** 75
to **record** [rɪ'kɔ:d] aufnehmen; aufzeichnen **III**
recordable disc [rɪ'kɔ:dəbl ˌdɪsk] beschreibbare CD ⟨**VT2,** 30⟩
to **recover** [rɪ'kʌvə] sich erholen **III**
red [red] rot **I**
to **redeem** [rɪ'di:m] erlösen ⟨**VT4,** 64⟩
to **reduce** [rɪ'dju:s] reduzieren; vermindern **IV**
reduction [rɪ'dʌkʃn] Reduzierung; Verminderung **VT5,** 79
to **refer (to)** [rɪ'fɜ:] (sich) beziehen (auf); sprechen (von) **IV**
referee [ˌrefr'i:] Schiedsrichter(in) **III**
reference ['refrnts] Referenz; Bezug **IV**
refrigerator [rɪ'frɪdʒreɪtə] Kühlschrank **VT3,** 49
refugee [ˌrefjʊ'dʒi:] Flüchtling **VT2,** 25; ⟨**VT3,** 50⟩
refusal [rɪ'fju:zl] Ablehnung; Weigerung ⟨**VT1,** 23⟩
to **refuse** [rɪ'fju:z] ablehnen; sich weigern **IV**
to **regain** [rɪ'geɪn] wiedererlangen; zurückgewinnen **IV**
region ['ri:dʒn] Region; Gegend **III**
regret [rɪ'gret] Bedauern **IV**
regular ['regjələ] regelmäßig; gleichmäßig **I**
regulation [ˌregjə'leɪʃn] Regelung; Verordnung; Vorschrift **VT5,** 79
reign [reɪn] Regierungszeit **III**
to **reinforce** [ˌri:ɪn'fɔ:s] verstärken **VT4,** 62
to **reject** [rɪ'dʒekt] zurückweisen; ablehnen ⟨**VT4,** 67⟩
*to be **related** to [bi: rɪ'leɪtɪd] verwandt sein mit; sich beziehen auf **IV**
race **relations** [ˌreɪs rɪ'leɪʃnz] Rassenbeziehungen **VT2,** 25
relationship [rɪ'leɪʃnʃɪp] Beziehung **III**
relative ['relətɪv] Verwandte(r) **I**
relative ['relətɪv] relativ **II**
defining relative clause [dɪˌfaɪnɪŋ ˌrelətɪv 'klɔ:z] notwendiger Relativsatz **IV**
non-defining relative clause [ˌnɒndɪfaɪnɪŋ ˌrelətɪv 'klɔ:z] nicht notwendiger Relativsatz **IV**
relative clause [ˌrelətɪv 'klɔ:z] Relativsatz **II**
relative pronoun [ˌrelətɪv 'prəʊnaʊn] Relativpronomen **II**
to **relax** [rɪ'læks] sich entspannen, sich ausruhen **I**
release [rɪ'li:s] Freigabe; Herausgabe; Freisetzung **VT4,** 61
to **release** [rɪ'li:s] freigeben; herausgeben; freisetzen; loslassen ⟨**VT2,** 32⟩
relentless [rɪ'lentləs] unerbittlich; unbarmherzig **IV**
relevant ['reləvənt] relevant; von Bedeutung **IV**
reliable [rɪ'laɪəbl] zuverlässig; vertrauenswürdig **IV**
relief [rɪ'li:f] Erleichterung; Linderung ⟨**VT4,** 70⟩
relief drive [rɪ'li:f ˌdraɪv] Hilfsaktion **VT2,** 26
religion [rɪ'lɪdʒn] Religion **III**
religious [rɪ'lɪdʒəs] religiös **II**
Religious Education [rɪˌlɪdʒəs‿edʒʊ'keɪʃn] Religionsunterricht **II**
to **relinquish** [rɪ'lɪŋkwɪʃ] aufgeben ⟨**VT1,** 23⟩
reluctant [rɪ'lʌktnt] zögernd; widerwillig **VT4,** 64
to **remain** [rɪ'meɪn] bleiben **IV**
remains [rɪ'meɪnz] Rest(e); Überbleibsel ⟨**VT2,** 30⟩

remedy ['remədi] Mittel; Abhilfe ⟨**VT4,** 67⟩
to **remember** [rɪ'membə] sich erinnern (an); sich merken **I**
to **remind** sb of sth/sb [rɪ'maɪnd] (jmdn an etw./jmdn) erinnern **III**
remote [rɪ'məʊt] fern; abgelegen ⟨**VT4,** 70⟩; **VT5,** 72
removal [rɪ'mu:vl] Beseitigung; Entfernung; Umzug **VT4,** 58
to **remove** [rɪ'mu:v] entfernen **IV**
to **rename** [ˌri:'neɪm] umbenennen **IV**
renewable [rɪ'nju:əbl] erneuerbar; verlängerbar **IV**
to **rent** [rent] mieten **III**
to **repair** [rɪ'peə] reparieren **III**
to **repeat** [rɪ'pi:t] wiederholen **II**
repetition [ˌrepɪ'tɪʃn] Wiederholung **IV**
repetitive [rɪ'petətɪv] sich wiederholend; monoton **VT5,** 72
to **replace (sth by/with sth)** [rɪ'pleɪs] ersetzen (etw. durch etw.) **IV**
reply [rɪ'plaɪ] Antwort **III**
to **reply** [rɪ'plaɪ] antworten, erwidern, entgegnen **II**
report [rɪ'pɔ:t] Bericht **III**; Knall ⟨**VT4,** 70⟩
to **report** [rɪ'pɔ:t] berichten; (sich) melden **II**; anzeigen; melden **VT3,** 43
representation [ˌreprɪzen'teɪʃn] Vertretung; Darstellung; Repräsentation; Repräsentanz **IV**
to **require** [rɪ'kwaɪə] benötigen; erfordern **IV**
rerun ['ri:rʌn] Wiederholung **VT2,** 26
rescue ['reskju:] Rettung **II**
Mountain Rescue [ˌmaʊntɪn 'reskju:] Bergwacht **II**
to **rescue** ['reskju:] retten **II**
research [rɪ'sɜ:tʃ] Recherche; Forschung; Untersuchung **IV**
to **research** [rɪ'sɜ:tʃ] recherchieren; erforschen; untersuchen **IV**
to **resemble** [rɪ'zembl] ähneln **VT3,** 40; **VT5,** 73
reservation [ˌrezə'veɪʃn] Reservat **IV**
reserve [rɪ'zɜ:v] Reserviertheit ⟨**VT4,** 70⟩
reservoir ['rezəvwɑ:] Stausee **IV**
resident ['rezɪdnt] Anwohner(in); Bewohner(in); Ortsansässige(r) **IV**
residential [ˌrezɪ'dentʃl] Wohn- ⟨**VT1,** 23⟩; **VT4,** 59
residue ['rezɪdju:] Rückstand; Überrest ⟨**VT2,** 30⟩
to **resign** [rɪ'zaɪn] resignieren; zurücktreten ⟨**VT2,** 30⟩
to **resist** [rɪ'zɪst] widerstehen; sich widersetzen **IV**
resistance (to) [rɪ'zɪstnts] Widerstand; Resistenz (gegen) **IV**
resolution [ˌrezl'u:ʃn] Entschluss; Vorsatz **IV**
natural **resource** [ˌnætʃrl rɪ'zɔ:s] Bodenschatz **IV**
to **respect** [rɪ'spekt] respektieren **IV**
to **respond** [rɪ'spɒnd] reagieren; erwidern; antworten ⟨**VT1,** 19⟩; ⟨**VT3,** 48⟩
respondent [rɪ'spɒndnt] Antwortende(r); Befragte(r) ⟨**VT3,** 48⟩
response [rɪ'spɒnts] Antwort; Erwiderung; Rückmeldung **VT1,** 9; **VT3,** 43
responsibility [rɪsˌpɒntsə'bɪləti] Verantwortung **IV**
responsible [rɪs'pɒntsəbl] verantwortlich; verantwortungsvoll **IV**
rest [rest] Rest **I**; Rast **VT2,** 28
to **rest** [rest] rasten; ausruhen; liegen **VT2,** 28; ⟨**VT3,** 51⟩; **VT5,** 76
restaurant ['restrənt] Restaurant, Gaststätte **I**
to **restore** [rɪ'stɔ:] wiederherstellen; restaurieren; zurückgeben **IV**
to **restrain** [rɪ'streɪn] zurückhalten; festhalten ⟨**VT3,** 50⟩; ⟨**VT4,** 70⟩
to **restrict** [rɪ'strɪkt] begrenzen; beschränken **VT2,** 25
result [rɪ'zʌlt] Ergebnis, Resultat **II**
as a result of [əz_ə rɪ'zʌlt_əv] infolge (von) **III**
résumé *(AE)* ['rəzju:meɪ] Lebenslauf **IV**
retailer ['ri:teɪlə] Einzelhändler(in) **VT2,** 33
to **retire** [rɪ'taɪə] sich zurückziehen; sich zur Ruhe setzen **III**
to **retrieve** [rɪ'tri:v] zurückholen; wieder auffinden ⟨**VT2,** 30⟩
in **return** [ɪn rɪ'tɜ:n] als Gegenleistung **IV**
to **return** [rɪ'tɜ:n] zurückgeben, zurückschlagen; zurückkehren **II**
to **rev** [rev] den Motor hochjagen; die Motordrehzahl erhöhen ⟨**VT4,** 62⟩
to **reveal** [rɪ'vi:l] enthüllen; offenbaren: preisgeben **VT5,** 77
revenge [rɪ'vendʒ] Rache, Revanche **III**
revenue ['revnju:] Erlös; Einnahmen ⟨**VT4,** 67⟩
to **reverse** [rɪ'vɜ:s] umkehren; rückgängig machen; rückwärts fahren **IV**
review [rɪ'vju:] Kritik **II**
to **revise** [rɪ'vaɪz] noch einmal durchsehen; korrigieren; sich auf eine Prüfung vorbereiten **IV**
*to do some **revision** [ˌdu: səm rɪ'vɪʒn] lernen (wiederholen) **IV**
revolting [rɪ'vɒltɪŋ] abscheulich ⟨**VT3,** 45⟩
revolution [ˌrevl'u:ʃn] Revolution **IV**
revolutionary [ˌrevl'u:ʃnri] revolutionär **IV**
*to **rewrite** [ˌri:'raɪt] umschreiben; neu schreiben **IV**
rhino ['raɪnəʊ] Rhinozeros; Nashorn ⟨**VT4,** 67⟩
rhyme [raɪm] Reim **IV**
to **rhyme** [raɪm] (sich) reimen **IV**
rhythm ['rɪðm] Rhythmus **IV**
rice [raɪs] Reis **II**
rich [rɪtʃ] reich **I**
*to get **rid** of [get 'rɪd_əv] loswerden **II**
ride [raɪd] Fahrt, Ritt **II**
*to **ride** [raɪd] fahren; reiten **I**
rider ['raɪdə] Reiter(in) **II**
ridiculous [rɪ'dɪkjələs] lächerlich **IV**
horseback **riding** [ˌhɔ:sbæk 'raɪdɪŋ] Reiten **II**
rifle ['raɪfl] Gewehr **VT4,** 62
right [raɪt] Recht **III**
Civil Rights Act [ˌsɪvl 'raɪts_ækt] Bürgerrechtsgesetz **VT2,** 24
human rights abuse [ˌhju:mən 'raɪts_əˌbju:s] Menschenrechtsverletzung **VT4,** 63
right [raɪt] richtig, korrekt **I**; rechts; rechte(-r/-s) **I**
all right [ɔ:l 'raɪt] in Ordnung; alles klar **II**; schon **VT5,** 74
on somebody's right/left [ɒn ˌsʌmbədiz 'raɪt/'left] zur Rechten/zur Linken von jemandem **I**
right away [raɪt_ə'weɪ] sofort, gleich **I**
right now [ˌraɪt 'naʊ] jetzt gleich **II**
righteous ['raɪtʃəs] rechtschaffen ⟨**VT3,** 43⟩
ring [rɪŋ] Ring **IV**
key ring ['ki: ˌrɪŋ] Schlüsselbund; Schlüsselanhänger **IV**
*to **ring** [rɪŋ] klingeln; anrufen **II**
The phone is ringing off the hook. [ðə ˌfəʊn_ɪz rɪŋɪŋ ɒf ðə 'hʊk] Das Telefon klingelt ohne Unterlass. ⟨**VT3,** 43⟩
riot [raɪət] Aufruhr; Ausschreitung; Unruhe **VT4,** 62
ripe [raɪp] reif **IV**
*to **rise** [raɪz] steigen; sich erheben; aufgehen *(Sonne)* **IV**
risk [rɪsk] Risiko **IV**
to **risk** [rɪsk] riskieren **III**
ritual ['rɪtjuəl] Ritual **IV**
rival ['raɪvl] Rivale, Rivalin; Konkurrent(in) **III**
river ['rɪvə] Fluss **I**
road [rəʊd] Straße **I**
robot ['rəʊbɒt] Roboter; Automat ⟨**VT3,** 44⟩; **VT5,** 72
rock [rɒk] Fels, Stein **I**
rock [rɒk] Rock *(Musik)* **II**
rodeo [rəʊ'deɪəʊ; 'rəʊdiəʊ] Rodeo **I**
role [rəʊl] Rolle **I**
role model ['rəʊl ˌmɒdl] Vorbild **VT3,** 48
role play ['rəʊl pleɪ] Rollenspiel **I**
roll [rəʊl] Brötchen **II**
to **roll** [rəʊl] rollen **III**
roller coaster ['rəʊləˌkəʊstə] Achterbahn ⟨**VT1,** 22⟩
roof [ru:f] Dach **I**
room [ru:m] Zimmer; Platz **I**
changing room ['tʃeɪndʒɪŋ ˌrʊm] Umkleideraum **III**
living room ['lɪvɪŋ ˌrʊm] Wohnzimmer **I**

sitting room ['sɪtɪŋ ˌrʊm] Wohnzimmer **IV**
staff room ['stɑːf rʊm] Lehrerzimmer **III**
root [ruːt] Wurzel **III**
rope [rəʊp] Seil **II**
to **know the ropes** [ˌnəʊ ðə 'rəʊps] die Spielregeln kennen ⟨**VT3,** 43⟩
rosary ['rəʊzri] Rosenkranz ⟨**VT3,** 41⟩
to **rot** [rɒt] verrotten; verfaulen; verfallen **VT5,** 77
rotor ['rəʊtə] Rotor; Walze ⟨**VT1,** 18⟩
rotten ['rɒtn] verfault; scheußlich **IV**
rough [rʌf] grob; rau; ungefähr **VT3,** 48; **VT5,** 77
to **sleep rough** [ˌsliːp 'rʌf] auf der Straße leben; im Freien übernachten ⟨**VT5,** 80⟩
round [raʊnd] Runde **II**
round [raʊnd] um … herum **I**
route [ruːt] Route **II**
routine ['ruːtiːn] Routine; regelmäßig anfallend **IV**
row [rəʊ] Sträßchen; Reihe **I**
row [raʊ] Streit; Krach **IV**
to **have a row** [ˌhæv‿ə 'raʊ] streiten; Krach haben **IV**
to **row** [rəʊ] rudern **I**
R-rated *(AE)* ['ɑːˌreɪtɪd] frei ab 17 ⟨**VT1,** 9⟩
to **rub** [rʌb] reiben **VT1,** 12
rubber ['rʌbə] Radiergummi **I**
rubbish ['rʌbɪʃ] Müll; Quatsch **II**
rubble ['rʌbl] Geröll; Schutt ⟨**VT5,** 77⟩
rude [ruːd] unhöflich; unverschämt **IV**
rugby ['rʌgbi] Rugby **I**
rugged ['rʌgɪd] rau; wild ⟨**VT5,** 76⟩
to **ruin** ['ruːɪn] ruinieren, zerstören **II**
rule [ruːl] Regel **I**
to **rule** [ruːl] herrschen **III**
ruler ['ruːlə] Lineal **I**
on the **run** [ɒn ðə 'rʌn] auf der Flucht **III**
*to **run** [rʌn] rennen, laufen **I**; führen, leiten **IV**
to **run down** [rʌn 'daʊn] leer werden **II**
to **run out** [ˌrʌn‿'aʊt] ausgehen **III**
to **run out of sth** [ˌrʌn‿'aʊt‿əv] bald kein … mehr haben; jmdm ausgehen **IV**
runaway ['rʌnəˌweɪ] Ausreißer(in) **III**
rural ['ruːrl] ländlich ⟨**VT4,** 67⟩; ⟨**VT4,** 69⟩
rush [rʌʃ] Rausch; Adrenalinstoß ⟨**VT1,** 17⟩
to **rush** [rʌʃ] sich beeilen **I**

S

sack [sæk] Sack **II**
sacred ['seɪkrɪd] heilig ⟨**VT4,** 69⟩
sad [sæd] traurig, schmerzlich **I**
saddle ['sædl] Sattel **II**
safe [seɪf] Safe; Tresor **III**
safe [seɪf] sicher **I**
safety ['seɪfti] Sicherheit **III**
to **sag** [sæg] durchhängen; durchsacken; sich durchbiegen ⟨**VT5,** 77⟩
to **sail** [seɪl] segeln **III**
sailor ['seɪlə] Seemann, Matrose; Segler **III**
saint [seɪnt] Heilige(r) **VT3,** 42
salad ['sæləd] Salat **II**
sale [seɪlz] Verkauf **IV**
sales [seɪlz] Vertrieb; Verkauf **IV**
salmon, *pl.* **salmon** ['sæmən] Lachs **III**
salt [sɔːlt] Salz **IV**
salute [sə'luːt] Salut; Gruß **VT2,** 29
to **sanction** ['sæŋktʃn] sanktionieren; billigen **VT2,** 27
sand [sænd] Sand **I**
sandwich ['sændwɪdʒ] Sandwich, belegtes Brot **I**
sanguine ['sæŋgwɪn] gesund *(Gesichtsfarbe)* ⟨**VT5,** 76⟩
satellite ['sætlaɪt] Satellit **IV**
satirical [sə'tɪrɪkl] satirisch; Spott- ⟨**VT2,** 38⟩; **VT5,** 77
to **satisfy** ['sætɪsfaɪ] zufriedenstellen ⟨**VT4,** 69⟩
sauce [sɔːs] Sauce **IV**
saucer ['sɔːsə] Untertasse **I**
to **saunter** ['sɔːntə] schlendern; bummeln ⟨**VT3,** 50⟩
sausage ['sɒsɪdʒ] Wurst **II**
to **save** [seɪv] retten, bergen **I**; sparen **III**
to **save up** [ˌseɪv‿'ʌp] zusammensparen **IV**
savings account ['seɪvɪŋz əˌkaʊnt] Sparkonto **IV**
Saxon ['sæksn] Sachse, Sächsin; sächsisch **II**
*to **say** [seɪ] sagen, sprechen **I**
needless to say ['niːdləs tə ˌseɪ] natürlich **VT1,** 12
to **say hello** [seɪ hə'ləʊ] Hallo sagen, sich begrüßen **I**
saying ['seɪɪŋ] Redensart; Sprichwort **IV**
scale [skeɪl] Skala; Maßstab **IV**
scar [skɑː] Narbe **II**
*to be **scared** [biː 'skeəd] Angst haben, erschrocken sein **I**
scary ['skeəri] unheimlich, gruselig; schreckhaft **II**
to **scatter** ['skætə] (sich) zerstreuen; auseinanderjagen ⟨**VT4,** 62⟩
scene [siːn] Szene; Schauplatz **I**
scenery ['siːnri] Landschaft **III**
scented ['sentɪd] parfümiert ⟨**VT3,** 47⟩
schedule ['ʃedjuːl; 'skedʒuːl] Stundenplan; Fahrplan **II**
scheme [skiːm] Programm; Plan; Maßnahme ⟨**VT4,** 67⟩
school [skuːl] Schule **I**
boarding school ['bɔːdɪŋ skuːl] Internat **VT3,** 52
comprehensive school [kɒmprɪ'hentsɪv ˌskuːl] Gesamtschule ⟨**VT3,** 55⟩
elementary school *(AE)* [elɪ'mentri ˌskuːl] Grundschule **II**
grammar school ['græmə ˌskuːl] Gymnasium *(BE)* **IV**
high school ['haɪ ˌskuːl] High School *(weiterführende Schule in den USA, Oberstufe)* **III**
jump school ['dʒʌmp ˌskuːl] Fallschirmspringerschule ⟨**VT1,** 12⟩
middle school ['mɪdl ˌskuːl] Mittelschule *(weiterführende Schule in den USA, Mittelstufe)* **II**
primary school ['praɪmri ˌskuːl] Grundschule ⟨**VT3,** 55⟩
public school [ˌpʌblɪk 'skuːl] Privatschule *(BE)*; staatliche Schule *(AE)* **VT3,** 52
school bag ['skuːl bæg] Schultasche **I**
science [saɪənts] (Natur-)Wissenschaft **II**
scientist ['saɪəntɪst] Wissenschaftler(in) **IV**
scooter ['skuːtə] Roller **I**
score [skɔː] Punktestand **III**
to **score** [skɔː] punkten; ein Tor schießen **III**
scorer ['skɔːrə] Torjäger(in); Korbjäger(in) **III**
Scot [skɒt] Schotte; Schottin **III**
scrambled egg [ˌskræmbld‿'eg] Rührei **IV**
scrapbook ['skræpbʊk] Sammelalbum **II**
scrapheap ['skræphiːp] Müllhaufen ⟨**VT3,** 44⟩
scratch [skrætʃ] Kratzer **III**
to **scream** [skriːm] schreien, kreischen **I**
screen [skriːn] Bildschirm **I**
to **screw** [skruː] schrauben ⟨**VT3,** 44⟩
to **scrutinize** ['skruːtɪnaɪz] eingehend untersuchen ⟨**VT5,** 77⟩
sculpture ['skʌlptʃə] Skulptur **III**
sea [siː] Meer **I**
seagull ['siːgʌl] Möwe ⟨**VT1,** 18⟩
seal [siːl] Seehund **I**
to **search** [sɜːtʃ] durchsuchen **III**
to **search for** ['sɜːtʃ fə] suchen (nach) **III**
seaside ['siːsaɪd] Küste, Meeresküste **I**
at the seaside [ət ðə 'siːsaɪd] am Meer **I**
season ['siːzn] Saison; Jahreszeit **III**
seat [siːt] Sitz, Sitzplatz **II**
second ['seknd] Sekunde **III**
split second [ˌsplɪt 'seknd] Sekundenbruchteil **VT1,** 17
second ['seknd] zweite(-r/-s) **I**
to **have second thoughts** [hæv ˌseknd 'θɔːts] Zweifel haben; es sich anders überlegen ⟨**VT1,** 19⟩
secondary school ['sekəndri ˌskuːl] weiterführende Schule ⟨**VT3,** 55⟩
second-hand [ˌseknd 'hænd] gebraucht **II**
second-hand shop [ˌseknd hænd 'ʃɒp] Gebrauchtwarenladen **II**
secret ['siːkrət] Geheimnis **I**
secretly ['siːkrətli] heimlich **IV**

section ['sekʃn] Sektion; Abschnitt **IV**
sector ['sektə] Sektor **VT4,** 56
security [sɪ'kjʊərəti] Sicherheit; Schutz ⟨**VT4,** 68⟩; **VT5,** 80
*to **see** [si:] sehen **I**
I see. [aɪ 'si:] aha; ach so **II**
See you! ['si: ju:] Bis dann!, Bis … **I**
to **seek** [si:k] suchen **VT4,** 59
to **seem** [si:m] scheinen **II**
to **seem familiar** [ˌsi:m fə'mɪliə] bekannt vorkommen **III**
segregation [ˌsegrɪ'geɪʃn] Trennung; Rassentrennung **VT2,** 24; **VT4,** 57
seldom ['seldəm] selten **VT5,** 76
to **select** [sɪ'lekt] auswählen; aussuchen **IV**
self-esteem [ˌselfɪs'ti:m] Selbstwertgefühl; Selbstachtung **VT4,** 66
self-sufficient [ˌselfsə'fɪʃnt] autark; unabhängig; selbstgenügsam **IV**
*to **sell** [sel] verkaufen **II**
*to **send** [send] schicken **I**
sense [sents] Sinn; Bedeutung **III**
common sense [ˌkɒmən 'sents] gesunder Menschenverstand **VT3,** 43
to **make sense** [ˌmeɪk 'sents] Sinn machen; einleuchten **III**
sensitive ['sentsɪtɪv] sensibel; empfindlich; empfindsam **IV**
sentence ['sentənts] Satz **I**; Verurteilung; Strafmaß **VT4,** 61
to **sentence** ['sentənts] verurteilen **VT4,** 61
sentience ['sentʃnts] empfindungsfähiges Wesen ⟨**VT5,** 74⟩
sentient ['sentʃnt] empfindungsfähig ⟨**VT5,** 74⟩
to **separate** ['sepreɪt] trennen **IV**
separate ['seprət] separat; getrennt; verschieden **II**
serial ['sɪəriəl] Serie; Fortsetzungsgeschichte **IV**
series, *pl.* **series** ['sɪəri:z] Serie **IV**
serious ['sɪəriəs] ernst **II**
to **take sth seriously** [ˌteɪk 'sɪəriəsli] etw. ernst nehmen **IV**
servant ['sɜ:vnt] Bedienstete(r); Diener(in) **III**
civil servant [ˌsɪvl 'sɜ:vnt] Beamter; Beamtin **VT4,** 61
to **serve** [sɜ:v] (be)dienen; aufschlagen *(Sport)* **II**
to serve it up double [tə ˌsɜ:v‿ɪt‿ʌp 'dʌbl] es doppelt so schlimm machen ⟨**VT3,** 45⟩
service ['sɜ:vɪs] Service, Dienst **II**; Militärdienst **VT1,** 12
session ['seʃn] Sitzung; Stunde; Versammlung **IV**
*to **set fire to** [set 'faɪə tə] in Brand stecken **II**
to **set off** [set‿'ɒf] aufbrechen **II**; auslösen ⟨**VT4,** 70⟩
to **set the table** [ˌset ðə 'teɪbl] den Tisch decken **I**
to **set up** [set‿'ʌp] einrichten; aufbauen; gründen **III**
setting ['setɪŋ] Schauplatz; Rahmen **IV**
to **settle** ['setl] siedeln; sich niederlassen **III**; festlegen; erledigen **IV**
settlement ['setlmənt] Siedlung **III**
settler ['setlə] Siedler(in) **III**
several ['sevrl] mehrere; verschiedene **IV**
severe [sɪ'vɪə] ernst; schwerwiegend **VT1,** 16
*to **sew** [səʊ] nähen **IV**
sewerage ['sʊərɪdʒ] Kanalisation ⟨**VT4,** 59⟩
sex [seks] Sexualität; Geschlecht **VT1,** 8
shack [ʃæk] Baracke; Bretterbude **VT4,** 58
shade [ʃeɪd] Schattierung; Schatten ⟨**VT2,** 30⟩
shadow ['ʃædəʊ] Schatten **IV**
*to **shake** [ʃeɪk] schütteln **I**; zittern **III**
shallow ['ʃæləʊ] seicht; flach **VT1,** 16
shantytown ['ʃæntitaʊn] Elendsviertel; Barackensiedlung ⟨**VT4,** 59⟩
shape [ʃeɪp] Form **IV**
to **shape** [ʃeɪp] formen ⟨**VT5,** 81⟩
to **share** [ʃeə] teilen **IV**
shark [ʃɑ:k] Hai **III**
sharp [ʃɑ:p] scharf; spitz ⟨**VT2,** 31⟩
to **shatter** ['ʃætə] zerschlagen; zertrümmern **VT1,** 17
to **shave** [ʃeɪv] (sich) rasieren **II**
she [ʃi:] sie **I**
shed [ʃed] Schuppen, Stall **I**
to **shed** [ʃed] abwerfen ⟨**VT2,** 26⟩
sheep, *pl.* **sheep** [ʃi:p] Schaf **I**
sheepdog ['ʃi:pdɒg] Hütehund; Schäferhund **I**
sheepish ['ʃi:pɪʃ] kleinlaut; schüchtern; verlegen **IV**
sheet [ʃi:t] Blatt; Bettlaken; Blech **IV**
shelf, *pl.* **shelves** [ʃelf; ʃelvz] Regal, Regalbrett **I**
shelter ['ʃeltə] Obdach; Schutz(hütte) **III**
sheriff ['ʃerɪf] Sheriff **II**
to **shield** [ʃi:ld] beschirmen; schützen **VT1,** 13
shift [ʃɪft] Schicht **IV**; Wechsel; Verschiebung **VT5,** 80
to **shift** [ʃɪft] verrutschen **VT1,** 13
*to **shine** [ʃaɪn] scheinen; glänzen **I**
shiny ['ʃaɪni] glänzend **II**
ship [ʃɪp] Schiff **I**
shirt [ʃɜ:t] Hemd; Shirt **I**
shit *(vulg)* [ʃɪt] Scheiße; Scheißdreck ⟨**VT2,** 31⟩
to **take no shit** *(vulg)* [ˌteɪk nəʊ 'ʃɪt] sich nichts gefallen lassen ⟨**VT3,** 42⟩
to **shiver** ['ʃɪvə] erschauern; frösteln **IV**
shock [ʃɒk] Schock **II**
to **shock** [ʃɒk] schockieren **IV**
shoe [ʃu:] Schuh **I**
*to **shoot (at)** [ʃu:t] schießen (auf) **II**
shop [ʃɒp] Geschäft, Laden **I**
junk shop ['dʒʌŋk ˌʃɒp] Ramschladen **VT2,** 36
second-hand shop [ˌseknd hænd 'ʃɒp] Gebrauchtwarenladen **II**
shop assistant ['ʃɒp‿əˌsɪstnt] Verkäufer(in) **I**
shopping ['ʃɒpɪŋ] Einkaufen; Einkäufe **I**
shopping centre ['ʃɒpɪŋ ˌsentə] Einkaufszentrum **I**
to **go shopping** [ˌgəʊ 'ʃɒpɪŋ] einkaufen gehen **I**
to **shore up** [ˌʃɔ:r‿'ʌp] abstützen ⟨**VT5,** 77⟩
short [ʃɔ:t] kurz **I**
short cut ['ʃɔ:t kʌt] Abkürzung **II**
shortage ['ʃɔ:tɪdʒ] Knappheit; Mangel **IV**
to **shorten** ['ʃɔ:tn] (ver)kürzen **IV**
shorts *(pl.)* [ʃɔ:ts] Shorts, kurze Hose **III**
shot [ʃɒt] Schuss, Schlag **II**
to **give sth a shot** [ˌgɪv‿ə 'ʃɒt] es mal probieren mit etw.; sein Glück versuchen mit etw. ⟨**VT3,** 48⟩
should [ʃʊd] sollte(n) **II**
shoulder ['ʃəʊldə] Schulter **I**
shout [ʃaʊt] Schrei, Ruf **III**
to **shout** [ʃaʊt] schreien, rufen **I**
to **shove** [ʃʌv] schieben; drängen **VT2,** 36
show [ʃəʊ] Show, Schau, Aufführung **II**
talk show ['tɔ:k ˌʃəʊ] Talkshow **III**
*to **show** [ʃəʊ] zeigen **I**
It just goes to show … [ɪt ˌdʒʌst gəʊz tə 'ʃəʊ] Das zeigt mal wieder … ⟨**VT4,** 68⟩
to **show sb around (a place)** [ʃəʊ] jmdn (an einem Ort) herumführen **II**
shower ['ʃaʊə] Schauer; Dusche **III**
show-off ['ʃəʊ‿ɒf] Angeber(in) **II**
Shsh! [ʃ] Pssst! **I**
*to **shut** [ʃʌt] zumachen, schließen **I**
to **shut off** [ʃʌt‿'ɒf] abschalten; herunterfahren ⟨**VT5,** 76⟩
to **shut up** *(rude)* [ʃʌt‿'ʌp] die Klappe halten ⟨**VT2,** 32⟩
shutdown ['ʃʌtdaʊn] Schließung; Stilllegung ⟨**VT3,** 50⟩
shy [ʃaɪ] schüchtern **III**
sick [sɪk] krank; unwohl **VT2,** 36
to **be sick** [bi: 'sɪk] sich übergeben **IV**
to **be sick of (+ noun/gerund)** [bi: 'sɪk‿əv] satt haben, (einer Sache) überdrüssig sein **IV**
to **feel sick** [ˌfi:l 'sɪk] Übelkeit verspüren; sich schlecht fühlen **III**
side [saɪd] Seite **II**
sidewalk *(AE)* ['saɪdwɔ:k] Gehweg; Gehsteig ⟨**VT2,** 32⟩
sierra [sɪ'erə] Gebirgskette ⟨**VT1,** 18⟩
Sierra Wave [sɪˌerə 'weɪv] Sierra Wave *(ein in der Sierra Nevada auftretendes außergewöhnliches Thermikphänomen)* ⟨**VT1,** 18⟩

to **sigh** [saɪ] seufzen **II**
sight [saɪt] Sehenswürdigkeit; Sicht, Anblick **II**
out of sight [ˌaʊt‿əv 'saɪt] außer Sicht **VT4,** 58
sightseeing ['saɪtsi:ɪŋ] Besichtigungstour **I**
sign [saɪn] Zeichen **II**
to **sign** [saɪn] unterzeichnen **IV**
signal ['sɪgnl] Signal, Zeichen **II**
signature ['sɪgnətʃə] Unterschrift **IV**
significant [sɪg'nɪfɪkənt] signifikant; bedeutend; wesentlich **VT2,** 33
silence ['saɪlənts] Stille **III**
silent ['saɪlənt] still **IV**
silly ['sɪli] Dummkopf **I**
silly ['sɪli] dumm, doof, albern **I**
silver ['sɪlvə] Silber **II**
similar ['sɪmɪlə] ähnlich **III**
simple ['sɪmpl] einfach, simpel **IV**
simultaneous [ˌsɪml'teɪniəs] simultan; gleichzeitig **VT5,** 77
sin [sɪn] Sünde **VT3,** 42
since [sɪnts] seit, seitdem **II**; da **III**
sincere [sɪn'sɪə] aufrichtig; seriös **VT3,** 42
Yours sincerely [jɔ:z sɪn'sɪəli] Mit freundlichen Grüßen **IV**
*to **sing** [sɪŋ] singen **I**
to **sing along** [ˌsɪŋ‿ə'lɒŋ] mitsingen **I**
singer ['sɪŋə] Sänger(in) **II**
single ['sɪŋgl] einzeln; einzig; alleinstehend **IV**
to **single sb out** [ˌsɪŋgl‿'aʊt] herausgreifen; aussondern ⟨**VT3,** 45⟩
singular ['sɪŋgjələ] Singular **IV**
*to **sink** [sɪŋk] sinken **IV**
sir [sɜ:] mein Herr *(Anrede)* **I**
Sir [sɜ:] Sir *(Anrede für einen Ritter)* **III**
sister ['sɪstə] Schwester **I**
*to **sit** [sɪt] sitzen **I**
sitting room ['sɪtɪŋ ˌrʊm] Wohnzimmer **IV**
to **sit (down)** [sɪt 'daʊn] sich (hin)setzen **I**
sitcom ['sɪtkɒm] Situationskomödie **IV**
site [saɪt] Ort; Gelände; Schauplatz **VT1,** 16; ⟨**VT4,** 67⟩; **VT5,** 77
sit-in ['sɪtɪn] Sitzstreik **VT2,** 29
situation [ˌsɪtju'eɪʃn] Situation **II**
sixteen-track [ˌsɪksti:n'træk] 16-Spur-Aufnahmegerät ⟨**VT2,** 31⟩
size [saɪz] Größe, Kleidergröße **I**
the next size down [ðə ˌnekst saɪz 'daʊn] eine Größe kleiner **III**
to **skate** [skeɪt] skaten; Skateboard fahren **IV**
skateboard ['skeɪtbɔ:d] Skateboard **I**
skates *pl.* [skeɪts] Inlineskates, Rollschuhe, Schlittschuhe **I**
skating ['skeɪtɪŋ] Inlineskate/Schlittschuh fahren **I**
skeletal ['skelɪtl] skelettartig ⟨**VT1,** 22⟩
to **ski** [ski:] Ski fahren **III**
skiing ['ski:ɪŋ] Skifahren **I**
skill [skɪl] Fertigkeit; Geschick **III**
computer skills [kəm'pju:tə ˌskɪlz] EDV-Kenntnisse **IV**
to **skim** [skɪm] überfliegen; abschöpfen **VT5,** 77
skin [skɪn] Haut, Fell **I**
to **skip sth** [skɪp] überspringen; auslassen; schwänzen **VT3,** 48
skirt [skɜ:t] Rock **I**
sky [skaɪ] Himmel **I**
skyscraper ['skaɪskreɪpə] Wolkenkratzer **I**
to **slap** [slæp] schlagen; einen Klaps geben **VT5,** 75
to **slash** [slæʃ] aufschlitzen ⟨**VT4,** 64⟩
slate [sleɪt] Schiefer **II**
slave [sleɪv] Sklave; Sklavin **IV**
slavery ['sleɪvri] Sklaverei **VT2,** 24; **VT5,** 77
sled [sled] Schlitten **II**
*to go to **sleep** [gəʊ tə 'sli:p] einschlafen **I**
*to **sleep** [sli:p] schlafen **I**
sleeping bag ['sli:pɪŋ ˌbæg] Schlafsack **III**
to **sleep over** ['sli:p‿əʊvə] übernachten ⟨**VT1,** 11⟩
to **sleep rough** [ˌsli:p 'rʌf] auf der Straße leben; im Freien übernachten ⟨**VT5,** 80⟩
sleepover ['sli:pəʊvə] Übernachtung ⟨**VT1,** 11⟩
slight [slaɪt] leicht; gering ⟨**VT3,** 44⟩
slim [slɪm] dünn; schlank; gering **VT5,** 75
to **slip** [slɪp] (aus)rutschen **III**; schlüpfen; gleiten **IV**
slippery ['slɪpri] rutschig, glitschig **II**
slogan ['sləʊgən] Slogan; Werbespruch **IV**
to **slow (sb) down** [ˌsləʊ 'daʊn] (jmdn) bremsen **VT1,** 12
slow [sləʊ] langsam **I**
slowly ['sləʊli] langsam **I**
slum clearance ['slʌm ˌklɪərnts] Slumbereinigung; Slumsanierung ⟨**VT4,** 58⟩
small [smɔ:l] klein **I**
the small of the back [ðə ˌsmɔ:l‿əv ðə 'bæk] Kreuz ⟨**VT1,** 12⟩
smart [smɑ:t] pfiffig; schlau **VT2,** 27; ⟨**VT5,** 81⟩
smart ass *(slang)* [ˌsmɑ:t‿'æs] Klugscheißer(in) ⟨**VT3,** 43⟩
The smart money says ... ['smɑ:t ˌmʌni] Die meisten wetten, dass ... ⟨**VT1,** 12⟩
smell [smel] Geruch, Gestank **I**
*to **smell** [smel] riechen (an) **II**
smile [smaɪl] Lächeln **I**
to **smile** [smaɪl] lächeln **I**
smog [smɒg] Smog **IV**
smoke [sməʊk] Rauch **III**
to **smoke** [sməʊk] rauchen **IV**
to **smooth out** [ˌsmu:ð‿'aʊt] ausgleichen; glatt streichen ⟨**VT5,** 75⟩
to **smuggle** ['smʌgl] schmuggeln **II**
smuggler ['smʌglə] Schmuggler(in) **II**
snack [snæk] Snack, Imbiss **III**
snake [sneɪk] Schlange **I**
to **snatch** [snætʃ] schnappen; ergreifen **VT2,** 36
to **sneak** [sni:k] schleichen; schmuggeln ⟨**VT1,** 22⟩; **VT4,** 60
to **sneer** [snɪə] spotten, spöttisch grinsen **II**
to **sneeze** [sni:z] niesen **II**
snigger ['snɪgə] Kichern ⟨**VT3,** 45⟩
to **snoop** [snu:p] schnüffeln ⟨**VT5,** 77⟩
snot *(infml)* [snɒt] Rotz ⟨**VT4,** 68⟩
snow [snəʊ] Schnee **II**
snowboarding ['snəʊbɔ:dɪŋ] Snowboarden **III**
so [səʊ] so **I**
so far ['səʊ fɑ:] bis jetzt **II**
so [səʊ] also, deshalb **I**
so (that) ['səʊ ðət] damit; so dass **I**
to **soak** [səʊk] tränken; durchweichen; durchnässen ⟨**VT4,** 71⟩
soap [səʊp] Seife **I**
to **soar** [sɔ:] aufsteigen; segeln ⟨**VT1,** 18⟩; ⟨**VT4,** 69⟩; ⟨**VT5,** 77⟩
to **sob** [sɒb] schluchzen ⟨**VT4,** 68⟩
soccer *(AE)* ['sɒkə] Fußball **I**
social ['səʊʃl] sozial, gesellschaftlich **II**
social engineering [ˌsəʊʃl endʒɪ'nɪərɪŋ] Sozialplanung ⟨**VT4,** 59⟩
society [sə'saɪəti] Gesellschaft **II**
burial society [ˌberiəl sə'saɪəti] Bestattungsverein ⟨**VT4,** 70⟩
sock [sɒk] Socke **I**
soft [sɒft] weich; sanft **III**
soft drink [ˌsɒft 'drɪŋk] alkoholfreies Getränk **IV**
software ['sɒftweə] Software *(Computerprogramme)* **IV**
solar energy [ˌsəʊlər‿'enədʒi] Solarenergie; Sonnenenergie **IV**
soldier ['səʊldʒə] Soldat(in) **II**
solemn ['sɒləm] ernst; feierlich ⟨**VT4,** 70⟩
to **solo** ['səʊləʊ] einen Alleingang machen ⟨**VT1,** 18⟩
solution [sə'lu:ʃn] Lösung **III**
to **solve** [sɒlv] lösen **VT1,** 11
some [sʌm] einige; etwas **I**
some day ['sʌm deɪ] eines Tages **II**
somebody ['sʌmbədi] jemand **I**
somehow ['sʌmhaʊ] irgendwie **IV**
someone ['sʌmwʌn] jemand **II**
something ['sʌmθɪŋ] etwas **I**
sometime ['sʌmtaɪm] irgendwann **II**
sometimes ['sʌmtaɪmz] manchmal **I**
somewhat ['sʌmwɒt] ein wenig; einigermaßen **VT5,** 76
somewhere ['sʌmweə] irgendwo **II**
son [sʌn] Sohn **II**
song [sɒŋ] Lied, Song **I**

soon [su:n] bald **I**
sordid ['sɔ:dɪd] schäbig; schmutzig; erbärmlich ⟨**VT5,** 77⟩
sore [sɔ:] wunde Stelle **III**
sorry ['sɒri] Tut mir leid, Entschuldigung **I**
to **feel sorry for** [ˌfi:l 'sɒri] Mitleid haben mit; bedauern **II**
sort [sɔ:t] Sorte; Art **IV**
to **sort** sth **out** [ˌsɔ:t‿'aʊt] etw. klären; etw. erledigen **VT1,** 10
soul [səʊl] Seele; Soul **III**
sound [saʊnd] Ton, Geräusch **I**
sound practice ['saʊnd ˌpræktɪs] *Hör-/ Ausspracheübung* **I**
to **sound** [saʊnd] klingen **II**
soup [su:p] Suppe **II**
sour [saʊə] sauer **IV**
source [sɔ:s] Quelle **III**
south [saʊθ] Süden **I**
southern ['sʌðən] südlich **II**
souvenir [ˌsu:və'nɪə] Souvenir, Andenken **I**
Soviet Union [ˌsəʊviət 'ju:njən] Sowjetunion ⟨**VT5,** 76⟩
space [speɪs] Raum; Weltraum **I**
spacecraft ['speɪskrɑ:ft] Raumschiff **VT5,** 73
span [spæn] Spanne **VT5,** 74
Spanish ['spænɪʃ] spanisch; Spanisch **I**
Spare me! [ˌspeə 'mi:] Verschonen Sie mich! ⟨**VT5,** 74⟩
spare [speə] übrig; Ersatz- **IV**
spark [spɑ:k] Funke **VT2,** 28
*to **speak** [spi:k] sprechen **I**
speaker ['spi:kə] Lautsprecher **II**; Sprecher(in) **III**
native speaker [ˌneɪtɪv‿'spi:kə] Muttersprachler(in) **IV**
spear [spɪə] Speer **III**
special ['speʃl] Sonderangebot; Spezialmenü **IV**
special ['speʃl] besonders, speziell **I**
special offer [ˌspeʃl‿'ɒfə] Sonderangebot **I**
specialty *(AE)* ['speʃlti] Spezialität; Besonderheit **III**
species, *pl.* **species** ['spi:ʃi:z] Spezies **VT4,** 56
specific [spə'sɪfɪk] spezifisch, speziell **VT2,** 26; **VT3,** 40
spectacular [spek'tækjələ] spektakulär **III**
speech [spi:tʃ] Sprache; Rede **III**
direct speech [dɪˌrekt 'spi:tʃ] direkte Rede **III**
indirect speech [ˌɪndɪrekt 'spi:tʃ] indirekte Rede **III**
part of speech [ˌpɑ:t‿əv 'spi:tʃ] Wortart **IV**
speed [spi:d] Geschwindigkeit **VT5,** 75
*to **spell** [spel] buchstabieren **I**
spelling ['spelɪŋ] Orthographie, Rechtschreibung **II**

*to **spend** [spend] ausgeben; verbringen **I**
spicy ['spaɪsi] würzig; pikant **IV**
spider ['spaɪdə] Spinne **II**
*to **spill** [spɪl] verschütten **III**
*to **spin** [spɪn] spinnen; (sich) schnell drehen **IV**
to **spiral** ['spaɪərl] spiralförmig aufsteigen ⟨**VT1,** 19⟩
spirit ['spɪrɪt] Geist; Stimmung ⟨**VT3,** 51⟩
spirits *(pl.)* ['spɪrɪts] Spirituosen **VT1,** 8
*to **spit** [spɪt] spucken **IV**
in **spite** of [ɪn 'spaɪt‿əv] trotz **III**
spiteful ['spaɪtfl] gehässig; schadenfroh ⟨**VT2,** 38⟩
splash [splæʃ] Spritzer, Planscher **I**
*to **split** [splɪt] spalten ⟨**VT5,** 87⟩
split second [ˌsplɪt 'seknd] Sekundenbruchteil **VT1,** 17
to **spoil** [spɔɪl] verderben ⟨**VT4,** 69⟩
to **sponsor** ['spɒntsə] sponsern; fördern **IV**
to **spook** sb **out** [ˌspu:k‿'aʊt] jmdm unheimlich werden ⟨**VT5,** 79⟩
spoon [spu:n] Löffel **I**
sport [spɔ:t] Sport **I**
sportsman, *pl.* **sportsmen** ['spɔ:tsmən] Sportler **III**
sportswear ['spɔ:tsweə] Sportbekleidung **IV**
sportswoman, *pl.***sportswomen** ['spɔ:tsˌwʊmən] Sportlerin **III**
spot [spɒt] Fleck; Ort **IV**
to **spray** [spreɪ] sprühen **VT5,** 85
*to **spread** [spred] (sich) verbreiten **IV**
spring [sprɪŋ] Frühling **II**
*to **spring** up [ˌsprɪŋ‿'ʌp] entspringen; hervorquellen **VT5,** 77
to **sprint** [sprɪnt] sprinten; spurten **VT1,** 13
spur [spɜ:] Sporn **II**
square [skweə] Platz **I**; Quadrat **III**
square dance ['skweə ˌdɑ:nts] Square Dance **II**
to **squeeze** [skwi:z] pressen; quetschen **VT5,** 77
to **squirt** [skwɜ:t] spritzen; sprühen ⟨**VT5,** 75⟩
to **stab (to death)** [stæb] (er)stechen ⟨**VT3,** 50⟩
stable ['steɪbl] Stall **I**
staff [stɑ:f] Personal; Kollegium **III**
staff room ['stɑ:f rʊm] Lehrerzimmer **III**
stage [steɪdʒ] Bühne **II**; Stadium **VT1,** 21; **VT3,** 55; **VT5,** 74
to **stagger (about)** ['stægə] (herum)torkeln **II**
to **stagger** ['stægə] staffeln ⟨**VT3,** 50⟩
stairs *(pl.)* [steəz] Treppe **III**
*to **stand** [stænd] ertragen, ausstehen **II**
to **stand (up)** [stænd‿'ʌp] (auf)stehen **I**

standard ['stændəd] Standard **III**
standard of living [ˌstændəd‿əv 'lɪvɪŋ] Lebensstandard **IV**
of such **standing** [əv ˌsʌtʃ 'stændɪŋ] von solchem Ansehen ⟨**VT4,** 69⟩
stanza ['stænzə] Strophe **IV**
star [stɑ:] Star; Stern **I**
pop star ['pɒp stɑ:] Popstar **I**
to **stare** [steə] starren **IV**
stark [stɑ:k] krass ⟨**VT2,** 26⟩
to **start** [stɑ:t] anfangen, starten **I**
Let's start! [lets 'stɑ:t] Lass(t) uns anfangen **I**
starter ['stɑ:tə] Vorspeise **II**
startling ['stɑ:tlɪŋ] alarmierend; verblüffend **VT5,** 77
to **starve** [stɑ:v] (ver)hungern **III**
state [steɪt] Staat, Land **I**; Zustand **IV**
to **state** [steɪt] feststellen; aussagen; darstellen **IV**
statement ['steɪtmənt] Aussage, Behauptung **II**
station ['steɪʃn] Haltestelle, Bahnhof **I**; Farm *(in Australien)* **III**
power station ['paʊə ˌsteɪʃn] Kraftwerk **VT5,** 85
station wagon ['steɪʃn ˌwægən] Kombi ⟨**VT2,** 26⟩
statistics *(pl.)* [stə'tɪstɪks] Statistik **IV**
statue ['stætʃu:] Statue, Standbild **I**
status ['steɪtəs] Status **II**
to **stay** [steɪ] bleiben **I**; übernachten **II**
to **stay put** [ˌsteɪ 'pʊt] an Ort und Stelle bleiben **VT1,** 13
steady on! [ˌstedi‿'ɒn] Immer mit der Ruhe! Sachte! ⟨**VT3,** 45⟩
steak [steɪk] Steak **II**
*to **steal** [sti:l] stehlen **II**
steam [sti:m] Dampf **III**
steam engine ['sti:m‿endʒɪn] Dampfmaschine **IV**
steel [sti:l] Stahl **IV**
steep [sti:p] steil **II**
step [step] Stufe; Schritt **III**
to **step** [step] treten; steigen **III**
stepmother ['stepmʌðə] Stiefmutter **II**
stepsister ['stepsɪstə] Stiefschwester **II**
stereo ['steriəʊ] Stereoanlage **I**
stereotype ['steriəʊtaɪp] Stereotyp **IV**
*to get **stick** *(infml)* [ˌget 'stɪk] schikaniert werden ⟨**VT2,** 33⟩
*to **stick** [stɪk] kleben; stecken ⟨**VT3,** 50⟩
to **be stuck** [bi: 'stʌk] stecken bleiben, festklemmen **II**
sticker ['stɪkə] Aufkleber ⟨**VT2,** 30⟩
sticky ['stɪki] klebrig ⟨**VT2,** 30⟩
still [stɪl] still **III**
still [stɪl] noch, immer noch **I**
to **stimulate** ['stɪmjəleɪt] stimulieren; anregen ⟨**VT4,** 67⟩
stimulus, *pl.* **stimuli** ['stɪmjələs] Stimulus; Reiz ⟨**VT5,** 81⟩

*to **stink** [stɪŋk] stinken **VT2,** 36
to **stir** [stɜː] sich regen; (sich) rühren; umrühren **VT1,** 14
stocking ['stɒkɪŋ] Strumpf **IV**
stockpile ['stɒkpaɪl] Vorrat; Stapelbestand ⟨**VT4,** 67⟩
stomach ['stʌmək] Magen ⟨**VT1,** 19⟩
stone [stəʊn] Stein **I**
stone dead [ˌstəʊn 'ded] mausetot ⟨**VT4,** 68⟩
stool [stuːl] Hocker **IV**
stop [stɒp] Haltestelle **II**
to **stop** [stɒp] aufhören; anhalten **I**
storage ['stɔːrɪdʒ] Speicherung; Lagerung **IV**
store [stɔː] Laden, Geschäft **II**
to **store** [stɔː] speichern; lagern **IV**
storm [stɔːm] Sturm **I**
story ['stɔːri] Geschichte, Erzählung **I**
storybook ['stɔːribʊk] Lesebuch; Märchenbuch **IV**
to **straggle** ['strægl] umherstreifen ⟨**VT5,** 77⟩
straight [streɪt] gerade, geradewegs, direkt **I**
to **strain** [streɪn] (sich) anstrengen; belasten ⟨**VT2,** 30⟩
strange [streɪndʒ] fremd; seltsam; merkwürdig **III**
stranger ['streɪndʒə] Fremde(r) **II**
stranglehold ['stræŋglhəʊld] Würgegriff; Umklammerung ⟨**VT3,** 47⟩
strap [stræp] Träger; Gurt **VT3,** 40
strawberry ['strɔːbri] Erdbeere **II**
stream [striːm] Bach **III**; Strom **IV**
street [striːt] Straße **I**
streetcar *(AE)* ['striːtkɑː] Straßenbahn; Tram **IV**
strength [streŋkθ] Stärke **VT5,** 73
stress [stres] Stress **II**; Betonung **IV**
to **stress** [stres] betonen **III**
to **stretch** [stretʃ] strecken; dehnen **VT2,** 35
strict [strɪkt] streng; strikt **III**
strike [straɪk] Streik **VT2,** 28
*to **strike** [straɪk] schlagen; anzünden *(ein Streichholz)* **IV**
string [strɪŋ] Schnur **II**
strip [strɪp] Streifen **III**
stripe [straɪp] Streifen **III**
strong [strɒŋ] stark **I**
structure ['strʌktʃə] Struktur; Aufbau **IV**
to **structure** ['strʌktʃə] strukturieren; gliedern **VT2,** 27
struggle (for sth) ['strʌgl] Kampf; Anstrengung **IV**
to **struggle** ['strʌgl] kämpfen; ringen **IV**
stubborn ['stʌbən] eigensinnig; störrisch **VT1,** 15
stud [stʌd] Ohrstecker ⟨**VT3,** 44⟩
student ['stjuːdnt] Student(in); Schüler(in) **II**
studies ['stʌdiz] Studium; Lernen; Arbeit für die Schule **IV**
studio ['stjuːdiəʊ] Studio; Atelier **IV**
to **study** ['stʌdi] studieren; lernen **III**
stuff [stʌf] Zeug **II**
to **stumble** ['stʌmbl] stolpern ⟨**VT4,** 70⟩
stupid ['stjuːpɪd] dumm, blöd **I**
style [staɪl] Stil **II**
stylistic device [staɪˌlɪstɪk dɪ'vaɪs] Stilmittel **VT2,** 29
sub *(AE: substitute teacher)* [sʌb] Aushilfslehrer(in) ⟨**VT1,** 12⟩
subconscious [ˌsʌb'kɒnʃəs] Unterbewusstsein ⟨**VT3,** 44⟩
subcontinent [sʌb'kɒntɪnənt] Subkontinent ⟨**VT2,** 25⟩
subject ['sʌbdʒɪkt] Schulfach; Thema **I**
to **subject (sb to sth)** [səb'dʒekt] unterwerfen **VT2,** 33
suburb ['sʌbɜːb] Vorort **III**
suburban [sə'bɜːbn] Vorstadt- **VT2,** 26
subway ['sʌbweɪ] Unterführung *(BE)*; U-Bahn *(AE)* ⟨**VT1,** 22⟩
to **succeed (in** *+ noun or gerund)* [sək'siːd] Erfolg haben; nachfolgen **VT1,** 10
success [sək'ses] Erfolg **II**
successful [sək'sesfl] erfolgreich **IV**
such [sʌtʃ] solch **III**
such as ['sʌtʃ‿əz] (solche) wie **III**
to **suck up** *(infml)* [ˌsʌk‿'ʌp] kriechen; sich einschleimen ⟨**VT3,** 44⟩
suddenly ['sʌdnli] plötzlich, auf einmal **I**
to **suffer** ['sʌfə] leiden **IV**
sugar ['ʃʊgə] Zucker **III**
sugar cane [ˌʃʊgə 'keɪn] Zuckerrohr ⟨**VT4,** 56⟩
to **suggest** [sə'dʒest] vorschlagen **II**; andeuten; nahe legen **IV**
suggestion [sə'dʒestʃn] Vorschlag, Anregung **I**
suicide ['suːɪsaɪd] Selbstmord **IV**
to **commit suicide** [kəˌmɪt 'suːɪsaɪd] Selbstmord begehen **VT1,** 11
bathing **suit** ['beɪðɪŋ ˌsuːt] Badeanzug **IV**
to **suit** [suːt] passen (zu); (jmdm) stehen **III**
suitable ['suːtəbl] geeignet; passend **IV**
suitcase ['suːtkeɪs] Koffer **III**
*to be **suited** (for/to) [biː 'suːtɪd] geeignet sein (für) **IV**
sum [sʌm] Summe; Betrag **IV**
to **summarize** ['sʌməraɪz] zusammenfassen **IV**
summary ['sʌmri] Zusammenfassung **II**
summer ['sʌmə] Sommer **I**
to **sum up** [ˌsʌm‿'ʌp] zusammenfassen **III**
sun [sʌn] Sonne **I**
Sunday ['sʌndeɪ] Sonntag **I**
sunny ['sʌni] sonnig **I**
sunscreen ['sʌnskriːn] Sonnencreme **I**
sunset ['sʌnset] Sonnenuntergang **IV**
sunshine ['sʌnʃaɪn] Sonnenschein **II**
super ['suːpə] super **II**
superlative [suː'pɜːlətɪv] Superlativ **II**
supermarket ['suːpəˌmɑːkɪt] Supermarkt **I**
to **supervise** ['suːpəvaɪz] beaufsichtigen; betreuen **IV**
supper ['sʌpə] spätes Abendessen **VT1,** 11
supplier [sə'plaɪə] Zulieferer; Anbieter **IV**
support [sə'pɔːt] Unterstützung; Hilfe ⟨**VT1,** 22⟩
to **support** [sə'pɔːt] unterstützen **IV**
supportive [sə'pɔːtɪv] unterstützend **VT1,** 10; ⟨**VT4,** 70⟩
to **suppose** [sə'pəʊz] vermuten; annehmen **VT1,** 17
to **be supposed to** *(+ infinitive)* [biː sə'pəʊzd tə] (etw. tun) sollen **IV**
sure [ʃʊə; ʃɔː] sicher **I**
surface ['sɜːfɪs] Oberfläche **VT5,** 76
surfing ['sɜːfɪŋ] Wellenreiten, Surfen **I**
surgeon ['sɜːdʒn] Chirurg(in) **VT5,** 73
surprise [sə'praɪz] Überraschung **I**
to **surprise** [sə'praɪz] überraschen **III**
*to be **surprised** [sə'praɪzd] überrascht sein **I**
to **surround** [sə'raʊnd] umgeben **III**
surveillance [sɜː'veɪlənts] Überwachung; Beobachtung; Beaufsichtigung **VT5,** 79
survey ['sɜːveɪ] Umfrage; Studie **IV**
survival [sə'vaɪvl] Überleben **IV**
to **survive** [sə'vaɪv] überleben **III**
suspense [sə'spents] Spannung **IV**
suspicion [sə'spɪʃn] Hauch; Anflug ⟨**VT3,** 45⟩
to **swallow** ['swɒləʊ] schlucken **IV**
to **swap** [swɒp] tauschen ⟨**VT2,** 31⟩; **VT5,** 74
to **swarm** [swɔːm] schwärmen; strömen; sich drängen ⟨**VT3,** 50⟩
*to **swear** [sweə] schwören; fluchen ⟨**VT2,** 30⟩; ⟨**VT3,** 50⟩; ⟨**VT4,** 69⟩
swearword ['sweəwɜːd] Schimpfwort ⟨**VT1,** 11⟩
sweater ['swetə] Pullover **IV**
sweatshirt ['swetʃɜːt] Sweatshirt **I**
*to **sweep** [swiːp] fegen ⟨**VT3,** 50⟩
to **sweep away** [ˌswiːp‿ə'weɪ] wegfegen; wegspülen **VT1,** 16
sweets *pl.* [swiːts] Süßigkeiten, Bonbons **I**
sweet [swiːt] süß **I**
sweetcorn ['swiːtkɔːn] Mais **IV**
*to **swell** [swel] anschwellen **IV**
*to **swim** [swɪm] schwimmen **I**
swimmer ['swɪmə] Schwimmer(in) **III**
swimming ['swɪmɪŋ] Schwimmen **I**
swimming pool ['swɪmɪŋ ˌpuːl] Schwimmbecken; Schwimmbad **I**
*to **swing** [swɪŋ] schwingen; schwenken **VT1,** 12; **VT4,** 60
to **swing opinion** [ˌswɪŋ‿ə'pɪnjən] eine Meinung ändern **VT4,** 60
swirl [swɜːl] Wirbel; Strudel **VT5,** 76

to swirl [swɜːl] wirbeln **VT5, 76**
switch [swɪtʃ] Schalter **VT5, 76**
to switch off [swɪtʃ ˈɒf] ausschalten **III**
to **switch on** [swɪtʃ ˈɒn] einschalten **III**
sword [sɔːd] Schwert **III**
syllable [ˈsɪləbl] Silbe **IV**
symbol [ˈsɪmbl] Symbol **III**
sympathetic [ˌsɪmpəˈθetɪk] mitfühlend **IV**
to sympathize [ˈsɪmpəθaɪz] mitfühlen; sympathisieren **VT2, 37**
system [ˈsɪstəm] System **II**
systematic [ˌsɪstəˈmætɪk] systematisch; gezielt **III**

T

table [ˈteɪbl] Tisch **I**; Tabelle **II**
tables *(pl.)* [ˈteɪblz] Einmaleins **IV**
table tennis [ˈteɪbl ˌtenɪs] Tischtennis **II**
to **set the table** [ˌset ðə ˈteɪbl] den Tisch decken **I**
tableau, *pl.* **tableaux** [ˈtæbləʊ] Bild ⟨**VT5, 77**⟩
to tack [tæk] heften **VT5, 76**
taco [ˈtɑːkəʊ] Taco *(mexikanische gefüllte Teigtasche)* **IV**
tactful [ˈtæktfl] taktvoll **III**
tactics *(pl.)* [ˈtæktɪks] Taktik **IV**
tag [tæg] Schildchen, Etikett **I**
question tag [ˈkwestʃən ˌtæg] Frageanhängsel, Bestätigungsfrage **I**
*__to take__ [teɪk] (mit)nehmen; bringen **I**; dauern, (Zeit) brauchen **II**
to **take ill** [ˌteɪk ˈɪl] krank werden **VT3, 47**
to **take no shit** *(vulg)* [ˌteɪk nəʊ ˈʃɪt] sich nichts gefallen lassen ⟨**VT3, 42**⟩
to **take off** [teɪk ˈɒf] abheben **I**; ausziehen **III**
to **take one's own life** [ˌteɪk wʌnz əʊn ˈlaɪf] sich das Leben nehmen **II**
to **take part (in)** [teɪk ˈpɑːt] teilnehmen (an) **II**
to **take photos** [teɪk ˈfəʊtəʊz] fotografieren, Fotos machen **I**
to **take place** [teɪk ˈpleɪs] stattfinden **II**
to **take sb to court** [ˌteɪk tə ˈkɔːt] jmdn verklagen **VT1, 8; VT3, 41**
to **take sb (time) to do sth** [teɪk] jmdn (Zeit) kosten **II**
to **take sth out on sb** [ˌteɪk ɪt ˈaʊt ɒn] etw. an jmdm auslassen **VT2, 35**
to **take sth seriously** [ˌteɪk ˈsɪəriəsli] etw. ernst nehmen **IV**
to **take to** *(+ gerund)* [ˈteɪk tə] sich angewöhnen zu ⟨**VT3, 45**⟩
to **take turns** [teɪk ˈtɜːnz] sich abwechseln **II**
whatever it takes [wɒtˌevər ɪt ˈteɪks] alles, was nötig ist **IV**
takeaway [ˈteɪkəweɪ] *(Restaurant, das Speisen zum Mitnehmen verkauft)* **II**
*__to take the helm__ [ˌteɪk ðə ˈhelm] das Heft in die Hand nehmen ⟨**VT3, 50**⟩
tale [teɪl] Geschichte, Erzählung **II**
fairy tale [ˈfeəri ˌteɪl] Märchen **II**
talent [ˈtælənt] Talent **IV**
talk [tɔːk] Vortrag; Rede **II**
talk show [ˈtɔːk ˌʃəʊ] Talkshow **III**
to **give a talk** [ˌgɪv ə ˈtɔːk] einen Vortrag halten **II**
to talk [tɔːk] sprechen, reden **I**
tall [tɔːl] groß; hoch **I**
tame [teɪm] zahm **IV**
tanker [ˈtæŋkə] Tanker **IV**
tap [tæp] Wasserhahn **III**
tape [teɪp] (Ton-)Band **II**
target [ˈtɑːgɪt] Ziel(scheibe) **II**
tarmac [ˈtɑːmæk] Asphalt ⟨**VT3, 50**⟩
tart [tɑːt] scharf; herb; schroff ⟨**VT2, 31**⟩
task [tɑːsk] Aufgabe; Auftrag **IV**
taste [teɪst] Geschmack **IV**
to taste [teɪst] schmecken **II**
tasty [ˈteɪsti] schmackhaft **IV**
tax [tæks] Steuer **IV**
poll tax [ˈpəʊl ˌtæks] Kopfsteuer ⟨**VT4, 61**⟩
taxation [tækˈseɪʃn] Besteuerung **IV**
taxi [ˈtæksi] Taxi **I**
tea [tiː] Tee; Abendessen **I**
*__to teach__ [tiːtʃ] unterrichten, lehren **I**
teacher [ˈtiːtʃə] Lehrer(in) **I**
head teacher *(BE)* [ˌhed ˈtiːtʃə] Schulleiter(in) **III**
team [tiːm] Gruppe, Team **I**
tear [tɪə] Träne **III**
*__to tear__ [teə] (zer)reißen **III**
to tease [tiːz] necken; quälen **VT1, 10**; ⟨**VT4, 70**⟩
teatime [ˈtiːtaɪm] Zeit für Nachmittagstee; Abendessen **I**
technical [ˈteknɪkl] technisch; handwerklich; fachlich **IV**
technician [tekˈnɪʃn] Techniker(in) ⟨**VT3, 51**⟩
technique [tekˈniːk] Methode; Technik **III**
techno [ˈteknəʊ] Techno **II**
technological [ˌteknəˈlɒdʒɪkl] technisch; technologisch **IV**
technology [tekˈnɒlədʒi] Technologie, Computerunterricht **II**
information technology [ɪnfəˌmeɪʃn tekˈnɒlədʒi] Informatik; Informationstechnik **IV**
teddy bear [ˈtedi ˌbeə] Teddybär **II**
teen [tiːn] Teenager; Jugendliche(r) **IV**
teenager [ˈtiːnˌeɪdʒə] Teenager; Jugendliche(r) **IV**
telephone [ˈtelɪfəʊn] Telefon **I**
telescope [ˈtelɪskəʊp] Teleskop; Fernrohr **I**
television [ˈtelɪvɪʒn] Fernsehen; Fernseher **I**
*__to tell (somebody)__ [tel] (jemandem) sagen, mitteilen **I**
telling [ˈtelɪŋ] aufschlussreich; vielsagend ⟨**VT5, 82**⟩
temperature [ˈtemprətʃə] Temperatur **IV**
template [ˈtempleɪt] Vorlage; Schablone; Muster ⟨**VT3, 50**⟩
temporary [ˈtemprəri] vorübergehend; temporär **VT1, 17; VT2, 26**
ten [ten] zehn **I**
to tend to [tend] (zu etw.) neigen **VT1, 11; VT2, 33**
tennis [ˈtenɪs] Tennis **I**
table tennis [ˈteɪbl ˌtenɪs] Tischtennis **II**
tense [tents] Zeit, Zeitform *(grammatisch)* **I**
tense [tents] angespannt; verkrampft ⟨**VT4, 62**⟩
tension [ˈtentʃn] Spannung **IV**
tent [tent] Zelt **II**
term [tɜːm] Trimester; Semester; Halbjahr **IV**; Begriff **IV**
in terms of [ɪn ˈtɜːmz əv] bezüglich **VT5, 80**
to **come to terms with** [ˌkʌm tə ˈtɜːmz wɪð] zurechtkommen mit; sich arrangieren mit ⟨**VT5, 81**⟩
terrace [ˈterɪs] Terrasse; Absatz; Häuserreihe **VT5, 77**
terraced house [ˌterɪst ˈhaʊs] Reihenhaus **IV**
terrible [ˈterəbl] schrecklich, furchtbar **I**
terrified [ˈterəfaɪd] außer sich vor Schrecken **II**
territory [ˈterɪtri] Territorium **IV**
terrorist [ˈterərɪst] Terrorist(in) **IV**
to terrorize [ˈterəraɪz] terrorisieren **VT2, 29**
test [test] Test; Klassenarbeit; Schulaufgabe **II**
text [tekst] Text; Textnachricht (SMS) **I**
textile [ˈtekstaɪl] textil; Textil- **IV**
than [ðæn; ðən] als *(bei Vergleichen)* **I**
to thank [θæŋk] danken **II**
thank God [ˌθæŋk ˈgɒd] Gott sei Dank **II**
thank you letter [ˈθæŋk juː ˌletə] Dankschreiben **I**
Thank you very much! [ˌθæŋk juː veri ˈmʌtʃ] Vielen Dank! Herzlichen Dank! **I**
thanks [θæŋks] danke **I**
that [ðæt; ðət] dass **I**
that [ðæt] das; jenes **I**
that [ðæt] der, dem, den, die, das *(Relativpronomen)* **II**
the [ðə; ði] der, die *(auch pl.)*, das **I**
the odd ... [ði ˈɒd] das ein oder andere ⟨**VT3, 44**⟩
theatre [ˈθɪətə] Theater **I**
theatrical [ˈθɪətrɪkl] theatralisch; Theater- ⟨**VT2, 31**⟩
thee [ðiː] dir; dich *(alt)* ⟨**VT2, 28**⟩

theft [θeft] Diebstahl **VT4,** 66
their [ðeə] ihr, ihre *(Plural)* **I**
them [ðem; ðəm] sie; ihnen **I**
theme [θi:m] Thema **IV**
theme park ['θi:m ˌpɑ:k] Freizeitpark; Themenpark **IV**
then [ðen] dann **I**
theory ['θɪəri] Theorie **IV**
there [ðeə] dort **I**
over there [ˌəʊvə 'ðeə] da drüben **I**
there are [ðeər‿'ɑ:] da sind; es gibt **I**
there's [ðeəz] **(= there is)** [] da ist, es gibt **I**
therefore ['ðeəfɔ:] deshalb; somit **VT3,** 41; **VT4,** 59
thermal ['θɜ:ml] Thermik ⟨**VT1,** 18⟩
the same [seɪm] derselbe (die-/das-) **I**
these [ði:z] diese (hier) **I**
these days ['ði:z ˌdeɪz] heutzutage **II**
they [ðeɪ] sie *(Plural)* **I**; man **II**
they're (= they are) ['ðeə] sie sind **I**
thick [θɪk] dick *(nicht für Personen)*; dumm *(für Personen)* **II**
thief, *pl.* **thieves** [θi:f; θi:vz] Dieb(in) **II**
thin [θɪn] dünn **II**
thing [θɪŋ] Sache, Ding **I**
*to **think** (of) ['θɪŋk‿əv] denken (an) **I**
to **think of** ['θɪŋk‿əv] halten von **II**
third [θɜ:d] Drittel **IV**
thirsty ['θɜ:sti] durstig **III**
thirteen [θɜ:'ti:n] dreizehn **I**
this [ðɪs] diese(-r/-s) **I**
this very afternoon [ðɪz ˌveri‿ɑ:ftə'nu:n] noch heute Nachmittag ⟨**VT3,** 44⟩
those [ðəʊz] diese dort, jene **I**
though [ðəʊ] obwohl **IV**
even though [ˌi:vn‿'ðəʊ] auch wenn; obwohl **IV**
thought [θɔ:t] Gedanke ⟨**VT1,** 19⟩; ⟨**VT1,** 23⟩; ⟨**VT5,** 77⟩
to **have second thoughts** [hæv ˌseknd 'θɔ:ts] Zweifel haben; es sich anders überlegen ⟨**VT1,** 19⟩
two **thousand** [ˌtu: 'θaʊznd] zweitausend **II**
thread [θred] Zwirn; Garn; Faden **IV**
threat [θret] Bedrohung; Gefahr **VT4,** 66
three cheers for … [ˌθri: 'tʃɪəz fə] ein dreifaches Hoch auf … ⟨**VT3,** 51⟩
throat [θrəʊt] Kehle; Hals **IV**
to **clear one's throat** [ˌklɪə wʌnz 'θrəʊt] sich räuspern **VT1,** 13
through [θru:] durch **I**
*to **throw** [θrəʊ] werfen **I**
to **throw a party** [ˌθrəʊ‿ə 'pɑ:ti] eine Party veranstalten **IV**
*to **throw up** [ˌθrəʊ‿'ʌp] erbrechen ⟨**VT1,** 22⟩
thud [θʌd] dumpfer Schlag ⟨**VT4,** 70⟩
thug [θʌg] Gangster; Schläger; Verbrecher ⟨**VT4,** 64⟩

thumb [θʌm] Daumen ⟨**VT2,** 32⟩; **VT3,** 49
to **thump** [θʌmp] klopfen ⟨**VT4,** 69⟩
thunder ['θʌndə] Donner **VT4,** 56; ⟨**VT5,** 87⟩
to **thunder** ['θʌndə] donnern **VT4,** 56
thus [ðʌs] dadurch; demnach; so **IV**
ticked off *(infml)* [ˌtɪkt 'ɒf] verärgert ⟨**VT1,** 11⟩
ticket ['tɪkɪt] Ticket, Fahrschein, Eintrittskarte **I**
tide [taɪd] Flut **VT4,** 60; ⟨**VT5,** 87⟩
to **tidy (up)** ['taɪdi] aufräumen, in Ordnung bringen **II**
tidy ['taɪdi] sauber, ordentlich **I**
to **tie** [taɪ] binden, fesseln **II**
tiger ['taɪgə] Tiger ⟨**VT4,** 67⟩
tight *(infml)* [taɪt] klasse, toll ⟨**VT2,** 31⟩
till [tɪl] Kasse **VT2,** 35
till [tɪl] bis **III**
timber ['tɪmbə] (Bau-)Holz ⟨**VT5,** 77⟩
time [taɪm] Zeit **I**; Mal **I**
all the time [ˌɔ:l ðə 'taɪm] die ganze Zeit **I**
in olden times [ɪn'əʊldən ˌtaɪmz] anno dazumal **VT3,** 42
in time for [ɪn 'taɪm fə] rechtzeitig zu **II**
most of the time ['məʊst‿əv ðə ˌtaɪm] meistens **III**
on time [ɒn 'taɪm] pünktlich **II**
time line ['taɪm laɪn] Zeitstrahl **II**
What time … ? [wɒt 'taɪm] (Um) wie viel Uhr … ? **I**
timetable ['taɪmteɪbl] Stundenplan; Fahrplan **II**
timid ['tɪmɪd] schüchtern; furchtsam **VT1,** 10
tin [tɪn] Dose, Büchse **I**; Blech **VT4,** 58
to **tingle** ['tɪŋgl] prickeln ⟨**VT1,** 18⟩
tiny ['taɪni] winzig **VT2,** 27; **VT4,** 64; **VT5,** 83
tip [tɪp] Tipp **I**; Trinkgeld **IV**
tired ['taɪəd] müde **I**
to **be tired of** *(+ gerund)* [bi: 'taɪəd] es müde/leid sein/satt haben, etwas zu tun **III**
tissue ['tɪsju:] Taschentuch ⟨**VT3,** 44⟩
title ['taɪtl] Titel, Überschrift **I**
to [tʊ; tə] bis **I**; in; nach; zu **I**
toast [təʊst] Toast **II**
to **reclaim a toast** [rɪˌkleɪm‿ə 'təʊst] *hier:* einen Toast aussprechen ⟨**VT5,** 87⟩
tobacco [tə'bækəʊ] Tabak **VT2,** 24; **VT3,** 40
today [tə'deɪ] heute **I**
toenail ['təʊneɪl] Zehennagel **VT2,** 36
together [tə'geðə] zusammen, miteinander **I**
toilet ['tɔɪlɪt] Toilette **VT4,** 58
to **tolerate** ['tɒlreɪt] tolerieren; dulden **VT3,** 42
to **loot** [lu:t] plündern; erbeuten ⟨**VT4,** 62⟩

tomato, *pl.* **tomatoes** [tə'mɑ:təʊ] Tomate **II**
tombstone ['tu:mstəʊn] Grabstein ⟨**VT1,** 16⟩
tomorrow [tə'mɒrəʊ] morgen **I**
ton [tʌn] Tonne *(Gewicht)* **I**
tone [təʊn] Ton **IV**
tongue [tʌŋ] Zunge; Sprache **IV**
mother tongue [ˌmʌðə 'tʌŋ] Muttersprache **VT4,** 57
tonight [tə'naɪt] heute Abend/Nacht **II**
too [tu:] auch **I**; zu **I**
Me, too. [ˌmi: 'tu:] Ich auch. **II**
tool [tu:l] Werkzeug, Gerät **II**
buck-**toothed** ['bʌkˌtu:θt] hasenzähnig ⟨**VT1,** 14⟩
tooth, pl. teeth [tu:θ; ti:θ] Zahn **I**
top [tɒp] Spitze, oberer Teil **II**; Top **III**
on top (of) [ɒn 'tɒp] obendrauf **II**
topic ['tɒpɪk] Thema **III**
topping ['tɒpɪŋ] Belag **IV**
to **topple** ['tɒpl] stürzen ⟨**VT4,** 70⟩
torch [tɔ:tʃ] Fackel; Taschenlampe **VT1,** 11
torture ['tɔ:tʃə] Folter **VT2,** 36
to **scan** [skæn] scannen; abtasten; nach Details durchsuchen **VT2,** 26
total ['təʊtl] Summe; Gesamtmenge **IV**
total ['təʊtl] total; gesamt; vollständig **IV**
*to get in **touch** (with) [ˌget‿ɪn 'tʌtʃ] in Verbindung treten (mit); kontaktieren **III**
to **touch** [tʌtʃ] berühren; antippen **I**
touching ['tʌtʃɪŋ] rührend; ergreifend ⟨**VT3,** 51⟩
tough [tʌf] hart; rau; zäh **III**
tour [tʊə] Tour, Fahrt, Reise **I**
tourism ['tʊərɪzm] Tourismus **IV**
tourist ['tʊərɪst] Tourist **I**
towards [tə'wɔ:dz] in Richtung; auf … zu, darauf zu **I**
towel ['taʊəl] Handtuch **I**
tower ['taʊə] Turm **II**
communications tower [ˌkəmju:nɪ'keɪʃnz ˌtaʊə] Fernmeldeturm; Sendemast **VT5,** 85
to **tower** [taʊə] hoch aufragen ⟨**VT3,** 50⟩; ⟨**VT5,** 77⟩
town [taʊn] Stadt **I**
township ['taʊnʃɪp] Gemeinde; von Farbigen oder Schwarzen bewohnte städtische Siedlung *(Südafrika)* **VT4,** 59
toy [tɔɪ] Spielzeug **II**
to **trace** [treɪs] verfolgen; nachspüren ⟨**VT3,** 48⟩
sixteen-**track** [ˌsɪksti:n'træk] 16-Spur-Aufnahmegerät ⟨**VT2,** 31⟩
track [træk] Spur; Fährte; Musiktitel ⟨**VT2,** 31⟩; ⟨**VT5,** 81⟩
dirt track ['dɜ:t ˌtræk] Feldweg; unbefestigte Straße ⟨**VT4,** 69⟩
track and field [ˌtræk‿ənd 'fi:ld] Leichtathletik **III**

to track sb [træk] aufspüren; verfolgen **VT5,** 79
trade [treɪd] Handel **VT2,** 24
trade union [ˌtreɪd ˈjuːnjən] Gewerkschaft **VT4,** 61
to trade [treɪd] Handel treiben **III**
tradition [trəˈdɪʃn] Tradition **I**
traditional [trəˈdɪʃnl] traditionell **II**
traffic [ˈtræfɪk] Verkehr **II**
traffic jam [ˈtræfɪk ˌdʒæm] Stau **II**
tragedy [ˈtrædʒədi] Tragödie ⟨**VT3,** 50⟩
trail [treɪl] Wanderweg **III**; Spur; Schleppe; Schweif **VT4,** 62
train [treɪn] Zug **I**
to train [treɪn] trainieren, ausbilden **II**
trainer [ˈtreɪnə] Turnschuh **IV**
training [ˈtreɪnɪŋ] Training, Ausbildung **II**
main **trait** [ˌmeɪn ˈtreɪt] Haupteigenschaft **VT1,** 15
tramp [træmp] Landstreicher ⟨**VT3,** 45⟩
to transfer [træntsˈfɜː] transferieren; übertragen **IV**
to transform [træntsˈfɔːm] transformieren; umwandeln; verwandeln **VT4,** 59; ⟨**VT5,** 81⟩;
to translate [trænzˈleɪt] übersetzen **II**
translation [trænzˈleɪʃn] Übersetzung **II**
to transmit [trænzˈmɪt] übertragen; senden **VT5,** 77
transparency [trænˈspærntsi] Folie **III**
transport [ˈtræntspɔːt] Transport **II**
means of transport *(sg. and pl.)* [ˌmiːnz‿əv ˈtræntspɔːt] Transportmittel, Verkehrsmittel **II**
to transport [trænˈspɔːt] transportieren **II**
trap [træp] Falle **II**
*__to be trapped__ [biː ˈtræpt] in der Falle sitzen **III**
trash *(AE)* [træʃ] Abfall, Müll **II**
trash can *(AE)* [ˈtræʃ kæn] Mülleimer **IV**
trauma, *pl.* **traumata** [ˈtrɔːmə] Trauma; seelischer Schock **VT4,** 63
travel [ˈtrævl] (das) Reisen **II**
travel agent's [ˈtrævl ˌeɪdʒnts] Reisebüro **II**
to travel [ˈtrævl] reisen **II**
treasure [ˈtreʒə] Schatz **IV**
treat [triːt] besondere Freude; Belohnung **II**
to treat [triːt] behandeln **II**
treatment [ˈtriːtmənt] Behandlung **IV**
treaty [ˈtriːti] Vertrag **IV**
tree [triː] Baum **I**
tree-fern [ˈtriːfɜːn] Baumfarn ⟨**VT4,** 69⟩
trek [trek] Wanderung; anstrengender Marsch **III**
to trek [trek] wandern, marschieren **II**
pony **trekking** [ˈpəʊni ˌtrekɪŋ] Ponyreiten im Gelände **II**

to tremble [ˈtrembl] zittern **II**
trend [trend] Trend; Entwicklung; Richtung **IV**
trial [traɪəl] Gerichtsverfahren; Gerichtsverhandlung **VT4,** 61
tribe [traɪb] Stamm **I**
trick [trɪk] Trick; Streich **I**
to trick [trɪk] austricksen, täuschen **I**
trifle [ˈtraɪfl] *englischer Nachtisch* **I**
trip [trɪp] Trip, Reise, Ausflug **I**
to trip (over) [trɪp] stolpern (über) **II**
troops *(pl.)* [truːps] Truppen **IV**
trouble [trʌbl] Ärger, Probleme **II**
troublesome [ˈtrʌblsəm] störend; lästig ⟨**VT3,** 50⟩
trousers *pl.* [ˈtraʊzəz] Hose **I**
trout, *pl.* **trout** [traʊt] Forelle **II**
truck [trʌk] Truck, Lastwagen **II**
true [truː] wahr **I**
to **come true** [ˌkʌm ˈtruː] wahr werden; in Erfüllung gehen **III**
trumpet [ˈtrʌmpɪt] Trompete **II**
to trust [trʌst] vertrauen **II**
truth [truːθ] Wahrheit **II**
to try (on) [traɪ‿ˈɒn] (an)probieren; versuchen **I**
T-shirt [ˈtiːʃɜːt] T-Shirt **II**
to tuck in [ˌtʌk‿ˈɪn] einstecken; einschlagen **VT3,** 40
tune [tjuːn] Melodie **II**
to tune out [ˌtjuːn‿ˈaʊt] abschalten ⟨**VT1,** 12⟩
tunnel [ˈtʌnl] Tunnel **IV**
to turf sb out *(BE) (slang)* [ˌtɜːf‿ˈaʊt] hinauswerfen ⟨**VT3,** 44⟩
turkey [ˈtɜːki] Truthahn, Pute **I**
It's your **turn.** [ˈjɔː tɜːn] Du bist/Sie sind dran. **I**
to **take turns** [teɪk ˈtɜːnz] sich abwechseln **II**
to turn [tɜːn] einbiegen, abbiegen; drehen, wenden **I**
to **turn (into)** [ˈtɜːn‿ɪntə] werden; (sich) verwandeln in **III**
to **turn off** [ˌtɜːn‿ˈɒf] ausschalten **IV**
to **turn on sb** [ˈtɜːn‿ɒn] sich gegen jmdn wenden; jmdn anfallen **VT2,** 35
to **turn out to be** [tɜːn‿ˈaʊt tə ˌbiː] sich herausstellen als **VT2,** 26; **VT4,** 64
to **turn up** [tɜːn‿ˈʌp] auftauchen; erscheinen ⟨**VT3,** 45⟩; **VT3,** 48
turning point [ˈtɜːnɪŋ ˌpɔɪnt] Wendepunkt **III**
turnover [ˈtɜːnˌəʊvə] Absatz; Umsatz ⟨**VT5,** 82⟩
tutor [ˈtjuːtə] Klassenlehrer(in) **I**
tutor group [ˈtjuːtə ˌgruːp] Klasse *(in einer englischen Schule)* **I**
TV [tiːˈviː] Fernsehen; Fernseher **I**
to **watch TV** [ˌwɒtʃ tiːˈviː] fernsehen **I**
twelve [twelv] zwölf **I**
twenty [ˈtwenti] zwanzig **I**

twice [twaɪs] zweimal **II**
*__to be twinned with__ [biː ˈtwɪnd wɪð] Partnerstadt sein von **IV**
to twist [twɪst] verdrehen; verzerren **III**
2-1 [ˌtuː ˈwʌn] zwei zu eins **II**
a two-minute walk away from ... [ˌtuːmɪnɪt ˈwɔːk] zwei Minuten zu Fuß von ... entfernt **II**
two thousand [ˌtuː ˈθaʊznd] zweitausend **II**
2.45 (point) [ˈtuː pɔɪnt ˌfɔː ˈfaɪv] Komma *(bei Zahlenangaben)* **I**
type [taɪp] Typ **III**
to type [taɪp] tippen **III**
typical (of) [ˈtɪpɪkl] typisch (für) **I**
tyranny [ˈtɪrni] Tyrannei; Gewaltherrschaft ⟨**VT1,** 22⟩

U

Ugh! [ɜː] Igitt! *(Ausruf des Ekels)* **I**
ugly [ˈʌgli] hässlich **IV**
varicose **ulcer** [ˌværɪkəʊs‿ˈʌlsə] Krampfadergeschwür ⟨**VT5,** 76⟩
ultimately [ˈʌltɪmətli] schließlich ⟨**VT4,** 67⟩
unable [ʌnˈeɪbl] unfähig **III**
unaccountable [ˌʌnəˈkaʊntəbl] ohne rechtliche Grundlage **VT5,** 80
unbelievable [ˌʌnbɪˈliːvəbl] unglaublich **III**
uncle [ˈʌŋkl] Onkel **I**
uncountable [ʌnˈkaʊntəbl] unzählbar **IV**
under [ˈʌndə] unter **I**
*__to undergo__ [ˌʌndəˈgəʊ] durchmachen; sich etw. unterziehen **IV**
undergraduate [ˌʌndəˈgrædjuət] Student(in) vor dem ersten akademischen Grad **VT3,** 54
to underline [ˌʌndəˈlaɪn] unterstreichen **III**
underneath [ˌʌndəˈniːθ] unterhalb; unten ⟨**VT3,** 50⟩
*__to understand__ [ˌʌndəˈstænd] verstehen **I**
underwear [ˈʌndəweə] Unterwäsche **VT3,** 40
undesirable [ˌʌndɪˈzaɪərəbl] unerwünscht **VT5,** 80
unemployed [ˌʌnɪmˈplɔɪd] arbeitslos **VT4,** 61
unemployment [ˌʌnɪmˈplɔɪmənt] Arbeitslosigkeit **IV**
unexpected [ˌʌnɪkˈspektɪd] unerwartet **IV**
unforgettable [ˌʌnfəˈgetəbl] unvergesslich **III**
unfortunately [ʌnˈfɔːtʃnətli] leider; unglücklicherweise **IV**
unhappy [ʌnˈhæpi] unglücklich **II**
uniform [ˈjuːnɪfɔːm] Uniform **I**
Soviet **Union** [ˌsəʊviət ˈjuːnjən] Sowjetunion ⟨**VT5,** 76⟩
trade union [ˌtreɪd ˈjuːnjən] Gewerkschaft **VT4,** 61

unit ['ju:nɪt] Kapitel; Einheit **I**
to **unite** [ju:'naɪt] vereinen; vereinigen **IV**
universal [ˌju:nɪ'vɜ:sl] universell **VT3,** 42
universe ['ju:nɪvɜ:s] Universum **III**
university [ˌju:nɪ'vɜ:səti] Universität **III**
unknown [ʌn'nəʊn] unbekannt **III**
unless [ˌən'les] wenn nicht; es sei denn, (dass) ... **IV**
unlike [ʌn'laɪk] anders als; im Gegensatz zu **III**
*to be **unlikely** (to) [bi:ˌʌn'laɪkli] unwahrscheinlich sein **III**
unlocked [ʌn'lɒkt] unverschlossen; entriegelt **IV**
unnecessary [ʌn'nesəsri] unnötig **III**
to **unpack** [ʌn'pæk] auspacken **III**
unpleasant [ˌʌn'pleznt] unangenehm ⟨**VT3,** 45⟩
unpopular [ʌn'pɒpjələ] unpopulär; unbeliebt **IV**
unprecedented [ˌʌn'presɪdentɪd] beispiellos; noch nie da gewesen ⟨**VT4,** 63⟩
unreasonable [ʌn'ri:znəbl] unvernünftig; unverschämt; unangemessen **IV**
unskilled [ʌn'skɪld] ungelernt **IV**
unthinkable [ʌn'θɪŋkəbl] undenkbar; unvorstellbar **IV**
until [ʌn'tɪl; n'tɪl] bis **I**
  not until [nɒtˌən'tɪl] nicht (be)vor; erst (wenn/als) **III**
unutterable [ʌn'ʌtrəbl] unsagbar ⟨**VT5,** 75⟩
up (to) [ʌp] herbei (zu); auf ... zu **III**
  It's up to you [ɪtsˌʌp tə 'ju:] Wie du willst **VT1,** 15
  to **be up in arms** [bi:ˌʌpˌɪnˌ'ɑ:mz] Sturm laufen; sich empören ⟨**VT3,** 43⟩
  up to ['ʌp tə] bis zu **III**
up [ʌp] (hin)auf, hoch **I**
upset [ʌp'set] aufgebracht; bestürzt **IV**
upstairs [ʌp'steəz] (nach) oben, im Obergeschoss **I**
urban ['ɜ:bn] städtisch **IV**
us [ʌs] wir; uns **I**
US [ju:'es] Vereinigte Staaten; US-amerikanisch **I**
It's no **use** *(+ gerund)* [ɪts 'nəʊ ˌju:s] Es nützt nichts ... **III**
to **use** [ju:z] benutzen, verwenden **I**
  to **be used to** *(+ gerund)* [bi: 'ju:st tə] gewöhnt sein an; gewohnt sein **III**
  to **get used to** *(+ gerund)* [ˌget 'ju:st tə] sich gewöhnen an **III**
  used to *(+ infinitive)* ['ju:st tə] pflegte(n) zu; tat(en) früher **IV**
useful ['ju:sfl] nützlich **II**
useless ['ju:sləs] nutzlos **III**
usual ['ju:ʒl] üblich **II**
usually ['ju:ʒli] normalerweise, gewöhnlich **I**
utter ['ʌtə] äußerst; völlig **IV**

V

vacation *(AE)* [və'keɪʃn] Ferien, Urlaub **II**
vague [veɪg] vage; unbestimmt; unklar **VT5,** 77
in **vain** [ɪn 'veɪn] umsonst; vergeblich ⟨**VT5,** 87⟩
Valentine's card ['væləntaɪnz ˌkɑ:d] Valentinskarte **III**
valley ['væli] Tal **II**
valuable ['væljuəbl] wertvoll **III**
value ['vælju:] Wert **III**
van [væn] Lieferwagen; Transporter **III**
varicose ulcer [ˌværɪkəʊsˌ'ʌlsə] Krampfadergeschwür ⟨**VT5,** 76⟩
various ['veərɪəs] verschieden(artig) **VT1,** 16
to **vary** ['veəri] variieren; (sich) ändern **IV**
vast [vɑ:st] ausgedehnt; riesig; unermesslich **VT4,** 56; **VT5,** 77
vegetable ['vedʒtəbl] Gemüse **I**
vegetarian [ˌvedʒɪ'teərɪən] Vegetarier(in) **II**
vehicle ['vɪəkl] Fahrzeug; Vehikel **VT4,** 62
venue ['venju:] Veranstaltungsort; Treffpunkt ⟨**VT5,** 83⟩
verb [vɜ:b] Verb **IV**
  phrasal verb [ˌfreɪzl 'vɜ:b] phrasal verb *(Verb + Präposition oder Partikel)* **IV**
  verb of perception [ˌvɜ:bˌəv pə'sepʃn] Verb der Wahrnehmung **IV**
verbal ['vɜ:bl] verbal ⟨**VT5,** 81⟩
verse [vɜ:s] Vers; Strophe **IV**
version ['vɜ:ʃn] Version **II**
vertebra, *pl.* **vertebrae** ['vɜ:tɪbrə] Wirbel ⟨**VT1,** 17⟩
this **very** afternoon [ðɪz ˌveriˌɑ:ftə'nu:n] noch heute Nachmittag ⟨**VT3,** 44⟩
very ['veri] sehr **I**
recon **vessel** [rɪ'kɒn ˌvesl] Aufklärungsschiff ⟨**VT5,** 74⟩
vet [vet] Tierarzt, Tierärztin **I**
vibrant ['vaɪbrənt] dynamisch; lebhaft; pulsierend ⟨**VT2,** 33⟩
to **vibrate** [vaɪ'breɪt] vibrieren **III**
victim ['vɪktɪm] Opfer **VT2,** 25; **VT4,** 62
victory ['vɪktri] Sieg **III**
video ['vɪdiəʊ] Video **I**
  video clip ['vɪdiəʊ klɪp] Videoclip **IV**
  video projector [ˌvɪdiəʊ prəʊ'dʒektə] Beamer *(Projektionsgerät)* **III**
view [vju:] Aussicht, Sicht **I**
  point of view [ˌpɔɪntˌəv 'vju:] Standpunkt; Perspektive **IV**
vile [vaɪl] gemein; widerwärtig ⟨**VT5,** 76⟩
village ['vɪlɪdʒ] Dorf **I**
violence ['vaɪələnts] Gewalt **IV**
violent ['vaɪəlnt] gewaltsam; gewalttätig; brutal **VT1,** 9; **VT4,** 61
virtual ['vɜ:tʃuəl] virtuell **IV**
visa *(pl.* **visas***)* ['vi:zə] Visum *(pl. Visa)*; Einreisebewilligung **IV**
vision ['vɪʒn] Vision; Vorstellung; Sicht **IV**
visit ['vɪzɪt] Besuch **II**
to **visit** ['vɪzɪt] besuchen; besichtigen **I**
visitor ['vɪzɪtə] Besucher **I**
vista ['vɪstə] Aussicht ⟨**VT5,** 77⟩
visual ['vɪʒuəl] visuell; optisch **III**
vocabulary [vəʊ'kæbjəlri] Vokabular; Wortschatz **IV**
vocational [ˌvəʊ'keɪʃnl] berufsbildend; beruflich ⟨**VT3,** 55⟩
voice [vɔɪs] Stimme **I**
volcano, *pl.* **volcanoes** [vɒl'keɪnəʊ] Vulkan **III**
volleyball ['vɒlibɔ:l] Volleyball **III**
volume ['vɒlju:m] Volumen; Lautstärke; Band *(Buch)* **IV**
voluntary ['vɒləntri] freiwillig; ehrenamtlich **IV**
volunteer [ˌvɒlən'tɪə] Freiwillige(r); ehrenamtliche(r) Helfer(in) **IV**
vomit ['vɒmɪt] Erbrochenes ⟨**VT1,** 22⟩
vote [vəʊt] Abstimmung; Stimme **IV**
to **vote** [vəʊt] abstimmen; wählen **IV**
vulnerable ['vʌlnrəbl] verletzlich; verwundbar **VT1,** 10

W

wages *(pl.)* ['weɪdʒɪz] Lohn **IV**
wagon ['wægən] Waggon; Planwagen **IV**
  station wagon ['steɪʃn ˌwægən] Kombi ⟨**VT2,** 26⟩
waist [weɪst] Bauch; Taille **VT1,** 17; **VT3,** 40
waistband ['weɪstbænd] Bund ⟨**VT2,** 31⟩
to **wait (for)** [weɪt] warten (auf) **I**
waiter ['weɪtə] Kellner, Bedienung **II**
waitress ['weɪtrəs] Kellnerin, Bedienung **IV**
*to **wake** (somebody) **up** [weɪkˌ'ʌp] (jemanden) aufwecken; aufwachen **I**
walk [wɔ:k] Spaziergang **I**
  a two-minute walk away from ... [ˌtu:mɪnɪt 'wɔ:k] zwei Minuten zu Fuß von ... entfernt **II**
  to **go for a walk** [ˌgəʊ fərˌə 'wɔ:k] spazieren gehen **I**
to **walk** [wɔ:k] gehen, laufen **I**
wall [wɔ:l] Wand; Mauer **I**
wallet ['wɒlɪt] Brieftasche; Geldbörse **VT4,** 64
wallpaper ['wɔ:lpeɪpə] Tapete **VT2,** 36
wannabe *(infml)* ['wɒnəbi:] Möchtegern ⟨**VT3,** 48⟩
to **want** (to) ['wɒnt tə] wollen, mögen **I**
  to **want sb to do sth** [wɒnt] wollen, dass jmd etw. tut **II**
war [wɔ:] Krieg **III**
  civil war [ˌsɪvl 'wɔ:] Bürgerkrieg **III**
warm [wɔ:m] warm **I**
to **warn** [wɔ:n] warnen **II**
wary ['weəri] wachsam; misstrauisch ⟨**VT5,** 80⟩
to **wash** [wɒʃ] (sich) waschen; spülen **I**

to **wash up** [wɒʃ'ʌp] abwaschen, abspülen **II**
waste [weɪst] Abfall; Verschwendung **III**
to **waste** [weɪst] verschwenden **III**
watch [wɒtʃ] Armbanduhr **II**
to **watch** [wɒtʃ] beobachten, (sich) ansehen **I**
to **watch TV** [ˌwɒtʃ ti:'vi:] fernsehen **I**
Watch out! [wɒtʃ'aʊt] Achtung! Pass(t) auf! **I**
water ['wɔ:tə] Wasser **I**
mineral water ['mɪnrl ˌwɔ:tə] Mineralwasser **III**
waterproof ['wɔ:təpru:f] wasserdicht **III**
wave [weɪv] Welle **I**
Sierra Wave [sɪˌerə 'weɪv] Sierra Wave *(ein in der Sierra Nevada auftretendes außergewöhnliches Thermikphänomen)* ⟨**VT1,** 18⟩
to **wave** [weɪv] winken; schwenken **I**
way [weɪ] Weg; Art und Weise **I**
by the way [ˌbaɪ ðə 'weɪ] übrigens **III**
Milky Way [ˌmɪlki 'weɪ] Milchstraße **II**
No way! [ˌnəʊ 'weɪ] Auf keinen Fall! **III**
the wrong way round [ðə ˌrɒŋ weɪ 'raʊnd] falsch herum **III**
to **be in a bad way** [ɪn ə 'bæd ˌweɪ] in schlechter Verfassung sein **I**
we [wi:] wir **I**
we're !wɪə? (= we are) [] wir sind **I**
weak [wi:k] schwach **I**
weakness ['wi:knəs] Schwäche **VT5,** 73
wealth [welθ] Wohlstand; Reichtum **III**
wealthy ['welθi] wohlhabend; reich **III**
weapon ['wepən] Waffe **III**
*to **wear** [weə] anhaben, tragen **I**
to **wear off** [ˌweər'ɒf] abgehen; sich abnutzen **IV**
weather ['weðə] Wetter **I**
weather forecast ['weðə ˌfɔ:kɑ:st] Wettervorhersage **II**
*to **weave** [wi:v] weben **IV**
web [web] (Spinnen-)Netz **III**
website ['websaɪt] Website, Internetauftritt **II**
wedding ['wedɪŋ] Hochzeit **IV**
to **weed** [wi:d] jäten ⟨**VT4,** 70⟩
week [wi:k] Woche **I**
a week [ə 'wi:k] pro Woche, in der Woche **II**
What a week! [ˌwɒt ə 'wi:k] Was für eine Woche! **II**
weekend ['wi:kend] Wochenende **I**
weekly ['wi:kli] wöchentlich ⟨**VT1,** 23⟩
*to **weep** [wi:p] weinen **IV**
to **weigh** [weɪ] wiegen **I**
weigh-in [ˌweɪ'ɪn] Wiegeaktion ⟨**VT1,** 23⟩
weight [weɪt] Gewicht **IV**
weird [wɪəd] sonderbar; merkwürdig **VT1,** 14; ⟨**VT3,** 44⟩
weirdo *(infml)* ['wɪədəʊ] Psychopath; komischer Kauz **VT2,** 33
to **welcome** ['welkəm] willkommen heißen **II**
You're **welcome.** [jɔ: 'welkəm] Bitte schön./Gern geschehen. **III**
Welcome! ['welkəm] Willkommen! **I**
to **weld** [weld] schweißen **VT5,** 73
welfare ['welfeə] Wohl(ergehen); Sozialhilfe **IV**
well [wel] gesund **III**
Get well soon! [get ˌwel 'su:n] Gute Besserung! **III**
to **get well** [get 'wel] gesund werden **III**
well [wel] gut **I**
as well [əz 'wel] auch **III**
... as well as ... [əz 'wel əz] sowohl ... als auch ... **IV**
to **mix well** [ˌmɪks 'wel] gut mit Menschen auskommen ⟨**VT4,** 70⟩
well [wel] also; na ja; nun gut **II**
well-known [ˌwel'nəʊn] wohl bekannt **IV**
welly ['weli] Gummistiefel **I**
Welsh [welʃ] walisisch; Walisisch; Waliser(in) **III**
west [west] Westen **I**
western ['westən] Western-; westlich **II**
westwards ['westwədz] westlich; westwärts **IV**
wet [wet] nass **I**
to **get wet** [get 'wet] nass werden **I**
wetter and wetter [ˌwetər ənd 'wetə] immer nasser, immer verregneter **II**
what [wɒt] was **I**
What about you? [ˌwɒt əbaʊt 'ju:] Und dir/euch/Ihnen? Und du/ihr/Sie? **I**
What a pity! [ˌwɒt ə 'pɪti] Wie schade! **II**
What a week! [ˌwɒt ə 'wi:k] Was für eine Woche! **II**
What colour is/are ... ? [ˌwɒt 'kʌlər ɪz/ ɑ:] Welche Farbe hat/haben ... ? **I**
what else [ˌwɒt 'els] was sonst/noch **II**
What's ... in English? [ˌwɒts ... ɪn 'ɪŋglɪʃ] Was heißt ... auf Englisch? **I**
What's it like? [ˌwɒts ɪt 'laɪk] Wie ist es? **II**
What's missing? [ˌwɒts 'mɪsɪŋ] Was fehlt? **I**
What's the matter? [ˌwɒts ðə 'mætə] Was ist los? Was hast du? **I**
What's your name? [ˌwɒts jə 'neɪm] Wie heißt du/heißen Sie? **I**
What time ... ? [wɒt 'taɪm] (Um) wie viel Uhr ... ? **I**
whatever [wɒt'evə] was auch immer; egal welche **IV**
whatever it takes [wɒtˌevər ɪt 'teɪks] alles, was nötig ist **IV**
wheat [wi:t] Weizen **I**
wheel [wi:l] Rad **I**
to **wheel** [wi:l] rollen **VT1,** 12
wheelchair ['wi:ltʃeə] Rollstuhl **III**
when [wen] wann; als; wenn **I**
whenever [wen'evə] wann immer; immer, wenn; so oft **IV**
where [weə] wo; wohin **I**
Where are you from? [ˌweər ə jə 'frɒm] Woher kommst du/kommt ihr/kommen Sie? **I**
Where ... from? [ˌweə ... 'frɒm] Woher ... ? **I**
whereas [weə'ræz] während; wohingegen **IV**
wherever [weə'revə] wo(hin) auch immer **III**
whether ['weðə] ob **III**
which [wɪtʃ] welche(-r/-s) **I**
which [wɪtʃ] der, dem, den, die, das *(Relativpronomen)* **II**
a **while** [ə 'waɪl] eine Weile **III**
while [waɪl] während **I**
to **whine** [waɪn] quengeln ⟨**VT4,** 70⟩
to **whip** [wɪp] schlagen **IV**
to **whirl** [wɜ:l] wirbeln; sich drehen ⟨**VT5,** 77⟩
whisky ['wɪski] Whisky **I**
to **whisper** ['wɪspə] flüstern **III**
whistle ['wɪsl] Trillerpfeife **III**
whistle-blowing ['wɪslˌbləʊɪŋ] verräterisch ⟨**VT1,** 22⟩
white [waɪt] weiß **I**
white-ripple-marked [ˌwaɪt rɪpl 'mɑ:kt] mit weißer Wellenzeichnung ⟨**VT4,** 69⟩
white horses [waɪt 'hɔ:sɪz] *hier*: Schaumkronen **I**
who [hu:] wem, wen **I**; wer **I**
who [hu:] der, dem, den, die *(Relativpronomen)* **II**
whole [həʊl] ganz **II**
the whole deal [ðə ˌhəʊl 'di:l] alles ⟨**VT5,** 74⟩
whose [hu:z] wessen **I**
whose [hu:z] dessen, deren *(Relativpronomen)* **II**
why [waɪ] warum **I**
wide [waɪd] groß; breit; weit **I**
widow ['wɪdəʊ] Witwe **IV**
wife, *pl.* **wives** [waɪf; waɪvz] Ehefrau **II**
wild [waɪld] wild **II**
wilderness ['wɪldənəs] Wildnis **III**
wildlife ['waɪldlaɪf] Tierwelt (in freier Wildbahn) **II**
will [wɪl] werden *(futurisch)* **II**
*to be **willing** to do sth [bi: 'wɪlɪŋ] gewillt sein, etw. zu tun **VT2,** 27
willow-herb ['wɪləʊhɜ:b] Weidenröschen ⟨**VT5,** 77⟩
wimp *(infml)* [wɪmp] Weichei; Schlappschwanz ⟨**VT3,** 45⟩
*to **win** [wɪn] gewinnen, siegen **I**
wind [wɪnd] Wind **I**
window ['wɪndəʊ] Fenster **I**
window pane ['wɪndəʊ ˌpeɪn] Fensterscheibe ⟨**VT5,** 77⟩

windsurfing ['wɪndsɜ:fɪŋ] Windsurfen **II**
wine [waɪn] Wein **II**
wing [wɪŋ] Flügel **IV**
to **wink** [wɪŋk] zwinkern ⟨**VT5,** 83⟩
winner ['wɪnə] Gewinner(in), Sieger(in) **II**
winter ['wɪntə] Winter **II**
wire [waɪə] Draht; Kabel **VT5,** 77
wish [wɪʃ] Wunsch **IV**
to **wish** [wɪʃ] wünschen **IV**
with [wɪð] mit **I**
within [wɪ'ðɪn] innerhalb **IV**
without [wɪ'ðaʊt] ohne **I**
  without fail [wɪˌðaʊt 'feɪl] unweigerlich; auf alle Fälle **VT2,** 28
to **witness** ['wɪtnəs] miterleben ⟨**VT4,** 70⟩
wizard ['wɪzəd] Zauberer **II**
woman, *pl.* **women** ['wʊmən; 'wɪmɪn] Frau **I**
wonder ['wʌndə] Wunder; Verwunderung **III**
to **wonder** ['wʌndə] sich Gedanken machen, sich fragen **III**
wonderful ['wʌndəfl] wunderbar **II**
won't [wəʊnt] nicht werden *(futurisch)* **II**
wood [wʊd] Holz **III**; Wald **IV**
wooden ['wʊdn] hölzern **III**
Woof! [wʊf] Wau! **I**
wool [wʊl] Wolle **VT4,** 56
word [wɜ:d] Wort **I**
  words *(pl.)* [wɜ:dz] Text(e) **II**
  Find the odd word out! [ˌɒd wɜ:d‿'aʊt] Finde das Wort, das nicht in die Gruppe passt! *(Wortschatzübung)* **I**
  key word ['ki: wɜ:d] Stichwort; Schlüsselbegriff **II**
  Word power ['wɜ:d ˌpaʊə] *Besondere Wortschatzübung* **I**
work [wɜ:k] Arbeit **I**
  out of work [ˌaʊt‿əv 'wɜ:k] arbeitslos **III**
  public works [ˌpʌblɪk 'wɜ:ks] öffentliche Bauarbeiten; staatliche Bauprojekte **IV**
  work experience ['wɜ:k‿ɪkˌspɪəriənts] Berufserfahrung **IV**
to **work** [wɜ:k] arbeiten **I**; funktionieren **II**
  to **work out** [ˌwɜ:k‿'aʊt] herausbringen, herausfinden; ausarbeiten **II**
  working class [ˌwɜ:kɪŋ 'klɑ:s] Arbeiterklasse **IV**
workman, *pl.* **workmen** ['wɜ:kmən] Handwerker **I**
workplace ['wɜ:kpleɪs] Arbeitsplatz; Arbeitsstätte **VT2,** 27
workshop ['wɜ:kʃɒp] Workshop, Werkstatt **III**
world [wɜ:ld] Erde, Welt **I**
worldwide [ˌwɜ:ld'waɪd] weltweit **IV**
*to be **worried** ['wʌrid] besorgt, beunruhigt sein **I**
worry ['wʌri] Sorge **III**
to **worry** ['wʌri] (sich) Sorgen machen **I**
*to be **worth** *(+ gerund)* [bi: 'wɜ:θ] (es) wert sein (zu) **III**
would [wʊd] würde(n) **II**
  I'd [aɪd] Ich würde **II**
  I'd rather [aɪd 'rɑ:ðə] ich würde lieber **IV**
  Would you like ...? [ˌwʊd jə 'laɪk] Möchtest du/möchten Sie/möchtet ihr ...? **II**
wound [wu:nd] Wunde; Verletzung **VT4,** 63
to **wound** [wu:nd] verwunden; verletzen **IV**
wow! [waʊ] Wow! Toll! **I**
to **wrap** [ræp] einwickeln; einpacken **IV**
wreck [rek] Wrack **I**
*to **write** [raɪt] schreiben **I**
writer ['raɪtə] Schriftsteller(in) **III**
wrong [rɒŋ] falsch **I**
  the wrong way round [ðə ˌrɒŋ weɪ 'raʊnd] falsch herum **III**
  to **be wrong** [bi: 'rɒŋ] Unrecht haben **II**
  to **go wrong** [gəʊ 'rɒŋ] schief gehen **II**
  to **prove sb wrong** [ˌpru:v 'rɒŋ] beweisen, dass jmd Unrecht hat ⟨**VT3,** 48⟩
wrongful ['rɒŋfl] unrechtmäßig **III**

Y

yard [jɑ:d] Hof **I**; Yard *(Längenmaß: 91,44 cm)* ⟨**VT2,** 30⟩
to **yawn** [jɔ:n] gähnen **IV**
yeah *(infml.)* [jeə] ja **I**
year [jɪə] Jahr; Jahrgang **I**
  a day/year off [ə ˌdeɪ‿'ɒf] ein freier Tag/ein freies Jahr **IV**
  for many years [fə ˌmæni 'jɪəz] viele Jahre lang **II**
yearbook ['jɪəbʊk] Jahrbuch **II**
to **yell** [jel] brüllen; laut schreien ⟨**VT3,** 45⟩
yellow ['jeləʊ] gelb **I**
yes [jes] ja **I**
yesterday ['jestədeɪ] gestern **I**
  the day before yesterday [ðə ˌdeɪ bɪfɔ: 'jestədeɪ] vorgestern **I**
yet [jet] schon; noch **II**; doch **IV**
yoghurt ['jɒgət] Joghurt **II**
you [ju:; jə] man **I**; du, ihr, Sie **I**
  bless you ['bles ju:] Gesundheit! **II**
  It's up to you [ɪts‿ʌp tə 'ju:] Wie du willst **VT1,** 15
  you lot ['ju: ˌlɒt] ihr alle **I**
  You're welcome. [jɔ: 'welkəm] Bitte schön./Gern geschehen. **III**
young [jʌŋ] jung **I**
your [jɔ:; jə] dein(e); euer/eure; Ihr(e) **I**
  It's your turn. ['jɔ: tɜ:n] Du bist/Sie sind dran. **I**
Yours sincerely [ˌjɔ:z sɪn'sɪəli] Mit freundlichen Grüßen **IV**
help **yourself** [ˌhelp jɔ:'self] bediene dich!/bedienen Sie sich! **II**
youth [ju:θ] Jugend; Jugendliche(r) **IV**
Yuk! [jʌk] Igitt! **I**
yummy ['jʌmi] lecker **I**

Z

to **zap** [zæp] knipsen ⟨**VT1,** 14⟩
zero ['zɪərəʊ] null **VT2,** 26
zip [zɪp] Schwirren ⟨**VT5,** 81⟩
zipper ['zɪpə] Reißverschluss **III**
zit *(infml)* [zɪt] Pickel **VT1,** 14
  zit-blasted *(infml)* ['zɪtˌblɑ:stɪd] mit Pickeln übersät ⟨**VT1,** 14⟩
zone [zəʊn] Zone **III**
zoo [zu:] Zoo, Tierpark **I**

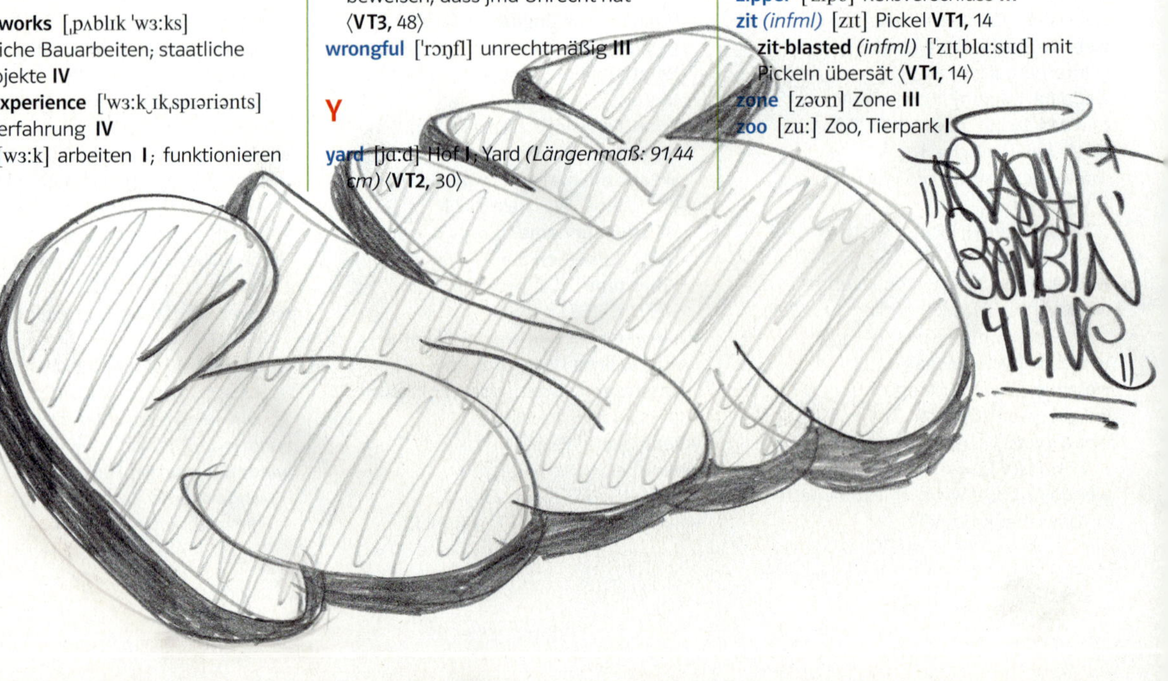

Grammar solutions for *Checking up*

B Talking about the past (page 114)

Checking up

1 I've been waiting • 2 rang • 3 was getting • 4 we'd finished • 5 came • 6 arrived • 7 was just disappearing • 8 You've got • 9 I've been thinking • 10 Have you seen • 11 saw • 12 had been looking • 13 liked • 14 I've talked

C Expressing conditions and consequences (page 117)

Checking up

1. You're lucky to live so near! If you **still lived/were still living** in Oxford Road, you **wouldn't be able to/couldn't** walk to school.
2. Don't worry about your exams next month. If you **revise** well, you **will pass** easily.
3. It was just bad luck. If I **hadn't been** ill last week, I **wouldn't have missed** those important lessons.

D Using modal auxiliaries (page 118)

Checking up

1. "**Can/May** I borrow that book?" – "OK, but I **have (got) to/must** take it back to the library next week, so you **mustn't** forget to give it back to me."
2. "Sorry I **couldn't/wasn't able to** come to the cinema last night." – "You **needn't** worry – the film wasn't worth seeing!"
3. "The menu was in Greek, so we **couldn't/weren't able to** understand much of it. We **had to** ask the waiter to translate it."
4. "If you take that big bag, you **won't be able/allowed to** take it on the plane with you. You'll **have to** hand it in at the check-in counter."

E Describing things (page 120)

Checking up

a) 1. "The concert was **really fantastic**. You played **beautifully**!" – "Thanks! I felt **pretty nervous** at the beginning. But **luckily** everything went **well**.
   2. "Be **careful**! I **absolutely** hate it when you drive so **fast**." – "Come on! You can't call me a **dangerous** driver. I just don't like driving **slowly** for no **real** reason."

b) 1. We had a great time at the barbecue down on the beach last Saturday.
   2. We always have breakfast rather late on Sundays.
   3. Frankly, I have never actually cooked a proper meal on my own.

c) 1. I don't agree with everything (that) you said.
   2. Most of the people (who) I talked to were Americans.
   3. Jane and Mike, who were both at the meeting, came up to us afterwards.
   4. Carlos spoke excellent English, which impressed me a lot.

F Linking ideas (page 123)

Checking up

1. He left the house without telling anyone where he was going.
2. Knowing the weather would be cold, we packed warm clothing.
3. Several houses destroyed in the floods had been built to near the river.
4. She's looking forward to spending next year in Paris.
5. Instead of using the underground, I decided to go by bus.

Glossary of literary terms

Some of the terms are used to explain others. They are underlined.

atmosphere ['ætməsfɪə]	The feeling a literary work creates in the reader (see mood).
biography [baɪ'ɒgrəfi]	Prose representation of parts or of the whole life of a person, written by another person. When somebody writes a representation of their own life, it is called an autobiography.
chapter ['tʃæptə]	One of the sections a book is divided into.
characterization [ˌkærəktraɪ'zeɪʃn]	Presentation of characters in a text. Direct characterization: The narrator of the text tells the reader what a person is like. Indirect characterization: The reader has to find out what a person is like through what this character does, says, thinks or feels.
climax ['klaɪmæks]	The moment in a play, novel, short story, narrative or poem at which the suspense reaches its highest point. It is usually the turning point in the action.
comedy ['kɒmədi]	Originally, comedy (as opposed to tragedy) was a genre of drama of ancient Athens. Since the 19th century comedy has been associated with humour.
conclusion [kən'klu:ʒn]	Last part of a literary work which sums up its content and finishes it.
drama ['drɑ:mə]	1. A type of play. 2. The art of writing and performing a play.
dystopia [dɪs'təʊpiə]	Opposite of utopia, describes an unpleasant imaginary world, usually of the future, e.g. *Nineteen Eighty-four* by George Orwell.
exaggeration [ɪgˌzædʒr'eɪʃn]	Making something greater, better or worse than it really is.
exposition [ˌekspəʊ'zɪʃn]	The first part of a play or short story which gives the information which is necessary to understand the conflict and events which follow.
fiction ['fɪkʃn]	Fiction is the general term for invented stories. It is now usually applied to novels, short stories and related genres.
flashback ['flæʃbæk]	Part of a film, novel or play in which the plot suddenly changes to events in the past.
foreshadowing [fɔ:'ʃædəʊɪŋ]	Suggesting or showing what will occur later in a narrative.
frame narrative ['freɪm ˌnærətɪv]	A story in which another story is enclosed.
genre ['ʒɑ̃:nrə]	Literary type or class. Some major genres are: tragedy, comedy, novel, short story, poetry.
imagery ['ɪmɪdʒri]	Use of language which represents objects, actions, feelings, thoughts, and ideas through the use of simile and metaphor.
irony ['aɪərəni]	Using the contrast between what is said and what is meant to create humour.
metaphor ['metəfə]	One thing is represented by a word which normally describes something different, e.g. *All the world's a stage*. Unlike a simile it contains no words of comparison *(like, as)*.
metre ['mi:tə]	The regular pattern of stressed and unstressed syllables in a poem.
monologue ['mɒnəlɒg]	Speech given by one speaker regardless of whether there is any audience.
mood [mu:d]	The feeling a literary work creates in the reader (see atmosphere).
narrative ['nærətɪv]	A story, prose or verse, involving events and characters.
narrator [nə'reɪtə]	The voice that tells a story.
non-fiction [ˌnɒn'fɪkʃn]	Non-fiction is a representation of a subject which is presented as fact (German: Sachliteratur).
novel ['nɒvl]	A long fictional prose text, often including a large number of characters, different settings and a complex plot.
personification [pəˌsɒnɪfɪ'keɪʃn]	Attribution of personality to an impersonal thing, e.g. *The wind cries softly outside the window.*
play [pleɪ]	A work designed to be presented on a stage and performed by actors and actresses.
plot [plɒt]	The sequence of events in a story.

poem/poetry ['pəʊɪm/'pəʊɪtri]	Piece of writing divided into single lines. It often expresses the speaker's experiences. Most poetry makes use of four important poetic devices: metre, rhyme, rhythm and stanza.
point of view [ˌpɔɪnt‿əv'vju:]	The perspective from which the narrator presents the story.
prose [prəʊz]	The kind of writing found in news articles, short stories, novels, etc. as opposed to poetry.
protagonist [prəʊ'tægənɪst]	The main character in a work of fiction.
pseudonym ['sju:dənɪm]	A 'false name' taken by a writer.
pun [pʌn]	A play on words, usually the humorous use of a word with two meanings or of different words that sound the same, e.g. *'I'm always ill on Tuesdays,' said Tom weakly.*
repetition [ˌrepɪ'tɪʃn]	Single words or phrases that appear several times in one text, a way of creating emphasis.
review [rɪ'vju:]	A short notice, discussion or a critical article about a text, a film, a play, etc.
rhyme [raɪm]	Similarity of sounds in two or more words. This often occurs at the end of lines (end rhyme), e.g. **teacher** – **preacher**. The pattern created is called a rhyme scheme.
rhythm ['rɪðm]	The sound pattern of a phrase. It is mainly based on metre.
satire ['sætaɪə]	Combines humour and criticism with the aim of making people laugh at the stupidity of individuals and institutions. It differs from comedy in that it seeks to correct or improve.
science fiction [ˌsaɪənts'fɪkʃn]	Novels or short stories set in the future or another world, which often focus on imaginary technological developments. Science fiction may be utopian or dystopian.
setting ['setɪŋ]	The time and place that characterize a work of literature.
short story ['ʃɔ:t ˌstɔ:ri]	A fictional prose narrative that is too short to be published as a volume on its own. A short story normally focuses on a single event and setting with only one or two characters.
simile ['sɪmɪli]	A comparison between objects or ideas, using *like, as or as if*, e.g. *He fought like a tiger.*
stanza ['stænzə]	The regular number of lines which form a unit of a poem.
stereotype ['steriəʊtaɪp]	Fixed ideas about other people or things. They may be positive or negative prejudices, e.g. *All Germans wear 'Lederhosen'.*
stream-of-consciousness [ˌstri:m‿əv 'kɒntʃəsnəs]	Refers to a technique of writing in which a character's perceptions, thoughts, and memories are presented in an apparently irregular form. It can appear as dreams, memories, imaginative thoughts or real perception.
style [staɪl]	How a writer uses language. It is the tone and the 'voice' of the writer, often typical of a certain period or genre.
suspense [sə'spents]	Suspense results mainly from two factors: 1. the reader's identification with and concern for the welfare of a character, and 2. an expectation of violence.
symbol ['sɪmbl]	Something concrete which stands for an abstract idea, e.g. a rose is a symbol for love.
theme [θi:m]	The theme of a novel, poem, short story, etc. is the central idea or 'message'. It may be demonstrated by the use of symbols, repetition and statements.
tone [təʊn]	The author's attitude towards his/her subject, characters and readers.
tragedy ['trædʒədi]	A form of drama representing the terrible downfall of a central character (protagonist). Shakespeare is famous for his tragedies, including *Macbeth, King Lear,* and *Hamlet.*
turning point ['tɜ.nɪŋ ˌpɔɪnt]	The moment in a story or a play when there is a change in direction which leads towards the end result. See also climax.
utopia [ju:'təʊpiə]	The term is based on the Greek words for 'no place' and 'good place'. It refers to literature which describes an imaginary ideal society and political state (opposite of dystopia).
verse [vɜ:s]	Another word for poetry, a single line of a poem, or a stanza.

Irregular verbs

infinitive	simple past	past participle	German
to **awake** [ə'weɪk]	**awoke** [ə'wəʊk]	**awoken** [ə'wəʊkn]	erwachen
to **be** [bi:]	**was/were** [wɒz; wɜ:]	**been** [bi:n]	sein
to **bear** [beə]	**bore** [bɔ:]	**borne** [bɔ:n]	(er)tragen
to **beat** [bi:t]	**beat** [bi:t]	**beaten** ['bi:tn]	besiegen, schlagen
to **become** [bɪ'kʌm]	**became** [bɪ'keɪm]	**become** [bɪ'kʌm]	werden
to **begin** [bɪ'gɪn]	**began** [bɪ'gæn]	**begun** [bɪ'gʌn]	beginnen
to **bend** [bend]	**bent** [bent]	**bent** [bent]	beugen
to **bet** [bet]	**bet** [bet]	**bet** [bet]	wetten
to **bid** [bɪd]	**bid** [bɪd]	**bid** [bɪd]	bieten (Auktion)
to **bite** [baɪt]	**bit** [bɪt]	**bitten** ['bɪtn]	beißen
to **bleed** [bli:d]	**bled** [bled]	**bled** [bled]	bluten
to **blow** [bləʊ]	**blew** [blu:]	**blown** [bləʊn]	blasen
to **break** [breɪk]	**broke** [brəʊk]	**broken** ['brəʊkn]	brechen
to **bring** [brɪŋ]	**brought** [brɔ:t]	**brought** [brɔ:t]	bringen
to **build** [bɪld]	**built** [bɪlt]	**built** [bɪlt]	bauen
to **burn** [bɜ:n]	**burned/burnt** [bɜ:nd; bɜ:nt]	**burned/burnt** [bɜ:nd; bɜ:nt]	brennen
to **burst** [bɜ:st]	**burst** [bɜ:st]	**burst** [bɜ:st]	bersten, platzen
to **buy** [baɪ]	**bought** [bɔ:t]	**bought** [bɔ:t]	kaufen
to **catch** [kætʃ]	**caught** [kɔ:t]	**caught** [kɔ:t]	fangen
to **choose** [tʃu:z]	**chose** [tʃəʊz]	**chosen** ['tʃəʊzn]	(aus)wählen
to **cling** [klɪŋ]	**clung** [klʌŋ]	**clung** [klʌŋ]	(sich) festhalten
to **come** [kʌm]	**came** [keɪm]	**come** [kʌm]	kommen
to **cost** [kɒst]	**cost** [kɒst]	**cost** [kɒst]	kosten
to **creep** [kri:p]	**crept** [krept]	**crept** [krept]	schleichen; kriechen
to **cut** [kʌt]	**cut** [kʌt]	**cut** [kʌt]	schneiden
to **deal (with)** [di:l]	**dealt** [delt]	**dealt** [delt]	(be)handeln
to **do** [du:]	**did** [dɪd]	**done** [dʌn]	tun, machen
to **draw** [drɔ:]	**drew** [dru:]	**drawn** [drɔ:n]	zeichnen
to **dream** [dri:m]	**dreamed/dreamt** [dri:md; dremt]	**dreamed/dreamt** [dri:md; dremt]	träumen
to **drink** [drɪŋk]	**drank** [dræŋk]	**drunk** [drʌŋk]	trinken
to **drive** [draɪv]	**drove** [drəʊv]	**driven** ['drɪvn]	fahren
to **eat** [i:t]	**ate** [et; eɪt]	**eaten** ['i:tn]	essen
to **fall** [fɔ:l]	**fell** [fel]	**fallen** ['fɔ:lən]	fallen
to **feed** [fi:d]	**fed** [fed]	**fed** [fed]	füttern
to **feel** [fi:l]	**felt** [felt]	**felt** [felt]	(sich) fühlen
to **fight** [faɪt]	**fought** [fɔ:t]	**fought** [fɔ:t]	streiten, kämpfen
to **find** [faɪnd]	**found** [faʊnd]	**found** [faʊnd]	finden
to **fly** [flaɪ]	**flew** [flu:]	**flown** [fləʊn]	fliegen
to **forget** [fə'get]	**forgot** [fə'gɒt]	**forgotten** [fə'gɒtn]	vergessen
to **freeze** [fri:z]	**froze** [frəʊz]	**frozen** ['frəʊzn]	erstarren, gefrieren
to **get** [get]	**got** [gɒt]	**got** [gɒt] *(BE)* **gotten** [gɒtn] *(AE)*	(be)kommen; werden
to **give** [gɪv]	**gave** [geɪv]	**given** ['gɪvn]	geben
to **go** [gəʊ]	**went** [went]	**gone** [gɒn]	gehen
to **grow** [grəʊ]	**grew** [gru:]	**grown** [grəʊn]	wachsen; anbauen
to **hang** [hæŋ]	**hung** [hʌŋ]	**hung** [hʌŋ]	hängen
to **have** [hæv]	**had** [hæd]	**had** [hæd]	haben
to **hear** [hɪə]	**heard** [hɜ:d]	**heard** [hɜ:d]	hören
to **hide** [haɪd]	**hid** [hɪd]	**hidden** ['hɪdn]	(sich) verstecken
to **hit** [hɪt]	**hit** [hɪt]	**hit** [hɪt]	schlagen; treffen
to **hold** [həʊld]	**held** [held]	**held** [held]	halten
to **hurt** [hɜ:t]	**hurt** [hɜ:t]	**hurt** [hɜ:t]	verletzen, weh tun
to **keep** [ki:p]	**kept** [kept]	**kept** [kept]	behalten; weitermachen
to **know** [nəʊ]	**knew** [nju:]	**known** [nəʊn]	wissen
to **lay** [leɪ]	**laid** [leɪd]	**laid** [leɪd]	legen
to **lead** [li:d]	**led** [led]	**led** [led]	führen
to **leap** [li:p]	**leaped/leapt** [li:pt; lept]	**leaped/leapt** [li:pt; lept]	springen
to **lean** [li:n]	**leaned/leant** [li:nd; lent]	**leaned/leant** [li:nd; lent]	(sich) lehnen
to **learn** [lɜ:n]	**learned/learnt** [lɜ:nd; lɜ:nt]	**learned/learnt** [lɜ:nd; lɜ:nt]	springen
to **leave** [li:v]	**left** [left]	**left** [left]	(ver)lassen
to **lend** [lend]	**lent** [lent]	**lent** [lent]	leihen
to **let** [let]	**let** [let]	**let** [let]	lassen

infinitive	simple past	past participle	German
to **lie** [laɪ]	**lay** [leɪ]	**lain** [leɪn]	liegen
to **light** [laɪt]	**lit** [lɪt]	**lit** [lɪt]	anzünden, beleuchten
to **lose** [lu:z]	**lost** [lɒst]	**lost** [lɒst]	verlieren
to **make** [meɪk]	**made** [meɪd]	**made** [meɪd]	machen
to **mean** [mi:n]	**meant** [ment]	**meant** [ment]	bedeuten; meinen
to **meet** [mi:t]	**met** [met]	**met** [met]	(sich) treffen
to **pay** [peɪ]	**paid** [peɪd]	**paid** [peɪd]	zahlen
to **put** [pʊt]	**put** [pʊt]	**put** [pʊt]	stellen, legen, setzen
to **read** [ri:d]	**read** [red]	**read** [red]	lesen
to **ride** [raɪd]	**rode** [rəʊd]	**ridden** ['rɪdn]	reiten; fahren
to **ring** [rɪŋ]	**rang** [ræŋ]	**rung** [rʌŋ]	klingeln; anrufen
to **rise** [raɪz]	**rose** [rəʊz]	**risen** ['rɪzn]	steigen; sich erheben
to **run** [rʌn]	**ran** [ræn]	**run** [rʌn]	rennen, laufen
to **say** [seɪ]	**said** [sed]	**said** [sed]	sagen
to **see** [si:]	**saw** [sɔ:]	**seen** [si:n]	sehen
to **sell** [sel]	**sold** [səʊld]	**sold** [səʊld]	verkaufen
to **send** [send]	**sent** [sent]	**sent** [sent]	schicken
to **set** [set]	**set** [set]	**set** [set]	setzen, legen, stellen
to **sew** [səʊ]	**sewed** [səʊd]	**sewn** [səʊn]	nähen
to **shake** [ʃeɪk]	**shook** [ʃʊk]	**shaken** ['ʃeɪkn]	schütteln
to **shine** [ʃaɪn]	**shone** [ʃɒn]	**shone** [ʃɒn]	scheinen, glänzen
to **shoot** [ʃu:t]	**shot** [ʃɒt]	**shot** [ʃɒt]	schießen
to **show** [ʃəʊ]	**showed** [ʃəʊd]	**shown** [ʃəʊn]	zeigen
to **shut** [ʃʌt]	**shut** [ʃʌt]	**shut** [ʃʌt]	schließen
to **sing** [sɪŋ]	**sang** [sæŋ]	**sung** [sʌŋ]	singen
to **sink** [sɪŋk]	**sank** [sæŋk]	**sunk** [sʌŋk]	sinken
to **sit** [sɪt]	**sat** [sæt]	**sat** [sæt]	sitzen
to **sleep** [sli:p]	**slept** [slept]	**slept** [slept]	schlafen
to **smell** [smel]	**smelled/smelt** [smeld; smelt]	**smelled/smelt** [smeld; smelt]	riechen
to **speak** [spi:k]	**spoke** [spəʊk]	**spoken** ['spəʊkn]	sprechen
to **spell** [spel]	**spelled/spelt** [speld; spelt]	**spelled/spelt** [speld; spelt]	buchstabieren
to **spend** [spend]	**spent** [spent]	**spent** [spent]	ausgeben; verbringen
to **spill** [spɪl]	**spilled/spilt** [spɪld; spɪlt]	**spilled/spilt** [spɪld; spɪlt]	verschütten
to **spin** [spɪn]	**spun/span** [spʌn; spæn]	**spun** [spʌn]	spinnen, schnell drehen
to **spit** [spɪt]	**spat** [spæt]	**spat** [spæt]	spucken
to **split** [splɪt]	**split** [splɪt]	**split** [splɪt]	spalten
to **spread** [spred]	**spread** [spred]	**spread** [spred]	(sich) verbreiten
to **spring** [sprɪng]	**sprang** [spræŋ]	**sprung** [sprʌŋ]	entspringen
to **stand** [stænd]	**stood** [stʊd]	**stood** [stʊd]	stehen
to **steal** [sti:l]	**stole** [stəʊl]	**stolen** ['stəʊlən]	stehlen
to **stick** [stɪk]	**stuck** [stʌk]	**stuck** [stʌk]	kleben; stecken
to **stink** [stɪŋk]	**stank** [stæŋk]	**stunk** [stʌŋk]	stinken
to **strike** [straɪk]	**struck** [strʌk]	**struck** [strʌk]	schlagen; anzünden
to **strive** [straɪv]	**strove** [streʊv]	**striven** ['strɪvn]	streben
to **swear** [sweə]	**swore** [swɔ:]	**sworn** [swɔ:n]	schwören, fluchen
to **sweep** [swi:p]	**swept** [swept]	**swept** [swept]	fegen
to **swell** [swel]	**swelled** [sweld]	**swollen** ['swəʊlən]	anschwellen
to **swim** [swɪm]	**swam** [swæm]	**swum** [swʌm]	schwimmen
to **swing** [swɪŋ]	**swung** [swʌŋ]	**swung** [swʌŋ]	schwingen, schwenken
to **take** [teɪk]	**took** [tʊk]	**taken** ['teɪkn]	nehmen
to **teach** [ti:tʃ]	**taught** [tɔ:t]	**taught** [tɔ:t]	lehren
to **tear** [teə]	**tore** [tɔ:]	**torn** [tɔ:n]	reißen
to **tell** [tel]	**told** [təʊld]	**told** [təʊld]	sagen, erzählen
to **think** [θɪŋk]	**thought** [θɔ:t]	**thought** [θɔ:t]]	denken
to **throw** [θrəʊ]	**threw** [θru:]	**thrown** [θrəʊn]	werfen
to **wake** [weɪk]	**woke** [wəʊk]	**woken** ['wəʊkn]	aufwachen; wecken
to **wear** [weə]	**wore** [wɔ:]	**worn** [wɔ:n]	tragen, anhaben
to **weave** [wi:v]	**weaved/wove** [wi:vd; wəʊv]	**woven** ['wəʊvn]	weben
to **weep** [wi:p]	**wept** [wept]	**wept** [wept]	weinen
to **win** [wɪn]	**won** [wʌn]	**won** [wʌn]	gewinnen
to **write** [raɪt]	**wrote** [rəʊt]	**written** ['rɪtn]	schreiben

Bild- und Textquellenverzeichnis

Bildquellenverzeichnis: UM1: Avenue Images GmbH/Fancy, Hamburg; UM2: Klett-Archiv; UM4: shutterstock/Mendenhall, NY; S. 3: Avenue Images GmbH/Stock4B, Hamburg; S. 8: (1) Alamy Images RF, Abingdon, Oxon; (2) Alamy Images RM/Mediacolors; (3) Picture-Alliance/Ruetschi, Frankfurt; S. 9: (1) Alamy Images RM/K. deWitt; (2) Avenue Images GmbH/Banana Stock, Hamburg; (3) images.de digital photo GmbH/Rolf Schulten, Berlin; S. 10: (1/2) URW, Hamburg; (3) Imageshop RF, Düsseldorf; (4) Fotosearch RF/PhotoDisc, Waukesha; (5) Avenue Images GmbH/imageshop, Hamburg; S. 11: (1) Fotosearch RF/Stockbyte, Waukesha; (2) Avenue Images GmbH/Stockbyte; (3) JupiterImages/photos.com, Tucson; S. 13: (1) DigitalVision, Maintal-Dörnigheim; S. 13: (2–3) Getty Images RF/Photodisc rot/PNC, München; S. 15: Richard Peck/Internet; S. 16: (1) iStockphoto/RF/Carsten Madsen, Calgary, Alberta; (2) iStockphoto/RF/lubilub; S. 17: (1) iStockphoto/RF/Habur; (2) shutterstock/RF/Varina and Jay Patel, NY; S. 19: shutterstock/Drazen Vukelic; S. 20: (1) CartoonStock/Bryant, Adeyl, Bath; (2) CartoonStock/Baldwin, Mike; S. 21: (1–3) Klett-Archiv/Holger Hill; S. 22: (1) Bridgeman Art Library, Berlin; (2) Corbis/Reuters/F. Prouser, Düsseldorf; S. 24: (1) Fotosearch RF/Brand X Pictures; (2) Bilderberg/Peter Schroeder, Hamburg; (3) Fotosearch RF/Maps Resources; S. 25: (1) Alamy Images RM/D. Hoffman; (2) Corbis/Barry Lewis, Düsseldorf; (3) Alamy Images RM/Janine Wiedel Photolibrary; S. 26: (1) Getty Images RF/Photodisc; (2) Das Fotoarchiv, Essen; S. 27: (1) laif/Hemis, Köln; (2) f1 online digitale Bildagentur/Prisma, Frankfurt; S. 28: (1) Corbis/Moebes, Düsseldorf; (2) Corbis/Bettmann; (3) Picture-Alliance/PA; S. 29: (1) Corbis/Hulton-Deutsch, Düsseldorf; (2–4) Corbis/Bettmann; S. 30: Corbis/Sygma/McPherson, Düsseldorf; S. 33: (1) Alamy Images RM/David Pearson, Abingdon, Oxon; (2) Corbis/Ashley Cooper, Düsseldorf; (3) Alamy Images RM/Photofusion Picture Library; S. 34: (1) Alamy Images RM/Jon Arnold, Abingdon, Oxon; (2) Alamy Images RM/P. Wolmuth; S. 35: Corbis/Sygma/McPherson, Düsseldorf; S. 36: Corbis/Bettmann), Düsseldorf; S. 37: (1–3) BBC Broadcasting Corporation South, Bristol; S. 38: (1) Picture-Alliance/Photoshot, Frankfurt; (2) Creativ Collection Verlag GmbH, Freiburg; (3) MEV, Augsburg; S. 39: (1) Corbis/Steve Crisp/Reuters, Düsseldorf; (2) Corbis/Ashley Cooper; (3, 5) Corbis, Düsseldorf; (4) Corbis/Eleanor Bentall; (6) Corbis/Trapper); S. 40: (1) Alamy Images RF, Abingdon, Oxon; (2) shutterstock/RF/M. Stout, NY; (3) Imageshop RF, Düsseldorf; S. 41: (1) iStockphoto/RF/Zulkifli, Calgary, Alberta; (2) Fotosearch RF/Design Pics, Waukesha; S. 42: Corbis/Rune Hellestad, Düsseldorf; S. 43: (1) iStockphoto/RF/Michel de Nijs, Calgary, Alberta; (2) JupiterImages/RF/photos.com, Tucson, AZ; S. 44: Alamy Images RM/stockwales, Abingdon, Oxon; S. 46: (1) CartoonStock/Mike Baldwin, Bath; (2) CartoonStock/Ralph Hagen; S. 47: (1/2) MEV,Augsburg; (3) Alamy Images RM/Wileman, Abingdon; (4) Klett-Archiv/Studio Leupold, Stuttgart; S. 48: (1/2) Corbis/Reuters/Fred Prouser, Düsseldorf; S. 49: (1) Fotosearch RF/PhotoDisc, Waukesha; (2) Avenue Images GmbH/Brand X Pictures, Hamburg; (3) Corbis/Preston, Düsseldorf; S. 51: (1) NI Syndication/The Sun, London; (2) John Murray Publisher, London; S. 52: (1) Alamy Images RM/Pictor, Abingdon, Oxon; (2) Alamy Images RF/photofrenetic; S. 53: CartoonStock/Andrew Toos, Bath; S. 55: © Richard Young; S. 56: (1) Corbis/Steve & Ann Toon/Robert Harding World Im., Düsseldorf; 56.2: laif/RF/Ken Sorrie, Köln; S. 57: laif/Emmler, Köln; (2) Picture-Alliance/Zieminski, Frankfurt; (3) Comstock, Luxemburg; S. 58: (1) Corbis/Sigheti/Reuters, Düsseldorf; (2) Corbis/Richard T. Nowitz; (3) Corbis/Tony Arruza, Düsseldorf; S. 59: (1) Ravan Press/Peter Kallaway/Patrick Pearson/ Buchtitel: Johannesburg: Images and Continuities: A history of Working Class, Life through Pictures 1885–1935; (2) Corbis/Gideon Mendel, Düsseldorf; S. 60: (19 Corbis7David Turnley; Düsseldorf; (2) Corbis/Cardinale, Stephane/Sygma; S. 61: (1) Corbis/Reuters/Shaun Best, Düsseldorf; (2) Getty Images/Tomasz Tomaszewski/National Geographic, München; (3) Corbis/D. G. Houser, Düsseldorf; S. 62: (1) Corbis/Bettmann, Düsseldorf; (2) Corbis/Gideon Mendel; S. 63: (1) pieter@proagri.co.za; (2) AP/Adil Bradlow POOL, Frankfurt am Main; (3) Getty Images/Walter Dhladhla München; S. 64: (1) AKG, Berlin; (2) Filmverleih; (3) Mauritius/africanpictures, Mittenwald; S. 65: (1) Getty Images/Rajesh Jantilal/AFP, München; (2) Corbis/Leo Mason, Düsseldorf; (3) Corbis/Mike Hutchings/Reuters; S. 66: (1) Getty Images/Pettersson, München; (2) Rapid Phase Ltd., Parktown North, Johannesburg; S. 67: (1) Corbis/Louise Gubb, Düsseldorf; (2) Corbis, Düsseldorf; (3) Getty Images/Stone, München; S. 69: (1) Creativ Collection Verlag GmbH, Freiburg; (2) iStockphoto/RF/Catherine Milton, Calgary, Alberta; (3) iStockphoto/RF/Daniel Rodriguez; S. 71: (1) Alamy Images RM/Images of Africa Photobank, Abingdon, Oxon; S. 72: (1) Cinetext, Frankfurt; (2) picturemaxx.net RF/defd, München; (3) Getty Images/Frederick M. Brown, München; (4) picturemaxx.net RF, München; S. 73: (1) Corbis, Düsseldorf; (2) Ford-Werke AG, Köln; (3) Corbis/Reuters/Max Rossi, Düsseldorf; (4) Riken Bio-Mimetic Control Research, Nagoya; (5) Corbis/Smithsonian Institution, Düsseldorf; (6) Wikimedia Foundation Inc./Public Domain, St. Petersburg FL; S. 74: CartoonStock/Royston-Robertson, Bath; S. 75: tb@terrybisson.com; S. 76: (1) Corbis/Swim Ink, Düsseldorf; (2) Corbis/Claro Cortes IV/Reuters, Düsseldorf; S. 77: Corbis/Sygma, Düsseldorf; S. 78: Klett-Archiv/Screenshot; (2) MEV, Augsburg; (3) Cinetext, Frankfurt; (4) AKG, Berlin; (5) Verleih/UIP; S. 79: Cartoon Stock/Carpenter, Dave, Bath; S. 80: (1) Alamy Images RF/Burke, Abingdon, Oxon; (2) shutterstock/RF/T. Large, NY; S. 81: (1) iStockphoto/RF/Ntousiopoulos, Calgary, Alberta; (2) iStockphoto/RF/10four; S. 83: (1) iStockphoto/Eliza Snow, Calgary, Alberta; (2) shutterstock/Lance Bellers, NY; (3) F1 Online/Johnér, Frankfurt; (4) CartoonStock/Bryant, Adey, Bath; S. 84: (1) shutterstock/RF/Yuri Arcurs, NY; (2) www.info-rfid.de/Pressebild; S. 85: (1, 5) Fotosearch RF/Digital Vision, Waukesha; (2) JupiterImages/RF/photos.com, Tucson; (3, 6) Avenue Images GmbH/PhotoDisc, Hamburg; (4) Klett-Archiv; (7) Fotolia LLC/RF/DanHzen, New York; (8) Wisconsin Department of Natural Resources; S. 86: Toronto City Planning/Environmental Policy Planner; S. 87: (1, 3) MEV, Augsburg; (2) iStockphoto/RF/Starfotograf, Calgary, Alberta; (4) Imago Stock & People/Seeliger, Berlin; S. 88: (1/2) Getty Images RF/PhotoDisc, München; (3) Avenue Images GmbH/Corbis RF, Hamburg; S. 89: Mauritius/age fotostock, Mittenwald; S. 90: Klett-Archiv/Aribert Jung, |Stuttgart; (2) iStockphoto/Alvarez, Calgary, Alberta; S. 91: (1, 3) Avenue Images GmbH/StockDisc, Hamburg; (2) Fotosearch RF/Big Cheese RF, Waukesha; (4–6) Fotosearch RF/PhotoDisc, Waukesha; S. 93: Corbis/Bob Rowan; Progressive Image, Düsseldorf; S. 94: CartoonStock/Dan Reynolds, Bath; S. 95: Corbis/Bettmann, Düsseldorf; S. 97: shutterstock/RF/Jozsef Szasz-Fabian, NY; S. 98: Picture-Alliance/EPA, Frankfurt; S. 99: (1/2) Avenue Images GmbH/RF/Corbis, Hamburg; S. 100: Imago Stock & People/Horst Rudel, Berlin; S. 101: Klett-Archiv/Hell, Stuttgart; S. 102: (1/2) Corbis/P. Camboulive/Sygma/Kipa, Düsseldorf; (3/4) Corbis/Bettmann, Düsseldorf; S. 103: (1) Klett-Archiv; (2) Image 100/RF; S. 104: (1/2) Image 100/RF, Berlin; S. 105: (1) ullstein bild/Lineair, Berlin; (2) Foto: akg-images/Erich Lessing, Berlin © The Munch Museum/The Munch; S. 106: (1) CartoonStock/Mike Shapiro, Bath; (2) Geoatlas, Hendaye; S. 107: Avenue Images GmbH/Digital Vision, Hamburg; S. 108: The Cartoon Bank/New Yorker/Drew Dernavich, Yonkers, NY; S. 109: MEV, Augsburg; S. 110: Klett-Archiv/Steinle, Stuttgart; S. 111: iStockphoto/RF/Amanda Rohde, Calgary, Alberta; S. 112: (1) Avenue Images GmbH/Stockbyte, Hamburg; (2) JupiterImages/photos.com, Tucson; S. 115: (1) Corbis/Bettmann, Düsseldorf; (2) Getty Images RF/Photodisc, München; S. 116: (1–4) Klett-Archiv/Alan Fletcher; S. 117: CartoonStock/Shirvanian, Vahan, Bath; S. 119: CartoonStock/Goddard, Clive, Bath; S. 121: Getty Images RF/Photodisc, München; S. 122: (1) Getty Images RF/Photodisc, München; (2) Getty Images RF/digital Vision; (3) Avenue Images GmbH/Brand X Pictures, Hamburg; S. 124: (1) Klett-Archiv/Wolfgang Riemer, Stuttgart; (2) Getty Images/Stone, München; (3) Fotosearch RF/Photodisc, Waukesha; S. 125: Punch Library, London; S. 131: (1) MEV, Augsburg; (2) Corbis/Stephen Welstead, Düsseldorf; S. 136: (1) Corbis/WildCountry, Düsseldorf; (2) Getty Images RF/Photodisc, München; S. 142: (1) CartoonStock/Mike Baldwin, Bath; (2) Robert Harding Picture Library Ltd./Robert Harding, London; (3) Avenue Images GmbH/image100, Hamburg; (4) iStockphoto/RF/ René Mansi, Calgary, Alberta; S. 148: (1/2) Corel Corporation, Unterschleissheim; S. 154: (1) CartoonStock/Noel Ford, Bath; (2) CartoonStock/Naf, Bath; S. 201: Avenue Images GmbH/RF/Comstock Select, Hamburg; (2) Avenue Images GmbH/Digital Vision, Hamburg

Song- und Textquellenverzeichnis: S. 9: The Western Courier by Joseph Lemanski; S. 10–11: www.childrens-express.org; S. 12–15: NTC Publishing Group "Coming of Age: Short stories about youth & adolescence" © 1989 by Richard Peck; S. 16-17: © Shout, D.C. Thompson 2006; S. 18/19: Sierra Wave from Good Rockin' Tonight: A Collection of Short Stories by William Hauptmann. © 1988 by William Hauptmann. Used by permission of Bantam Books, a division of Random House, Inc.; S. 20: Song: © Story Songs Ltd., Neue Welt Musikverlag GmbH, Hamburg; S 21: © Die Zeit/Lara Fritzsche; S. 22/23: The Globe and Mail, Toronto by Joanne Kates; S. 26/27: International Herald Tribune by Joan Venocchi; S. 28: Song: © Neville Music Publishing Company/Irving Music Inc., Rondor Musikverlag GmbH, Hamburg; S. 30–32: On Beauty by Zadie Smith, Penguin 2006; S. 33: (1) © by Ian Herbert, Independent Newspapers (UK) Ltd.; (2) © by Sarfraz Manzoor, The Week; S. 34: © by Zia Haider Rahman, The Sunday Times; S. 35: adapted form The Buddah of Suburbia by Hanif Kureishi, Faber & Faber, 1990; S. 38: © by John Agard; S. 40: © www.hcbe.net; S. 42/43: © by Frank McCourt, Harper Perennial 2006; S. 44–46: © by Malachy Doyle, Bloomsbury Publishing, 2002; S. 47: © by Brian Patten, 2000, www.poetryarchve.org; S. 48: © by Hannah Frankel, Times Educational Supplement, 2007; S. 49: Song: © 1985 by chariscourt Ltd./GM Summer, Rondor Musikverlag GmbH, Berlin, EMI Music Publishing Germany GmbH & Co. KG, Hamburg; S. 50/51: © Marie Stubbs, extract from Ahead of the Class, published by John Murray 2003 in The Week, 2003; S. 56/57: www.go2africa.com; S. 58: © Nadine Gordimer, Jump and other stories, Penguin London; S. 60: Song: © 1988 by Greenheart Music LTD.; Für D: Hanseatic Musikverlag GmbH, Hamburg; S. 61: Nelson Mandela, © Abacus London, 1995; S. 62: by Milton Nkosi, www.bbc.co.uk; S. 63: (1) by Christopher van Wyk, ETONSA; (2) by Greg Barrow, www.news.bbc.co.uk; S. 64: by Julie Rigg, Movie Time, ABC Radio National; S. 65: www.suedafrika.net; S. 66: © Mail & Guardian, 2006; S. 67: © Rolf Hogan, The Daily Mail; S. 68–71: © Nadine Gordimer – Jump and other stories, Penguin London; S. 74/75: © by Terry Bisson; S. 76/77: © by George Orwell; S. 79/80: The Independent, 2004; S. 81/82: © by Richard Woods, The Sunday Times, 2006; S. 84: www.ctv.ca; S. 87: Song: © Intersong Music Ltd., Hanseatic Musikverlag GmbH, Hamburg; S. 95: School report: © HumourHub.com

JOHANNESBURG

Administrative regions and main roads

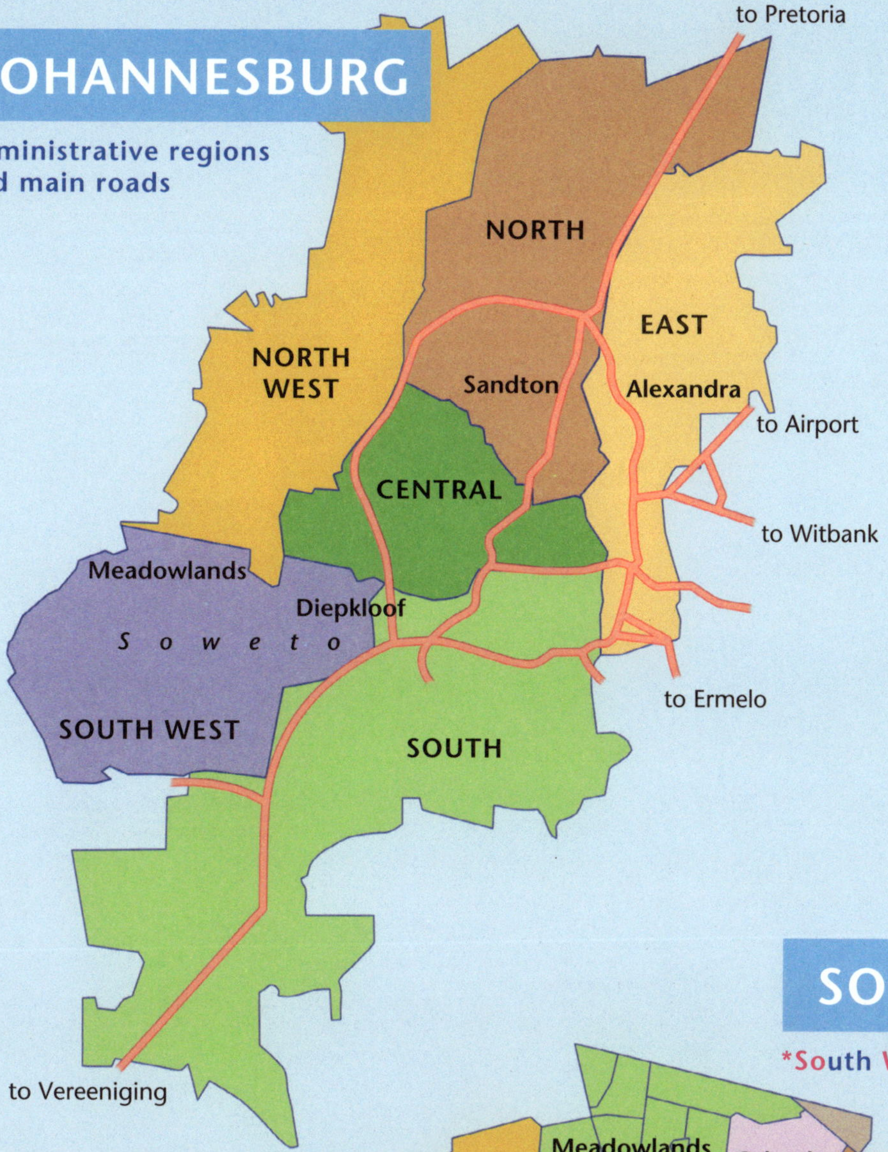

SOWETO*

*South Western Townships

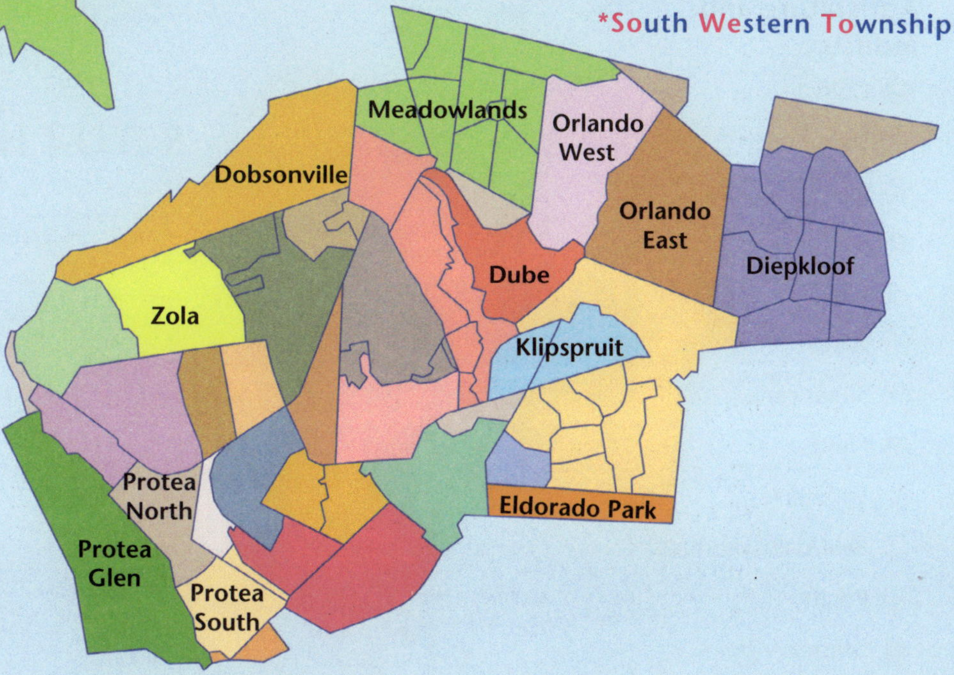

REPUBLIC OF
SOUTH AFRICA
NAMIBIA
BOTS
SOUTH ATLANTIC
OCEAN
Orange
SOUTH AFRICA
TABLE MOUNTAIN
NATIONAL PARK
Cape Town
Agriculture and industry
Gold
Diamonds
Other metals
Machinery
Maize
Wheat
Sugar cane
Fruits
Vegetables
Beef/dairy products
Poultry
Mutton/wool
Wine